NORTH CAROLINA

JASON FRYE

Contents

Although every effort was made to make sure the information in this book was accurate when going to press, research was impacted by the COVID-19 pandemic and things may have changed since the time of writing. Be sure to confirm specific details, like opening hours, closures, and travel guidelines and restrictions, when making your travel plans. For more detailed information, see page 526.

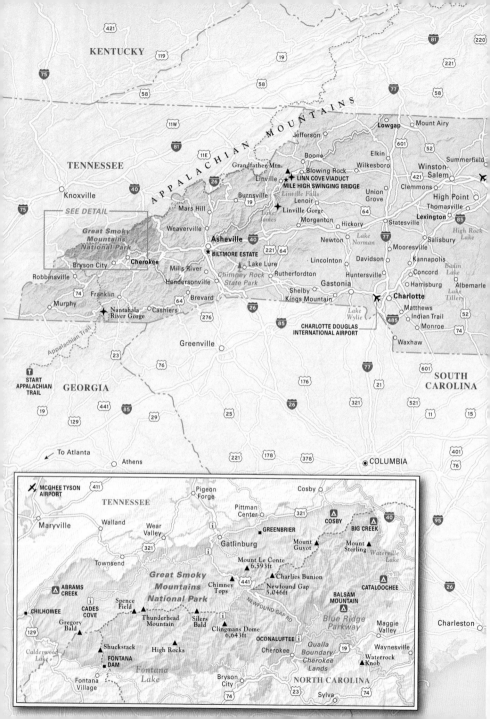

DISCOVER

North Carolina

Stay here long enough and North Carolina will start to color everything you see. It won't take more than a minute or two, but somewhere between a sip of sweet tea and a bite of barbecue sandwich, you'll see blue everywhere. The sky, more often than not, is Tarheel Blue. The Atlantic Ocean: turquoise near shore but growing to a deeper sapphire as it approaches the horizon, a line invisible in the evenings when the sky and sea seem as one. On maps, blue veins of rivers and creeks draw the unseen contours of the land. And west, where the mountains rise high and rugged, you can see their crenellations grow blue with distance.

We're bracketed by blue here—surrounded by it. Inside, it's a paint-by-numbers picture of geography, history, culture, and personalities. The palette changes by the season, but it's always vivid and it's always up to you just how to color it in. Red clay and the bright and tiny fire of flame azaleas in bloom. White sands on the shore and winter's snowy cap topping the tallest mountains. A hundred shades of autumn jeweling the mountainsides and a hundred more in spring's wildflower bloom. The pink of a salamander's belly and the coral sunset over Pamlico Sound. The green of leaf—oak, pecan, longleaf pine—and the

Clockwise from top left: hang gliding at Jockey's Ridge State Park; craft beer; the Elizabethan Gardens on Roanoke Island; riverwalk at the Cape Fear River in Wilmington; hiking in Great Smoky Mountains National Park; Linn Cove Viaduct on the Blue Ridge Parkway.

green of the envy you feel when a friend says, "We're headed to North Carolina for the weekend."

Don't get too jealous, though. You can come to North Carolina any time. There's a map of the state waiting for you to fill it in with your colored pencils. We've gone ahead and colored in the borders, defined our edges with gradations of blue; the rest is up to you. A visit during every season is enjoyable, all you need to bring is a sense of adventure—how else will you explore our trails and tracks, rivers and rapids, cities and country roads? How else will you find a favorite bite to eat, a new beer to crave, a new town to fill your daydreams?

Clockwise from top left: surfing off Hatteras Island; Clingmans Dome; Wilmington's Azalea Festival; Wright Brothers National Memorial.

8 TOP EXPERIENCES

1 **Hike in Great Smoky Mountains National Park:** The best way to explore the woods, peaks, and waterfalls in this beautiful park is by foot (page 452).

2 **Take a Scenic Drive:** Get your camera ready—there are some lovely drives in North Carolina. The **Blue Ridge Parkway** may even be the best scenic drive in America (page 31).

3 **Escape to the Outer Banks:** This gorgeous stretch of coast has **wild horses** (page 43), historic **lighthouses** (page 62), and remote islands, like **Ocracoke** (page 70), which feel worlds away. Enjoy all three at **Cape Lookout National Seashore** (page 121).

4 **Get Your 'Cue On:** North Carolina has two distinct barbecue styles and hundreds of places claiming to be the best. Better come hungry (page 22).

5 **Make a Splash:** Kayak around **Kitty Hawk** (page 43) or the black-water rivers of **Merchant's Millpond State Park** (page 76). For even more excitement, go white-water rafting in the wild **Nantahala River Gorge** (page 471) or at the **U.S. National Whitewater Center** (page 298).

6 **Sip Craft Brews:** You can't go far without passing a brewery in North Carolina. Don't miss the brews around Wilmington and Cape Fear (page 152), the High Country (page 349), and Asheville (page 405).

<<<

7 **Jam to Local Music:** However you get your kicks—whether bluegrass twang or electronic beats—you'll find great music across the state (page 206).

>>>

8 **Get Away to Cool Towns:** Spend a weekend enjoying both the natural beauty and cosmopolitan flare of these hip towns (page 28).

<<<

15

Planning Your Trip

Where to Go

The Outer Banks

This ribbon of shore is rich with ecological wonders, centuries-old traditions, and historical mysteries. Around **Nags Head** and the **Cape Hatteras National Seashore**, surfers, hang gliders, and kiteboarders ride the wind and waves. One of the first English settlements appeared and then disappeared on **Roanoke Island**, Blackbeard roamed these waters before losing his head near **Ocracoke**, and the Wright Brothers changed the world in a windswept field in **Kill Devil Hills**. Along the vast **Pamlico and Albemarle Sounds**, colonial towns and fishing villages stand along deep still rivers. **The Great Dismal Swamp**, an eerie unforgettable place perfect for kayaking and canoeing, once harbored the colonial rebels who birthed our country and thousands of enslaved people seeking freedom and a life of their own.

Beaufort and the Crystal Coast

Quaint **beach towns** line the Crystal Coast. **Beaufort** and **New Bern**, two of early North Carolina's most important cities, have some of the South's most stunning early architecture. **Morehead City** is a hot spot for scuba diving the offshore wrecks in **The Graveyard of the Atlantic**, and **Cape Lookout National Seashore** has 56 miles of undeveloped shoreline inhabited only by wild horses, shorebirds, and one of the state's **iconic lighthouses**. Inland, **New Bern** and **Tryon Palace** speak to the state's early history served with a refreshing side of hospitality.

ferry on its way from Cape Hatteras to Ocracoke Island

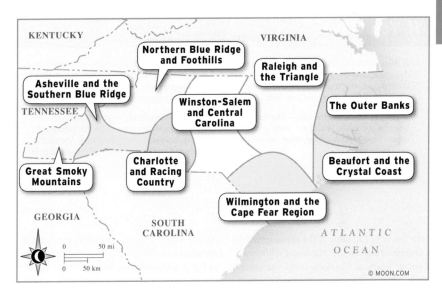

Wilmington and the Cape Fear Region

The towns surrounding the mouth of the Cape Fear River are year-round knockouts. The port city of **Wilmington,** known for its **antebellum homes and gardens** and the annual **Azalea Festival,** has a food and craft beer scene to rival almost any other in the state. **Topsail Island, Wrightsville Beach,** and **the Beaches of Brunswick County** offer some of the most beautiful stretches of sand in the nation. Inland, the **Waccamaw** and **Lumber Rivers** creep through black-water swamps, while the **Cape Fear River** leads upstream to **Fayetteville,** a city full of surprises.

Raleigh and the Triangle

College towns **Raleigh, Durham,** and **Chapel Hill** share a creative verve and intellectual vibe and a richness that comes from a diverse student and faculty population. Visitors enjoy rich **music and literary scenes** and volcanically exciting **college sports.** Great **museums;** plenty of **greenways and parks** where you can play the day away; and a bevy of fantastic restaurants, bars, and breweries make this region a must-visit.

Winston-Salem and Central Carolina

History, art, and culture collide in **Winston-Salem,** where an array of galleries, museums, restaurants, and breweries show the city's creative flair, and **Old Salem** preserves the village built by 18th-century religious pilgrims. This is the gateway to the Yadkin Valley, the heart of North Carolina's wine country. Nearby **Greensboro** is home to the **International Civil Rights Center and Museum.** In the southeastern corner of the region, the **Sandhills** are a golfing epicenter, thanks to the famed **Pinehurst Resort** and one of the best-known courses in the world, and the nearby town of **Seagrove** is renowned for its pottery. The ancient, creepy **Uwharrie Mountains** shelter deep forests and mountain lakes, drawing hikers, explorers, and off-road enthusiasts from far and wide.

Charlotte and Racing Country

The Old South, New South, and Global South come together to make Charlotte unmatched in its cultural vitality. The **diverse restaurants** alone show this: you'll find everything from fried chicken to *phô* to enchiladas. There's plenty to do

If You Have . . .

- **A Weekend:** Nature calls. Pick a natural wonder to explore: the Outer Banks, beaches near Wilmington, the Blue Ridge Parkway, or the Great Smoky Mountains National Park.

- **5 Days:** Add a nearby city—Charlotte, the Triangle, Asheville, Winston-Salem, and Wilmington have fantastic food, drink, and cultural sites to discover.

- **7 Days:** Add a festival—check out www.visitnc.com or www.ncfestivals.com to find out what's happening during your visit—a concert or a can't-miss happening.

- **10 Days:** Go camping—across the state, North Carolina's parks preserve some spectacular natural environments, great hiking trails, and boating spots, and they're rife with wildlife-watching opportunities.

here: South of Charlotte is the amusement park **Carowinds** and the **U.S. National Whitewater Center;** north of Charlotte is the epicenter of NASCAR at the **Charlotte Motor Speedway;** in every neighborhood and corner of town there's exceptional food, drink, and shopping. The surrounding towns are filled with fun shops and historic sites.

Northern Blue Ridge and Foothills

The **Blue Ridge Parkway** winds through the South's stunning mountain scenery, ranging from rolling hills near the Virginia border to the tall, rough mountains on our border with Tennessee. Friendly foothills towns like **Mount Airy** and **Wilkesboro** are rich with mountain music, moonshine, and wine. **Blowing Rock** retains the feel of an elite yesteryear mountain retreat, while nearby college town **Boone** is progressive and eclectic. Yadkin Valley **wineries** wait for tasters, and outdoor recreation—hiking, whitewater rafting, and the highest ski resort in the East—is abundant.

Asheville and the Southern Blue Ridge

Asheville's a town chock-full of creative types: Artists, chefs, brewers, and musicians find inspiration here. A top **beer destination** and one of the South's **premier food cities,** Asheville is filled with **galleries, boutiques,** and the general weirdness you expect from bigger cities. **Art deco architecture,** the famed and lovely **Biltmore Estate,** the wildly creative **River Arts District,** and a renewed embrace of **Black creators** and entrepreneurs are a few of the reasons to visit. Its location between the Blue Ridge and Smokies gives easy access to the mountains, especially the **Great Smoky Mountains National Park,** where recreation opportunities abound.

Great Smoky Mountains

Straddling the border with Tennessee, **Great Smoky Mountains National Park** is a land of ridges, rocky rivers, virgin forests, and tumbling waterfalls. The **most-visited national park** in the United States, it's a hot spot of trails, **waterfalls,** mountain vistas, and 500,000 acres of wilderness to explore. Visit appealing little towns like **Bryson City, Dillsboro and Sylva,** and **Maggie Valley** as well as the tribal seat of the Eastern Band of the **Cherokee,** a **casino,** and the first (and only) **fly-fishing trail** in the United States.

Know Before You Go

Spring debuts in the Southeast as early as late February, then creeps into central North Carolina and up the coast, reaching the mountains a little later. Temperatures are a consistent 60-70°F by mid-April. The weather's nice, but some regional events are so large that entire cities or corners of the state may be booked. April is the most challenging month, with Wilmington's **Azalea Festival,** Durham's **Full Frame Documentary Festival,** and North Wilkesboro's **MerleFest.**

Summer is high season: beaches are jam-packed, traffic is slow in the mountains, and across the state you'll find festivals, farmers markets, and events. Heat and humidity can be brutal, so the cooler mountains and breezy coastline draw visitors from far and wide. Rent your beach houses and mountain cabins far in advance for the choicest of stays.

Autumn begins in the mountains and spreads across the state. **Fall foliage** accounts for the mountains' second high season, running late September-early November; it's busiest in October, when cooler weather offers relief after sweltering September. Near the coast, fall doesn't begin until after hurricane season has passed, in early November. Water along the coast stays swimmably warm past Halloween. It's also time for barbecue and bluegrass, both of which you'll find in Raleigh at the **Wide Open Bluegrass** fan festival in early October; for more modern music try the city's **Hopscotch Music Festival** in September.

Winter is milder here than in many parts of the country, but many businesses in the mountains and along the coast reduce their hours or close entirely. West of I-95, the Piedmont gets a few snow showers, and the coast gets one or two every couple of years. In the mountains, temperatures are much colder, and snow falls a few times a year. You'll hear no complaints

autumn foliage along the Blue Ridge Parkway

In winter, Beech Mountain serves skiers, but the rest of the year mountain bikers rule the mountain.

from skiers hitting the slopes at **Appalachian Ski Mountain, Beech Mountain** (a ski resort that's a mile high), and **Sugar Mountain.** If you plan to visit the beach or the deep mountains in January, book accommodations in advance.

Weather can change on a whim. It pays to layer, as temperatures in the 80s can drop into the 60s at night. **Pack** for chilly weather in the mountains, even in the summer. On the coast, it can be breezy and cool on the water even on warm days, and you may want a light long-sleeved layer to protect you from the sun.

Cell phone signals are consistent, but there are rural pockets on the extreme coast or in the deep mountains where cell service and 4G, 5G, and LTET connectivity is spotty.

North Carolina Getaways

From the mountains to the sea, North Carolina sweeps across some 560 miles of wildlands, woodlands, and wetlands. Explore towns and cities, shores and summits, the Sandhills and the Blue Ridge foothills, eating, drinking, and playing your way into nearly every corner of the state.

This day-by-day route takes you from the **Great Smoky Mountains** in the west to **pristine beaches** in the east, crossing through rural and metropolitan North Carolina along the way. You could easily reverse the route or start in **Charlotte, Raleigh,** or **Winston-Salem.** You need at least two weeks for this epic road trip, but each region stands as its own **two- to five-day getaway,** allowing you to discover the state on your own terms.

Adventure in the Smokies

Hiking, rafting, waterfalls, fly-fishing, sightseeing trains, and the western end of the North Carolina Barbecue Trail are just some of the attractions waiting around the next mountain curve.

DAY 1

Begin your journey in the southwestern part of the state where **Bryson City** sits surrounded by the Smoky Mountains. A train ride on **Great Smoky Mountains Railroad** or a **hike** along **Deep Creek** to a trio of **waterfalls** gives you a great introduction to the region. Make the time for a drive on the **Cherohala Skyway,** a 43-mile scenic highway whose curves and views draw sports-car and motorcycle enthusiasts from far and wide, before settling in to your boutique hotel or **mountain cabin** for the night.

DAY 2

Start your day in Bryson City white-water rafting the **Nantahala River,** then enjoy a riverside

a trail bridge in Great Smoky Mountains National Park

Get Your 'Cue On

In North Carolina, barbecue can be a divisive topic, yet it always brings people back together. There are two primary styles within the state and hundreds of regional and family recipe variations on seasonings, sauce, and sides, but let's keep it simple and say that in North Carolina, barbecue is either Eastern-style or Lexington-style.

True barbecue is cooked the traditional way—low and slow over a pile of wood coals—in fancy pits with computer temperature monitoring, or right out back in a low cinderblock pit covered with a piece of tin. Eastern-style barbecue uses whole hogs that, once cooked over oak wood coals (sometimes as long as overnight), are chopped or pulled apart, seasoned with a dash or splash of thin sauce made from vinegar and peppers, then served on sandwiches and platters. You'll find the highest concentration of Eastern-style 'cue restaurants east of I-95. Lexington-style barbecue uses shoulders and butts, cooks them over a hickory-dominant blend of woods, and is chopped coarsely before being served on platters and sandwiches. The sauce builds off the vinegar and pepper from the East and adds something thick and sweet—sometimes tomato paste, other times brown sugar, and still other times molasses—to give it body. You'll hear friendly, even borderline heated, discussions on the merits of each style and how sides like slaw, hush puppies, or potato salad should be prepared, but despite all the bluster and all the declarations of this style's superiority, you'll never find someone turning down a plate of 'cue.

I'm a fan of barbecue. I make my own sauce, have cooked a few whole hogs, know how I like my cornbread and collards, and toss a butt or 10 on the smoker throughout the year. But I always love trying a new barbecue restaurant. Here are a few of the best barbecue joints you'll find. They represent traditional approaches and chef-driven takes on one of the state's favorite foods.

- **Skylight Inn** (page 109), one of the oldest and most lauded barbecue joints in the state, uses the whole hog all the time. Dishes are served with dense fried cornbread and slaw.

- **Sam Jones BBQ** (page 211) serves a fantastic pulled pork sandwich. Sam, the son of the Skylight Inn family, has put his twist on barbecue traditions.

- **Southern Smoke BBQ** (page 184) is the next generation of North Carolina barbecue. There's

Lexington No. 1

traditional 'cue and sides taken from granny's cookbook with a twist.

- **Picnic** (page 225) in Durham is elevating barbecue with traditional and new approaches to the state's favorite food.

- **Lexington No. 1** (page 278) is the pinnacle of Lexington-style barbecue. Order a plate of coarse chopped brown—the crispy, barky bit on the outside of the meat—and you'll be hooked.

- **Stamey's Old Fashioned Barbecue** (page 273) is family-run, and they've been running for a long time, so you know their barbecue game is strong. Traditional, rootsy, and delicious, Stamey's is a must.

- **Buxton Hall Barbecue** (page 404) is an Asheville joint that cooks whole hogs with a high-concept twist to the sides. Intent on honoring the barbecue traditions coming from both of the Carolinas, the sauces and sides tell a story about history and culture.

- **Luella's Bar-B-Que** (page 409) puts a new spin on barbecue—you'll find plenty of pork here, but also barbecued tempeh and veggie (even vegan) sides.

lunch at the **Nantahala Outdoor Center.** Take U.S. 74 southeast to Sylva for prime trout fishing on the **Western North Carolina Fly-Fishing Trail,** or continue past Sylva on to Highway 107 for about an hour to view several waterfalls near the town of **Cashiers. Sliding Rock, Silver Run Falls,** and **Whitewater Falls** are beautiful year-round, but stunning in the fall. Reverse course, make the hour's trip northwest to Cherokee, and spend the night at **Harrah's Cherokee Casino and Hotel.**

DAY 3

Book a massage at Harrah's **Mandara Spa** or spend a few hours at the gaming tables. Next, admire Native American art at the **Qualla Arts and Crafts Mutual,** and visit the **Museum of the Cherokee Indian,** across the street, and the **Oconaluftee Indian Village,** just up the hill. During the summer months, catch an evening performance of *Unto These Hills.* Anglers love the **trophy waters** here, and mountain bikers are flocking to **Fire Mountain Trails,** but a drive along the **Blue Ridge Parkway** or a hike

in **Great Smoky Mountains National Park** give many visitors the dose of nature they've been seeking.

DAY 4

Take the 30-mile **Newfound Gap Road** through the park into Gatlinburg, Tennessee, eat lunch, and head back to North Carolina. You're as likely to see a bear as a deer on this stunning scenic road, and you'll also pass a number of trailheads. Trails range from short jaunts to overnight hikes leading deep into the forest. The trails in **Cades Cove** and around **Clingmans Dome**—the highest point in the Smokies—are popular. The **Appalachian Trail** crosses Clingmans Dome, so take a stroll here if for no other reason than to say you've hiked on the AT. Beat a retreat back to your campsite or Harrah's and rest up; tomorrow, you're heading to Asheville.

Art and Beauty: Asheville and the Blue Ridge

In **Asheville,** you'll find streets lined with **galleries,** one of the nation's largest collections

a cabin along the Blue Ridge Parkway

Asheville

of **art deco architecture,** and a growing array of chefs, brewers, and mixologists. Farther north, around **Boone** and **Blowing Rock,** winter sports abound, but there's plenty to do year-round.

DAY 1

If you're leaving Cherokee, hop on the **Blue Ridge Parkway.** The first section takes about 30 minutes before you traverse unforgettable mountain passes en route to U.S. 19. From here, it's a 45-minute drive east to Asheville, not counting an essential stop for breakfast at Maggie Valley's lauded **Joey's Pancake House.**

In Asheville, head directly to the **Biltmore Estate.** Tour the **Biltmore Winery,** watch the **blacksmith** at Antler Hill Village make music with the anvil, and find lunch at **Cedric's Tavern.** Head downtown and check into **The Foundry Hotel,** freshen up, and get ready to roam.

Dine downtown at **Cucina 24** or at **Benne on Eagle,** then head to nearby **Orange Peel, Rabbit Rabbit,** or **Salvage Station** for live music. Make one last stop at **Sovereign Remedies** for a nightcap.

DAY 2

A few blocks away on Wall Street, breakfast awaits at **Early Girl Eatery.** Window shop at **Malaprop's Bookstore** and **Woolworth Walk** art gallery, and don't sweat lunch: A food tour with **Eating Asheville** will fill you up and point you in a direction for dinner. Walk off your food tour at the **Asheville Art Museum** while you debate whether to dine at **The Admiral, Cúrate,** or **Jettie Rae's.**

DAY 3

Eat breakfast at West Asheville's **Sunny Point Café** before hitting the road. Travel east on I-40 for one hour until you reach Morganton. Check out the gorgeous pottery at **Hamilton Williams Gallery,** then grab lunch at **Root and Vine** before heading north on Highway 181 until you reach the **Blue Ridge Parkway** (about 45 minutes). Slow your pace and follow the parkway past **Grandfather Mountain** and across the precariously perched **Linn Cove Viaduct** until you come to the town of **Blowing Rock,** about a 40-minute drive if you don't stop to take pictures.

In Blowing Rock, tour the antiques shops and galleries downtown, making your way to the **Blowing Rock Art and History Museum,** also home to the Blowing Rock Visitors Center. Sleep in a **bed-and-breakfast** in the heart of downtown.

DAY 4

Visit the namesake **Blowing Rock** before taking a short drive to **Boone.** Eat a late breakfast at **Sunrise Grill** and walk next door to **River and Earth Adventures** to schedule a guided hike, rafting trip, or caving expedition, then spend the afternoon exploring. Clean up at your bed-and-breakfast, and then revisit Boone for dinner at **Lost Province.**

Racing Around Charlotte

In addition to its storied racing sights, Charlotte offers outstanding art museums, first-class dining, and professional sports galore. It's no wonder that its status as a must-visit Southern city seems to be written in stone.

DAY 1

If you're leaving Blowing Rock, drive two hours south along U.S. 321 through Hickory and some beautiful North Carolina countryside until you connect with I-85 outside Gastonia. Once you arrive in Charlotte, take a break from your windshield time at the **NASCAR Hall of Fame** in the heart of downtown. Great restaurants are located within a few blocks, or you can check into **Kimpton Tryon Park Hotel** and explore nearby eateries like **Church and Union, Angeline's,** or **The King's Kitchen.** After lunch, visit the **Mint Museum's** uptown location at the **Levine Center for the Arts.** Here you'll also find the **Bechtler Museum of Modern Art,** the **Harvey B. Gantt Center for African-American Arts + Culture,** and the **John S. and James L. Knight Theatre,**

where you might catch a ballet or concert. Dinner at **The Goodyear House** will leave you speechless.

DAY 2

Northeast of Charlotte in nearby Concord is the **Charlotte Motor Speedway,** a mecca for racing fans. Take a ride-along in a stock car or even take one for a spin yourself. After visiting the track, visit one of the many **breweries** around town. **Triple C, Wooden Robot, Birdsong, and Olde Mecklenburg Breweries** keep this town from going thirsty, and they're just a drop in the bucket of beer here. If you're in Charlotte during sports season, take in a **Panthers** or **Hornets** game, some **minor league baseball,** maybe even a race at the Speedway.

DAY 3

Carowinds, a few minutes south of downtown Charlotte, straddles the South Carolina state line and is home to an impressive collection of roller coasters, including the Dale Earnhardt-themed Intimidator. Get your thrills here, or spend the morning shopping, snacking, and wandering through **Camp North End** and **Optimist Hall,** two destinations filled with eclectic shops and restaurants.

Wining and Dining in Winston-Salem

The Moravian village of Salem and the industry town of Winston merged to form one hardworking town that honors its past as it evolves into a city known for food, arts, and innovation. It's also the gateway to the **Yadkin Valley Wine Trail,** so come thirsty.

DAY 1

From Charlotte, drive an hour northeast on I-85 to Lexington, home of a tremendous **Barbecue Festival** each October. Take a tour of the winemaking process at **Childress Vineyards** and taste to your heart's content, then enjoy a meal on-site. Continue north on U.S. 52 for 30 minutes and check in to one of Winston-Salem's

If you want to get your adrenaline flowing or keep things on the milder side, there's plenty to experience in North Carolina, no matter where your visit takes you.

MOUNTAINS

Go big on a monster **zip line** that goes as fast as a car at **Navitat,** or try one of the longest zip courses in the state at **The Gorge.** There are hundreds of miles of hiking trails in the **Great Smoky Mountains National Park,** or you can hike to a number of waterfalls in the **DuPont State Recreational Forest** near Brevard. **Whitewater rafting** with Nantahala Outdoor Center gives big thrills, or you can calm it down with a **river tube float** in **Asheville, Todd,** and **Deep Creek.**

PIEDMONT

In Greensboro, **SKYWILD** offers up one of the most challenging high ropes and challenge courses you'll find in North Carolina. It's adjacent to the aquarium if you get tired. The **North Carolina Zoo** in Asheboro and the **Carolina Tiger Rescue** in Pittsboro will give you a look at some exotic wildlife. Around Charlotte, **Carowinds** delivers those roller coaster thrills, or you can face some world-class rapids at the **U.S. National Whitewater Center;** you can also hop in a race car for a **NASCAR Ride Along** at the Charlotte Motor Speedway.

COAST

On the Outer Banks, go **hang gliding** not far from where the Wright Brothers first flew. If you

tubing at Deep Creek

like it, go higher and try a **tandem hang glide** over the coast. Get close to nature with a **wild horse tour** and see the Banker ponies in Corolla and on the Crystal Coast. For a real thrill, and the best coastal views you'll find, try **skydiving.** And, of course, there's a day of **deep-sea fishing** and the excitement of reeling in the big one. If water sports are to your taste, a **guided kayak or paddleboard tour** may be to your liking, or even a **dive off one of hundreds of shipwrecks.**

beautiful inns, like the luxurious **Graylyn** or the possibly haunted **Brookstown Inn.** For dinner, go for Modern Southern at **Spring House Restaurant, Kitchen & Bar;** try the next-level bites at **Mojito Latin Soul Food;** or some pizza pie from **Cugino Forno** and a beer from neighboring **Incendiary Brewing.**

DAY 2

After breakfast at **Krankies,** hit the Yadkin Valley Wine Trail. Head west on U.S. 421 for 45 minutes to **Raffaldini Vineyards and Winery.** Make a meal of their gourmet snack selection, then go to your next winery—**Medaloni Cellars, Westbend Winery and Brewhouse,** and **Shelton Vineyards** are all good options—working your way back east to Winston-Salem. Dinner at **Jeffrey Adams Restaurant on 4th** and a bottle from their great wine list makes for a perfect end to the day.

DAY 3

After a day of decadence, enjoy some quiet in the colonial Quaker village of **Old Salem.** Take a self-guided tour through cobblestone streets and colonial homes before visiting the **Museum of Early Southern Decorative Arts.** Lunch at **Mojito Latin Soul Food** for excellent ceviche, Cuban sandwiches, and empanadas, among other tasty offerings. Visit the **Southeastern Center for Contemporary Art,** then contrast the pieces there with those at the **Reynolda House Museum of American Art.** After a day of art and history, relax with a beer and pub food at **Foothills Brewing Company** downtown.

DAY 4

Travel east on I-40 to Greensboro to see one of the most important sites in civil rights history: the Woolworth's Lunch Counter, where a peaceful sit-in ignited the civil rights movement in North Carolina. The **International Civil Rights Center and Museum** is housed in the former F. W. Woolworth building where the protest took place. After exploring the museum, stop by **Natty Greene's Pub** to sample ales and IPAs and grab a bite to eat. Spend the afternoon exploring galleries and gardens, then eat dinner at **1618 West Seafood Grill.**

College Town Antics in Raleigh and the Triangle

The Triangle—Raleigh, Durham, and Chapel Hill—is a hotbed of intellectual activity and home to a number of major universities. It's a lively international scene with many ethnic and ethnic-fusion restaurants and a trio of fantastic museums in Raleigh, the state capital.

DAY 1

Chapel Hill, about an hour east of Greensboro, is home to the **University of North Carolina.** This progressive little college town is great to walk in and filled with fun eateries. Walk around campus, cruise the streets, and pop into vintage shops, galleries, and boutiques. Thirsty? Point yourself toward **The Crunkleton** to sample an

Old Salem in Winston-Salem

North Carolina's Coolest Towns

If you're trying to figure out where to base yourself for a weekend getaway, look no further than these sweet spots. These neat towns feature great recreation and natural beauty as well as urban pursuits like live music venues and great breweries.

ASHEVILLE

The heartbeat of North Carolina's culinary and brewery scene, Asheville is cool for the food and drink alone, but the arts, culture, and natural beauty make it one of the best. Drive the Blue Ridge Parkway, explore the architecture and gardens of the Biltmore Estate, visit countless art galleries and studios, then take in a concert—from a big-name act or an unbelievable busker—and you'll get it.

the Wide Open Bluegrass Festival in Raleigh

WILMINGTON

Three beaches within a 15-minute drive; hundreds of miles of rivers, waterways, and marsh creeks to explore by boat; a fantastic (and growing) brewery scene with heavy hitters like Flytrap and New Anthem; restaurants like Seabird, Savorez, Dram Yard, and Catch showing off on the plate; spring's Azalea Festival and a bevy of outdoor concerts throughout summer all put Wilmington on the list of coolest towns.

OCRACOKE

This isolated artsy island was once home to Blackbeard, but now you'll have its beautiful beaches to yourself, along with art galleries, fresh seafood restaurants, sailing and fishing the days away, and stargazing at night. Unexpected and surprising, Ocracoke's the epitome of low-key cool.

BOONE

With a pair of great breweries (both of which serve great pizza); a chic boutique hotel; miles of hiking and mountain biking trails, ski runs, and the Blue Ridge Parkway nearby; plus the energy of a college town, it's beautiful in every season and cool to the core.

RALEIGH

The state capitol is packed with history and architecture, home to a fabulous art museum and a greenway that will deliver you right to its door. Dine on Indian cuisine at Garland or southern fare at Poole's Diner or modern American at Crawford & Son, and slake your thirst at Trophy Brewing or one of the

dozen breweries in town. In fall, college football, music festivals, and the state fair make the city even more lively.

SOUTHERN PINES AND PINEHURST

These two neighboring towns complement one another so well, they could be one. Golf courses to write home about, horseback riding, a mix of shopping that includes high-end boutiques and local specialty shops, and some fine restaurants show the charm of the Sandhills.

DURHAM

Home of the Durham Bulls, that fabled AAA baseball team, this town has got it all: great breweries (looking at you Fullsteam and Ponysaurus) and cocktail lounges (like Bar Virgile), restaurants that run the gamut from sushi to reimagined tapas to Southern cuisine, Duke University's vibrant art and music scene, off-Broadway performances at DPAC, and the town's creative reuse of old tobacco factory architecture. Spend a weekend in Durham and you'll be ready to come back for a week.

CHARLOTTE

Can a city this big be a cool town? Absolutely. Each neighborhood feels distinct, there are loads of breweries, and dining options like Heirloom Restaurant showcase what's great about Charlotte food. Throw in NBA and NFL franchises, an amusement park, the U.S. National Whitewater Center, and a light-rail system that will carry you to just about every corner of the city, and you'll see Charlotte's got a lot.

impressive selection of bourbon. Retire to **The Carolina Inn,** where you'll find dinner and a bed for the night.

DAY 2

Raleigh, a short drive east from Chapel Hill, is home to the **North Carolina Museum of History, North Carolina Museum of Natural Sciences,** and **North Carolina Museum of Art.** The history and natural sciences museums are right across from the capitol downtown, perfect for a morning visit. Head to the Museum of Art, not far from downtown, for lunch at **Iris,** the museum's top-notch restaurant. Splurge and spend the night at **The Umstead Luxury Hotel and Spa,** a few minutes northwest of downtown Raleigh. Dine there or at one of the great restaurants downtown, like **Beasley's Chicken + Honey** or **The Fiction Kitchen.** Then make your way to **Raleigh Beer Garden** for an astounding array of beer.

DAY 3

Wake up early to hike or bike the miles of trails in **William B. Umstead State Park,** just outside the bustle of Raleigh. Drive 20 minutes northwest to Durham and take in some baseball, if the **Durham Bulls** are playing. Downtown, stroll the storied **Duke University** campus or shop the markets and boutiques before heading to **Fullsteam Brewery** to find distinctly Southern beers. Dinner downtown at **Mateo Bar de Tapas, Pizzeria Toro,** or **M Sushi** is in order.

DAY 4

Travel 1.5 hours northeast along U.S. 64 and I-95 to the historic town of **Halifax,** birthplace of the documents that inspired the Declaration of Independence. Visit the museum and colonial sites, then head south and east to the **Sylvan Heights Bird Park** in Scotland Neck. Continue south along U.S. 258 to U.S. 64 east, which you'll follow through wetlands and swamps until you reach the **Croatan Sound** and **Roanoke Island,** the gateway to the Outer Banks and North Carolina's coast. Check into a beachfront motel and get ready to put your toes in the sand.

North Carolina Museum of Natural Sciences

Duke University

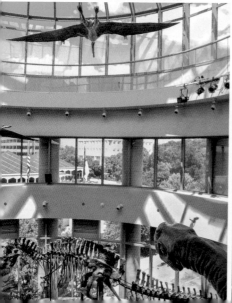

Cruise the Coast

North Carolina has more than 300 miles of coastline stretching from Virginia to South Carolina. You'll find storied lighthouses, pristine beaches, pirate havens, and places you won't want to leave.

DAY 1

In Nags Head, grab breakfast at **Sam & Omie's,** an Outer Banks institution, and head to the beach for a brisk morning walk. Brush the sand off your feet, then start traveling north, past the huge sand dune known as Jockey's Ridge and the Wright Brothers National Memorial. Stop in the village of Duck to shop at beach boutiques and enjoy lunch on the sound at **Aqua Restaurant and Spa.** Check in to **Sanderling Resort and Spa** before continuing north to Corolla for a **wild horse tour** and a glimpse at some of the Outer Banks' oldest residents: a herd of wild mustangs known as the Banker ponies. Farther north, climb to the top of **Currituck Beach Lighthouse,** then head back to the Sanderling for a dip in the ocean and dinner at **Kimball's Kitchen.**

DAY 2

Head south to visit the **Wright Brothers National Memorial.** Make a first flight of your own with a hang-gliding lesson at **Jockey's Ridge State Park,** or walk out on the dunes and watch others take to the sky. Head back across the sound to the north end of Roanoke Island and tour the **Elizabethan Gardens,** or catch a performance of *The Lost Colony,* a seasonal outdoor drama. Continue south to Manteo to dine on the waterfront and claim a room at one of Manteo's quaint bed-and-breakfasts.

DAY 3

Cross back onto the mainland and take U.S. 264 south along the Pamlico Sound and through haunting marshlands. Passing through small towns and the **Alligator River National Wildlife Refuge,** you'll be in a desolate but verdant landscape. As you near civilization again, head toward Kinston. Nearby, the legendary **Skylight Inn** serves some of the best barbecue in the state, and Kinston's **Chef & the Farmer** dishes up fine dining in this former tobacco town. After dinner, make the 1.5-hour drive to Wrightsville Beach. Take Highway 41 to I-40, and head to the shore. Check in at **Blockade Runner** and grab a bite at **EAST Oceanfront Dining** before taking an evening stroll on the beach.

DAY 4

Soak up some morning sun at sandy Wrightsville Beach before heading toward Wilmington. Grab lunch at **Sealevel City Gourmet** for vegan fare, or upscale pub grub at downtown's **Front Street Brewery** or a fat burger from **The Fork n Cork** before browsing at **Art in Bloom, New Elements Art Gallery,** or the other **boutiques** downtown. Grab a beer at **Flytrap Brewing, New Anthem Beer Project,** or **Cape Fear Wine and Beer** while you wait for dinner. And when it's time, be sure you made a reservation for **Seabird** or **Dram Yard** if you're looking for fine and fancy faire, or heading to a dog-friendly spot like **Mess Hall** for a burger with a side of barks.

DAY 5

Travel south along Highway 133 to **Southport** with a stop by **Brunswick Town and Fort Anderson,** the remains a colonial town and Civil War fort steeped in history. In Southport, head to the waterfront where the Cape Fear River and Intracoastal Waterway provide access to the Atlantic Ocean under the watchful eyes of a pair of lighthouses. Dine on piles of steamed shrimp at **Yacht Basin Provision Company,** wander the oak-lined streets, and stop by boutiques, antiques shops, and one of the **North Carolina Maritime Museums** before tucking into a memorable meal at **Ports of Call Bistro.**

Best Scenic Drives

Blue Ridge Parkway

Running more than 450 miles between Shenandoah National Park in Virginia and Great Smoky Mountains National Park in North Carolina, the Blue Ridge Parkway is the mother of all scenic roads. It covers more than 200 miles in North Carolina, from Lowgap at the state line to Cherokee in the Smokies, and passes by many major destinations in western North Carolina, including **Linville Falls, Mount Mitchell,** and the **Biltmore Estate.** There are great places to stay on and near the parkway.

Traveling the parkway from the North Carolina line to **Great Smoky Mountains National Park** in one day requires a pretty rigorous schedule. Plan at least two days to enjoy sights along the way. Traffic on the parkway is always slow—the maximum speed limit never exceeds 45 mph, and along many stretches driving that fast would be reckless. Traffic can be congested in summer, particularly on weekends, and during leaf season. In any season, drive slowly and be ready to hit the brakes. The twisty road can get incredibly foggy, and you never know when a deer or other beast will leap out of the trees.

Sections of the parkway sometimes close due to weather or other conditions. Snow and ice are considerations three seasons of the year; rockslides are also possible. To find out about current closures, contact the office of the National Park Service's **Blue Ridge Parkway** (828/298-0398, www.nps.gov/blri).

Down East on U.S. 70

U.S. 70 runs almost the entire length of North Carolina, from Asheville to Core Sound. The farthest-east section, a dogleg through Craven, Jones, and Carteret Counties, gives you a taste of life Down East. This is a great drive to take if you're staying in **New Bern** because you can pick up U.S.

viewpoint along the Blue Ridge Parkway

North Carolina is a big state with a varied geography. From the shores and swamps in the east to the foothills of the Blue Ridge Mountains and the cloud-veiled Smoky Mountains in the west, it's possible to find a patch of nature so teeming with wildlife that you'll think you're the first human to set foot there.

So, what can you see here? Wild horses, salamanders so big they seem surreal, elk, black bear, white squirrels, birds galore, lemurs and lions, sharks, sea turtles, and even red wolves.

WHERE TO SEE WILDLIFE

- **Great Smoky Mountains National Park** (page 442) is where you can see elk at the Oconaluftee Visitors Center and in Cataloochee Valley, spot bears along Newfound Gap Road and in Cades Cove, and watch the streams for hellbenders—salamanders of an unreal size.

- **Cape Lookout National Seashore** (page 121) is home to one herd of the famed Banker ponies—wild horses believed to have been shipwrecked here centuries ago that still roam the islands and marshes just offshore.

wild horses on the beach at the Outer Banks

- **Bald Head Island** (page 173) hosts spectacular year-round birding. It's also a great place to watch loggerhead sea turtles nest and even see a turtle nest hatch.

- **Alligator River National Wildlife Refuge** (page 85), a wild patch of coastal marsh and woods, is home to black bears, red wolves, and—you guessed it—alligators.

- **Kuralt Trail** (page 80) is a coastal bird-watching hot spot directly in the path of dozens of migratory birds.

- **Pettigrew State Park** (page 84) is where thousands of migratory waterfowl roost in the trees and crowd the waters, making for an astonishing sight.

WHERE TO GET EDUCATED

- **North Carolina Aquariums** on the Outer Banks (page 55), Crystal Coast (page 127), and Wilmington (page 167), are filled with tanks of sharks, alligators, salt and freshwater fish, and touch tanks where you can get a feel for some of the wildlife.

- **Duke Lemur Center** (page 218) at Duke University studies lemurs, and you can see several types and even interact with them here.

- **Carolina Tiger Rescue** (page 242), a rescue and rehab facility just outside of Raleigh, is a great place to learn more about big cats.

- **Karen Beasley Sea Turtle Rescue and Rehabilitation Center** (page 163) is where injured turtles come to get patched up and released. You can visit them while they convalesce, and, if the timing is right, see them returned to the wild.

- **North Carolina Zoo** (page 279), in the Piedmont, is a zoo that distinguishes itself in one big way: It's the world's largest natural habitat zoo, which means animals have plenty of room to explore.

70 here. Drive southeast through the **Croatan National Forest,** then east through seafood central—**Morehead City.** When you cross the bridge into the colonial port of **Beaufort,** leave U.S. 70 for a few blocks by turning right onto a side street. This takes you into historic downtown Beaufort and down to the waterfront along Front Street, where most of the attractions and 18th-century architecture are found.

From Beaufort, U.S. 70 winds up along **Core Sound** through fishing communities and marshes full of herons and egrets. Just past Stacy, you can either backtrack on U.S. 70 or proceed to the **Cedar Island National Wildlife Refuge** at the end of the peninsula and catch the Ocracoke Ferry at Cedar Island.

This drive is just over 70 miles. Driving quickly, it could be done in about 1.5 hours. But the point is to dawdle and enjoy the scenery and small towns, so it's more fun to set aside a whole day. It's an attractive drive any time of year, but old coastal cities like New Bern and Beaufort are most gorgeous in spring, especially in late March-early April when the azaleas are in bloom.

Cherohala Skyway

On the opposite end of the state, the Cherohala Skyway was built for beauty. For 43 miles between Robbinsville and the town of Tellico Plains, Tennessee, the road winds along the top of the **Smoky Mountains,** sometimes at elevations well over 5,000 feet. The vistas are incredible, and the road is legendary for motorcyclists and pleasure trippers. Avoid the route in wintry weather, and fill your gas tank and stomach before leaving; there are no facilities other than restrooms along the way. You'll feel like you're in the wilderness on top of the world.

The prettiest times for this drive are summer and fall, but the road is often extremely crowded during leaf season. The Cherohala Skyway website (www.cherohala.com) lists current road conditions.

Highway 12: A Serene Seascape

Highway 12 traces the **Outer Banks** from the mainland onto the barrier islands and all the way up to the Virginia border. It's a 160-mile trip that shows you nearly every square inch of the Banks.

Start at sea level (technically on U.S. 70, but a great place to start a beachside drive) and connect with Highway 12. Take the ferry at Cedar Island across to **Ocracoke,** home to one of the state's oldest lighthouses, and the place where pirate Blackbeard held an epic party before losing his head, literally, in a nearby inlet. Continue through scenery that's surreally beautiful and serene. Another ferry takes you to the village of Hatteras at the southern end of Hatteras Island, part of the **Cape Hatteras National Seashore.** This landscape is desolate and beautiful, although you'll find tiny villages along with a legion of surfers and kite-surfers. Crossing Oregon Inlet, you're approaching the touristed section of the Outer Banks and stellar options for food and lodging. You'll travel from Whalebone Junction into Nags Head and the dunes of **Jockey's Ridge,** then on to **Kill Devil Hills,** where the Wright Brothers took their first flight, and the towns of **Duck** and **Corolla,** where the paved highway ends. If you're adventurous and have a four-wheel-drive vehicle and beach driving experience, head north a few miles toward the Virginia border. A herd of wild horses (and not much else) lives here.

The Outer Banks

This series of islands traces a path along the northeastern coast some 125 miles long. You'll find lighthouses and pirate lore, wild horses, stretches of untamed shore, and enough beach to go around.

From the Virginia border in the north to Ocracoke Island in the south, The Outer Banks stand guard against the incessant grind of wind and wave and the powerful force of a single storm. As barrier islands, it's their job to protect the mainland, marshlands, and towns of the Inner Banks from a storm's brunt. As they do so, a centuries-old inlet may be filled in a night and a new channel opened a hundred yards away. In 2012, Hatteras Island was cut off from the rest of the Outer Banks as Hurricane Sandy washed out Highway 12—the only

Highlights

Look for ★ to find recommended sights, activities, dining, and lodging.

★ **Wright Brothers National Memorial:** See where North Carolina earned the slogan "First in Flight" and view a replica of the famed *Wright Flyer* (page 39).

★ **Wild Horse Tours:** See wild horses in the dunes, along the shore, and even swimming in the surf along the northernmost portion of the Outer Banks (page 43).

★ **Fort Raleigh National Historic Site:** See where the Lost Colony, the first English settlement in the New World, mysteriously disappeared in the 1580s (page 53).

★ **Cape Hatteras Lighthouse:** Climb to the top of this iconic lighthouse (page 63).

★ **Ocracoke Island:** On this remote island, you'll find a historic village home to one of the country's most unique communities, along with the waters where Blackbeard met his fate and one of the oldest lighthouses in the nation (page 70).

★ **Somerset Place Historic Site:** The graceful architecture and impressive setting of this early plantation contrast with the tragic history of its involvement in the enslavement of people (page 84).

★ **Pettigrew State Park:** Lake Phelps, the park's centerpiece, is an attractive enigma, a body of shallow water with a deep history (page 84).

★ **Mattamuskeet National Wildlife Refuge:** This dramatic waterscape that attracts tens of thousands of migratory birds (page 87).

The Outer Banks

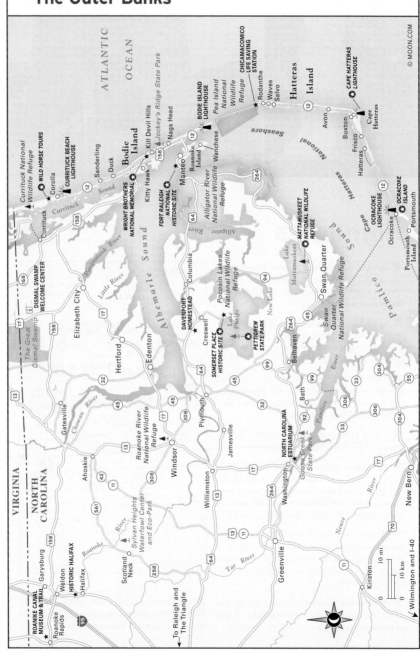

© MOON.COM

road to follow the length of the Banks—and damaged bridges, filling roadways with several feet of sand and changing, once more, the face of the Outer Banks.

Between the Outer Banks and the mainland in the Inner Banks is a collection of sounds known as the Albemarle-Pamlico Estuary. Many travelers ignore the sounds, giving them little more than a glance as they cross on a bridge or a ferry, but they play a crucial role in the region. The Albemarle-Pamlico Estuary is the second-largest estuarine system in the country after Chesapeake Bay to the north, and it includes Albemarle, Pamlico, Core, Croatan, Roanoke, and Currituck Sounds. Covering more than 3,000 square miles, the sounds drain more than 30,000 square miles and provide diverse marine and terrestrial environments that shelter essential plant and animal life. The vast and beautiful marshlands and wide, shallow sounds protect the mainland from storm surges and the Atlantic Ocean from toxins and sediment, all the while providing nursery grounds to countless fish and bird species.

Sheltered from the Atlantic, the Inner Banks are a much more accommodating (ecologically speaking) and familiar landscape than the Outer Banks. Along the marshes and wetlands, hundreds of thousands of migratory birds shelter and rest on their annual journeys, while pocosins (a kind of bog) and maritime forests have nurtured innumerable generations of animals and people. This is where you'll find North Carolina's oldest colonial towns—Bath, New Bern, and Edenton. Settlers established their roots here, and the towns have survived for more than 300 years. In Washington County, a rural expanse of farms and wetlands, 4,000-year-old canoes pulled out of Lake Phelps stand witness to the region's unplumbed depths of history. Rivers flow from farther inland, with towns like Roanoke Rapids and Halifax that played a vital role in North Carolina's history and development from colony to state.

PLANNING YOUR TIME

Most visitors plan to come to the coast during late spring and summer, and the reasons are obvious: the beaches, restaurants, and attractions that are only open in season as well as numerous warm-weather festivals and goings-on. However, don't overlook midspring and early fall. During the fall, the water is still warm, most of the restaurants and attractions are still open, and the crowds are smaller. Perhaps surprisingly, winter is picking up in popularity too. To many, the solitude offered by a winter beach is hard to beat.

Agriculture affects eastern North Carolina in a unique way. In fall, the area's second-busiest season, the tobacco harvest fills the nostrils of visitors. In rural areas, trucks laden with huge yellow-green tobacco leaves head for the curing barns. The smell of curing tobacco, and later the tight bales of golden leaves, is like none other, and once you smell it, you'll have a taste for fall in this part of the state. Early autumn also brings intermittent clouds of smoke as farmers and backyard-garden hobbyists clear their summer gardens and prepare the ground for cool-weather crops. Beds of lettuce and onions and patches of mustard greens and collards begin to appear alongside houses. Cotton comes in late in the year; as the bolls ripen, the fields appear snow-covered and quite beautiful.

Water sports should also be considered when planning your trip. Spring and fall, and even the occasional winter warm spell, offer many ideal days for exploring eastern North Carolina's rivers, creeks, and swamps in a kayak, canoe, or stand-up paddleboard. In the fall, mild temperatures are comfortable enough for a day of paddling, and though the foliage is still green, the absence of summer's leafiness means you can see deeper into the landscape and spy on wildlife from a safe distance. Keep in mind, though, that you can see alligators or even snakes in late fall and throughout the winter.

Previous: fishing along the shore of Cape Hatteras; Virginia Dare statue in the Elizabethan Gardens; the entrance to Cape Hatteras Lighthouse.

Pronunciation Primer

North Carolina is full of oddly pronounced place-names, and the far northeast corner is a good place to pause for a lesson in talking like a native. The Outer Banks are a garland of peculiar names as well as names that look straightforward but are in fact pronounced in unexpectedly quirky ways. If you make reference publicly to the town of **Corolla** and pronounce it like the Toyota, you'll be recognized right away as someone "from off." It's pronounced "ker-AH-luh." Similarly, **Bodie Island,** site of the striped lighthouse, is pronounced "body." That same pattern of pronouncing *o* as *ah* is repeated farther down the coast at **Chicamacomico,** which comes out "chick-uh-muh-CAH-muh-co." But just to keep you on your toes, the rule doesn't apply to **Ocracoke,** which is pronounced like the Southern vegetable and the soft drink: "O-kra-coke."

Farther south along the banks is the town of **Rodanthe,** pronounced "ro-DAN-thee." On Roanoke Island, **Manteo** might resemble a Spanish word but is in fact front-loaded, like so many Carolina words and names. It's pronounced "MAN-tee-oh" or "MAN-nee-oh." Next door is the town of **Wanchese,** pronounced like a pallid dairy product, "WAN-cheese." Inland, the **Cashie River** is pronounced "cuh-SHY," **Bertie County** is "ber-TEE," and **Chowan County** is "chuh-WAHN."

While fall can be ideal to visit the coast, remember that autumn is peak hurricane season in North Carolina. Surfers may love the waves before and after storms, but even people with lots of experience avoid hurricanes. These storms can be beautiful in their ferocity and violence, but anyone who's been through even a weak hurricane will tell you they're no joke. About a week before a fall visit, check the long-term forecasts and call to confirm the weather where you're staying. If authorities issue evacuation orders during your visit, don't hesitate; just pack up and head to safety on the mainland.

INFORMATION AND SERVICES

The **Aycock Brown Welcome Center** (Milepost 1, Kitty Hawk, 877/629-4386, www.outerbanks.org, 9am-5pm daily, closed Thanksgiving Day and Dec. 25) at Kitty Hawk and the **Sarah Owens Welcome Center** (1 Visitors Center Circle, Manteo, 252/473-2138 or 877/629-4386, www.outerbanks.org, 9am-5pm daily, closed Thanksgiving Day and Dec. 25) are the main welcome centers in the Outer Banks, with smaller welcome centers at Hatteras and Whalebone Junction (RV drivers take note, there's a dump station available

24 hours daily at the Sarah Owens welcome center).

Major hospitals include **The Outer Banks Hospital** (Milepost 14, 4800 S. Croatan Hwy., Nags Head, 252/449-4500, www.theouterbankshospital.com) in Nags Head, **Sentara Albemarle Medical Center** (1144 N. Road St., Elizabeth City, 252/335-0531, www.sentara.com) in Elizabeth City, **Vidant Roanoke-Chowan Hospital** (500 S. Academy St., Ahoskie, 252/209-3000, www.vidanthealth.com) in Ahoskie, **Vidant Chowan Hospital** (211 Virginia Rd., Edenton, 252/482-8451, www.vidanthealth.com) in Edenton, **Vidant Beaufort Hospital** (628 E. 12th St., Washington, 252/975-4100, www.vidanthealth.com) in Washington, **Vidant Bertie Hospital** (1403 S. King St., Windsor, 252/794-6600, www.vidanthealth.com) in Windsor, and **Vidant North Hospital** (250 Smith Church Rd., Roanoke Rapids, 252/535-8011, www.vidanthealth.com) in Roanoke Rapids. On Ocracoke, which is only accessible by air or water, nonemergency medical situations can be addressed by **Ocracoke Health Center** (305 Back Rd., Ocracoke, 252/928-1511, www.ocracokeisland.com). Note that 911 emergency service is available on Ocracoke, as it is throughout the state.

Nags Head and Vicinity

Coral reefs anchor most barrier islands, lending them a bit of strength and permanence; not so on North Carolina's Outer Banks. Here, no reef helps shape the islands, and they're more like enormous sandbars, susceptible to the whims of the wind, the sea, and storms. But that's part of their beauty. These natural forces shape the land as well as its history and culture.

Jockey's Ridge, a 100-foot-high dune visible far out to sea, has been used as a navigational aide for hundreds of years. Legend has it that Nags Head earned its name because of these dunes and the passing ships. Islanders known as proggers (a shipwreck scavenger or land pirate) would lead a nag or mule along the beach and dune ridge with a lantern hung around its neck, luring ships into the shallows and shoals where they'd wreck, making their cargo easy pickings. Likewise, the shoals, shallows, and currents gave birth to the heroic members of the United States Lifesaving Service, predecessor to the Coast Guard, who braved many storms to save those shipwrecked.

The relentless wind on the Outer Banks lured Orville and Wilbur Wright to Kill Devil Hills, where they became the first people in history to take flight. It also drew Francis Rogallo, a NASA engineer and the inventor of hang gliding. Today, thousands flock to the Wright Brothers Memorial to see where history was made, and even more visit Jockey's Ridge to watch hang gliders or even to take to the sky themselves. With kite-flying, kiteboarding, skydiving, parasailing, and even paragliding, flight enthusiasts love the Outer Banks. Add to this sailing, diving, surfing, paddling, hiking, bird-watching, and, of course, visits to beaches like Duck, which is lovely at sunset, and Corolla, where you can spot wild ponies, and it's obvious that the northern Outer Banks are among the most promising areas in North Carolina for outdoor adventure.

SIGHTS
★ Wright Brothers National Memorial

In 1903, Orville and Wilbur Wright changed the world in just 12 seconds. Their first flight was short, but it was the culmination of more than three years of failed designs, tests, and travels between their Dayton, Ohio, home and Kitty Hawk, North Carolina, where they tested their gliders on Kill Devil Hill, then the tallest dune on the Outer Banks. A number of Banker families fed and housed them, built them hangars, and assisted with countless trial runs. On the morning of December 17, 1903, several local people were on hand to help that famous first powered flight get into the air. John Daniels, a lifesaver from a nearby station, took the iconic photo of the airplane lifting off. It was the only photograph he ever took. He was later quoted in a newspaper saying of the flight, "I didn't think it amounted to much." Even though he was unimpressed, the feat is honored at the **Wright Brothers National Memorial** (Milepost 7.5, U.S. 158, 1000 N. Croatan Hwy., Kill Devil Hills, 252/473-2111, www.nps.gov, tickets www.recreation.gov, park and visitors center 9am-5pm daily year-round, $10 over age 15, free under age 16). Replica gliders, artifacts from the original flight, and tools the Wright brothers used are on display. In the adjacent field a wooden runner and stone markers show their runway, takeoff point, and the spots where their first four flights landed. Climb nearby Kill Devil Hill to see the 60-foot monument honoring their achievement and marking the spot where they launched hundreds of gliders that preceded that first powered flight. At the foot of the hill, a life-size bronze sculpture of the *Wright Flyer* seconds after liftoff lets you get a sense of the excitement of the moment.

Jockey's Ridge State Park

Jockey's Ridge State Park (Milepost 12,

U.S. 158, 300 W. Carolista Dr., Nags Head, 252/441-7132, http://ncparks.gov, park 8am-6pm daily Nov.-Feb., 8am-8pm daily Mar., Apr., and Oct., 8am-9pm daily May-Sept., visitors center 9am-5pm daily Nov.-Feb., 9am-6pm daily Mar.-Oct.), contains 420 acres of recreational opportunities in an array of environments. With the big dune, which shifts between 80 and 100 feet high, the smaller dunes surrounding it, the maritime forest, and the sound, you can sand-board (think snow-boarding at the beach), fly kites, hike, go for a swim, or even learn to hang glide. Another resource is www.jockeysridgestatepark.com, a site operated by Friends of Jockey's Ridge State Park, where you'll find a few additional notices of outings and activities.

Nags Head Woods Ecological Preserve

Adjacent to Jockey's Ridge, the Nature Conservancy maintains the 1,111-acre **Nags Head Woods Ecological Preserve** (701 W. Ocean Acres Dr., 1 mile from Milepost 9.5 on U.S. 158, 252/441-2525, www.nature.org, dawn-dusk daily year-round). The landscape includes deciduous maritime forest, dunes, wetlands, and interdune ponds, providing a compact look at the diverse environments found on the Outer Banks. It's a bird-watcher's paradise, as more than 50 species nest here in season. Ruby-throated hummingbirds, green herons, and red-shouldered hawks are among the easiest to spot, but don't just look for winged wildlife; a number of land animals and reptiles and even some unusual plants call this place home. Five miles of public trails wind through the property, starting at the visitors center. Dogs are welcome on several trails, provided they are on leash.

Kitty Hawk Woods Coastal Reserve

Kitty Hawk Woods Coastal Reserve (trail access from Woods Rd. and Birch Lane, off Treasure St., south of U.S. 158, Kitty Hawk, 252/261-8891, www.deq.nc.gov, dawn-dusk daily year-round), a 1,824-acre nature

Nags Head and Vicinity

To Duck, Corolla, and Currituck
National Wildlife Refuge
12

WRIGHT MEMORIAL BRIDGE — 158

CYPRUS
MOON INN ●

Currituck
Sound

AYCOCK BROWN
WELCOME CENTER [i]

● OCEAN BOULEVARD

SEA SCAPE ⛳
GOLF LINKS

ATLANTIC OCEAN

BYP 158

Kitty Hawk   BAD ▼
                BEAN

W KITTY

— MILE POST 4

Kitty Hawk Woods
Coastal Reserve   HAWK RD

▼ GROWLERS
  TO GO

▼ TRIO

Kitty Hawk Bay

CHIP'S WINE
& BEER ▼
MARKET

— MILE POST 6
— AVALON PIER

Kill   ● DRIFTIN' SANDS
Devil   MOTEL
Hills 12

WRIGHT BROTHERS
NATIONAL MEMORIAL

— MILE POST 8

COLINGTON   RD

Colington   COLINGTON
             CREEK INN

● CYPRESS
  HOUSE INN

SHUTTERS
ON THE BEACH

OUTER BANKS ▼
BREWING STATION

▼ BRONZER SHACK
— MILE POST 9

Albemarle

Nags Head
Woods ▲
Ecological
Preserve

● ATLANTIC
  STREET INN

Sound

— MILE POST 10

▼ MAMA KWAN'S
  GRILL & TIKI BAR

BUFFALO CITY ▼
JUG SHOP

Nags Head   ▼ TORTUGA'S LIE

BYP 158   — NAGS HEAD
           FISHING PIER

0   1 mi
US 158/S. CROATAN HWY
(THE BYPASS)   — MILE POST 12

0   1 km
NC 12/VIRGINIA DARE TR   ● LUCKY 12
(BEACH ROAD)

Jockey's Ridge
State Park

OUTER BANKS
DIVE CENTER/
▼ KITTY HAWK
  KITES

© MOON.COM

preserve maintained by the North Carolina Coastal Reserve, contains one of the largest remaining maritime forests in the Outer Banks. Maritime forests help barrier islands absorb the brunt of powerful storms, and Kitty Hawk Woods contains unusual examples of maritime swale ecosystems, swampy forest sheltered between coastal ridges. Hiking and birding opportunities are abundant, and exploring it from the water via canoe, kayak, or stand-up paddleboard is easy thanks to a put-in. Hunting is permitted in Kitty Hawk Woods, so exercise caution while hiking or paddling during the spring and fall hunting seasons.

Jennette's Pier

My family vacationed on the Outer Banks for years, and **Jennette's Pier** (Milepost 16.5, 7223 S. Virginia Dare Trail, Nags Head, 252/255-1501, www.ncaquariums.com, 9am-5pm daily Dec.-Mar., 7am-9pm Apr. and Nov., 6am-10pm May-Oct., fishing $14 adults, $7 children, walk-on $2 adults, $1 under age 13) was a fixture on each trip. The then-wooden pier, originally built in 1939, was picturesque but fragile; the owners repaired it after each storm until 2003, when the North Carolina Aquariums bought the pier and Hurricane Isabel demolished 540 feet of the pier structure. Many thought it was the end of the beachside institution, but a friend of mine—Chip Hemingway of Bowman Murray Hemingway Architects—designed a new 1,000-foot concrete pier. The LEED Platinum-certified facility is beautiful and will stand to serve countless vacationing families. The North Carolina Aquarium manages Jennette's Pier as an educational and recreational platform, and activities in peak season include summer day camps and nighttime seashore expeditions that teach kids and adults about the ecology of the area.

Currituck Heritage Park

We've come to expect grand, ostentatious beachside homes, but on the shore of Currituck Sound, you'll find what may be the original one on the Outer Banks: the **Whalehead Club** (1100 Club Rd., Corolla, 252/453-9040, www.whaleheadclub.org, tours 10am-4pm Mon.-Sat. year-round, $7 adults, $5 seniors and ages 6-12, free under age 6). This art deco home was built in the 1920s as a summer cottage for Edward Collings Knight Jr., an industrialist whose wealth was made in railroads and sugar. The beautiful, simple yellow house is the centerpiece of **Currituck Heritage Park,** where visitors can picnic, wade, launch from the boat ramp, or learn about the ghosts (yes, it's rumored to be haunted, and it's no wonder, with so many shipwrecks just off shore).

Next to the Whalehead Club is the **Outer Banks Center for Wildlife Education** (1160 Village Lane, Corolla, 252/453-0221, www.nc-wildlife.org, 9am-4:30pm Mon.-Fri.). Exhibits focus on native birds, fish, and other creatures in Currituck Sound as well as a huge collection of antique decoys. These decoys represent an important folk-art tradition and way of life for many along the Carolina coast. They're beautiful not just for their design but also for their utility. Naturalists put on a number of nature and art programs throughout the year; check the calendar on the website before you go.

A favorite spot here is the **Currituck Beach Lighthouse** (1101 Corolla Village Rd., 252/453-4939, www.obcinc.org, 9am-5pm daily Mar.-Nov., 9am-8pm Wed.-Thurs. Memorial Day-Labor Day, $10, free under age 8) and its grounds. Built in 1875, this 158-foot-tall redbrick lighthouse is open to ascend much of the year. As you climb the 214 steps to the top, think about the lighthouse keepers, who for years carried pails of lard and then later kerosene to the top to fuel the light. Once at the observation deck, take a moment to catch your breath and take in the scenery (and hold on to your hat; it can be windy). The Currituck light is a twin to the Bodie Island Lighthouse, 32 miles south. Upon its completion it lit the last "dark spot" on the North Carolina coast, making for safer navigation.

Corolla Wild Horse Museum

In the town of Corolla you'll find a museum dedicated to some of the more unexpected residents of the Outer Banks. The **Corolla Wild Horse Museum** (520 B Old Stoney Rd., Corolla, 252/453-8002, www.corollawild-horses.com, 10am-4pm Mon.-Fri. and 10am-4pm Sat.-Sun.) tells the history of the herd of horses that has lived on the Outer Banks from Corolla to Cape Lookout since the 1600s. The Corolla herd now lives in a preserve north of

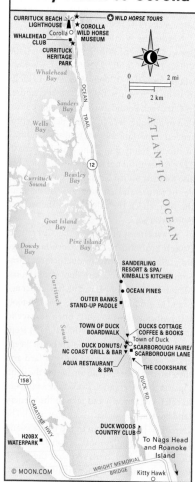

Kitty Hawk to Corolla

CURRITUCK BEACH
LIGHTHOUSE
WHALEHEAD
CLUB
CURRITUCK
HERITAGE
PARK
*Whalehead
Bay*

WILD HORSE TOURS
COROLLA
Corolla WILD HORSE
MUSEUM

*Sanders
Bay*

*Wells
Bay*

OCEAN TRAIL

0   2 mi

0   2 km

12

*Currituck
Sound*

*Beasley
Bay*

ATLANTIC OCEAN

*Goat Island
Bay*

*Dowdy
Bay*

*Pine Island
Bay*

SANDERLING
RESORT & SPA/
KIMBALL'S KITCHEN

OCEAN PINES

Currituck Sound

OUTER BANKS
STAND-UP PADDLE

TOWN OF DUCK
BOARDWALK

DUCKS COTTAGE
COFFEE & BOOKS
Town of Duck
SCARBOROUGH FAIRE/
SCARBOROUGH LANE

DUCK DONUTS/
NC COAST GRILL & BAR

AQUA RESTAURANT
& SPA

THE COOKSHARK

DUCK RD.

158

CARATOKE HWY.

DUCK WOODS
COUNTRY CLUB

To Nags Head
and Roanoke
Island

H2OBX
WATERPARK

© MOON.COM

WRIGHT MEMORIAL
BRIDGE   Kitty Hawk

the town, and several guides offer tours to see the horses in their native habitat.

SPORTS AND RECREATION

Beaches

Beaches along the Outer Banks are easily accessible. Highway 12, which many call the "Road to Nowhere," is the main, and usually the only, route to travel, though in a few places where the barrier islands widen enough

to warrant it, you'll find a beachfront road as well as one skirting the sound. The Outer Banks is divided into several smaller beach towns and communities. From the north the towns are Corolla, Duck, Southern Shores, Kitty Hawk, Kill Devil Hills, and Nags Head. South of Nags Head you have Whalebone Junction and the Oregon Inlet, then Hatteras Island and its collection of towns. Just west of Nags Head and Whalebone Junction is Roanoke Island, where two towns—Manteo and Wanchese—make up the population centers.

Though these towns abut one another in a seamless transition of beachiness, each has a different character. Corolla is still a little wild, which is fitting, as Highway 12 terminates here (though you can drive to the Virginia border in a 4WD vehicle, provided you have some knowledge of driving in sand and have a plan of what to do once you arrive at our northern neighbor), and a herd of wild horses known as Banker ponies calls the marshes, dunes, and scrubby forests here home. Duck has grown up since my family stayed here, and it has now become a shopping destination. Kitty Hawk, Kill Devil Hills, and Nags Head have row upon row of homes marching from the sea to the sound; it's here that you'll find much of the commercial activity—shops for beach towels, fudge, and taffy; bars and restaurants; and grocery stores.

The beaches can be separated into three categories: wild, sparse, and blanket-to-blanket. Corolla is the wild beach, where you'll get a real sense of isolation (save the occasional wild horse tour). Along Duck, Southern Shores, and the southern reaches of Nags Head (minus the area around Jennette's Pier), the crowds are thinner, and you can spread out for a leisurely day on the shore. Starting in Kitty Hawk and running south through Kill Devil Hills to Nags Head, you find the blanket-to-blanket area. The beaches here are significantly more populated than those at Duck, and you'll find pockets of beachgoers near public access points, piers, and the like.

Kayaking and Stand-Up Paddleboarding

The Outer Banks combines two very different paddle-sport opportunities, kayaking and stand-up paddleboarding (SUP), in two very different environments—the challenge of ocean paddling and even surfing, and the leisurely drifting tours of salt marshes and creeks. **Kitty Hawk Kites** (Milepost 12.5, 3925 S. Croatan Hwy./U.S. 158, Nags Head, 877/395-8447, www.kittyhawk.com, kayak tours $30-55, SUP lessons $65) has 10 locations up and down the Outer Banks offering kayak tours, SUP lessons and rentals, and a range of other recreational activities—like dolphin cruises ($15-35) as well as kayak fishing ($275 for 1 angler, $225 pp for 2, $200 pp for 3, $175 pp for 4) and a crabbing and fishing excursion (from $299 for a 2-hour trip, from $499 for a 6-hour trip), among others—and equipment. *National Geographic Adventure* magazine called them one of the "best adventure travel companies on earth," and it has been in business since the early 1990s.

Kitty Hawk Kayak & Surf School (Milepost 1, 6150 N. Croatan Hwy./U.S. 158, Kitty Hawk, 252/261-0145, www.khkss.com, tours $40-55, kayak rentals from $69 per week, SUP rentals from $150 per week) teaches kayaking and SUP, rents equipment for paddling and surfing, and leads group and private tours, including overnighters. Many of the tours take you to seldom-seen marsh habitats and gorgeous creeks, or even back to the mainland to explore the waterways of the Alligator River National Wildlife Refuge.

Coastal Kayak Touring Company (reservations at North Beach Outfitters, 1240 Duck Rd., Duck, 252/441-3393, www.outerbankskayaktours.com, kayak tours $35-70, SUP tours $70) leads groups through some of the beautiful nature reserves on the Outer Banks, namely Kitty Hawk Woods Coastal Reserve and the Pine Island Audubon Sanctuary, but one of the coolest they offer is back on the mainland in the Alligator River

National Wildlife Refuge. Tours range 1.5-3 hours.

Outer Banks Paddleboard (1578 Duck Rd., Duck, 252/371-1661, www.outerbanks-paddleboard.com, lessons $65, ecotour $65, night lighted tour $79, rentals from $59 per day) helps beginners find their footing and love this sport, and gives practiced paddlers an idea of the ecology and environment around the Outer Banks while you paddle. Their light-up nighttime paddle—where the boards are lit from beneath—is a one-of-a-kind activity.

★ Wild Horse Tours

You can hike in any park and most of the preserves on the Outer Banks, but nothing compares to seeing the wild horses—affectionately called Banker ponies—in Corolla. The Banker ponies are descended from Spanish Mustangs. Legend says those mustangs were shipwrecked here, which makes sense given all the wrecks, but no one really knows. **Wild Horse Adventure Tours** (610 Currituck Clubhouse Dr., Corolla, 252/489-2020, www.wildhorsetour.com, from $60) will take you out onto the beach in search of the famed Banker ponies, and you'll ride in style in their custom-built open-top Hummer. For the best chance of spotting the horses, and maybe some dolphins, book the sunrise tour (it's early, but totally worth it) or the one nearest sunset, when the horses are active in the dunes and maybe even the surf. Another tour operator, **Corolla Wild Horse Tours** (1159 Austin St., Corolla, 252/453-0877, www.outerbankstours.com, 8am-8pm daily, $55 over age 12, $50 seniors and military, $35 ages 3-12, $35 infants—car seat required), also runs excursions searching for the horses.

Hiking

At **Jockey's Ridge State Park** (Milepost 12, U.S. 158, 252/441-7132, http://ncparks.gov, park 8am-9pm daily May-Sept., 8am-7pm daily Oct., 8am-6pm daily Nov.-Feb.,

8am-8pm daily Mar.-Apr., visitors center 9am-6pm daily Mar.-Oct., 9am-5pm daily Nov.-Feb.), explore the dunes freely or follow one of the trails. The Soundside Nature Trail is about one mile long and takes you through maritime thickets and grassy dunes on a walk through a seldom-seen part of the park. Follow the Tracks in the Sand trail on its 1.5-mile course early in the morning to see animal tracks left during the night. Remember, the sand can be downright hot, especially during summer. Bring sunscreen, shoes, and plenty of water if you're trekking around this park.

The **Currituck Banks National Estuarine Preserve** (Hwy. 12, 877/623-6748, www.nccoastalreserve.net) protects some 1,000 acres of woods and water, extending far out into Currituck Sound. A short boardwalk runs from the parking lot to the sound, and a primitive trail runs 1.5 miles through the maritime forest.

Surfing

North Carolina has a reputation for having some of the best waves on the East Coast, making this a top destination for experienced surfers and those new to the sport.

Kitty Hawk Kites (Milepost 12.5, S. Croatan Hwy./U.S. 158, Nags Head, 252/449-2210, www.kittyhawk.com) provides lessons and board rentals. **Farmdog Surf School** (2500 S. Virginia Dare Trail, Nags Head, 252/255-2233, http://farmdogsurfschool. com, lessons from $75, surfboard and paddleboard rentals from $75 per week) has lessons and gear rentals, and they have a service to set up your beach cabana (from $650 per week) and beach umbrella and chair (from $299 per week). **Corolla Surf Shop** (807 Ocean Trail, Corolla, 252/453-9283, www.corollasurfshop. com, lessons from $70, rentals from $25 per day) also offers lessons, rentals, and advice, and has kiteboarding lessons ($275).

If you're a veteran surfer and you're bringing your own board, several online resources will help you find the best conditions and the perfect breaks. The websites **OBXLiveSurf**

(www.obxlivesurf.com), **Surfline** (www. surfline.com), and **SwellInfo** (www.swell-info.com) describe the best places to suit up and drop in.

Hang Gliding

With all the wind on the Outer Banks, everyone thinks about flying a kite, but how about flying a hang glider? **Kitty Hawk Kites** (Milepost 12.5, S. Croatan Hwy./U.S. 158, Nags Head, 252/251-4341, www.kittyhawk. com, $109) offers hang gliding lessons that will give you a taste of the thrill of flight as you lift off over the face of dunes on Jockey's Ridge. More than 300,000 people have learned to hang glide here since the company's Hang Gliding Training Center opened in 1974. You can also up the thrill factor and try a tandem flight that will have you and an instructor towed up to a mile high before being released to fly back to earth. If you want to pursue advanced certification through the U.S. Hang Gliding Association, you can do that on the dunes or on a tandem flight; you can even buy a glider and all the accessories you need to get started at the Kitty Hawk Kites retail store across the road from the school.

Fishing Piers

The Outer Banks is home to three classic wooden fishing piers and one stunning concrete pier that's carrying on the long-held traditions of its wooden brethren. I have an affinity for Jennette's Pier, the 1,000-foot concrete pier in Nags Head, but there's something elegant to the way the wooden piers weather over the years. Barnacles appear on their lower legs; the wood shrinks and cracks, and turns gray; the handrail warp and the whole deck grows curvy or rises and falls; and you can feel every wave push and pull as they race to shore. The odd beauty of the things aside, they're here because the fishing is outstanding on the Outer Banks and it's somehow better

---

1: Wild horses roam freely on the sand dunes of the Outer Banks. **2:** Wright Brothers National Memorial by sculptor Stephen Smith **3:** sunrise over Jennette's Pier **4:** the shore in Nags Head

out on the pier, but if you just want to go hang out, you're welcome to.

The northernmost pier is **Avalon Pier** (Milepost 6, Kill Devil Hills, 252/441-7494, www.avalonpier.com, 5am-2am daily summer, 6am-10pm daily fall-spring, fishing day rate $12 adults, $6 under age 13, 3-day pass $33, 7-day pass $69), a 696-foot pier where they carry tackle and bait as well as the usual pier assortment of arcade games, souvenir shorts and shirts, and snacks. Next is **Nags Head Fishing Pier** (Milepost 11.5, 3335 S. Virginia Dare Trail, Nags Head, 252/441-5141, www.nagsheadpier.com, 5am-midnight daily, day pass $14 adults, $7.50 under age 13, 3-day pass $39, 7-day pass $84, sightseeing $2) stretches out 750 feet to where folks gather to try to catch the biggest fish; in the pier house they have a tiki bar and restaurant serving sandwiches and such, and a decently outfitted tackle shop.

Next is **Jennette's Pier** (Milepost 16.5, 7223 S. Virginia Dare Trail, Nags Head, 252/255-1501, www.ncaquariums.com, fishing $14 adults, $7 under age 13, sightseers, $2 adults, $1 under age 13), a 1,000-foot long concrete pier that replaced the wooden version that stood here until hurricanes rendered it unusable; there's a North Carolina Aquarium outpost here and their staff offers classes and activities throughout the year in addition to the fishing you can do. Then **Outer Banks Fishing Pier** (Milepost 18.5, 8901 S. Old Oregon Inlet Rd., Nags Head, 252/441-5740, www.fishingunlimited.net, 24 hours daily, $10 adults, $5 under age 13, 3-day passes $25, 7-day passes $50), which is just about as far south as you can go and still be in Nags Head, reaches 600 feet over the Atlantic to give anglers a shot at hooking a big one.

Water Park

H2OBX Waterpark (8526 Caratoke Hwy., Powells Point, 252/491-3000, www.hwobxwaterpark.com, 10am-7pm daily late-May-early-Sept., $42 adults, $30 seniors and children under 42 inches tall, discounts for online ticket purchases) is on the mainland just 12 minutes from Kitty Hawk, and it's packed with more than 30 watery attractions—splash pads, waterslides, a Flowrider, a wave pool, and more—for the daring and those who just want to bob around in the pool. Family rides using giant rafts, lighting-quick racing slides, and even a watery obstacle course deliver a day's worth of fun.

ENTERTAINMENT AND EVENTS

My favorite spot for wine and beer on the Outer Banks is **Trio** (Milepost 4.5, 3708 N. Croatan Hwy., 252/261-0277, www.obxtrio.com, 11am-9pm Mon.-Sat., $6-25), a name that refers to wine, beer, and cheese, the passions of the four owners. The selection here encompasses a wide range of wine and beer styles, nations and regions, and grape varietals. Tastings include the Trio Passport (focusing on wine from different nations) as well as varietal- and style-specific tastings. Nearly two dozen beers are on tap, and self-serve wine vending stations give you the chance to try tasting-size samples or even full glasses of expensive, hard-to-find, or interesting wines. Trio serves a selection of small plates, including paninis, salads, cheese plates, and other nibbles that go well with a glass of whatever you're drinking.

I like being able to stop in a place and sample some new beers. Maybe they're local brews, maybe it's a curated selection from afar; it makes no difference to me. The selection at **Buffalo City Jug Shop** (1900 S. Croatan Hwy., Suite B, Kill Devil Hills, 252/255-2347, www.buffalocitybeer.com, 2pm-8pm Mon.-Tues., noon-9pm Wed.-Sat.), the first growler shop on the beach, is great whether you're getting a pint or some cans to go. They've got 24 rotating taps, a crowler machine (it fills enormous can-like crowlers and is pretty cool to watch), and a staff who knows their suds. In Duck and Kitty Hawk, **Growlers to Go** (3723 N. Croatan Hwy., Kitty Hawk; 1187 Duck Rd., Duck, www.craftbeerobx.com, 11am-7pm daily, hours vary in winter) has an enormous selection on draft and in bottles and cans. The

Kitty Hawk location is larger and has more taps and cans to go, so if you're looking for something the Duck location doesn't have, head south and check the selection there.

Food Festivals

As food-centered travel has gained momentum, four festivals taking advantage of this trend have emerged on the Outer Banks. Each draws visitors during the shoulder seasons and showcases something different about the area and its cuisine.

In March, **Taste of the Beach** (www.obx-tasteofthebeach.com) features wine tastings, cooking classes by local chefs, cook-offs, dine-arounds, and more, hosted by more than 50 restaurants, breweries, wine shops, and food purveyors on the Banks. The four-day festival culminates with the OBX Grand Tasting, where restaurants compete for the best overall dish, best local seafood dish, Chefs Award, and People's Choice Award. *Coastal Living* magazine named Taste of the Beach one of the top seafood and wine festivals in the country in 2008, and it has been on the list ever since.

The **Duck and Wine Festival** (www.duckandwine.com), a one-day cook-off held in mid-late April, brings foodies together in the town of Duck to sample dishes that local chefs have created using, you guessed it, duck. The town shines again in mid-October for the one-day **Duck Jazz Festival** (www.townofduck.com), which features talented national jazz artists and alfresco dining from some of Duck's best restaurants.

Mid-October is also the time for the **Outer Banks Seafood Festival** (www.outerbanksseafoodfestival.org). Although oyster roasts, shrimparoos, and other informal seafood celebrations have been the norm on the Outer Banks for more than a century, 2012 was the first year for this formal seafood festival. More than a dozen restaurants participate in the one-day event, and organizers plan to grow the festival into a marquee event.

Nightlife

Part beach dive bar, part sports bar, **Lucky 12** (Milepost 12, 3308 S. Virginia Dare Trail/Hwy. 12, Nags Head, 252/255-5825, www.lucky12tavern.com, 11:30am-2am daily, $8-28) is a hit with locals and visitors alike. With 20 beers on tap, another 90 in bottles or cans, a staggering 40-martini drink menu, and more than a dozen TVs, it's perfect to watch a game, hang out with friends, and order a pizza or, better yet, the burger (served until 2am).

Fish Heads Bar & Grill (Milepost 18.5, 8901 S. Old Oregon Inlet Rd., Nags Head, 252/441-5740, www.fishheadsobx.com, 11am-9pm daily, $7-14) never closes, and since it's at the Outer Banks Fishing Pier, it makes sense that a snack and a cold beer go well with all-night fishing. They have a small food menu—sandwiches, tacos, a few salads, some good appetizers—and an incredible beer selection of around 30 brews, many from North Carolina. Throw in live music just about every night during summer and most nights in the off-season, the crash of waves, and a pier to explore, and you've got a recipe for a fun evening.

Ocean Boulevard Bistro & Martini Bar (Milepost 2.5, 4700 N. Virginia Dare Trail, Kitty Hawk, 252/261-2546, www.obbistro.com, 5pm-late daily, entrées $21-34), an upscale but casual martini bar and bistro, features live music Friday-Saturday during the season, and with the impressive drink menu, it's easy to see why the place is popular with locals and visitors. If you're looking for an excellent spot to stop by after a late round of golf, this is it.

A weird-in-the-best-way place to grab a drink and listen to some music is **Bonzer Shack Bar & Grill** (1200 S. Virginia Dare Trail, Kill Devil Hills, 252/480-1010, www.bonzershack.com, 11:30am-10pm Wed.-Sat. and 11:30am-9pm Sun., $9-15). They call themselves a surf shack hangout, and that's just about right. Music nearly every night (two shows: afternoon and late night), a decent beer selection, and some boozy cocktails add to the atmosphere, but it's the people—a collection of characters you'll tell stories about later—that make it special.

SHOPPING

Much of the shopping on the Outer Banks is focused on souvenir T-shirts or beach supplies such as towels, boogie boards, and rash guards. These mass-market beachwear clearing houses are so prolific that they're easy to find. There are also some boutiques carrying bathing suits, art, and jewelry, though most of the shopping (not of the overly touristy variety) is found in towns like Duck, to the north, and Hatteras, to the south.

Kitty Hawk Kites (Milepost 12.5, 3925 S. Croatan Hwy., Nags Head, 252/251-4314, www.kittyhawk.com, call for hours) carries swimwear and beach supplies as well as kites, toys, and an assortment of beach games and sports equipment; they have 10 shops on the Outer Banks, so you're never far from one. **Birthday Suits** (Milepost 10, 2000 S. Croatan Hwy., Kill Devil Hills, 252/441-5338, http://birthday-suits.com, 10am-6pm daily) has been in the business of outfitting Bankers and visitors in the best bathing suits for more than 25 years. They have two other locations on the Outer Banks: in Duck (1171 Duck Rd., Duck, 252/261-7297) at Scarborough Lane Shops, and in Corolla (801 Ocean Trail, Monterey Plaza, Corolla, 252/453-4862).

In Duck, **The Town of Duck Boardwalk** (www.townofduck.com) follows the Albemarle Sound for nearly a mile, passing countless scenic spots and cool shops. The Duck Merchants Association (www.DoDuckNC.com) provides a map and list of shops. Shops along this stretch run quite a range. You can grab fresh seafood or a ready-to-cook steamer pot at a **Dockside 'N Duck Seafood Market** (Wee Winks Square, 1216 Duck Rd., 252/261-8687, www.docksideduckseafood.com, 10am-6pm Mon.-Sat.), pick up doughnuts at the fantastic **Duck Donuts** (Osprey Landing Shops, 1190 Duck Rd., 252/480-3304, www.duckdonuts.com, 7am-1pm daily), and pick up a handcrafted gift at **SeaDragon Gallery** (Waterfront Shops, 1240 Duck Rd., 252/261-4224, www.

seadragongallery.com, 10am-9pm Mon.-Fri., 10am-7pm Sat., 10am-5pm Sun. summer, hours vary in shoulder seasons and winter).

One of those spots on the map is **Scarborough Faire** (1177 Duck Rd., Duck, 540/272-0975, www.scarboroughfaireinducknc.com, 1am-8pm Mon.-Sat., 1pm-5pm Sun.), which has served the boutique shopping needs of visitors and residents for more than 30 years. More than a dozen shops call Scarborough Faire home, including **Island Bookstore** (252/261-8981, www.islandbooksobx.com, 9am-9pm daily, hours vary in winter), which carries a good selection of best-sellers and books for kids and teens; **The Island Attic** (252/489-1919, www.theislandattic.com, 10:30am-4:30pm Tues.-Sat.), a shop with assorted gifts and goods from around the world; and **Treehouse Coffee** (252/722-3606, www.treehousecoffeenc.com, 8am-1pm Wed.-Sat., 8am-noon Sun., $6.50-15) where you'll get a great coffee drink and a fantastic breakfast (seriously, show up early or you'll wait for an hour to get your biscuit).

Next door is **Scarborough Lane** (1171 Duck Rd., 757/222-9411, hours vary by store), a collection of shops and eateries including **Flip Flop Shops** (252/441-1757, www.flipflopshops.com, 10am-4pm daily), which sells summer footwear; and **Duck Pizza Company** (252/255-0099, www.duckpizza.com, 11:30am-9pm Tues.-Sun., $10-25), which revamped the pizza menu and has some great pies on offer.

Duck's Cottage Coffee & Books (Waterfront Shops, 1240 Duck Rd., 252/261-5510, www.duckscottage.com, 7am-6pm daily) lives up to its name as you'll find both books and coffee in this cute little cottage in Duck. In all seriousness, they serve a fine cup of coffee and have bags of ground and whole-bean (including their sought-after Coconut Crunch) coffee available. And the bookstore has an excellent selection. In the mornings it's busy with folks out for their first cup and a copy of the paper to peruse.

FOOD

When I first started visiting the Outer Banks, it seemed that every other restaurant was a seafood buffet. Today, buffets still abound, but a number of notable independent restaurants have taken root. The selection varies from gourmet to down-home, including pizza and burgers along with barbecue, fine dining, and a decent representation of international cuisines.

One of my current favorite spots for a bite is ★ **Bad Bean Baja Grill** (4146 N. Croatan Hwy., Kitty Hawk, 252/261-1300, www.badbeanobx.com, 11am-8pm Tues.-Sat., $4-16), where they serve Latin-inspired food and use local seafood in all their tacos and burritos. The fish taco and pork belly taco are excellent choices, as long as you start with some chips (spring for the dip sampler; the roasted tomato and habanero salsa gets two thumbs up, but it's hot). The burritos are great (try the shrimp or the roasted sweet potato and onion burrito), but before you decide, have a look at the specials menu, there may be a top 10 dish hiding there.

Single Fin Thai and Sushi (2424 S. Croatan Hwy., Nags Head, 252/715-3983, www.singlefinobx.com, 11:30am-9pm Mon.-Thurs., 11:30am-9:30pm Fri.-Sun., $12-24) has a number of Thai dishes, a few Chinese plates, and some general pan-Asian bites on the menu, but, honestly, I've never looked past the sushi menu, and it's fantastic start to finish. Local fish means every bite is super fresh.

★ **Mama Kwan's Grill and Tiki Bar** (1701 S. Croatan Hwy., Kill Devil Hills, 252/441-7889, www.mamakwans.com, 11:30am-8:30pm daily, $9-24) serves killer fish tacos (especially the jerk-seasoned ones), but their sashimi tuna appetizer is fantastic. A little divey, always delicious, Mama Kwan's is a fun spot to stop for a bite.

Sam & Omie's (7728 S. Virginia Dare Trail, Nags Head, 252/441-7366, www.samandomies.net, 8am-9pm Thurs.-Tues., $4.25-38) opened in the summer of 1937 as a place for charter fishing customers and guides to catch breakfast before heading out to sea. They still serve a hearty breakfast heavy on the classics—two eggs your way, pancakes, grits, and the like—but take a look at the specialties, such as crab benedict or the chef's special. Sam & Omie's also serves lunch and dinner, and, as you may expect, both menus emphasize seafood. Sure, you can get a burger, steak, or chicken breast, but why would you when you can get a clam dog?

The **Outer Banks Brewing Station** (Milepost 8.5, 600 S. Croatan Hwy., Kill Devil Hills, 252/449-2739, www.obbrewing.com, 11:30am-2am Mon.-Fri., 11am-1pm Sat., 11am-midnight Sun., entrées $15-31) is an innovative and interesting spot to eat, not just because the food presses beyond expected seafood and the beers are adventurous, but because they're wind-powered. A group of friends who met in the Peace Corps combined their love of food, beer, and sustainability to create a hot spot on the Outer Banks' dining and nightlife scenes.

AQUA Restaurant and Spa (1174 Duck Rd., Duck, 252/261-9700, www.aquaobx.com, 11:30am-2pm and 4:30pm-8:30pm daily, $18-32) has an interesting concept, with a day spa upstairs and an excellent restaurant downstairs, creating flavorful food using community-sourced organic ingredients that will, as the owner puts it, "nourish your body and spirit." Grab a table by the windows or on the deck (weather permitting) and enjoy views of the sound while you dine. The food is a fusion of regional dishes and international flavors and techniques. The *fruits de mer* pasta is Italian in nature but uses all fresh and local seafood. Their seared duck breast uses local ducks (when possible) and seasonal produce. Dishes like the fish-and-chips, shrimp or fish tacos, and crab cakes are—you guessed it—caught nearby.

In Duck you'll also find **NC Coast Bar & Grill** (1184 Duck Rd., Duck, 252/261-8666, www.nccoastobx.com, lunch 11:30am-2:30pm Tues.-Sun., dinner 4pm-9pm daily, $11-37). Reserve a seat on their deck overlooking Pamlico Sound and dine on a steam pot full of shrimp, crab, and clams; get the pasta with scallops, shrimp, and lobster; go for duck with a Thai chili glaze, or a delicious vegetarian coconut curry bowl.

You can grab a slice of pizza, a burger, or a sandwich at many places in Duck, but I'd be remiss if I didn't mention a restaurant that serves one of my favorite foods of all times: chicken tenders. I know chicken tendies seem like a thing only kids love, but that's wrong, as adults love them too; one bite of the all-white-meat tenders from **The Cookshak Fried Chicken** (Loblolly Pines Shops, 1187 Duck Rd., Duck, 252/261-1156, www.thecookshakfriedchicken.com, 11:30am-8:30pm daily, $10-25) and you'll be convinced these are the best tenders ever. They also have regular fried chicken (up to a whole bird served with slaw and mac-and-cheese) and fries, and a second location in **Nags Head** (2515 S. Croatan Hwy., Unit A, Nags Head, 255/441-1156) if you're down that way and notice you're dangerously low on tenders.

Blue Moon Beach Grill (4104 S. Virginia Dare Trail, Nags Head, 252/261-2583, www.bluemoonbeachgrill.com, $10-30) has a fantastic lunch and a dinner that stands up to almost any place on the Outer Banks. Fish-and-chips, fish tacos, fried oysters, bucatini loaded with shrimp and scallops and veggies, and salads topped with blackened shrimp (or not, your call) are favorites among my crew.

Basnight's Lone Cedar Café (7623 S. Virginia Dare Trail on the Nags Head-Manteo Causeway, 252/441-5405, www.lonecedarcafe.com, dinner 4:30pm-9pm daily, brunch 11am-3pm Sun., dinner $14-32, brunch $8-14) is a water-view bistro that specializes in local food—oysters from Hyde and Dare Counties, fresh-caught local fish, and North Carolina chicken, pork, and vegetables. It's one of the most popular restaurants on the Outer Banks, and they don't take reservations, so be sure to arrive early. The full bar is open until midnight.

To satisfy your sweet tooth, visit one of the many locations of **Duck Donuts** (Osprey Landing Shops, 1190 Duck Rd., 252/480-3304, www.duckdonuts.com, 7am-1pm daily). My friend who lives on the Outer Banks calls eating them "a rite of passage," and I have to agree; these things are tasty, like carnival fritters, but made more delicious by the salt air. If you want something cold and sweet, try **Surfin' Spoon** (3408 S. Virginia Dare Trail, Nags Head, 252/441-7873, www.surfinspoon.com, noon-11pm Mon.-Sat.), a frozen yogurt bar where you fill a bowl with your chosen flavor and then pile it high with toppings (cookies, candy, sprinkles, fruit, gummy bears—you get the picture). The owners—pro surfer Jesse Hines and his wife, Whitney—go out of their way to make Surfin' Spoon an experience through surf movies, a game room, and tons of surf photos on the walls.

There is one more place to grab a bite that you should know about, but it requires a couple of caveats. First, it's in a Quick Stop gas station. Second, their biscuits are a thing of beauty. Third, if you're easily offended, just get in line and don't avert your eyes. That's almost all you need to know about **Biscuits N' Porn** (2122 S. Croatan Hwy., Nags Head, 252/441-6446, 6am-9pm Sun.-Thurs., 6am-10pm Fri.-Sat., $1.50-8), except that their biscuits are great and they do indeed have a whole magazine rack full of *those* kinds of magazines. I like a plain biscuit (with some butter and honey or jam) and a ham, egg, and cheese biscuit, but friends swear by the biscuits and gravy, the fried chicken, and their cheeseburger.

ACCOMMODATIONS

Depending on the Outer Banks experience you want, you have a choice of where to stay. Hatteras Island (in the next section) offers the least busy, most remote stay; the beach towns from Nags Head to Southern Shores put you in or near the thick of shopping, restaurants, and the beach; and staying in Duck or farther north offers a slower pace and a less busy beach experience (there are no public beach access in Duck, only private entrances from homes and neighborhoods, but you'll always have a way to the beach if you're staying here). If you want to stay in Duck, rental homes are always a good option, but so are the condos at Ocean Pines (1445 Duck Rd., Duck, reservations 855/978-3777 office 252/255-0459, www.oceanpinesresort.com, from $217). Ocean Pines has 1- and 2-bedroom suites, a bevy of resort amenities (pool, tennis court, play area for kids), private beach access, and a walking, jogging, and cycling path that leads north to Duck and south to Southern Shores and the rest of the Outer Banks.

If you're looking for that classic beach-motel feel, you've come to the right place, the Outer Banks has several. Keep in mind, these are motels built to serve travelers of 50 to 70 years ago, so they're smaller, and you might have issues finding enough outlets to keep all of your electronics plugged in at once. But there's a trade-off: these spots are charming, historic, family-owned, and often pet-friendly. The bargain Sea Foam Motel (7111 S. Virginia Dare Trail, Nags Head, 252/441-7320, www.seafoam.com, $68-149) is a no-frills motel with so much wood paneling and throwback charm it's on the National Register of Historic Places. There are pet-friendly rooms here and a pool. At Driftin' Sands Motel (109 N. Virginia Dare Trail, Kill Devil Hills, 252/715-4100, www.driftin-sandsmotel.com, winter from $69, summer from $129), you'll step back in time as soon as you see the sign with its proper, but now antiquated, cursive script; they're pet friendly, convenient to the ocean and to Avalon Pier, and the price is right.

The ★ First Colony Inn (6715 S. Croatan Hwy., Nags Head, 855/207-2262, www.first-colonyinn.com, $99-364) is a beautiful little 1932 beachfront hotel. This regional landmark has won historic preservation and landscaping awards for its 1988 renovation, which involved moving the entire building, in three pieces, three miles south of its original location. Of the 27 guest rooms, all are exceedingly comfortable and give guests a taste of luxury accommodations at an affordable rate.

In Duck, the ★ Sanderling Resort and Spa (1461 Duck Rd., Duck, 855/412-7866, www.sanderling-resort.com, $200-790) is a mainstay for luxury travel on the Outer Banks. A 2013 renovation—totaling more than $6 million—added more guest rooms and an adults-only pool, upgraded public spaces, and gave the resort's dining options a real boost. In 2015, they continued their quest for the ultimate guest experience and added 28 new rooms ranging from suites with unobstructed ocean and sound views to queen rooms with ocean views. Sanderling has a renowned spa and one of the best restaurants on the Outer Banks, ★ Kimball's Kitchen (entrées $24-40). Kimball's serves a menu centered around local seafood and grass-fed steaks, but the view of the sound from the dining room is unparalleled. The view, when combined with the food and level of service, makes Kimball's Kitchen a spectacular dining experience.

There are many bed-and-breakfasts, including the Cypress Moon Inn (1206 Harbor Court, Kitty Hawk, 252/262-2731, www.cypressmooninn.com, no children, $135-210), a small but beautiful sound-side home featuring three guest rooms. The owners also have three cottages nearby that are perfect for secluded getaways.

The Cypress House Inn (Milepost 8, Beach Rd., 500 N. Virginia Dare Trail, Kill Devil Hills, 252/441-6127, www.cypresshouse-inn.com, from $179) is only 125 yards from the ocean, and that, combined with its central location and undeniable charm, makes it a desirable B&B. Guests staying in each of the six guest rooms at the 1940s-style inn are treated to complimentary beach chairs and towels. The Atlantic Street Inn (Milepost 9.5, 205 E. Atlantic St., Kill Devil Hills, 252/305-0246, www.atlanticstreetinn.com, $69-159) offers similar treatment, with bicycles available for guest use; reserve its six guest rooms individually or, if you book far enough ahead, reserve the entire inn or the nearby beach house. One thing you'll find at Atlantic Street that most other accommodations are lacking: a lawn. Their backyard is a lovely spot to relax and spend some time outside, but in the shade.

The Colington Creek Inn (1293

Colington Rd., Kill Devil Hills, 252/449-4124, www.colingtoncreekinn.com, no children or pets, $200-365) has four guest rooms and a standalone cottage, all with water views of the sound and its namesake creek, along with porches perfect for morning coffee or an evening drink. Perched on a little patch of land and nearly surrounded by water, you'll have beautiful views wherever you are in the house.

In Nags Head, the **Oasis Suites Hotel** (7721 S. Virginia Dare Trail, Nags Head Causeway, 252/441-5211, www.oasissuites. com, $200-375) features 17 all-suite rooms with waterfront views, private balconies, full kitchens, saltwater pool, and a number of ADA Accessible rooms. In the mornings, grab a quick cup of coffee and head to the waterside gazebo for one of those incredible Outer Banks sunrises.

Big rooms, plenty of oceanfront balconies, and two pools are some of what makes **Shutters on the Banks** (405 S. Virginia Dare Trail, Kill Devil Hills, 252/441-5581 or 800/848-3728, www.shuttersonthebanks.com, from $209) a great stay. This 86-room hotel has 8 suites and easy access to one of the wider spots on the beach. It's always clean, the folks are always friendly, and from your room you can take in the sunrise and watch for dolphins without even getting out of your pj's.

Vacation Rentals

Many groups—families, bridal parties, bachelor parties, anglers, surfers—who need a place with plenty of space turn to rental homes, and on the Outer Banks there are a number of rental agencies to choose from. **Seaside Vacations** (3620 N. Croatan Hwy., Kitty Hawk, 252/261-5500 or 800/395-2525, www. outerbanksvacations.com) rents houses in every little town from Corolla to Nags Head and has a large selection of sizes, styles, locations (oceanfront, ocean view, sound-side), and prices in their catalog of homes. **KEES Vacations** (101 Pan Ridge Court, Suite A, Point Harbor, 866/316-1843, www.keesouterbanks.com) has more than 300 homes and rentals in their portfolio and have homes in

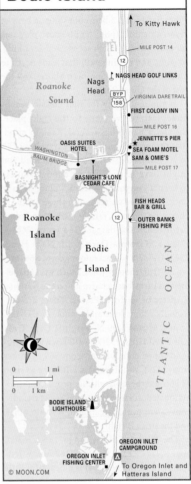

every town from the Virginia state line to Ocracoke Island. **Outer Banks Blue** (3732 N. Croatan Hwy., Kitty Hawk, 252/255-1220 or 888/623-2583, www.outerbanksblue.com) has 250 properties in their growing portfolio, including plenty of options with pools, private beach accesses, family-friendly homes, and more. And at **Carolina Designs Realty & Vacation Rentals** (1197 Duck Rd., Duck, 252/261-3934 or 800/368-3825, www.

carolinadesigns.com) they use that local insight to help vacationers find the right property for their trip.

GETTING THERE AND AROUND

The closest major airport is **Norfolk International Airport** (ORF, 2200 Norview Ave., Norfolk, VA, 757/857-3351, www.norfolkairport.com), approximately 1 hour from the northern Outer Banks. **Raleigh-Durham**

International Airport (RDU, 2400 John Brantley Blvd., Morrisville, 919/840-2123, www.rdu.com) is 3-5 hours' drive from most Outer Banks destinations.

Only two bridges exist between the mainland and the northern Outer Banks. U.S. 64/264 crosses over Roanoke Island to Whalebone, just south of Nags Head. Not too far north of there, U.S. 158 crosses from Point Harbor to Southern Shores. Highway 12 is the main road all along the Outer Banks.

Roanoke Island

In the 1580s, the first nonnative residents of the Outer Banks, and perhaps their most famous denizens, moved in. These intrepid English colonists found Roanoke Island—protected from the brunt of storms by the Albemarle, Roanoke, and Croatan Sounds and the mass of Bodie Island—a fine place to call home. They established Fort Raleigh, and there, Virginia Dare, the first European born on the new continent, came into the world. Shortly thereafter, the community vanished, earning the name many now know them by: The Lost Colony. Where they went and the specifics of how and when they met their collective fate is unknown to this day, but one that's explored in the aptly named outdoor drama, *The Lost Colony*.

Visitors to Roanoke Island today will find what the colonists found: a beautiful, welcoming island ripe for exploration. The relative abundance of bed-and-breakfasts, restaurants, and shops make staying on Roanoke Island much easier than it was four centuries ago. At the northern end of Roanoke Island, Fort Raleigh National Historic Site marks the last known location of the Lost Colony, and the nearby town of Manteo offers a day or two of dining and distractions. Most of the island's offerings for visitors are concentrated here. It's a short and beautiful 15-minute drive across the causeway in Nags Head to Manteo.

★ FORT RALEIGH NATIONAL HISTORIC SITE

Fort Raleigh National Historic Site (1401 National Park Dr., Manteo, 252/473-2111, www.nps.gov/fora, grounds 24 hours daily, visitors center 9am-5pm daily, closed Dec. 25, free) includes much of the original site of the first English settlement in the New World. Archaeologists still conduct digs here, regularly unearthing new artifacts and assembling clues about the Lost Colony's fate, but sections of the earthworks associated with the original 1580s fort remain and have been preserved, making it easy to imagine the site as a working fort on the frontier of an unknown land. In the visitors center, artifacts and interactive displays tell the story of the fort, the missing colonists, and the freedman's colony—a colony of freed and displaced enslaved people established on the island during the Civil War. Two nature trails in the park allow you to explore the natural landscape and the site of a Civil War battle. Within the National Historic Site, two of Manteo's most famous attractions operate autonomously.

Elizabethan Gardens

Nearly 60 years ago, **Elizabethan Gardens** (1411 National Park Dr., Manteo, 252/473-3234, http://elizabethangardens.org, 10am-3pm daily Jan., 9am-5pm daily Mar. and Oct.,

Roanoke Island

9am-6pm Apr.-Sept., 9am-4pm Nov., 11am-4pm and 6pm-9pm Dec., closed Feb., $10 adults, $7 ages 6-17, $3 under age 6, $3 pets) was conceived by the Garden Club of North Carolina as a permanent memorial to the settlers of Roanoke Island. As a tribute, they planted the types of gardens and plants that would have been common in the colonists' native England in the 16th century. There are many corners to explore in this 10.5-acre garden and many treasures, both natural and artificial, to discover: an ancient live oak so huge that many believe it has been standing since the colonists' days; a sunken garden containing Renaissance-era statuary; an impressive display of camellias and azaleas; and a 19th-century statue of Virginia Dare. The statue was underwater off the coast of Spain for two years, was salvaged, and made it to Massachusetts, where it was nearly lost in a fire. It finally arrived in North Carolina in the 1920s, where modest residents, shocked by the statue's nudity, passed it around the state for years until it found a permanent home in Elizabethan Gardens.

The Lost Colony

Also within the park is the Waterside Theatre. North Carolina has a long history of outdoor performances celebrating regional heritage and history, and the best-known of these is Roanoke Island's *The Lost Colony* (1409 National Park Dr., Manteo, 252/473-6000, http://thelostcolony.org, $25-40 adults, $22-37 seniors and military, half price ages 6-12, free under age 6). Playwright Paul Green was commissioned to write a drama about the colony in 1937 to celebrate the 350th anniversary of the birth of Virginia Dare. What he thought would be a single-season production has turned into a fixture, with performances every year since, except when extraordinary circumstances, like German U-boats prowling off the coast during World War II, interrupted the production schedule. An impressive list of actors has performed in the play, including Andy Griffith and current director Ira David Wood III.

© MOON.COM

OTHER SIGHTS

The Roanoke Island Maritime Museum (104 Fernando St., Manteo, 252/475-1750, www.manteonc.gov, 8:30am-5pm Mon.-Fri., free) is a unique working boat shop and repository for artifacts that offers a look at local and regional maritime heritage. Traditional boat builders offer classes in boat building and handling at the George Washington Creef Boathouse, but visitors not enrolled in the classes are still welcome to come and observe. Also on the grounds is the Roanoke Marshes Lighthouse. The large lighthouses protecting the outer Atlantic coast are well known, but a number of smaller river and marsh lighthouses also once dotted the coast. This structure is a reconstruction of the square cottage-style lighthouse that was decommissioned in 1955.

Both the Maritime Museum and the Marshes Lighthouse are part of Roanoke Island Festival Park (1 Festival Park, Manteo, 252/475-1500, www.roanokeisland. com, 9am-5pm daily Mar.-Dec., $11 adults, $8 ages 3-17, free under age 3, tickets good for two days), which has a lot to offer. The living history museum portion of the park features costumed interpreters demonstrating skills (blacksmithing, carpentry, maybe basketry or weaving) showing what colonists' lives were like when they arrived. The highlight for many is the *Elizabeth II*, a ship built to represent one of the seven English merchant vessels from the voyage of 1585. A staff of sailors is onboard in costume to show visitors a bit about living and working on such a ship.

Island Farm (1140 U.S. 64, Manteo, 252/473-6500, www.obcinc.org, 9am-3pm Tues.-Fri. Apr.-late-Nov., closed Thanksgiving Day, $10 adults, free under age 3) is a living-history site that transports you back to a Roanoke Island farm circa 1850. Reproduction outbuildings include the smokehouse, cookhouse, and quarters for enslaved people alongside the original farmhouse, built between 1845 and 1850. Period interpreters lead tours and talks that focus on gardening, cooking, and other day-to-day doings on a farm in the pre-Civil War Outer Banks. Take a look at one of the most surprising things on the Outer Banks—their windmill. These were common sights all over the Outer Banks until the late 1800s. If you're lucky you might also be able to see one of the Banker ponies that lives here as part of an outreach and education program.

The North Carolina Aquarium on Roanoke Island (374 Airport Rd., Manteo, 252/475-2300, www.ncaquariums.com, 9am-5pm daily year-round, closed Thanksgiving Day and Dec. 25, $13 adults, $12 seniors and military, $11 ages 3-12, free under age 3) is one of three state aquariums on the North Carolina coast. A great place for kids, the aquarium is home to all sorts of marine fauna and tells the aquatic story of North Carolina from the deep sea to freshwater tributaries. See river otters, alligators, freshwater fish, sharks, and more in traditional and touch-tank aquariums. Don't miss the daily dive shows in the huge 285,000-gallon Graveyard of the Atlantic tank. Displays in the aquarium detail the U.S. Lifesaving Service, and outside is the grave of Richard Etheridge, the first African American to captain a Lifesaving Station on Pea Island, just south of the Bodie Island Lighthouse.

SPORTS AND RECREATION

Roanoke Island Outfitters and Dive Center (627 U.S. 64, Manteo, 252/473-1356, www.roanokeislandoutfittersanddivecenter. com, 10am-5:30pm Mon.-Fri., 10am-3pm Sat.) offers scuba diving classes (from $100) and courses in everything from spearfishing and freediving to advanced and specialist scuba courses and more ($175-800). There's also a snorkeling expedition to explore a shipwreck ($49); the ship sits 20 feet down and is loaded with crabs and fish, so if you're a diver or want to give it a try, this is a fantastic thing to do.

Spearfishing is just one way to catch a big one on the Outer Banks. On Roanoke Island it's easy to catch fish with a rod and a reel, thanks to a number of inshore and offshore charters that are available year-round. **The Outer Banks Visitors Bureau** (www.outer-banks.org) has a comprehensive list of charter operators and rates.

Fishing is a critical industry on the Outer Banks whether you're talking about commercial fishing and shrimping or charter boats taking folks out to catch a few. In Wanchese you can get a closer look at the commercial side with a pair of trips unlike anything I've seen. **OBX Crabbing & Shrimping Charters** (4457 Mill Landing Rd., Wanchese, 252/423-0421, www.obxcrabbing.com, 4-hour crabbing and shrimping trip $600, 3-hour shrimping $500, 2-hour crabbing $300) and **Hallie M Charters** (4457 Mill Landing Rd., Wanchese, www.halliemcharters.com, 3.5-hour shrimping trips $480) will take you out on a shrimp boat and teach you to trawl. Well, at least they'll show you how it works and let you help haul in the nets and sort the catch. On both trips, anything you catch of legal limit and in season, you get to keep, and you're likely to come away with a cooler full of shrimp, crabs, and maybe even a few fish. Since shrimp are pretty abundant in the sound, you don't have to go out onto the ocean on either of these trips.

TOURS

The *Downeast Rover* (sails from Manteo waterfront, 252/473-4866, www.downeastrover.com, daytime sails $45 adults, sunset cruises $60) is a 55-foot reproduction of a 19th-century schooner. Cruises last two hours; departure times vary. If you sail with the Rover, be sure to bring something to eat and drink (even alcohol, but be sensible, especially if you've never sailed before) and make your sunset sail something special.

The gardens and quaint waterfronts on Roanoke Island are charming for adult visitors, but there's a good bit for kids to do too. On **Captain Johnny's Outer Banks Dolphin Tours** (400 Queen Elizabeth Ave., Manteo, 252/473-1475, www.outerbankscruises.com, daytime cruises $30 adults, $20 ages 2-12, $10 under18 months, sunset

cruises $35 adults, $25 ages 2-18, $10 under 18 months), you'll get up close to bottlenose dolphins in their native habitat and watch as they swim, leap, and sometimes even inspect the boat on each tour. Cruises last two hours and depart five times daily, at 8:30am, 10:30am, 1:30pm, 3:30pm, and 2 hours prior to sunset. You can also charter the whole boat for $800 during the day or $1,300 for a private sunset sail.

Stroll the streets of Manteo with a real pirate (adult talk: it's not a real pirate) on an **OBX Pirate Walk** (meeting place varies, 252/305-2976, www.obxwalkingtours.com, $25 over age 12, $18 ages 4-12, free under age 4) hearing some true stories, some tall tales, and some things that fall in between. At the end there's a round or two of Treasure Trivia where your pirate guide shares their riches. This one might not exactly be for the kids, but the pirate folks also run an **Outer Banks Ghost Tour** ($25 over age 12, $20 ages 6-12, free under age 6) in Manteo where they reveal, among other spooky things, why the Outer Banks is the most haunted stretch of beach in all of America. And if you're a Wright Brothers superfan, a real history aficionado, or need to do some research on the birth of aviation, the pirate and ghost folks can take you on a **First in Flight Walking Tour** ($25 over age 12, $20 ages 4-12, free under age 4) at the Wright Brothers National Memorial (you'll need to buy your own entry ticket).

If you don't mind a scare, take a 90-minute stroll through Manteo with **Ghost Tours of the OBX** (399 Queen Elizabeth Ave., at Budleigh St., Manteo, 252/573-1450, www.ghosttoursoftheobx.com, $40 adults, $10 ages 6-12). Visit the village cemetery, look for the ghosts of pirates and lost sailors along the shore and waterfront, and learn about supernatural creatures in the surrounding woods on one of three chilling but kid-friendly tours. They also offer a tour of homes,

1: Elizabethan Gardens 2: soft shell crab sandwich at O'Neal's SeaHarvest 3: Manteo's Roanoke Island Inn 4: Waterside Theatre at the Fort Raleigh National Historic Site

a pirate-focused tour, and a tour centered around adult beverages.

BREWERIES AND DISTILLERIES

The **Lost Colony Brewery & Cafe** (208 Queen Elizabeth St., 252/473-6666, www.lost-colonybrewery.com, 11am-9pm Thurs.-Sun., $10-30) dishes up crab cakes, fish-and-chips, fried oysters, and a fried seafood platter that you may need a friend to help you eat. In addition, they have burgers, po' boys, and barbecue sandwiches. Their beers—they brew eight—include an imperial stout, a red ale, and an IPA; order a flight and find your favorite.

If that's not enough to lift your spirits, pay a visit to **Outer Banks Distilling** (510 Budleigh St., Manteo, 252/423-3011, www.out-erbanksdistilling.com, noon-9pm Thurs.-Sat.) for some Kill Devil Rum. They only make rum here, and it's great. You can get silver and aged rums, rums infused with pecans or named after different shipwrecks, spiced dark and light rum, and a rum that benefits local charities (a portion of each bottle purchase goes into the charity pot). Stop by for a tasting or a couple of rum cocktails, or just dash in, buy a bottle, and head on your merry way.

In May, the **Outer Banks Bluegrass Island Festival** (www.bluegrassisland.com, single-day $55, three-day pass $110) sees Roanoke Island Festival Park transformed into a bluegrass bonanza. Three days of music, from acts like Rhonda Vincent & the Rage, Seldom Scene, and The SteelDrivers, as well as a fantastic location, have made this into a premier event on the Outer Banks.

ENTERTAINMENT AND EVENTS

Roanoke Island is a pretty tame place, with most of the events and activities of a family-oriented nature. To that end, on the first Friday of the month April-November, the town of Manteo celebrates **First Friday** (6pm-8pm 1st Fri. Apr.-Nov.) a free downtown festival that brings locals and visitors out for live music, street performers, and more. In addition to live music on the streets, many restaurants and shops feature their own musical acts, sales, and refreshments. The **Dare County Arts Council Gallery** (300 Queen Elizabeth Ave., Manteo, 252/473-5558, www.darearts.org, 10am-5pm Tues.-Fri., 10am-4pm Sat.) has lovely exhibits by local artists and hosts a reception during First Friday that showcases a new exhibit by a local or regional artist.

SHOPPING

Roanoke Island is small but has its fair share of shopping. The **Manteo Downtown Market** (104 Fernando St., 252/473-4040, 8am-noon Sat.) brings a number of makers, artisans, and craftspeople together at George Washington Creef Park for a morning of mingling, haggling, and going home happy. **Silver Bonsai Jewelry & Art Gallery** (905 U.S. 64, Manteo, 252/475-1413, www.silverbonsai.com, call for hours) has a gorgeous selection of jewelry and a great collection of fine and functional artwork. The **Phoenix Shops** (Budleigh St. and Queen Elizabeth Ave., 252/473-2133) are home to an eclectic mix of boutiques, galleries, and home-goods stores. **Downtown Books** (105 Sir Walter Raleigh St., Manteo, 252/473-1056, www.duckscottage.com, 10am-5pm Mon.-Sat., 11am-4pm Sun.) is a small but well-stocked bookstore, with more than just the best-sellers; there is quite a selection of books by local and regional authors. The staff are friendly and knowledgeable and can point out easy summer reads.

FOOD

Hands down one of my favorite restaurants on the Outer Banks and one of my favorite in the state is located in an unlikely spot: the commercial harbor at Wanchese at the south end of Roanoke Island. ★ **O'Neal's SeaHarvest** (622 Harbor Rd., Wanchese, 252/473-4535, www.onealsseaharvest.com) is where you'll find a seafood market (10am-4pm Mon.-Sat.) and restaurant (11am-3:30pm Mon.-Sat., $9-17). You order at the same counter whether you're buying fish or lunch, so when you say "soft-shelled crab sandwich" they say "which crab do you want?" and point to the seafood case. OK, maybe they only do that if it's not crowded, but you get the idea—the seafood they serve here is the same as they sell, so it's high quality. Order up some shrimp to munch on while you wait for a fried fish sandwich, an oyster po' boy, or a basket of seafood so good you'll make this a permanent stop on future trips to the Outer Banks.

For a quick but filling bite, a sandwich or wrap from **The Hungry Pelican** (205 Budleigh St., Manteo, 252/473-9303, www. thehungrypelican.com, 11am-7pm Mon.-Fri., 11am-3pm Sat., $7-9) will do the trick. They have a long list of hot and cold deli sandwiches, all the potato salad, chips, and pickle spears you could want, plus ice cream scoops, cones, and shakes. What's not to love?

You'll find a great cup of coffee and some light bites for breakfast at **Front Porch Café** (300 U.S. 62 S., Manteo, 252/473-3160, www. frontporchcafe.com, 6am-5pm Mon.-Fri., 6am-3pm Sat., 7am-3pm Sun., $2-6), a coffee shop that has two other locations in Nags Head and Kill Devil Hills. If you need to go get your caffeine fix, want to escape for a few minutes of solitude or to do a crossword in peace, or need a mid-afternoon pick-me-up, this is the place. Plus it's totally adorable.

Poor Richard's Sandwich Shop (303 Queen Elizabeth St., Manteo, 252/473-3333, www.poorrichardsmanteo.com, 11am-3pm Mon.-Sat., bar 5pm-11pm daily, $8-12) is more than a great place to eat (and it is—their burgers and sandwiches are legendary around here). During the summer season they have trivia on Wednesday and live entertainment in the bar most other nights.

Shaddai Peruvian & Mexican Grill (112 U.S. 64, Manteo, 252/423-3013, 11am-9pm Mon.-Sat., $9-22) is a departure from the seafood-rich menus at restaurants around, and that's one of the reasons it's so popular with locals. The Peruvian half of their menu is a taste of Lima on the Outer Banks, and if you doubt it one bite of their *lomo saltado* (Peruvian stir-fry) or their *pollo a la brasa* (rotisserie chicken) served with Inca Kola will convince you. There is seafood here in the form of ceviche (Peruvians invented the dish, so it's fitting) and the *jalea mixta* (a South American spin on the fried fish you find along the North Carolina coast).

ACCOMMODATIONS

The ★ **White Doe Inn** (319 Sir Walter Raleigh St., Manteo, 252/473-9851, www. whitedoeinn.com, from $250) is one of North Carolina's premier inns. The 1910 Queen Anne is the largest house on the island and is listed on the National Register of Historic Places. Guest rooms are exquisitely furnished in turn-of-the-20th-century finery. Guests enjoy a four-course breakfast, evening sherry, espresso and cappuccino anytime, and a 24-hour wine cellar. Spa services are available on-site (by reservation only), and you need only step out to the lawn to play croquet or boccie.

The ★ **Roanoke Island Inn** (305 Fernando St., Manteo, 252/473-5511, www. roanokeislandinn.com) has been in the owner's family since the 1860s and I'm certain it's been a charmer since then too. This beautiful old place has a big porch that overlooks the marsh, garden areas and a koi pond in back, and plenty of comfortable rooms (even some that are pet-friendly and that welcome kids). They have eight rooms in the inn (from $250), two of which are family suites, two of which are pet friendly; a lovely pet-friendly 2-bedroom cottage (from $310); an immaculately restored Sears Kit home perfect for families and travelers with pets (from $380); and a spacious 1920s cottage (from $377) that's pet-friendly too.

For a hotel with an ideal location, take a look at **Tranquil House Inn** (405 Queen Elizabeth Ave., 252/473-1404, www.tranquilhouseinn.com, from $200 winter, from $295 summer). It's right across the harbor from Roanoke Island Festival Park and right on the edge of downtown, and downstairs is **1587 Lounge** ($8-16), a restaurant and lounge where you can order an assortment of small plates (baked brie, hummus, crab dip, pimento cheese, and the like) to share. **Burrus House Inn** (509 U.S. 64/264, 252/475-1636, www.burrushouse.com, $175-250) has direct waterfront access, which, surprisingly, makes it a rare find in Outer Banks B&Bs; the waterfront suites feature double showers and soaking tubs as well as private decks.

You'll find 14 comfortable rooms at **Scarborough Inn** (524 U.S. 64, Manteo, 252/473-3979, www.scarboroughinnmanteo.com, $145-165 summer, $105-125 spring and fall, closed mid-Nov.-Apr.), located in a central spot 10 minutes from the beaches at Nags Head and a short drive or medium-length walk from Manteo's downtown and waterfront.

At **The Roanoke Bungalow** (511 Ananias Dare St., Manteo, 252/305-4473, www.roanokebungalow.com) you'll be well taken care of while you stay in an absolutely lovely place. There are only two rooms, and they can be rented individually ($275) or as one suite ($525). The home was built in the 1930s by the owner's grandparents. It's been on the Roanoke Island Home & Garden Tour and Holiday Tour of Homes, and it's an enchanting little walk to the heart of downtown from here—if you want to leave, that is.

GETTING THERE AND AROUND

Coming from the mainland, you first reach the town of Mann's Harbor on the inland side of the Croatan Sound; from there you have two choices to cross to Roanoke Island. If you take U.S. 64/264 to the north (left), you'll cross the sound to the north, arriving in Manteo. If you drive straight ahead at Mann's Harbor, you'll be on the U.S. 64/264 Bypass, which crosses to the middle of the island, south of Manteo. Proceed until you get to the main intersection with Highway 345, where you can turn left onto U.S. 64/264 to go to Manteo, or right onto Highway 345 to Wanchese.

To reach Roanoke Island from the Outer Banks, take U.S. 158 or Highway 12 to Whalebone Junction, south of Nags Head, and cross Roanoke Sound on the U.S. 64/264 bridge.

Cape Hatteras National Seashore

Cape Hatteras stretches farther south and east than any other part of the United States, jutting out into the Atlantic and brushing the warm waters of the Gulf Stream. Hatteras draws surfers, anglers, divers, and beach-loving vacationers by the thousands. It's also a haven to migratory birds, home to important inshore and offshore fisheries, making it popular for bird-watching. In Hatteras Village, Waves, Salvo, and Avon, museums and historic sites tell the history of the Outer Banks as well as the story of the birth of the Coast Guard. In these towns, there are also galleries packed with the work of local artists and fish markets with trays and coolers full of today's catch.

Due to Hatteras' position so close to the strong currents of the Gulf Stream, a shifting set of sandbars called Diamond Shoals extends from the cape's pristine beaches far out into the Atlantic. While the lighthouses at Cape Hatteras and Bodie Island provide guidance for ships, in years past, many ran afoul of the shoals, sinking outright or beaching on the sandbars. These ships are part of what's called the Graveyard of the Atlantic, an incredible number of shipwrecks that line the coast of North Carolina but congregate here. Ships range from colonial sailboats to Civil War blockade runners to German U-boats sent to harass supply and troop ships in World War II. Hundreds of species of fish are drawn to the wrecks, as are divers and anglers. There's a ton of information on Hatteras Island and the National Seashore, including details on off-road driving, recreational opportunities, and history, on www.outerbanks.org.

BODIE ISLAND

Bodie Island hasn't been a true island in decades, but the name stuck around. Today Bodie Island sits at the southern tip of the thin peninsula that constitutes the most recognizable (and populous) portion of the Outer Banks, just north of Oregon Inlet and Hatteras Island. It is the northern end of the Cape Hatteras National Seashore, which runs the length of the islands from Whalebone Junction, where U.S. 64/264 joins Highway 12, to Hatteras Inlet and separates Hatteras and Ocracoke Islands.

You'll spot the horizontal black-and-white stripes of the 170-foot **Bodie Island Lighthouse** (8210 Bodie Island Lighthouse Rd., 6 miles south of Whalebone Junction, 252/473-2111, www.nps.gov/caha, visitors center 9am-5pm daily) from several miles away. The Bodie Light's huge Fresnel lens first beamed in 1872, but this is the third lighthouse on this location. The first iteration of the Bodie Light (pronounced "body") was built in the 1830s, but due to engineering errors and shifting sand it leaned like the Tower of Pisa and didn't last too long. The next one stood straight but proved such a tempting target for the Yankee Navy during the Civil War that the Confederates blew it up themselves. The third light still stands, although a flock of geese nearly put it out of commission soon after its first lighting when they collided with and damaged the lens.

The Bodie Island Lighthouse opened to the public for climbs in 2013 and remains popular. Self-guided tours (tickets available only at www.recreation.gov, daily late Apr.-early Oct., $10 adults, $5 seniors and under age 12) take you on a strenuous climb up the lighthouse, but it is worth it for the view. Solid shoes are required to climb the lighthouse, so no heels, flip-flops, or bare feet.

The nearby Lighthouse Keeper's Cottage serves as a visitors center, and it is also the trailhead for self-guided nature trails to Roanoke Sound. These trails wind through beautiful marsh on the sound side of Bodie Island.

The **Oregon Inlet Campground** (12001 Hwy. 12, reservations 877/444-6777, campground information 252/441-6246, www.recreation.gov, year-round), operated by the National Park Service, offers tent ($28) and RV camping ($28 with no hookup, $35 with electric hookup) behind the sand dunes, with cold-water showers, potable water, and restrooms. A dump station and water are at Oregon Inlet Fishing Center, across Highway 12.

Getting There

To get to the Bodie Island Lighthouse from the northern Outer Banks towns of Corolla, Duck, Kitty Hawk, Kill Devil Hills, and Nags Head, go south along U.S. 158 or Highway 12; it's a trip of 70 minutes from Corolla or 20 minutes from Nags Head without traffic, or considerably longer with traffic. From any of the Hatteras Island towns south of Bodie Island, head north along Highway 12; it's a 25-minute drive from Rodanthe, the northernmost Hatteras Island town.

HATTERAS ISLAND

As Cape Hatteras arches dramatically along the North Carolina coast, it shelters Pamlico Sound from the ocean like a giant cradling arm. The cape itself is the point of the elbow, an exposed and vulnerable spit of land that's nearly irresistible to passing hurricanes. Most of the island is included in Cape Hatteras National Seashore, the first of its kind in the country, although a handful of small towns—Rodanthe, Waves, Salvo, Avon, Buxton, Frisco, and the village of Hatteras—dot the coastline. For the most part Hatteras Island isn't much wider than the dune line and Highway 12, which makes for a great deal of dramatic scenery on all sides.

One of the first things you'll notice about Hatteras Island is its wildness. Since most of the island is part of the Cape Hatteras National Seashore, there's little permanent human habitation here, save the seven communities of Rodanthe, Waves, Salvo, Avon, Buxton, Frisco, and Hatteras Village. This makes it a favorite spot for those seeking a

Historic Lighthouses

Centuries of mariners have plied the waters off North Carolina's coast, harvesting its aquatic beasts, protecting or prowling the shore, and skirting or foundering on its dangerous shoals. As beautiful as North Carolina's lighthouses are, they were built to perform a service of life-and-death importance. Today, the historic lights—some still in operation—are popular destinations for visitors. Most are open for climbing and offer fantastic views. The following are some of North Carolina's favorites.

Cape Hatteras Lighthouse

- Visitors willing to climb the 214 spiral steps to the top of **Currituck Beach Lighthouse** are treated to a dazzling view of Currituck Sound.

- Climb to the top of **Bodie Island Lighthouse,** which overlooks Lighthouse Bay and the Atlantic Ocean. This striking structure has been sending its signal out to sea since 1872 but was closed to the public until 2013.

- **Cape Hatteras Lighthouse,** the tallest brick lighthouse in the United States, has a black-and-white spiral exterior that makes it visible from miles away. Pay a small admission price to climb all the way to the top.

- Whale oil originally powered the beam of **Ocracoke Lighthouse,** the second-oldest working lighthouse in the United States. Because it's still on duty, visitors can't go inside, but there are lovely places to walk on the grounds.

- The black-and-white diamond-spangled **Cape Lookout Lighthouse,** one of the most iconic symbols of North Carolina, has stood watch since 1859. The nearby keeper's quarters give an intriguing glimpse into the isolated and meditative life of the light keeper. While you're there, explore Cape Lookout's 56 miles of unspoiled beach, where you may have a close encounter with one of the Outer Banks' famous wild horses.

- Commissioned by Thomas Jefferson and built in 1817, **Old Baldy Lighthouse** is North Carolina's oldest lighthouse. From its strategic point on the southern coast of Bald Head Island, Old Baldy has seen nearly two centuries of commerce, war, and peace.

little solitude, especially surfers and kiteboarders hoping to take advantage of wind and wave without worrying about knocking into beachgoers, beachcombers, nature lovers, and anglers.

Rodanthe, a town made notable by North Carolina author Nicholas Sparks's novel *Nights in Rodanthe* and the Richard Gere film of the same name based on the book, is the first community on Hatteras Island as you travel south on Highway 12 from Nags Head. It's a small attractive beach town, home

to the Chicamacomico Life-Saving Station (the first such established along the North Carolina coast) and a lovely stretch of beach where fans of the namesake novel and film still come to visit.

Waves and **Salvo** are similarly small, though Salvo has an interesting story behind its name. It's said that during the Civil War, a Union ship's captain spied the town, couldn't identify it on his map, ordered his gunners to "Give it a salvo anyway," then jotted "Salvo" on his map, and the name stuck. Life in Salvo is geared a little more toward crabbing and fishing, and this is the spot where many travelers will pull off the road to take a few pictures of colorful crab pots stacked and piled on docks just a few feet from the road.

Avon, about halfway down Hatteras Island, is known for being a surf fishing destination. The beaches are stunning, and in the sound on the west side of town you'll see kiteboarders galore.

Buxton is home to the famous Cape Hatteras Lighthouse and an immensely popular surf fishing spot called Cape Point. Hatteras Island begins to make a turn to the west and south here, growing a little fatter and sporting a bit of maritime forest. Frisco, just south of Buxton on the edge of Buxton Woods, is a quiet little town with two identities: seaside retreat and maritime forest escape.

Hatteras Village, on the southernmost tip of the island, is a little bigger than the other towns, but not by much. Here you'll find the Ocracoke Ferry and a decent sized charter fishing fleet. There are a few showy rental homes in the Village, but more often than not, visitors stay in condos or motels when they come here.

Chicamacomico Life-Saving Station

Lifesaving operations are an important part of North Carolina's maritime heritage. Corps of brave men occupied remote stations along the coast, ready at a moment's notice to risk their lives to save foundering sailors in the relentlessly dangerous waters off the Outer Banks. In Rodanthe, the **Chicamacomico Life-Saving Station** (Milepost 39.5, 23645 Hwy. 12, Rodanthe, 252/987-1552, www.chicamacomico.org, 10am-4pm Mon.-Fri., $8 adults, $7 over age 64 and students, $6 ages 4-17, free under age 4) preserves the original station, a handsome gray-shingled 1874 building, the 1911 building that replaced it and now houses a museum of fascinating artifacts from maritime rescue operations, and a complex of other buildings and exhibits depicting the

lives of lifesavers and their families. The antique lifesaving drill demonstrations (2pm Thurs. Memorial Day-Labor Day) are fascinating to see; try to stop by and check it out.

★ Cape Hatteras Lighthouse

At 210 feet tall, **Cape Hatteras Lighthouse** (46379 Lighthouse Rd., Buxton, 252/473-2111, www.nps.gov/caha, lighthouse 9am-5pm daily, children under 42 inches tall not permitted, grounds $8, $4 children and seniors) is the tallest brick lighthouse in the United States, and its distinctive black-and-white spiral paint job makes it easy to see from miles away on land or sea. Built in 1870, it stood in its original spot until 1999 when rising sea levels caused waves to encroach on the site and endanger the lighthouse. Over 23 days it was moved 2,900 feet in an incredible accomplishment of engineering prowess (I remember going down to watch it creep foot-by-foot from its old seaside location to its current spot; it was an amazing sight and one of the things that convinced my cousin she should become an engineer). In typical years, the lighthouse is open for climbing during summer months, but deferred maintenance and the wear from salt spray and the constant wind means the lighthouse will be closed to climbing for 2022 and possibly parts of the 2023 season. When it returns, climbing works like this: get a ticket (around $10 adults, $4 children and seniors), get in line, and make the hike to the top. It's a long way up—257 steps—and once you get there, you'll have awesome views and some insane winds (sometimes it's so breezy they delay or cancel climbs).

Graveyard of the Atlantic Museum

The Outer Banks has a rather fearsome nickname: the Graveyard of the Atlantic. This nickname comes well earned thanks to the treacherous shoals and currents off the Outer Banks, and thanks to a pair of world wars that saw German naval forces torpedoing ships here, and thanks also to the storms and hurricanes that send ships to the bottom. At the **Graveyard of the Atlantic Museum** (59200 Museum Dr., Hatteras, 252/986-0720, www.graveyardoftheatlantic.com, 10am-4pm Mon.-Sat., free) in Hatteras Village, one of the North Carolina Maritime Museums, you'll find exhibits that deal with the maritime history of the Outer Banks, including pirates, the prevalence of fishing as a way of life, battles fought during the Civil War, shipwrecks from Colonial days to just last year, the evolution of the U.S. Lifesaving Service's evolution into the U.S. Coast Guard, diving, and more. Geared for all ages, it's a fascinating stop at the southernmost tip of Hatteras Island and well worth the drive.

Sports and Recreation

Pea Island National Wildlife Refuge (Hwy. 12, 10 miles south of Nags Head, 252/987-2394, www.fws.gov) occupies the northern reach of Hatteras Island. Much of the island is covered by ponds, making this an exceptional place for watching migratory waterfowl. Two nature trails link some of the best bird-watching spots, including the 0.5-mile fully wheelchair-accessible North Pond Wildlife Trail. Viewing and photography blinds are scattered along the trails for extended observation. Throughout the year, guided bird walks, canoe trips, and walking lectures on the wildlife of Pea Island take place.

Waterfowl hunting is permitted on Cape Hatteras National Seashore, but only in designated areas on Bodie Island. There the National Park Service maintains 20 hunting blinds including the ADA-accessible Bodie Island Marsh Blind, though conditions and availability of blinds vary, and hunters should be prepared to construct a temporary blind if necessary. To hunt, you'll need a valid North Carolina hunting license with waterfowl privileges, a Federal Harvest Program (HIP) certification, and a Ducks Unlimited stamp. Hunters must register at the Whalebone Junction Information Station at 4:30am to be assigned a hunt area. Full hunting procedures and regulations—including maximum party size, firearm and ammunition limitations, rules for retriever dogs, and hunting area entrance and exit procedures—are available and regularly updated on the Cape Hatteras National Seashore website (www.nps.gov/caha).

BEACH DRIVING

Many folks come to the Outer Banks, specifically to Hatteras Island, because of the incredible beach access. All along Cape Hatteras National Seashore, and at a few spots in the towns on the northern end of the Outer Banks, you'll see people driving on the sand. It's easy to do if you have a little know-how and confidence, and more than 50 off-road vehicle (ORV) entrance ramps provide access to the beach and the sound all along the National Seashore. Anglers come to cast a line in their favorite hole, surfers come in pursuit of a great session in the waves, and the adventurous just like to tool around on the shore. Certain sections of the shore are open to ORVs, some year-round, other seasonally, but both require a permit from the National Park Service. To obtain an ORV permit you'll need to pay the **fee** ($50 for 10 days, $120 annually) and fill out the paperwork online (www.recreation.gov). There's a full rundown of the procedures and vehicle requirements at www.nps.gov/caha under the "Plan Your Visit" heading.

Before you drive out onto the sand, let me provide a cautionary tale. If you don't know what you're doing, you'll get stuck, as the family who drove their minivan was stuck on my last visit to the National Seashore. Their van had bottomed out and was blocking the onramp. They didn't have the gear or tools they needed to extricate themselves and after taking a look at the situation, we decided it was best for them to call a very expensive tow truck that likely came with a fine from the National Park Service for driving on the beach with no permit.

Driving in the sand can be easy if you

1: Avon Fishing Pier 2: Bodie Island Lighthouse
3: wildlife along Cape Hatteras National Seashore
4: Cape Hatteras shipwreck

follow some guidelines. Lower your tire pressure to around 20 psi (it helps the tires grip deep, loose sand more easily). A 4WD vehicle works better than all-wheel drive (AWD) or standard two-wheel drive. Stay in the tire tracks you see when possible. Stay off the dunes and out of marked areas. Avoid the salt water and wash your car as soon as you're off the beach as salt water is pretty corrosive. When you get off the sand, reinflate your tires as soon as possible. Otherwise, take a look at the regulations posted on the national seashore's website or at www.outerbanks.org before you hit the sand.

SURFING AND KITEBOARDING

The Outer Banks owe their existence to the volatile action of the tides, and the same forces that created this habitable sandbar also make it an incredible place for water sports. **Canadian Hole,** a spot in the sound between Avon and Buxton, is one of the most famous windsurfing and kiteboarding places in the world (and, of course, it's perfect for flying kites). The island is extraordinarily narrow at Canadian Hole, so it's easy to tote your board from the sound side over to the ocean for a change of scene.

Hatteras Island is a major East Coast destination for kiteboarders and surfers, and at **REAL Watersports** (25706 Hwy. 12, Waves, 252/987-6000 or 866/732-5548, www.realwatersports.com), the largest kite-surfing school in the world, they offer lessons (from $350) and camps (from $1,495); you can also rent kiteboarding gear (from $150 per day for a full kit). If kiteboarding isn't your thing, the staff at REAL also offer surfing lessons (from $250) and rentals (from $25 per half day) as well as stand-up paddleboard rentals (from $20 per hour, $50 per day). They also offer instruction in using foils: underwater wings that give you more speed and maneuverability while riding your board in the waves or wakes (lessons from $175, 3-day camp $1,695).

Among the ways to tour Hatteras, **Equine Adventures** (52193 Piney Ridge Rd., Frisco, 252/995-4897, www.equineadventures.com)

leads two-hour horseback tours along the beaches of Cape Hatteras ($135), often giving experience riders the chance to gallop off through the sand and surf for an exhilarating experience.

Hatteras Watersports (Milepost 42.5, 27130 Hwy. 12, Salvo, 252/987-2306, www.hatteraswatersports.com, by reservation only, Mon.-Sat.) offers Jet Skis ($99), stand-up paddleboards (from $25 per hour, $125 for a 3-day rental), and kayak rentals (from $15 per hour) as well as guided and self-guided kayak tours (rates vary). Their location on shallow Pamlico Sound is a perfect spot to head out in any of their watercraft, even for novices.

FISHING

The Outer Banks is renowned for its fishing. The Gulf Stream is nearby, the sounds and inland waters are rife with fishing opportunities, and there are an incredible number of fishing guides who will take you out on the water for a day you won't forget. The **Oregon Inlet Fishing Center** (8770 S. Old Oregon Inlet Rd., Nags Head, 252/441-6301, www.oregoninlet.com, 9am-4pm Mon.-Sat.) is home to the largest, most modern fleet of charter boats on the East Coast, and is a full-service marina with all the stuff you need (camping gear, fuel, ice, oil, bait, and more), and the site of some NC Wildlife boat ramps. But the draw is the charter fleet. At last count, there were 43 charter boats based at Oregon Inlet, but that number swells in summer and by season. Offshore charters (which will stay near shore or head out to the Gulf Stream, depending on what's biting and what you're hoping to catch) run $2,200 per boat, but near-shore and inshore fishing is less expensive, starting at $450 per half day, $800 full day. The Oregon Inlet Fishing Center maintains a list and booking service for all the boats in the fleet, making it an easy one-stop-shop when you need to scratch that fishing itch.

You can also go fishing from the shore along Cape Hatteras National Seashore as long as you have a **Coastal Recreational Fishing License** (www.ncwildlife.org, 10-day license

$11) or you can head to one of the piers where you can fish without a license as long as you pay the small admission fee. The **Rodanthe Pier** (2451 Atlantic Dr., Rodanthe, 252/987-0030, www.rodanthepierllc.com, 7am-sunset daily Apr.-May, 6am-midnight daily June-mid-Sept., 7am-midnight daily mid-Sept-late-Nov., closed Thanksgiving-weekend before Easter) is a classic wooden pier with all the twists, turns, and rocking with the waves that you expect. It's nearly 700 feet long, and you'll find locals and loyal visitors posted up on either side waiting to get a bite. At the **Avon Fishing Pier** (41001 Hwy. 12, Avon, 252/995-5480, www.avonfishingpier.com, 6am-midnight daily summer, 6am-10pm daily spring and fall, closed winter), another wooden relic and the last of the wooden piers built on Hatteras Island, you might just reel in a record: Dozens of anglers over the years have set records for the fish they've hauled in, so good luck! At each pier there's a small **fee** (around $12 per day adults, $7 under age 11, $2 sightseers, $10 pole rental) to fish.

Shopping

Down here on Hatteras Island you're surrounded by Cape Hatteras National Seashore, and it's not exactly the place if you want rows of T-shirt shops, souvenir stands, and beach goodies. You'll find a few of the brightly-colored beach marts here, but much of the shopping is focused on serving locals (grocery stores and small convenience stores), the sporting community (tackle shops, gun and rod stores), and water sports enthusiasts (surf shops large and small).

Many of the shops here are actually galleries packed with the works of local and regional artists. The **Pea Island Art Gallery** (27766 Hwy. 12, Salvo, 252/987-2879, www.peaislandartgallery.com, 10am-5pm Mon.-Sat.) has works from more than 100 artists in a range of media in a gallery that's a replica of a 19th-century lifesaving station. **SeaWorthy Gallery** (58401 Hwy. 12, Hatteras, 252/986-6510, www.seaworthygallery.com, 10am-5pm Tues.-Sat.) carries pieces ranging from

fun cartoonish folk art representations of area wildlife to painstaking paintings of area landmarks, seascapes, and landscapes. **Blue Pelican Gallery** (57762 Hwy. 12, Hatteras, 252/986-2244, www.bluepelicangallery.com, 10am-5pm Thurs.-Sat.) carries jewelry from local glassblowers, lockets filled with objects found on and inspired by the shore, jewelry, and a beautiful selection of yarn and supplies for knitting and other needle arts.

The indie bookshop **Buxton Village Books** (47918 Hwy. 12, Buxton, 252/995-4240, www.buxtonvillagebooks.com, 10am-6pm daily) carries a large selection of books about the Outer Banks and by regional authors, along with the latest in contemporary and Southern fiction. If you need a recommendation, the staff has great taste and are broad readers, so they'll help you no matter what you're looking for. Their collection of Outer Banks cookbooks will help you bring some of the flavors of your vacation home with you, and gifts from maps to art to nautical-inspired tote bags give you even more to browse when you stop by.

Food

Dining options are limited on Hatteras Island, but there are plenty of places to eat. **Café Pamlico at the Inn on Pamlico Sound** (49684 Hwy. 12, Buxton, 866/726-5426, www.innonpamlicosound.com, 5pm-9pm Mon.-Sat., $10-40) caters to guests of the inn, but if you call in advance, you may be able to get a reservation for dinner, even if you're staying elsewhere. The chef likes to use fresh-caught seafood, sometimes brought in by the guests themselves earlier in the day. Vegetarian fare and other special requests are available.

Every meal I've had at **Hatteras Sol Waterside Grill** (58646 Hwy. 12, Hatteras, 252/986-1414, www.hatterassol.com, 5pm-9pm Tues.-Sun., $12-37) has been great, and that includes a few I carried away in to-go containers and ate at a picnic table or in my hotel room. Their hot-and-sour shrimp soup is a favorite, but others may want to try the Hatteras-style clam chowder (it's brothy, not creamy), and their crabcakes and Mediterranean shrimp and scallop pasta are especially good.

In Avon you can get your pizza fix thanks to the outstanding pies from **Gidget's Pizza and Pasta** (41934 Hwy. 12, Avon, 252/995-3109, www.gidgetspizza.com, 11:30am-9pm Tues.-Sat., $5-20). I'm on the Outer Banks quite a lot, and in the last few years, Gidget's has become a go-to when I'm on Hatteras Island. Their pies come in all sorts of toppings—a veggie deluxe, meatball, one topped with crab—but my favorites are the margherita (simple and perfect) and the five-cheese pie. They also offer up salads (big and filling), pasta, hot subs, great breadsticks (I mean, they're just weirdly cut pizza; of course they're good!) and starters.

There aren't a lot of coffee shops on Hatteras, and no chain coffee shops at all, so when you find a good one, you tend to go back. The coffee at **Uglie Mugs Coffee Shop** (40534 Hwy. 12, Avon, 252/995-5990, 7am-2pm daily, $2-8) in Avon keeps me coming back because they make a good latte, their pastries are just enough to get me started in the morning, and the people are friendly and open with recommendations for places to eat or things to do.

If you want to get your day started with a massive one-of-a-kind pastry, try the apple uglies—monstrous apple fritters—from **Orange Blossom Bakery** (47206 Hwy. 12, Buxton, www.orangeblossombakery.com, 6:30am-11am daily, $1-8), take it across the way to the Cape Hatteras Lighthouse, and devour it while you watch the waves roll in.

Watermen's Bar & Grill (25706 Hwy. 12, Waves, 252/987-2000, www.watermensbarandgrill.com, noon-8pm Mon.-Sat., $8-34) offers smoothies to get you started, sandwiches and wraps for lunch (try the grilled mahimahi wrap or the blackened tuna sandwich, both with fish caught locally), and a short list of tasty dinner entrées. They run specials every night of the week; Fajita Tuesday and Barbecue Rib Thursday are popular.

Accommodations

Among the lodging choices on Hatteras Island is the very fine ★ **Inn on Pamlico Sound** (49684 Hwy. 12, Buxton, 866/726-5426, www.innonpamlicosound.com, from $220). The inn is right on the sound, with a private dock and easy waterfront access. The dozen suites are sumptuous and relaxing, many with their own decks or private porches. Small gardens throughout the property provide ingredients to the inn's kitchen, where you can—actually, should—dine, as it's exceptional. Mornings and evenings, the light is absolutely incredible looking west across the sound, be sure you make the time to catch a sunrise or sunset or two while you're here.

You'll find **The Atlantic Inn** (573212 Hwy. 12, 252/986-2700, www.theatlanticinn.com, from $109) a lovely place to stay and just as pretty in person as it is on the antique postcards you'll see on display. This is a pretty important place. Back in 1928 it was the first hotel built on Hatteras Island, and over the years it has been just that: a welcoming place for visitors to come when they want to fall in love with the Outer Banks. New owners gave it a bit of love and attention, and in 2021 reintroduced it to the world. Now, in addition to the rooms and general hospitality, they host several retreats and events throughout the year.

There's a wide array of accommodations available with **Lighthouse View Oceanfront Lodging** (46677 Hwy. 12, Buxton, 800/225-7651, www.lighthouseview.com), near the lighthouse in Buxton. They have everything from oceanfront rooms and suites ($88-363) to poolside rooms and efficiencies ($74-240) to small cottages ($118-303) to houses that sleep six or more ($103-650).

Breakwater Inn (57896 Hwy. 12, Hatteras, 252/986-2565, www.unwind.breakwaterhatteras.com, $109-169) is in the heart of Hatteras, next to the marina. It's convenient, spacious, and affordable, and anglers or surfers headed to the area should definitely take note: It's close to some great breaks and fishing holes. On-site there's also **Breakwater Restaurant** (252/986-2733, www.breakwaterhatteras.com, 5pm-9pm daily, $14-38), where the seafood is outstanding and dishes like the potato-crusted crab cakes are a crowd pleaser.

Koru Village Resort and Spa (40920 Hwy. 12, Avon, 252/995-3125, www.koruvillage.com, $175-240, 3-night minimum in summer) is an oceanfront resort focused on health and wellness, and as such, they have a yoga studio, a killer fitness center, and a series of programs from beachfront yoga to fire dancing to keep you fit and feeling fine. Their 15-acre campus includes the **Avon Fishing Pier** (252/995-5480, www.avonfishingpier. com, 6am-midnight daily summer, 6am-10pm daily spring and fall, closed winter), a 665-foot pier that's the only one remaining in operation along the Cape Hatteras National Seashore; a **Spa** (252/995-3125, treatments $55-155); and **Pangea Tavern** (252/995-3800, www.pangeatavern.com, 5pm-9pm Tues.-Sat., $12-28), where the menu is seafood-centric and dishes like the fish tacos, seafood-and-chips (a mix of fish and shrimp), and sesame-seared tuna stand out as favorites.

CAMPING

The National Park Service operates two campgrounds in this stretch of the National Seashore: **Frisco Campground** (53415 Billy Mitchell Rd., Frisco, reservations 877/444-6777, campground information 252/995-5101, Apr.-Nov., $28), where you actually camp in the dunes, and **Cape Point Campground** (46700 Lighthouse Rd., Buxton, reservations 877/444-6777, campground information 252/465-9602, Apr.-Nov., $20), with level campsites located behind the dunes. Both have cold showers, restrooms, and potable water.

Rodanthe Watersports and Campground (24170 Hwy. 12, 252/987-1431, www.rodanthewatersports.com) has a number of camping options, waterside and not. Tent sites are primitive (from $57) and waterside with water and electric (from $77); RV sites are standard (from $77) with electric, water, and Wi-Fi or waterfront (from

$97). They can only take campers up to 25 feet long, so if you're longer, look at one of the other campgrounds nearby.

At **Camp Hatteras** (24789 Hwy. 12, Rodanthe, 252/987-2777, www.camphatteras. com), RVers and tent campers will find more than 400 sites with concrete pads, plenty of full hookups, campsites available from the sound to the ocean, bathhouses, laundry, a dog park, a camp store, and just about any other thing you might want.

Cape Hatteras KOA (2509 Hwy. 12, Rodanthe, 252/987-2307, www.capehatteraskoa.com) offers campsites, RV sites, and small cabins along with a pool, a play area for kids, a small commissary, and direct beach access. Rates vary by season and location, with tent sites ($40-98) and RV sites ($56-165). Additional charges are for cable TV ($3), pets, ($3), additional adults ($8), and kids ages 6-18 ($4). They also have RV units for rent if you're in town without your home on wheels; rates vary by season ($103 late-Nov.-Mar., $115 Apr. and Oct.-late-Nov., $150 May and Sept., $287 late-May-early-Sept.).

VACATION RENTAL HOMES

At **Midgett Realty—Hatteras** (57783 Hwy. 12, Hatteras Village, 252/986-2841 or 866/348-8819, www.midgettrealty.com), you'll find tons of homes, from charming forest cottages to giant beachfront escapes, including pet-friendly stays, flexible dates, and more. **Surf or Sound Realty** (40974 Hwy. 12, Avon, 252/995-5801 or 800/237-1138, www. surforsound.com) has been renting homes to families, anglers, surfers, weddings, and groups of all sorts since 1978, and their portfolio of homes ranges from the simple to the elegant. Looking for pet-friendly? A pool? A hot tub? An elevator? Check and check. And if you're looking to have your wedding on Hatteras Island, they have an event coordinator who can help direct you to the perfect home or homes for a beach wedding.

Getting There

Hatteras Island can be reached by car,

following Highway 12 for 17 miles south from Nags Head, but it's another 50 miles to get to Hatteras Village at the south end of the island. Along Highway 12 you'll go through the towns of Rodanthe, Waves, Salvo, and Avon, and then around the tip of the cape to Buxton, Frisco, and Hatteras, where the highway ends. From here, you have two choices: backtrack or take a ferry to Ocracoke (free, 60 minutes), which runs hourly 5am–midnight in the off-season and three times hourly during peak season.

TOP EXPERIENCE

★ OCRACOKE ISLAND

Ocracoke Island, one of the most geographically isolated places in the state, is the southernmost part of the Cape Hatteras National Seashore. Accessible only by water and air, this 16-mile-long island seems charmingly anchored in the past. Regular ferry service didn't start until 1960, as most residents were content to stay on their island, separate from the rest of the state, and they didn't have a paved highway until 1963. The natural beauty of the island is mostly intact, and some areas look much like they did in 1585 when the first English colonists ran aground. It may have been during their time on Ocracoke (called Wococon at the time) that the ancestors of today's wild ponies first set hoof on the Outer Banks. Theirs was not the last shipwreck at Ocracoke, nor was it the first; Spanish explorers reportedly ran aground here too, and it's possible the now feral Banker ponies came from their ships. As on the northern stretches of the Outer Banks, Ocracokers subsisted partially on the flotsam and goods that would wash up after shipwrecks, so wherever the wild horses came from, like other gifts from the sea, they have become part of the island's history and lifestyle.

In some ways, Ocracoke is a little creepy. Its isolation has something to do with that, but so do its legends and ghosts. During the early 18th century, Ocracoke was a favorite haunt of the pirate Edward Teach, better known as Blackbeard. He lived here from time to time, married his 14th wife here, and died here. He met his fate in Teach's Hole, a spot just off the island, when a band of privateers (pirate hunters) hired by Virginia's Governor Spottswood finally cornered and killed him. According to legend, he didn't go down without a fight; it took five musket shots, more than 20 stab wounds, and a near beheading before his fight was over. Afterward, Spottswood's privateers took Blackbeard's head as a trophy and dumped his body overboard where, legend says, it swam around the ship seven times before going under.

All of **Ocracoke Village** (www.visitocracokenc.com), near the southern end of the island, is on the National Register of Historic Places. While the historical sites of the island are highly distinctive, the most unique thing about the island and its people is the culture that has developed over the centuries. Ocracokers have a "brogue" or dialect of their own, similar to those of other Outer Banks communities but distinctive and unique to the island.

Ocracoke Lighthouse

A lighthouse has stood on Ocracoke since at least 1798, but due to the constantly shifting sands, the inlet that it protected kept sneaking away. Barely 20 years after that first tower was built, it was almost a mile from the water. The current **Ocracoke Lighthouse** (Lighthouse Rd., Ocracoke) was built in 1823 and originally burned whale oil to power the beam. It is still in operation, the oldest continuously operating light in North Carolina and the second-oldest in the nation. Because it's on active duty, it is not publicly accessible, but a boardwalk nearby gives nice views.

British Cemetery

The **British Cemetery** (243 British Cemetery Rd.) is not a colonial graveyard but rather a vestige of World War II, when the Carolina coast was lousy with German U-boats. Defending the Outer Banks became a pressing concern, and on May 11, 1942, the HMS

Ocracoke Island

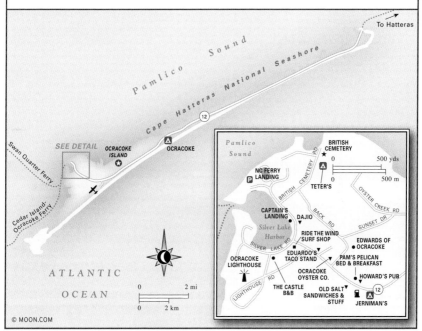

Bedfordshire, a British trawler sent to aid the U.S. Navy, was torpedoed by the German *U-558*. The *Bedfordshire* sank, killing all 37 men on board. Over the course of the next week, four bodies washed up on Ocracoke. An island family donated a burial plot, where the four men lie today.

Sports and Recreation

Ride the Wind Surf Shop (486 Irvin Garrish Hwy., 252/928-6311, www.surfocracoke.com, 10am-5pm daily) gives individual and group surfing lessons for adults and children ($95 per hour 1 person, $185 per hour 2 people), covering ocean safety and surfing etiquette in addition to board handling. Ride the Wind also leads sunrise, sunset, and full-moon kayak tours ($40, $18 under age 13) around the marshes of Ocracoke. Kayak, stand-up paddleboard, surfboard, and boogie-board rentals ($12-59 per day, $28-150 per week) are available.

The *Windfall II* (departs from Community Store Dock, Ocracoke, 252/928-7245, www.schoonerwindfall.com, sunset charter for 6 $250, shared trip $50 pp, daytime sail with 6 $200, shared trip $35 pp), a beautiful 32-foot lazy jack schooner, sails out into the Pamlico Sound to visit Teach's Hole, where Blackbeard was brought to justice, and conducts daily sunset cruises.

Tradewinds Tackle Shop (1094 Irvin Garrish Hwy., 252/928-5491, www.tradewindstackle.com, 7am-7pm daily Apr.-Dec.) offers fishing tips and sells all the gear you'll need, including licenses, to land a big one. The Ocracoke Island fishing experts at Tradewinds can tell you where to catch what and how, or they can simply send you to a good fishing guide.

Food

Ocracoke's isolation and size have kept it a small, close-knit community; its dining

scene is likewise small. Restaurants tend to be old-guard seafood but new places break through and become island go-tos. One is ★ **Eduardo's Taco Stand** (950 Irvin Garrish Hwy., 252/928-0234, www.eduardo-socracoke.com, 8am-3pm daily, dinner 5pm-9pm Mon.-Sat., $7-18), a place that's not much to look at due to the fact that it's somewhere between a food truck and a semi-permanent trailer restaurant. An order of fish tacos—always made with local seafood—is to die for, and when the crab tacos are on special, you'd better get there quick or you're missing out. Don't fret if you prefer a burrito or bowl; they serve plenty of both every day.

Howard's Pub & Raw Bar Restaurant (1175 Irvin Garrish Hwy., 252/928-4441, www.howardspub.com, 11am-10pm daily, entrées $15-26) is a cross between a divey beach bar-restaurant and a sports bar; it's fun-loving and relaxing, but not fine dining. They serve steaks, burgers, salads, sandwiches, and a wide assortment of tasty seaside bites, of which you should try the hush puppies, conch fritters, and crab cakes.

Since the weather on Ocracoke makes for pleasant picnic weather for most of the year and there are miles and miles of beach and waterfront where you can spread out for a meal, I'm not hesitant to recommend another food truck. **Old Salt Sandwiches & Such** (800 Irvin Garrish Hwy., 252/340-0245, 11am-2pm Tues.-Sat. Apr.-Dec., $8-14, cash only) has burgers, a chicken sandwich, and a fried fish sandwich that can't be beat, but what intrigues me is the NC Shrimpburger, a burger endemic to the North Carolina Coast (generally the Crystal Coast, but I'll talk about that in the next chapter) that's a real treat when done right, and Old Salt does it the right way.

Get your fill of oysters at **Ocracoke Oyster Company** (621 Irvin Garrish Hwy., 252/928-0200, 4pm-2am Sun.-Mon., 11am-2am Tues.-Sat., $11-30) where they serve the bivalves a half-dozen ways and send tacos, burgers, platters, and sandwiches to tables full of hungry diners. Order some oysters on the half shell or baked, get a fried seafood plater, have some fish or blackened shrimp tacos, or make a feast of starters (peel-and-eat shrimp, a pile of nachos, and a hushpuppy basket qualifies for a meal when you're on vacation).

There's plenty of excellent seafood as well as pizzas and steak at **Dajio** (305 Irvin Garrish Hwy., 252/928-7119, www.dajiores-taurant.com, 5pm-11pm Tues.-Sat. Apr.-Dec., $12-30). They're all about local seafood (in a fishing village, you kind of have to be) and they treat it right. Chargrilled oysters and the calamari *fritti* (fried calamari) make good starters, the fried green tomato sandwich is a great break from seafood, and a dish like pap-pardelle and clams is a filling and tasty meal.

Accommodations

The **Captain's Landing** (324 Hwy. 12, 252/928-1999, www.thecaptainslanding.com, from $230 summer, from $130 off-season), with a perch right on the harbor (called Silver Lake) looking toward the lighthouse, is a modern hotel owned by a descendant of Ocracoke's oldest families. Suites have 1.5 baths, full kitchens, comfortable sleeper sofas for extra guests, and decks with beautiful views. Also available is a bright airy penthouse ($2,700 per week) with two bedrooms, an office, a gourmet kitchen, and even a laundry room. The Captain's Cottage ($2,600 per week) is a private two-bedroom house, also right on the water, with great decks and its own courtyard.

Edwards of Ocracoke (216 Old Beach Rd., 252/928-4801 or 800/254-1359, www.ed-wardsofocracoke.com, from $70 spring and fall, from $115 summer, $460-875 weekly) has several cozy bungalows typical of coastal Carolina, referred to here as "vintage accommodations." The mid-20th-century vacation ambiance is pleasant, the cabins are clean and well-kept, and the rates are great. Private cottages are available, as are two homes perfect for larger groups traveling together.

Pam's Pelican Bed & Breakfast (1021

1: playing in the surf on Ocracoke Island
2: Ocracoke Lighthouse

Irvin Garrish Hwy., 252/928-1661, www.pamspelican.com, $129-199) is a dog-friendly spot not far from the marina. They offer free pickup service from both the marina and airport, so getting here is easy if you've come over car-free. Pam's Pelican is laid-back, and they have bikes, coolers, and grills for guests to use, making for some communal evenings.

The Castle B&B (155 Silver Lake Rd., 252/928-3505, www.thecastlebb.com, $85-240) is a beautiful home with well-appointed guest rooms, spectacular views, a pool, and, of course, breakfast. Get to breakfast early, when the biscuits are hot; they're legendary around these parts.

There are also cottages and vacation homes for rent (typically by the week) all over Ocracoke. To find a vacation property that fits your needs—it allows pets, can accommodate a large group, is ideal for a romantic getaway—take a look at what's on offer from **Ocracoke Island Realty** (1075 Irvin Garrish Hwy., 252/928-6261 or 866/806-0782, www.ocracokeislandrealty.com) and **Blue Heron Realty** (585B Irvin Garrish Hwy., 252/928-7117, www.blueheronvacations.com).

CAMPING

The National Park Service operates the **Ocracoke Campground** (4352 Irvin Garrish Hwy., Ocracoke, campground 252/928-6671, reservations 877/444-6777, www.recreation.gov, $28), where campsites are right by the beach and behind the dunes (bring extra-long stakes or sand anchors for your tent), and the campground has flush toilets, potable water, cold showers, and grilling stations.

There are two other campgrounds on the island. **Jerniman's Campground** (990 Irvin Garrish Hwy., Ocracoke, 252/928-0308, www.jernimans.com) has tent sites with electric and water hookups starting at $40, and RV sites for 30-foot (from $70) and 40-foot (from $80) RVs. If you're a longtime Ocracoke visitor, Jerniman's is on the site of the former Beachcomber Campground, which was devastated during Hurricane Matthew in 2016 and revitalized in 2019.

Teeter's Campground (200 British Cemetery Rd., 252/588-2030, www.teeterscampground.com) has been serving visitors to Ocracoke since 1976, and this lovely spot is a dream for RVers, with shady trees, inviting patches of lawn, and plenty of campsites. Tent sites (primitive $30, with electricity $40) and RV sites (30-amp $50, 50-amp $60) are perfect little getaways, and with the complimentary Wi-Fi, it's a place you can stay connected to the outside world—or pretend to be on "island time" and use the remoteness of Ocracoke Island as an excuse to stay off grid.

Getting There

Ocracoke can only be reached by ferry. The **Hatteras-Ocracoke Ferry** (800/293-3379, www.ncdot.gov/ferry, 1 hour, $5 pp) is the shortest route to Ocracoke. On some maps, Highway 12 is shown crossing from Ocracoke to Cedar Island, as if there were an impossibly long bridge over Pamlico Sound. In fact, that stretch is a ferry route too. The **Cedar Island-Ocracoke Ferry** (800/293-3379, www.ncdot.gov/ferry), a 2.25-hour ride, costs $15 one-way for a regular-size vehicle. There's also an **Ocracoke-Swan Quarter Ferry** (800/293-3379, www.ncdot.gov/ferry, 2.5 hours, regular-size vehicle $15 one-way).

Across the Sounds

Traditionally called the Albemarle, although today sometimes called the Inner Banks, the mainland portion of northeastern North Carolina is the heart and hearth of the state's colonial history, the site of its first colonial towns and earliest plantations, and the seat of power for the largely maritime economy.

Inland, early European Carolinians and Virginians named a region they thought of as a diseased and haunted wasteland "the Great Dismal Swamp." They planned to drain it and create more hospitable places to settle, and to a point they succeeded in doing so. But enough of the swamp remains today that it is recognized it as one of the state's prettiest places, valued by human visitors almost as much as by the bears and wolves that live there.

Early cities like Edenton and Bath were influential centers of commerce and government, and today they preserve some of the finest examples of colonial and early Federal architecture in the Southeast. Inland, along the Roanoke River, the small town of Halifax played a key role in American history; in a tavern in Halifax, representatives from North Carolina wrote and ratified the Halifax Accords, the first documents to denounce British rule over the colonies and to declare American independence. The Halifax Accords were read at the Continental Congress in Philadelphia, which led to the Declaration of Independence and the Revolutionary War.

The vast networks of rivers and creeks feeding the Roanoke River and other major waterways include some of the state's best places for inland canoeing and kayaking. Along the Albemarle Regional Canoe-Kayak Trail, a number of camping platforms allow paddlers to spend an unforgettable night listening to owls hoot and otters splash. The abundant water also irrigates the vast farms in this corner of the state, and if a small town has a restaurant, it'll be either a country kitchen or a fish shack. Either way, you'll get to sample the region's inland seafood traditions.

THE GREAT DISMAL SWAMP

Thought of for centuries as an impediment to progress, the Great Dismal Swamp is now recognized for the national treasure that it is, and tens of thousands of its acres are protected. There are several points to access the interior of the Dismal Swamp. On U.S. 17, a few miles south of the Virginia-North Carolina border, is the **Dismal Swamp Welcome Center at Dismal Swamp State Park** (2294 U.S. 17 N., South Mills, 252/771-6593, www.ncparks.gov, 8am-6pm daily Mar.-Oct., 8am-5pm daily Nov.-Feb., closed Dec. 25, visitors center 9am-4:30pm Mon.-Fri., 9:30am-4:30pm Sat.-Sun., bike, canoe, and kayak rentals $7 per hour) as well as the **Dismal Swamp Visitors Center** (2356 U.S. 17 N., South Mills, 877/771-8333, www.dismalswampwelcomecenter.com, 9am-5pm daily). Arriving by water, you'll find the Welcome Center at mile 28 on the Intracoastal Waterway. You can tie up to the dock and spend the night, or wait for one of the four daily lock openings (8:30am, 11am, 1:30pm, and 3:30pm) to proceed. There are also picnic tables, grills, and restrooms open 24 hours daily.

Another area of the swamp to explore is the **Great Dismal Swamp National Wildlife Refuge** (3100 Desert Rd., Suffolk, VA, 757/986-3705, www.fws.gov, trails dawn-dusk daily, auto tour 7:30am-3pm Mon.-Sat., $5), which straddles the state line. Two main entrances, Washington Ditch and Jericho Lane (7am-7pm daily Apr.-Sept., 7:30am-5pm daily Oct.-Mar.), are outside of Suffolk, Virginia, off White Marsh Road (U.S. 642). In the middle of the refuge is Lake Drummond, an eerie 3,100-acre natural lake that's a wonderful place for canoeing. Contact refuge headquarters for directions on navigating the feeder ditch into Lake Drummond. You may see all sorts of wildlife in the swamp, including poisonous snakes like cottonmouths, canebrake rattlers, and copperheads, and possibly even black bears. Controlled hunting is permitted on certain days October-December, so if you visit in the fall, wear bright-colored clothing and contact refuge staff before your visit to find out about closures.

GATESVILLE

Near the town of Gatesville, west of South Mills on U.S. 158, is another gorgeous natural swamp area, **Merchant's Millpond State Park** (176 Millpond Rd., Gatesville, 252/357-1191, http://ncparks.gov, visitors center 8am-6:30pm Mon.-Fri. Mar.-Oct., 8am-5pm Mon.-Fri. Nov.-Feb., park 8am-6pm daily Nov.-Feb., 8am-8pm daily Mar.-May and Sept.-Oct., 8am-9pm daily June-Aug.). There is an amazing variety of wildlife, particularly reptiles, with many species of snakes (most are harmless), turtles (harmless, except for the snappers), and, despite the relatively northerly clime, alligators (most emphatically not harmless). Other denizens include salamanders, mink, and nutrias.

TOP EXPERIENCE

Kayaking

This is a great spot for canoeing or kayaking, with miles of beautiful black-water backwaters. For those unfamiliar with black water, it looks like it sounds: Tannins from decaying vegetation leech into the water, turning it a dark tea or coffee color and creating a beautiful, but eerie, effect. The park has canoe rentals ($7). There are nine miles of hiking trails, all classified as easy, but rangers strongly caution hikers to avoid ticks. Wear bug spray, tuck your pant legs into your socks, wear light-colored clothing to see the ticks better, and when you return, do a tick check by running your fingers over every inch of your body.

Merchant's Millpond has several campsites (www.northcarolinastateparks.reserveamerica.com, $12-23). The family campground, near the park office, is easily accessible, accommodates tents and RVs, and has a washhouse with restrooms, showers, and drinking water. Off the park's Lassiter Trail are five backpack campsites, where all supplies, including water, must be packed in; there is a pit toilet nearby. There are also two canoe camping areas accessed by canoe trails, with pit toilets; campers must bring water and other supplies.

ELIZABETH CITY

The free **Museum of the Albemarle** (501 S. Water St., 252/335-1453, www.museumofthealbemarle.com, 9am-5pm Mon.-Sat.) covers the four centuries since the first English settlers arrived at Roanoke. Come to learn about the Lost Colonists, the pirates who swarmed the region, and the folkways of the sound country. At **Arts of the Albemarle** (516 E. Main St., 252/338-6455, www.artsaoa. org, 10am-4pm Tues.-Sat.), more than 250 artists have their work on display and for sale in this community gallery and center for the arts; this is a great launch point if you're in town for **First Friday ArtWalk** (4pm-7pm 1st Fri. of the month).

Shopping

There are several places to shop that show off the creative and entrepreneurial spirits of Elizabeth City. Arts of the Albemarle has you covered when it comes to fine art with a coastal focus, but where do you go if you need a good book or some fresh threads? Pick up something to read at **Page After Page Bookstore** (111 S. Water St., 252/335-7243, www.pageafterpagebookstore.indielite. org, 10am-4pm Tues., 10am-6pm Wed.-Fri., 10am-4pm Sat.) whether you're looking for an exciting new release, an esoteric staff pic, or something focused on tales from nearby. **Lazzy Frog** (603 E. Fearing St., 252/338-2328, www.lazzyfrog.com, 10am-5:30pm Tues.-Fri., 10am-3pm Sat.) carries chic clothes and sassy T-shirts for women, cute clothes for kids, and an assortment of gifts and accessories.

Craft Brewing

Elizabeth City is getting in on North Carolina's obsession with beer, and **Ghost Harbor Brewing Company** (602 E. Colonial Ave., 252/599-1030, www.ghostharborbrewing.com, 3pm-10pm Tues.-Thurs., 1pm-11pm Fri.-Sat., 1pm-7pm Sun.) not only has an awesome name and logo, they make some very good beer. Like a lot of young breweries, they're settling into their style, and their focus on pale ales, from their American pale ale to a wheat spin on that to their IPA and double IPA, they deliver clean, hop-centric pints.

Food

For something fun, go over to **Big Boss Burritos** (110 N. Poindexter St., 252/202-7155, 11am-9pm Mon.-Sat., $10) and see if you can handle their namesake burrito. The Big Boss Burrito is huge—a flour tortilla stuffed with steak, french fries (say no more, I'll eat it), cheesy white rice, black beans, sour cream lettuce, *pico de gallo,* and a tomatillo sauce— good luck finishing it in one go. You can also get your giant burrito as a bowl, go for tacos (chicken, ground beef, steak, grilled tuna, barbacoa), and grab dessert—you'll be tempted by the fried Oreos, and that's not a bad call, but go for the churros; they're killer.

Cypress Creek Grill (113 Water St., 252/334-9915, www.cypresscreekgrill.com, 11am-9pm Mon.-Fri., 5pm-9pm Sat., entrées $11-27) is close to downtown and serves gulf-style seafood, Tex-Mex cuisine, and a few creole dishes. The owners are from Texas, and they've blended their native flavors with the local ingredients of eastern North Carolina to make for some tasty dining.

It doesn't matter if you have lunch, dinner, or a weekend brunch, **The Mills Downtown Bistro** (200 N. Poindexter St., 252/621-1471, www.millsbistro.com, 11am-3pm and 5pm-9pm Tues.-Fri., 10am-2pm and 5pm-9pm Sat., 10am-2pm Sun., $14-25) has a something to quell your hunger. At brunch, you'll struggle to decide between the Monte Cristo and the breakfast burger, while the rest of the time it's a battle between binging on small plates (the clams are dreamy, as are the mussels) or going for a crepe, flatbread, or sandwich.

Accommodations

To stay in Elizabeth City and get a feel for the charm here, opt for a bed-and-breakfast. **Foreman House Bed & Breakfast** (311 W. Church St., 252/562-6690, www.foremanhousebedandbreakfast.com, $120-150) was built in 1899. Each of its four rooms is perfectly lovely, but what makes this place is the openness of the innkeepers; their friendly nature, ease around guests, and devotion to ensuring an exceptional stay make this B&B quite the experience. **Blue Ruby at Grice-Fearing House Bed and Breakfast** (200 S. Road St., 252/333-1792, www.bluerubygricefearing.com, $115-200) is the oldest home in the city, dating back to around 1798. The house was expanded in 1840 and again in 1885, was transformed a bed-and-breakfast in 2004, and in 2020 it was refreshed by the new owner. There are three suites at Blue Ruby, but that only adds to the homey feel (it's dog-friendly, which can also add to the hominess). Weather permitting, breakfast is served on the brick patio, a lovely place to start the day. Built in the 1930s, the **Culpepper Inn** (609 W. Main St., 252/335-9235, www.culpepperinn.com, from $119), just a few blocks from Albemarle Sound, has several comfortable guest rooms in the main house as well as cozy accommodations in a carriage house and a cottage.

EDENTON

Incorporated in 1722, Edenton is North Carolina's second-oldest town, even though it was the state's first permanent colonial settlement. For 50 years prior to incorporation, colonists called the lovely waterside town home. Edenton, as one of the largest ports in the colony, served as the first colonial capital until 1743. It's home to a beautiful collection of historic homes and sites along the Maritime Underground Railroad; in the historic district, more than 250 years of architectural styles are on display, including the state's oldest courthouse. The Chowan County Courthouse, built in 1767, is still in use today.

The folks around here are proud of their town and are ready to give you a recommendation on what to see and where to eat. While you could ask just about anyone on the street, the best place for questions is the **Penelope Barker House** (505 S. Broad St., 252/482-7800, www.ehcnc.org, 10am-5pm Mon.-Sat., 10am-4pm Sun.), part of the town's Historic Site and the home of the Edenton Welcome Center. You can also contact the **Chowan County Tourism Development Authority** (800/775-0111, www.visitedenton.com, 9am-5pm Mon.-Fri.) with travel inquiries.

Historic District

All of Edenton is lined with historic buildings, and several especially important sites are clustered within a few blocks of the waterfront. The easiest starting point for a walking tour is the headquarters of the **Edenton State Historic Site** (108 N. Broad St., 252/482-2637, www.nchistoricsites.org, 9am-4pm Tues.-Sat., guided tours $5 adults, $2.50 ages 3-15). From here, it's a short walk to any of a number of historic sites, including the **1886 Roanoke River Lighthouse** (10am-4pm daily, $2.50 adults, $1.50 ages 3-15), an exquisitely restored original river lighthouse. The 1758 **Cupola House** (408 S. Broad St., tickets and information at Edenton Visitors Center, 108 N. Broad St., 252/482-2637, www.cupolahouse.org, 10am-4pm Tues.-Sat., $5 adults, $2.50 ages 3-15) is a home of great architectural significance and a National Historic Landmark. Although much of the original interior woodwork was removed in 1918 and sold to the Brooklyn Museum in New York, where it remains, Cupola House has been meticulously restored inside and out and its colonial gardens recreated. Also a designated National Historic Landmark is the **Chowan County Courthouse** (117 E. King St., 252/482-2637, www.nchistoricsites.org, 10am-4pm Tues.-Sat., $2.50 adults, $1.50 ages 3-15), a superb 1767 brick building in the Georgian style. It's the best-preserved colonial courthouse in the United States and the oldest in-use courthouse in the nation.

Downtown you'll find yourself surrounded by beautiful examples of Jacobean, Georgian, Federal, and Victorian homes as well as a number of other important historical sites, including **St. Paul's Episcopal Church** (W. Church St. and N. Broad St., 252/482-3522, www.spedenton.org), the second-oldest church structure in the state, and **Colonial Waterfront Park** (Edenton waterfront, parking on W. Water St. and S. Broad St.), a stop on the **Maritime Underground Railroad** (www.harrietjacobs.org). African American workers would find sailors willing to assist enslaved people and arrange their passage on ships to a free state. Harriet Jacobs's description of her 1842 escape by sea from Edenton is one of the few existing written accounts. Learn more about her story at http://harrietjacobs.org or on a guided or self-guided walking tour that highlights her years in Edenton.

Leisurely guided **trolley tours** (10:30am, 11:30am, 1:30pm, and 2:30pm Mon.-Sat., 11:30am and 1pm Sun. Apr.-Nov., 11:30am Sun. Dec.-Mar., $12.50 over age 11, $2.25 ages 6-11, free under age 5) depart from the Penelope Barker House Welcome Center, and there are discounts for groups of more than 10.

Food and Accommodations

★ **The Inner Banks Inn & Restaurant** (103 E. Albemarle St., 252/482-3641, www.innerbanksinn.com, from $139), formerly known as The Pack House Inn, occupies three exceptional historic buildings: the 1900 grand Victorian mansion known as the Lords Proprietor's; the 1915 Pack House, which started its life as a tobacco packing house on a nearby plantation; and the 1879 Tillie Bond House cottage. Each is artfully restored with soft and restful furnishings.

1: Merchant's Millpond State Park 2: the 1758 Cupola House 3: the 1886 Roanoke River Lighthouse

A three-course breakfast, which features gluten-free and vegetarian selections if arranged in advance, is served every morning in the Tillie Bond Dining Rooms, and their restaurant, **The Table at Inner Banks** (by reservation only, 4:30pm-8pm Thurs.-Sun., $22-38), serves a wonderful selection of dishes that include seasonal seafood dishes as well as duck and beef dishes. Grab a bite at **Edenton Bay Oyster Bar** (621 W. Queen St., Edenton, 252/482-1128, www.edentonbayoysterbar.co, 5pm-9pm Wed.-Thurs., 5pm-10pm Fri., 4pm-8pm Sun., $12-29) and celebrate the seafood of the Outer Banks and Sounds on the plate. You can get a pork chop or a steak here, but focus on the seafood—the oysters (raw, steamed, broiled, or fried), crab cakes, seared scallops, and the fried seafood platter—and you'll go home happy. The Chef at **Old Colony Smokehouse** (802 W. Queen St., Edenton, 252/482-2400, www.oldcolonysmokehouse. com, 11am-2pm Thurs.-Sat., $5-27) knows his way around the kitchen, and he's got the chops to prove it; specifically, he won an episode of *Chopped,* the "use whatever oddball ingredients we throw at you" competition on Food Network. But you don't come here to eat a Cap'n Crunch and kimchi Stromboli; you come here for barbecue. Chopped pork, brisket, pulled chicken, smoked turkey, ribs, sandwiches with your meat of choice, and all those sides (collards, slaw, and loaded potato salad are stars) will make you a happy eater.

WINDSOR

A small historic town on the Cashie (cuh-SHY) River, Windsor is the seat of Bertie (ber-TEE) County. Historic architecture, good food, and wetlands exploration are equally compelling reasons to visit this lesser-known treasure of the Albemarle region.

Sights

Hope Plantation (132 Hope House Rd., 252/794-3140, www.hopeplantation.org, visitors center 10am-2pm Mon. and Wed., $15 adults, $14 seniors, $8 students and children) was built in 1803 for David Stone. Stone did not live to see his 50th birthday, but by the time of his death he had been governor of North Carolina, a U.S. senator and representative, a state senator, and a superior court judge, and had been elected seven times to the State House. He graduated from Princeton and passed the bar when he was 20, fathered 11 children, and was one of the founders of the University of North Carolina. As busy as he was, he also managed to oversee the construction of this impressive house. Characterized by a mixture of Georgian and Federal styles with significant twists of regional and individual aesthetics, Hope House is on the National Register of Historic Places. Also on the register, and now on the grounds of the plantation, is the brick-end, gambrel roof **King-Bazemore House,** built in 1763 and also a significant example of its type.

The **Roanoke-Cashie River Center** (112 W. Water St., Windsor, 252/794-2001, www. partnershipforthesounds.net, 10am-4pm Tues.-Fri., $2, $1 children) has interpretive exhibits about this region's history and ecology. There is a canoe ramp outside where you can access the Cashie River, and canoe rentals ($10 per hour, $25 half day, $35 full day) are available.

Recreation

The **Roanoke River National Wildlife Refuge** (visitor contact station at 114 W. Water St., Windsor, www.fws.gov, 8am-4:30pm Mon.-Fri.) stretches over nearly 21,000 acres in Bertie County, through the hardwood bottomlands and cypress-tupelo wetlands of the Roanoke River Valley, an environment that the Nature Conservancy calls "one of the last great places." The refuge is an exceptional place for bird-watching, with the largest inland heron rookery in North Carolina, a large population of bald eagles, and many wintering waterfowl and neotropical migratory species. There's only one designated hiking trail, The **Kuralt Trail** (2 miles north of Williamston, off U.S. 17/13), though there are several other access points along forest roads, so you'll do a little bushwhacking along with your bird-watching. If you're here in fall and spring, wear some bright orange and be safe in the woods, as they're open to hunters for small game and deer.

Food

Bunn's Bar-B-Q (127 N. King St., 252/794-2274, 9am-5pm Mon.-Tues. and Thurs.-Fri., 9am-2pm Wed. and Sat., from $5) is a barbecue joint of renown, an early gas station converted in 1938 to its present use. Service here is blazing fast, primarily because there are just a few choices on the menu. Superfinely chopped barbecue is the specialty, and you get it on a plate or a sandwich, with tart or creamy coleslaw and cornbread. It comes lightly sauced, the way the locals like it, but if you want more, or hotter, sauce, you'll find a bottle close at hand. Any time you're passing by a barbecue joint, pick up a pint or pound and a bottle of sauce; it's fun to do a barbecue taste test and find your favorite.

SCOTLAND NECK

In the little Halifax County community of Scotland Neck, west of Windsor, is the **Sylvan Heights Bird Park** (500 Sylvan Heights Park Way, off Lees Meadow Rd., 252/826-3186, www.shwpark.com, 9am-4pm Tues.-Sun., $12 adults, $11 over age 62, $9 ages 3-12, free under age 2), a center for the conservation of rare species of birds and home to the world's largest collection of waterfowl, comprising more than 1,000 birds of 170 different species. You'll see birds native to every continent except Antarctica; it gets a little hot here for penguins. A visit to Sylvan Heights is an unbeatable opportunity to get up close to birds you won't encounter elsewhere and a great spot for wildlife photography—you won't even need your zoom lens.

HISTORIC HALIFAX AND ROANOKE RAPIDS

Sometimes the biggest things come from the smallest places. Fewer than 300 people call the tiny hamlet of Halifax home, but it is the birthplace of a nation, where the first official documents calling for independence from British rule were written. Once an important town due to its proximity to the river and trade routes, Halifax dwindled as nearby Roanoke Rapids rose in significance. Today, Halifax is not much more than a state historic site, with the vast majority of local shopping, dining, and infrastructure located in Roanoke Rapids.

In its heyday Roanoke Rapids was home to several textile mills. But, as in so many other Southern towns, the mill jobs left, and the town suffered. Once part of a complex series of locks allowing river traffic to bypass the falls on the Roanoke River, the Roanoke Canal Museum and Trail has become a historical sight and a well-used walking and cycling path.

Sights

The main attraction is **Historic Halifax** (25 St. David St., Halifax, 252/583-7191, www.nchistoricsites.org, 9am-5pm Tues.-Sat., free). Several colonial-era buildings still stand, including a prominent merchant's home and the Tap Room tavern, both from 1760, and the 1790 Eagle Tavern; there are also several early-19th-century buildings, including a home, an attorney's office, the clerk's office, and the jail. Five tours run throughout the day and take 30-60 minutes. On April 12, the Halifax Day celebration commemorates the date of the 1776 Halifax Resolves, which are believed to have been signed in the Eagle Tavern. Events, speakers, tours, and usually costumed Colonial-era reenactors fill the day with the sights, sounds, smells, and activities that would have given the community so much energy so long ago.

In Roanoke Rapids, the **Roanoke Canal Museum and Trail** (15 Jackson St. Ext., Roanoke Rapids, 252/537-2769, www.roanokecanal.com, museum 10am-4pm Tues.-Sat., trail dawn-dusk daily, museum $4 over age 8, free under age 9, trail free) is more than a museum; it includes a 7.5-mile nature trail. At the trailhead, a museum tells the story of this 200-year-old canal, originally opened to allow river traffic to bypass the falls, and all its subsequent incarnations. In 1882 investors developed it into an early hydroelectric power source, and by 1900, two powerhouses were in full operation. The investors couldn't maintain it, and it was sold to a power company that operated it for several decades; in 1976 what remained of the canal was placed on the National Register of Historic Places. Learn about this in greater detail in the museum, which also provides an overall feel for the history of the Roanoke River Valley.

For one of the weirdest sights around, you need to head to nearby Littleton, where the **Cryptozoology & Paranormal Museum** (300 N. Main St., Littleton, 631/220-1231, www.crypto-para.org, 1pm-7pm daily, free) takes a deeper look into the creatures and happenings that defy explanations offered by traditional science. They've got plaster casts, photos, and stories of a bigfoot, or a similarly inexplicable cryptid, captured in nearby Medoc Mountain State Park; ghost-hunting tools and equipment (which they'll be happy to discuss in detail); info on UFO sightings from near and far; and more.

Sports and Recreation

The **Roanoke Canal Trail** (15 Jackson St. Ext., trailheads at Roanoke Rapids Lake, near Oakwood Ave., Roanoke Rapids; and Rockfish Dr., near U.S. 158/301, Weldon, dawn-dusk daily) runs for 7.5 miles along the tow path beside the 19th-century canal. Expect river views and secluded woodsy sections along the path; bring water and bug spray.

You can jog, hike, or ride bikes on the Roanoke Canal Trail, but there are even more trails to explore at **Medoc Mountain State Park** (1541 Medoc State Park Rd., Hollister, 525/586-6588, www.ncparks.gov, 8am-6pm daily Nov.-Feb., 8am-8pm daily Mar.-May and Sept.-Oct., 8am-9pm daily June-Aug., visitors center 8am-5pm daily, closed Christmas Day). They have 10 miles each of hiking and bridle trails, and 9 miles of mountain biking trails, plus fishing and paddling along Little Fishing Creek. Camping

(www.northcarolinastateparks.reserveamerica.com) is available, and they have primitive sites ($12), sites with electrical hookups ($28) and without ($23), and even equestrian-only backcountry sites ($12).

Every spring, anglers from around the country come to nearby Weldon to catch striped bass, known here as rockfish; as they travel up the river to spawn, the fishing is excellent. The Roanoke River's other fish species include shad, largemouth bass, and catfish. Outfitters can provide gear as well as the requisite fishing license. A comprehensive list of outfitters and guides is maintained by the **Halifax County Convention and Visitors Bureau** (www.visithalifax.com).

If kayaking is more your speed, **Roanoke River Partners** (www.roanokeriverpartners.org) maintains an index of outfitters and guides happy to help you with a solo or guided exploration of the river.

Shopping

At the western end of the Roanoke Canal Trail is **Riverside Mill** (200 Mill St., Weldon, 252/536-3100, www.riversidemill.net, 10am-6pm daily), an antiques mall and artisans gallery in a historic cotton mill. It's a fun place to explore because of the eclectic mix of local pottery, paintings, crafts, and antiques.

An odd and strangely fun thing to do is hook up with the **U.S. 301 Endless Yard Sale** (www.301endlessyardsale.com, typically 3rd Fri.-Sat. of June), a 100-mile yard sale stretching across five counties and lining the roads, parks, parking lots, fields, and any available space along U.S. 301 from Halifax to Johnston County with stuff. It's a two-day affair occurring in June, and it's your chance to find some unusual—read: treasure, trash, junk, oddities, and everything in between—items to take home. At the very least, it's quality people-watching.

Food and Accommodations

The Hen & The Hog (16 S. King St., Halifax, 252/583-1017, www.thehenthehog.com, 11am-2:30pm Tues.-Fri., 5:30pm-9:30pm Thurs.,

5:30pm-9pm Fri.-Sat., $10-45) uses local farms and ranches to supply the ingredients for tremendous Southern dishes that stay focused on regional cuisine, but strays to include other Southern specialties. The pork chop with seasonal veggies and the shrimp and grits are dinner favorites, and the shrimp po' boy is a lunchtime crowd-pleaser.

When you're ready to head out for some antiquing or you just need a caffeinated pick-me-up, swing by **The Mill Coffee & Eatery** (1020 Roanoke Ave., Roanoke Rapids, 252/308-6849, www.themillcoffeeandeatery. com, 8am-8pm Mon.-Fri., 11am-3pm Sat., $2-12) for a cup of coffee and a bite. You can get a bagel, biscuit, and breakfast burrito in the mornings, switch to a baked potato (or its loaded cousin) or a sandwich for lunch, and grab a cookie to go so you're equipped with a road snack.

Accommodations in the area consist mostly of chain hotels and a few mom-and-pop motels that open and close periodically. One reliable option is the **Country Inn & Suites by Radisson, Roanoke Rapids** (101 Hampton Blvd., Roanoke Rapids, 252/537-3141 or 800/333-3333, www.radissonhotelsamericas. com, from $85); another is the **Baymont by Wyndham Roanoke Rapids** (1001 Old Farm Rd. S., Roanoke Rapids, 252/507-4958, www.wyndhamhotels.com, from $70).

Nearby Enfield, just a few miles south of Roanoke Rapids, is home to one B&B. **Bellamy Manor and Gardens Bed and Breakfast** (613 Glenview Rd., Enfield, 252/445-2234, www.manorbnb.com, from $125) has four charming guest rooms in a beautiful home. Extensive gardens provide a place to walk and unwind, and if you're the sporting type, request a skeet-shooting outing when you make your reservation.

Getting There and Around

From the Outer Banks, Halifax is a 2.5-hour drive west. Follow U.S. 64 across Roanoke Island and onto the mainland, then continue along this route for approximately 53 miles. Turn right on Highway 45 north, and follow this road for 13 miles until it meets U.S. 17. Turn left onto U.S. 17 and then take the U.S. 17 Bypass to Highway 308, approximately 11 miles. Follow Highway 308 for 28 miles until you reach U.S. 258/Highway 561, where you'll turn left. After 7 miles, turn right onto Highway 561 and take it the rest of the way to Halifax.

Weldon is approximately 10 minutes north along U.S. 301, and Roanoke Rapids is 10 minutes west of Weldon via U.S. 158.

WILLIAMSTON AND VICINITY

Williamston is at the junction of U.S. 17 and U.S. 64. If you're passing through town, Williamston is a great place to stop for barbecue or a fresh seafood meal at one of the few remaining traditional seafood houses.

Sights

One of the oddest sights in eastern North Carolina may be **Deadwood** (2302 Ed's Grocery Rd., 252/792-8938, www.deadwood. live, 5pm-9pm Thurs., 5pm-10pm Fri., noon-11pm Sat., noon-9pm Sun.), a tiny amusement park with an Old West flair. The owner calls this 10-acre park "a weird, out-of-hand backyard project" inspired by Dolly Parton's Dollywood in Tennessee. Amusements here include miniature golf, a miniature train ride, a kid-friendly roller coaster, and a murder-mystery dinner show (1st Sat. of the month, $30, $15 under age 13), complete with pratfalls, a gunfight, and a hearty dinner. It's well worth the stop, even if all you do is play a round of mini golf and eat ice cream.

Food

The ★ **Sunny Side Oyster Bar** (1102 Washington St., 252/792-3416, 5:30pm-8:30pm Mon.-Thurs., 5:30pm-10pm Fri.-Sat., 5:30pm-8pm Sun., $7-25), a seasonal oyster joint open during the months which have names that contain the letter *R*—that is, oyster season—draws diners from hundreds of miles away. It has been in business since 1935 and is a historic and gastronomic landmark. Oysters are steamed behind the restaurant and then hauled inside and shucked at the bar. Visit the restaurant's website to meet the shuckers. In eastern North Carolina, a good oyster shucker is as highly regarded as a good artist or athlete, and rightly so.

The Smokehouse Grill (252/792-8516, www.deadwoodnc.com, 5pm-9pm Thurs., 5pm-10pm Fri., noon-11pm Sat., noon-9pm Sun., $9-23), in the Deadwood amusement park, serves steaks, ribs, chicken, shrimp, and Tex-Mex specialties in a kitschy but charming Old West venue.

EAST ON U.S. 64

The eastern stretch of U.S. 64 runs along the Albemarle Sound between Williamston and the Outer Banks, passing through the towns of Plymouth, Creswell, and Columbia before it crosses to Roanoke Island. Here you'll encounter evidence of North Carolina's ancient past in old-growth forests, its recent past in the form of a plantation with a long history of enslavement, and its present in art galleries and abundant wildlife-watching and recreational opportunities.

Plymouth

Plymouth is an attractive little town on the Roanoke River with a rich maritime and military history. Most notably it was the site of the 1864 Battle of Plymouth, the second-largest Civil War battle in North Carolina, fought by more than 20,000 soldiers. At the **Roanoke River Lighthouse and Maritime Museum** (W. Water St., 252/217-2204, www.roanokeriverlighthouse.org, 11am-3pm Wed.-Sat., 2pm-4pm Sun. and by appointment, $3 adults, $2 students), visitors can explore a pretty replica of Plymouth's 1866 screw-pile lighthouse. Across the street in an old car dealership, the maritime museum features artifacts and photographs from the region's water-faring heritage. On East Water Street is the **Port O'Plymouth Museum** (302 E. Water St., 252/793-1377, www.portoplymouthmuseum. org, 9am-4pm Tues.-Fri., 9am-3pm Sat., $3.50 adults, $2.50 ages 12-17, $1.50 ages 8-12, free

under age 8, guided tour $5 adults, $3 ages 12-17). This tiny museum is packed with Civil War artifacts, including a collection of beautiful pistols, telling the story of the Battle of Plymouth, the last major Confederate victory of the Civil War and the third-largest battle in North Carolina. Surprisingly, some 5,000 North Carolinians from around here joined the Union navy. On-site there's a fully functioning scale replica of the ironclad CSS *Albemarle;* see it and more at a living history event held the last weekend in April.

★ Somerset Place Historic Site

Somerset Place Historic Site (2572 Lake Shore Rd., Creswell, 252/797-6020, www. nchistoricsites.org, 9am-5pm Tues.-Sat., free) was one of North Carolina's largest and most profitable plantations for the 80 years leading up to the Civil War. In the late 18th and early 19th centuries, 80 African-born men, women, and children were enslaved and brought to Somerset to labor in the fields. The grief and disorientation they experienced and the subsequent trials of the enslaved people, whose numbers grew to more than 300, are told by the historian Dorothy Spruill Redford in the book *Somerset Homecoming.* Somerset is a significant historical place for many reasons, but the story of its African Americans makes it one of this state's most important historic sites. Visitors can walk around the estate at their leisure. A small bookshop on the grounds is a good source for books about North Carolina history in general and African American history in particular.

★ Pettigrew State Park

Pettigrew State Park (2252 Lakeshore Rd., Creswell, 252/797-4475, http://ncparks. gov, 8am-6pm daily Nov.-Feb., 8am-8pm daily Mar.-May and Sept.-Oct., 8am-9pm daily June-Aug., closed Dec. 25, park office 8:30am-6pm Mon.-Fri.), on the banks of **Lake Phelps,** preserves an unusual ancient waterscape that's unlike anything else in the state. Archaeology reveals that there was a human presence here at least 10,000 years ago. The lake, which is five miles across and never more than nine feet deep, is only fed by rainfall and has yielded more than 30 ancient dugout canoes, some as old as 4,400 years and measuring more than 30 feet. The natural surroundings are ancient too, encompassing some of eastern North Carolina's only remaining old-growth forests. **Pungo Lake,** a smaller body of water within the park, is visited by 50,000 migrating snow geese over the course of the year, an unforgettable sight for wildlife watchers. Visitors can camp (www.northcarolinastateparks.reserveamerica.com) at the family campground ($23), which has drive-in sites and access to restrooms and hot showers, or at primitive group campsites (from $42).

Sports and Recreation

Palmetto-Peartree Preserve (entrance on Pot Licker Rd./Loop Rd./State Rd. 1220, east of Columbia, 252/796-0723 or 919/967-2223, www.conservationfund.org) is a 10,000-acre natural area, wrapped in 14 miles of shoreline along Albemarle Sound and Little Alligator Creek. Originally established as a sanctuary for the red cockaded woodpecker, this is a great location for bird-watching and spotting other wildlife, including alligators, wolves, bears, and bobcats, as well as hiking, cycling, and horseback riding along the old logging trails through the forest or canoeing and kayaking. The preserve's excellent paddle trail passes by Hidden Lake, a secluded cypress-swamp black-water lake.

Once the southern edge of the Great Dismal Swamp, **Pocosin Lakes National Wildlife Refuge** (205 S. Ludington Dr., 6 miles south of Columbia, 252/796-3004, www.fws.gov) is an important haven for many species of animals, including migratory waterfowl and reintroduced red wolves. Five important bodies of water lie within the refuge: Pungo Lake, New Lake, the 16,600-acre Lake Phelps, and stretches of the Scuppernong and Alligator Rivers. All of these areas are good spots for observing migratory waterfowl, but Pungo Lake is special in the fall and winter, when snow geese and tundra swans visit in massive numbers—approaching 100,000—on their arctic journeys.

Also east of Columbia on U.S. 64 is the **Alligator River National Wildlife Refuge** (between Columbia and Roanoke Island, 252/473-1131, www.fws.gov). The large refuge covers most of the peninsula bounded by the Alligator River to the west, Albemarle Sound to the north, Croatan Sound to the east, and Pamlico Sound to the southeast. This large swath of woods and pocosin represents one of the most important wildlife habitats in the state, home to more than 200 species of birds as well as alligators, red wolves, and more black bears than anywhere in the coastal Mid-Atlantic. In the 1980s, red wolves were introduced into the Alligator River Refuge as they became extinct in the wild elsewhere in their original range. The Columbia-based **Red Wolf Coalition** (252/796-5600, http://redwolves.com) works to educate the public about the wolves in the hope of helping to establish free-ranging, self-sustaining red wolf populations at a number of sites. Alligator River National Wildlife Refuge has a **Visitor Center** (100 Conservation Way, Manteo, 252/473-1131, 9am-4pm Mon.-Sat., noon-4pm Sun.) on Roanoke Island where you can learn more about the flora, fauna, natural, and human history of the place, pick up maps, and inquire with the folks there about wildlife sightings and any ranger-led programming.

There are many other ways to enjoy the Alligator River National Wildlife Refuge, including hiking, kayaking, and bird-watching. The refuge does not have a physical headquarters or traditional visitors center, but detailed directions and visitor information are available on the website.

Art Galleries

Eastern North Carolina has always had a folk-art tradition. **Pocosin Arts** (201 Main St., Columbia, 252/796-2787, www.pocosinarts.org, 9am-5pm Mon.-Fri.) has helped keep the tradition of arts and crafts alive, teaching community classes in ceramics, fiber arts, sculpture, jewelry making, metalwork, and other media. The sales gallery has beautiful handmade items, and the main gallery displays many examples of folk art from eastern North Carolina.

WASHINGTON, BATH, AND BELHAVEN

North of the Pamlico River, as you head toward the Mattamuskeet National Wildlife Refuge and the Outer Banks, the towns of Washington, Bath, and Belhaven offer brief but beautiful diversions into the nature and history of the region.

North Carolina Estuarium

The **North Carolina Estuarium** (223 E. Water St., Washington, 252/948-0000, www.partnershipforthesounds.net, 10:30am-3:30pm Tues.-Sat., $5, $3 children, free under age 5) is a museum dedicated to both the natural and cultural history of the Tar-Pamlico River basin. In addition to the exhibits, which include live native animals, historic artifacts, a 0.75-mile boardwalk along the Pamlico River, and hands-on displays, the Estuarium operates pontoon boat tours (10:30am and 1:30pm Wed.-Fri., 10:30am Sat., reservations required, free).

Elmwood 1820

These small coastal towns exude charm, and when you get to a B&B like **Elmwood 1820** (731 W. Main St., 252/623-1466, www.elmwood1820.com, $209-259), you'll absolutely fall in love with a place, maybe even think to yourself, "I could retire here, run a B&B . . ." This 200-year-old home (built in 1820, hence the name) is steeped in history, and the architecture is spectacular. There's a big lawn and a porch you'll miss sitting on as soon as you leave, and the guest rooms are tastefully decorated with works by local artists and pieces the owners collected over years of travel. Five rooms, three of which are suites, have king or queen beds so comfy you might see if you can just move in.

From Elmwood 1820 you've got a lovely 10-minute walk to a dining institution: **Bill's Hot Dogs** (109 Gladden St., 252/946-3343, 8:30am-5pm Mon.-Sat., $1.50-2.25). This longtime local favorite has been around since 1928, so they've got their process down—you can only order when they ask for your order—and they know how to produce the dogs on the double.

Goose Creek State Park

Goose Creek State Park (2190 Camp Leach Rd., 252/923-2191, http://ncparks.gov, 8am-6pm daily Nov.-Feb., 8am-8pm daily Mar.-May and Sept.-Oct., 8am-9pm daily June-Aug., closed Dec. 25, park office 8am-5pm daily) is on the banks of the Pamlico River where Goose Creek joins it. It's an exotic environment of brackish marshes, freshwater swamps, and tall pine forests that are home to a variety of wildlife, including bears, a multitude of bird species, and lots of snakes. Eight miles of hiking trails as well as boardwalks and paddle trails traverse the hardwood swamp environment, and miles of shoreline and creek await exploration from a kayak or canoe (bring your own). Camping is available (reserve at 877/722-6762, www.northcarolinastateparks.reserveamerica.com, year-round) and they welcome RVers ($36), tent campers ($15, group campsite $45), and folks who want to stay in their cabins ($58).

Historic Bath

North Carolina's oldest colonial town, Bath was chartered in 1705. The town has changed so little that even today it is mostly contained within the original boundaries laid out by the explorer John Lawson. For its first 70 years, Bath enjoyed the spotlight as one of North Carolina's most important centers of trade and politics, home to governors, a refuge from the Indian Wars, and frequently host to and victim of the pirate Blackbeard. Bath faded into obscurity as the town of Washington grew in the years after the Revolution, and today almost all of Bath is designated as **Historic Bath** (252/923-0525, www.nchistoricsites.org, visitors center and tours 9am-5pm Tues.-Sat., admission charged for both the Palmer-Marsh and Bonner Houses, $2 adults, $1 students). Important sites on the tour of the village are the 1734 St. Thomas Church, the 1751 Palmer-Marsh House, the 1790 Van Der Veer House, and the 1830 Bonner House, which overlooks a plot of land where Blackbeard once had a house. Bath has its fair share of legends, including a set of indelible hoof prints said to have been made by the devil's horse and "Teach's light"—supposedly ghostly remnants of the pirate Blackbeard.

If you decide to stay the night, try the **Inn on Bath Creek** (116 S. Main St., 252/923-9571, www.innonbathcreek.com, 2-night minimum Fri.-Sat. Apr.-Nov., $145-150). This bed-and-breakfast, built on the site of the former Buzzard Hotel, fits in nicely with the old architecture of the historic town, but because it was built in 1999, it has modern conveniences to make your stay comfortable. Breakfast is big—think scratch-made blueberry pancakes, scrambled-egg wraps, and quiche along with the usual fruit, coffee, and pastries—and vegetarian options are available.

Belhaven

The little town of Belhaven sits on the Pungo River and is about as adorable as adorable can be. There's not a ton to do in town, but folks love it for that. You can find more visitors information at www.visitbelhavennc.com.

Belying its innocuous name, **Belhaven Memorial Museum** (210 E. Main St., www. beaufort-county.com, 1pm-5pm Thurs.-Tues., free) is actually a very strange little institution that houses the collection of Miss Eva Blount Way, who died in 1962 at the age of 92, a collector of oddities. She was described in a 1951 newspaper article as "housewife, snake killer, curator, trapper, dramatic actress, philosopher, and preserver of all the riches of mankind." Among her earthly treasures is a collection of pickled tumors (one weighs 10 pounds), a pickled one-eyed pig, a pickled two-headed kitten, cataracts (pickled),

and three human infants (also pickled). It is without a doubt one of the weirdest museums you'll find.

Belhaven is a stopover for folks driving to or cruising to the Outer Banks or making their way along the Intracoastal Waterway (a sort of water highway running from Maine to Key West; naturally, life on the North Carolina coast revolves in some way around the Intracoastal), and **Between Water and Main** (367 E. Water St., 252/943-0367, www. betweenwaterandmain.com, $140-175) is a B&B catering to those travelers and travelers of any stripe. Five spacious rooms, each with an en suite bath, and walkable to the water and everything downtown, it's a lovely spot to spend a night or two.

One place you must stop to dine is ★ **Spoon River Artworks & Market** (263 Pamlico St., 252/945-3899, www.spoonrivernc.com, 5:30pm-10pm Thurs.-Sat., 11:30am-2pm Sat., 10:30am-2pm Sun., $16-38). Known for their artful plating of delicious farm-to-fork food, Spoon River is a great find in this corner of the state, where an excellent meal is hard to find. Seafood, in particular oysters and shrimp, are excellent, but you'll see almost as many steaks coming out of the kitchen.

★ MATTAMUSKEET NATIONAL WILDLIFE REFUGE

Near the tiny town of Swan Quarter, **Mattamuskeet National Wildlife Refuge** (856 Mattamuskeet Rd., off Hwy. 94, between Swan Quarter and Englehard, 252/926-4021, www.fws.gov) preserves one of North Carolina's most remarkable natural features as well as one of its most famous buildings. Lake Mattamuskeet, 18 miles long by 6 miles wide, is the state's largest natural lake, and at an average of 1.5 feet deep—5 feet at its deepest point—it is a most unusual environment. The hundreds of thousands of waterfowl who rest here on their seasonal rounds make this a world-famous location for bird-watching and wildlife photography.

Hiking and biking trails thread through the refuge, but camping is not permitted. In hunting season, which runs during spring and autumn months, beware of hunters (wearing a bright color like safety orange isn't a bad idea), and keep an eye out for copperheads, cottonmouths, two kinds of rattlesnakes, and alligators. Bears and red wolves abound here as well.

Within the administration of the Mattamuskeet Refuge is the **Swanquarter National Wildlife Refuge** (252/926-4021, www.fws.gov), located along the north shore of the Pamlico Sound, and accessible only by water. It is a gorgeous waterscape full of wildlife and worth exploring if you have the time and the means to get here. In spring, songbirds like robins, warblers, and red-winged blackbirds return by the thousands to nest and breed, and summer brings fledgling and juvenile birds like great blue herons, green herons, and great and snowy egrets. During fall, the refuge is thick with ducks and geese, and it stays that way for much of winter. In colder weather, and for the annual waterfowl hunts in December-January, you'll spot green-winged teal, northern pintail, American coots, gadwalls, and ring-necked ducks, among others.

GREENVILLE

Thirty minutes west of Washington is Greenville, a college town that's home of East Carolina University and one of eastern North Carolina's legendary barbecue joints, B's Barbecue. This city of 95,000 is the largest in this part of the state, and the energetic, relatively young populace takes a great deal of pride in their home, building an eclectic art and cultural scene. The **Greenville-Pitt County Convention & Visitors Bureau** (www.visitgreenvillenc.com) operates a **Visitors Center** (417 Cotanche St., Suite 100, 252/329-4200, 8am-5pm Mon.-Fri.) in Uptown Greenville to help point visitors, and

the families of prospective college students, to some of the best things the city has to offer.

Sights

Uptown Greenville is a lively spot; you'll find many shops, galleries, and eateries. Among the best galleries are the Greenville Museum of Art and Emerge Gallery and Art Center. On the small side, fine-art **Greenville Museum of Art** (802 S. Evans St., 252/758-1946, www.goma.org, 10am-4:30pm Tues.-Sat., free) has a permanent collection that includes 19th- and 20th-century works by American artists, along with galleries dedicated to showing works and artists of particular local and regional interest. The Pitt County Arts Council operates **Emerge Gallery and Art Center** (404 S. Evans St., 252/551-6947, www.pittcountyarts.org, 10am-9pm Tues.-Fri., 10am-4pm Sat., 1pm-4pm Sun. Sept.-May, 10am-9pm Tues.-Thurs., 10am-4pm Fri.-Sat. June-Aug., free), a combo workshop and gallery space. Its two galleries show rotating exhibits and pieces for sale, often featuring local works or works created on-site. The public can take a number of art classes, including a few one-day studio classes.

The **African American Cultural Trail of Greenville-Pitt County** (www.visitgreenvillenc.com) celebrates Black culture, history, and contributions to the community on a six-stop tour around town. Visit the original site of the Sycamore Hill Church, a Black worship center that began in 1860 in a member's home but moved to a proper church post-Emancipation; the two-room (in a private home, mind you) hospital serving "colored" patients back in the 1920s; The Block, a onetime center for Black business; and others. Each stop is accompanied by narration and oral histories you can listen to via the Visit Greenville app.

Pitt Street Brewing Company (630 S. Pitt St., 252/227-4151, www.pittstreetbrewing.com, 2pm-10pm Mon.-Thurs., noon-midnight Fri.-Sat., 1pm-7pm Sun.) is a popular spot, not just because the beer is good, but because it welcomes well-behaved children and dogs,

1: Alligator River National Wildlife Refuge
2: Mattamuskeet National Wildlife Refuge

brings in food trucks, hosts open-mike comedy and music, and is just a good spot to hang out. The menu is IPA-heavy, but they also have a gose, a molasses-loaded Baltic porter, and other styles available.

At **Uptown Brewing Company** (418 Evans St., 252/689-6487, www.uptownbeers.com, 2pm-10pm Tues.-Thurs., 2pm-1am Fri., noon-1am Sat.) you'll find a big taproom where they play good music, host frequent events and musical guests, and serve some excellent beer. They may have a wide range of styles, from the expected IPAs and wheat ales to porters, lagers, and even barley wines and sours. The gose is excellent, as is their cerveza, a Mexican-style lager that's perfect for the long summers.

Sports and Recreation

The Tar River flows by the city, and some of the best recreational opportunities are tied to the water. **Knee Deep Adventures** (2800 E. 10th St., 252/714-5836, www.kneedeepadventures.com, noon-6pm Thurs.-Mon.) rents kayaks and paddleboards (from $35 for 4 hours), allowing you to explore the Tar River on your own. **River Park North** (1000 Mumford Rd., 252/329-4560, www.greenvillenc.gov, 6am-8pm daily May-Aug., 7am-7pm daily Sept.-Oct. and Mar.-Apr., 8am-5pm daily Nov.-Feb., free) has 1.2 miles of Tar River frontage, five ponds for fishing and pedal boating ($7 per half hour), a handful of campsites in the campground ($15) and on a riverside camping platform ($30), hiking trails, and plenty of space for picnicking; you can also rent a Jon boat ($12 for 3 hours) or kayak ($12 for 3 hours) if you want to get out on the river. There's also a small nature center here; the **Walter L. Stasavich Science & Nature Center** (252/329-4560, 9:30am-5pm Tues.-Sat., 1pm-5pm Sun., $3 over age 12, $1.50 under age 13, discount for city residents) has a 10,000-gallon freshwater aquarium, live animals of the kind you'd find around Greenville, and displays on the fauna and flora of the area.

A favorite way for locals to enjoy the Tar River is by taking a stroll, jog, or bike ride along the nine-mile **South Tar River Greenway** (www.greenvillenc.gov). Part of Greenville's larger greenway system, the South Tar River Greenway links the Town Common to the Tar River on a wide, well-maintained, and well-used path. The Greenway winds across town, taking you through the town common, past a university-centric neighborhood and along creeks, through parks and more of the university, and to several spots for picnics or just soaking up the view.

Food

You can't come to eastern North Carolina and not try some barbecue, and you can't come to Greenville without trying B's, a giant in the world of eastern North Carolina 'cue. **B's Barbecue** (751 B's Barbecue Rd., 252/758-7126, 11am-2pm Tues.-Wed. and Fri.-Sat., 11am-1pm Thurs., under $10) does it right: whole hog, pepper-laced vinegar sauce and sides like what you'd eat at home. From the outside B's could use a coat of paint and some TLC, but they focus all of their efforts on the plate, and that's why they sell out of barbecue every day they're open. B's claims to be open until 2pm, but I've never known them to last much longer than 12:30, so if you have a hankering for barbecue, fried chicken, and country sides, get in line early; it'll be out the door.

One of the most lauded barbecue joints in North Carolina is Skylight Inn, in Ayden, between Greenville and Kinston, but the son of the famous Jones barbecue family has opened his own spot in Winterville. ★ **Sam Jones BBQ** (715 W. Fire Tower Rd., Winterville, 252/689-6449, www.samjonesbbq.com, 11am-9pm Mon.-Sat., 11am-8:30pm Sun., $8-22) serves chopped whole-hog 'cue in trays, plates, and sandwiches, but he pushes out into other barbecue territory too. Smoked chicken and turkey, ribs (which, surprising to many, aren't a part of North Carolina's barbecue tradition), wings, catfish, and burgers. A barbecue sandwich is a must, but don't miss the fried pork skins and pimento cheese.

Greenville is a college town and there are loads of places specializing in the cheap eats that college kids survive on—burgers, hot dogs, wraps and bowls, pizza—but you can find a full meal and some good drinks at **Dickenson Avenue Public House** (703 Dickinson Ave., 252/689-6388, www.daphousenc.com, 5:30pm-9pm Tues.-Thurs., 5:30pm-9:30pm Fri.-Sat., bar open late, $13-32). The Korean BBQ Beef Fries can feed a solo diner, but then you'd miss out on the braised pork shoulder, their hot fried chicken sandwich, or their DAP Burger, and that'd be a crime, so come hungry or come with folks who like to share.

Accommodations

The 5th Street Inn (1105 E. 5th St., 252/277-0364, www.the5thstreetmanor.com, $180-244) is the only bed-and-breakfast in town, and fortunately it's a lovely one. Located in the College View Historic District, the white three-story home cuts a fine figure on its lot across the street from ECU. Elegant and well-appointed without feeling like one of those antique-filled, not-sure-if-I-can-touch-anything B&Bs, 5th Street Manor ticks all the boxes when it comes to a comfortable, welcoming stay.

If you're traveling with or in your RV, check out **Whispering Oaks RV Resort** (2773 Sunny Side Rd., 252/752-8886, www.whisperingoaksrvresort.com, $55, $275 per week, $600 per month). There are 14 fully-kitted sites (50- and 110-amp electric, city water and sanitation hookups), a private fishing pond, and 30 acres to explore, plus a canopy of oak trees more than a century old, making this a charming spot to call home for a bit. Owner Wayne Mayhew lives on-site

and he knows the area, so he's quick with a recommendation or an answer if you've got questions or need to know which direction to head.

There are several choices when it comes to chain hotels in Greenville, but the best of them are the **Fairfield Inn & Suites** (908 Moye Blvd., 252/353-0606, www.marriot.com, from $124) and the **Hampton Inn Greenville** (305 SW Greenville Blvd., 252/355-7400, www.hilton.com, from $154).

GETTING THERE AND AROUND

This remote corner of North Carolina is crossed by two major north-south routes, U.S. 17 and U.S. 168, both from Chesapeake, Virginia. U.S. 168 passes to the east through Currituck, and U.S. 17 is the westerly route, closest to the Dismal Swamp and Elizabeth City, passing through Edenton, Windsor, and Williamston. At Williamston, U.S. 17 meets U.S. 64, a major east-west route that leads east to Plymouth, Creswell, and Columbia.

If you continue south on U.S. 17 from Williamston, the next major town is Washington, where you can turn east on U.S. 264 to reach Bath and Belhaven. Alternately, you can reach U.S. 264 from the other direction, taking Highway 94 at Columbia and crossing Lake Mattamuskeet. West of Washington along U.S. 264 is the town of Greenville; from Greenville you have easy access to I-95 by following U.S. 264 west.

There is one state ferry route in this region, at the far northwest corner, between Currituck and Knotts Island (800/293-3779, www.ferry.ncdot.gov, 45 minutes, 6 trips daily, free).

Beaufort and the Crystal Coast

Long before you smell the ocean salt on the air,

you can feel the ocean drawing near. The sky seems wider, and it takes on a deeper shade of blue.

Hardwoods and hills give way to towering pines and flat fields, and then more and more water—creeks, wetlands, and widening rivers. Somewhere between Kinston and New Bern, still an hour's drive from the beaches and sounds of Carteret County, you can sense the Atlantic.

Along the Crystal Coast, as North Carolina's central coast is known in these parts, you'll find New Bern and Beaufort, two old North Carolina towns that were centers of colonial commerce and provided access to the Atlantic. Beautifully preserved, these two towns have great examples of historic commercial and residential architecture

Highlights

Look for ★ to find recommended sights, activities, dining, and lodging.

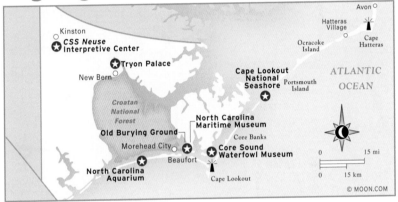

© MOON.COM

★ **Tryon Palace:** The splendid, and in its day controversial, seat of colonial government is worthy of a day's leisurely exploration (page 97).

★ **CSS *Neuse* Interpretive Center:** Far up the Neuse River, a Confederate ironclad was built, scuttled, and burned to prevent its capture. It stayed in the river for nearly a century before being salvaged for historic preservation. This museum tells its story, complete with the recovered hull (page 105).

★ **North Carolina Maritime Museum:** The state's seafaring heritage, ranging from pirate history to its current maritime culture, is represented by fascinating exhibits and activities (page 110).

★ **Old Burying Ground:** One of the prettiest and most storied cemeteries in the South, this Beaufort churchyard is home to the "Little Girl Buried in a Barrel of Rum" and other fascinating residents (page 112).

★ **Core Sound Waterfowl Museum:** Actually a museum about people rather than ducks, the Waterfowl Museum eloquently tells of the everyday lives of past generations of Down Easterners while bringing their descendants together to reforge community bonds (page 119).

★ **Cape Lookout National Seashore:** The more than 50 miles of coastline along Core and Shackleford Banks, now home only to wild horses and turtle nests, were once also the home of Bankers who made their livings in the fishing, whaling, and shipping trades (page 121).

★ **North Carolina Aquarium:** Sharks, jellies, otters, and their aquatic kin show their true beauty in underwater habitats at the aquarium (page 127).

Beaufort and the Crystal Coast

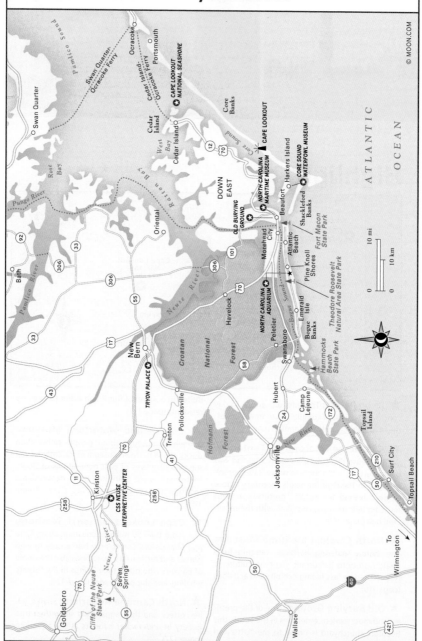

© MOON.COM

dating as far back as three centuries, including one home that belonged to the dreaded pirate Blackbeard.

The Neuse River winds through pine forests, passing Kinston—a town with an unusual Civil War past and a food scene that's worth the visit—and widening as it enters the coastal plain, feeding the primeval forest, creeks, hidden lakes, and tiny towns in the Croatan National Forest. To the northeast, the Cedar Island National Wildlife Refuge is a vast swath of marshes, gradually easing into the Pamlico Sound, where Cape Lookout National Seashore shelters the mainland from storms. Along the seashore are miles of beach where the only occupants are wild horses, the Banker ponies, and the beautiful diamond-patterned Cape Lookout Lighthouse. You won't find homes here. Portsmouth Village, a once-thriving whaling port washed away by a series of storms, is a ghost town and administered by the National Park Service.

Sometimes people in North Carolina refer to any part of the coast, from Wilmington to Nags Head, as "Down East." In the truest sense of the term, Down East refers to northeast Carteret County, the area north of Beaufort. Here the islands, marshes, and towns bordering Core Sound are undergoing colossal cultural shifts as people from "Up North" (meaning "anywhere but here") move into the area and local youth leave generations of family life for greener economic pastures. Changes in global trade and in the environment have made traditional maritime occupations like fishing and shrimping untenable. Nonetheless, Down Easterners work to preserve the treasure of their home, the Core Sound, with conservation and historic preservation as well as folkways education. Witness the Core Sound Waterfowl Museum on Harkers Island, where community members have assembled an interesting collection of family photos, quilts, baseball uniforms, oyster knives, net hooks, and other treasures to tell their story.

PLANNING YOUR TIME

Beach-season rules apply along the coastal areas and river towns, meaning that prices and crowds increase dramatically between Memorial Day in May and Labor Day in early September; conversely, they drop to rock bottom during the off-season. Visiting during shoulder seasons can mean warm water, empty beaches, and no waiting for restaurant tables, but your accommodations and dining choices can be limited, particularly in smaller towns.

When you visit, try the fresh local seafood. To ensure you're getting the best local catch, Carteret Catch (www.carteretcatch.org) provides downloadable cards and information on the seasonally fresh seafood caught in the area.

Across the Southeast, late summer and early autumn are hurricane season. The paths of hurricanes can be quite unpredictable. Even if reports say a storm will dissipate over Cuba, that doesn't mean it won't turn into a hurricane and head for the Carolina coast. Chances are that you'll have sufficient warning before any major storm, but it's advisable to keep an eye on the weather forecast. A storm that stays offshore, even at some distance, can cause foul beach conditions; surfers love the big waves that precede a storm, but they know the danger of powerful tides, strong undertow, rip currents, and the general unpredictability that storms bring. Not unique to this region, the risk is the same anywhere on the North Carolina coast.

Barring storms, fall is a fabulous time to visit. Days and nights are still warm, the ocean is swimmable, and the crowds are smaller. Mild weather often holds through the end of October into November, but the water becomes chilly for swimming then, although

---

Previous: a popular dock; the Cape Lookout Lighthouse; Spanish moss in New Bern.

air temperatures are still nice for strolling on the sand.

INFORMATION AND SERVICES

Hospitals in the area include **Carteret Health Care** (3500 Arendell St., Morehead City, 252/499-6000, www.carterethealth.org) in Morehead City, **CarolinaEast Medical Center** (2000 Neuse Blvd., New Bern, 252/633-8111, www.carolinaeasthealth.com) in New Bern, **Vidant Duplin Hospital** (401 N. Main St., Kenansville, 910/296-0941, www.vidanthealth.com) in Kenansville, **UNC Lenoir Health Care** (100 Airport Rd., Kinston, 252/522-7000, www.unclenoir.org) in Kinston, and **Wayne UNC Health Care** (2700 Wayne Memorial Dr., Goldsboro, 919/736-1110, www.waynehealth.org) in Goldsboro.

Extensive travel information is available from the **Crystal Coast Tourism Authority** (3409 Arendell St., 252/726-8148, www.crystalcoastnc.org) in Morehead City.

New Bern

New Bern's history attracts visitors, but the natural beauty of this artistic community keeps many of them returning year after year. Situated at the confluence of the Trent and Neuse Rivers, it's a prime spot for sightseeing and retirement living. Despite the attention it gets and the consequent traffic, New Bern has retained its charm and is still a small and enormously pleasant town. An important note: It's pronounced "NYEW bern" or "NOO bern," sometimes even like "neighbor," but never "new BERN."

At the junction of two major highways, New Bern is easily reached by car. U.S. 17 passes through New Bern north-south, and U.S. 70 crosses east-west, with Beaufort and Morehead City an hour to the southeast and Kinston 45 minutes to the west; Wilmington is 2.5 hours to the southwest via Highway 17, and Raleigh 2.5 hours west-northwest.

HISTORY

New Bern's early days were marked by tragedy. It was settled in 1710 by a community of Swiss and German colonists under the leadership of English surveyor John Lawson (author of the 1709 *A New Voyage to Carolina*, available today in reprint) and Swiss entrepreneur Christoph von Graffenried (from Bern, Switzerland). More than half of the settlers died en route to the New World, and those who made it alive suffered tremendous hardship in the first years. Lawson and Graffenried were both detained in 1711 by the Indigenous Tuscarora people, whom the colonists had evicted from their land without compensation. Graffenried was released, according to some accounts because he wore such fancy clothes that the Tuscarora feared executing such a high-ranking official. Lawson was tried and burned at the stake, and the conflict escalated into the Tuscarora War.

Despite early disasters, New Bern was on its feet again by the mid-18th century, when it was home to the colony's first newspaper and its first chartered academy. It also became North Carolina's capital, an era symbolized by the splendor of Tryon Palace, one of the most recognizable architectural landmarks in the state.

During the Civil War, New Bern was captured early on by Ambrose Burnside's forces. Despite multiple Confederate attempts to retake the city, it remained a Union stronghold for the balance of the war. It became a center for African American resistance and political organization through the Reconstruction years, a story grippingly told in historian David Cecelski's book *The Waterman's Song*.

New Bern

SIGHTS
★ Tryon Palace

Tryon Palace (529 S. Front St., 800/767-1560, www.tryonpalace.org, 10am-5pm Mon.-Sat., noon-5pm Sun., last guided tour 4pm, gardens 9am-6pm Mon.-Sat. and noon-6pm Sun. Mar.-Nov., 9am-5pm Mon.-Sat. and noon-5pm Sun. Nov.-Mar., museum shop 9am-5pm Mon.-Sat., 1pm-5pm Sun., day pass $20 adults, $10 ages 6-14, galleries and gardens $12 adults, $6 ages 6-14, gardens pass $6 adults, $3 ages 6-14) is a remarkable feat of historic re-creation, a reconstruction of the 1770 colonial capitol and governor's mansion

done from the ground up. It was a magnificent project the first time around too, when Governor William Tryon bucked the preferences of Piedmont Carolinians and had the colonial government's new home built here on the coastal plain. He hired English architect John Hawks to design the complex, a Georgian house on an estate laid out in the Palladian style. The palace's first incarnation was short-lived, standing for a scant 25 years before burning down in 1798. As the new state had relocated its governmental operations to Raleigh, there was no need to rebuild the New Bern estate, but it was not forgotten.

In the early 20th century a movement arose to rebuild Tryon Palace. By the 1950s both the funds and, incredibly, Hawks's original drawings and plans had been secured, and the palace was rebuilt over a period of seven years using the drawings as well as the stables, the only original building not destroyed in the fire, as a model. Today, it is once again one of the most striking and recognizable buildings in the state.

Tryon Palace is open for tours year-round, and it hosts various lectures and living-history events throughout the year. One of the best times to visit is during the December holiday season, when the estate is decorated beautifully and a recreated **Jonkonnu,** a colonial African American celebration once seen throughout the Caribbean and Southeast, is celebrated. Also known by the name Junkanoo, John Canoe, and several other variations, it was a Mardi Gras-like festival with deep African roots, involving a parade through plantations with music and outlandish costumes, some representing folk characters associated with the celebration. Like Mardi Gras, it was a sort of upside-down day, when the social order was temporarily inverted and enslaved people could demand gifts or money. Some enslavers participated. It was a tradition fraught with both joy and sorrow. Tryon Palace puts on a lively and enlightening re-creation.

Tryon's living-history interpreters do a wonderful job of enlightening visitors to certain aspects of colonial life, on a guided tour of the palace and on a walk through the nearby kitchen. In the kitchen, costumed interpreters show what was involved in running an 18th-century household, utilizing the nearby kitchen garden for most of what they cook with during the demonstrations. Lately the cooking demonstrations have expanded, pairing the beauty of the palace with the talents of a local chef to put on dinner events, including the on-site Savoring Spring event that makes use of the bounty of the kitchen garden.

At the Tryon Palace ticket office is the **North Carolina History Center,** a collection of galleries and exhibits that illustrate the history of the region and New Bern in particular. The **Pepsi Family Center** is a hit with kids as interactive displays transport you back to 1835, when the region was busy producing valuable things like turpentine for the nation's young navy. Visitors interested in Jonkonnu will find enlightening exhibits on the festival, and art lovers will appreciate the best of the region in the **Duffy Exhibit Gallery.** Admission to the Pepsi Family Center, Duffy Exhibit Gallery, and Regional History Museum are included in the admission cost for Tryon Palace.

Visiting Tryon Palace and its gardens along with the North Carolina History Center can fill an afternoon or even a full day. When you're done exploring, the surrounding neighborhood contains some wonderful old homes.

New Bern Firemen's Museum

The **New Bern Firemen's Museum** (420 Broad St., 252/636-4087, www.newbernfiremuseum.com, 10am-3pm Wed.-Sat., $7 adults, $4 students, free under age 6) is a fun museum for gearheads that has an antiquarian bent. The museum—in an old fire station—houses a collection of 19th- and early-20th-century fire wagons and trucks and chronicles the lively and contentious history of firefighting in New Bern. The city was the first in North Carolina and one of the first in the country to charter a fire department. After the Civil War, three fire companies operated in New Bern; one was founded before the war, one was founded after, and the third was a boys bucket brigade, a training program for junior firefighters. They competed, even fought, to put out fires. Learn their stories and the tale of the disastrous fire of 1922 that left more than 1,800 residents homeless.

Attmore-Oliver House

The beautiful 1790 **Attmore-Oliver House** (511 Broad St., 252/638-8558, www.

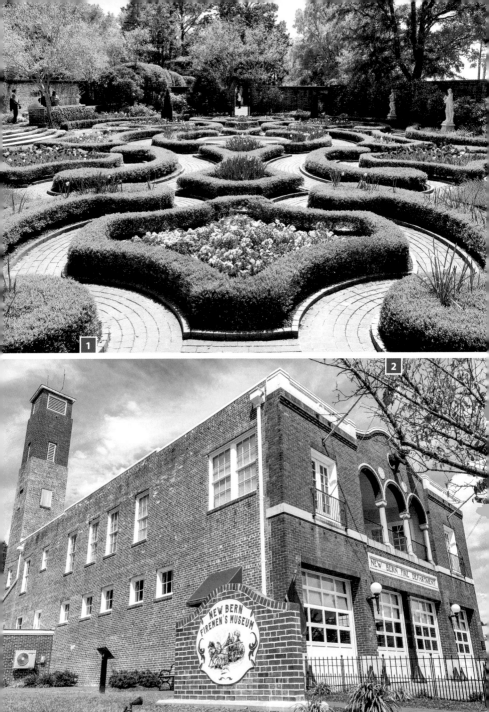

newbernhistorical.org, 10am-4pm Mon.-Fri., guided tours by appointment, free) is a historic house museum with exhibits about New Bern's Civil War history, the stories of the veterans interred in Greenwood Cemetery, and more. They also hold lectures and tours about different topics pertaining to New Bern history. It's also the headquarters of the New Bern Historical Society.

Birthplace of Pepsi

We often think of Coca-Cola as the quintessential Southern drink, but it was here in New Bern that Caleb Bradham, a drugstore owner, put together what he called Brad's Drink—later Pepsi-Cola. The Pepsi-Cola Bottling Company operates a soda fountain and gift shop at the location of Bradham's pharmacy, called the **Birthplace of Pepsi** (256 Middle St., 252/636-5898, www.pepsistore.com, 10am-6pm Mon.-Sat., noon-4pm Sun.). A few Pepsi antiques sit in display cases, and there's a mural showing the original recipe, but aside from some T-shirts and souvenirs, there's little else here.

SPORTS AND RECREATION

Given the town's location right on the river and near miles of tributaries to explore by boat, it's no surprise that water sports dominate New Bern's outdoor offerings. **Palm Coast Tours** (252/288-1244 or 949/433-5556, www.palmcoasttours.com, $35) offer daily eco tours on their 20-foot pontoon, *River Glide.* Tours depart daily at 10am and 2:30pm, with one more sunset cruise leaving 30-45 minutes before sunset. **Cruise the Neuse Boat Tours** (departing from New Bern Grand Marina Dock D, 101 Craven St., 252/876-7232, www.cruisetheneuse.com) offers daytime (10am, noon, 2pm) and sunset cruises. Tours are narrated, and you're free to bring a snack onboard.

This part of North Carolina is home to some of the oldest towns and cities in the state, and the things that went on here from the colonial era through the pirates, the Revolution, the Civil War, and up to today have left it a pretty haunted place. But don't take my word for it; take a **Ghosts of New Bern tour** (252/635-1410, www.haunted-newbern.com, 7:30pm Tues.-Sat. Mar.-Oct., 6:30pm Fri.-Sat. Nov.-Feb., $17 adults, $15 seniors, military, and ages 7-13, free under age 7) and learn about the spooky side of this town for yourself. Tours meet at **The Black Cat Shoppe** (246 Middle St.) to start and end, but along the way you'll see many of the beautiful (and haunted) homes, streets, alleys, and more around town.

ENTERTAINMENT AND EVENTS

For a fun hangout, check **The Garage** (1209 U.S. 70 E., 252/288-6077, www.thegaragenc.com, 5pm-8pm Mon.-Tues., 5pm-9pm Wed.-Thurs., 5pm-midnight Fri., 1pm-midnight Sat., noon-7pm Sun.), a little taphouse and bar with room for live music, a handful of retro arcade games, and space to spread out with your people. The 10 beers on their rotating tap list are always solid choices, and in all but a few instances they're from craft breweries from North Carolina or nearby.

Another solid option is **Tap That Craft Beer and Wine Bar** (901 Pollock St., 252/288-5853, www.tapthatnewbern.com, 3pm-11pm Tues.-Wed., 3pm-midnight Thurs.-Fri., noon-midnight Sat. noon-11pm Sun., $10-12), a big bar, restaurant, and events space. They have music, pulled pork nachos, a big beer list with lots of regional breweries represented, trivia night, karaoke, and something going on any time they're open. In a similar vein, **Captain Ratty's Seafood Restaurant** (202-206 Middle St., 252/633-2088 or 800/633-5292, www.captainrattys.com, 11am-9pm Mon.-Thurs., 8am-9:30pm Fri.-Sat., $10-30) has a rooftop bar that's a popular gathering spot for locals and travelers alike, and the combo of friends, drinks, and appetizers makes this a great place to watch the sun go down.

SHOPPING

You'll find a wearable souvenir at **Surf, Wind and Fire** (230 Middle St., 252/288-5823, www.surfwindandfire.com, 10am-6pm Mon.-Thurs. and Sat., 10am-7pm Fri., noon-4pm Sun.), a surf-inspired outdoor lifestyle and gear shop downtown. Their logo is fun: a cartoon pig on a surfboard, and, fittingly, they've got The Surfing Pig Tap Room, where you can get a coffee or a pint of local beer, so you can do a little sip-and-shop. You'll find the seasonal gear from brands you know (The North Face, Kuhl, Patagonia, Life is Good) and a few seaside essentials that'll make your travel here a little more comfortable.

Things are a little less focused at **The Black Cat Shoppe** (246 Middle St., 252/635-1410, www.theblackcatshoppe.com, 10am-6pm Mon.-Thurs., 10am-9pm Fri., 9am-9pm Sat., 11am-6pm Sun.) where they say they carry "randomly inspired fun." And it's a fun, weird shop stocked with fun, weird things.

Tryon Palace is a fun shopping spot for history buffs and home-and-garden fanciers. The historical site's **Museum Shop** (Jones House, Eden St. and Pollock St., 252/639-3532, 10am-5pm Tues.-Sat., noon-5pm Sun.) has a nice variety of books about history and architecture as well as handicrafts and children's toys and games.

Strolling the streets of New Bern, you'll notice a number of art galleries, including the **Craven Arts Council & Gallery's Bank of the Arts** (317 Middle St., 252/638-2577, www.cravenarts.org, 11am-5pm Tues.-Sat., free), a onetime bank that's now a great exhibition space. **Community Artists Gallery & Studio** (309 Middle St., 252/633-3715, www.communityartistsgallery.org, 10am-5pm Tues.-Sat., 11am-3pm Sun.) is a gallery and studio space exclusively for local artists. It really shows the diversity of media, styles, and interpretations of the landscapes and inspiring points in this part of North Carolina. **Carolina Creations** (317-A Pollock St., 252/633-4369, www.carolinacreations.com, 10am-5pm Mon.-Sat., 11am-3pm Sun.) carries pottery, jewelry, textiles, paintings, and more from local and national artists.

FOOD

The food and the space at ★ **The Chelsea** (335 Middle St., 252/637-5469, www.thechelsea.com, 11am-9pm Mon.-Thurs., 11am-10pm Fri.-Sat., $11-36) are interesting and refined. For starters, the space dates to 1912 and was used for a while by Caleb Bradham, inventor of Pepsi-Cola, and original features like the mosaic tile floor, the tin ceiling, and some of the stained glass were preserved when this place became The Chelsea. On the menu you've got crab cake sandwiches, shrimp and grits, steaks, and excellent fish dishes. I've seen some interesting specials pop up from time to time, like smoked ribs with a Pepsi-Cola barbecue sauce, so keep an eye on the specials board.

One of the top restaurants in New Bern also happens to have the best view. At **Persimmons Restaurant** (100 Pollock St., 252/514-0033, www.persimmonsrestaurant.net, 11am-9pm Thurs.-Sun., $13-35) you can take in the water views from a seat in the comfortable dining room or outside on the dockside deck. There's an excellent chef at Persimmons, and the dishes are seafood-centric and executed at a much higher level than at other restaurants in town.

Crema Brew (914 Broad St., 225/288-5381, www.cremabrew.com, 7am-3pm Mon.-Sat., $2-6) is a fair-trade coffee shop that makes all the café concoctions, smoothies, and baked goods you expect, plus lunch (soup of the day and a chicken, egg, or tuna salad sandwich), a few slices of cake, and pies. The pies are really good, as is the German Chocolate Cake, but it's the café latte and cinnamon roll, two simple things done just right, that's won them so many loyal fans.

For a down-home breakfast, the **Country Biscuit Restaurant** (809 Broad St., 252/638-5151, http://thecountrybiscuit.com, 5am-2:30pm Mon.-Sat., $2-12), is popular, not surprisingly, for its biscuits. They say they serve "real food for real folks," and indeed, the food is simple, homey, and filling. The trout breakfast plate is a locals' favorite, but I'm still inclined toward a biscuit (maybe it's because I'm trying to perfect my own recipe, or maybe I'm just genetically predisposed to love a biscuit).

The Cow Café (319 Middle St., 252/672-9269, www.cowcafenewbern.com, 11am-8pm Mon.-Thurs., 11am-9pm Fri.-Sat., 11:30pm-6pm Sun., $2-10) is a pleasant downtown creamery and restaurant with some unusual and classic homemade ice cream flavors you can't find anywhere else in town. Expect cones and cups, banana splits, and shakes on the sweet side, and barbecue, turkey, and chicken sandwiches for something heartier. The fun logo and Holstein cow decor make it hard to miss.

If your sweet tooth is calling, ★ Mayte Sweets Patisserie & Café (901 Broad St., 571/414-7025, http://maytesweets.com, 8am-6pm Tues.-Fri., 9am-3pm Sat., 8am-1pm Sun., $2-13) will definitely be able to help, and help in style. This is a real-deal patisserie with all the macarons, éclairs, profiteroles, madeleines, and full-size tarts and cakes ($40-100) to feed a crowd. The work is gorgeous, almost so good looking you don't want to eat it. But you'll take a moment to admire it, eat it, then go back inside and order more.

What I like about Thai Angel (247 Craven St., 252/631-5461, www.thaiangelnewbern. com, 3:30pm-8:30pm Tues.-Sat., $12-27) is how they develop deep Thai flavors and bring in some seasonal and local flavors in a dish like soft-shell crab and shrimp curry. Everything here hits the right notes, from the smoky, tamarind-sharp pad thai to the hint of heat in the red curry. They're a great addition to the downtown dining scene.

The Veteran-owned Beer Army Gastropub (313 Pollock St., 252/288-5814, www.beerarmy.com, 11am-10pm daily, kitchen until 9pm, $10-14) has more relaxed enlistment standards than any traditional branch of the military; as they say, "If you drink beer, then you're in the beer army." If that's true, I've been a happy solider for a few years now, calling on Beer Army every time I pass through New Bern. They keep more than a dozen taps flowing with great craft beer from across the state, and they keep twice that number in cans. In true gastropub fashion it's the assortment of tacos (with fish and shrimp tacos this close to the water), fish-and-chips, dressed up mac-and-cheese, wings, and fried things, and burgers. But the burger truly is a favorite of mine in town, and I've never turned down any of their wings or spicy sriracha shrimp.

ACCOMMODATIONS

Pollock Street is lined with charming 19th-century houses decorated in classic bed-and-breakfast style. The ★ Benjamin Ellis House Bed & Breakfast (215 Pollock St., 252/259-2311, www.benjaminellishouse. com, $115-169) has seven well-appointed guest rooms and three suites. Two of the suites feature king beds and two-person jetted tubs, while the third offers a queen bed and a separate living room with a queen sleeper sofa. Breakfast is exceptional as the owners draw on their love of Southern food and culinary influences from their world travels and put out a spread that includes eggs florentine with mornay sauce, grits soufflé, and muesli.

Meadows Inn Bed & Breakfast (212 Pollock St., 252/634-1776, www. meadowsinn-nc.com, $125-219) was built in 1847 and has been one of the town's best B&Bs since it opened as one in 1980. Room options include the Bern Bear Suite, which is a two-bedroom unit that's actually the whole third floor of the house; the cozy nature-inspired Croatan Suite, and other rooms just as tranquil and relaxing. They have a number of special options—wine, champagne, and treats in the room; flowers; vouchers to local restaurants—and even have an elopement package if you and your significant other wanted to make a little more than a weekend getaway of things.

At the **Hanna House Bed and Breakfast** (218 Pollock St., 252/635-3209 or 866/830-4371, http://hannahousenc.net, no children under age 6, $119-169), expect one of the best breakfasts you can get at a B&B. The owners take pride in their morning spread and offer a selection of dishes ranging from eggs *en croûte* to a variety of frittatas and my favorite, stuffed french toast. Hanna House isn't all breakfast; each of the five guest rooms is comfortable and spacious for both single travelers and couples.

Several hotels can be found around New Bern as well, including **Clarion Pointe New Bern** (3455 Dr. MLK Jr. Blvd., 252/649-2214, www.choicehotels.com, from $105), **SpringHill Suites** (300 Hotel Dr., 252/637-0017, www.marriott.com, from $135), and **DoubleTree by Hilton** (100 Middle St., 252/658-9000, www.hilton.com, from $215), has a great waterfront location and is easily walkable to most of what you'll want to see, do, and taste in town.

Camping

New Bern's **KOA Campground** (1565 B St., reservations 800/562-3341, information 252/638-2556, www.koacamping.com, tent sites from $40, RV sites from $55, cabins from $89) is on the other side of the Neuse River from town, right on the riverbank. Choices include 20-, 30-, and 40-amp RV sites; "Kamping Kabins and Lodges"; and tent sites. Pets are allowed, and there is a dog park on-site. The campground has free wireless internet access. Stop by the New Bern Convention Center's visitor information center before checking in and pick up a KOA brochure for some valuable coupons.

GETTING THERE AND AROUND

New Bern is located on the Neuse River, at the point where the river opens wide and prepares to meet the Pamlico Sound. A pair of recognizable roads run through town, including U.S. 70 from the east and U.S. 17 from the south. U.S. 70 continues through New Bern down to Morehead City on the coast, an hour-long drive through the Croatan National Forest. New Bern is 2 hours north of Wilmington via U.S. 17, and 2.25 hours southeast of Raleigh via U.S. 70. Nags Head and the Outer Banks are 2.75 hours from New Bern via U.S. 17 and U.S. 64.

Croatan National Forest and Vicinity

A huge swath of swampy wilderness, the Croatan National Forest is all the land bounded by the Neuse, Trent, and White Oak Rivers and Bogue Sound, from New Bern to Morehead City and almost all the way to Jacksonville. Despite its size, Croatan is one of the lesser-known and least developed federal preserves in the state. All three nearby towns in Jones County (population just over 10,000) enjoy a similar atmosphere of sequestration, where barely traveled roads lead to dark expanses of forest and swamp as well as narrow old village streets.

CROATAN NATIONAL FOREST

Headquartered just off U.S. 70 south of New Bern, the **Croatan National Forest** (141 E. Fisher Ave., New Bern, 252/638-5628, www.fs.usda.gov) has few amenities for visitors but plenty of land and water trails to explore.

Hiking and Biking

The main hiking route is the **Neusiok Trail,** which begins at the Newport River Parking area and ends at the Pinecliff Recreation Area on the Neuse River. It traverses 20 miles of beach, salt marsh, swamp, pocosin, and pine woods. Part of North Carolina's Mountains to Sea Trail (a 900-mile route from Jockey's Ridge on the Outer Banks to Great Smoky Mountains National Park in the west), Neusiok is blazed with white circles and is quite an old trail, used by everyone from Indigenous people to hunters, woodsmen, and even moonshiners. Dogs are permitted as long as they're leashed. This long trail is a popular hike for backpackers; you can camp anywhere, but a trio of shelters offers a dry spot to sleep in this otherwise wet forest. The 1.3-mile **Cedar Point Tideland National Recreation Trail** covers estuary marshes and woods, starting at the Cedar Point boat ramp near Cape Carteret. The 0.5-mile **Island Creek Forest Walk** passes through virgin hardwood forests and includes interpretative signage installed as part of an Eagle Scout project. If you want to bike, the best place is at the Neuse River Campground, where there are two miles of bike trails.

Boating

The spectacular **Saltwater Adventure Trail** is a water route nearly 100 miles in length that starts at Brice's Creek, south of New Bern, and winds north to the Neuse River, following the Neuse River to the Harlowe Canal. The route then leads down to Beaufort and Bogue Sound, turning back inland on the White Oak River and ending at Haywood Landing north of Swansboro. If you're up for the challenge, it's an incredible trip.

There are eight popular boat launches in Croatan National Forest: Brices Creek, Catfish Lake, Great Lake, Siddie Fields, Cahooque Lake, Cedar Point, Haywood Landing, and Oyster Point. You can launch a shallow-drafting motor boat from any of these as well as use them as launch points for kayaks, canoes, and stand-up paddleboards.

For boat rentals, not many outfitters serve the national forest. **White Oak River Outfitters** (7660 New Bern Hwy., Maysville, 910/743-2744, www.whiteoakrivercampground.com, reservations required, single

kayaks $40 half day, $50 full day, double kayaks and canoes $50 half day, $60 full day) rents out canoes and kayaks, has a shuttle service that makes trips a lot easier, and offers guided tours on the White Oak River and other waters in the area. They also have **camping available** (reservations 910/595-4163), with tent ($20) and RV ($30) sites.

Great Lake is a popular spot to explore via canoe, kayak, or small flat-bottomed boat. Surrounded by centuries-old cypress trees, it's easy to feel like you're in another world or another time. A handful of campsites lets you extend your stay or just enjoy the day paddling around or fishing for crappie, perch, and bullhead, all easy catches.

The **Oyster Point Campground,** which is also the trailhead for the Neusiok Trail, offers a boat launch suitable for both motorized and paddle watercraft. It's easy to explore the marshy fringes of the forest from here or head into one of the tributaries or winding marsh creeks nearby.

Camping

There are four developed campsites in the Croatan Forest (877/444-6777, www.recreation.gov). Also called Flanners Beach Campground, **Neuse River** ($20 no electricity, $25 with electricity, $50 double site with electricity) has 41 sites with showers and flush toilets. **Cedar Point** ($27 single sites, $54 double sites) has 40 campsites with electricity, showers, and flush toilets. **Oyster Point Campground** ($10 single site, $20 double site) is small, with only 16 sites, but **Fisher's Landing** (free) is smaller with only nine sites and no facilities other than vault toilets. Primitive camping areas are at Great Lake, Catfish Lake, and Long Point.

OHV Area

Off-highway vehicle (OHV) trails are growing more popular in forests and recreation areas across the United States. Here in Croatan National Forest, the designated, and only permitted, OHV riding area is the **Black Swamp OHV Trail** ($5 per day, purchased at the Croatan District Office in New Bern), and it's a hot one. The easy to intermediate trails are suited for ATVs, trail bikes, and SUVs with a small wheelbase (50 inches or less). At Black Swamp, there are several miles of trails completed with many more in the planning and developmental stages.

Getting There and Around

The main highway running through Croatan National Forest is U.S. 70. It runs south and east through the forest, connecting New Bern (to the north) with Morehead City (to the south). U.S. 17 forms the western boundary of the National Forest, and inside the forest proper, there are dozens of state routes and roads crisscrossing the land. Detailed maps are available from the Croatan National Forest Office or online (www.fs.usda.gov/nfsnc).

KINSTON

In years past you wouldn't find Kinston on many must-see lists, but this formerly prosperous tobacco town two hours northwest of Wilmington has made quite a turnaround in recent years. A couple of locals have spearheaded renewal, opening a renowned restaurant and a brewery with a growing reputation for great craft beer and changing the face of downtown. Add to that a top-of-the-line museum dedicated to the town's Civil War history and a community that's passionate about preserving its past.

Sights

Like many towns that were once prosperous and suddenly experienced a downturn, Kinston is an architectural time capsule. Driving, or better, walking the several downtown blocks of **Queen Street,** the town's main artery, is an education in early-20th-century commercial architecture. The Hotel Kinston is the town's tallest building, an 11-story structure with a ground level that's a crazy blend of art deco and Moorish motifs. The 1914 post office is a big heavy beaux arts beauty, and the Queen Street Methodist Church is turreted to within an inch of its life. The People's Bank building testifies to the heyday of early-20th-century African American commerce. With its many strange and daring experiments in building styles, Queen Street is a crazy quilt, but the buildings are beautifully complementary in their diversity. In the Heritage Street neighborhood, near the bend of the river, block after block of grand old houses stand in threadbare glory. On the other side of town are shotgun houses, the icon of Southern folk housing, lining the alleys of the old working-class neighborhood.

★ CSS *NEUSE* INTERPRETIVE CENTER

The remains of the Confederate ironclad gunboat CSS *Neuse* are on display in Kinston in a museum located near the spot where she was scuttled in 1865 to keep her out of the hands of the advancing Union Army. All that remains is the core of the 158- by 34-foot hull, but even in such deteriorated condition the *Neuse* is a striking feat of boatbuilding. At the **CSS *Neuse* Interpretive Center** (100 N. Queen St., 252/522-2107, www.cssneuse.org, 9am-5pm Tues.-Sat., $5 adults, $4 seniors and military, $3 ages 3-12, free under age 3) you can see what remains of the hull, which sat in the river for more than 100 years before it was salvaged. If you're lucky, one of the volunteers will be a Kinston old-timer who can tell you stories about using the *Neuse* as a diving board for summer swims. On display are artifacts including the ironclad's bell, cannonballs and shells, coal rakes, and other small items. The centerpiece is the overhead view of the ironclad's hull. Now outfitted with a ghostly shape showing the original form of the ship, it's an impressive sight. For a full-scale look at the CSS *Neuse,* check out the **CSS *Neuse II*** (Herritage St. and Gordon St., 252/560-2150, www.cssneuseii.org, 10am-4pm Sat. or by appointment, free), a 158-foot facsimile of the gunboat. Climb aboard to feel how tight the quarters were, peer out the gun ports, and imagine sleeping, eating, and fighting on board.

MOTHER EARTH BREWING

Mother Earth Brewing (311 N. Herritage St., 252/208-2437, www.motherearthbrewing.com, taproom and trading post 3pm-10pm Mon.-Thurs., noon-10pm Fri.-Sat., 1pm-8pm Sun.) has been making craft beer in Kinston since 2008 and racking up awards ever since. In 2013, they became the first brewery to attain LEED Gold Certification, and their taproom and distillery are solar-powered. Brewery tours are free, but as it is a working brewery, some days the tours may be crowded, limited to certain areas, or canceled altogether. When brewery tours return, they'll start and end in the solar-powered **Mother Earth Brewing Tap Room,** serving up the best Mother Earth brews. A mix of original art, exposed brick walls, sleek modern lines, and contemporary lighting makes this room one of a kind. Cozy up to the bar or grab a pint to take to a nearby table or to the patio out back. I'm fond of the Dark Cloud Dunkel and Old Neighborhood Oatmeal Porter, but the kölsch, witbier, and IPA are also popular.

At the same location, Mother Earth also operates **Mother Earth Spirits** (call for tour information), where they make gin, rum, and whiskey. As North Carolina laws change regarding distilled spirits, you may be able to purchase on-site, but until then, you can find Mother Earth Spirits in ABC Stores across the state; locally you'll find their spirits in cocktails at The Boiler Room, Chef & the Farmer, and The Red Room.

Sports and Recreation

The first time I came to Kinston, I was in college and a friend from high school was playing baseball here for the Kinston Indians, the first stop on his short career in professional baseball. A few years after he was moved up, the Kinston Indians were no more, moved on to another city, and Kinston was left without baseball for the first time since 1925. Happily, baseball returned—and with a much more appropriate name. Now the **Down East Wood Ducks** (www.woodducksbaseball.com), a Low-A affiliate of the Texas Rangers, plays at Grainger Stadium (400 E. Grainger Ave., 252/686-5164, box office 10am-4pm Mon.-Fri. and in-season, tickets $7-15), an easy walk from downtown. They're a fun team to watch, the hometown fans love the Ducks, and if you're one of those rabid baseball fans, this is your chance to check out the next crop of MLBers.

Oddly, there's a water park in Kinston. **Lions Water Adventure** (2602 W. Vernon Ave., 252/939-1330, www.lionswateradventure.com, 11:30am-5:30pm Mon.-Sat., 12:30pm-5:30pm Sun., $15), has three three-story high slides—the zebra slide, a twisty tube ride; the lion slide, a straightforward waterslide with a decent drop at the end; and the low-splash slide. There's a 5,000-square-foot kiddie lagoon, a lazy river longer than a football field, a lap pool, and a heated therapeutic pool. They serve food, mainly kid-friendly bites and snacks, but the water park is close enough to town that you can head out for a real meal with little effort.

In Kinston you can enjoy disc golf or a traditional round. At the **Barnet Disc Golf Course** (100 Sand Clay Rd., 252/939-3332, http://kinstondiscgolf.com, dawn-dusk daily, free), you'll need to bring your own discs, but this fun course layout rewards aggressive but accurate players. For a day on a regular, albeit short, golf course, at Bill Fay Park there's a fun **Par 3 Course** (1007 Phillips Rd., 252/939-3356, www.kinstonrec.com, 18 holes, par 54, $2 for 18 holes, $5 to play all day) where you can work on your short game.

Entertainment and Events

Kinston is fortunate to have a great local arts engine, the **Kinston Community Council for the Arts** (KCCA, 400 N. Queen St., 252/527-2517, www.kinstoncca.com, 10am-6pm Tues.-Fri., 10am-2pm Sat.), which has the kind of energy and artistic vision one would expect to find in a much larger city. It

---

1: the Croatan National Forest **2:** Mother Earth Brewing **3:** Cedar Point Tideland National Recreation Trail **4:** Kinston's kitschy-cool Mother Earth Motor Lodge

occupies an old storefront on Queen Street, remodeled into a gorgeous gallery and studio space. In addition to the many community events hosted here, KCCA has consistently hosted innovative exhibits in the main gallery, including avant-garde photography and collage art, and a recent exhibition of dozens of custom motorcycles.

Every spring, barbecue enthusiasts flock to Kinston for the **BBQ Festival on the Neuse** (last weekend in Apr. or 1st weekend in May). This four-day festival features competitions pitting barbecue teams against one another in categories such as showmanship, quality, and sauce. During the festival, downtown is crowded with food, smoke from a dozen barbecue cookers, carnival rides, concerts, a wine garden, and beer from Mother Earth Brewing. Many artists come for the opening day's **Plein Air Paint Out,** a competitive painting event, which awards the winner with an image of their painting for the next upcoming year's festival poster. The Art Fest event invites everyone to create art inspired by the festival; it's a hit with kids as well as adults who shake off their artistic inhibitions. With concerts, fireworks, and heaping plates of 'cue, there's plenty to do, see, and eat.

Food

Kinston's reputation as a food town has been on the rise lately, thanks in large part to a trio of locals—chef Vivian Howard Knight and brewery owners Stephen Hill and Trent Mooring. They collectively opened a renowned restaurant, a top-notch brewery and taproom, and an oyster bar. Though these may be the best known, they're not the only food options in town.

You might know ★ **Chef & the Farmer** (120 W. Gordon St., 252/208-2433, www.chefandthefarmer.com, 4pm-9pm Wed.-Sat., $13-48) from the PBS show *A Chef's Life.* Here, chef-owner Vivian Howard Knight elevates the simple Southern food she grew up eating on a farm not far from here into true fine-dining dishes that have been recognized by the James Beard Foundation. This restaurant

has evolved several times since opening in 2006, and every new iteration is more delicious than the last. It's simple dishes to start—butterbean hummus, fried collards, a creative charcuterie dish, a seasonal salad—and elegant but hearty dishes as mains—chicken confit with Carolina Gold rice, a cauliflower steak with curried peanut butter sweet potato, North Carolina trout, a great rib-eye. For dessert, the chocolate chess pie gets two thumbs up.

Queen Street Deli (117 S. Queen St., 252/527-1900, www.queenstreetdeli.com, 8:30am-3pm Mon.-Fri., $6-11) bakes vegan and nonvegan cookies and makes great sandwiches. Go for the filling Queen's Chicken Salad, which comes with toasted pecans and cranberries. Their take on the BLT, called Prides Pimento, is another good option made with pimento cheese, sliced tomatoes, and bacon.

Lovick's Cafe (320 N. Herritage St., 151/523-6854, www.lovickscafe.com, 6am-2pm Tues.-Fri., 6am-11am Sat., $3-12) has been a Kinston fixture since 1941, when Milton and Eva Lovick borrowed $180 (a monumental sum at the time) and opened Lovick's Quick Lunch. Since then, not much has changed except the prices. Bacon and eggs, pancakes, biscuits, and breakfast sandwiches are served until 1:30pm on weekdays; lunch consists of pork chops, hamburger steak, barbecue and barbecue chicken, and the Dough Burger, a flour- and spice-laced hamburger, on the original menu as a way to make meat, a precious commodity during World War II, go a little further. Strange as it sounds to us today, it's pretty tasty.

FatBaby's Country Cooking (1215 Greene Haynes Rd., 252/527-9779, 5pm-1:30pm Mon.-Sat., $0.75-8.50) keeps up the diner-like tradition of Lovick's, opening before sun-up to ensure farmers and folks can get a bite to eat before the day begins in earnest. The food is simple and filling and absolutely dirt cheap—a plain or jelly biscuit is only $0.75 and the most expensive thing on the menu, the FatBaby triple cheeseburger, is a shade under $8.50—so stop by and tuck into some great grub while you listen to the locals discuss anything and everything. Biscuits are a must, and the biscuit sandwiches are awesome, and the burgers are solid options even if you don't go for that triple stack.

Jessie Bell's Soul Food Restaurant (106 E. Vernon Ave., 252/686-5209, 11am-6:30pm Tues. and Thurs.-Sun.) gives culinary attention to the often overlooked soul food traditions in this part of the country. Smoked or fried turkey wings, fried chicken, collards, a gravy-drenched hamburger steak, pigs feet (also called trotters) all get the care and attention they always have in soul food and the Southern Black food tradition, which means a lot of flavor coaxed out of overlooked cuts of meat and seasonal vegetables.

Just outside Kinston you'll find the James Beard Award-winning world-famous ★ **Skylight Inn** (4618 S. Lee St., Ayden, 252/746-4113, www.skylightinnbbq.com, 10am-7pm Mon.-Sat., under $10). For many, this is the end-all-be-all of barbecue. It's where eastern North Carolina-style barbecue is done up right: chopped and served with a vinegary sauce that brings out the flavor in the pork like no other sauce can. When you pull into the gravel parking lot, you'll notice a mountain of wood waiting to become the coals in the huge smokehouse just a few steps away. The Jones family has been cooking 'cue since 1830, so they know their way around a hog; their current location dates to 1947, and son Sam Jones is carrying on the tradition, overseeing the smokehouse here and at his own restaurant, Same Jones BBQ, which has locations in Winterville (north a little ways) and in Raleigh.

Accommodations

The O'Neil (200 N. Queen St., 252/208-1130, www.the-oneil.com, from $189), a boutique hotel in the former Farmers & Merchants Bank, stands in the heart of downtown. Construction on this building ran from 1919 to 1924, and it's got that powerful early-20th-century look about it. The hotel was the vision of Mother Earth's Stephen Hill, and the renovation kept much of the building's character by preserving elements like the main vault and teller windows. There are only a few rooms, but it's an absolutely lovely place.

Another of Hill's visions was the retro-sexy ★ **Mother Earth Motor Lodge** (501 N. Herritage St., 252/520-2000, www.motherearthmotorlodge.com, from $109). This massive remodel converted a derelict motel from a beautiful homage to motels from the 1950s through the 1970s. Bold colors, a kidney-shaped pool, and modern furniture in each room highlight this cozy lodge, and Mother Earth Brewery, Chef & the Farmer, and everything else in Kinston are within easy walking distance.

There are a few chain hotels around, and one of the newest is **Fairfield Inn & Suites Kinston** (667 Sheffield Dr., 252/208-7878, www.marriott.com, from $132), a good spot to earn or burn some loyalty points. It's in a good location that makes it easy to get into town for dinner and back on the road to continue your travels tomorrow.

CLIFFS OF THE NEUSE STATE PARK

In Seven Springs, a historic little town about 30 minutes' drive southwest of Kinston, is **Cliffs of the Neuse State Park** (240 Park Entrance Rd., Seven Springs, 919/778-6234, http://ncparks.gov, visitors center 9am-5pm daily, park 7am-6pm daily Nov.-Feb., 7am-8pm daily Mar.-Apr. and Sept.-Oct., 7am-9pm daily May-Aug.), a highly unusual blend of environments, including high red bluffs overlooking the Neuse River, hardwood and pine forests, and cypress swamps. Hiking trails follow the cliff line through Spanish moss-draped forests. Boating and swimming (11am-6:45pm daily late May-early Sept.) are permitted at the park's artificial lake during summer; swimming ($6 adults, $4 ages 3-12) is allowed only when a lifeguard is on duty. Boats must be rented ($7 per hour) as no private watercraft are permitted.

Camping (877/772-6762, https://northcarolinastateparks.reserveamerica.com) is available year-round in campsites for tents and RVs ($23 without electricity, $30 with electricity) as well as tiny house-style cabins ($55). There is a washhouse with hot showers and electricity, and several water stations are located in the campsite. Note that unless you have a medical emergency, when you're camping you must stay inside the park from the time the gates close until 8am the next morning—so no slipping out for a late supper.

GETTING THERE AND AROUND

Kinston is at the junction of U.S. 70, U.S. 258, and Highway 58. Raleigh is 80 minutes west along U.S. 70, New Bern is 36 miles east on U.S. 70, and Greenville is 30 minutes north on Highway 11. You can be in Atlantic Beach in 80 minutes by following U.S. 70 east.

Beaufort and Vicinity

The small waterside town of Beaufort has unusual problems stemming from its geography—there's also a Beaufort in South Carolina—and the idiosyncrasies of regional Southern dialects. This Beaufort is pronounced in the French way, "BO-fert," while the name of town in South Carolina is pronounced "BYEW-fert." Pronunciation notwithstanding, Beaufort is a beautiful little town. The third-oldest colonial settlement in North Carolina, it matches its elders, Bath and New Bern, in the charm department. Once North Carolina's window to the world, Beaufort was a surprisingly cosmopolitan place that would often receive news from London or Barbados sooner than from other colonies. Today you'll find the streets crowded with old homes, many built in that double-porch steep-sided roof style that shows off the early cultural ties to the Caribbean.

It was long rumored that the pirate Blackbeard ran his ship aground in the inlet here, which is plausible because he did frequent Beaufort, and his pirate base at Ocracoke Island isn't far away. In the late 1990s the rumor was proved to be true: In Beaufort Inlet the *Queen Anne's Revenge*, the French slave ship that Blackbeard captured in 1717 and made into the flagship of his dreaded fleet, was found mired in nearly three centuries of silt. Blackbeard had increased his ship's arsenal to 40 cannons, a fact that helped confirm the identity of the wreck. A few months after he ran his flagship aground, Blackbeard himself was killed at Ocracoke after putting up a tremendous fight with privateers (pirate hunters) sent from Virginia. In the intervening time between the shipwreck and its discovery, incredible artifacts from the *Queen Anne's Revenge* washed up on the shores here, a number of which are on display at the North Carolina Maritime Museum.

From the Maritime Museum, a short walk leads to Beaufort's cafés, boutiques, antiques shops, restaurants, and dock. Across the waterway you can see Carrot Island, home to a herd of wild horses, one of the few remaining in eastern North Carolina. You can also catch a ride on a ferry or tour boat to Cape Lookout National Seashore, where the stunning Cape Lookout Lighthouse has guarded the coast for more than 150 years. Or simply tour the marshes for a close-up glimpse of the area's wildlife.

SIGHTS
★ North Carolina Maritime Museum

The **North Carolina Maritime Museum at Beaufort** (315 Front St., 252/540-7740, www.ncmaritimemuseums.com, 10am-5pm Mon.-Sat., noon-5pm Sun., free) is among the best museums in the state and one of three state maritime museums; the others are in

Beaufort and Vicinity

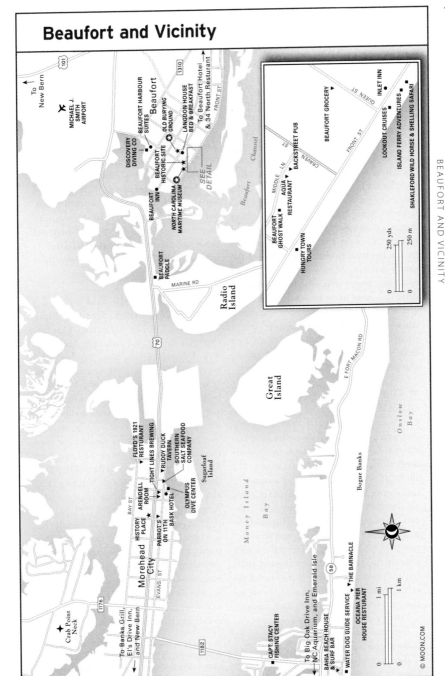

© MOON.COM

Southport and on Roanoke Island. Even if you don't think you're interested in boatbuilding or maritime history, you'll get caught up in the exhibits here. Historic watercraft, reconstructions, and models of boats are on display, well presented in rich historical and cultural context. The display of artifacts and weapons recovered from Blackbeard's *Queen Anne's Revenge* wows visitors and excites curators and their preservation specialist. There's also a lot about the state's fishing history, including related occupations, such as the highly complex skill of net-hanging. Far from being limited to the few species caught by today's fisheries, early North Carolinians did big business hunting sea turtles, porpoises, and whales. One of their most interesting exhibits reaches back to the earliest days of the state's seafaring history when Portsmouth and other towns were whaling villages; to drive this point home they have a complete articulated sperm whale skeleton and even a whale heart you can touch (it was preserved using the same plasticization methods used in the famed Bodies exhibits showing human anatomy).

★ Old Burying Ground

One of the most beautiful places in North Carolina is Beaufort's **Old Burying Ground** (Anne St., www.beauforthistoricsite.org, dawn-dusk daily, tours by appointment through Beaufort Historic Site, $12 adults, $6 ages 6-12), a picturesque cemetery that's quite small by the standards of some old Carolina towns and crowded with 18th- and 19th-century headstones. Huge old live oaks, Spanish moss, wisteria, and resurrection ferns, which unfurl and turn green after a rainstorm, give the Burying Ground an irresistibly Gothic feel. Many of the headstones reflect the maritime heritage of the town, including a sea captain whose epitaph reads:

> The form that fills this silent grave
> Once tossed on ocean's rolling wave
> But in a port securely fast
> He's dropped his anchor here at last.

Captain Otway Burns, an early privateer

who spent much time in Beaufort, is buried here; his grave is easy to spot, as it is topped by a cannon from his ship, the *Snap Dragon*. Nearby is another of the graveyard's famous burials, the "Little Girl Buried in a Barrel of Rum." This unfortunate child died at sea and was placed in a cask of rum to preserve her body for burial on land. Visitors often bring toys and trinkets to leave on her grave, which is marked by a simple wooden plank. Though hers is the most gaudily festooned, you'll see evidence of this old tradition of funerary gifts on other graves here as well, most often coins and shells. This is a tradition found throughout the coastal South and the Caribbean, with roots tracing back to Africa. Feel free to add to her haul of goodies, but beliefs hold that it's not karmically advisable to tamper with those already here.

Beaufort Historic Site

The **Beaufort Historic Site** (100 Block Turner St., 252/728-5225, www.beauforthistoricsite.org, 9:30am-5pm Mon.-Sat. Mar.-Dec., 10am-4pm Mon.-Sat. Jan.-Feb.) recreates life in late-18th and early-19th-century Beaufort in several restored historic buildings. The 1770s "jump and a half" (1.5-story) Leffers Cottage reflects middle-class life in its day; a merchant, whaler, or, as in this case, a schoolmaster would have lived in such a home. The Josiah Bell and John Manson Houses, both from the 1820s, reflect the Caribbean-influenced architecture prevalent in the early days of the coastal South. A restored apothecary shop, a 1790s wooden courthouse, and a haunted 1820s jail that was used into the 1950s are among the other important structures. There are tours led by costumed interpreters (10:30am and 2pm Mon.-Sat. Dec.-Mar., 10am and 2:30pm Mon.-Sat. Apr.-Nov., $12 adults, $6 ages 6-12) as well as driving tours of the old town on a double-decker bus (1:30pm Mon.-Sat. Apr.-Oct., $12

1: Beaufort's Old Burying Ground **2:** Beaufort Historic Site **3:** a ghost tour in Beaufort **4:** getting ready to go paddling to the Rachel Carson Reserve

adults, $6 ages 6-12), and tours of the Old Burying Ground (by reservation only, $12 adults, $6 ages 6-12).

SPORTS AND RECREATION
Diving and Fishing
North Carolina's coast is a surprisingly good place for scuba diving. The **Discovery Diving Company** (414 Orange St., 252/728-2265, www.discoverydiving.com, $75-460) leads half-day, full-day, and multi-dive scuba trips to explore the reefs and dozens of fascinating shipwrecks nearby. The water here is often exceptional—hence the name Crystal Coast—and warm, both of which make for a great day underwater. If you need rental gear, they have some on hand, and if you're new to scuba and want to give it a try, they have a starter package that'll introduce you to the basics ($195 pp).

Anglers should give **Bounty Hunter Guide Service** (919/218-8451, www.bountyhunterguidenc.com) a call and arrange for some time on the water. Captain Will's been fishing here since the 1970s when he was just a tyke, earned a degree in ecology, environmental, and evolutionary biology, and worked for the North Carolina Division of Marine Fisheries, so he knows the waters, the spots, and all about the fish you'll find. Join him for some **inshore fishing** ($450 half day, $600 three-quarter day, $750 full day), **nearshore fishing** ($500 half day, $650 three-quarter day, $800 full day), search for huge **redfish** ($550 half day, $800 full day, $900 split day with morning and evening fishing), and fall-only trips to catch **albacore tuna** ($600 three-quarter day, $800 full day).

Cruises and Tours
Hungry Town Tours (400 Front St., 252/648-1011, www.hungrytowntours.com) offers bicycle and walking tours of Beaufort on a number of themes. Culinary bike tours ($75) take you through town for a mini history tour and stops at several restaurants. Sightseeing bike tours ($25) get you out and about to see

some of the town's prettiest spots, including locations from and inspired by Beaufort author Nicholas Sparks. Walking tours ($25) range from sightseeing and history tours to culinary-themed walks. And even a tour pointed at folks who want to relocate to this bucolic corner of North Carolina. Combined with the bus tour from the Historic Site, you'll have a good sense of the town's past and present by the time you're through.

Port City Tour Company leads one of my favorite tours on the coast: the **Beaufort Ghost Walk** (108 Middle Lane, 252/772-9925, http://pctourco.com, $17 over age 9, $12 ages 3-9), which wanders through town led by a "pirate" in character. Highlights include supposedly haunted homes, tales of Blackbeard and other ghost pirates, ghost ships, mysterious murders, and more. Many people report taking photos in the cemetery and seeing ghostly figures, orbs, and other unexplained phenomena in the resulting images.

Island Express Ferry Service (252/728-7433, www.islandexpressferryservices.com) runs trips to and from Cape Lookout from its locations on **Harkers Island** (1800 Island Rd., Harkers Island, $20 adults, $13 ages 3-11, times vary but summer departures every 30 minutes 8:15am-5:45pm) and the **Beaufort Waterfront** ($45 adults, $25 ages 3-11, tours operated as staffing allows, departure times vary) on a spacious, 49-person catamaran. From Harkers Island the trip takes 20-25 minutes round-trip, and they drop you off on the island to explore (and catch the return ferry) on your own. Departures from Beaufort are four-hour tours and visits to Cape Lookout, combining a bit of history and environmental narration, a quick look for the wild horses and dolphins, and a couple of hours on Cape Lookout.

Island Ferry Adventures (610 Front St., 252/728-4129, www.islandferryadventures.com, $10-15 adults, $5-8 children) runs dolphin-watching tours; trips to Carrot Island, Bird Shoal, and Sand Dollar Island; and trips to look for the wild ponies of Shackleford Banks. **Lookout Cruises** (600

Front St., 252/504-7245, www.lookoutcruises. com, $40-89 adults, $30-75 under age 13) carries sightseers on lovely catamaran rides in the Beaufort and Core Sound region, sightseeing trips out to Cape Lookout, and dolphin-watching trips.

Take a **Shackleford Wild Horse and Shelling Safari** (252/838-1167, www.shacklefordwildhorseandshellingsafari.com, from $34 over age 11, $33 senior and military, $24 ages 3-11, free under age 3), departing from Grayden Paul Park (702 Front St.), to catch sight of the Banker ponies on the small islands here. Your tour starts with a talk about the history of the Banker ponies and of the area, then you'll search the dunes and woods and shoreline for the horses. After, you'll spend time shelling: searching for conchs, whelks, and more.

FOOD

For generations, local families have plied the waters off Beaufort to earn a living and catch fish for their families. To ensure residents and visitors dine at eateries utilizing locally caught seafood when possible, **Carteret Catch** (www.carteretcatch.com) provides a list of such restaurants and a list of retail fish markets where you can pick up the fresh catch, some harvested-today oysters, and more (be sure to bring a cooler). Not only does this help the local fishing industry, it allows chefs and home cooks to provide the best and freshest seafood possible, meaning your dinner tastes even better.

★ **Aqua Restaurant** (114 Middle Lane, 252/728-7777, www.aquaexperience.com, 5:30pm-9pm Tues.-Sat., small plates $5-30, big plates $37-43) uses local seafood in a number of their dishes, including a fresh-catch tostada, shrimp and grits, and bouillabaisse. Along with local seafood, they use locally and regionally sourced produce and meats. The menu changes frequently, but structurally it's always composed of tapas, small plates, salads, and big plates. With a number of vegetarian and gluten-free items, the menu is amenable to most dietary needs.

Beaufort Grocery (117 Queen St., 252/728-3899, www.beaufortgrocery.com, 11:30am-2:30pm and 5:30pm-9pm Mon. and Thurs.-Sat., 10am-2pm and 5:30pm-9pm Sun., $12-49), despite its humble name, is a sophisticated little eatery. Lunch features salads and crusty sandwiches along with specialty soups. In the evening the café atmosphere gives way to that of a more formal gourmet dining room. For starters, the ahi tuna napoleon is both beautiful and delicious, and Aunt Marion's Apple and Onion Salad makes an interesting plate to share. Some of the best entrées include duck two ways (seared and leg confit); a whole rack of lamb, served with a chèvre and mint *gremolata;* a stuffed double-cut pork chop; and, of course, the daily fish preparation. Try the cheesecake for dessert.

Go for a tasty pizza and a feast of appetizers at ★ **Black Sheep** (510 Front St., 252/269-7272, www.blacksheepbeaufort.con, 11am-9pm Wed.-Sun., $9-18), right on the water in Beaufort. The Wenny pizza—a white pie with fontina, caramelized onions, arugula, and prosciutto—and the meaty Charcuterie Pie will disappear within moments of arriving at the table, but so will any other pizza they have—pepperoni, roasted veggie, even the anchovy pizza. Start with a spread of burrata, the Mediterranean Platter, and the anchovy crostini (these salty little fish are delicious and used sparingly, so don't be afraid to try them here), all choices that'll please your palate.

In what was a turn-of-the-20th-century bakery you'll find a pub that's been called the friendliest, funkiest bar in the United States: **Backstreet Pub** (124 Middle Lane, 252/728-7108, www.historicbeaufort.com, noon-2am Mon.-Sat., 5pm-2am Sun., $8-20). They serve up live music most nights along with cold pints, mixed drinks, and a menu that runs the gamut from steamed oysters to sandwiches and burgers to pizzas that'll help you pass the time and tell your hunger to beat it.

ACCOMMODATIONS

Catty-corner to the Old Burying Grounds is the ★ **Langdon House Bed and**

Breakfast (135 Craven St., 252/728-5499, www.langdonhouse.com, from $155). One of the oldest buildings in town, this gorgeous house was built in the 1730s on a foundation of English ballast stones and has been added onto or renovated several times: in the 1790s, 1860s, and 1920s. Unlike most other B&Bs, Langdon House allows guests to customize their breakfast (and overall room rate) by selecting from options that range from coffee and tea only to the two-course Hallmark Breakfast, which includes fresh fruit, waffles, french toast, omelets, and more; it's quite a production.

The **Beaufort Inn** (101 Ann St., 252/728-2600 or 800/726-0321, www.beaufort-inn.com, from $209) is a large hotel on Gallants Channel, along one side of the colonial district. It's an easy walk to the main downtown attractions, and the hotel's outdoor hot tub and balconies have great views. The **Inlet Inn** (601 Front St., 252/728-3600 or 800/554-5466, www.inlet-inn.com, from 219 summer, from $85 winter) has one of the best locations in town, right on the waterfront. If you're planning to go dolphin-watching or hop the ferry to Cape Lookout, you can get ready at a leisurely pace and just step outside to the docks.

★ **Beaufort Hotel** (2440 Lennoxville Rd., 252/728-3000, www.beauforthotelnc.com) brings something a little different to the Crystal Cost: the resort hotel. This 133-room hotel sits on 10 acres overlooking Taylors Creek for some views that would be the highlight of any trip. A North Carolina Wildlife boat launch and the full-service **Boathouse Marina** (2400 Lennoxville Rd., 252/838-1524, www.boathousemarinanc.com) nearby makes it easy to get on the water when you stay here. The on-site **34° North Restaurant** (252/838-7250, www.34degreesnorthrestaurant.com, 7am-3pm and 5pm-9pm daily, bar 11am-11pm Sun.-Thurs., 11am-midnight Fri.-Sat., $10-42, weekend brunch $10-25), serves cuts of certified Angus beef, great seafood (how could you not?), and some really fun appetizers (the wahoo fish spread is a must, as is the cracklin' shrimp); breakfast is the usual eggs and accompaniments, and lunch is all about the handheld (the fried chicken sandwich and blackened mahimahi tacos are the way to go).

Beaufort Harbour Suites (313 Cedar St., 252/728-3483, www.beaufortharboursuites.com, from $130 weeknights, $190 weekends summer, from $79 weeknights, $110 weekends winter, pet-friendly rooms from $160 weeknights, $220 weekends summer, from $110 weeknights, $140 weekends winter) has 16 suites with full kitchens and pet-friendly rooms. If you're arriving by boat (don't laugh, plenty of folks do; the Intracoastal Waterway connects Key West with Maine and goes right by the Beaufort Waterfront), they have rooms and slip packages.

MOREHEAD CITY

Giovanni da Verrazzano may have been the first European to set foot in present-day Morehead City when he sailed into Bogue Inlet. It wasn't until the mid-19th century that the town came into being, built as the terminus of the North Carolina Railroad to connect the state's overland commerce to the sea. Despite its late start, Morehead City has been a busy place. During the Civil War it was the site of major encampments by both armies. A series of horrible hurricanes in the 1890s, culminating in the 1899 San Ciriaco Hurricane, brought hundreds of refugees from the towns along what is now the Cape Lookout National Seashore. They settled in a neighborhood that they called Promise Land, and many of their descendants are still here. The Atlantic and North Carolina Railroad operated a large hotel here in the 1880s, ushering in Morehead's role as a tourism spot, and the bridge to the Bogue Banks a few decades later increased holiday traffic considerably.

Morehead is also an official state port, one of the best deepwater harbors on the Atlantic Coast. This mixture of tourism and gritty commerce gives Morehead City a likeable real-life feel missing in many coastal towns today.

Sights

Morehead City's history is on display at the **History Museum of Carteret County** (1008 Arendell St., 252/247-7533, www.carterethistory.org, 10am-4pm Tues.-Fri., 10am-4pm 1st Sat. of the month). There are many interesting and eye-catching historical artifacts on display, but the most striking exhibit is that of a carriage, clothes, and other items pertaining to Morehead City's Emeline Piggott, considered a heroine by the traitorous Confederacy but whose bold actions can't help but elicit a grin. She was a busy woman all through the Civil War, working as a nurse, a spy, and a smuggler. The day she was captured, they found 30 pounds of contraband hidden in her skirts, including Union troop movement plans, a collection of gloves, several dozen skeins of silk, needles, toothbrushes, a pair of boots, and five pounds of candy.

Sports and Recreation

Many of this region's most important historic and natural sites are underwater. From Morehead City's **Olympus Dive Center** (713 Shepard St., 252/726-9432, www.olympusdiving.com, 8am-6pm Mon.-Sat., intro lessons from $75, open-water lessons from $495, advanced lessons from $150, half-day charters from $85, full day from $155), scuba divers of all levels of experience can take charter trips to dozens of natural and artificial reefs that teem with fish, including the ferocious-looking but not terribly dangerous eight-foot-long sand tiger shark. This is the Graveyard of the Atlantic, so there are many shipwrecks to choose from, including an 18th-century schooner, a luxury liner, a German U-boat, and many Allied commercial and military ships that fell victim to the U-boats that infested this coast during World War II.

Inshore fishing has its own fans, and **Water Dog Guide Service** (252/728-7907 or 919/423-6310, www.waterdogguideservice.com, tours from $450) knows where to find the fish, including speckled trout, flounder, and red drum, in the sounds, marshes, and creeks. They venture to some inland waters, offering striped bass fishing trips on the Roanoke River near Weldon (from $500), northeast of Raleigh, but here they fish at near-shore wrecks and reefs for bluefish, mahimahi, and Spanish mackerel. Check their website to see what's biting, and plan a trip around the red drum spawn, when red drum invade the marsh in huge numbers. Or try fly fishing for false albacore.

Taking a kayak or stand-up paddleboard tour with **Beaufort Paddle** (424 Old Causeway Rd., 252/725-3065, www.beaufortpaddle.com) will give you about a thousand great photo opportunities, so come with something waterproof or come with an iron grip so you don't lose your phone or camera in the drink. Tours ($55 adults, $30 under age 13) head out to the Rachel Carson Reserve (where you'll have a chance to see the Banker Ponies, those wild horses that live here, from a distance), Bird Shoals (a haven for migratory and year-round waterfowl and shorebirds), and along the waterfront in Beaufort. They also rent kayaks (single kayaks $20 per hour, $65 half day, $65 full day, $45 additional days, tandem kayaks $30 per hour, $70 half day, $80 full day, $45 additional days) and paddleboards ($30 per hour, $70 half day, $80 full day, $45 additional days) and offer lessons on the stand-up paddleboard (group lessons $55 pp, private lessons $75 per hour).

Entertainment and Nightlife

Seafood is a serious art in Morehead City. The enormous **North Carolina Seafood Festival** (252/726-6273, www.ncseafoodfestival.org), the state's second-largest fair after the State Fair in Raleigh, takes place here the first weekend in October. The city's streets shut down, and some 150,000 visitors descend on the waterfront. Festivities kick off with a blessing of the fleet, followed by music, fireworks, competitions such as the flounder fling (where you compete for distance by flinging a frozen flounder), fishing tourneys, and, of course, loads of food to sample.

Arendell Room (715 Arendell St., 252/240-2753, www.arendellroom.com,

5pm-midnight Mon.-Thurs., 5pm-2am Fri.-Sat.) is an unexpected find here: an upscale cocktail bar. They make drinks both classic and nouveau, and although they open at 5pm, the bartender is here most of the day, squeezing, juicing, peeling, slicing, dicing, and macerating all of their garnishes, mixes, bitters, and cocktail accouterments. Order off the menu, or do what I do and opt for the Bartender's Choice; after a few questions about what you like in a cocktail, the barkeep will whip up something just for you.

Just next door to Arendell Room is **Tight Lines Brewing** (709 Arendell St., 252/622-4618, www.tightlinesbrewing.com, 11:30am-9pm Sun.-Mon. and Wed.-Thurs., 11:30am-10pm Fri.-Sat., $10-24), a brewpub with some good pub grub (try the fish-and-chips, sesame tuna nachos, or loaded tater tots) and has more than a dozen beers on tap. IPAs, sours, Vienna lagers, seasonal porters, and one-off brews keep beer fans happy, and their flagship, Carterican, a Vienna lager, does a good job of showing their skills in the brewhouse.

Food

The Banks Grill (2900 Arendell St., Suite 3, 252/499-9044, www.thebanksgrill.com, 7am-2pm Mon.- Fri., 7:30am-2pm Sat.-Sun., $3-12) serves breakfast and lunch of the stick-to-your-ribs variety. The jumbo breakfast sandwich is served on the XXL Biscuit, one of the biggest biscuits I've ever seen, and if you want, you can get it smothered in gravy. The Lighthouse Breakfast takes that XXL Biscuit and uses it as part of an eggs benedict setup. Lunch is all about the shrimp burger or the fish sandwich; they're awesome choices.

El's Drive-In (3706 Arendell St., 252/726-3002, www.elsdrivein.com, 10:30am-10pm Sun.-Thurs., 10:30am-11pm Fri.-Sat., around $7), a tiny place across from Carteret Community College, seems like it has been around almost as long as the town. It's most famous for its shrimp burgers but serves all sorts of fried delights. It's a hit among locals and road-food fans, and most everyone agrees that the shakes are great, as are the onion rings. Be forewarned: It's car-side service, and the place is mobbed with gulls at times; they'll swoop down and snatch a french fry.

★ **Parrott's on Eleventh** (105 S. 11th St., Morehead City, 252/773-0532, 5pm-8pm Tues.-Sat., $15-34) has long been one of the top restaurants on this little strip of coast, and they continue to impress. The menu is small—a dozen items split between entrées and small plates, plus a couple of specials—but there's not a bad choice on it. Their preparations of fish—seared, grilled, blackened, or glazed catch of the day, crabcakes, shrimp—are impeccable, as is their seasonal duck dish, the fillet, and the current pork dish. The service here is the best in town, so you're in for a stupendous evening.

Ruddy Duck Tavern (509 Evans St., 252/726-7500, www.ruddyducktavern.com, 11am-9pm Thurs.-Sun., $9-24) has a fun bar, a few waterside tables, and a menu that takes a playful international approach to seafood and area delicacies. Shrimp tossed in Thai chili sauce, a seafood-packed jambalaya, and fish and shrimp tacos are table-pleasing entrées, but you can pass some time here in the early afternoon with a drink and a couple of appetizers—the duck drumettes, small hill of smothered nachos, and the Cajun fish bites make a good snack.

Southern Salt Seafood Company (701 Evans St., 252/499-9528, www.southern-saltseafood.com, 11am-10pm Sat.-Mon. and Thurs., 4pm-10pm Tues.-Wed. and Fri., $14-39) sticks to the spirt of the seafood menu along this part of the coast but adds some fun accents. The Down East Egg Roll, with collards, pimento cheese, and andouille, or the extra-spicy Buffalo shrimp, or the fresh oysters on the half shell are among the best starters; when it comes to dinner, the combo platter of blackened, broiled, or fried seafood is the way to go. They do fun things in the winter and shoulder seasons, like all-you-can-eat steamed oysters and shrimp, taking the backyard oyster roast party to their waterside restaurant.

Floyd's 1921 Restaurant (400 Bridges St., 252/727-1921, www.floyds1921.com, 4pm-9pm Tues.-Sat., $10-50) serves a blend of Southern classics and contemporary Southern cuisine. The appetizers are so big they warn you about them on the menu, and you can easily make dinner out of the Shrimp Napoleon. But then you'd miss out on the rest of the menu. Shrimpburgers and a Thai-spiced version, blackened tuna, shrimp étouffée, ribs, chicken and biscuits; the list is endless.

Accommodations

Morehead City has several chain hotels where you can stay, but a great option is **Bask Hotel at Big Rock Landing** (814 Shepard St., Morehead City, 252/499-9200, www.baskhotel.com, around $230). It's a short walk to the waterfront and the dock where the Big Rock Fishing Tournament weighs in, and it's right around the corner from Arendell Room and Parrott's on Eleventh, so it's in a prime location. The hotel is full of huge suites and generous studios, giving you and your traveling companions room to spread out a little.

HARKERS ISLAND

The Core Sound region stretches east-northeast from Beaufort, many miles up to the Pamlico Sound. Filled with birds, boats, and not much else, it's a hauntingly beautiful landscape. As along much of the North Carolina coast, the marshes and pocosins serve as way stations for countless flocks of migratory birds as they migrate, adding greatly to the year-round bird population. Fishing has always been a way of life here, but so has hunting, particularly hunting waterfowl. In earlier generations, men who earned a living fishing most of the year had sideline businesses hunting birds. They ate the birds they shot, sold the feathers for women's hats, trained bird dogs, and worked as birding outfitters to visiting hunters. Consequentially, many Down Easterners became expert decoy carvers. The beautifully carved decoys started as functional pieces, but today most are produced as art for art's sake; either way, the tradition survives.

Woodworking on a much grander scale has defined the culture of the people of Harkers Island, as it is home to generations of boat builders whose creations are as elegant as they are reliable. Keep an eye out as you drive through; you may see boats under construction in backyards and garages—not canoes or dinghies, but full-size fishing boats.

To get to Harkers Island, follow U.S. 70 east from Beaufort around the dogleg that skirts the North River. East of the town of Otway, you'll see Harkers Island Road; go right and head south toward Straits. Straits Road will take you through the town of Straits and then across a bridge over the straits themselves, finally ending up on Harkers Island.

★ Core Sound Waterfowl Museum

The **Core Sound Waterfowl Museum** (1785 Island Rd., 252/728-1500, www.coresound.com, 10am-5pm Mon.-Sat., 2pm-5pm Sun., $5), which occupies a modern building on Shell Point next to the Cape Lookout National Seashore headquarters, is a community-wide labor of love. The museum is home to exhibits crafted by members of the communities it represents, depicting the Down East maritime life through decoys, nets, and other tools of the trades as well as everyday household objects, beautiful quilts, and other utilitarian folk arts. This is a sophisticated modern institution, but its community roots are evident in touching details like the index-card labels, written in the careful script of elderly women, explaining what certain objects are, what they were used for, and who made them. The museum hosts Core Sound Community Nights (2nd Tues. every month). These get-togethers are a taste of the old home days when families and long-lost friends reunite over home-cooked food to reminisce about community history and talk about their hopes and concerns for the future.

The museum's gift shop has a nice selection of books and other items related to Down East culture. Be sure to pick up a copy of *Island Born and Bred: A Collection of Harkers Island Food, Fun, Fact and Fiction* by the Harkers

Island United Methodist Women. This cookbook has become a regional classic for its wonderful blend of authentic family recipes and community stories. You may also be able to find a Core Sound Christmas Tree, made by Harvey and Sons in nearby Davis. This old family fishery has made a hit in recent years manufacturing small Christmas trees out of recycled crab pots. It's a fun playful item, but it carries significant messages about the culture of the Core Sound region.

Core Sound Decoy Carvers Guild

Twenty years ago, over a pot of stewed clams, some decoy-carving friends Down East decided to found the **Core Sound Decoy Carvers Guild** (1575 Harkers Island Rd., 252-838-8818, www.decoyguild.com, call for hours). The guild is open to the public and gives demonstrations, competitions, and classes for grown-ups and children; the museum shop is a nice place to browse. It's also a cultural spot akin to the Appalachian craft guilds you find in the mountains: members preserve and celebrate history and a deep-rooted way of life for families around here. Spend a little time talking with decoy artists old and young and see for yourself just how far down the family tree this art goes.

Events

The Core Sound Decoy Carvers Guild also hosts the **Core Sound Decoy Festival,** usually held in the early winter. Several thousand people come to this annual event—more than the number of permanent residents on Harkers Island—to buy, swap, and teach the art of making decoys.

Food

Bay Breeze Restaurant and Bar (3557 Cedar Island Rd., near the Cedar Island-Ocracoke Ferry Terminal, 252-225-0248, www.baybreezerestaurantbar.business.site, 11am-9pm Sun.-Wed., 11am-10pm Thurs., 11am-midnight Fri.-Sat., $9-27) is a stone's throw from the ferry terminal on Cedar Island, so you can grab a bite before you hop on the ferry to Ocracoke or as soon as you hit the mainland after crossing back. In years past they've served a small breakfast menu (around $5) but their lunch and dinner have remained steady over the years. Go for the catch of the day or the Fishermen's Feast (which has some of all of their fried seafood on one table-size platter), but be sure to try the Down East Clam Chowder, a brothy, tasty chowder that comes served with dumplings the way it has been for generations.

Fish Hook Grill (980 Island Rd., Harkers Island, 252-728-1790, 11:30am-2:30pm and 4:30pm-9pm Wed.-Thurs. and Sat., 11:30am-2:30pm and 4:30pm-10pm Fri., noon-3pm Sun., $9-24) is a small-town restaurant serving big portions of seafood, burgers, and more. They're known locally for their chowder, crab cakes, potato salad, hush puppies, fried oysters, coleslaw, and, well, just about everything on the menu.

VILLAGE OF CEDAR ISLAND

For a beautiful afternoon's drive, head back to the mainland and follow U.S. 70 north. You'll go through some tiny communities—Williston, Davis, Stacy—and if you keep bearing north on Highway 12 when U.S. 70 heads south to the town of Atlantic, you'll eventually reach the tip of the peninsula and the village of Cedar Island. This little fishing town has the amazing ambience of being at the end of the earth. From the peninsula's shore you can barely see land across the sounds. The ferry to Ocracoke departs from Cedar Island, a two-hour-plus ride across Pamlico Sound. The beach here is absolutely gorgeous, and horses roam on it; they're not the famous wild horses of the Outer Banks, but they move around freely as if they were.

A spectacular location for bird-watching is the **Cedar Island National Wildlife Refuge** (U.S. 70, east of Atlantic, 252-926-4021, www.fws.gov). Nearly all of its 14,500 acres are brackish marshland, and it's often visited in season by redhead ducks, buffleheads, surf scoters, and many other species. While there are trails for hiking and cycling, this refuge is primarily intended as a haven for the birds. That said, they do allow hunting here and have a 200-acre area designated for waterfowl hunts. Fishing is allowed here too, but both activities are closely regulated, so check on rules, seasons, permits, and other information before you head out.

GETTING THERE AND AROUND
Car

One of the state's main east-west routes, U.S. 70 provides easy access to most of the destinations in this chapter. From Raleigh to Beaufort is a little over 150 miles, but keep in mind that long stretches of the highway are in commercial areas with plenty of traffic and red lights. U.S. 70 continues past Beaufort, snaking up along Core Sound through little Down East towns like Otway and Davis and finally ending in the town of Atlantic. At Sea Level, Highway 12 branches to the north, across the Cedar Island Wildlife Refuge and ending at the Cedar Island-Ocracoke Ferry.

Down south, to reach the Bogue Banks (Atlantic Beach, Emerald Isle, and neighboring beaches) by road, bridges cross Bogue Sound on Highway 58 at both Morehead City and Cedar Point (not to be confused with Cedar Island).

Ferry

Inland, a 20-minute passenger and vehicle ferry (800/339-9156, free, pets allowed) crosses the Neuse River between Cherry Branch (near Cherry Point) and Minesott Beach in Pamlico County every 30 minutes.

Lower Outer Banks

The southern stretch of the Outer Banks of North Carolina contains some of the region's most diverse destinations. Core and Shackleford Banks lie within Cape Lookout National Seashore, the fifth national seashore established in the country and the second in North Carolina (Cape Hatteras National Seashore to the north was the first in the country). It's a wild place, a maritime environment populated by birds, herds of wild horses, and not a single human. The towns of Bogue Banks—Atlantic Beach, Salter Path, Pine Knoll Shores, Indian Beach, and Emerald Isle—are classic beach towns with clusters of motels and restaurants and even a few towel shops and miniature golf courses. Both areas are great fun; Cape Lookout especially so for ecotours and history, and Bogue Banks for those looking for a day on the beach followed by an evening chowing down on good fried seafood.

TOP EXPERIENCE

★ CAPE LOOKOUT NATIONAL SEASHORE

Cape Lookout National Seashore (visitors center 1800 Islands Rd., Harkers Island, 252/728-2250, www.nps.gov/calo) is an otherworldly place: 56 miles of beach stretched out across four barrier islands, a long strip of sand seemingly so vulnerable to nature that it's hard to believe there were ever any towns on its banks. There were; Cape Lookout was settled in the early 1700s, and people in the towns of the south Core Banks made their living in fisheries that might seem brutal by today's terms: whaling and catching dolphins and sea turtles, among the more mundane species. Portsmouth was an important port to the early economy of North Carolina. Portsmouth declined slowly, but catastrophe rained down all at once on the people of the southerly Shackleford Banks, who were driven out of their own long-established communities to start new lives on the mainland when a series of terrible hurricanes decimated the islands in the 1890s.

Among the dunes, patches of maritime forest fight for each drop of fresh water, while ghost forests of trees that were defeated by advancing saltwater look on. Along the endless beach, loggerhead turtles come ashore to lay their eggs, and in the waters just off the strand, three other species of sea turtles are sometimes seen. Wild horses roam the beaches and dunes, and dolphins frequent both the ocean and sound sides of the islands. Other mammals are all of the small and scrappy variety: raccoons, rodents, otters, and rabbits. Like all of coastal North Carolina, it's a great place for bird-watching as it's located in a heavily traveled migratory flyway. Pets are allowed on a leash; the wild ponies on Shackleford Banks can pose a threat to dogs that get among them, and the dogs can frighten the horses, so be careful not to let them mingle.

Portsmouth Village

Portsmouth Village, at the northern tip of the Cape Lookout National Seashore, is a peaceful but eerie place. The village looks much as it did 100 years ago, with the handsome houses and churches all tidy and in good repair. But with the exception of caretakers and summer volunteers, no one has lived here since 1970 when the last two residents moved away. What had once been a town of 700 people and one of the most important shipping ports in North Carolina died. Founded before the Revolution, Portsmouth was a lightering station, a port where huge seagoing ships that had traveled across the ocean would stop and have their cargo removed for transport across the shallow sounds in smaller boats. There is a visitors center at Portsmouth (hours vary Apr.-Oct.), where you can learn about the village before embarking on a stroll to explore the quiet streets.

In its busy history, Portsmouth was captured by the British during the War of 1812

and by Union troops in the Civil War, underscoring its strategic importance. By the time of the Civil War, though, its utility as a way station was already declining. An 1846 hurricane opened a new inlet at Hatteras, which quickly became a busy shipping channel. After abolition, the town's lightering trade was no longer profitable without enslaved people to perform much of the labor. The fishing and lifesaving businesses kept the town afloat for a few more generations, but Portsmouth was never the same.

Once a year, an unusual thing happens: Boatloads of people arrive on shore, the church bell rings, and the sound of hymns come through the open church doors. At the Portsmouth Homecoming, descendants of the people who lived here come from all over to pay tribute to their ancestral home. They have an old-time dinner on the grounds and then tour the little village together. It's like a family reunion with the town itself as the matriarch. The rest of the year, Portsmouth receives visitors and National Park Service caretakers, but one senses that it's already looking forward to the next spring, when its children will come home again.

Shackleford Banks

The once-busy villages of Diamond City and Shackleford Banks are like Portsmouth in that, although they have not been occupied for many years, its residents' descendants retain a profound attachment to their ancestors' homes. Diamond City and nearby communities met a spectacular end. The hurricane season of 1899 culminated in the San Ciriaco Hurricane, a disastrous storm that destroyed homes and forests, killed livestock, flooded gardens with salt water, and washed the Shackleford dead out of their graves. The Bankers saw the writing on the wall and moved to the mainland en masse, carrying as much of their property as would fit on boats. Some actually floated their houses

1: aerial view of Cape Lookout National Seashore
2: the Cape Lookout Lighthouse

across Core Sound. Harkers Island absorbed most of the refugee population, and many went to Morehead City; their traditions are still an important part of Down East culture. Daily and weekly programs held at the Light Station Pavilion and the porch of the Keepers Quarters during the summer months teach visitors about the natural and human history of Cape Lookout, including what day-to-day life was like for the keeper of the lighthouse and the keeper's family.

Descendants of the Bankers feel a spiritual bond to their ancestors' home, and for years they would return, occupying fish camps that they constructed along the beach. When the federal government bought the Banks, it was made known that the fish camps would soon be off-limits to their deedless owners. The outcry and bitterness that ensued reflected the depth of the Core Sounders' love of their ancestral grounds. The National Park Service may have thought that the fish camps were ephemeral and purely recreational structures, but to the campers, the Banks were still home, even if they had been born on the mainland and had never lived here for longer than a fishing season. Retaining their sense of righteous, if not legal, ownership, many burned down their own fish camps rather than let the government take them down.

Cape Lookout Lighthouse

By the time you arrive at the 1859 **Cape Lookout Lighthouse** (252/728-2250, www. nps.gov/calo, visitors center and Keeper's Quarters Museum 9am-5pm daily Apr.-Nov., lighthouse climbs 10am-3:45pm Wed.-Sat. early May-mid-Sept., $8 adults, $4 seniors and under age 12), you will have seen it portrayed on dozens of brochures, menus, signs, and souvenirs. With its striking diamond pattern, it looks like a rattlesnake standing at attention. This 163-foot-tall lighthouse was first lit in 1859. Like the other lighthouses along the coast, it's built of brick. At its base, the walls are nine feet thick, narrowing to two feet at the top. The present lighthouse isn't the first to guard this section of the coast; originally a

lighthouse was built only a few yards away, but it was plagued with problems and replaced by the current structure.

Recreation

There's a lot to do on Cape Lookout. Visits to the lighthouse are a must, and climbing to the top (when it's open and available) will make it an even more memorable experience. Lots of folks come over to camp and fish, driving their trucks, SUVs, and off-road vehicles (ORVs) onto the sand (permit required, www. recreation.gov, $25) for a little adventure or to carry them to prime fishing spots. More come over just to check out the beach (the swimming is great), go shelling (these virtually untouched beaches are riddled with cool shells), or just to satisfy their own curiosity. Fishing is excellent here, and with so many miles of unspoiled shoreline to choose from, anglers will find it easy to settle into a spot where they can cast from shore and reel in a big one. Other anglers bring their kayaks, canoes, and fishing kayaks or stand-up paddleboards and wet a line in the marshes and creeks on the back side of the island for a totally different fishing experience.

You can also have a rare national park experience at Cape Lookout by driving an ATV or UTV on the beach. These vehicles aren't allowed on most national park land, but the size and remoteness of Cape Lookout make these vehicles ideal for getting to and from campsites and fishing holes, the ferry dock, and the lighthouse. A growing number of visitors to the island bring their UTVs with them, but you can rent one from **Island Express Ferry Service** (252/728-7433, www.island-expressferryservices.com), who keeps a small fleet of three-passenger ($100 half day, $150 full day) and 6-passenger ($150 half day, $250 full day) rides available. Driving these is fun, but it's not the kind of freewheeling, off-road, doughnut-doing, dune-jumping, do-it-yourself X-Games experience some folks want; instead, it's reasonable, responsible driving: staying off dunes, being mindful of wildlife habitats and nesting areas (sea turtles, migratory birds, and other critters call this place home), and generally displaying a bit of courtesy to your fellow humans and this amazing place.

And in an exciting development for stargazers, astrophotographers, and dark-sky enthusiasts, in December 2021, Cape Lookout National Seashore was certified as an International Dark Sky Park. This is the first place in the National Park Service's Atlantic Coast District to receive this certification, and it's a testament to the quality and clarity of the air, the lack of light pollution, and the absolutely astounding stargazing opportunities you'll find here. If you have a telescope, bring it, but if not, a decent pair of binoculars and a stargazing app on your smartphone or tablet will help you find some celestial sights that'll leave you speechless.

Accommodations

There are **cabins** (877/444-6777, information www.nps.gov/calo, reservations www. recreation.gov, Mar.-Nov.) to rent on Cape Lookout, but you must reserve well in advance to obtain one. At **Great Island** ($80-180), you can rent cabins with hot and cold water, gas stoves, and furniture, but in some cases visitors must bring their own generators for lighting as well as linens and utensils. Before you make a reservation, remember that with no air-conditioning, fall and spring are far more comfortable than summer. For decades, a second set of cabins, at Long Point near Portsmouth Village at the north end of the island, were available, but as happens on the North Carolina coast, a hurricane took them out and the National Park Service completed the demolition. Plans are in place to rebuilt cabins in a similar location around Portsmouth Village, but as of mid-2022, no plans have been released.

CAMPING

Camping is permitted within Cape Lookout National Seashore. There are no designated campsites or camping amenities, and everything you bring must be carried back out when you leave. Campers can stay for up to 14 days, and large groups (25 or more campers) require special permits. The National Park Service website for Cape Lookout (www.nps. gov/calo) has full details on camping regulations and permits.

Getting There

Except for the visitors center at Harkers Island, Cape Lookout National Seashore can

driving ORVs on Cape Lookout

only be reached by ferry. Portsmouth, at the northern end of the park, is a short ferry ride from Ocracoke, but Ocracoke is a very long ferry ride from Cedar Island. The Cedar Island-Ocracoke Ferry (800/293-3779, www.ferry.ncdot.gov) is part of the state ferry system and costs $15 one way for regular-size vehicles (pets allowed). It takes 2.25 hours to cross Pamlico Sound, but the ride is fun, and embarking from Cedar Island feels like sailing off the edge of the earth. The Ocracoke-Portsmouth Ferry is a passenger-only commercial route, licensed to Captain Rudy Austin of Austin Boat Tours (252/928-4361 or 252/928-5431, daily as weather permits, $20 pp, 3-person minimum). Call to ensure a seat. Most ferries operate April-November, with some exceptions.

Commercial ferries cross every day from mainland Carteret County to the southern parts of the national seashore. There is generally a ferry route between Davis and Great Island, but service can be variable; check the Cape Lookout National Seashore website (www.nps.gov/calo) for updates.

Island Express Ferry Service (252/728-7433, www.islandexpressferryservices.com) runs trips to and from Cape Lookout from its locations on Harkers Island (1800 Island Rd., Harkers Island, times vary, summer departures every 30 minutes 8:15am-5:45pm, $20 adults, $13 ages 3-11) and the Beaufort Waterfront (tours operate as staffing allows, departure times vary, $45 adults, $25 ages 3-11) on a spacious 49-person catamaran. From Harkers Island the trip takes 20-25 minutes round-trip, and they drop you off on the island to explore (and catch the return ferry) on your own. Departures from Beaufort are four-hour tours and visits to Cape Lookout, combining a bit of history and environmental narration, a quick look for the wild horses and dolphins, and a couple of hours on Cape Lookout. At the ferry terminal on Harkers Island you'll also find Shark Island Eats (11am-6pm Wed.-Sun. Apr.-Oct., $4-10), a food truck operated by the Island Express Ferry folks. It's a seafood-centric truck, but

they do have a burger, a hot dog, and nachos if that's more your style. The softshell crab burger, the mound of fried oysters in the oyster basket, and the shrimp tacos are especially good.

Cape Lookout Cabins and Camps (125 Davis Lane, Davis, 252/729-9751 or 252/729-9752, www.cape-lookout-cabins-camps-ferry-davis-nc.com), 30 minutes east of Beaufort on U.S. 70, midway to Cedar Island, runs regular ferries from Davis to the South Core Banks and Cape Lookout. Trips run mid-March to the end of the year, and prices range from $16 over age 10 to $350 for trucks hauling a camper or trailer. You can also rent a 4WD vehicle for $200 per day.

The Morehead City Ferry Service (709 Shepherd St., 252/504-2488, www.moreheadcityferryservice.com) takes folks on tours to several nearby islands. Sand Dollar Island (from $20) takes you out to a beach filled with sand dollars. The Sunset Dolphin Watch Cruise (from $25) is a 90-minute tour in search of dolphins and a beautiful sunset (it's not hard to find either). And Special Sand Dollar Island and Dolphin Watch Tour (from $27) combines the two in one 3.5-hour tour.

BOGUE BANKS

Most folks around here call the long island off the coast of Morehead City and Beaufort by the wrong name: Emerald Isle. Emerald Isle is the name of one of the beach towns on the island known officially as Bogue Banks. But if you, and they, get it wrong, no one is going to hold it against anyone. The Bogue Banks are home to several beach towns, the most prominent of which are the aforementioned Emerald Isle and Atlantic Beach. These two towns, and their smaller counterparts, have the typical North Carolina Coast laid-back feel. There's a quieter, slower pace here, as opposed to the fun-fun-fun neon jungles of beaches elsewhere. The major attractions, Fort Macon State Park and the North Carolina Aquarium at Pine Knoll Shores, are a bit more cerebral than, say, amusement parks and bikini contests. The other major draw is the beach itself, a long south-facing stretch of sand that's perfect for surfing, fishing, beachcombing, or just relaxing.

★ North Carolina Aquarium

The **North Carolina Aquarium at Pine Knoll Shores** (1 Roosevelt Blvd., Pine Knoll Shores, 252/247-4003, www.ncaquariums.com, 9am-5pm daily, closed Thanksgiving Day and Dec. 25, $13 adults, $12 seniors and military, $11 ages 3-12, free under age 3) is one of the state's three great coastal aquariums. Here at Pine Knoll Shores, exhibit highlights include a 300,000-gallon aquarium in which sharks and other aquatic beasts go about their business in and around a replica German U-boat (plenty of originals lie right off the coast and form homes for reef creatures); a "jelly gallery" (I think they're mesmerizing); a tank filled with the beautiful but invasive lionfish; a pair of river otters; and many other wonderful animals and habitats.

Trails from the parking lot lead into the maritime forests of the 273-acre **Theodore Roosevelt Natural Area,** where a network of trails takes your through secluded marshes, on a high dune ridge, and under a coastal forest canopy, providing plenty of opportunities for bird-watching and wildlife viewing. The trails close at 4:30pm, so get an early start.

Fort Macon State Park

At the eastern tip of Atlantic Beach is **Fort Macon State Park** (2303 E. Fort Macon Rd., 252/726-3775, http://ncparks.gov, visitors center and bookstore 9am-5pm daily, fort 9am-5:30pm daily, bathhouse area 8am-5:30pm daily Nov.-Feb., 8am-8pm daily Mar.-May and Sept., 8am-7pm daily Oct., swimming area 10am-5:45pm daily May-Sept. as staffing allows, free). The central feature of the park is Fort Macon, an 1820s federal fort that was a Confederate garrison for one year during the Civil War. Guided tours are offered, and there are exhibits inside the casemates. For such a stern and martial building, some of the interior spaces are surprisingly pretty. The park has 1.5 miles of beach, perfect for fishing,

swimming, sunbathing, or simply strolling. At different times throughout the year, the park is filled with costumed Civil War reenactors.

Beaches

The 21-mile-long island known as the Bogue Banks on maps, and Emerald Isle by locals, is actually made up of five beach towns and communities. From west to east they are Emerald Isle, Indian Beach, Salter Path, Pine Knoll Shores, and Atlantic Beach. The two most prominent of these communities are Emerald Isle and Atlantic Beach. Atlantic Beach, on the eastern end of the island due south from Morehead City, is the more developed of the communities in terms of commercial spots—shops, restaurants, and outfitters—but it's still a quiet little beach town. At the western end, Emerald Isle is larger, but less commercial; there are many more homes on this end of the island, however. Beaches along the length of the Bogue Banks are south-facing, so waves and winds are slightly different than at other beaches, but unless you surf or sail, the only difference you'll notice is that the sun rises and sets over the Atlantic Ocean. Families flock to the Bogue Banks because it's what the Outer Banks was 25 years ago—beautiful beaches, great houses, no crowds—and the distractions offered by the kayak and bike outfitters, fishing and sightseeing charters, and the mix of seafood and family restaurants that deliver on that ideal beach vacation.

Sports and Recreation

The ocean side of Bogue Banks offers plenty of public beach access. In each of the towns—Atlantic Beach, Pine Knoll Shores, Salter Path, Indian Beach, and Emerald Isle—are parking lots, some free and some paid. The beach at **Fort Macon** is bounded by the ocean, Bogue Sound, and Beaufort Inlet. Because there's a Coast Guard station on the Sound side and a jetty along the inlet, swimming is permitted only along one stretch of the ocean beach. A concession stand and bathhouse are located at the swimming beach.

Atlantic Beach Surf Shop (515 W. Fort

Macon Rd., Atlantic Beach, 252/726-9382, www.absurfshop.com, surf rentals $25 per day) opened in 1964 because the 14-year-old owner loved surfing so much, he had to help others get into the sport. Now they sell and rent surfboards and stand-up paddleboards and carry a big line of surf lifestyle clothing. They offer instruction in partnership with local pros and instructors. Rates and arrangements vary.

There's a small store stocked with all the gear you'll need for a day on the water at **Hot Wax Surf Shop** (200 Mallard Dr., Emerald Isle, 252/354-6466, www.hotwaxsurf.com, 10am-5pm Mon.-Sat.). Here you can arrange for surfing and stand-up paddleboard lessons ($100-125); rent kayaks, surf, and SUP equipment (from $30 full day); join a guided kayak fishing excursion (from $125); or go on a guided excursion to the Cedar Point Recreation Area (check for availability and prices), where there are several paddle trails to explore.

AB Watersports (612 Atlantic Beach Causeway, 252/422-0520, www.abwatersport. com, 9am-6pm daily) has tours and rentals for just about every water sport you can imagine. Get out on the water via jet skis ($65 half hour, $125 per hour, Cape Lookout Tour $195), stand-up paddleboards ($50 half day, $75 full day, $25 additional day), single kayaks ($40 half day, $60 full day, $25 additional day), double kayaks ($50 half day, $70 full day, $30 additional day), or a pontoon boat ($425 half day, $252 plus fuel full day).

Anglers love this part of the coast for its inshore and offshore fishing; find an up-to-date list of Morehead City charter boats at www.downtownmoreheadcity.com. Just over the bridge from Morehead City, **Captain Stacy Fishing Center** (416 Atlantic Beach Causeway, Atlantic Beach, 252/726-4675 or 800/533-9417, www.captstacy.com, from $70 adults, $65 children) has been hauling in big fish off the coast for decades. Charter options include a nighttime shark fishing expedition. Full-day and half-day bottom-fishing excursions take you offshore into deep water.

Pelagic Sportfishing (212 Smith St., 252/904-3361, www.pelagicsportfishing.com) has a 61-foot boat at Atlantic Beach for half-day, three-quarter day ($1,750), and full-day ($2,225) charters for tuna, mahimahi, and redfish. These are experienced anglers, fishing here and in Guatemala (Feb.-Mar.), and entering just about every local tournament that pops up, so they know where to put you on the fish.

Food

You'll find one of North Carolina's food icons at ★ **Big Oak Drive-In and Bar-B-Q** (1167 Salter Path, 252/247-2588, www.bigoakdrivein.com, 11am-3pm Tues.-Thurs. and Sun., 11am-8pm Fri.-Sat., around $6), a classic beach drive-in: a little red, white, and blue-striped building with a walk-up counter and drive-up spaces. They're best known for their shrimp burgers ($5), a fried affair slathered with Big Oak's signature red sauce, coleslaw, and tartar sauce. Then there are the scallop burgers, oyster burgers, clam burgers, hamburgers, and barbecue, all cheap and made for easy eating. You can dine at the handful of picnic tables out back under the big oaks, off the hood of your car (I've eaten a dozen shrimpburgers this way) or tailgate of your truck, or you can whip out a couple of camping chairs and chow down wherever you can sit.

★ **The Island Grille** (401 Money Island Dr., Atlantic Beach, 252/240-0000, www.islandgrillenc.com, 5pm-9pm daily, $14-41) came highly recommended from a friend who grew up nearby, and I'm glad I listened. They bill themselves as "Atlantic Beach's gourmet hole in the wall" and I can't think of any way to say it better. The food is southern coastal—scallops and shrimp sautéed in butter and served with mushrooms and fresh vegetables, crab cakes, pork chops—and outstanding. Do yourself a favor and make a reservation now, then plan your trip around it.

Bahia Beach House & Surf Bar (208 West Dr., Atlantic Beach, 252/499-9033, https://bahiabeachhouseab.com, 5pm-9pm

Wed.-Thurs., 11:30am-3pm and 5pm-9pm Fri.-Sun., $11-40) is just a few paces from the beach and Idle Hour Biergarten, and the food here is decidedly upscale. The Chili Dusted Shrimp and Grits could use a little more spice for my taste but were a crowd pleaser on my last visit; the spicy shrimp tacos delivered a bit of heat. You can make a meal of appetizers here, with exceptional yellowfin tuna ceviche, crab croquettes, and my favorite, the Oysters Oaxafeller (a playful twist on oysters Rockefeller that bring poblano peppers, chorizo, and manchego to the oyster for great results).

★ **Caribesa Restaurant** (8921 Crew Dr., Emerald Isle, 252/424-8400, https://caribsearestaurant.com, 5pm-9pm or later daily, $12-58) delivers an upscale experience from their charming dining room, but the setting and the fine folks who work here aren't the only things you'll love; the rest is on the menu. Huge crabcakes (almost entirely crab, very little cake), amazing scallops (served over a kimchi-sweet potato puree and roasted mushrooms), a massive 28 ounce bone-in rib-eye, a sushi roll of the day, and a perfectly-paired wine list make this an awesome night out.

A community institution you should check out is the **Crab Shack** (146 Headen Lane, Salter Path, 252/247-3444, www.thecrabshacksalterpath.com, 11am-8:30pm Mon., 11am-8pm Wed. and Sun., 11am-9pm Thurs.-Sat., $16-47), a small waterfront restaurant tucked away behind Salter Path United Methodist Church. Operated by the Guthries—a family name that dates back to the early colonists in this area—the restaurant was wiped out in 2005 by Hurricane Ophelia but was rebuilt, much to the joy of loyal diners of the local and vacationer variety.

Before dinner, or after, or both, grab a drink at one of the coolest bars in Atlantic Beach, **The Barnacle** (700 E. Ft. Macon Rd., 252/726-0863, www.oceananapier.com, 4pm-10pm Wed.-Fri., noon-10pm Sat.-Sun.). The Barnacle is a sort of boozy hut at the end of Oceanana Pier, and it has the sunset view you're looking for. Perched as it is hundreds of feet out into the Atlantic, you can capture the sun, clouds, waves, and shore in one stunning glance. Cocktails are simple but good, and the selection of beer and wine is limited, but out here they all taste great. The sister to The Barnacle is **Oceana Pier House Restaurant** (252/726-0863, www.oceananapier.com, 7am-8pm Mon. and Thurs., 7am-9pm Fri.-Sat., 7am-5pm Sun., $6-30), where you can grab breakfast, lunch, or dinner. Breakfast is simple

The shrimp burger from Big Oak Drive-In and Bar-B-Q is a regional favorite.

eggs and bacon, but lunch gets into burgers, hot dogs, and chicken sandwiches as well as shrimp burgers and fresh seafood platters.

Accommodations

The Inn at Pine Knoll Shores (511 Salter Path Rd., Atlantic Beach, 252/247-4155 or 800/338-1533, http://theinnatpks.com, $139-329) is another reliable option with all-oceanfront guest rooms. You'll find beach chairs and umbrellas to use as well as a game room, a poolside bar, and wireless internet. Pets are not allowed. The **Atlantis Lodge** (123 Salter Path Rd., Atlantic Beach, 252/726-5168 or 800/682-7057, www.atlantislodge.com, $119-354) is an established family-run motel. It has simple and reasonably priced efficiencies in a great beachfront location; the hotel's private boardwalk puts you on the beach in two minutes. Well-behaved pets are welcome for an additional fee. The **Windjammer Inn** (103 Salter Path Rd., Atlantic Beach, 252/247-7123 or 800/233-6466, www.windjammerinn. com, $142-228) is another simple, comfortable motel with decent rates through the high season and great rates in the off-season.

VACATION RENTALS

In beach towns like these, many vacationers opt for a whole house or a condo rather than a hotel room. I think this is the way to go, as it gives you the chance to dig into that local seafood and cook for yourself or hire a personal chef, like Chef Patrick Hogan of Carlton's Catering Company (910/381-4846, www.carlotonscateringcompany.com), to cook for you. If you're looking for a house, **Emerald Isle Realty** (7501 Emerald Dr., Emerald Isle, 888/974-0511, www.emeraldislerealty.com) is one of the largest rental companies in the region and has a broad portfolio of homes and accommodations in a variety of sizes, configurations, locations, and prices. **Sun-Surf Realty** (7701 Emerald Dr., Emerald Isle, 800/553-7873, www.sunsurfrealty.com) has a smaller selection of homes and condos, but their list is loaded with great places to stay. **Shorewood Real Estate** (7703 Emerald Dr., Emerald Isle, 252/354-7873 or 888/557-0172, www.shorewoodrealestate.com) has a number of options, from pet-friendly stays to the five-plus-bedroom beach palaces and luxury cottages.

GETTING THERE AND AROUND

The Bogue Banks extend from the Bogue Inlet in the west to Fort Macon to the east. Morehead City and Beaufort sit across the sound a short drive away. Along the length of the Banks are several small towns, anchored by Emerald Isle and Atlantic Beach. One road, Highway 58, runs the length of the island and goes through several name changes as it does, so whether you find yourself on Fort Macon Road, Salter Path Road, or Emerald Drive, it's all the same. Emerald Isle is 24 minutes from Morehead City, a testimony of the length of the Bogue Banks, but with summer traffic, that drive can stretch to 34 or even 44 minutes, so leave in plenty of time if you've made reservations for dinner or an excursion. The B. Cameron Langston Bridge enters Bogue Banks (from Cape Carteret on the mainland) at the west, and the Atlantic Beach-Morehead City Bridge crosses the Bogue Sound from Morehead City on the east side of the island.

Wilmington and Cape Fear

In 1524, the first known European explorer ar-rived on these shores of North Carolina at the mouth of the Cape Fear River.

Giovanni da Verrazzano wrote to the king of France that the land here was "as pleasant and delectable to behold as is possible to imagine."

The southeastern corner of North Carolina is indeed a natural beauty: Barrier islands here contain the largest intact piece of maritime forest in the state. There are stunning beaches and miles of river, marsh, and creek to explore, plus, as you move inland, the gentle rising of the Sandhills and hardwood forests. Pleasant and delectable indeed.

As enthusiasm for the New World built in Europe, the influence of England, Spain, and France profoundly changed the cultural and

Highlights

Look for ★ to find recommended sights, activities, dining, and lodging.

© MOON.COM

★ **Wilmington's Historic District:** Downtown reflects its glory days of commerce and high society in the state's largest 19th-century historic district, a gorgeous collection of antebellum and late-Victorian townhouses and commercial buildings (page 139).

★ **Wrightsville Beach:** North Carolina has many wonderful beaches, but few can compare with Wrightsville for its pretty sand, easy public access, clear waters, and overall beauty (page 141).

★ **Hammocks Beach State Park:** One of the wildest and least disturbed Atlantic coast beaches, accessible only by boat, Bear Island is a popular stopover for migrating waterfowl and turtles (page 165).

★ **Southport:** From this picturesque fishing town you can see the oldest and newest lighthouses in North Carolina, enjoy dinner on the water, and celebrate your independence on the Fourth of July (page 170).

★ **Cape Fear Botanical Garden:** This gorgeous botanical garden in Fayetteville provides a place for locals and visitors to stretch their legs while admiring the flora of the region (page 184).

Wilmington and Cape Fear

© MOON.COM

ATLANTIC OCEAN

Richlands

Jacksonville

New River

HAMMOCKS BEACH STATE PARK

Folkstone

North Topsail Beach

Topsail Island

Surf City

Topsail Beach

WRIGHTSVILLE BEACH

Wilmington

HISTORIC DISTRICT

Hampstead

Masonboro Island

Carolina Beach State Park

Carolina Beach

Kure Beach

Pleasure Island

Fort Fisher State Park

SOUTHPORT

Smith Island

Cape Fear

Holly Shelter Swamp

Wallace

Currie

MOORE'S CREEK NATIONAL BATTLEFIELD

Cape Fear River

BRUNSWICK TOWN/ FORT ANDERSON

Caswell Beach

Bald Head Island

EV-HENWOOD NATURE PRESERVE

Boiling Spring Lakes

Long Beach

Oak Island

Yaupon Beach

Clinton

Jones Lake State Park

Black River

Green Swamp

Supply

Holden Beach

Shallotte

Ocean Isle Beach

Waccamaw State Park

Lake Waccamaw

BIG CATS

Sunset Beach

Calabash

Clarkton

Whiteville

Waccamaw River

Little River

CAPE FEAR BOTANICAL GARDEN

Fayetteville

Elizabethtown

Tabor City

To Myrtle Beach

NORTH CAROLINA

Lumberton

Fair Bluff

SOUTH CAROLINA

Conway

Raeford

Pembroke

Laurinburg

Dillon

Mullins

Marion

10 mi

10 km

physical landscapes of the Caribbean and the southern Atlantic coast of North America. Towns and forts sprung up where Indigenous people once lived. Then came plantations built by enslaved Africans for their European enslavers. Wilmington shares this legacy with other cities in the Atlantic-Caribbean region such as Havana, Nassau, New Orleans, Savannah, and Charleston. The architecture of these cities shows European influence, and the culture—language, food, and folkways—shows the influence of Africans.

The Lumbee people, Indigenous people historically and spiritually tied to the blackwater Lumber River, now make their home in Pembroke. They are the largest Indigenous community east of the Mississippi River, though their name is not widely known. This is due in part to the fact that they've been denied federal status, a complex and contentious issue that continues to cast a shadow for members of the community. They don't have a reservation and for centuries have lived a rural existence and practiced deeply rooted Christianity. Their little-known history can be explored in and around Pembroke.

Between Wilmington and Lumberton the landscape of the state's southeast corner becomes a waterscape comprising black-water creeks and seductive, even eerie swamps, bays, marshes, and rivers. It's the world's only native habitat of the Venus flytrap. Many visitors wrinkle their noses at the marsh's distinctive smell as the tide recedes and the mudflats are exposed, but to locals the mingled scent of marsh and salt water is the scent of home. The cypress knees, tannic creeks, marsh birds, and occasional alligator make this region worth staying a little longer.

The greatest draw is the water: the beautiful beaches of Brunswick, New Hanover, Pender, and Onslow Counties and the well-known Wrightsville and Topsail beaches as well as other hidden gems just north of bustling Myrtle Beach, South Carolina. You can find the same mini golf and beach-towel vendors peppering the beach towns of North Carolina, but the state's coast mostly seems downright bucolic compared to its southern neighbor.

Inland, the landscape changes but the water is no less important. At the edge of this region is Fayetteville, with a long history that includes Revolutionary War standoffs, Civil War battles, and ties to the Cape Fear River. At Fayetteville the marshes give way to rolling hills with a mix of pines and hardwoods. Home to Fort Bragg, Fayetteville has a longstanding military presence and history, dating to the colonial era when immigrant Scots called these hills home.

PLANNING YOUR TIME

There's a lot to do in the Cape Fear region and, depending on your interests, a wide range of choices for a home base. Wilmington is the obvious choice: Centrally located on the coast, it's minutes from Wrightsville, Kure, and Carolina Beaches and only a little farther from Topsail and the beaches of Brunswick County. Fayetteville and Raleigh are only a couple of hours away, making day trips a possibility. The town of Wilmington is full of activities and sights, and you'll want a day or two to explore this historic river city. For inland adventures in the region, Fayetteville offers a good selection of motels, and it's still a reasonable drive to the coast for a day at the beach.

Weather across the region is mostly mild, with a short winter on the coast and a slightly longer winter around Fayetteville. Spring is a beautiful time to visit, when the Southern gardens fill with azaleas. Summer starts early, with warm waters (courtesy of the Gulf Stream) and sunny days growing warmer throughout summer months and sticking around until October or later. Fall is short along the coast, and there are few fall leaves to see, however, the hills around Fayetteville see a true autumn color show. Hurricanes are a concern along the coast of the Carolinas, and although hurricane season runs June-November, the biggest threat is during the latter months of the season, usually September-October. On the coast, the dangers are the expected rain, wind, and strong surf and tide, but inland, wind, rain, and flooding are a concern. Keep an eye on the long-range forecast when planning a trip during hurricane season, and be sure to follow the instructions of local authorities if one pops up while you're here.

HISTORY

Giovanni da Verrazzano's 1524 visit started a land race that took two centuries to take off. Lucas Vásquez de Ayllón and his crew, which possibly included the first enslaved Africans brought to what is now the United States, walked the shores here in 1526 scouting for resources and settlement sites before their shipwreck in South Carolina. A number of other colonial parties were warded off, likely by the frightening name given to the river and shoals here: Cape Fear. The shoals and currents at the mouth of the Cape Fear River gave Sir Richard Greenville fits in 1585, and he nearly wrecked; consequently, he gave it the name it has today. Perhaps the name is why it took 140 years for someone to settle here. A couple of failed settlements appeared on the banks of the river, but colonists cited the humidity, hurricanes, and bugs, among other things, as reason to abandon these attempts.

It wasn't until 1726 that European settlement finally took hold in the region. Maurice Moore and his brother Roger established their family's domain at Brunswick Town and Orton Plantation, a half mile north. Today, only ruins remain at Brunswick Town in the form of ballast-stone house foundations and the brick walls of an Anglican church, but Orton Plantation still stands and is once again owned by Moore descendants. The machinations of the Moores and Brunswick Town residents led to the demise of the indigenous Cape Fear people. Many of them were driven off, and the remainder were rounded up and later murdered.

Brunswick Town was an important port, as the only inland deepwater access on the river, but it was soon eclipsed by Wilmington to the north once dredging technology allowed the shoals between the two towns to be cleared. As Brunswick Town declined, the American Revolution heated up, and the small port town played important roles in defying George III's taxes and harrying General Cornwallis and his troops as they raided the area. At the same time, the large population of Scottish immigrants around Fayetteville grew even larger, making their living in the forests preparing tar, pitch, and turpentine for naval stores.

In the lower Cape Fear Region, especially present-day Brunswick, New Hanover, Bladen, and Onslow Counties, the concentration of enslaved laborers was significantly larger than in many other parts of the state. The naval stores industry demanded workers, as did the large rice and indigo plantations—including Orton—that once dominated the local agricultural industry. The same was true along the coasts of South Carolina, Georgia, and parts of northern Florida, where many of the enslaved people had been taken from the same part of Africa. These large communities of African-born and first-generation American-born people shared ideas, memories, and culture, which became what is known today as Gullah or Geechee culture. Most prominent around Charleston and Savannah, the Gullah dialect and cultural influence still exist in and around Wilmington. The dialect is reminiscent of English as spoken in the Caribbean, and cultural traditions still in evidence include the cuisine, heavy with gumbo, peanuts, and okra, and folklore, in which houses are painted bright blue to keep bad luck away and bottle trees are used to capture evil spirits.

Another cultural group in the Cape Fear region is the indigenous Lumbee people. Also called the Croatan Indians, Pembroke Indians, and Indians of Robeson County, they're the largest indigenous community in the eastern United States. During the time of enslavement and the Civil War they were called "free people of color," and they had no right to vote or to bear arms. The Lumbee people have a long history of resistance and defending their land. Most famously, in the 19th century the Lowry (sometimes spelled Lowrie) Band of outlaws defined the Lumbee cause for future generations. Another transformative moment in Lumbee history was a 1958 armed conflict near Maxton. Ku Klux Klan grand wizard "Catfish" Cole and about 40 other armed Klansmen held a rally at Hayes Pond. Fed up with a recent wave of vicious intimidation, 1,500 armed Lumbee showed up at the rally and shot out the lone electric light. Although no one was killed in the exchange of gunfire, the Klansmen fled. The confrontation was reported around the country, energizing the cause of Native American civil rights.

In the late 20th and early 21st centuries, southeastern North Carolina's role as a military center expanded. Fort Bragg in Fayetteville is one of the country's largest Army installations and home to thousands of the soldiers who were stationed in Iraq and Afghanistan; the base continues to grow. Nearby Pope Air Field is the home of the 440th Airlift Wing, and there is a major Marine Corps presence nearby at Camp Lejeune in Jacksonville. Numerous museums in Fayetteville and Jacksonville tell the history of the military in southeastern North Carolina.

One of the most important developments in the region's recent history is the arrival of the film industry. Wilmington's EUE/Screen Gems Studios' 50-acre studio lot is the largest outside Los Angeles, and on this lot, more than 350 film, television, and commercial projects have come to life. Productions like *Iron Man 3, Dawson's Creek, One Tree Hill, Under the Dome, Eastbound and Down,* and *Firestarter,* which started the film craze, were shot here. Although the film industry was once thriving, today it's a shell of its former self as decisions by state legislators forced productions to shoot elsewhere.

INFORMATION AND SERVICES

Area hospitals include two in Wilmington, **New Hanover Regional Medical Center Orthopedic Hospital** (formerly Cape Fear Hospital, 5301 Wrightsville Ave., Wilmington, 910/667-8100, www.nhrmc.org) and the **New Hanover Regional Medical Center** (2131 S. 17th St., Wilmington, 910/667-7000, www.nhrmc.org); two in Brunswick County, **Brunswick Novant Medical Center** (240 Hospital Dr. NE, Bolivia, 910/721-1000, www.novanthealth.org) and **Dosher Memorial Hospital** (924 N. Howe St., Southport, 910/457-3800, www.dosher.org); in Onslow County, **Onslow Memorial Hospital** (317 Western Blvd., Jacksonville, 910/577-2345, www.onslow.org); in Pender County, **Pender Memorial Hospital** (507 E. Fremont St., Burgaw, 910/259-5451, www.nhrmc.org); and Fayetteville's **Cape Fear Valley Medical Center** (1638 Owen Dr., Fayetteville, 910/615-4000, www.capefearvalley.com). Myrtle Beach, South Carolina, has the **Grand Strand Regional Medical Center** (809 82nd Pkwy., Myrtle Beach, SC, 843/692-1000, www.mygrandstrandhealth.com), not far from the southernmost communities in Brunswick County. In an emergency, of course, call 911.

More information on dining, attractions, and lodging is available through local convention and visitors bureaus: the **Wilmington, NC River District & Island Beaches** (1 Estell Lee Place, Suite 101, Wilmington, 877/406-2356, www.wilmingtonandbeaches.com, 8:30am-5pm Mon.-Fri.) with a **Visitors Information Booth** (Market St. and Water St., 9am-4:30pm daily Mar.-May and Sept.-Oct., 9:30am-5pm daily June-Aug., 10am-4pm Fri.-Sun. Nov.-mid-Mar.), **North Carolina's Brunswick Islands** (712 Village Rd. SW, 910/755-5517, www.ncbrunswick.com), and the **Fayetteville Area CVB** (245 Person St., Fayetteville, 910/483-5311, www.visitfayettevillenc.com, 8am-5pm Mon.-Fri.).

Wilmington

In some ways, Wilmington is a town where time has stood still. During the Civil War, General Sherman's fiery march that razed so many Southern towns missed Wilmington. For most of the 20th century the economy moved in fits and starts, with long slumps and standstills punctuated by short boom periods. Surviving the Civil War combined with a slow economy provided Wilmington's architecture with an unexpected benefit: historic preservation. Much of the downtown remains a museum of beautiful buildings dating to the town's first heyday, and that historic appeal accounts for much of its popularity as a destination today.

HISTORY

Founded in the early 1730s, Wilmington went through a short identity crisis as New Carthage, New Liverpool, and New Town before settling on Wilmington in 1739. Early on it was a deepwater port and quickly became a bustling shipping center for the export of lumber, rice, and naval stores, including turpentine and tar tapped from longleaf pine trees, lumber for ships' keels, and ribbing from live oak branches. By 1769, the town had grown from a collection of wharves, warehouses, and homes into a respectable colonial city, included on a map drawn by acclaimed French cartographer C. J. Sauthier. By 1840 the city was booming and positioned as the southern terminus of the Wilmington and Weldon Railroad (the 161-mile track was the longest in the world at the time).

During the Civil War the Wilmington and Weldon Railroad line was an essential Confederate artery for trade and troop transport. The Union navy attempted a blockade of the Cape Fear River and inlets up and down the coast, but Wilmington's port was a hive of blockade runners bringing in arms, food, medicine, and materials from Europe and the Caribbean. In January 1865 the Union took nearby Fort Fisher, the key gun emplacement guarding the river's mouth, and Wilmington soon fell. It was a crushing blow to the failing Confederacy. Continued commerce at the port allowed Wilmington to thrive during the Civil War and Reconstruction, unlike many towns in the South; by 1890 the population hit 20,000, making it the largest city in North Carolina.

Political tensions ran high during Reconstruction, and there were conflicts between white people and Black people, Democrats and Republicans, and staunch Confederate supporters and carpetbaggers (Northerners who came to the South for economic opportunities) and copperheads (their Southern supporters). In 1898 the only successful coup d'état on American soil took place in the Wilmington Race Riot. White Democrats loyal to the long-dead Confederacy threatened to overthrow the city government if their candidate lost. He did, and two days after the election, a mob of white Democrats and their supporters overthrew the city's Republican government, destroyed the city's African American newspaper, the *Daily Record,* and killed at least 22 African American citizens.

In the early 20th century, North Carolina's power center shifted from the agriculture and shipping at coastal towns like Wilmington to the textile mills and manufacturing of the Piedmont region. Charlotte surpassed Wilmington in population, interstate highways joined larger cities to the rest of the nation, and economically Wilmington stood still. In 1960 the Atlantic Coast Line Railroad relocated its headquarters to Florida, and the city experienced several decades of decline. After I-40 was completed, connecting Wilmington to the rest of the country, the tourism industry began to rise. Wilmington and surrounding towns had a real estate boom in the late 1990s that lasted for several

Wilmington

© MOON.COM

ATLANTIC OCEAN

2 mi

2 km

0

0

SCOTTS HILL LOOP RD

POPLAR GROVE PLANTATION

Intracoastal Waterway

BEACH RD

POPTERS NECK RD

CAST IRON KITCHEN

PHO VANHY

MARKET ST

MILITARY CUTOFF RD

FISHHOUSE GRILL/ DOCKSIDE

AQUATIC SAFARIS

BENTO BOX

LUMINA AVE

WRIGHTSVILLE BEACH

SOUTH BEACH GRILL
BLOCKADE RUNNER
EAST OCEANFRONT DINING

WB SURF CAMP

AIRLIE GARDENS

ARBORETUM

SIDBURY RD

SIDBURY RD

EASTWOOD DR

MAYFAIRE TOWN CENTER

LUMINA STATION

MILITARY CUTOFF RD

CATCH

GORDON RD

COLLEGE RD

AROMAS OF PERU

UNIVERSITY OF NORTH CAROLINA AT WILMINGTON

OLEANDER DR

GREENVILLE LOOP

Masonboro Island

Masonboro Island Coastal Reserve

Intracoastal Waterway

MASONBORO LOOP RD

MOHICAN TRAIL

COLLEGE RD

KERR AVE

CLAY RD

KERR RD

BLUE CLAY RD

M.L.K. JR. BLVD

PRINCESS PL DR

HOLIDAY INN

FLEA BODY'S ANTIQUE MALL

INDOCHINE/ THE IVY COTTAGE

COLLEGE RD

LA TAPATIA

SEALEVEL CITY GOURMET

REGIONAL MEDICAL CENTER

SHIPYARD BLVD

CAMERON ART MUSEUM

Halyburton Park

17TH ST

BEACH RD

LongleafPark

INDEPENDENCE BLVD

CAROLINA BEACH RD

SANDERS RD

WILMINGTON INTERNATIONAL AIRPORT

Smith Creek

N 23RD ST

MARKET ST

17TH ST

16TH ST

OAKDALE CEMETERY

LIVE OAK BANK PAVILLION

NE Cape Fear River

HISTORIC DISTRICT

Wilmington

Cape Fear River

RIVER RD SE

RIVER RD SE

SEE "HISTORIC DISTRICT" MAP

BENNY'S BIGTIME PIZZA/MARIPOSA/ SATELLITE LOUNGE/THE SECOND GLASS/ NEW ANTHEM BEER PROJECT

CAPE FEAR NATIONAL AT BRUNSWICK FOREST

Lake Sutton

Cape Fear River

CEDAR HILL RD

OLD MILL RD

VILLAGE RD

OLD FAYETTEVILLE RD

MT MISERY RD

LANVALE RD

OCEAN HWY

Town Creek

CREEK RD

GOVERNORS RD

DAWS

years. At the same time, the film industry grew, boosting the local economy and influencing local culture. Like most of the country, Wilmington was hit hard by the end of the real estate bubble in 2006, and the city is still climbing out from under the wreckage of that widespread economic collapse. Of late, the film industry is in decline, although there is growth in Wilmington—in high-tech and industrial sectors—and the city continues to make strides in terms of identity and economy, thanks, largely, to the resilience of its people.

SIGHTS
★ Historic District

Wilmington's historic district, which includes some 200 blocks, is among the largest in North Carolina. You'll find shady tree-lined streets and a gorgeous collection of antebellum and late Victorian homes, mansions, and commercial buildings. Wilmington is home to the state's largest 19th-century historic district, which includes beautiful examples of pre-Civil War Italianate architecture as well as influences from the French and English Caribbean. Until 1910, Wilmington was the state's most populous city; the earlier boom and subsequent decline are reflected in the architecture, as the city lacks the fine examples of early-20th-century buildings found in cities like Asheville and Charlotte.

BELLAMY MANSION

The **Bellamy Mansion** (503 Market St., 910/251-3700, www.bellamymansion.org, tours hourly 10am-4pm daily, $14 adults, $12 seniors, military, and students, $7 ages 6-18, free under age 6) is a superb example of Wilmington's late-antebellum mansions. This porticoed, four-story, 22-room home shows both Greek Revival and Italianate architectural influences and stands as one of the most beautiful Southern city homes of its era. Just two months before North Carolina seceded from the Union in 1861, planter and physician John Bellamy and his family

moved into their city home, where they lived until the fall of Fort Fisher and the ensuing fall of Wilmington to the Union. After the war, Bellamy traveled to Washington to ask President Andrew Johnson, a fellow North Carolinian, for a pardon, and used his pardon to recover the home from federal ownership.

In addition to the mansion, another significant building stands on the property: the quarters for enslaved people who lived at the estate. This two-story brick building is a rare surviving example of urban dwellings for enslaved people, and the interior, which remained largely unchanged through the years, is an important part of the historical record of enslavement in the South.

BURGWIN-WRIGHT HOUSE

The **Burgwin-Wright House** (224 Market St., 910/762-0570, www.burgwinwright-house.com, tours 10am-4pm Mon.-Sat., final tour 3pm, $14 adults, $12 seniors, military, and students, $7 ages 6-18, free under age 6) is older than the Bellamy Mansion by nearly a century, but it has an oddly similar history. John Burgwin ("ber-GWIN"), a planter and treasurer of the North Carolina colony, built the home in 1770 atop the city's early jail. Soon after, British forces commandeered the home as their headquarters during the Revolutionary War. In 1781, General Cornwallis took the house as his headquarters. Joshua Grainger Wright purchased the house in 1799, and it was his residence until 1937, when the National Society of the Colonial Dames of America purchased the home because of its historic significance.

Like the Bellamy Mansion, the Burgwin-Wright House is a version of the classic white-columned, magnolia-shaded Southern home of the wealthy merchant-planter class, but it's not overly ostentatious. Seven terraced gardens filled with native plants and those grown in the 18th century surround the house; through the years, restoration efforts have helped preserve many original garden structures, including walls, paths, steps, and gates.

Historic District

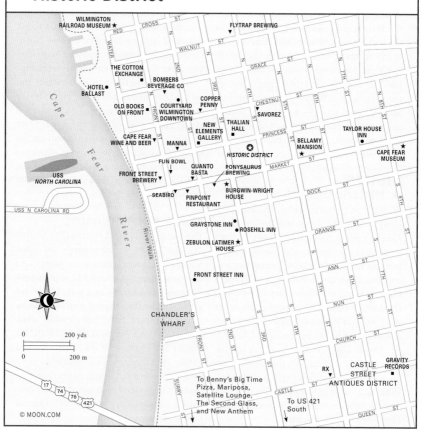

ZEBULON LATIMER HOUSE

Another beautiful home in Wilmington's historic district is the **Zebulon Latimer House** (126 S. 3rd St., 910/762-0492, www.lcfhs.org, tours hourly 10am-3pm Tues.-Sat., $14 adults, $12 seniors, military, and students, $7 ages 6-18, free under age 6). Merchant Zebulon Latimer built this home in 1852, and it housed three generations of Latimers until 1963, when it became a museum and the headquarters of the Lower Cape Fear Historical Society. In its day the Latimer House was a little more fashion-forward, architecturally speaking, than its neighbors; delicate cast-iron cornices and porch railings speak to both the Italianate

and emerging Victorian influences. Also located on the grounds are a two-story brick dwelling for enslaved people and gardens planted with period-authentic plants. Join the **Historic Wilmington Guided Walking Tour** (reservations required, 910/762-0492, 10:30am Sat., $14 adults, $12 military and students, $7 youths), departing from the Latimer House, for a deeper dive into Wilmington history.

WILMINGTON RIVERWALK

Just three blocks from the Latimer House is the **Wilmington Riverwalk,** a mile-long riverside promenade that stretches the length of downtown Wilmington, overlooking the Cape Fear River and the battleship USS *North Carolina*. Most of the boutiques, dining, and nightlife in Wilmington are on the Riverwalk or a block from it. A **Visitors Information Booth** (Market St. and Water St., 9am-4:30pm daily Mar.-May and Sept.-Oct., 9:30am-5pm daily June-Aug., 10am-4pm Fri.-Sun. Nov.-mid-Mar.) or friendly locals can steer you in the right direction.

★ Wrightsville Beach

A few miles east of Wilmington is one of the nicest beaches on the Carolina coast: **Wrightsville Beach.** Wide and easily accessible, it is one of the most visitor- and family-friendly beaches you'll find. Wrightsville benefits from proximity of the Gulf Stream; here the warm ocean current sweeping up the Atlantic seaboard is only 30-40 miles offshore, which means warmer waters that are colored more like the Caribbean. Getting to Wrightsville Beach is easy from downtown Wilmington. Take 3rd Street north out of downtown; it will soon turn into Martin Luther King Parkway. Martin Luther King becomes Eastwood Road when it crosses Market Street and leads straight to Wrightsville Beach, a journey of 11.4 miles.

A number of lodging and rental choices along the beach make it an easy place to stay, and numerous public beach access points (www.towb.org), some of which are disabled-accessible and some with showers or restrooms, line Lumina Avenue. The largest public parking lot, with 99 spaces, disabled access, showers, and restrooms, is at **Beach Access 4** (2398 N. Lumina Ave.). **Beach Access 36** (650 S. Lumina Ave.) has 86 parking spaces, disabled access, showers, and restrooms. On busy days the parking lots can fill up, but trekking from one access point to the next will often yield a spot. To avoid the rush, plan to arrive before 9am.

Poplar Grove Plantation

North of the city, about halfway between Wilmington and Topsail Island, is **Poplar Grove Plantation** (10200 U.S. 17 N., 910/686-9518, www.poplargrove.org, 9:30am-3:30pm Wed.-Sat. Mar.-Nov., closed Easter Sun., Memorial Day, July 4, Labor Day, Thanksgiving Day, $14 adults $12 seniors, military, and students, $7 ages 6-18, free under age 6). This pre-Civil War peanut plantation preserves the homestead of a successful farming family, including the beautiful main house, a restored tenant farmer's cabin, a blacksmith's shop, and a barn. The 67-acre Abbey Nature Preserve maintains an extensive network of hiking trails winding through coastal forests and wetlands adjacent to the house; a **Farmers Market** (8am-1pm Wed. Apr.-Oct.) shows off the bounty of the area's agriculture.

Moore's Creek National Battlefield

In Wilmington and the surrounding area are a number of significant military sites, most dating to the Revolutionary War and the Civil War. About 20 miles northwest of Wilmington, outside the town of Currie, near Burgaw, is the **Moore's Creek National Battlefield** (40 Patriots Hall Dr., Currie, 910/283-5591, www.nps.gov/mocr, grounds 9am-5pm daily, visitors center 9am-5pm Tues.-Sat., closed federal holidays, free). The site commemorates the brief but bloody battle of February 1776 between Loyalist Scottish highlanders, kilted and piping and brandishing broadswords, and Patriot colonists. The Patriots fired on the Scotsmen with cannons and muskets as they crossed a bridge over Moore's Creek. Some 30 Loyalists died in the attack, and the remainder scattered into the surrounding swamps and woods. The battle marked an important moment in the Revolutionary War, as the Scottish Loyalists were unable to join General Cornwallis's army in Southport and mount an attack on Patriots nearby. It also marks an important moment in Scottish military history, as the battle was the last major broadsword charge in Scottish history, led by the last Scottish clan army.

USS *North Carolina*

Don't be alarmed if you notice a battleship across the Cape Fear River from Wilmington; it's the **USS *North Carolina*** (1 Battleship Rd., Eagles Island, 910/399-9100, www.battleshipnc.com, 8am-5pm daily, $14 adults, $10 seniors and active or retired military, $6 ages 6-11, free under age 6), a decommissioned World War II warship that now serves as a museum and memorial to North Carolinians who died in the war. This hulking gray colossus participated in every major naval offensive in the Pacific, earning 15 battle stars, and was falsely reported to have sunk six times.

Tours are self-guided and start with a short film providing an overview of the museum, then proceed onto the one-acre deck of the battleship. Nine levels of the battleship are open to explore, including the 16-inch gun turrets on the deck, the bridge, crew quarters, ship's hospital, kitchens, and the magazine, where munitions were stored. It gets tight belowdecks, and stairways are quite steep, so visitors prone to claustrophobia, and those unable to traverse steep steps may want to stay topside. A walkway and coffer dam now encircles the ship, allowing you to see it from all angles.

The USS *North Carolina* is also one of North Carolina's most famous haunted houses—reputedly home to several ghosts, seen and heard by staff and visitors alike. The SyFy Channel has featured the ship on various ghost-hunting and paranormal shows, and it has been the subject of extensive investigations. Check out **Haunted NC** (www.hauntednc.com) to hear some chilling and unexplained voices recorded by investigators.

Oakdale Cemetery

By the mid-19th century, Wilmington was experiencing growing pains as the bustling shipping and railroad center of North Carolina. The city's old cemeteries were becoming overcrowded with former residents, and **Oakdale Cemetery** (520 N. 15th St., 910/762-5682, www.oakdalecemetery.org, 8am-5pm daily year-round) was founded some distance from downtown to ease the graveyard congestion. Designed in the parklike style of graveyards popular at the time, it was soon filled with superb examples of funerary art—weeping angels, obelisks, willow trees—set off against the natural beauty of the place. Separate sections were reserved for Jewish burials and for victims of the 1862 yellow fever epidemic. Oakdale's website has an interesting guide to Victorian grave art symbolism.

Cape Fear Museum

The **Cape Fear Museum** (814 Market St., 910/798-4370, www.capefearmuseum.com, 9am-5pm Mon.-Sat., 1pm-5pm Sun. Memorial Day-Labor Day, 9am-5pm Tues.-Sat., and 1pm Sun. Labor Day-Memorial Day, $8 adults, $7 seniors, military, and students, $5 ages 6-17) has exhibits showing the history and ecology of Wilmington and the region, including locally important historical perspectives and the fossil skeleton of a giant ground sloth unearthed in town.

Cameron Art Museum

The **Cameron Art Museum** (3201 S. 17th St., 910/395-5999, www.cameronartmuseum.com, 10am-5pm Tues.-Wed. and Fri.-Sun., 10am-9pm Thurs., closed July 4, Thanksgiving, Dec. 24-25, and Jan. 1, $10 adults, $8 seniors, military, and students, free under age 17) is one of the major art museums in North Carolina. This 42,000-square-foot facility includes a permanent collection in a range of styles and media, but with an emphasis on North Carolina artists. Classes and event are held. There's also a delightful café.

Wilmington Railroad Museum

The **Wilmington Railroad Museum** (505 Nutt St., 910/763-2634, www.wrrm.org, 10am-5pm Mon.-Sat., 1pm-5pm Sun. Labor Day-Memorial Day, 10am-4pm Mon.-Sat. Memorial Day-Labor Day, $10 adults, $9 senior and military, $6 ages 2-12, free under

1: Wilmington Riverwalk 2: Bellamy Mansion 3: aircraft on the USS *North Carolina* 4: Wrightsville Beach

age 2) sheds light on a largely forgotten part of Wilmington's history: its role as a railroad town. In 1840, Wilmington became the southern terminus for the world's longest continuous rail line, The Wilmington and Weldon (W&W) Railroad; in 1900 the Atlantic Coast Line Railroad absorbed W&W and kept its headquarters in Wilmington until the 1960s. On display at the museum are a number of railroad artifacts, including timetables, tools, and locomotives.

Gardens and Parks
AIRLIE GARDENS

Airlie Gardens (300 Airlie Rd., 910/798-7700, www.airliegardens.org, 9am-5pm daily Mar.-Dec., 9am-5pm Tues.-Sun. Jan.-Feb., closed July 30, Thanksgiving Day, Dec. 24-25, and Jan. 1, $9 adults, $5 military and New Hanover County residents, $3 ages 4-12), a formal garden park dating to 1901, features more than 50,000 azaleas, several miles of walking trails, and grassy areas perfect for picnics and park concerts, including the Summer Concert Series (1st and 3rd Fri. May-Sept., call for hours). Highlights of Airlie Gardens include the Airlie Oak, a massive live oak believed to be 500 years old, and the Minnie Evans Sculpture Garden and Bottle Chapel. Evans, a visionary African American artist whose mystical work is among the best examples of outsider art, was the gatekeeper here for 25 of her 95 years; examples of her work can also be seen at the Cameron Art Museum. Most of the paths and walkways comply with federal disabled-access rules, but for visitors not mobile enough to walk the gardens, trams are available; the tram schedule is listed on the website.

BLUETHENTHAL WILDFLOWER PRESERVE

On the campus of the University of North Carolina Wilmington, you'll find the **Bluethenthal Wildflower Preserve** (601 S. College Rd., behind the Fisher University Union on Price Dr., 910/962-3000, http://uncw.edu, dawn-dusk daily, free), a small nature preserve with a rich bed of wildflowers and, more importantly, carnivorous plants like the Venus flytrap. It's a lovely walk any time of year, though a little buggy if the wind is still.

LONG LEAF PARK

There are a number of parks in and around Wilmington, but locals and visitors stop by **Long Leaf Park** (314 Pine Grove Dr., 910/798-7620, www.parks.nhcgov.com, 8am-10pm daily) for the playground, the splash pad, tennis courts and baseball fields, the dog park, and the 1.5-mile walking trail. Centrally located, loaded with facilities like picnic areas and the playground, it's a big draw. You're just as likely to find someone lounging in a hammock strung between two longleaf pines as you are to find them playing tennis or watching the action on the kids ball fields. This park underwent a name change in summer 2020, in part as a response to the Black Lives Matter movement and in part as a response for the community's long-held desire to drop the former name (it was named in honor of one of the perpetrators of the 1898 massacre in which white supremacist mobs and their political allies attacked Black business owners, residents, and political figures) in exchange for something everyone could feel proud of. If you're wondering what a long leaf pine looks like, they're everywhere in the park, making it a fitting name.

NEW HANOVER COUNTY ARBORETUM

The **New Hanover County Arboretum** (6206 Oleander Dr., 910/798-7660, www.arboretum.nhcgov.com, 8am-5pm daily, free) is another popular spot for a stroll or a picnic. The five-acre gardens are also home to a Cooperative Extension horticulture laboratory. Most of the gardens use native plants and showcase the floral variety of the area.

Anoles of Carolina

anole, dewlap extended

While you're in the Wilmington area, you'll almost certainly run across a few anoles. These tiny bright-green lizards skitter up and down trees and walls and dash along railings—impossibly fast and improbably green. You may hear locals call them "chameleons" because anoles can change their color from bright green to dirt brown as a way to camouflage themselves against the background and guard against predators. If you watch them long enough, you'll see a fascinating courtship and territorial dominance ritual: A male anole will spread his forelegs wide, do several "push-ups," and then puff out his little crescent-shaped dewlap, the scarlet pouch beneath the chin. When you see one do this, keep still and keep watching; they often repeat the act several times.

SPORTS AND RECREATION
Land Tours

There are a number of land-based tours of Wilmington that dive into the history, food, and brewery scenes. **Wilmington History** (www.wilmingtonhistory.com, tours from $25 pp) offers walking tours of downtown that cover the town's history, Civil War happenings, African-American history, and more; they also offer tours via smartphone app ($6). **Taste Carolina** (919/237-2254, www.tastecarolina.net) offers daytime tasting tours ($78) on Saturday that visit 5-6 restaurants, as well as an evening drinks and tasting tour ($77) which pairs drinks and bites on Friday and Saturday nights; Saturday they offer a farmers

market tour and cooking class ($77). Beer lovers should hop on the **Port City Brew Bus** (www.portcitybrewbus.com, $55-65); their tours visit breweries in different areas of Wilmington and the beach towns and even include a beer and brunch tour. Guides are brewers, bartenders, and members of the **Cape Fear Craft Beer Alliance** (www.capefearcraft.org), so they know their way around a pint.

Masonboro Island

Just a few minutes' boat ride or a 30-minute paddleboard or kayak ride from Wrightsville Beach brings you to Masonboro Island. Masonboro is an 8.5-mile-long undeveloped barrier island that is fantastic for shelling, birding, surfing, and camping. Get here via your own boat, kayak, or paddleboard, or catch a lift with **Wrightsville Beach Scenic Tours** (109 Causeway Dr., Wrightsville Beach, 910/200-4002, www.wrightsville-beachscenictours.com, Masonboro Island Shuttle $35), who runs a shuttle to and from the island (Mon.-Sat. summer) three times daily. The boat leaves Wrightsville Beach at 9am, 10:30am, 12:30pm, and 2pm, and departs Masonboro at 11am, 1pm, 2:30pm, and 4:30pm. If you go over, you'll be there for a while, so pack a cooler with plenty of water, and remember your sunscreen and bug spray. Wrightsville Beach Scenic Tours also offers a number of other tours for adults and for families, including birding tours ($45) in and around Masonboro Island, a Masonboro Island guided beach tour ($45), eco-tour ($35), shelling tours ($45), pirate tours ($35), sunset tours ($40), and more.

In Wilmington you can tour the Cape Fear River with **Wilmington Water Tours** (212 S. Water St., Cape Fear Riverwalk, 910/338-3134, www.wilmingtonwatertours.net, $15-55 adults, $7-15 kids). From the comfort of the 46-foot catamaran *Wilmington* you can learn more about the Cape Fear River, its tributaries, and the history of the surrounding land. Tours take you by the Wilmington waterfront, multiple branches of the Cape Fear River, and the Black River. Bring your binoculars and a zoom lens for your camera because you'll spot ospreys, eagles, and other birds on your trip.

Surfing

East Coast surfers love Wrightsville Beach because the waves are consistent and the surf is fun year-round. If you've never tried hanging 10, join one of the many surf camps in the area. **WB Surf Camp** (222 Causeway Dr., 866/844-7873, www.wbsurfcamp.com, $440-1,590) is one of the largest surfing schools in the area, including one-day, week-long, kids-only, teens-only, women-only, and family camps, even overnight and international surf camps ($2,900-4,500). **Crystal South Surf Camp** (Public Access 39, Wrightsville

Beach, 910/465-9638, www.crystalsouthsurf-camp.com) offers individual and group lessons ($85 90-minute individual lesson, $65 2-hour group lesson).

Tony Silvagni Surf School (107 Charlotte Ave., Carolina Beach, 910/232-1592, www.surfschoolnc.com, private lessons $65 one-hour lesson, group lessons $55 pp per hour, surf camps $330) receives rave reviews. He's well respected in the local surf community, and his private and group lessons and camps in Carolina Beach are geared toward helping new surfers catch their first wave and advanced surfers refine their techniques.

Kayaking and Stand-Up Paddleboarding

With miles of winding marsh creeks around Masonboro Island and lining the shores of the Intracoastal Waterway, there's no shortage of areas to explore by kayak or stand-up paddleboard. Several outfitters lead tours, provide lessons, and rent out all the gear you'll need to get on the water. **Hook, Line and Paddle** (435 Eastwood Rd., 910/792-6945, www.hook-lineandpaddle.com, fishing kayaks $60 half-day, $200 per week, single kayaks $50 half-day, $180 per week, double kayaks $70 half-day, $210 per week, tours from $65, fishing guide $250 for 5 hours) leads group tours around Wrightsville Beach and Masonboro Island and has a variety of kayaks for rent, including fishing kayaks, sit-in and sit-on kayaks, and double kayaks.

Mahanaim Adventures (910/547-8252, www.mahanaimadventures.com, from $55 half-day, $65 full day, overnight trips from $150) offers kayak trips on the rivers and in the swamps and creeks inland from the area's beaches. **Town Creek, Three Sisters Swamp,** and **Black River** expeditions are fun and take you into parts of the coastal landscape you'd otherwise never see.

For a different type of paddling experience, **Wrightsville SUP** (96 W. Salisbury St.,

1: kayaking marsh creeks 2: stand-up paddleboarders going out for a morning session

910/378-9283, www.wrightsvillesup.com, lessons from $65) rents and provides tours on paddleboards ($35 for 2 hours, $75 per day), kayaks (tours $65, rental from $20 per hour), and outrigger canoes ($50), and provides lessons, as does **Hook, Line and Paddle** (rentals $50 half-day, $180 per week). It looks difficult at first, but once you get the hang of it, you'll gain confidence quickly.

You can also get a stand-up paddleboard or kayak from **Wrightsville Beach Kayak Company** (910/599-0076, www.wrightsvillebeachkayak.com, kayak or paddleboard rentals $40 for 2 hours, $80 per day, $180 per week, tandem and fishing kayaks $50 for 2 hours, $90 per day, $225 per week); they deliver to beach houses or meet you at one of the area kayak launches and rend beach supplies (chairs $10 per day, $30 per week, umbrella $15 per day, $45 per week, boogie board $10 per day, $25 per week, beach cruisers $25 per day, $75 per week).

Diving

The warm, clear water along North Carolina's coast beckons divers from the world over, and the abundance of shipwrecks, ledges, and natural formations off the coast of Wrightsville Beach make it an ideal location for diving. **Aquatic Safaris** (7041 Wrightsville Ave., Suite A, 910/392-4386, www.aquaticsafaris.com, 10am-6pm Mon.-Fri., 10am-5pm Sat., noon-5pm Sun., discover scuba diving program $50, beginner open water classes $395, rental gear $10-66, charters $55-170) has been getting divers in the water since 1988, visiting sites from 3 to 59 miles offshore in water as shallow as 25 feet or as deep as 130 feet. They rent out gear, give classes that will have beginners in open water in as few as three days, and provide charter services to two dozen offshore sites.

Golf

One of the best things about the Wilmington region is the weather, perfect for both the beach and the golf course. In the winter the weather is mild enough to play anytime; in the summer the courses are immaculate, and it doesn't get all that hot on the greens. Hit the links at **Beau Rivage** (649 Rivage Promenade, 800/628-7080, www.beaurivagegolf.com, 18 holes, par 72, greens fees $35-69), just south of Wilmington, halfway to Kure Beach; it's a lovely and reasonably priced course with challenging holes. Risk-taking players will enjoy taking shots over water hazards on several holes, including one par 3 that will put your ball in the drink if you don't land it just right.

The Donald Ross-designed **Wilmington Municipal Golf Course** (311 Donald Ross Dr., 910/791-0558, 18 holes, par 71, greens fees $24-40) features forgiving fairways and on more than one hole raises the classic question "Can I carry that bunker?" North of Wilmington, **Castle Bay** (107 Links Court, 910/821-3603, www.castlebaycc.com, 18 holes, par 72, greens fees $27-58 Mon.-Thurs., $31-62 Fri.-Sun., includes cart) offers a different round of golf. As a Scottish links-style course, it's level, open, and full of deep bunkers, water, and waste areas. The wind can be a factor here, but it's a beautiful course where you can play a round unlike any other in the area.

Spectator Sports

Most spectator sports in Wilmington revolve around cheering on your friend who's running one of the many marathons and road races in town, watching your kids play softball, baseball, soccer, or another youth sport, or cheering on the **University of North Carolina Wilmington Seahawks** (www.uncwsports.com). UNCW fields 18 varsity sports, including baseball, softball, basketball, diving, and soccer. Always popular here in town, after the men's basketball team have made a few NCAA tournament appearances in the last few years, it seems everyone has become a fan. The local baseball team, the **Wilmington Sharks** (910/343-5621, www.wilmingtonsharks.com, reserved seats $10-12) play in the Coastal Plain League. Home games are played at **Legion Sports Complex** (2149 Carolina Beach Rd.).

ENTERTAINMENT AND EVENTS

Performing Arts

Thalian Hall (310 Chestnut St., 910/632-2285, www.thalianhall.org), the only surviving theater designed by prominent architect John Montague Trimble, has been in near-continuous operation since it opened in 1858. Once serving as the city hall, a library, and an opera house, at the time of its construction it could seat one-tenth of the population of Wilmington, North Carolina's largest city. In its heyday, Thalian Hall was an important stop for theater troupes, productions, and artists touring the country, and today it serves as a major arts venue in the region, hosting a variety of musical acts, ballet, children's theater, and art-house and limited-release films. The resident theatre company, the **Thalian Association** (910/251-1788, www.thalian.org), can trace its roots back to 1788 and is North Carolina's official community theater company.

A number of other theater groups call Thalian Hall home: the **Opera House Theatre Company** (910/762-4234, www.operahousetheatrecompany.org). Opera House has produced annual big-name musicals and dramas as well as works by important North Carolinians and other Southern playwrights at Thalian Hall. **Cape Fear Shakespeare on the Green** (910/399-2878, www.capefearshakespeare.com) puts on free plays by the Bard at Thalian Hall and at Greenfield Lake Amphitheater.

Wilmington being an artsy town with a flair for stage and screen performances, it's no surprise to learn that a lot of theater is produced "off Thalian," as it were. **Big Dawg Productions** (910/367-5237, www.bigdawgproductions.org) puts on several plays each year at their 50-seat Cape Fear Playhouse (613 Castle St.). Plays range from classical to contemporary works. They also host the **New Play Festival** each year, a celebration of first-time productions authored by playwrights under age 18. The festival is approaching its 20th anniversary and has seen many works

that premiered here go on to wider audiences and acclaim.

The **Wilson Center** (703 N. 3rd St., 910/362-7999, www.wilsoncentertickets.com), a Cape Fear Community College performing arts venue, sits at the north end of downtown Wilmington and hosts dozens of concerts, plays and stage productions throughout the year. Past performers include Brian Wilson, Lily Tomlin, Chris Isaak, Frankie Valli, Monty Python's *Spamalot*, and *Jersey Boys*. Another place to catch a concert is **Greenfield Lake Amphitheater** (1941 Amphitheater Dr., www.greenfieldlakeamphitheater.com), with a bevy of concerts spring-fall. Shows are improv-rock heavy, and past performers include Bob Weir and RatDog, Tedeschi Trucks Band, Les Claypool, G. Love & Special Sauce, Thievery Corporation, and more. Seating around 800, it's an intimate venue with great sound and awesome sight lines.

The biggest venue in town is a fantastic one. **Live Oak Bank Pavilion** (10 Cowan St., www.livenation.com) opened with a bang—three nights by Widespread Panic—and kept it rolling with shows from Trey Anastasio Band, Santana, Counting Crows, Trevor Noah, Glass Animals, The Avett Brothers, and Miranda Lambert, among others. With a huge lawn, loads of food and drink vendors, and an easy walk from anywhere downtown, this 7,200-seat venue is drawing big acts to Wilmington, making this an even more appealing place to visit for a few days.

Festivals

Wilmington plays host to a number of small festivals throughout the year, but the crown jewel is the **Azalea Festival** (910/794-4650, www.ncazaleafestival.org), held at venues around the city each April and hopefully coinciding with the blooming of the namesake flowering shrubs. Tours of azalea-laden historic and contemporary homes and gardens draw many visitors, but the street fair, which takes over much of Water Street and a good portion of Front Street, draws many more. With more than 200 arts and crafts vendors,

countless food vendors, a dedicated children's area, and four stages of entertainment from national and local acts, the street fair is quite a party. But garden tours and the street fair are just a small part of what the Azalea Festival has to offer: a parade, a circus, dance competitions, gospel concerts, boxing matches, and fireworks round out Azalea Festival events. Like any self-respecting Southern town, it crowns royalty—in this case, the North Carolina Azalea Festival Queen, a Princess, the Queen's Court, a phalanx of cadets from The Citadel, and 100 Azalea Belles. The Azalea Festival draws more than 300,000 visitors annually, so if you decide to visit the area on a weekend trip in early April, be prepared to find Wilmington far more bustling than normal.

Each October, **Riverfest** (www.wilmingtonriverfest.com) takes over part of downtown for a street fair that includes art shows; art, crafts, and food vendors; and car shows. It's smaller than the Azalea Festival, but many downtown venues coordinate concerts and events with Riverfest, making downtown more vibrant for the weekend.

What would a film town be without a film festival? The **Cucalorus Film Festival** (910/343-5995, www.cucalorus.org) celebrates independent films and filmmakers each November. About 150 films from national and international indie filmmakers are shown, along with panels featuring filmmakers, writers, and actors, at Thalian Hall and other venues around town. In a short time Cucalorus has garnered the attention of major film-industry publications.

Burgaw, a tiny town 30 minutes north of Wilmington, is home to the **North Carolina Blueberry Festival** (www.ncblueberryfestival.com) each June. Live music, food vendors, and loads of products featuring blueberries— soap, barbecue sauce, ice cream, muffins— make up this festival.

The **Cape Fear Craft Beer Alliance** (www.capefearcraft.org) puts on a number of events each year, but the best is **Cape Fear Craft and Cuisine** (www.capefearcraftandcuisine.com), a one-evening event in late March-early April pairing local breweries and restaurants that's become one of the best food events in town.

Another great food event takes place in March: the **Beer, Bourbon & Barbecue Festival** (www.wilmington.beerandbourbon.com, $42, VIP $75). More than 60 beers from across the state and nation, 40-some bourbons and spirits to taste (including Wilmington favorite, End of Days Distillery), and barbecue representing a range of styles and flavors. If you're around and attending, chances are you'll spot me chatting up the pit masters or discussing the merits of whatever beer, bourbon, or barbecue my friends and I happen to be tasting.

Nightlife

Craft beer fans will want to pull up a barstool at **Cape Fear Wine and Beer** (139 N. Front St., 910/763-3377, www.capefearwineandbeer.com, 1pm-2am daily), a spot that's more punk than trendy, but one that welcomes beer lovers of any ilk. The bartenders are beer experts and can guide even the choosiest of drinkers to a bottle or draft they'll love. You'll find rare microbrews, meads, and barley wines from around the world, but you'll also find a strong emphasis on the best North Carolina beers.

Just down the street, **Front Street Brewery** (9 N. Front St., 910/251-1935, www.frontstreetbrewery.com, 11:30am-10pm Tues.-Sat., noon-8pm Sun.) serves lunch and dinner ($9-16). As good as the pulled-chicken nachos are, the best part about Front Street Brewery is the IPAs, pilsners, and seasonal beers brewed on-site; you can tour the brewery and get a sample to wet your whistle 3pm-5pm daily. And if that's not enough, take a look at their selection of bourbon—it's tremendous.

When I'm in town, you'll find me at **Flying Machine Brewing Company** (3130 Randall Pkwy., 910/769-8173, www.flyingmachine.

1: Wilmington's Azalea Festival 2: Ricky Evans Art Gallery 3: Seabird restaurant 4: TAB performing at Live Oak Bank Pavilion

Craft Brews in Cape Fear

Just a few years ago there was only one brewery in Wilmington, but times have changed and there are nearly two-dozen in town. Wilmington breweries have racked up accolades, awards, and stellar write-ups, and the city's now on the map as one of North Carolina's great beer destinations. Every bartender in town has their favorite brewery, and everyone at the bar will have their favorite beer, so ask for a recommendation. But let us do a little of the work for you. Here's a list of some of our favorite breweries in town (and just for good measure, a *kombucha* brewery):

- **Flying Machine Brewing Company** (3130 Randall Pkwy., www.flyingmachine.beer) has a huge taproom and brew house where they have live music and plenty of events. Their Patersbier—a light, hoppy Belgian Pale Ale—is not to be missed.

- **Flytrap Brewing** (319 Walnut St., 910/769-2881, www.flytrapbrewing.com) pours Belgian- and American-style beer from their taproom and brewery a short walk from downtown. Their ongoing saison series is noteworthy.

- **New Anthem Beer Project** (116 Dock St., 910/399-4683, www.newanthembeer.com) makes some of the tastiest IPAs in Wilmington. Don't miss Throwing Shade or Kill the Head-lights, two of their hazy IPAs that remain some of the most popular brews in town.

- **Broomtail Craft Brewery** (6404 Amsterdam Way, 910/264-1369, www.broomtailcraft-brewery.com), an equestrian-themed brewery, has Elysium, a French-style *bière de garde* that's malty and high gravity, and their **Barcade** (7211 Market St., 844/768-7275) features their beer, a full bar, and arcade games.

- **Bill's Front Porch Pub & Brewery** (4238 Market St., 910/762-6333, www.billsfrontporch.com) serves an excellent breakfast stout—laced with coffee, a bit of toasted oats, and maple syrup—and the kitchen makes some of the best fried chicken in town.

beer, 4pm-10pm Mon.-Thurs., noon-11pm Fri., 11am-11pm Sat., 11am-9pm Sun.). With more than two dozen beers on tap and a brew house that stays busy cranking out new recipes, they keep beer lovers busy. They make my favorite IPA—Ink Jet, a Double IPA that's rich in tropical notes—and Chuck, their American Corn Lager, is an exceptional (and crushable) brew. But more often than not I find myself with at Du Globe (an amber ale that's some-how an under-the-radar beer), one of their sours, or, if it's hot, one of their sours turned slushy. There are food trucks here most every night, and the River to Sea Trail (a mixed-use biking and walking path) goes right by. They have a second spot out at Wrightsville Beach, **Flying Machine at Wrightsville Beach Taproom + Kitchen** (530 Causeway Dr., 910/239-9474, www.flyingmachinewb.com,

11am-10pm Wed.-Thurs., 11am-11pm Fri.-Sat., 11am-9pm Sun., $13-25) with a full bar, a selection of their beers, and a kitchen dishing up creative coastal cuisine like crispy shrimp and smoked cheddar grits, fried oysters, and fish-and-chips.

At **Flytrap Brewing** (319 Walnut St., 910/769-2881, www.flytrapbrewing.com, 3pm-10pm Mon.-Thurs., 3pm-11pm Fri., noon-11pm Sat., 1pm-8pm Sun.) they have a small operation but make some delicious American- and Belgian-style ales. Wilmington's food trucks make this a regular stop, so check the calendar to see if there will be a bite to eat when you get there.

New on the Wilmington scene are two breweries that opened outposts here. Asheville's **Hi-Wire Brewing** (1020 Princess St., 910/933-5500, www.hiwirebrewing.com,

- **Wilmington Brewing Company** (824 S. Kerr Ave., 910/392-3315, www.wilmingtonbrewingcompany.com) brews one of the most popular IPAs in town: Tropical Lightning. You'll bring a crowler or two home with you.

- **Hi-Wire Brewing** (1020 Princess St., 910/933-5500, www.hiwirebrewing.com) brings their Hi-Pitch and Lo-Pitch IPAs, Pink Lemonade sour, and other brew to the Port City from Asheville.

- **Ponysaurus Brewing** (214 Market St., www.ponysaurusbrewing.com) brought their biergarten and pizza concept down from Durham and are delivering with great 'za and tasty brews (The Golden Rule Saison is aces).

- **Salty Turtle Beer Company** (103 Triton Lane, Surf City, 910/803-2019, www.saltyturtlebeer.com) keeps the brews flowing and the food trucks coming to Topsail Island and Surf City.

Flying Machine Brewing Company

- **Waterman's Brewing Company** (1610 Pavilion Place, 910/839-3103, www.watermansbrewing.com) brews Brilliant Sunshine, a great citrus-forward IPA complete with tropical notes and a big alcohol bill.

- **Panacea Brewing Company** (102 Old Eastwood Rd., Suite A5, 910/769-5591, www.panaceabrewingcompany.com) served *kombucha*—fermented, but low alcohol, tea leaves with added herbal and floral flavors; the Pineapple Ginger Turmeric is excellent.

3pm-10pm Mon.-Thurs., noon-11pm Fri.-Sat., noon-9pm Sun.) has a taproom pouring their beer (Pink Lemonade, a session sour ale, is excellent, as is the Lo-Pitch Hazy IPA); food trucks frequent this spot and there have been rumors around town that a pizza place is opening next door. Close to the heart of downtown, Durham's **Ponysaurus Brewing** (214 Market St., www.ponysaurusbrewing.com, 3pm-10pm Mon.-Thurs., 3pm-11pm Fri., noon-11pm Sat., noon-10pm Sun.) showed up and opened a *biergarten* and **pizzeria** (4pm-9pm Mon. and Wed.-Fri., noon-9pm Sat.-Sun., $8.50-15); their Rye Pale Ale and Golden Rule Saison are favorites.

In the South Front neighborhood are a collection of restaurants (Benny's Big Time Pizzeria and the excellent tapas joint, Mariposa) and bars. For a full bar, a good lineup of beer, and the chance to hear some live music or get into some other kind of happening, make **Satellite Lounge** (120 Greenfield St., 910/399-2796, 4pm-2am Mon.-Fri., 2pm-2am Sat.-Sun.) your destination. Right next door is **The Second Glass** (1540 S. 2nd St., Suite 110, 910/399-7486, www.secondglasswinebar.com, 4pm-10pm Wed.-Sat., 10am-3pm Sun., $7-45), a wine bar and restaurant where they pour from more than 30 wines by the glass and have triple that by the bottle, and where you can grab a bite ranging from an exceptional steak to sharable wine-time snacks. **New Anthem Beer Project** (110 Greenfield St., 910/399-3100, www.newanthembeer.com, 2pm-9pm Tues.-Thurs., noon-9pm Fri.-Sat., noon-8pm Sun.) has a huge space here, just around the corner from Satellite and Second Glass, and their IPAs are the draw. Neon God and The Vapors are two IPAs that hop heads should try, but they have other brews too, like Hillbilly Prophet (a stout aged in Willet bourbon barrels), Suddenly Beautiful (a sour IPA), plus barley wines, *festbier,* milk stouts, and more.

To back up the breweries, there are several great bottle shops in and around town. The first is **HEY!BEER** (4405 Wrightsville Ave., 910/547-6707, www.heybeernc.com, noon-9pm Mon., 10am-9pm Tues.-Thurs., 10am-10pm Fri.-Sat., 10am-8pm Sun.), where they keep an awesome selection of local beers and a sizable curated selection of the best beers from across the state. There's a dozen taps with a rotating selection of local and statewide suds, and whether it's Charles or someone else who helps you (tell Charles that the guidebook guy says hi), they'll be able to guide you to a tasty brew to enjoy here or elsewhere. And on North 4th Street, not far from Live Oak Pavilion, is **Palate Bottle Shop & Reserve** (1007 N. 4th St., 910/399-1081, www.palatenc.com, 1pm-9pm Mon.-Tues., 1pm-10pm Wed.-Thurs., 1pm-11pm Fri.-Sat., noon-9pm Sun.), a perfect spot for pre- or post-gaming your concert. They have a dozen taps of well-curated beer and walls lined with coolers and shelves filled with some hard-to-find beer, including one cooler dedicated to North Carolina beer. Their wine list is equally impressive, with a small but excellent selection. On top of that, Palate is a fun spot to hang out, whether at the bar, outside, or on their covered patio, and **The Kitchen at Palate** (5pm-8pm Wed.-Sat., noon-4pm Sun., $4-14), a food truck that's found a permanent home; they always have a vegetarian option on the menu alongside fried chicken, pulled pork sandwiches, tacos, and other small bites.

It's not all cocktails. Over at **End of Days Distillery** (1815 Castle St., 910/399-1133, www.eoddistillery.com, 11am-9pm Wed.-Sat., noon-6pm Sun.), they produce vodka, gin, bourbon, and rum, and in their tasting room you can sample cocktails, hang out and grab a bite from a food truck, grab a table inside or out and hang with friends, and listen to live

music. It's a lively spot at the north end of the Cargo District and definitely worth the visit.

Dead Crow Comedy Room (511 N. 3rd St., 910/399-1750, www.deadcrowcomedy.com, doors open 7pm Tues.-Thurs., for early and late shows 7pm and 10pm Fri.-Sat.) is the only full-time comedy club in the region, and they draw some big national acts—think Todd Glass, Brian Posehn, Monroe Martin—and some crazy-funny regional comedians like Cliff Cash and Matt White. There's also improv night (Wed.) and open-mike night (Thurs.). They have a full bar, and the area's best food trucks frequent the spot.

SHOPPING
Shopping Centers

The group of buildings known as **The Cotton Exchange** (Front St. and Grace St., 910/343-9896, www.shopcottonexchange.com, 10am-5:30pm Mon.-Sat., noon-4pm Sun.) has housed a variety of businesses in 150 years of continuous operation: the largest flour and hominy mill in the South, a printing company, a Chinese laundry, a "mariners saloon" (where they served more refreshment than just beer), and, of course, a cotton exchange. Today, dozens of boutiques and restaurants call these historic buildings home. **Heart of Carolina** (910/343-0500) carries all sorts of products made by locals, celebrating North Carolina; **Down to Earth** (910/251-0041) carries essential oils and will make custom blends in-house for you; and **Olde Wilmington Toy and Candy Company** (910/399-3594) carries candy, toys, and gifts.

Near Wrightsville Beach, the boutique shops and restaurants of **Lumina Station** (1900 Eastwood Rd., 910/256-0900, www.luminastation.com, 10am-6pm Mon.-Sat.) can keep shoppers busy for an afternoon. Some of Wilmington's nicest boutiques call Lumina Station home, including **Ziabird** (Suite 9, 910/352-6338, www.ziabird.com), which carries beautiful jewelry and accessories from local designers; **figgy co.** (Suite 107, 910/239-9144, www.figgyco.com), specializing natural, ethically made, and good-for-you beauty and wellness goods; and **Airlie Moon** (Suite 114, 910/256-0655, www.airliemoon.com), a purveyor of chic coastal home goods, including art by area artists.

Antiques and Consignment Stores

Just out of downtown on Market Street, **The Ivy Cottage** (3020, 3030, and 3100 Market St., 910/815-0907, www.threecottages.com, 10am-5:30pm Mon.-Sat., noon-5pm Sun.) occupies a trio of buildings and an overflow warehouse, all filled with antiques and consignment furniture. In Cottage 2, you'll find antique jewelry as well as an extensive collection of crystal stemware and decanters. At Cottage 3, you'll find more beachy, shabby-chic furniture and home goods, while Cottage 1 carries more armoires, dressers, and knickknacks.

Take a look inside **Flea Body's Antique Mall** (3405-1 Market St., 910/399-4010, www.fleabodyshop.com, 10am-5pm Mon.-Sat., noon-5pm Sun.), where 40 collectors and vendors have everything from furniture and upcycled goods—and a selection of paint and hardware for DIY projects—to vintage and retro-era items. Downtown on Front Street, **Antiques of Old Wilmington** (25 S. Front St., 910/763-6011, 10am-5pm Mon.-Sat., noon-4pm Sun.) has a large array of antique lighting, bookcases, and thousands of small collectibles. And if you want a selection of upcycled furniture, cool antiques, and salvaged goods, go to **Legacy Architectural Salvage** (1831 Dawson St., Unit B, 910/338-6443, www.historicwilmington.org, 10am-2pm Wed. and Fri.-Sat., 9am-5pm Thurs.), a spot operated by the Historic Wilmington Foundation.

There are a few vintage shops around, but make your first stop **Divine Vintage Boutique** (22 N. Front St., 910/399-6776, www.divinevintageboutique.com, 11am-5pm Tues.-Thurs., 11am-7pm Fri.-Sat., noon-5pm Sun.). Divine Vintage carries luxury vintage and consignment goods, so expect to see brands like Gucci, Louis Vuitton, and Prada on the racks and shelves. In the Cargo District there's a pair of cool vintage shops among the other interesting places to browse. **The Vintage Cellar** (1605 Queen St., Unit 102, 11am-6pm Tues.-Sat., 11am-4pm Sun.) always has a cool selection of concert and graphic-print T-shirts, jeans, and jackets, and their selection has a sense of humor (a Grave Digger monster truck shirt and a vivid teal Charlotte Hornets warmup jacket are just the starters here).

Last Stop (707 S. 16th St., 11am-8pm daily) sells streetwear, sneakers, and vintage clothes, and if you're a sneakerhead, this is the place to stop in town. Near Vintage Cellar and Last Stop there's one more spot I have to mention if only because my in-laws' dogs love treats from there. **Bones Pet Boutique** (1605 Queen St., Unit 113, 919/369-0331, 11am-6pm Wed., noon-6pm Thurs.-Sat., noon-3pm Sun.) has healthy pet treats and a selection of homemade toys the dogs I know personally love to gnaw on.

Books and Games

Wilmington has an active and vibrant literary culture. The University of North Carolina Wilmington is home to a creative writing program of national renown, with a growing number of authors (including this one) graduating and producing novels, memoirs, screenplays, and more. The town has several good bookstores that carry their works and works by local authors as well as the expected selections. **Pomegranate Books** (4418 Park Ave., 910/452-1107, www.pomegranatebooks.wordpress.com, 9am-4pm Tues.-Sat.) has a close relationship with local authors and the faculty, students, and alumni from UNCW's Creative Writing BFA and MFA Programs (I earned my MFA there a while back), and because of those relationships, they have tons of signed copies, host readings and events, and have books from authors like National Book Award Winner Jason Mott, Nina de Gramont, David Gessner, Wiley Cash, and more. **Old Books on Front Street** (249 N. Front St., 910/762-6657, www.oldbooksonfrontst.com, 11am-6pm Mon.-Tues. and

Thurs.-Sat., noon-5pm Sun.) is a used book-store with nearly two miles of books on their floor-to-ceiling shelves. Knowledgeable staff and extensive selection make this a must-stop for book lovers.

Ghost Hill Press (1605 Queen St., Container 105, www.ghosthillpress.com, 11am-6pm Wed.-Sat., 11am-4pm Sun.) was inspired by the founder's time in Scotland where she was impressed by the independent bookshops she found everywhere she went. The vibe here reflects that passion, and the selection of fiction runs from the general to historical to Gothic and horror, and there's poetry, plays, short stories, and nonfiction as well. You'll find books from local writ-ers like Wiley Cash, National Book Award Winner Jason Mott (who earned his BFA and MFA from UNC Wilmington), Taylor Brown, Ashleigh Bryant Phillips (another UNCW alumna), Nina de Gramont, yours truly, and others (and a lot of books are signed).

Cape Fear Games (4107 Oleander Dr., Suite D, 910/798-6006, www.capefeargames. com, 10am-10pm Mon.-Sat., 10am-9pm Sun.) carries a large selection of board games, card games, and tabletop role-playing games. They have a number of games to try out, and they host Magic: The Gathering and Pokémon tournaments as well as adults-only brews-and-board game nights pairing craft beer with tabletop games.

Galleries and Art Studios

The ArtWorks (200 Willard St., 910/352-1822, www.theartworks.co, 11am-5pm Thurs.-Sat., noon-5pm Sun.) is a 7,000-square-foot "art village" including more than 50 working artists' studios and space for public art classes. Artists include jewelers, oil and acrylic paint-ers, potters, glass artists, sculptors, and illus-trators; individual artists have their work for sale. Many of the artists open their studios for the monthly Fourth Friday Gallery Nights (6pm-9pm 4th Fri. of each month).

At **Art in Bloom** (210 Princess St., 910/763-8341 or 484/885-3037, www.aibgallery.com, 10am-4pm Mon.-Thurs., 10am-5pm Fri.-Sat.

and by appointment) you'll find a gallery in a repurposed 19th-century horse stable. The walls are filled with paintings, photography, mixed media, charcoal, and other pieces, and they have a collection of ceramics, sculpture, glasswork, jewelry, and more in this inviting spot.

New Elements Art Gallery (271 N. Front St., 910/343-8997, www.newelementsgallery. com, noon-5pm Wed.-Sat. or by appointment) has been showcasing works by local and re-gional artists since 1985. Featuring contem-porary art in a wide range of styles and media, New Elements remains an influential gallery today, and openings are well attended. With art that includes the avant-garde, classical plein air oil paintings, and wire or ceramic sculptures, they always have something you'll want to take home.

Between Wilmington and Wrightsville is **Blue Moon Gift Shops** (203 Racine Dr., 910/799-5793, www.bluemoongiftshops.com, 10am-6pm Mon.-Fri., 10am-5pm Sat., noon-5pm Sun.), a huge gallery with works from more than 100 artists and artisans, ranging in style from folk art to fine metalwork.

Music

Even with the advent of digital music, Wilmington's love of vinyl kept a handful of shops in operation. One of the best is **Gravity Records** (612 Castle St., 910/343-1000, 9am-6pm Mon.-Sat., 10am-5pm Sun.), a spot where record fans head to pick up new, vintage, and reissued LPs, and to browse the selection of new and used CDs. **Record Bar** (5751-11 Oleander Dr., 910/859-0072, www.record-barilm.com, 10am-5pm Mon.-Thurs., 10am-6pm Fri.-Sat., noon-5pm Sun.) carries a wide selection of vinyl that has local DJs happy. Deep cuts, weird corners of music, vintage and used LPs, CDs, and tapes (yes, tapes) make this an interesting place to browse.

FOOD

Dining out in Wilmington means a lot of things. For some visitors, it's a meal in some-place familiar like a nationally recognized chain (there are plenty of those in town); for others it's a quick bite that'll let them get back to the beach; and others want a real taste of the place, exploring local restaurants one meal at a time. No matter what you want—white tablecloth, waterside dining at the beach or downtown, international cuisine, Southern food—you can find it here, and you just might need to make a reservation first.

South American

There are plenty of taquerias, *tiendas,* and taco trucks in Wilmington, but two in particular have become my favorites. **Los Portales Taqueria** (1207 S. Kerr Ave., 910/799-5255, www.taquerialosportales.com, 10am-9pm Sun.-Thurs., 10am-10pm Fri.-Sat., $2.50-17) is one of those spots where speaking a little Spanish might help you out, but if you're not multilingual, don't worry, those *sopes* (delicious), huaraches (delicious and big), tacos (order three, and don't forget the fried fish tacos) and whatever else you order are going to be great. Just up the street, **La Tapatia** (820 S. College Rd., Suite 1, 910/397-7707, www.latapatiawilmington.com, 10:30am-9:30pm Sun.-Thurs., 10:30am-10pm Fri.-Sat., $2.50-14) serves up a great burrito as well as a burrito bowl (perfect for lunch), some awesome fish tacos, and the usual assortment of tacos, *sopes,* and the like.

A few years ago I went to Peru and had some of the most amazing food, so when I got back home I immediately went to **Aromas of Peru** (417 S. College Rd., Suite 23, 910/839-3030, 11:30am-7:30pm Wed.-Thurs., 11:30am-8pm Fri., noon-8pm Sat., noon-7pm Sun., $8-23) to see how it stacked up. One bite of *lomo saltado* and I was right back in Lima having it for the first time. The ceviche is spot on (I mean, the Peruvians invented it, so it stands to reason a Peruvian restaurant would make a great version) and the Miraflores burger is great, but my go-to order is the rotisserie chicken.

Indian

Nawab Fine Indian Cuisine (6828 Market St., 940/769-7418, www.nawabfineindian.com,

11am-2:30pm and 5pm-9:15pm Wed.-Mon., $13-21) serves up bold flavors in a broad menu that includes just about anything you'd like from the subcontinent. Our vegetarian friends love the huge selection here (*bhindi masala*—with okra—is a great option, as is the *malai kofta nawab*—a paneer and potato dumpling), but they've got plenty of chicken, fish, goat, and lamb on offer too. Word of advice: don't brag to your friends about how spicy you like your food and then order the spiciest thing on the menu; it's a scorcher.

Italian

Benny's Big Time Pizzeria (206 Greenfield St., 910/550-2525, www.vivianhoward.com, 5pm-9pm Sun.-Thurs., 5pm-10pm Fri.-Sat., $9-17), from chef Vivian Howard and her husband, Ben Knight, is their homage to the checked-tablecloth Italian restaurants that Ben grew up with. A departure from the exceptional nouveau Southern the couple dishes up at Chef & the Farmer in Kinston (about 90 minutes north), Benny's is no less exceptional. House-made pasta, hand-tossed pizza, and hot honey (a tantalizing blend of honey and Calabrian peppers), plus a slate of creative pies (the Talk'in Shiitake is a mushroom and sausage pie to die for, and The Little Greenie, a pie with brussels sprouts, guindilla peppers, and nutritional yeast) grace the plates. Unless you want to wait for a while (which is fine; there are a couple of bars and breweries within a two-minute walk), make a reservation.

I was pretty excited when one of my favorite chefs from Winston-Salem decided to bring his Italian concept to Wilmington. **Quanto Basta Italian Eatery & Wine Bar** (107 N. 2nd St., 910/395-6120, www.qbwilmington.com, 4pm-9pm Mon.-Thurs., 4pm-10pm Fri.-Sat., $12-24), Quanto Basta for short, serves high-caliber Italian food inspired by chef-owner Tim Grandinetti's own food heritage (Grandinetti spends most of his time in Winston-Salem, leaving the Wilmington kitchen under the command of a talented executive chef). Italian classics—spaghetti with Sunday sauce, Nonna's Baked Ziti, chicken and eggplant parmesan—are served alongside pizzas and some great starters (the calamari and stuffed peppers are excellent). When you're here, go for whatever looks good to you, but don't overlook the seafood bianco pizza, a pie loaded with shrimp, clams, and alfredo sauce that'll have you wondering why you don't order a shrimp pizza more often.

Seafood

I don't exaggerate when I say that one of the top five restaurants in North Carolina sits in the heart of downtown Wilmington. ★ **Seabird** (1 S. Front St., 910/769-5996, www.seabirdnc.com, 9am-2pm and 5pm-10pm Mon. and Thurs.-Sat., 9am-2pm and 5pm-9pm Sun., $13-30), under the helm of Chef Dean Neff (remember that name; he'll have a James Beard Award soon), makes meals that are delightful from the moment you read the description on the menu to the last forkful. I was astounded by the swordfish schnitzel, two delicious things I'd not thought to combine, and I dream about eating the smoke catfish & oyster pie (think loose interpretation of a pot pie, and make it exquisite). You cannot go wrong with the oysters here; in fact, I insist you buy a dozen (and tell your server to tell the chef I said to); and if you're feeding a crowd, or just want to impress someone, go for the Seafood Tower ($85), a gorgeous tower of smoked, pickled, deviled, and preserved fish, raw oysters, and more. Make reservations well in advance.

The seafood from ★ **South Beach Grill** (100 Lumina Ave. S., 910/256-4646, www.southbeachgrillwb.com, 11am-10pm Tues.-Sat., 11am-4pm Sun., $13-31) may just be the best in Wilmington. It's fresh, perfectly prepared, and the menu has enough variety to keep you coming back every meal for a week. Whether you're in the mood for blackened fish tacos or fried oyster tacos, shrimp and grits or a pulled pork sandwich, the fresh catch or a sweet potato-crusted flounder, you'll go home raving about it.

Wilmington native Keith Rhodes, a James Beard Award semifinalist and a *Top Chef*

contender, owns one of the top restaurants in town, **Catch** (6623 Market St., 910/799-3847, www.catchwilmington.com, 5:30pm-9pm Tues.-Sat., $28). At Catch, Rhodes serves his "Viet-South" cuisine, a fusion of Vietnamese flavors with Southern ingredients and techniques that has won fans that include celebrities like Gwyneth Paltrow and renowned chefs.

Near Wrightsville Beach, the **Fish House Grill** (1410 Airlie Rd., 910/256-3693, www.thefishhousegrill.com, 11:30am-9pm Tues.-Sat., $6-20) and **Dockside** (1308 Airlie Rd., 910/256-2752, www.thedockside.com, 11:30am-9pm daily, $7-24), two restaurants only steps apart on the Intracoastal Waterway, deliver good food and great views. At the Fish House, the food is a little more casual, with a menu that focuses on burgers and sandwiches; Dockside focuses more on seafood, and their elevated deck gives you a bird's-eye view of passing boats while you dine.

At **three10** (1022 N. 4th St., 910/399-5428, www.three10wilmington.com, 5pm-9pm Mon.-Sat., $12-27) order the country-fried grouper with Carolina Gold dirty rice, sweet potato-sunchoke cream, and crispy leek, and you'll have a great idea of what this place is about: fresh bites that allow the ingredients to shine. Fresh fish (including a seafood boudin), raw and broiled oysters, and some great buttermilk cornbread are the stars on this small menu, but the kitchen puts a lot of care into everything they create.

Barbecue and Comfort Food

One of Wilmington's best restaurants from opening day to its current iteration, **PinPoint Restaurant** (114 Market St., 910/769-2972, www.pinpointrestaurant.com, 5:30pm-9:30pm Sun.-Thurs., 5:30pm-10:30pm Fri.-Sat., brunch 10:30am-2pm Sun., dinner $16-38, brunch $7-15) celebrates Southern United States cuisine in a restrained, refined, surprising way that few other restaurants can pull off. Start with a round of oysters on the half shell or the sweet potato hummus before moving on to the mains. The pan-seared flounder has earned a permanent place in my heart, as has the steak—this kitchen nails it every time—and the seasonally shifting vegetarian dish (sometimes a curry, sometimes a platter).

A new arrival on Wilmington's culinary scene made a splashy entrance. ★ **Dram Yard** (121 S. 2nd St., 910/782-2400, www.dramyard.com, 5pm-9pm Tues.-Sun., $14-45) initially opened at an inopportune time: in the midst of the pandemic. But after a brief hiatus they returned under the direction of chef Joe Wolfson, and he's quickly become the talk of the town. The menu is all small-plate sharable style, but the larger dishes—like the whole black bass with tamarind sauce or the Italian-inspired duck breast—are more traditional entrée size. The *uni* carbonara, which uses luxurious and creamy *uni* and the rich flavor of bottarga (cured tuna or mullet roe) for a fresh take on the Italian classic, is a phenomenal dish. And the charred brussels sprouts with garlic fondue and *nam jim jaew* (a pleasantly spiced Thai sauce) are transformative.

For gussied-up Southern food, head to **Rx** (421 Castle St., 910/399-3080, www.rxwilmington.com, 5pm-9pm Tues.-Sat., 10am-2pm Sun., $10-33). Their cast-iron skillet-fried chicken is hard to beat, and their innovative takes on classic Southern dishes (buffalo-style pig ears? Indeed!) will make you look at the region's cuisine in a new light.

One of the best in town (expect a wait here too) is **Cast Iron Kitchen** (8024 Market St., 910/821-8461, www.castiron-kitchen.com, 8am-2pm Wed.-Sun., $6-15). This is stick-to-your-ribs comfort food done right. Go-to dishes are biscuits and gravy that make you want to high five the next table, a burger that makes you want to stop making them yourself because you'll never make one this good, and a chicken biscuit with a runny egg and peppery cheese that landed them a spot on TV's *Diners, Drive-Ins and Dives*.

Creative Fusion

I'm neither vegetarian nor vegan, but I can't get enough of the vegan diner ★ **Sealevel**

City Gourmet (1015 S. Kerr Ave., 910/833-7196, www.sealevelcitygourmet.com, 11am-9pm Tues.-Sat., $3-18). The lentil patty melt is a favorite, but my go-to order varies between the tempeh kimchi reuben and the shrimp-burger (easy, it's made with a mung bean-based curlicue of "shrimp"). Seriously, it absolutely nails one of my favorite sandwiches in North Carolina in vegan form. People go wild for their hot dogs. The homemade cookies are silly good (go ahead and add one or two to your order, you won't regret it). Most of all you'll come away loving this place from the music (it varies wildly and is always surprising) to the folks who work here to what's on the plate.

★ **manna** (123 Princess St., 910/763-5252, www.mannaavenue.com, 5:30pm-close Tues.-Sat., $28-55) came onto Wilmington's dining scene and made a mark: This is where you come when you want to be wowed by what's on the plate, the thought behind it, and the techniques that made it possible. From the bar service (best cocktails in town, period) to the wine list (oenophiles rejoice) to the menu, it's perfection. The kitchen approaches food with a sense of humor, serving a massive rib-eye for two as the Fred Flynn-Stone alongside their Bobby Filet and Hook, Line & Sinker, a roasted fish with Carolina Gold rice. Start with Knead to Know Basis, the bread service, and a cocktail before you settle into a few oysters, an entrée, and dessert (don't you dare skip dessert at a place like this). Reservations are advised.

To say **The Fork n Cork** (122 Market St., 910/228-5247, www.theforkncork.com, 11am-10pm Sun.-Thurs., 11am-11pm Fri.-Sat., $9-16) serves burgers, sandwiches, and bar food is a disservice. It serves some of the best burgers you'll eat and spun-up takes on dishes you expect (like wings) in a bar. Two of my favorites aren't even burgers. The Texas poutine (a pile of fries topped with smoked brisket, cheese, and barbecue sauce), and duck wings (think chicken wings, but from a duck) have never let me down, but for burgers, The Hot Mess—it's got everything on it—is the way to go.

Chef-owner Sam Cahoon made a name for himself at another restaurant in town, but he's making his mark on Wilmington with **Savorez** (402 Chestnut St., 910/833-8894, www.savorez.com, 11:30am-10pm Mon.-Fri., noon-10pm Sat., 10am-2pm Sun., lunch and dinner $9-20, brunch $5-10), a restaurant that blends his love for Latin flavors and local ingredients. Everything here is fresh—it has to be when you regularly feature ceviche on the menu—and packed with flavor. Never too spicy but never dull, the seasoning brings out the best in every ingredient, making a forkful into something special.

Mess Hall (2136 Wrightsville Ave., 910/604-4927, www.messhallilm.com, 11am-9pm Mon.-Sat., $6-12) used to be the best burger place in Wilmington, then they moved and added a dog park and a bar, and now they're the best burger place in Wilmington *and* you can bring the dog, have a beer, and have plenty of room to spread out. Their burgers are serious business. Potato roll, double smashburger, cheese, maybe secret sauce, maybe onion straws and mess sauce. Or maybe you get the McWhat?, a patty with chicken tenders and all the toppings. At their **dog park** (day pass $5, purchase pass and upload vaccination records at www.messhallilm.com), you'll find a well maintained area where the dogs can frolic and do their thing while you do some damage to a pile of tots; a big, juicy burger; and a pint of local beer.

At **The Greeks** (5120 S. College Rd., Suite 107, 910/313-3000, www.thegreeksnc.weebly.com, 11am-8pm Mon.-Sat., noon-6pm Sun., entrées around $9) the menu includes classic Greek dishes and street food. One of their best dishes is The Authentic, a pork gyro made just like the owner used to have growing up in Greece: loaded down with tomato, onion, french fries, and mustard. But if you love falafel, theirs is the best in town, hands down.

The South Front neighborhood has become a destination unto itself, and you could easily spend an evening as you have two exceptional dinner options here: Benny's Big Time Pizzeria and **Mariposa** (1502 S. 3rd St., 910/769-0763, www.mariposatapas.com, 11am-9pm Mon.-Thurs., 11am-11pm Fri.-Sat., 10:30am-9pm Sun., $7-43). Mariposa goes the tapas route, and their menu is full of dishes that'll satisfy two or a party of a half dozen. The Albondigas (beef and chorizo meatballs), Tortilla Espanola (a potato-onion omelet), and olive assortment are all great, but give their cheeseburger a try (it's topped with manchego and 'nduja) and don't overlook the simple and perfect Pan con Tomate (toasted bread with tomato, garlic, and olive oil), the Conservas (tuna belly, sardines, razor clams, and more), or Carrilleras de Cerdo (pork cheeks, fennel, garlic, peppers). Make your reservation before you leave; that way you can get a table on the night you want.

One of Wilmington's most beloved food trucks decided to turn brick-and-mortar, and now **CheeseSmith** (624 S. 17th St., 910/231-0808, www.cheesesmithco.com, 11am-8pm Tues.-Sat., 11am-7pm Sun.) is one of the key components to the Cargo District Neighborhood (which also includes a cool barber shop, a coffee shop, neighborhood market, a plant shop, a bookstore, and more). When I was a kid, this was the restaurant of my dreams: one devoted to the grilled cheese. The OG is the classic; The New G adds brie and tomato jam. Things get interesting from there. The KimCheese adds, you guessed it, kimchi, but you can also get pimento cheese, buffalo chicken, pulled pork, fresh mozzarella, and so much more on your sandwich. And that's before you get into the fries (the Smith Fries, topped with beer cheese sauce, smoked pork belly, and pickled red onions, are a dream).

At **The Half Sandwich & Beverage** (510 1/2 Red Cross St., https://thehalfbev.com, 11am-9pm Wed.-Mon., $8-12) was opened by a trio of brewers and food and beverage pros, and their experience shows. A simple sandwich like the caprese (basil, balsamic, fresh tomatoes, and even fresher mozzarella) delivers more flavor than you expect, and whether you're all about a pimento cheese sandwich, a meaty or veggie-filled Italian sandwich, or something like a chickpea salad, you'll find a lunch to love here. In keeping with their brewing backgrounds, they have a great selection of craft beer and small-producer wines on hand, and they're working as a nomad brewery, collaborating with breweries up and down the East Coast to create beers that are perfect pairs for their menu.

Asian

Where Catch takes Asian cuisine and blends it with Southern food culture, a number of Asian restaurants in Wilmington stay true to their roots. ★ **Indochine** (7 Wayne Dr., at Market St., 910/251-9229, www.indochinewilmington.com, 11am-2pm and 5pm-10pm Tues.-Fri., noon-3pm and 5pm-10pm Sat., 5pm-10pm Sun.-Mon., $11-20) serves an expansive menu of Thai and Vietnamese dishes as well as a number of vegetarian options. Entrées are huge, so sharing is encouraged, but even then, be prepared for leftovers.

Bento Box (1121-L Military Cutoff Rd., 910/509-0774, www.bentoboxsushi.com, 11:30am-9pm Mon.-Wed., 11:30am-10pm Thurs.-Fri., 5pm-10pm Sat., $5-18) is hands down the best sushi in Wilmington. Chef Lee goes to great lengths to bring in the highest-quality fish he can find, and it pays off. Sit inside, where dark mica-flecked granite tops the bar and the atmosphere is a little cooler, or go to a more chill spot outside on the patio, weather permitting.

When a pair of local chefs send you a message and say, "Do yourself a favor and go to Pho Vanhly Noodle House now," you listen. **Pho Vanhly Noodle House** (208 Porter's Neck Rd., Suite 120, 910/821-0127, www.phovanhly.com, 11am-3pm Tues.-Sun. and 5pm-9pm Tues.-Sat., $9-22) lives up to their hype, and possibly exceeds it. Order a *bánh mì* if you want something handheld, but go for the *moo palow* (pork belly, tofu, and boiled egg in a killer broth), the *khao piek* (a rice noodle soup that's a Lao comfort food and delicious to the last drop), or the *bánh cuốn* (like a spring roll) if you want to experience Lao cuisine.

Downtown, Wilmington's only dedicated ramen shop, **Fun Bowl** (24 N. Front St., 910/769-3794, www.funbowlramen.com, 11am-9pm Tues.-Sun., $10-16), stays busy with folks slurping the delicious broth and gobbling down noodles by the bucketful. In addition to having *chashu,* miso, *tonkatsu,* and vegetarian broth to choose from, you can add anything from kimchi to mushrooms to a boiled egg to seaweed to your bowl, and you can get an extra order of noodles (do it) or broth (do it if it's cold out) if you're in the mood.

ACCOMMODATIONS
Bed-and-Breakfasts

Wilmington's Historic District is large and filled with historic bed-and-breakfasts. Check with the **Wilmington NC River District & Island Beaches** (www.wilmingtonandbeaches.com), the visitors bureau for the area, for a comprehensive listing of lodging, shopping, and dining.

★ **Front Street Inn** (215 S. Front St., 800/336-8184, www.frontstreetinn.com, $149-299) is a tiny boutique B&B only a block from the Riverwalk and a short stroll to a number of notable restaurants and charming shops. It occupies an old Salvation Army building and offers bright airy guest rooms in a great location. The **Rosehill Inn Bed and Breakfast** (114 S. 3rd St., 910/815-0250, www.rosehill.com, $149-338) occupies a gorgeous 1848 home only three blocks from the river. The flowery high-B&B-style decor suits the house.

The **Taylor House Inn** (14 N. 7th St., 910/763-7581, www.taylorhousebb.com, $147-165) is in a newer home that dates to 1905. Despite this relative novelty, it's a pretty but not ostentatious building, unlike some of the homes nearby. The famous **Graystone Inn** (100 S. 3rd St., 888/763-4773, www.graystoneinn.com, $209-645) was built in the same year as the Taylor House Inn but with a very different aesthetic. Solid stone and castle-like, the Graystone has beautiful guest rooms only blocks from good restaurants, shopping, and nightlife.

Hotels

An upscale place to stay is the **Hotel Ballast** (301 N. Water St., 910/763-5900, www.hotelballast.com, from $165), which overlooks the Cape Fear River. Part of the Tapestry Collection by Hilton, Hotel Ballast has 272 rooms that underwent a massive renovation and rebranding in 2017. The Riverwalk is right out the door, putting the restaurants and nightlife of downtown Wilmington only a short walk away, along with the on-site Ruth's Chris Steakhouse, a coffee shop, and **Board & Barrel Coastal Kitchen** (910/343-6130, 6:30am-10pm daily, $9-25), a bar and restaurant serving breakfast, lunch, and dinner.

At Wrightsville Beach, it's hard to beat the **Blockade Runner** (275 Waynick Blvd., 877/684-8009, www.blockade-runner.com, $150-800). From the outside it looks like any other 1960s hotel, but inside it's chic, stylish, and comfortable. Every guest room has a great view, with the Atlantic Ocean and sunrise on one side, the Intracoastal Waterway and sunsets on the other. With several adventure outfitters operating in the hotel, recreation options abound. The hotel restaurant, **EAST Oceanfront Dining** (breakfast 7am-11am Mon.-Sat., 7am-10am Sun., lunch 11am-5pm Mon.-Sat., 2pm-5pm Sun., dinner 5pm-9pm Sun.-Thurs., 5pm-10pm Fri.-Sat., jazz bunch 10:30am-2pm Sun., $10-35), is a hidden gem in Wilmington's dining scene thanks to the vision of chef Jess Cabo and her talented kitchen. What to order? Any of the specials; they're bubbling with creativity and inspired by the seasonal flavors that grab chef Cabo.

On the north end of downtown, **Embassy Suites by Hilton Wilmington Riverfront** (9 Estell Lee Place, 910/765-1131, www.embassysuites3.hilton.com, $165-366) serves the city's convention center, concertgoers, and other visitors. With the **Cloud 9 Rooftop Bar** (4pm-10pm Sun.-Thurs., 4pm-11pm Fri.-Sat.) giving you a great view, and with the Riverwalk and downtown's shops and restaurants nearby, and with Live Oak Bank Pavilion only a short walk away, it's a prime spot. If you're hungry and don't want to go far,

grab a bite to eat at **Steam** (5pm-9pm Sun.-Thurs., 5pm-10pm Fri.-Sat., $10-35), the in-house restaurant.

Brand-new in 2022, **Aloft Wilmington** (501 Nutt St., 910/377-7600, $175-369), connected to the Coastline Convention Center, adjacent to the Wilmington Convention Center, and a short walk to Live Oak Bank Pavilion, is a great hotel in a great location. Their WXYZ Bar offers cocktails, snacks, and lounging. You can grab a bite at aView, their rooftop tapas bar connected to WXYZ Bar, or you can always head downtown; you'll reach your first restaurant about three minutes from the hotel.

The boutique **ARRIVE Wilmington** (101 S. 2nd St., 910/726-3870, www.arrivehotels.com, from $205) is elevating the town's hospitality game with luxurious but accessible and affordable touches that make a stay something to look forward to. Whether it's the styling of the rooms, grounds, or the attached Dram Yard restaurant; the distinct spaces like the former convent on-site; or the effort they put into ensuring each guest falls in love with Wilmington, it's an exceptional place to spend the night when you head to this pocket of North Carolina.

There are plenty of more affordable options available just a couple of miles out of downtown. The **Holiday Inn** (5032 Market St., 910/392-1101, www.wilmingtonhi.com, $97) on Market Street is clean, comfortable, close to downtown, and minutes from the beach. The **SpringHill Suites by Wilmington Mayfaire Town Center** (1014 Ashes Dr., 910/239-9975, www.marriott.com, from $166) is an affordable option that's a short drive to both Wrightsville Beach and downtown Wilmington, and it's across the street from Mayfaire, a large shopping center.

Vacation Rentals

As in any good beach town, there are plenty of vacation rental agencies handling beach house and condo rentals at the beaches near Wilmington. Prices vary by season, size, amenity, and proximity to the waves, but you should be able to find a house that suits your travel style. Bryant Real Estate (855/760-7005, www.bryantre.com) and Intracoastal Vacation Rentals (855/346-2463, www.intracoastalrentals.com) are two of the bigger rental agencies, though the smaller companies—Wrightsville Sands Realty (910/679-4082, www.wrightsvillesands.com) and Sea Scape Properties (910/332-7284, www.seascapevacationhomes.com)—also have some gems to rent. The beauty of the beaches around Wilmington is this: If you can travel in September-October, the water is perfect, the crowds are somewhere else, and the rental rates go down.

NORTH OF WILMINGTON
Topsail Island

If you want to say it like a local, Topsail is pronounced "TOP-sul," so called because legend has it that pirates once hid behind the island and only their topsails were visible to passing ships. There are three towns on Topsail Island—Topsail Beach, North Topsail Beach, and Surf City. All are popular beach destinations and are less commercial than many beach communities but still have enough beach shops and souvenir shacks to keep that beach town charm. A swing bridge spans the

Intracoastal Waterway at Surf City, and it opens on the hour for passing ships (expect traffic backups when it opens). At the north end of the island, a tall bridge between Sneads Ferry and North Topsail Beach eliminates the traffic backups from passing ships and provides an unheralded view of the 26-mile-long island and the marshes around it.

Among Topsail's claims to fame is its importance in the conservation of sea turtles. The Karen Beasley Sea Turtle Rescue and Rehabilitation Center (302 Tortuga Lane, Surf City, 910/329-0222, www.seaturtlehospital.org, visiting hours noon-4pm Mon.-Tues. and Thurs.-Sat., tours $7 adults, $6 active military, $5 under age 13) treats sea turtles that have been injured by sharks or boats, or that have fallen ill or become stranded. Its 24 enormous tubs, which look something like the vats at a brewery, provide safe places for the animals to recover from their injuries and recoup their strength before being released back into the ocean. Hospital staff also patrol the full shoreline of Topsail Island every morning in the summertime, before the crowds arrive, to identify and protect any new clutches of eggs that were laid overnight. Founder Jean Beasley has been featured as a Hero of the Year on the Animal Planet TV channel. Unlike most

beach houses on Topsail Island

wildlife rehabilitation centers, this hospital allows visitors.

If you're staying in a beach house, do yourself a favor and bring dinner in one night. Call up **Topsail Steamer** (302 S. Topsail Dr., Surf City, 910/328-2645, www.topsailsteamer.com, noon-6pm daily, $57-213) and have them put together a steamer pot for you. These things feed two to six and include things like shrimp, clams, crab legs, scallops, sausage, corn, potatoes. There are instructions in each pot, but it's easy: heat and eat and clean up.

Head over to **Shaka Taco** (107 N. Shore Dr., Surf City, 910/616-3118, www.shakataconc.com, 11am-7pm Mon.-Sat., 11am-3pm Sun., $4-9) and get filled up on some great tacos, bowls, wings, and more. Tacos can be corn or flour, and these sizable, foldable, craveable bites are great whether you get yours with shrimp, fried fish, meat, or veggies. The wings are great—get them naked (no sauce) and sauce on the side—and the shaka nachos can help your whole table get their appetizers in gear for a feast.

One of my favorite restaurants in the region closed a few years ago, but the chef has returned with **CBT Burger Food Truck** (www.cbtburger.com, $10-14). The burgers are smashburger-style, and each hot dog purchase sees $1 donated to a local animal charity. You can find this truck at breweries around the area, including Wilmington's Flying Machine Brewery.

Here on Topsail, you can catch the CBT food truck and find a tasty pint of beer at **Salty Turtle Beer Company** (103 Triton Lane, Surf City, 910/803-2019, www.saltyturtlebeer.com, noon-10pm Mon.-Thurs., 11am-11pm Fri.-Sat., 11am-9pm Sun.). This cool little spot always keeps four flagship beers and a pair of flagship hard seltzers on hand, so you can enjoy their American Stout, their Coastline Kölsch, IPA, or Brown Ale whenever you go. Other beers, like their Key Lime gose, a super-dank IPA, and specialty brews the likes of which they're cooking up all the time, are great options too.

VACATION RENTALS

As with any beach town, there are plenty of vacation homes to rent. To find one that meets your needs, whether it's got a pool, is pet-friendly, or is only a few steps to the water, take a look at what's on offer from **Ward Realty** (910/328-3221, www.wardrealty.com) and **Carolina Retreats** (844/567-9779, www.carolinaretreats.com).

Jacksonville

Jacksonville, only 62 miles northeast of Wilmington on U.S. 17, is best known as the home of **Camp Lejeune,** a massive Marine Corps installation that dates to 1941. Lejeune is the home base of the II Marine Expeditionary Force and MARSOC, the Marine Corps division of U.S. Special Operations Command. The base's nearly 250 square miles include extensive beaches where service members receive training in amphibious assault skills.

Camp Johnson, a satellite installation of Camp Lejeune, used to be known as Montford Point and was the home of the famous Montford Point Marines, the first African Americans to serve in the United States Marine Corps. Their history, a crucial chapter in the integration of the U.S. Armed Forces, is paid tribute at the **Montford Point Marine Museum** (Bldg. M-101, East Wing, Camp Gilbert Johnson, 910/554-0808, www.montfordpointmarines.org, 11am-4pm Tues. and Thurs., other times by appointment, free).

Jacksonville is a town still growing into its identity, and as with any such town, especially a military town, you'll find a lot of places catering to the young men and women in the armed forces, making it a perfect stopping place when I'm driving up the coast and need a quick lunch. But there are restaurants beyond the fast-food variety. Take a look at **Marrakesh Mediterranean Cuisine** (409 Western Blvd., Jacksonville, 910/219-0229, www.marrakeshjax.wixsite.com, 10:30am-9pm Mon.-Sat., 10:30am-4:30pm Sun., $5-22), serving a taste of food from across the

Mediterranean, even going with some huge family-style meals (around $44). Lamb chops, shawarma, kebabs, gyros, and those incredible desserts are guaranteed to please a hungry traveler.

Duck's Grille & Bar (1207 Gum Branch Rd., 910/455-9128, www.ducksgrilleandbar.com, 11:30am-11pm Mon.-Thurs., 11:30am-2am Fri.-Sat., 10am-11pm Sun., $18-35) is the best steak place in town, and it's an old-school steak house with Caesar salad, lamb lollipops, seared duck breast, and killer rib-eye. Don't be surprised if you see a few Marines in here celebrating a return home, a promotion, or any old thing; there's a bunch of them that live nearby.

★ Hammocks Beach State Park

At the appealing little fishing town of Swansboro, you'll find the mainland side of **Hammocks Beach State Park** (1572 Hammocks Beach Rd., 910/326-4881, http://ncparks.gov, 8am-6pm daily Sept.-May, 8am-7pm daily June-Aug., park office 8am-5pm daily Sept-May, 8am-6pm daily June-Aug.). Most of the park lies on the other side of a maze of marshes on Bear and Huggins Islands. These wild, totally undeveloped islands are important havens for migratory waterfowl and nesting loggerhead sea turtles. Bear Island is 3.5 miles long and less than 1 mile wide, surrounded by the Atlantic Ocean, Intracoastal Waterway, Bogue and Bear Inlets, and wild salt marshes. A great place to swim, Bear Island has a bathhouse complex with a snack bar, restrooms, and outdoor showers. Huggins Island, by contrast, is significantly smaller and covered in ecologically significant maritime forest and lowland marshes. Two paddle trails, one just over 2.5 miles long and the other 6 miles long, weave through the marshes that surround the islands. **Paddle**

NC (910/612-3297, www.paddlenc.com) leads kayak and stand-up paddleboard tours ($50-60) of the islands. Camping (reservations 877/722-6762, www.northcarolinastateparks.reserveamerica.com, $12) is permitted on Bear Island in reserved and first-come, first-served sites near the beach and inlet, with restrooms and showers available nearby.

A private boat or **passenger ferry** (910/326-4881, http://ncparks.gov, round-trip $6 over age 12, $4 seniors and children) are the only ways to reach the islands. The ferry's schedule varies by the day of the week and the season, but it generally departs from the mainland and the islands every 30-60 minutes mid-morning until late afternoon; ferries don't run every day in the off-season, and there's no ferry service to Bear Island December-March. Check the website for current ferry times.

GETTING THERE AND AROUND

Wilmington is the eastern terminus of I-40, more than 300 miles east of Asheville and 120 miles south and east of Raleigh. The Cape Fear region is also crossed by a major north-south route, U.S. 17, the old Kings Highway of colonial times. Wilmington is roughly equidistant along U.S. 17 between Jacksonville to the north and Myrtle Beach, South Carolina, to the south; both cities are about an hour's drive away.

Wilmington International Airport (ILM, 1740 Airport Blvd., Wilmington, 910/341-4125, www.flyilm.com) serves the region with flights on American Airlines and Delta. It's a small airport, and flights can be limited, but flying into the two nearest airports—RDU in Raleigh, North Carolina, and MYR in Myrtle Beach, South Carolina—will add anywhere from 2 to 2.25 hours to your trip, plus the expense of a rental car.

The Southern Coast

From the beaches of Brunswick and New Hanover County to the swampy subtropical fringes of land behind the dunes, this little corner of the state is special. South of Wrightsville Beach, a series of barrier islands and quiet low-key beaches extends to the South Carolina border. Starting with Pleasure Island, which includes Kure and Carolina Beach, and ending with the Brunswick Islands, including Oak Island, Holden Beach, Sunset Beach, and Ocean Isle, these beaches are family-friendly places where you're more likely to find rental homes than high-rise hotels.

You'll see some distinctive wildlife here, including the ubiquitous green anole, called "chameleons" by many locals. These tiny lizards, normally bright lime green, are able to fade to brown. They're everywhere—skittering up porch columns and along balcony railings, peering around corners, and hiding in the fronds of palmetto trees. The males put on a big show by puffing out their strawberry-colored dewlaps.

This part of the state has the largest population of the anole's distant cousin: alligators. Unlike their tiny cousins, alligators have the potential to be deadly. All along river and creek banks and in bays and swamps, you'll see their scaly hulks basking in the sun. If you're in a kayak or canoe or on a paddleboard, you may mistake them for a log until you see their eyes and nostrils poking out of the water. Be aware of where you, children, and pets step when hiking, and avoid swimming in fresh water in places where alligators are prone to lurk. All that said, alligators are thrilling to see and generally will vacate the area if you come too close.

If you're in the area during the early part of summer, you could see a sea turtle dragging herself into the dunes to lay a clutch of eggs. Huge loggerhead sea turtles, tiny Kemp's ridley sea turtles, greens, and even the occasional leatherback make their nests along the beaches here. Nesting season runs mid-May-August, and they hatch 60-90 days later, depending on the species. Organizations such as the **Bald Head Island Conservancy** (700 Federal Rd., Bald Head Island, 910/457-0089, www.bhic.org) help protect nests and educate area residents and visitors on issues relevant to protecting sea turtles.

In certain highly specialized environments, mainly in and around Carolina bays, which have both moist and nutrient-poor soil, the Venus flytrap and other carnivorous plants thrive. The flytrap and some of its cousins are endangered, but in this region—and nowhere else in the world—you'll have plenty of opportunities to see them growing wild.

KURE BEACH AND CAROLINA BEACH

Kure is a two-syllable name, pronounced "KYUR-ee" like the physicist Marie Curie, not like "curry." This is a small beach community without the neon lights and towel shops of larger beaches. Kure abuts Carolina Beach, where the boardwalk and beach shops are part of the charm. This island is known as Pleasure Island, and it's a mix of full-time residences and vacation homes—some second homes, many rentals. You'll find a few motels scattered throughout, a state park and state historic site (like a lot of coastal towns, there's a Confederate gun emplacement here), as well as an excellent aquarium. Kure and Carolina Beaches are classic beach towns, the likes of which you don't often see today. A short drive from Wilmington—only 30 minutes—and you've stepped back in time.

Carolina Beach State Park

Just to the north of Kure is **Carolina Beach State Park** (1010 State Park Rd., off U.S. 421, Carolina Beach, 910/458-8206, http://ncparks. gov, office and visitors center 8am-5pm daily, park 7am-10pm daily May-Sept., 7am-9pm daily Mar.-Apr. and Oct., 7am-7pm daily Feb. and Nov., 7am-6pm daily Dec.-Jan.). Of all the state parks in the coastal region, this may be the one with the greatest ecological diversity. Within its boundaries are coastal pine and oak forests, pocosins between the dunes, saltwater marshes, a 50-foot sand dune known as Sugarloaf Dune, and lime-sink ponds. Of the ponds, one is a deep cypress swamp, one is a natural garden of water lilies, and one is an ephemeral pond that dries into a swampy field every year, an ideal home for carnivorous plants. You'll see Venus flytraps and their ferocious cousins, but resist the urge to dig them up, pick them, or tempt them with your fingertips. Sort of like stinging insects that die after delivering their payload, the flytraps' traps can wither and fall off once they're sprung.

The park (reservations 877/722-6762, www. northcarolinastateparks.reserveamerica.com, year-round, closed Dec. 24-25) has six cabins ($55) and 83 drive-in and walk-in campsites ($23-33), each with a grill and a picnic table. Two are wheelchair-accessible, and restrooms and hot showers are nearby. **Paddle NC** (910/612-3297, www.paddlenc.com) offers kayak and stand-up paddleboard tours ($55-80) departing from the marina.

Fort Fisher State Park

At the southern end of Kure Beach is **Fort Fisher State Recreation Area** (1000 Loggerhead Rd., off U.S. 421, 910/458-5798, http://ncparks.gov, 8am-9pm daily June-Aug., 8am-8pm daily Apr.-May and Sept., 8am-7pm daily Mar. and Oct., 8am-6pm daily Nov.-Feb.), with six miles of beautiful beach; it's a less crowded and less commercial alternative to the other beaches of the area. In summer a lifeguard is on duty (10am-5:45pm daily late May-early Sept.). The park also includes a 1.1-mile hiking trail that winds through marshes and along the sound, ending at an observation deck where visitors can watch wildlife.

Fort Fisher is also a significant historic site, a Civil War earthwork stronghold designed to withstand massive assault. Modeled in part on the Crimean War's Malakhoff Tower, Fort Fisher's construction was an epic saga as hundreds of Confederate soldiers, enslaved African Americans, and conscripted indigenous Lumbee people were brought here to build what became the Confederacy's largest fort. After the fall of Norfolk in 1862, Wilmington became the most important open port in the South, a vital harbor for blockade-runners and military vessels. Fort Fisher held until nearly the end of the war. On December 24, 1864, U.S. General Benjamin Butler attacked the fort with 1,000 troops but was repulsed; his retreat led to him being relieved of his command. A few weeks later, in January 1865, Fort Fisher was finally taken, but it required a Union force of 9,000 troops and 56 ships in what was the largest amphibious assault by Americans until World War II. Without its defenses at Fort Fisher, Wilmington soon fell, hastening the end of the war, which came just three months later. Due to the final assault by the Union forces and 150 years of wind, tides, and hurricanes, not much of the massive earthworks survive, but the remains of this vital Civil War site are preserved in an oddly peaceful and pretty seaside park that contains a restored gun emplacement and a visitors center with interpretive exhibits.

The **North Carolina Aquarium at Fort Fisher** (900 Loggerhead Rd., 910/772-0500, www.ncaquariums.com, 9am-5pm daily year-round, closed Thanksgiving Day and Dec. 25, $13 adults, $12 military and seniors, $11 ages 3-12) is one of three aquariums operated by the state; this is a beautiful facility that shows all manner of marinelife native to North Carolina waters. The aquarium follows the path of the Cape Fear River from its headwaters to the ocean. Along the way you'll meet Luna, an albino alligator; have the opportunity to touch horseshoe crabs, sea stars, and even bamboo sharks; and see a variety of sharks, fish, eels, and rays in a two-story, 235,000-gallon aquarium. Dive shows and daily feedings complement the exhibits. It's hard to miss the megalodon exhibit, dedicated to the huge prehistoric shark—it was bigger than a school bus—with teeth the size of dinner plates and a jaw eight feet across. Fortunately, all that remains are fossil relics of this two-million-year-old animal, many of which are found at dive sites nearby in less than 100 feet of water. Pose for a picture behind the massive set of jaws as proof of the ultimate fish story.

Food

Seafood is a staple all along Kure and Carolina Beaches, and I happen to absolutely love everything on the menu at ★ **Coast Craft Cocktails & Calabash** (604 N. Lake Park Blvd., 910/707-0422, www.eatatcoast.com, 5pm-close Tues.-Sat., $14-32). Don't be surprised: in a couple of visits you and your crew can eat this dozen-item menu too, making your way through the hush puppies and Old Bay fries, the shrimp and grits, a curried-coconut-broth bowl loaded with fresh fish, and their fried chicken sando (oh, it's a good one). Drinks are great, the kitchen likes to throw a couple of specials in the mix, and it's one of the best restaurants on this side of town, so make a reservation and show up hungry.

Heralded by many locals as the best Thai food around, **Ida Thai** (304 N. Lake Park Blvd., 910/458-8136, www.idathairestaurant.com, 11am-9pm Mon. and Wed.-Thurs., 11am-9:30pm Fri.-Sat., 4pm-9pm Sun., $12-24) has the crowd pleasers you'd expect—pad thai, pineapple fried rice, yellow curry—and daily specials that are just as delicious. Try the seafood *tom yum* or *tom kha khi*, the whole fried fish, or the spicy basil mixed seafood dish.

Southern California-inspired tacos, burritos, and quesadillas are the order of the day at **Nollies Taco Joint** (3 Pelican Lane, Carolina Beach, 910/707-0455, www.nolliestacojoint.com, $4-15). Choose from ground beef, marinated skirt steak, seasoned tofu, and fresh fish or shrimp for your taco, 'dilla, or burrito; they get all of them right and really work to ensure

you can get a good bite here whether you're a vegetarian or an omnivore. Like the name of the place, most of the menu items have skateboard-inspired names, making it a little more fun for those in the know.

Freddie's Restaurant (111 K Ave., Kure Beach, 910/458-5979, www.freddiesrestaurant.com, 5pm-close daily, $12-25) in Kure Beach has a big menu and serves even bigger portions. With seafood, pasta, and an exceptional specialty pork chop menu, it's not hard to find something to eat (if you want a real kick here, go check out the restaurant review on the wall; it was one of the first I wrote for the local newspaper).

After dinner, for breakfast, or for a snack, stop by **Britt's Donuts** (13 Boardwalk, 910/707-0755, www.brittsdonutshop.com, 8:30am-10pm daily Apr.-Oct.), a Carolina Beach institution since 1939. They use a secret recipe for their doughnut batter, and they come out salty, sweet, airy, crispy, and perfect in every way. Pull up a seat at the bar and order half a dozen to enjoy—and if you don't like them, find me and I'll gladly take any leftovers off your hands.

Accommodations

The beaches of the Carolinas used to be lined with boardinghouses, the old-time choice in lodging for generations. Hurricane Hazel razed countless boardinghouses when it pummeled the coast in 1954, ushering in the epoch of the family motel. The **Beacon House** (715 Carolina Beach Ave. N., 877/232-2666 or 910/458-6244, www.beaconhouseinnb-b.com, some pets allowed in cottages, rooms $169-219, cottages $225-299) at Carolina Beach, just north of Kure, is a rare survivor. The early-1950s boardinghouse has the typical upstairs and downstairs porches and dark wood paneling indoors; nearby cottages have a similar aesthetic. You'll be treated to a lodging experience from a long-gone era.

1: sunset over Southport **2:** Southport's Yacht Basin Provision Company **3:** on the dock after a day of fishing **4:** Kure Beach boardwalk and pier

Vacation rentals make the best accommodations here, and through rental agencies like **Carolina Retreats** (844/567-9779, www.carolinaretreats.com), **Carolina Beach Realty** (877/456-4311, www.carolinabeachrealty.net), and **Sea Coast Rentals** (800/334-5806, www.seacoastrentals.com) you'll be able to find a house or condo that has a pool, allows pets, or meets just about any need you've got.

★ SOUTHPORT

Without a doubt, Southport is one of North Carolina's most picturesque coastal towns; it's been named America's Happiest Seaside Town and is constantly in the running for best small town, best small coastal town, and best small seaside town from magazines and blogs across the country. The Cape Fear River, Intracoastal Waterway, and Atlantic Ocean meet here, and the water is almost always crowded with watercraft of all sizes and shapes. Wilmington is 45 minutes north via Highway 133 and U.S. 17, but you can reach this charming town via the Southport-Fort Fisher Ferry if you want to admire the water a little as you travel.

The town's history is rooted in the water, and there are still several multigenerational fishing and shrimping families around. River pilots who know the shoals and tides like no one else operate out of Southport, heading offshore in speedy boats to the container ships and tankers making their way to Wilmington; they help navigate the cumbersome ships safely to the port and back out to sea, just as people from local families have for 200-plus years. Throughout the town, historic buildings, including Fort Johnson, a British fort built in 1745, line the oak-shaded streets. The Old Smithville Burying Ground, a community cemetery dating to before the founding of the town, is a beautiful spot, and many of the headstones are inscribed with epitaphs for sea captains and their widows. Stop in at the **Fort Johnston-Southport Museum and Visitors Center** (203 E. Bay St., 910/457-7927, www.cityofsouthport.com, 10am-4pm Mon.-Sat., free) for more information on the town, although Southport is small enough to explore and discover on your own. While you're at the visitors center, ask about the history of four of the town's street names: Lord, Howe, Dry, and I Am.

Sights

The **North Carolina Maritime Museum at Southport** (204 E. Moore St., 910/457-5150, www.ncmaritimemuseumsouthport.com, 10am-4pm Tues.-Sat., free) tells the story of Southport as a maritime town in some detail. The pirate Blackbeard and his compatriot Stede Bonnet prowled these waters, and Stede Bonnet was captured on the river about a mile from the museum, then sent to Charleston, where he was hanged for his crimes. Other subjects include a 2,000-year-old Indigenous canoe fragment, information on the blockade of the river during the Civil War, and many artifacts brought up from nearby shipwrecks. Parents take note: The Maritime Museum at Southport is the first Certified Autism Center in the whole state, and that means their staff and volunteers have been trained on how to help those on the autism spectrum get the most out of their visit. The first Saturday of the month they hold **Sensory Saturdays** (9am-11am 1st Sat. of each month), where they dim the lights, mute the music, and make other accommodations to make the museum a welcoming place to any and everyone.

Given the beauty of the town and its proximity to Wilmington, it's no surprise that Southport has been the setting of several television shows and films. *Safe Haven,* an adaptation of North Carolina literary son Nicholas Sparks's novel of the same name, takes place here; one reviewer called the movie "an extended infomercial for the lulling charms of Southport," and comedian Paul Scheer said Southport was the "star of *Safe Haven.*" Since the movie's 2012 debut, a steady stream of fans has been touring the town. If you want to see Southport and the area by boat, or if you're on the lookout for dolphins and exceptional sunsets, arrange for a ride with **Southport By Seaside** (910/269-8674, www.southportbyseaside.com, $50 adults, $40 under age 13).

If you'd rather keep it land-based and history- and film-focused, try **Southport Fun Tours** (910/713-3373, www.southportfuntours.com, $12 adults, $5 under age 12).

Golf

In the vicinity of Southport, golfers will find several courses that are both challenging and beautiful. The **Oak Island Golf Club** (928 Caswell Beach Rd., Oak Island, 910/278-5275, www.oakislandgolf.com, 18 holes, par 72, greens fees from $52) is a 6,720-yard George Cobb-designed course that provides seren- ity with occasional ocean views and ocean breezes. In Boiling Spring Lakes, you can walk or ride **The Lakes Country Club** (591 S. Shore Dr., Boiling Spring Lakes, 910/845- 2625, www.thelakescountryclub.com, 18 holes, par 72, greens fees from $24 walking, from $34 with cart), the oldest golf course in Brunswick County.

Kayaking

The Adventure Kayak Company (807 N. Howe St., 910/454-0607, www.theadventu- recompany.net, kayak tours from $49, bike tours from $20, kayak rentals from $45 per day, bike rentals $18 per day) does tours of the Intracoastal Waterway, black-water creeks around Southport, sunset and full moon tours, and even trips to some of the uninhab- ited islands in the river and waterway.

Festivals

Southport has its share of fairs and festivals throughout the year, and one that's had the community—especially the art-lovers here, and there are lots of folks who love art in this town—buzzing is the **Southport Plein Air Festival** (www.upyourarts.org, mid-May), a two-day affair that sees nearly 100 artists painting scenes in and around Southport, then holding a publicly juried show (where you can also purchase pieces you can't live without) in the town park.

The can't-miss festival is the **North Carolina 4th of July Festival** (910/457- 5578, www.nc4thofjuly.com), the official

Independence Day celebration for the state. Some 50,000 people attend the parade, the fes- tival park, the street fair, and the fireworks in the evening. Launched from a barge on the river, the fireworks are a special treat as they reflect on the water. Perhaps the most moving of the events is the naturalization ceremony for new Americans as they declare their loy- alty and enjoy their first 4th of July celebra- tion as citizens.

Shopping

There are a number of cute boutiques, an- tiques stores, and kids' shops in Southport, and the local business alliance, **Downtown Southport Inc.** (www.downtownsouth- port.com) works to keep storefronts full and visitors shopping. A few of my favor- ites are **Ocean Outfitters** (121 E. Moore St., 910/457-0433, www.oceanoutfitters. com, 10am-5:30pm Mon.-Fri., 10am-6pm Sat., 11am-4pm Sun. summer, 10am-5pm Mon.-Sat., 11am-4pm Sun. winter), a sports- wear outfitter that carries clothing and gear perfect for enjoying and exploring the area. **Franklin Square Gallery** (130 E. West St., 910/457-5450, www.franklinsquaregallery. com, 10am-5pm Mon.-Sat., Mar.-late-Dec.) is a community art gallery and classroom space where you can catch a lecture, buy a painting or some pottery in the gallery, or join them for the **First Friday** gallery walks (1st Fri. of the month). The **Ricky Evans Art Gallery** (211 N. Howe St., 910/457-1129, www.rickyevans- gallery.com, 10am-5pm Tues.-Fri., 10am-4pm Sat.) features art by Ricky Evans and select local artists; Ricky's pen and ink drawings and his paintings of coastal scenes, especially North Carolina's lighthouses, are exceptional.

Southport has several antiques shops, and you can start your antiquing shopping spree at **Northrop Antiques Mall** (111 E. Moore St., 910/457-9569, 10am-5pm Mon.-Sat., noon- 5pm Sun.) where more than 30 vendors and collectors have their wares: coastal antiques, weird medical antiques (Civil War bone saw, anyone?), decanters and bottles, jewelry, and ephemera.

Food

For a town this size, Southport has a surprising number of good restaurants. I love to dine on the water at ★ **Yacht Basin Provision Company** (130 Yacht Basin Dr., Southport, 910/457-0654, www.provisioncompany.com, 11am-9pm daily mid-Mar.-late-Oct., $6-18), to enjoy a plate of peel-and-eat shrimp or a grouper sandwich. **Frying Pan** (319 W. Bay St., Southport, 910/363-4382, www.fryingpansouthport.com, 11am-9pm Mon.-Sat., 11am-8pm Sun., $12-30) serves fried seafood and local delicacies from a dining room elevated 18 feet off the ground, offering commanding water views.

Along this waterside strip (where the high tide sometimes covers the road by an inch or two; if it's high tide, don't wear your good shoes), you'll find another local favorite, **Fishy Fishy Café** (106 Yacht Basin Dr., Southport, 910/457-1881, www.fishyfishycafe.com, 11am-8pm Sun.-Thurs., 11am-9pm Fri.-Sat., $12-30), serving steam pots, seafood platters, fish-and-chips, burgers, and more from their beautiful dockside location. And up on Howe Street a few blocks from the river you'll find my in-laws' favorite date-night restaurant, **Ports of Call Bistro** (116 N. Howe St., Southport, 910/457-4544, www.portsofcallbistro.com, 1:30am-2:30pm and 5pm-9pm Tues.-Sat., 10am-2pm Sun., $12-40, brunch $10-22). This spot serves tapas-style sharable dishes as well as full-sized entrées, so order a crab galette, some fried oysters, and seared tuna to start, then decide if you're going surf, turf, or vegetarian; it's hard to go wrong.

Moore Street Market (130 E. Moore St., 910/363-4203, www.moorestreetmarket.net, 8am-3pm Mon. and Wed.-Thurs., 8am-4pm Fri.-Sat., 9am03pm Sun., $1-10), a small coffee shop and deli that makes a good lunch and serves the best cup of coffee in town. Its central location is steps from antiques shops and historic sites in Southport. Dinner is always good at **Ports of Call Bistro and Market** (116 N. Howe St., 910/457-4544, www.portsofcallbistro.com, 11:30am-3pm and 5pm-9pm Tues.-Sat., 10am-2pm Sun., lunch $8-21, dinner $15-31, brunch $11-18), a Mediterranean-inspired restaurant serving both tapas and entrées. Their menu changes seasonally and always features local seafood.

In South Harbor Marina, between Southport and Oak Island, are a trio of eateries that always deliver great food. **Joseph's Italian Bistro** (5003 O'Quinn Blvd., 910/454-4440, www.josephsitalianbistro.com, 5pm-9pm Mon.-Sat., $13-30) serves classic pasta dishes, some of the best veal around, and an excellent array of local and regional seafood; it's perfect for date night or an evening when all the grown-ups have secured a babysitter and need a night out. On Oak Island proper, sit down for a refined meal at the oceanfront restaurant, **Island Way** (1407 E. Beach Dr., Oak Island, 910/278-7770, www.islandwayres.com, 4:30pm-9pm Tues.-Sun., $11-35), where you'll find steaks, an awesome selection of seafood dishes, and a spectacular view to go along with the meal.

At the Oak Island Pier you'll find **KoKo Cabana** (405 Ocean Dr., Oak Island, 910/933-6222, www.islandgrindznc.com, 11am-8pm Tues.-Sun. Feb.-Nov., $10-16), where the ceviche and peel-and-eat shrimp are always delicious and you can't go wrong with an order of fish tacos or some nachos piled high with tofu, chicken, or the fresh catch. Also on the Oak Island Pier you'll find a sister restaurant, **Ruby's Coffeehouse & Eatery** (705 Ocean Dr., Oak Island, 910/933-6133, www.islandgrindznc.com, 7am-3pm Tues.-Sat., 9am-2pm Sun., $2-8), serving coffee and specialty coffee drinks and a small menu of breakfast and lunch bites perfect for your morning walk on the beach or to get you going for a day of fishing from the pier. Yet another sister restaurant, **Kai-Joe's** (4722 E. Oak Island Dr., Oak Island, 910/933-1073, www.islandgrindznc.com, 11am-8pm Tues.-Sun., $3-13), specializes in nachos, tacos, and burritos, and their Long Beach Burrito with shrimp, their North Shore Taco with grilled shrimp and chili sauce, and their overstuffed quesadillas are great.

Accommodations

There's a spot to stay where the views are spectacular: **River Hotel of Southport** (704 E. Moore St., 910/294-6070, www.riverhotelofsouthport.com, $129-259). Across the Cape Fear River you'll see the Old Baldy lighthouse on Bald Head Island and the Oak Island lighthouse on Oak Island, and you're a short pleasant walk from downtown. Built in the early 1950s and located on the river in the heart of downtown, **Riverside Motel** (103 W. Bay St., 910/457-6701, www.riversidemotel.net, from $120) has throwback charm. Another lovely bed-and-breakfast in Southport is **Captain Newton's Inn** (120 W. Moore St., 910/477-2743, www.captainnewtonsinn.com, $235), in the heart of Southport's historic district and walkable to the river, restaurants, and shops.

At Oak Island, west of Southport, **The Beach House at Oak Island** (500 Ocean Dr., Oak Island, 910/278-5644, www.carolinaretreats.com) sits a block away from the Oak Island Pier and across the street from the beach; throw in the outdoor pool and this pet-friendly, 22-room motel makes for a great home-away-from-home. They have motel-style units ($165 summer, $145 off-season), one-bedroom suites ($275 summer, $250 off-season), and two-bedroom suites ($315 summer, $285 off-season), but if you call the office in the off-season, you can often find lower rates; pets are welcome ($25 for two pets) with no weight limits; just don't get cute and bring a horse. The **Ocean Crest Motel** (1417 E. Beach Dr., Oak Island, 910/278-3333, www.oceancrestmotel.com, $120-225), a large condo-style motel, is also right on the beach.

As with most seaside towns, vacation rentals are the norm. On Oak Island and Caswell Beach, the two beach towns near Southport, **Oak Island Accommodations** (888/297-8066, www.rentalsatthebeach.com) and **Coastal Vacation Resorts at Oak Island** (8118 E. Oak Island Dr., 888/703-5469, www.coastalvacationresortsoakisland.com) have houses and condos all along the island, from beachfront castles to cozy cottages, that are pet-friendly, kid-friendly, and more.

BALD HEAD ISLAND

Two miles off the coast of Southport is Bald Head Island. From the mainland you can see the most prominent feature, Old Baldy, the oldest lighthouse in North Carolina, poking above the trees. Accessible only by a 20-minute ferry ride or private boat, the island is limited to golf carts, bicycles, and pedestrians; the only larger vehicles permitted are for emergency services, deliveries, or construction. Combined with the largest intact section of maritime forest in North Carolina, Bald Head Island seems like it's a world away. A true island resort, this is a community that is seasonal to the core. Restaurants and shops can have wildly different hours from month to month and season to season, so use the hours here as a guideline, but check www.baldheadisland.com, where you'll find a monthly bulletin with hours, specials, events (you'll also find events at www.celebratebhi.com), and announcements; you'll find the bulletin under "Guest Resources," "Hours of Operation."

Sights

Old Baldy was commissioned by Thomas Jefferson and built in 1817. You can climb to the top of the 109-foot lighthouse with admission to the **Smith Island Museum** (101 Lighthouse Wynd, 910/457-7481, www.oldbaldy.org, 9am-5pm Mon.-Sat., 11am-5pm Sun. summer, 10am-4pm Tues.-Sat. fall, $8 adults, $5 ages 3-12). The museum, housed in the former lighthouse keeper's cottage, tells the story of Old Baldy and the other lighthouses that have stood on the island. **The Old Baldy Foundation** (910/457-7481, tours 10:30am Tues. and Fri.-Sat., $30 adults, $20 ages 3-12, tickets include lighthouse admission) also conducts historic tours that reveal the island's long and surprising past.

Sports and Recreation

There are 14 miles of beaches to explore on Bald Head Island, several hundred acres of maritime forest with marked trails, miles of creeks that wind through the marsh behind the island, and ample opportunities to explore with one of the island's outfitters. You won't be able to see much of it on foot, so unless you brought a bike over, you'll need to rent a ride; fortunately, it's easy to get a golf cart or a bike.

At **Cary Cart Company** (261 Edward Teach Wynd, 910/457-7333, www.carycartco. com, 8:30am-4pm Mon.-Sat., 10:30am-4pm Sun., 4-passenger cart $72 per day, $350 per week, 6-passenger cart $102 per day, $500 per week) you can rent golf carts by the day or additional carts (they're included in nearly every rental on the island) for the week.

Riverside Adventure Company (10 Marina Wynd, 910/457-4944, www.riversideadventure.com, 8:30am-5pm daily, rentals from $20, tours $25 adults, $12 under age 13) offers bike rentals and a frightening but family-fun-focused ghost walk. Their sister outfitter, **The Sail Shop** (96 Keelson Row, 910/457-6844, www.thesailshop.com, 8:30am-5pm daily) provides surfing rentals ($50 per day) and lessons ($74) and sailing rentals ($75 pp) and lessons (from $150 pp), and offers kayak rentals (from $50 per day) and tours (from $65 guided, from $50 self-guided). If you want to try stand-up paddleboarding on the marsh or ocean, **Coastal Urge** (12-B Maritime Way, 800/383-4443, www.rentals.

coastalurge.com, 9am-5pm daily, SUP rentals $60 per day, tours $30-60, bike rentals $25-45 per day) supplies all the gear and lessons you need to get on the water.

The **Bald Head Island Conservancy** (700 Federal Rd., 910/457-0089, www.bhic. org), a group dedicated to preserving the flora and fauna of the island, leads programs (dates and times vary, call or check the website for a weekly schedule, $10-50) like kayak tours, birding walks, stargazing, kids camps, and, in the summer, turtle walks, giving Conservancy members (you can join while you're here) the chance to see a sea turtle make her nest. The ongoing sea turtle program is one of the crown jewels for the BHI Conservancy, and on tours with their interns and naturalists you might find yourself looking for turtle tracks in the dark (showing where a mama turtle has crawled from the tide to the dunes), watching as they take measurements and notes on a nesting turtle, see nest protection efforts like caging or even excavating nests (when weather or placement or other factors threaten these sensitive eggs), and, in mid-late summer, you might even see a nest "boil" as the hatchlings crawl free from their shells, emerge through the sand, and make their way to the ocean.

Exploring Bald Head Island with one of the

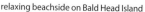

relaxing beachside on Bald Head Island

outfitters is a must-do, but most folks come for the beach. The island has three distinct beaches: West Beach, South Beach, and East Beach. Seeing how the island has east- and west-facing beaches, it's one of a few spots where you can watch the sun both rise and set over the ocean from your beach house. Along West Beach, the Cape Fear River and Intracoastal Waterway meet the Atlantic Ocean, so it's more of a strolling or fishing beach than a swimming one, as currents here can get a little gnarly. Often-secluded South Beach is excellent for surfing, swimming, shelling, sunning, and strolling. East Beach is likewise perfect for swimming, playing in the waves, and soaking up some sun.

GOLF

Without a doubt, **The Bald Head Island Club** (1 Salt Meadow Trail, 910/457-7300, www.bhiclub.net) delivers the most premier golf experience you'll have on the North Carolina coast. The **course** (par 72, 18 holes $195 May-Oct., $145 Mar.-Apr. and Nov., $125 Dec.-Feb., 9 holes $100 May-Oct., $75 Mar.-Apr. and Nov., $65 Dec.-Feb.), designed and built in 1974 by George Cobb, got a refresh in the 2010s from Tim Cate, and it's immaculate. Fairways are wide and can be generous, if you can control your landing zone, but the greens can get tricky and can negate a great drive unless you spent a little extra time on the practice green. Highlights include seeing Old Baldy standing above the trees on holes 1, 5, and 7, and the signature hole 16, a par-3 shot from an elevated green, from which you have a gorgeous vantage of the island and course. You'll face the ocean breeze, adding to the challenge. There are other activities on offer at The Bald Head Island Club, from tennis to croquet to a fitness center and pool; to play golf or use the recreational or dining facilities, you need to be a member, the guest of a member, or your rental unit needs a temporary membership. Often those memberships are rolled into the rental fees, but in case they're not, get a **temporary membership** ($125 per bedroom June-Aug., $95-125 per bedroom Apr.-May and Sept.-Oct., $40-75 per bedroom Nov.-Mar.).

Food

There are only a few places to eat on the island, but fortunately they're good. In the harbor, **Delphina Cantina** (8 Marina Wynd, 910/457-1222, www.delphinabhi.com, 11:30am-9:15pm daily, $6-37) serves some good Latin American food. At Delphina you'll find **Sandpiper Sweets and Ice Cream** (inside Delphina, 7:30am-11am daily, under $10) and **Marina Pizza to Go** ($12-22), which are great options for families. **Will O' the Wisp** (8:30am-10pm Mon.-Sat., 8:30am-6pm Sun., under $10), from the same owners, provides a great outdoor space to enjoy your pizza or a dish from Delphina, to sip a drink, or to play games with your family, because they do have activities like family bingo night, trivia night, and concerts on Friday during summer.

The **Maritime Market** (8 Maritime Way, 910/457-7450, www.maritimemarketbhi.com, 8am-6pm Mon.-Sat., 9am-2pm Sun. Oct.-Mar., 8am-9pm daily Mar.-Oct, $4-22) sits in the center of the island and is the only grocery store there, so you'll be here a lot when you visit Bald Head Island. They've got a pair of eateries—**Maritime Market Café** and **Copper's Wood-Fired Kitchen**—serving breakfast, lunch, dinner, and pizza pies in addition to the small but well-stocked grocery store (the market will deliver groceries to your house if you're hoping to arrive to a well-stocked pantry). Monthly they hold **Howl at the Moon** parties on East Beach. These community-wide gatherings bring locals and vacationers together to celebrate the full moon with a potluck feast; details and a schedule are available on the website.

Jules' Salty Grub and Island Pub (10 Marina Wynd, 910/457-7217, www.julessaltygrubbhi.com, noon-8pm Tues., noon-9pm Wed.-Sun., $15-40) sits right on the harbor, so it's got nothing but fantastic views. The menu is Southern coastal through and through. Smoked fish dip or steamed peel-and-eat shrimp make great starters, then go for something zesty like the Nashville Hot Chicken Plate, a low country classic in the Eb & Flo's Famous Steampot (crab legs, mussels, crawfish, shrimp, sausage, corn, and potatoes in a big pot), some seared scallops, or even a rib-eye. Lunch is a little lighter, with more emphasis on sandwiches and salads. It's a fun spot, and the sometimes scheduled, sometimes impromptu karaoke in the bar is always entertaining.

Accommodations

Most of the houses on Bald Head Island are rental homes, ranging from one-bedroom cottages to massive beachside homes ideal for family reunions. Rentals are available through **Intracoastal Realty** (www.baldheadisland.com/vacation) and **Tiffany's Rentals** (910/457-0544, www.tiffanysbeachproperties. com); rates range $2,000-12,000 per week. There are two inns on the island: **The Marsh Harbour Inn** (21 Keelson Row, 833/644-2441, www.marshharbourinn.com, $275-575) has beautiful harbor and marsh views, free use of golf carts for guests, and membership privileges to the private Bald Head Island Club; this is a great option for visitors not in a large group. **The Inn at Bald Head Island** (2 Keelson Row, 888/367-7091, www.theinnatbaldheadisland.com, from $275) has ten rooms, daily continental breakfast and afternoon wine and snacks, plus temporary membership to the Bald Head Island Club, bikes, and beach gear.

Getting There

As the billboards proclaim, getting to Bald Head Island is half the fun thanks to a 20-minute ferry ride that carries you three miles out to the island. I like to think I have more fun on Bald Head Island than what a ferry ride can deliver, but maybe that's just me because I do love the ferry. The **ferry** (1301 Ferry Rd. SE, Southport, 910/457-5003, www. baldheadislandferry.com, $23 adults, $12 ages 3-12) takes about 20 minutes to travel the Intracoastal Waterway to the marina; you'll want to call and reserve tickets, as the ferry

can get crowded, especially in summer. This passenger-only ferry (no cars are allowed on Bald Head Island except work and emergency vehicles) is the perfect mental reset you need to go from mainland work and life mode to vacation mode, or as some folks on Bald Head call it: turtle time.

OCEAN ISLE AND SUNSET BEACH

Ocean Isle is one of the most southerly beaches in North Carolina, separated from South Carolina only by Sunset Beach, Bird Island, and the town of Calabash. It's midway between Wilmington and Myrtle Beach, South Carolina, about an hour's drive from each. In October, Ocean Isle is the site of the **North Carolina Oyster Festival** (www. ncoysterfestival.com), a huge event that's been happening for nearly 30 years. In addition to an oyster stew cook-off, a surfing competition, and entertainment, this event features the North Carolina Oyster Shucking Competition.

Once, Sunset Beach and Bird Island were separated by a narrow tidal inlet; this has since filled in, creating one contiguous island. At Sunset Beach, stay at **The Sunset Inn** (9 N. Shore Dr., Sunset Beach, 910/575-1000, www. thesunsetinn.net, $143-299), a 14-room inn where every room has a king bed, a wet bar, and a screened porch facing the marsh—and it's only a five-minute walk to the beach.

While you're here, you should pay a visit to the **Kindred Spirits Mailbox** (www.the-kindredspirit.net), a touching but odd attraction—a mailbox set in the dunes where people come from all over the world to leave letters for the cosmos. Sometimes these letters and notes are fond memories of a visit to the shore, other times they're prayers or dreams, wishes, reflections, or sorrows, but almost every one is intriguing. And yes, you can read them. In the mailbox are several notebooks that are distributed, collected, and catalogued by volunteers. Write your own note or simply reflect on the thoughts of others. To get here, park at West 40th Street on Sunset Beach, take the beach access, and walk southwest (away from the pier) about 1.5 miles; you'll see an American flag waving in the dunes, marking the mailbox.

There are several places to dine on Sunset Beach, Ocean Isle, and nearby Holden Beach, and everywhere you go you're going to find some fantastic seafood. Longtime favorite **Causeway Gourmet** (100-7 Causeway Dr., Ocean Isle Beach, 910/575-1084, www.causewaygourmetoib.com, 11am-8:30pm Wed.-Sat., delivery after 5pm, $5-25) has something for everyone. Seriously, the menu is sweeping, but it all makes sense. The mood is casual, the food familiar and homey and delicious, and with a big menu—nearly two dozen sandwiches to choose from, but that's before you get to the entrées like the shrimp and grits or the sautéed local flounder—you'll find a great bite no matter what you're after.

Casual dining is all the thing at the beach, and two waterside restaurants give you a perfect menu to go with a perfect view. First, **Sharky's Waterfront Restaurant** (61 Causeway Dr., Ocean Isle Beach, 910/579-9177, www.sharkysoceanisle.com, 11am-10pm Mon.-Sat.) has a fun menu if you keep it focused, and I like to keep it focused on the local seafood. Start with the grouper bites or tuna tower, then go for the grouper sandwich or tacos (the burger's a good call too), and from there it's fried seafood baskets (shrimp, oyster; you can't go wrong) then the fish of the day special. One other place to dine is **Provision Company** (1343 Cedar Landing Rd. SW, Holden Beach, 910/842-7205, 11am-9pm daily, $6-20) in Holden Beach. Yes, it shares a name with the restaurant in Southport, and yes, the menu is markedly similar—steamed shrimp; crab cakes; quick, greasy, and delicious burgers—but it has different owners and a different vibe. The view of the Intracoastal Waterway is great, and the food—especially the grouper or tuna steak sandwiches—holds its own.

Makai Brewing Company (5850 Ocean Hwy. W., 910/579-2739, www.makaibrewing.com, noon-6pm Mon.-Thurs., noon-7pm Fri.-Sat., 1pm-6pm Sun.) has more than a dozen taps featuring their own beer as well as guest taps featuring other area breweries. They keep at least a pair of IPAs on draft, including their popular Carolina Tropical IPA, and those guest taps feature the best of Wilmington breweries.

SOUTH ALONG U.S. 17

U.S. 17 is an old colonial road; its original name, still used in some places, is the King's Highway. George Washington passed this way on his 1791 Southern tour, staying with the prominent planters in the area and leaving in his wake the proverbial legends about where he lay his head of an evening. Today, the King's Highway, following roughly its original course, is still the main thoroughfare through Brunswick County into South Carolina.

Brunswick Town and Fort Anderson

Near Orton is the **Brunswick Town-Fort Anderson State Historic Site** (8884 St. Philip's Rd. SE, Winnabow, 910/371-6613, www.nchistoricsites.org, 9am-5pm Tues.-Sat., free), the site of what was a bustling little port town in the early and mid-1700s. In its brief life, Brunswick saw quite a bit of action. It was attacked in 1748 by a Spanish ship that, to residents' delight, blew up in the river. One of that ship's cannons was dragged out of the river and is on display. In 1765, the town's refusal to observe royal tax stamps was a successful precursor to the Boston Tea Party eight years later. But by the end of the Revolutionary War, Brunswick Town was gone, burned by the British but also made obsolete by the growth of Wilmington.

Today, nothing remains of the colonial port except the lovely ruins of the 1754 **St. Philip's Anglican Church** and some building foundations uncovered by archaeologists. During the Civil War, Fort Anderson was built on this site; some of its walls also survive. It was a series of sand earthworks that were part of the crucial defenses of the Cape Fear, protecting the blockade-runners who came and went from Wilmington. A visitors center at the historic site tells the story of this significant stretch of riverbank. The grounds, with the town's foundations exposed and interpreted, are an intriguing vestige of a forgotten community.

Perhaps the most interesting artifact on display at the visitors center at Brunswick Town is the Fort Anderson battle flag that Confederate soldiers flew over the fort during their final battle. Once the fort fell, the flag was captured by a regiment from Illinois. They gave it to their commander, who gave it to the Illinois governor, who gave it to Abraham Lincoln in a ceremony at the National Hotel where John Wilkes Booth lived, which was reportedly witnessed by Booth. A number of Civil War and Lincoln scholars believe that this moment was when Booth's plan changed from kidnapping to assassinating the president.

Nature Preserves

The Nature Conservancy's **Green Swamp Preserve** (Hwy. 211, 5.5 miles north of Supply, 910/395-5000, www.nature.org) contains more than 17,000 acres of some of North Carolina's most precious coastal ecosystems, the longleaf pine savanna and evergreen shrub pocosin. Hiking is allowed in the preserve, but the paths are primitive. It's important to stay on the trails and not dive into the wilds because this is an intensely fragile ecosystem. In this preserve are communities of rare carnivorous plants, including the monstrous little pink-mawed Venus flytrap, four kinds of pitcher plant, and sticky-fingered sundew. It's also a habitat for the rare red-cockaded woodpecker, which is partial to diseased old-growth longleaf pines.

The Nature Conservancy maintains another nature preserve nearby, the **Boiling Spring Lakes Preserve** (1 Leeds Rd., Boiling Spring Lakes, 910/395-5000, www.ncbrunswick.org), with a trail that begins at the community center. Brunswick County contains the state's greatest concentration of rare plant species and the most diverse plant communities anywhere on the East Coast north of

Florida. This preserve is owned by the Plant Conservation Program and includes over half the acreage of the town of Boiling Spring Lakes. The ecosystem is made up of Carolina bays, pocosins, and longleaf pine forests.

The University of North Carolina Wilmington maintains a 174-acre nature preserve in Brunswick County, the **Ev-Henwood Nature Preserve** (6150 Rock Creek Rd. NE, near Town Creek, www.uncw.edu, dawn-dusk daily). Ev-Henwood (pronounced like "heaven wood" without the initial *h*) is named after the surnames of the former owner's grandparents: Evans and Henry. The property had been owned by the family since 1799 and was the site of turpentine stills, tar kilns, and a working farm. Now several miles of hiking trails wind through the property past barns and home sites, across fields, beside the beautiful and eerie black-water Town Creek, and through longleaf pine woods. Pick up a trail map at the parking lot and head out for a few hours in the woods. Bring water, bug spray, and your camera; if you're quiet enough, you may see otters playing in Town Creek or deer in the woods at the edge of a field.

Outdoor Adventure

Shallotte River Swamp Park (5550 Watts Rd., Ocean Isle Beach, 910/687-6100, www.shallotteriverswamppark.com, 9am-5pm Thurs.-Sun. off-season, 9am-7pm Wed.-Sun. Apr.) is a high-adventure wonderland. A 90-foot tower is your starting point for a cypress canopy tour ($79) and a three-line zip-line course ($32), each of which takes you through the trees and over sections of swamp; there's a swamp boat tour ($30) and an adventure park ($42 adults, $32 ages 7-13, $22 ages 4-6), which challenges your strength, agility, and nerve in an elevated obstacle course.

Another option for adventure is **Cape Fearless Extreme** (1571 Neils Eddy Rd., Rieglewood, 910/655-2555, www.capefearless.com), an aerial adventure course that sits in the middle of 25 acres of pine forest. Cape Fearless has three challenging courses, one just for kids ages 7-11 ($30) that's a good intro to the higher courses, and two open to ages 10 and up: the Full Aerial Adventure Course (from $55), a 3-4 hour mix of zip lines, swings, nets, and aerial challenges; and the Half Adventure Course (from $45), a 2-hour mix of zip lines and aerial obstacles that'll have your heart pounding. You can also play paintball ($28) here on a wooded course; rental equipment is available.

Golf

Brunswick County is a golf mecca, where more than 30 championship courses appeal to all skill levels and playing styles. The website **Brunswick Islands** (www.ncbrunswick. com) maintains a list of golf courses, among them the notable **Cape Fear National at Brunswick Forest** (1281 Cape Fear National Dr., Brunswick Forest, 910/383-3283, www. brunswickforest.com, greens fees $44-60), named one of the "Top 18 Course Openings in the World 2010" by *Links* magazine when it opened. The course is beautifully maintained and fun to play from any tee. **Crow Creek** (240 Hickman Rd. NW, Calabash, 910/287-3081, www.crowcreekgolf.com, greens fees from $70), is almost on the South Carolina state line. About 45 minutes south of Wilmington, the **Big Cats** (351 Ocean Ridge Pkwy. SW, 800/233-1801, www.bigcatsgolf. com, greens fees $35-100) is at Ocean Ridge Plantation with five stunning courses—Tiger's Eye, Leopard's Chase, Panther's Run, Lion's Paw, and Jaguar's Lair.

Calabash and Vicinity

The tiny fishing village of Calabash, just above the South Carolina state line and only 15 minutes from Ocean Isle, was founded in the early 18th century as Pea Landing, a shipping point for the local peanut crop. Local legend holds that calabash gourds were used as dippers in the town drinking water supply, explaining the town's 1873 renaming. Others hold that the crooked marsh creek that leads to the sea inspired the name. Either way, Calabash is home to some world-famous seafood.

In the early 1940s, Lucy High Coleman began frying fish for the local fisheries workers in a kettle of oil by the dock. Later she used a tent, which in turn became a lean-to and eventually a full-fledged restaurant, The Original, which was, well, the original Calabash-style seafood restaurant. Calabash-style seafood is marked by its light, crispy batter and the freshness of the seafood, and Coleman's descendants carry on the family tradition at several restaurants in town. Locals like to say that like champagne, which can only come from one region in France, or bourbon, only distilled in a single Kentucky county, you can only get Calabash seafood in Calabash; everything else is just an imitation.

For a long while Coleman's descendants ran restaurants just like their mother's, and now there are fewer, but there are still a good number of places where you can get Calabash seafood. Calabash is a style, named for this town, where freshly caught seafood is battered, flash fried, and served piping hot. Shrimp, flounder, oysters, clams, deviled crab, and even scallops appear on the menu, along with a few standards (burgers, a barbecue plate) and seasonal favorites like chowder. Calabash style seafood is often duplicated, but this is the only place in the world you can get the real thing.

Beck's Restaurant (1014 River Rd., 910/579-6776, www.becksrestaurant.com, 11am-9pm daily, $5-19) is one of the original Calabash restaurants run by the descendants of Lucy High Coleman, and they do a great job of capturing a down-home vibe in the restaurant and on the plate. **Calabash Seafood Hut** (1125 River Rd., 910/579-6723, www.calabashseafoodhut.net, 11am-8pm Tues.-Thurs. and Sun., 11am-8:30pm Fri.-Sat., $5-22) has the perfect name and some perfectly fried shrimp to go along with it. ★ **Waterfront Seafood Shack** (9945 Nance St., 910/575-0017, www.calabashfishingfleet.com, 11am-9pm Mon.-Sat., $4-22), is my favorite. Here, you can sit outside and watch the fishing fleet if they're working or just gaze at the river and order local freshly caught seafood to be fried, Calabash style, or grilled or broiled. Don't miss the grilled pound cake for dessert; with a scoop of ice cream it's nearly perfect.

The Oyster Rock (9931 Nance St., 910/579-6875, www.theoysterrock.com, 4pm-10pm Wed.-Mon., $13-64) takes a playful approach to fine dining, Southern cuisine, and local seafood. They serve Calabash fried seafood, iced seafood towers, oysters on the half-shell, smoked oysters, fresh catch, pork chops, and excellent soups. Cheeky names to dishes—The Hummus Dinger (a hummus sampler), Certified Nut Cases (coconut fried shrimp), and Slip Slidin' Away (pork barbecue sliders)—and a fun selection of craft beer make dinner that much better.

Indigo Farms (1542 Hickman Rd. NW, 910/287-6794, www.indigofarmsmarket.com, 8:30am-5pm Mon.-Sat., longer hours in summer), three miles north of the South Carolina line in Calabash, is a superb farm market, selling all manner of produce, preserves, and baked goods. They also have corn mazes and farm activities in the fall.

In the town of Shallotte, the Red Hare Brewing and Distilling's **34° North Experiment Station** (4802 Main St., Shallotte, 678/401-0600, ext. 4, www.redharebrewing.com, 1pm-9pm Tues.-Sat., 1pm-7pm Sun.)—which is a roundabout way of saying taproom—hosts food trucks, comedy shows, yoga classes, and more, but mostly they make and sell beer. Their focus tends toward the IPA, which is fine because the sharp hoppy bite from their brew is a good match for many of the food trucks that come here and for a bite from **Wing & Fish Company** (4764-1 Main St., Shallotte, 910/754-9858, www.wingandfishco.com, 11am-9pm Sun.-Thurs., 11am-11pm Fri.-Sat., $10-24) next door. Buffalo wings, local seafood, burgers, wraps, and all those great greasy bar sides are on order here, and whether you grab some to-go and take them next door, or eat here and catch some of the game, those wings will be just as good.

GETTING THERE AND AROUND

The Brunswick County beaches like Holden, Ocean Isle, and Sunset are easily accessed on U.S. 17. The beaches and islands along the cape, due south of Wilmington, can be reached by taking U.S. 76 south from Wilmington, then turning onto Highway 133 (closest to Wilmington), Highway 87, or Highway 211 (closer to the South Carolina border), or by ferry from Southport.

The **Southport-Fort Fisher Ferry** (1650 Ferry Rd. SE, Southport, 800/368-8969 or 800/293-3779, www.ncdot.gov, 5:30am-7pm daily, $1 pedestrians, $2 bicycles, $3 motorcycles, $7 cars, $14-28 longer vehicles) is popular as a sightseeing jaunt as well as a means to get across the river. Ferries depart from Southport and Fort Fisher year-round. It's a 30-minute crossing; most departures are 45 minutes apart. Pets are permitted if leashed or in a vehicle, and there are restrooms on all ferries.

A small airport near Oak Island, **Cape Fear Regional Jetport** (SUT, 4019 Long Beach Rd., Oak Island, 910/457-6483, www.capefearjetport.com) has no scheduled passenger service but is suitable for small private aircraft.

Inland from Wilmington

Driving inland from the Wilmington area, you first pass through a lush world of wetlands distinguished by the peculiar Carolina bays. Not necessarily bodies of water, as the name would suggest, bays are actually ovoid depressions in the earth of unknown and much debated origin. They are often water-filled but by definition are fed by rainwater rather than creeks or groundwater. They create unique environments and are often surrounded by bay laurel trees (hence the name) and home to a variety of carnivorous plants.

The next zone, bounded by the Waccamaw and Lumber Rivers, largely comprises farmland and small towns. For generations this was prime tobacco country, and that heritage is still very much evident in towns like Whiteville, where old tobacco warehouses line the railroad tracks. Culturally, this area—mostly in Columbus County and extending into Robeson County to the west and Brunswick County to the east—is linked with Horry, Marion, and Dillon Counties in South Carolina, with many of the same family names still found on both sides of the state line.

The area around the Lumber River, especially in Robeson County, is home to the Lumbee people, Native Americans with a long history of steadfast resistance to oppression and a heritage of devotion to faith and family. If you turn on the radio while driving through the area, you'll hear Lumbee gospel programming and get a sense of the cadences of Lumbee English. Its distinguishing characteristics are subtle and different among Lumbee families and towns.

At the edge of the region is Fayetteville. From its early days as the center of Cape Fear Scottish settlement to its current role as one of the most important military communities in the United States, Fayetteville has always been a significant city.

ALONG U.S. 74

A short distance inland from Calabash, the countryside is threaded by the Waccamaw River, a gorgeous dark channel full of cypress knees and dangerous reptiles. The name is pronounced "WAW-cuh-MAW," with more emphasis on the first syllable than on the third. It winds its way down from Lake Waccamaw through a swampy portion of North Carolina and crossing Horry County, South Carolina (unofficial motto: "The H is Silent"), before joining the Pee Dee and Lumber Rivers in South Carolina. The Waccamaw crosses through this little fringe of North Carolina, paralleling the much longer Lumber River, surrounding rural Columbus County and part of Robeson County in an environment of deep subtropical wetlands. From Wilmington it's at least an hour's drive west to the heart of this area.

Sights

Pembroke is the principal town of the Lumbee people, and at the center of life here is the University of North Carolina at Pembroke (UNCP). Founded in 1887 as the Indian Normal School, UNCP's population is now only about one-quarter Native American, but it's still an important site in the history of North Carolina's indigenous people. The **Museum of the Southeast American Indian** (1369 Old Main Rd., UNCP, University Rd., Pembroke, 910/521-6282, www.uncp.edu, 9am-5pm Mon.-Fri., free) is on campus, occupying Old Main, a 1923 building that's a source of pride for Pembroke. The Resource Center has a small but very good collection of artifacts and contemporary Native American art.

Laurinburg's **John Blue House** (13040 X-Way Rd., Laurinburg, 910/277-2456, www.nc-rural-heritage.com, grounds open daily, house and grounds tours 10am-4pm Sat.,

1pm-4pm Sun., by appointment Mon.-Fri., free) is a spectacle of Victorian design, a polygonal house built entirely of heart pine harvested from the surrounding property and done up like a wedding cake with endless decorative devices. John Blue, the builder and original owner, was an inventor of machinery used in the processing of cotton. A pre-Civil War cotton gin stands on the property, used today for educational demonstrations throughout the year. In October this is the site of the **John Blue Cotton Festival** (www.johnbluecottonfestival.com), which showcases not only the ingenuity of the home's famous resident and the process of ginning cotton but also lots of local and regional musicians and other artists.

After friends took a romantic weekend out of town, they came back raving about **Cape Fear Vineyard & Winery** (195 Vineyard Dr., Elizabethtown, 844/846-3386, www.capefearwinery.com), so I had to check it out. They were right: It's excellent. They produce four whites and four reds, and sampling a flight while you listen to a little live music makes for an excellent afternoon. You can stay in **The Cottages at Cape Fear Winery** (from $239); packages include dinner, a tasting flight, and a bottle; roses, champagne, and in-room gifts; golf vouchers; and more. Dinner and tastings are in **The Cork Room Restaurant and Winery** (910/645-4291 or 910/247-6587, 11:30am-9pm Wed.-Sat., 11:30am-4pm Sun., $10-30), which serves cheese platters, salads and sandwiches, and entrées like steak frites, a fried pork chop, and vegetarian pasta. And they have the **Tipsy Toad Gallery Gift Shop** (910/645-4291 or 910/645-4308, 10am-5pm Mon.-Tues., 10am-8pm Wed.-Sat., 10am-4pm Sun.), where art meets whimsy meets things for your home. They also own **Cape Fear Distillery** (277 Bourbon St., Elizabethtown, 910/645-4291, 9am-4pm Mon.-Fri.) on-site, and you can take a tasting tour ($10), sample cocktails using their spirits at The Cork Room, and pick up bottles to take home (or back to your cottage for more intense study).

Sports and Recreation

Several beautiful state parks line the Waccamaw and Lumber Rivers. **Lake Waccamaw State Park** (1866 State Park Dr., Lake Waccamaw, 910/646-4748, http://ncparks.gov, office 8am-5pm daily, park 7am-7pm daily Dec.-Feb., 7am-9pm daily Mar.-Apr. and Oct., 7am-10pm daily May-Sept., 7am-8pm daily Nov.) encompasses the 9,000-acre lake. The lake is technically a Carolina bay. Carolina bays are large, oval depressions in the ground, many of which are boggy and filled with water but which are named for the bay trees that typically grow around them. Lake Waccamaw has geological and hydrological characteristics that make it unique even within the odd category of Carolina bays. There are several aquatic creatures that live only in Lake Waccamaw, including the Waccamaw fatmucket (a mollusk) and the silverside (a fish). The park draws boaters and paddlers, but the only launches are outside the grounds. Primitive campsites (www.northcarolinastateparks.reserveamerica.com, $12-17) are available in the park.

North of Whiteville on U.S. 701 is Elizabethtown, home to **Jones Lake State Park** (4117 Hwy. 242, Elizabethtown, 910/588-4550, http://ncparks.gov, office and visitors center 8am-5pm Mon.-Fri., park 8am-6pm daily Nov.-Feb., 8am-8pm daily Mar.-May and Sept.-Oct., 8am-9pm daily June-Aug., closed Dec. 25). You can boat on Jones Lake either in your own craft (no motors over 10 hp) or in canoes or paddleboats ($7 per hour) rented from the park. The lake is also great for swimming late May-early September, with shallow cool water and a sandy beach. There are camping spaces (www.northcarolinastateparks.reserveamerica.com) with primitive sites ($15), sites with electric hookups ($27), and improved group campsites ($62) available.

Singletary Lake State Park (6707 Hwy. 53 E., Kelly, 910/669-2928, http://ncparks.gov, 8am-5pm daily), north of Lake Waccamaw in Kelly, has one of the largest of the Carolina bays, the 572-acre Singletary Lake, which lies within Bladen Lakes State Forest. There is no individual camping allowed, although there are facilities for large groups (including the entrancingly named Camp Ipecac, for the purgative herb that grows here) that date from the Civilian Conservation Corps (CCC) era. There is a nice one-mile hiking trail, the CCC-Carolina Bay Loop Trail, and a 500-foot pier extending over the bay.

Lumber River State Park (2819 Princess Ann Rd., Orrum, 910/628-4564, http://ncparks.gov, Princess Ann access: 7am-7pm daily Dec.-Feb., 7am-9pm daily Mar.-Apr. and Oct., 7am-10pm daily May-Sept., 7am-8pm daily Nov., Chalk Banks access: 8am-6pm daily Dec.-Feb., 8am-8pm daily Mar.-Apr. and Oct., 8am-9pm daily May-Sept., 8am-7pm daily Nov.) has 115 miles of waterways with numerous put-ins for canoes and kayaks. Referred to as both the Lumber River and Lumbee River, and farther upstream as Drowning Creek, the river traverses both the coastal plain region and the eastern edge of the Sandhills. Camping (www.northcarolina-stateparks.reserveamerica.com, $12) is available at unimproved walk-in and canoe-in sites and at group sites.

Yogi Bear's Jellystone Park (626 Richard Wright Rd., Tabor City, 877/668-8586, www.taborcityjellystone.com, RVs $40-84, tents $40-72, cabins $145-245, yurts $70-140) is a popular campground with RV and tent spaces, rental cabins, and yurts. The facilities are clean and well maintained, and there are tons of children's activities on-site. Some of the camping is in wooded areas, but for the most part expect direct sun.

Entertainment and Events

Several of the state's big agricultural festivals are held in this area. If you're in the little town of Fair Bluff in late July, you may be lucky enough to witness the coronation of the newest Watermelon Queen. The **North Carolina Watermelon Festival** (www.ncwatermelonfestival.org) began as an annual competition between two friends, local farmers whose watermelons grew to over 100 pounds. The competition expanded into this festival that celebrates watermelon growing throughout the state; a new court of watermelon royalty is crowned every year.

When spring rolls around, Chadbourn holds its annual **Strawberry Festival** (www.ncstrawberryfestival.com), at which the coronation of the Strawberry Queen takes place. If this seems a strange sort of royalty, bear in mind that across the state line in South Carolina, they have a Little Miss Hell Hole Swamp competition.

Food

The Chef & The Frog (607 S. Madison St., Whiteville, 910/640-5550, www.chefnc.com, lunch 11am-2pm Tues.-Fri., dinner 5pm-9pm Thurs.-Sat., brunch 11:30am-1:30pm Sun., $10-45, high-end steaks up to $96) is a bit of a surprise. The chef's family fled Cambodia when the Khmer Rouge took power, settling in France, where she learned to cook French and Cambodian cuisine; she married a French American and emigrated to the United States, eventually landing in Whiteville, where her menu features French dishes, American comfort dishes, and a good number of Asian and Cambodian-inspired plates.

There's a take-out counter in Whiteville that chowhounds will drive an hour out of their way to reach because it's said to have the best burgers around. Next to the railroad tracks, **Ward's Grill** (706 S. Madison St., Whiteville, 910/642-2004, 7am-1:30pm Mon.-Sat., under $10) has no seating, just a walk-up counter. The burgers and chili dogs are the go-to items here.

In Pembroke, try **Fuller's Old-Fashioned BBQ** (100 E. 3rd St., Pembroke, 910/521-4667, www.fullersbbq.com, 11am-9pm Mon.-Sat., 11am-6pm Wed. and Sun., 11am-7pm Thurs., 11am-9pm Fri.-Sat., lunch buffet $9, dinner buffet $11, Sun. buffet $13, entrées $4-14.50, ages 3-9 half price). Fuller's has a great reputation for its barbecue, but it also makes all sorts of country specialties like chicken gizzards, chitterlings, and a 12-layer cake.

If barbecue is what you have your heart set on, make the trip to Garland and visit

★ **Southern Smoke BBQ** (29 Warren St., Garland, 910/549-7484, www.southern-smokebbqnc.com, 11:30am until they sell out Thurs.-Fri., $5-18); it's a 1.25-hour drive from Wilmington, and worth every mile; keep an eye out for the **Southern Smoke Food Truck,** which you'll find at Flying Machine Brewery and others around town. Chef Matthew Register takes an interesting approach to barbecue—which is practically a religion in North Carolina—and provides an array of sauces that represent the state's sauce styles and even reaches beyond our borders for inspiration. Like any good pit master, he has a couple of secret tricks he uses when preparing his pork and ribs, and, of course, he builds sides and desserts off old family recipes. Keep an eye on the website and look out for the **South Supper Series,** a ticketed dinner event (typically $45) held three or four times a year; it features his barbecue, of course, but also dishes reflecting his influences and favorite styles from across the South, and, on special occasions, guest chefs from around the state.

Getting There and Around

This section of southeastern North Carolina is bisected by I-95, the largest highway on the East Coast. I-95 passes near Fayetteville and Lumberton. Major east-west routes include U.S. 74, which crosses Cape Fear at Wilmington and proceeds through Lake Waccamaw and Whiteville to pass just south of Lumberton and Pembroke to Laurinburg. Highway 87 goes through Elizabethtown, where you can choose to branch off onto Highway 211 to Lumberton, or bear north on Highway 87 to Fayetteville. Highway 87 and Highway 211 are quite rural and beautiful, especially in the spring, when azaleas are in bloom and the country is greening up, as well as in the fall, when cotton fields will make you do a double take, thinking you just sped past a field of snow. Take your time on these roads, and be ready to pull off to take photos of farmhouses, fields, and other pastoral scenes.

FAYETTEVILLE

Fayetteville is North Carolina's sixth-largest city and in its own quiet way has always been one of the state's most powerful engines of growth and change. In the early 1700s it became a hub for settlement by Scottish immigrants, who helped build it into a major commercial center. From the 1818 initiation of steamboat travel between Fayetteville and Wilmington along Cape Fear—initially a voyage of six days—to the building of Plank Road, which was a huge boon to intrastate commerce, Fayetteville was well connected to commercial resources in the Carolinas. Two hours northwest of Wilmington by highway, Fayetteville sits a little higher in elevation in an area that's part Sandhills, part hardwood forest.

Fayetteville serves as the location of two high-level military installations. Fort Bragg is home to the XVIII Airborne Corps, the 82nd Airborne, the Delta Force, and the John F. Kennedy Special Warfare Center and School. It's also home to many military families, and the community has a vibrant international community. Pope Field, home of the 440th Airlift Wing, is nearby.

Sights
★ **CAPE FEAR BOTANICAL GARDEN**

The 79-acre **Cape Fear Botanical Garden** (536 N. Eastern Blvd., 910/486-0221, www.capefearbg.org, 9am-5pm Mon.-Wed. and Fri.-Sat., 9am-7pm Thurs., and noon-5pm Sun. mid-Mar.-Sept., 9am-5pm Mon.-Sat. and noon-5pm Sun. Sept.-early Nov., 10am-5pm Mon.-Sat., noon-5pm Sun. Nov.-mid-Mar., $10 adults, $9 military and seniors, $5 ages 6-12, free under age 6) is one of the loveliest horticultural sites in North Carolina. The camellia and azalea gardens are spectacular sights in the early spring, but the variety of plantings and environments represented makes the whole park a delight. Along the banks of the Paw Paw River and Cross Creek, visitors will find dozens of garden environments, including lily gardens, hosta gardens, woods, a bog, and an 1880s farmhouse garden. This is the prettiest place in Fayetteville, and a fantastic spot for a picnic lunch on a long road trip down I-95.

AIRBORNE AND SPECIAL OPERATIONS MUSEUM

The **Airborne and Special Operations Museum** (100 Bragg Blvd., 910/643-2778, www.asomf.org, 10am-4pm Tues.-Sat., noon-4pm Sun., free, motion simulator $10) is an impressive facility that presents the history of Special Ops paratroopers, from the first jump in 1940 to the divisions' present-day roles abroad in peacekeeping missions and war. Vivid dioramas and displays put artifacts like Airborne uniforms, arms, and equipment on display with arms, equipment, and uniforms from enemy and friendly forces bring the story of the Airborne to life from its roots in World War II through today. As you come into the museum, you'll see two "parachuting" figures descending from the ceiling, one with a silk chute and the uniform and gear from World War II, the other in modern gear; it's quite striking to see them beside each other. As you explore the museum, be sure to engage the docents. Most of them are Airborne veterans, and they've got stories galore if you ask. In the museum's theater you can watch a film of what it looks like when a paratrooper makes a jump, and the 24-seat Pitch, Roll, and Yaw Vista-Dome Motion Simulator makes the experience even more exciting.

OTHER SIGHTS

The **Museum of the Cape Fear Regional Complex** (801 Arsenal Ave., 910/500-4240, www.musrumofthecapefear.ncdcr.gov, 10am-5pm Tues.-Sat., 1pm-5pm Sun., free) has three components, each telling different stories of Fayetteville's history. The museum has exhibits on the history and prehistory of the region, including its vital role in developing transportation in the state, as well as its military role. There is an 1897 house museum, the **Poe House,** which belonged to an Edgar Allen Poe—not the writer; this one was a brickyard

owner. The third section is the 4.5-acre **Arsenal Park,** site of a federal arms magazine built in 1836, claimed by the Confederacy in 1861, and destroyed by General Sherman in 1865.

Market House (intersection of Person, Hay, Green, and Gillespie Streets) is a beautiful and surprisingly important building in downtown Fayetteville. It was in this building that North Carolina ratified the U.S. Constitution in 1789 and chartered the University of North Carolina. The building that stands there now is not the original—that burned in 1831—but was rebuilt in 1865, supposedly by brick mason Thomas Grimes, a free African American known to be one of the most skilled masons in the area.

Given Fayetteville's deep and ongoing ties to the military, it's no surprise to learn the first park in the state dedicated to all military veterans is right here beside the Airborne and Special Operations Museum. **North Carolina Veterans Park** (300 Bragg Blvd., 910/433-1457, www.ncveteranspark.org, 10am-4pm Tues.-Sat., noon-4pm Sun. Mar.-Oct., noon-4pm Tues.-Sun. Nov.-Feb., free) is a touching tribute to veterans, living and passed. One of the most moving elements is the Oath of Service Wall, a long curved wall made of soil from each of the state's 100 counties, with the bronze-casted hands of 100 of North Carolina's veterans raised as if taking their induction oath.

The **JFK Special Warfare Museum** (Ardennes St. and Zabitosky St., Bldg. D-2815, Fort Bragg, 910/432-4272, www.jfkwebstore.com, 11am-4pm Mon.-Fri., free) tells the story of unconventional U.S. military projects, including Special Ops and Psychological Ops. The museum focuses on the Vietnam War era but chronicles warfare from colonial times to the present. Note that ID is required to enter the base.

Looking farther back in time, the **Fayetteville Independent Light Infantry Armory and Museum** (210 Burgess St., 910/323-5936, by appointment, free) displays artifacts from the history of the Fayetteville

Independent Light Infantry (FILI). FILI is still dedicated as North Carolina's official historic military command, which is a ceremonial duty. In its active-duty days, which began in 1793, FILI had some exciting times, particularly during the Civil War. In addition to military artifacts, the museum also exhibits a carriage in which the Marquis de Lafayette was shown around Fayetteville—the only one of the towns bearing his name that he actually visited.

Cross Creek Cemetery (N. Cool Spring St. and Grove St., 910/433-1457, dawn-dusk daily) is an attractive and sad spot, the resting place of many Scottish men and women who crossed the ocean to settle Cape Fear. People of other ethnicities and times are buried here, but the oldest section of the cemetery is the most poignant, where one stone after another commemorates early Scots colonists. The cemetery was founded in 1785, and the wall along the southern boundary is believed to be the oldest construction still standing in Fayetteville.

Sports and Recreation

There are several parks around Fayetteville that serve a dose of the great outdoors to locals and visitors. Near the Cape Fear Botanical Gardens and easily accessible from I-95, the **Riverside Dog Park** (555 N. Eastern Blvd., dawn-dusk daily) gives the pooches a chance to run around and get a little energy out. **Cross Creek Linear Park** (324 Ray Ave.) connects the Riverside Dog Park with the 14-acre **Festival Park** (Ray Ave. and Rowan St.) on a 2.8-mile route. The most popular walking, jogging, dog-walking route may be the **Cape Fear River Trail** (access at 631 Sherman Dr.), a 5.3-mile one-way park that'll have you out exploring Fayetteville from the edges of neighborhoods to the relative wilds of the bluffs overlooking the Cape Fear River. There's a long boardwalk across some marsh and wetlands, some terrain variations, and a ton of interpretive signs introducing the flora and fauna to trail users.

In Fayetteville you can attend a dizzying array of sporting events, from drag races to ice hockey. The **Fayetteville Marksmen** (1960 Coliseum Dr., 910/321-0123, www.marksmenhockey.com, $10-30) are an ice hockey team in the Southern Professional Hockey League, unusual for this warm climate. The **Rogue Rollergirls** (www.fayettevillerollerderby.com, $10 adults, $6 ages 9-16) is an up-and-coming all-female flat-track Roller Derby team participating in this fun fringe sport that had its heyday in the 1970s. The **Fayetteville Woodpeckers** (910/339-1989, www.milb.com/fayetteville, $6-10), the Class A Minor League affiliate of the Houston Astros, play home games at **Segra Stadium** (460 Hay St.). Games are inexpensive and fun, and there's plenty to eat and drink as you watch the game, so if you're in town and you hear "Play Ball" and a cheer erupt from Segra Stadium, you've got time to get to the box office, buy tickets, and get to your seat without missing more than a pitch or two.

If motors and mud are your thing, or if you just want to check it out, the **Deep Creek ATV Park** (2601 Slocomb Rd., Linden, 910/929-0658, 9am-midnight Fri., 8am-midnight Sat., 8am-6pm Sun., $20 pp daily, $15 veterans, active-duty military, first responders) has everything from mud bogs to sandy trails to explore on a UTV, ATV, dirt bike, or off-road vehicle. There are no rentals available on-site, so it's BYOR (bring your own ride). You can also go camping at a dry (primitive) site ($5) or at a site with water and electrical hookups for RVs ($40) if you're planning on doing a lot of riding.

At **Carvers Creek State Park** (2505 Long Valley Rd., Spring Lake, 910/436-4681, www.ncparks.gov, 8am-8pm daily Mar.-May and Sept.-Oct, 8am-9pm daily June-Aug., 8am-6pm daily Nov.-Feb., free) you can fish (with a license) on the 100-acre Millpond, go for an easy hike on the two completed trails in

1: *Iron Mike* statue by Leah Hiebert at the Airborne and Special Operations Museum 2: Cape Fear Botanical Garden 3: a baseball game at Segra Stadium

the park, and picnic. One of the newer parks in the North Carolina Parks system, it's still growing, so look for more developments—camping, new trails—as time goes on.

GOLF

The Sandhills of North Carolina are dotted with golf courses, and the countryside around Fayetteville is no exception: try **Anderson Creek Golf Club** (125 Whispering Pines Dr., Spring Lake, 910/814-2115, www.andersoncreekclub.com, 18 holes, par 72, greens fees from $60), **Bayonet at Puppy Creek** (349 S. Parker Church Rd., Raeford, 888/229-6638, www.bayonetgolf.com, greens fees from $49), and **Cypress Lakes** (2126 Cypress Lakes Rd., Hope Mills, 910/483-0359, www.cypresslakesnc.com, greens fees from $30).

ZIP LINE

If you want outdoor adventure, **ZipQuest** (533 Carvers Falls Rd., 910/488-8787, www.zipquest.com, 9am-5pm daily, $55-85) gives you a different sort of outdoor experience: flying through the trees on a zip line. The tour takes you on eight zip lines around and over Carver's Creek and even 20-foot Carver's Falls, the only waterfall in the area. There's an abbreviated tour—the Treetop Excursion—which includes five zip lines and a bevy of platforms, but at $55 it's a great intro to zipping. At the end of the run, you have the opportunity to get on the Swingshot, a swing that flies out over a four-story drop into the ravine below. Both the zip-line tour and Swingshot are exciting but not for the faint of heart.

INDOOR SKYDIVING

Paraclete XP SkyVenture (190 Paraclete Dr., Raeford, 910/848-2600, www.paracletexp.com, from $64) offers one of the most thrilling experiences you can have in the area: indoor skydiving. After a brief flight school, you'll step into a vertical wind tunnel with an instructor and take your first flight. If you show a little aptitude, they'll let you fly on your own (don't worry, they're never more than a couple of feet away) and even take you soaring to the top of the 51-foot tower and then rushing back down, giving you a real taste of what it's like to free fall. If you're lucky, you'll see the Golden Knights, the U.S. Army's parachute team, practicing aerial maneuvers, or maybe get to fly with world-class and even world-champion competitive skydivers, or see one of Paraclete's teams practice their wild aerial ballet.

Shopping

There are several antiques stores, a few big-box stores, and a mall in Fayetteville, but if you're shopping, keep it local. One of my favorites is **Bath Snob** (3505 N. Main St., Hope Mills, 910/568-3238, www.bathsnob.com, 10am-6pm Tues.-Sat.), where their handmade soap, beard and body oil, bath bombs, and other bath and home goods are made with high-quality products (by high-quality people; seriously, they're so nice), and they include unscented and allergy-sensitive bath products too. **Leclair's General Store** (1212 Fort Bragg Rd., Fayetteville, 910/305-5378, www.leclairsgeneralstore.com, 8am-7pm Mon.-Sat., 10am-5pm Sun.) has a collection of antiques, jewelry, art, vintage home goods, and a selection of coffee, wine, and craft beer to help lubricate your wallet as you shop. Grab your souvenir shirt or something local and tasty from **A Bit of Carolina** (306 Hay St., Fayetteville, 910/551-6537, www.abitofcarolina.com, 11am-6pm Mon.-Thurs., 11am-7pm Fri.-Sat., noon-6pm Sun.). They stock goods from more than 120 local food vendors, artisans, and artists, so for the perfect memento of your time in town, look here first.

Entertainment and Events

The **Cameo Theatre** (225 Hay St., 910/486-6633, www.cameoarthouse.com) is a cool old early-20th-century movie house, originally known as the New Dixie. Today it is "Fayetteville's alternative cinematic experience," a place for independent and art-house movies.

Cape Fear Regional Theatre (1209 Hay St., 910/323-4233, www.cfrt.org) began in 1962 as a tiny company with a bunch of borrowed equipment. Today it is a major regional theater with a wide reputation. Putting on several major productions each season and specializing in popular musicals, it draws actors and directors from around the country but maintains its heart here in the Fayetteville arts community. Its annual summertime Blue 'N' Brews is a one-day beer festival featuring some fine blues music.

The Gilbert Theater (116 Green St., 910/678-7186, www.gilberttheater.com, around $10) is a small company that puts on a variety of productions throughout the year, with emphasis on classic drama and multicultural offerings.

Fayetteville's late-April Dogwood Festival (www.thedogwoodfestival.com) features rock, pop, and beach-music bands; a dog show; a recycled art show; a "hogs and rags spring rally"; and the selection and coronation of Miss, Teen Miss, Young Miss, and Junior Miss Dogwood Festival. There's an October counterpart, the Dogwood Fall Festival, featuring concerts, hay rides, craft beer, and all the festival goodness you expect. In September, the International Folk Festival (www.theartscouncil.com) celebrates the many cultures that make up this community through food, music, art, and other cultural expressions.

The Arts Council of Fayetteville/Cumberland County (910/323-1776, www.theartscouncil.com) is in charge of the 4th Friday celebrations, a downtown celebration of arts and an excuse to get out and get friendly with the community. Various galleries and museums are open late, there are concerts, and everyone has a grand time. At the end of November (check for exact dates), A Dickens Holiday takes over downtown. Characters from A Christmas Carol roam downtown, and there are performances and Victorian pubs, a candlelight procession to the Market House, and horse-drawn carriages along with a holiday street fair.

Food and Accommodations

The city's dining choices once tended toward the highway chain restaurants, but Fayetteville has grown up, and there are a dozen great restaurants in town, another dozen good ones, and at least two dozen of those highway chain joints. For some of the best food in town, go to ★ Fowler's Southern Gourmet (723 W. Rowan St., 910/491-5721, www.fowlerssoutherngourmet.com, 11am-2pm Wed.-Sat., $4.25-24). This place is not strictly barbecue, but it's mostly barbecue, and in true barbecue joint fashion, it's open only for lunch and only as long as they've got food; when it's gone, they lock the doors, clean up, and go home. But while its open, oh, boy, you're in for a treat. *Our State Magazine* (which you really should check out while you're in North Carolina, and not just because you might run across my byline in there) called the Burnt Burnt Ends Here "beef candy," and that's a perfect description. You'll find burnt ends, brisket, and pork belly burnt ends on the menu alongside North Carolina barbecue staples like pulled pork, pulled smoked chicken, and sides (slaw, collards, potato salad), but then the menu turns to the "gourmet" part. Jerk chicken or pork tacos, a Philly cheesesteak-like sandwich with brisket or chicken, The Cluck Norris (their answer for a hot chicken sandwich), and the Carolina Bee Sting (pulled pork, honey sriracha sauce, and pickled jalapeños on a bun). It's a great bite of food, and if you want your choice of what's available, get there early; folks around here love it.

Beer lovers will find plenty to drink in Fayetteville, and Dirtbag Ales (5435 Corporation Dr., Hope Mills, 910/426-2537, www.dirtbagales.com, 11:30am-10pm Tues.-Thurs., 11:30am-11pm Fri., noon-11pm Sat., 10am-4pm Sun.) should be the first stop. A huge indoor space and an even bigger outdoor area give you plenty of room to spread out and sip a pint, enjoy a flight, or grab something to eat from Napkins (910/489-4857, $4-11), their on-site kitchen. Napkins' smashburgers are killer, but their Nashville Hot Chicken Sandwich and a basket of tots is my perfect order to pair with their IPA. Beers are small-batch but they stick pretty close to the core recipes, so even though you'll find plays on their IPA or kölsch on the menu, the backbone is the same, which is to say, excellent. The brewers at this veteran-owned spot are all about quality and consistency, and they deliver in every pint.

There are a dozen breweries around, but two you should check out are **Gaston Brewing Company** (124 Hay St., 910/748-0580, www.gastonbrewing.com, noon-10pm Tues.-Wed., noon-11pm Thurs.-Sat., noon-7pm Sun.) and **Bright Light Brewing Company** (444 W. Russel St., Suite 102, 910/339-0464, www.brightlightbrewco.com, 4pm-9pm Mon.-Wed., 4pm-10:30pm Thurs.-Fri., 1pm-10:30pm Sat., 1pm-8pm Sun.). Gaston is a dog-friendly spot with a small menu ($8-14) of burgers, salads, and apps to share at the table; their beers include a great Belgian *tripel* and a super clean lager as well as IPAs, porters, and other sudsy sips. Bright Light, which is also dog-friendly, keeps a tap list of house brews and guest taps, so they've always got something tasty on.

Fayetteville, being home to Fort Bragg, the massive U.S. Army post, is quite the international community. Deployed soldiers have returned home from overseas postings with new spouses and new families in tow, and interpreters and other workers assisting the armed forces have emigrated to Fayetteville, all of which makes an interesting international influence in the sandhills of eastern North Carolina. Take advantage of the multinational flair and grab a meal from elsewhere. **La Fogata** (500-C N. McPherson Church Rd., 910/864-8598, 10:30am-8:20pm Mon.-Thurs., 10:20am-9:30pm Fri.-Sat., 10:30am-7:30pm Sun., $11-27) delivers bold Colombian dishes that'll transport you to Bogotá. At **Zorba's Gyro on a Spit** (2919 Raeford Rd., 910/484-1010, www.zorbasgyro.com, 6am-9pm Mon.-Sat., 7am-2pm Sun., $4-18) you'll get a taste of Greece, the Mediterranean, and the Middle East, with a dash of American diner thrown in for good measure. And **Grilled Ginger**

Vietnamese Restaurant (5052 Yadkin Rd., 910/867-2227, www.grilledginger.com, 11am-8pm Mon.-Sat., $8-14) makes some of the best *phô* and *bánh mì* I've found stateside.

For breakfast, you need to head to **Vicky's Famous Biscuits & Chicken** (128 Grove St., 910/491-2681, 6am-2:30pm Mon.-Wed. and Fri., 11am-2:30pm Thurs., 7am-2pm Sun., $2-10). They put biscuits first because they're the star of the show. Get a biscuit with butter for just $1 to see just how good these things are unadorned, but you really should go for one with some toppings. Double ham, a bacon-egg-and-cheese biscuit, even one with a chicken fillet on there will make your tongue happy, but the homemade cinnamon roll—a thing the size of a softball—is one of those "we'll take one for the table to split" orders that's too much for one diner but just right to share.

If you want well-made familiar flavors and a solid selection of beer and cocktails, take your pub-grub cravings up a notch and try **Scrub Oaks Contemporary American Pub** (5780 Ramsey St., Suite 108, 910/884-3072, www.scruboaks.com, 11am-10pm Sun. and Wed.-Thurs., 11am-11pm Fri.-Sat., $10-25). Po' boys, burgers, and hot sandwiches, meal-worthy appetizers like wings or chicken tenders and a salad, and entrées like shepherd's pie, spicy fried shrimp, or a steak leave you filled without breaking the bank.

The charming **MacPherson House Bed & Breakfast** (701 Hay St., 910/302-7153, www.macphersonhouse.com, $159-199) has five rooms and a private cottage. Built in 1920 as part of the MacPherson Estate, it was disassembled and moved across town in the 1990s and restored to its former charm. The current owners opened it as a B&B in 2020, hosting the grandson of the original owners soon after. The rooms are spacious and well decorated, and breakfast satisfies, so consider this spot instead of one of the many chain hotels in town.

Fayetteville's lodging options are mostly chain motels, a multitude of which can be found at the Fayetteville exits along I-95.

Among the best of the chain offerings are the refreshed-in-2021 Embassy Suites by Hilton Fayetteville Fort Bragg (4760 Lake Valley Dr., 910/826-3600, www.hilton.com, standard rooms from $155, suites from $187, Presidential suite from $448); the all-suites Holiday Inn & Suites Fayetteville W-Fort Bragg (2501 Two Bale Lane, 910/236-6633, www.hiwestfortbragg.com, from $142), with an outdoor pool and a cocktail lounge; and the pet-friendly Home2 Suites by Hilton-Fayetteville, NC (4035 Sycamore Dairy Rd., 910/748-5281, www.hilton.com, from $155).

Information and Services

Cape Fear Valley Medical Center (1638 Owen Dr., 910/615-4000, www.capefearvalley.com) is a large hospital complex with full services, including acute care and a major cardiac care program.

The website of the Fayetteville Area Convention and Visitors Bureau (245 Person St., 910/483-5311, www.visitfayettevillenc.com, 8am-5pm Mon.-Fri.) is an excellent source of visitor information for the city. You'll find not only the basics but also detailed driving tours and extensive historical information.

Getting There and Around

Fayetteville Regional Airport (FAY, 400 Airport Rd., 910/433-1160, www.fly-fay.com) has daily flights to Charlotte and Dallas (American Airlines), Atlanta (Delta), and Washington DC (Delta and American). Amtrak (472 Hay St., 800/872-7245, www.amtrak.com, 10am-5:45pm and 10pm-5:45am daily) runs the *Silver Meteor* between New York City and Miami and the *Palmetto* between New York City and Savannah, Georgia; each train stops in Fayetteville once daily in each direction.

Fayetteville is near I-95; it is easily reached via Highway 24 from Jacksonville, Warsaw, and Clinton and via Highway 87 from points south.

Raleigh and the Triangle

The Raleigh-Durham-Chapel Hill area is called

"the Triangle," which originally referred to the three major universities here, the University of North Carolina at Chapel Hill, Duke University in Durham, and North Carolina State University at Raleigh. A map or aerial photo of the region shows that these three cities are a uniform urban mass, but lumping them together overlooks the unique personality, quirks, and scene of each.

That said, there is a spirit that unites the communities of the Triangle. The intense concentration of colleges and universities—there are more than a dozen, including several prominent historically African American universities—results in a well-educated population with shared interests and sensibilities. By some counts, there are

Highlights

Look for ★ to find recommended sights, activities, dining, and lodging.

★ **North Carolina Museum of Natural Sciences:** Get breathtakingly close to massive whale and dinosaur skeletons at this excellent nature museum (page 196).

★ **North Carolina Museum of History:** The state boasts centuries of remarkable history, literature, art, and sports—and there's no better place to explore it than here (page 196).

★ **North Carolina Museum of Art:** Amazingly varied collections encompass art from ancient Greece, Egypt, and the Americas as well as Judaica and pop art (page 197).

★ **William B. Umstead State Park:** Central to all the Triangle towns, this state park delivers hiking, mountain biking, and boating just a few minutes away (page 200).

★ **Beautiful Campuses:** Stroll past pretty gardens and ornate collegiate buildings on the scenic campuses of **University of North Carolina at Chapel Hill** (page 229) and the "Ivy League of the South," **Duke University** (page 215).

★ **Historic Stagville:** One of the South's largest enslaved populations lived and worked on this plantation immediately prior to the Civil War. The story of their community is preserved here (page 217).

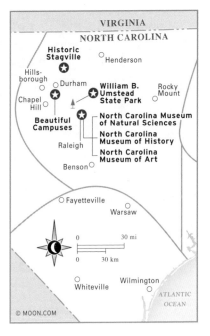

Raleigh and the Triangle

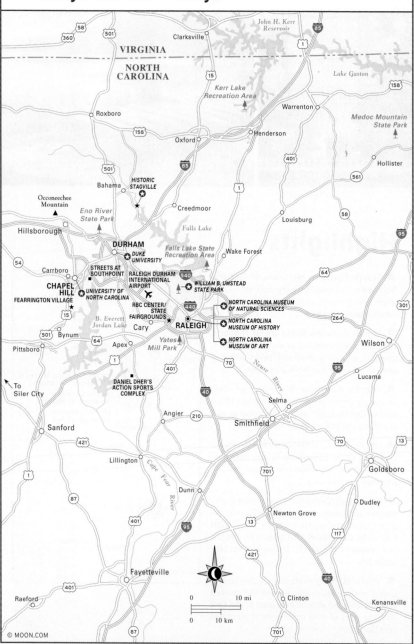

© MOON.COM

more PhDs per capita in the Triangle than anywhere in the country, partly due to the booming local biotech, pharmaceutical, and high-tech industries.

The Triangle has a deeply liberal bent, much to the frustration and befuddlement of many in this sometimes red state. Archconservative U.S. Senator Jesse Helms once remarked that there was no need to build a zoo in North Carolina; we could simply put a fence around Chapel Hill and achieve the same purpose. Gibes aside, Chapel Hill is a menagerie of all walks of humanity, making it the epicenter of progressive politics in the state, most intensely concentrated in the left-wing town of Carrboro, which elected North Carolina's first openly gay mayor in 1995. Carrboro was also the state's first community to extend domestic partnership benefits of to same-sex couples in 1994.

The Triangle is an area with deep roots in the arts, mostly of the literary and musical variety. Writers like David Sedaris and Charles Kuralt have called this area home, and it ranks with New Orleans and Oxford, Mississippi, as one of the literary capitals of the South. It seems that every writer in North Carolina is obliged to give a reading or a lecture or lead a workshop in Raleigh, Durham, Chapel Hill, or a satellite community. The music scene is just as lively, with Chapel Hill, the most collegiate of the local college towns, as its center. Acts like the Squirrel Nut Zippers, Corrosion of Conformity, Southern Culture on the Skids, Ben Folds Five, and Chatham County Line hail from here, and that's just Chapel Hill. Genres are widely flung, and you'll find everything from great chamber groups and orchestras to modern-day jug bands, dubstep DJs, and a rich bluegrass and alt-country scene.

PLANNING YOUR TIME

The area covered in this chapter is best approached as three destinations. From east to west, Wilson and other towns east of I-95 are an hour or less driving from Raleigh, and this region merits at least a day on its own. Raleigh and its suburbs, such as Zebulon, Cary, and Wake Forest, all radiating from the Beltline (the I-440 ring road), call for another full day. Durham and Chapel Hill are only nine miles apart, so together they are the third region of this chapter. Carrboro is so closely linked to Chapel Hill—it's actually difficult to tell exactly which block of Franklin Street or Main Street demarcates their city boundary—that they're treated here as one entity. Hillsborough is an easy drive from both Chapel Hill and Durham, and Pittsboro is about 20 minutes south of Chapel Hill.

If you decide to choose one town in the Triangle to stay in while exploring the wider area during the day, Durham is the most centrally located of the three cities. But I-40 and U.S. 70 link the whole Triangle area quite efficiently, and there are few points in the Triangle that are more than 30 minutes' drive from any other point.

Previous: North Carolina Museum of Natural Sciences in downtown Raleigh; Duke University; William B. Umstead State Park.

Raleigh and Vicinity

The first time I heard of Raleigh was on *The Andy Griffith Show*. Any time trouble found Mayberry, it either came from "Up North" or from Raleigh. Even though many of Andy's observations of life in North Carolina are accurate, his assertion that Raleigh is a hive of citified depravity is just wrong. It is a great city, home to a number of universities and the state government (granted, many would agree that involves its own kind of depravity). Raleigh is one of the sparks that helps power the cultural engine of North Carolina.

North Carolina State University is here, along with two historically African American universities, Shaw and Saint Augustine's, and two small but well-known women's colleges, Peace and Meredith. The North Carolina Museum of History is excellent, as are the Natural Sciences Museum and the North Carolina Museum of Art. There are a number of music and art festivals as well as the must-see event of the year, the State Fair.

SIGHTS

★ North Carolina Museum of Natural Sciences

The **North Carolina Museum of Natural Sciences** (Bicentennial Plaza, 11 W. Jones St., 919/707-9800, www.naturalsciences. org, 10am-5pm Tues.-Sun., closed Jan. 1-2, Thanksgiving Day, and Dec. 24-26, free) hosts national traveling exhibitions and is home to excellent permanent exhibits. "Mountains to the Sea" is a re-creation of the regional environments of the state, populated with live and mounted animals and plants. Stars of "Prehistoric North Carolina" include the world's only publicly displayed skeleton of an *Acrocanthosaurus*, a 38-foot, 4.5-ton predatory dinosaur, and the remains of "Willo," a 66-million-year-old small vegetarian dinosaur whose fossilized heart is a rare boon to paleontology. The whales whose skeletons hang in the Coastal Carolina exhibit are celebrities, each with its own interesting story, including "Trouble," a sperm whale who washed up at Wrightsville Beach in 1928, and "Mayflower," a right whale killed in a legendary 1874 struggle with Carolina whalers off Shackleford Banks. The 80,000-square-foot **Nature Research Center** allows visitors to watch scientists conduct research and experiments in the "Window on Research" areas. A three-story multimedia space provides plenty of room to show films, clips, and presentations. Other exhibits in this wing include displays on aquatics, astronomy, microbiology, and genetics. There's a great remote facility too, the **Prairie Ridge Ecostation** (1671 Gold Star Dr., 919/707-8888, 9am-4pm Tues.-Sat., closed New Years Day, Election Day, Thanksgiving Day, Dec. 24-25, and state holidays, free), a 45-acre Piedmont prairie with ponds, trails, and wildlife viewing opportunities.

★ North Carolina Museum of History

Also on Bicentennial Plaza is the **North Carolina Museum of History** (5 E. Edenton St., 919/814-7000, http://ncmuseumofhistory.org, 9am-5pm Mon.-Sat., noon-5pm Sun., closed New Years Day, Election Day, Thanksgiving, Dec. 24-25, and state holidays, free), where visitors learn about the history of the state's contributions to the military, from the Revolutionary War to the Iraq War; about the musicians and genres that make this state one of the wellsprings of American music; about the handicrafts, including pieces created by centuries of renowned artisans; and about medicine in North Carolina, from traditional African American root medicine and Native American herbal treatments to the pharmaceutical and medical technology businesses of today. You can also see a uniform worn by Harlem Globetrotter and Wilmington native Meadowlark Lemon and

Raleigh and Vicinity

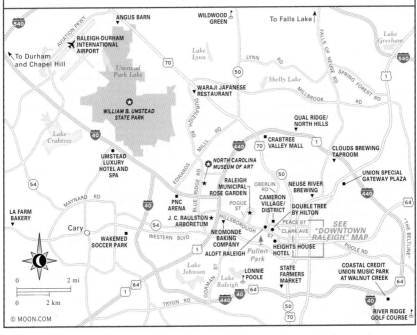

a stock car driven by Carolina legend Richard Petty. The Museum of History hosts concerts and many educational events throughout the year.

★ North Carolina Museum of Art

The **North Carolina Museum of Art** (2110 Blue Ridge Rd., 919/839-6262, http://ncartmuseum.org, 10am-5pm Wed.-Sun., closed New Years Day, Easter, Veterans Day, Thanksgiving Day, and Dec 24-26, free) is just outside the Beltline. Its collections include masterpieces from many eras and regions of the world, including ancient Egyptian, Greek, Roman, and pre-Columbian American art and the work of Botticelli, Giotto, Raphael, Monet, Georgia O'Keeffe, Thomas Hart Benton, and many more. The gallery is also home to one of the nation's two Jewish ceremonial art collections and to collections of 19th- and 20th-century African art. Perhaps most impressive is the collection of sculptures by the French master Auguste Rodin.

A 160-acre **outdoor gallery** (dusk-dawn daily) has miles of trails looping through it from one enormous outdoor art installation to the next; these trails connect to the **Raleigh Greenway System**, making the museum an ideal start or endpoint for a ride or an excellent break in the middle of a long ride. Art installations include a metal tree so organic that many visitors ask if the artist painted a real tree or wrapped one in foil. Throughout the park are opportunities to interact with the art pieces and the environment. A couple of the trails lead to the large outdoor amphitheater, which hosts concerts and film screenings during summer and fall.

Historic Homes

The 1770s **Joel Lane Museum House** (St. Mary's St. and W. Hargett St., 919/833-3431, www.joellane.org, 10am-5pm Tues.-Fri., tours hourly 10am-1pm Wed.-Fri., $8 adults, $7 seniors, $4 students, free under age 7) is Wake County's oldest extant home. Costumed docents lead tours of the house and period gardens.

Mordecai Historic Park (1 Mimosa St., 919/996-4364, www.raleighnc.gov, grounds dawn-dusk daily, hourly house tours 10am-3pm Tues.-Sun., $7 adults, $4 seniors and ages 7-17, free under age 7) includes a plantation house dating from the late 18th and early 19th centuries. It has restored dependencies and other buildings, including the birthplace of President Andrew Johnson.

More historic homes can be seen in Raleigh's historic **Oakwood Neighborhood,** listed on the National Register of Historic Places. Structures mostly date from the late 19th century in this neighborhood, bounded by Franklin, Watauga, Linden, Jones, and Person Streets. Self-guided walking and driving tour brochures can be picked up at the Capital Area Visitor Information center inside the Museum of History on Bicentennial Plaza. **Historic Oakwood Cemetery** (701 Oakwood Ave., 919/832-6077. www.historicoakwoodcemetery.org, 8am-6pm daily spring-fall, 8am-5pm daily winter), a beautiful and historic plot of land where you'll find the final resting places of a pretty interesting group of the area's onetime citizens. Some 1,000 Confederate soldiers, five Civil War generals, seven governors, and a number of U.S. senators are interred here.

North Carolina State Capitol

The **North Carolina State Capitol** (1 E. Edenton St., 919/733-4994, www.ncstatecapitol.org, 9am-5pm Mon.-Sat., closed most state holidays, tours 11am and 2pm Sat., free), built in the 1830s, is a Greek Revival structure that has been restored to its antebellum appearance. Outside there are some statues and memorials to the various veterans throughout the state's history. Be alert when you visit the library; this is where the capitol's many reported ghosts are allegedly most active. Guided tours last approximately 45 minutes.

Executive Mansion

The **Executive Mansion** (200 N. Blount St., 919/715-3962, www.ncdcr.gov), built in the 1890s, is a lovely example of Victorian architecture, once described by President Franklin D. Roosevelt as possessing "the most beautiful governor's residence interior in America." Tours are available, but the hours vary according to state functions—it is still the home of the governor. It's necessary to be with an official tour group; phone for more information.

Gardens

The **J. C. Raulston Arboretum** (4415 Beryl Rd., 919/515-3132, www.jcra.ncsu.edu, 9am-4:30pm Mon.-Fri. and 10am-5pm Sat.-Sun. Nov.-Feb., 9am-4:30pm Mon.-Fri. and 10am-6pm Sat.-Sun. Mar.-Oct., free) is a public garden focused on the development of ornamental plants suitable to the Southern climate. You can visit highly specialized areas devoted to white flowers, roses, and border plants; the 300- by 18-foot perennial border may cause some serious yard envy. Near North Carolina State University, the **Raleigh Municipal Rose Garden** (301 Pogue St., 919/821-4579, https://raleighlittletheatre.org, dawn-dusk daily, free) is home to more than 1,000 roses of 60 varieties. Carolina roses are blessed with an extra-long growing season, and the Municipal Rose Garden also features bulbs and other ornamental plants, so a visit to the garden is special any time of year. Another place for a scenic walk is **Historic Yates Mill County Park** (4620 Lake Wheeler Rd., 919/856-6675, www.wakegov.com, 8am-sunset daily), a few miles south of downtown. The gristmill that presides over the millrace is nearly 200 years old. Hiking trails encircle the millpond.

State Farmers Market

A favorite place to visit in Raleigh is the **State Farmers Market** (1201 Agricultural St., 919/733-7417, www.ncfarmfresh.gov, 9am-5pm daily, free), where you'll find the best produce, the finest meats, and all sorts of arts, crafts, candies, baked goods, bedding plants, garden plants, pots, and pretty things.

Downtown Raleigh

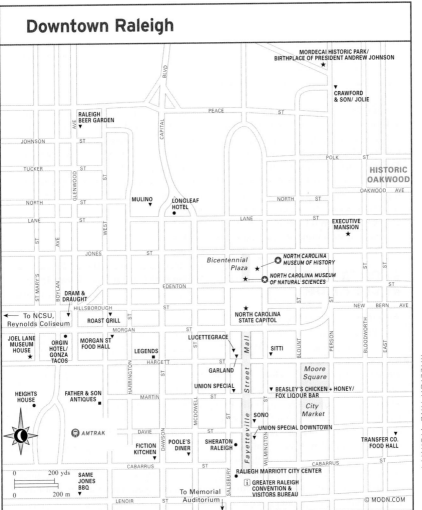

A 30,000-square foot-pavilion, where most of the farmers set up to sell their wares, is the central focal point, but the Market Shoppes, at around half the size, are where you'll find candy, baked goods, and other assorted North Carolina gifts, notions, soaps, and lotions. Across the street from the State Farmers Market is a restaurant that serves a big country breakfast and lunch; fittingly, a good deal of what they serve comes from right next door.

The **State Farmers Market Restaurant** (1240 Farmers Market Dr., 919/755-1550, www.realbiscuits.com, 6am-3pm Mon.-Sat., 8am-3pm Sun., $3-12) has excellent biscuits and hot cakes, but if you're there for breakfast, go big with Granny Cone's Sampler: two eggs, a sample of three breakfast meats, molasses, sausage gravy, spiced apples, a trio of silver dollar hot cakes, home fries or grits (go with the grits), and biscuits.

Wake Forest

The small town of **Wake Forest** in northern Wake County is the original home of Wake Forest University, which is now located 100 miles west in Winston-Salem. Wake Forest is an attractive town with pretty, historic architecture—including the pre-1820 **Calvin Jones House** (414 N. Main St., Wake Forest, 919/556-2911, www.wakeforestmuseum.org, 9am-noon and 1:30pm-4:30pm Tues.-Fri., free) as well as cafés, shops, and **Falls Lake State Recreation Area** (13304 Creedmoor Rd., Wake Forest, 984/867-8000, http://ncparks.gov, 8am-dusk daily, closed Dec. 25). At Falls Lake, you'll find 13 miles of mountain biking trails, several miles of hiking trails, fishing, and swimming at Sandling Beach and Beaverdam.

SPORTS AND RECREATION

Hiking

★ **WILLIAM B. UMSTEAD STATE PARK**

Between Raleigh and Durham, **William B. Umstead State Park** (8801 Glenwood Ave., 919/571-4170, http://ncparks.gov, 8am-dusk daily, closed Dec. 25, visitors center 8am-5pm daily) offers 20 miles of hiking trails, boat rentals ($7), and mountain bike trails. For an easy hike, try Sal's Branch Trail, a 2.7-mile trip that usually takes about an hour to complete; the trailhead is right behind the visitors center. There are also 13 miles of equestrian-friendly trails. Horses are not permitted on hiking trails, but hikers and cyclists often interact with equestrian enthusiasts at trailheads and on certain multiuse paths. The deep forest and creek banks feature flora normally found at higher elevations, including mountain laurel, and are frequented by a variety of wildlife. The Crabtree Creek entrance, where you'll find the visitors center, is 10 miles northwest of Raleigh along U.S. 70.

Raleigh also has a wonderful series of hiking trails in the **Capital Area Greenway Trail System** (www.raleighnc.gov). Currently there are around 100 miles of trails in the city.

They're not all interconnected, but plans are to join them to make a huge urban trail system. Pets, bicyclists, skaters, and skateboarders are all welcome on the Greenway Trail System.

Paddling

If your canoe or kayak is already strapped onto your car and all you need is a place to put in, try the **Neuse River Canoe Trail.** Over a stretch of 17 miles of the Neuse are five different launches, beginning at the Falls Lake Dam. Visit the City of Raleigh (www.raleighnc.gov) website for downloadable maps of the river.

Parks

There are several parks around Raleigh, but one that stands out is the wildly popular **Pullen Park** (520 Ashe Ave., www.raleighnc. gov, grounds and playground dawn-dusk daily, free), North Carolina's first public park, dating from 1887. The **Amusement Center** (919/996-6472, 8am-8pm daily) has a spectacular Gustav A. Dentzel Carousel from 1911, listed on the National Register of Historic Places, as well as a miniature train, a small lake with pedal-boat rentals, and picnic shelters galore. Rides take tickets ($1.50 each).

Mountain Biking

Daniel Dhers Action Sports Complex (171 Tradition Trail, Suite 301, Holly Springs, 919/557-8088, www.ddasc.com, 3pm-10pm Mon.-Fri., 10am-10pm Sat.-Sun.), just outside of town, is a BMX and mountain bike park with 17,500 square feet of riding areas, tracks, jumps, and obstacles indoors and 17,000 square feet of the same outdoors. Founded in 2013 by Daniel Dhers, a five-time X-Games Gold Medalist and four-time DewTour Champion, the facility is ideal for young athletes to practice their racing, tricks, and general course competency. You can come

---

1: the North Carolina Museum of History **2:** hiking in William B. Umstead State Park **3:** Historic Yates Mill County Park **4:** State Farmers Market

out and ride for the day ($16-20), take lessons ($50 per hour), or join a skills camp (from $70 per day, $300 per week). Rental gear is available ($3-15), and you can host a birthday party here ($200).

Golf

At North Carolina State University, the **Lonnie Poole Golf Course** (1509 Main Campus Dr., 919/515-6527, www.lonniepoolegolfcourse.com, 18 holes, par 72, tee-time reservation required, made up to one week in advance, greens fees $42-85, replays $25-35) is simply spectacular. A superb layout by Arnold Palmer includes views of the Raleigh skyline while offering a challenging but playable course. Be warned, though, that the first hole is a monster (578 yards from championship tees, par 5), requiring a long carry to a narrow bunker-guarded fairway.

Wildwood Green Golf Club (3000 Ballybunion Way, 919/846-8376, www.wildwoodgreen.com, 18 holes, par 70, greens fees $25-69) has four sets of tees that help even the distance between experienced and novice golfers. Generously wide fairways on most holes help beginners build some confidence and reward aggressive players who try long drives and green-seeking second shots. It's a pretty course with a little water throughout but nothing too intimidating.

At **River Ridge Golf Club** (3224 Auburn-Knightdale Rd., 919/661-8374, www.golfriverridge.com, 18 holes, par 72 men, par 71 women, greens fees $28-68), they like to brag that you'll get "private club golf course conditions at a daily-fee price." There's not a lot of water on the course, but there is some elevation change, causing you to club up or down, depending on your position, the wind, and the slope of the course.

Spectator Sports

North Carolina State University is the southern terminus of Tobacco Road, the zone of legendary college sports traditions in the Atlantic Coast Conference. Although the rivalry between the University of North Carolina and Duke may score more media attention, North Carolina State University's **Wolfpack Athletics** (919/865-1510, www.gopack.com) are worthwhile. Men's basketball games take place at the 20,000-seat **PNC Arena** (1400 Edwards Mill Rd., 919/861-2300, www.thepncarena.com), and football is next door at **Carter-Finley Stadium** (4600 Trinity Rd.). Women's basketball and other Wolfpack sporting events take place at **Reynolds Coliseum** (2411 Dunn Ave., 919/865-1510) and **Doak Field** (1081 Varsity Dr.).

During ice hockey season, PNC Arena is home to the **Carolina Hurricanes** (www.nhl.com/hurricanes). North Carolina may seem an unlikely place for a National Hockey League franchise, but the Canes proved themselves in the 2005-2006 season, beating the Edmonton Oilers to win the Stanley Cup. Tickets can be purchased in person at the Time Warner Cable Box Office inside PNC Arena (1400 Edwards Mill Rd., no phone sales) or through Ticketmaster (www.ticketmaster.com).

Formerly the Carolina Railhawks, the **North Carolina FC** (919/459-8144, www.northcarolinafc.com)—that's North Carolina Football Club, if you're not up on your soccer lingo—plays soccer in the USL League One. They play at WakeMed Soccer Park (101 Soccer Park Dr., Cary). The Triangle's soccer talent is broad, and there's good reason to think MLS will award the area with an expansion team, from the fans—who pack the stadium for every home game—to **NC Courage** (www.nccourage.com), the stellar National Women's Soccer League team under the same ownership; their games are as exciting and their fanbase just as loyal.

ENTERTAINMENT AND EVENTS

Performing Arts

The **North Carolina Symphony** (919/733-2750, www.ncsymphony.org), a full-time 66-member orchestra under the direction of conductors Grant Llewellyn, Carlos

Miguel Prieto, and Michelle Di Russo, tours throughout the state and beyond. Its home venue is the wonderful Meymandi Concert Hall at **Duke Energy Center for the Performing Arts** (2 E. South St., 919/996-8700, www.dukeenergycenterraleigh.com). The **North Carolina Opera** (919/792-3853, www.ncopera.org) has its home stage at Memorial Auditorium, also in the Duke Energy Center. The opera's rehearsals, held at a nearby church, are sometimes open to the public (see the website for details). The **Carolina Ballet** (919/719-0900, www.carolinaballet.com) performs a season of about 10 shows at the Duke Energy Center. At the **North Carolina Theatre** (1 E. South St., 919/831-6941 www.nctheatre.com) you can see productions like *Grease, Dirty Dancing, Into the Woods,* and other contemporary stage productions as well as classics.

Coastal Credit Union Music Park (3801 Rock Quarry Rd., 919/831-6400, www.coastalcreditunionmusicpark.com), formerly known as Walnut Creek, attracts top pop and country acts. Given the A-list artists who play here, concerts can sell out quickly. The **Lincoln Theatre** (126 E. Cabarrus St., 919/821-4111, www.lincolntheatre.com, all ages) is another important local performing arts institution where major rock, blues, jazz, and other bands fill the schedule.

In the heart of downtown, the **Red Hat Amphitheater** (500 S. McDowell St., 919/996-8800, www.redhatamphitheater.com) has room for around 5,500 concertgoers and draws big names; Widespread Panic, The National, and Bob Dylan have played here. Major headliners sell out quickly at this relatively small venue, so check their schedule ahead of time.

Cary's **Booth Amphitheatre** (8003 Regency Pkwy., 919/462-2025, http://booth-amphitheatre.com) hosts a number of concerts, movies, and events throughout the year in a beautiful lakeside facility. I was impressed not only with the size and arrangement of the place but with the food options, the outstanding concessions, and the beer selection. Check their website for upcoming concerts and events.

Nightlife

The best place to find out what's going on at Triangle-area clubs on any given night of the week is the *Independent Weekly,* a free newspaper that's available at restaurants and shops throughout the region. By state law, establishments that serve liquor and make no more than 30 percent of their revenue from food must be private-membership clubs, but every club has ways of getting first-time visitors through the doors. Some clubs must be joined a few days in advance, while others accept applications with nominal dues at the door. Raleigh's popular nightspots are dance clubs, lots of live-music venues, and gay clubs with great drag events.

Cocktails at **Dram & Draught** (1 Glenwood Ave., Suite 101, 919/607-8501, www.dramanddraught.com, 3pm-2am Mon.-Fri., noon-2am Sat.-Sun.) are made for cocktail enthusiasts, those who want their drinks to taste like something other than college happy-hour mixed well drinks. Barman Ian Murray is just one of the talented bar staff here, and he consistently wins cocktail competitions with his interpretations of classics and with drinks of his own devising. They carry more than 300 whiskeys from around the world, as well as a dozen beers on tap, but their cocktails are exceptional, and something so simple and elegant as a vieux carré is transformational.

Fox Liquor Bar (237 S. Wilmington St., 919/322-0128, www.ac-restaurants.com, 5pm-midnight Mon.-Thurs., 5pm-2am Fri.-Sat.) serves some of the best cocktails in Raleigh. The mixologists here aren't just bartenders, they're artists who take pride in the cocktails they create. The menu explains each cocktail down to the type of glass it's served in and the shape of the ice that goes in it. You'll find a lot of bourbon, rye, and gin but little vodka used in their classic, reimagined, and newly minted drinks, along with a number of house-made and exotic bitters. Best of all, if you get hungry, head upstairs to Fox's sister restaurants:

Chuck's for a burger, or for fried chicken and waffles, Beasley's Chicken + Honey.

The ambience and live jazz add to the experience of the cocktails at the dim and cozy **Watts and Ward** (200 S. Blount St., 919/896-8016, www.wattsandward.com, 4pm-2am daily). Classic and nouveau cocktails are on offer here, and whether you go for a Carolina lily (vodka, fresh strawberries, lemon-rhubarb, and sparkling rose), a brown derby (bourbon, grapefruit, and honey), or go for one of their craft beers on draft, you'll be coming back for more.

Go visit **Aunty Betty's Gin & Absinthe Bar** (411 W. Morgan St., 4pm-2am daily) in Morgan Street Food Hall for a totally different cocktail experience. Focusing on some flavor-forward spirits that many Americans are just discovering, the cocktails here are fascinating and unreal good. Cocktail mastermind Greg Ewan is a longtime friend, so I always trust him with a dealer's choice (but I have an affinity for both absinthe and gin, so I'm happy to roll the dice), but if you're nervous for a gin- or absinthe-forward drink, they'll help ease you into this new, delicious world of booze.

LGBTQ+ visitors to Raleigh will find a welcome seat at any brewery, bar, or cocktail lounge, but an active and visible LGBTQ+ community will point you in several directions when you're looking for where to go on a night out. One place they'll recommend is **The Green Monkey** (1217 Hillsborough St., 984/200-5682, www.greenmonkeyraleigh.com, noon-9pm Tues. and Thurs., noon-10pm Wed. and Fri.-Sat., 2pm-7pm Sun.), a friendly spot that's open to any and all people regardless of creed, race, pronoun, preference, or "ism," as long as you're nice. They have a big selection of wine and beer and gifts, host events, and get-togethers, and everyone here is as friendly as can be. Other LGBTQ+ hangouts have different vibes. **Legends** (330 W. Hargett St., 919/831-8888, www.legends-club.com, 9pm-3am Fri.-Sat.) is one of the most popular gay and lesbian clubs in the state, a fun bar that is also ground zero for the area's pageant circuit. Call for membership details.

Nearby is **Flex Club** (2 S. West St., 919/832-8855, www.flex-club.com, 7:30pm-1am Tues.-Thurs., 5pm-1am Tues.-Sun., membership $15), which is primarily a men's bar.

Players' Retreat (105 Oberlin Rd., 919/755-9589, www.playersretreat.net, 11:30am-midnight Mon.-Thurs., 11:30am-1am Fri., 11am-1am Sat., 11am-midnight Sun.) has been a favorite Raleigh bar since 1951, which means it's got that local dive feel down pat, probably because that's exactly and unashamedly what it is.

Goodnight's Comedy Club (861 W. Morgan St., 919/828-5233, www.goodnightscomedy.com) has a national reputation as a great place to see major and emerging stand-up comedians.

Breweries and Taprooms

Trophy Brewing Company (www.trophybrewing.com) has a trio of locations in Raleigh, each one serving great beer. Their vibe is fun-loving—they get their name from hundreds of trophies adorning walls and shelves. **Trophy Brewery and Pizza** (827 W. Morgan St., 919/803-4849, 4pm-10pm Mon.-Fri., noon-2am Sat.-Sun., $10-24) makes pizzas almost as good as their beer, which is to say you will want all of it. Seriously, the pies are on point and perfect with their beer, which ranges in style from American pale ales to imperial IPAs to an awesome gose and salted caramel stout (aptly called Milky Way). **Trophy Brewery and Taproom** (665 Maywood Ave., 919/803-1333, 3pm-10pm Mon.-Thurs., noon-midnight Fri.-Sat., noon-10pm Sun.) is the main production facility, and they carry cans, growlers, and flights. Food trucks stop by regularly; it's a fun spot and their beers—like the New England IPA called Sounds of Science and their hefeweizen, Hefe D and the Boys—illustrate their creativity on the menu and the glass.

The **Raleigh Beer Garden** (614 Glenwood Ave., 919/324-3415, www.theraleighbeergarden.com, 11am-2am Mon.-Fri., 10am-2am Sat.-Sun.) isn't just for brews, although they have a world-record-setting number of taps, at 366 and growing; they also have some outstanding food. It's all bar food—wings, pizzas, burgers, and sandwiches—but it's taken to a far tastier place than other bar bites. Of course, the beer is the real star of the show. In the back of the first floor is the North Carolina bar, 144 taps of North Carolina-only brews. Upstairs you'll find the 222 taps of domestic and import craft beer and a few old favorites in the mix for good measure. This place can become a zoo, but you can get here early, stake out a spot, get some beer, have a pizza or two (they're made to share), get another beer, eat some fries, have a final beer, and take a ride-share home, all while enjoying live music and the company of friends.

Neuse River Brewing Company (518 Pershing Rd., 984/232-8479, wwwneuseriverbrewing.com, 5pm-9pm Wed.-Thurs., 4pm-10pm Fri., noon-10pm Sat., noon-9pm Sun., $8-29) sits a little ways out of downtown, but it's worth the few minutes' drive, if not for the beer (totally worth it for the beer) then for the food from their Brasserie (add in the beer, and it's irresistible). As you dine on some fish-and-chips, duck poutine, or steak tartare, enjoy their Belgian brews, IPAs, and experimental quaffs.

I was really impressed by **Clouds Brewing** (www.cloudsbrewing.com) on a brewery tour in Raleigh several year ago, and I've kept an eye out for their name on tap lists ever since. They have a **Tap Room** (1233 Front St., 919/747-4836, 4:30pm-11pm Thurs., 3pm-9pm Fri., 1pm-7pm Sat.) where they cook up all sorts of German- and European-inspired lagers and ales and keep 18 fresh beers on tap (the Belgian Dark and Doppelbock are personal favorites), and **Downtown Restaurant and Tap Room** (126 N. West St., 919/307-8335, noon-9pm Tues., noon-10pm Wed.-Thurs., noon-11pm Fri., 11am-11pm Sat., 11am-8pm Sun., $8-17), where they have more than 40 of their own and area breweries' beers on offer, along with specials like flights paired with Girl Scout cookies and some tasty grub.

At the rate North Carolina keeps adding breweries, it's impossible to keep up with who is where and brewing what, so I lean on two sources for beer-related information, the **North Carolina Brewers Guild** (www.ncbeer.org) and the **NC Beer Guys** (www.ncbeerguys.com). The Brewers Guild is a professional organization and represents members well; the NC Beer Guys are two awesome dudes who travel across the state writing and making videos about breweries (and drinking beer). The other way I keep up with what's going on in Raleigh is with a beer tour from a spot like **City Brew Tours** (984/249-2337, www.citybrewtours.com, $70-99), which leads a pair of tours across the city, making 4-5 stops, plying you with a dozen or more beer samples, some food (even a full meal in the case of the high-end tour), and giving you an idea of what breweries you need to hit one more time before you head home.

Festivals and Events

The 10-day **North Carolina State Fair** (1025 Blue Ridge Rd., 919/821-7400, www.ncstatefair.org), held each October, is the nation's largest agricultural fair, with an annual attendance of about 800,000. Plan on going back several times to take it all in: livestock and produce competitions, big-name bluegrass concerts, carnival rides, fighter-jet flyovers, and lots of deep-fried food.

Raleigh ends the year right with the celebration of **First Night** (919/832-8699, www.firstnightraleigh.com, $16, $12 in advance). From dusk until midnight, when the Raleigh Acorn drops (Raleigh is known as the City of Oaks), downtown stays open on New Year's Eve for a night of home-grown jazz, rock and roll, traditional, country, and blues music at a variety of wonderful venues. First Night also features art exhibits, dance competitions, magic shows, clowns, comedians, circus acrobats, yoga, flue choirs, and fashion shows. Downtown streets, still twinkly with Christmas lights, are closed off to allow for relaxed pedestrian traffic. The First Night Tram offers comfortable transportation among the venues for those who prefer to ride.

May's **Out! Raleigh** (Fayetteville St.,

Jammin'

With fiddlers conventions, renowned symphony orchestras, busy indie-rock scenes, and a thriving gospel-music industry, there is no escaping good music here. Here are a couple of options to catch a great show:

RALEIGH

In September Raleigh is filled with music as the **Hopscotch Music Festival** (various venues, http://hopscotchmusicfest.com, 3-day pass $179, day pass $79-99, single events vary, early Sept.) delivers a genre-rich lineup of artists and the **Wide Open Bluegrass Festival** (Downtown Raleigh, passes $15-140, free lawn admission under age 15, late Sept.) brings hundreds of banjo pickers into the state capitol.

CHAPEL HILL

Chapel Hill-Carrboro is one of the best places to hear live music; a staple is **Cat's Cradle** (300 E. Main St., Carrboro, 919/967-9053, www.catscradle.com), where you can find a new favorite band or rediscover a long-lost musical love.

the Wide Open Bluegrass Festival in Raleigh

DURHAM

Durham is rich in music, with national and international touring acts playing at **Durham Performing Arts Center** (123 Vivian St., 919/680-2787, www.dpacnc.com).

ASHEVILLE

Asheville's a music-loving town if ever there was one, and the music scene revolves around the lauded, almost legendary, **Orange Peel Social Aid and Pleasure Club** (101 Biltmore Ave., Asheville, 828/398-1837, www.theorangepeel.net, noon-midnight or later daily). **Rabbit Rabbit** (75 Coxe Ave., Asheville, 828/255-4077, www.rabbitrabbitavl.com) adds another great venue to Asheville, bringing in an excellent lineup of jam and improvisational music, blues, Americana, hard rock, rap, and more to the mountains.

NORTHERN BLUE RIDGE

In the Northern Blue Ridge you'll find a few great fiddlers conventions, including the **Historic Happy Valley Old-Time Fiddlers Convention** (828/758-9448, www.happyvalleyfiddlers.org, Labor Day weekend) in Caldwell County, the **Bluegrass and Old-Time Fiddlers Convention** (691 W. Lebanon St., 336/488-8774, www.mountairyfiddlersconvention.com, first full weekend in June) in Mount Airy.

downtown Raleigh, 919/832-4484, www.outraleigh.org), a family-friendly festival celebrating the LGBTQ+ community, is a young festival—the first was held in 2011—but one that's growing as Raleigh and the Triangle continue to grow more LGBTQ-friendly. The one-day event features a number of activities for kids as well as concerts and speakers.

Raleigh has two fantastic events for music lovers. The annual **Hopscotch Music Festival** (various venues, http://hopscotch-musicfest.com, 3-day pass $179, day pass

$79-99, single events vary) brings more than 150 bands into downtown Raleigh for a three-day extravaganza. Expect street parties, outdoor and indoor concerts, impromptu jams, odd collaborations, and all sorts of nuttiness at this early-September gathering.

In late September, the **Wide Open Bluegrass Festival** (various location in Downtown Raleigh, http://wideopenbluegrass.com, passes $15-140, free lawn admission under age 15), the official fan festival for the International Bluegrass Music Association (IBMA), has a number of top-shelf bluegrass musicians playing around town in front of crowds large and small. There are a number of free concerts on Fayetteville Street, but larger acts perform at the Red Hat Amphitheater.

SPARKcon (www.sparkcon.com), also held in September, is the city's celebration of creativity. There are dance troupes, talks, and activities centered around comedy and poetry. You can get with circus folk, fashion folk, or filmmakers and pretty much find like-minded creative people engaged in whatever endeavor you're currently exploring.

Artsplosure (www.raleighartsfestival.com) celebrates Raleigh's arts in all shapes and forms. Held in May, this event has been growing every year since it began in 1980. Today it features a large marketplace, interactive art installations, exhibitions by students, and music and dance performances.

SHOPPING

The **Village District** (Oberlin Rd. between Hillsborough St. and Wade Ave., 919/821-1350, www.shopcameronvillage.com) was one of the earliest shopping centers in the Southeast. Formerly known as Cameron Village and built on the site of a onetime plantation, they changed their name in an effort to move away from its unpleasant past. The complex opened with three stores, but today there are exponentially more than that. It tends toward independent boutiques and high-end chains and is a fun place to splurge.

Some of the notable shops are **Great Outdoor Provision Company** (2017 Cameron St., 919/833-1741, http://greatoutdoorprovision.com, 10am-6pm Mon.-Sat., noon-5pm Sun.), a favorite outdoor-gear retailer; **Ivy & Leo** (2010 Cameron St., 919/821-7899, www.ivyandleo.com, 10am-7pm Mon.-Sat., noon-5pm Sun.), a fun boutique that brings in top styles, much to the delight of Raleigh's fashionistas; and **Cheshire Cat Antique Gallery** (2050 Clark Ave., 919/835-9595, https://cheshirecatgallery.org, 10am-5pm Mon.-Sat., 1pm-5pm Sun.) has a selection of antiques and estate pieces including jewelry, clothing and home decor; but wander around, there's plenty more to find here.

The 1914 **City Market** (215 Wolfe St., 919/232-8661, www.citymarketraleigh.com, hours vary by vendor) complex is another collection of nifty little shops and restaurants in a historic setting. **Lafayette Village** (8450 Honeycutt Rd., 919/714-7447, https://lafayettevillageraleigh.com) is a six-acre outdoor shopping center built to look like the winding streets and central courtyard plaza of a European village. Indeed, window shopping here is reminiscent of quaint little French or German villages, and their shops and restaurants offer an array of gifts and sundries in the boutiques, and tasty bites for any meal in the restaurants. **North Hills** (4321 Lassiter Mill Rd., at North Hills Ave., 919/369-4089, https://visitnorthhills.com) is a popular outdoor shopping center with a variety of shops and restaurants, a small green space for kids to play, and a movie theater. There's an REI outdoor gear shop, a number of clothing boutiques and jewelers, several good restaurants, a Starbucks, and a Ben and Jerry's ice cream shop. Park underground for an easy spot out of the weather.

Two of my favorite independent bookstores in North Carolina are in the Triangle. **Quail Ridge Books** (North Hills, 4321 Lassiter Mill Rd., at North Hills Ave., 919/828-1588, www.quailridgebooks.com, 10am-9pm Mon.-Sat., 10am-6pm Sun.) carries a solid selection of popular fiction and nonfiction and an especially nice selection of regional writers; they also host readings and events on a regular basis, giving you the chance to get to know some of the authors they carry. **Page 158 Books** (415 S. Brooks St., Wake Forest, 919/435-1843, www.page158books.com, 11am-6pm Mon.-Sat., 1pm-5pm Sun.) serves the nearby town of Wake Forest a similar platter of best-sellers as well as local and regional authors; like any good bookstore, they host readings and events like the two-day Wake Forest Lit Fest in mid-October where there are readings, workshops, and book signings.

I like checking out an antique shop, flea market, or vintage store when I'm in a new town, and even if I make a trip to Raleigh for the day, I end up exploring for some dusty treasures. **Father & Son Antiques** (302 S. West St., 919/832-3030, www.fatherandson-raleigh.com, noon-6pm Wed.-Sat., 1pm-5pm Sun.) is a longtime favorite here. More than 10,000 square feet of vintage clothing and accessories, weird records and books, cool modern furniture, and all sorts of knickknacks and goodies will keep you busy for a while. **Raleigh Flea Market** (1025 Blue Ridge Rd., 919/899-3532, www.raleighfleamarket. net, 9am-6pm Sat.-Sun.), held at the North Carolina State Fairgrounds, is a bazaar packed with everything from antiques to strange art to furniture. On every visit I've found something weird, something cool, and something totally unexpected.

FOOD
Eclectic

★ **Crawford & Son** (618 N. Pearson St., 919/307-4647, www.crawfordandsonrestaurant.com, 5pm-10pm Tues.-Sat., $15-30), from chef Scott Crawford, is the kind of dining I love: The food's accessible but impeccable, drinks are creative without sacrificing on flavor or technique, and the vibe is just right—jacket and no tie, you're fine; nice T-shirt and jeans, you're fine—and the focus is what's on the plate. Chef Crawford has the rare ability to elicit as much flavor and potential out of each ingredient as possible but not intrude on the identity of each component. Order the

seasonal vegetables, fresh catch, any chicken dish, or anything, really, and you'll go home happy.

I'd be remiss if I didn't mention a favorite—and deservedly so—steakhouse, **The Angus Barn** (9401 Glenwood Ave., 919/781-2444, www.angusbarn.com, 5pm-10pm Mon.-Fri., 4pm-10pm Sat., 5pm-10pm Sun., $20-107). This place serves around 20,000 steaks a month and the wine list has racked up numerous awards. Chef Walter Royal won his appearance on TV's *Iron Chef America,* so you can only imagine what he can do in his home kitchen.

Cameron Bar & Grill (2018 Clarke Ave., 919/755-2231, www.cameronbarandgrill. com, 11am-10pm Mon.-Wed., 11am-midnight Thurs.-Sat., 10am-10pm Sun., $9-20) serves dishes that are simpler but no less delicious. This place has burgers and chicken sandwiches that are topped with everything from an over-medium egg to pickled fried green tomato to ghost pepper jack cheese.

Vegetarians, vegans, and those inclined to give up meat for a meal or two will like **The Fiction Kitchen** (428 S. Dawson St., 919/831-4177, www.thefictionkitchen.com, 4:30pm-9pm Wed.-Sat., $12-20). Like every good North Carolina restaurant, they have barbecue on the menu—sure, it's pulled "pork," not pulled pork, but the sauce is spot on. They also make a curry that's big on flavor and is vegan, gluten free, and served as spicy as you want. Many rave over the NC Peanut Noodle Bowl, loaded with shiitake mushrooms and in-season veggies and topped with peanuts.

Earth to Us (2893 Jones Franklin Rd., 919/809-8622, www.shopearthtous.com, 11am-8pm Thurs., 11am-9pm Fri.-Sat., 11am-5pm Sun., $11-17), which also has a location in Durham, specializes in American and Latin American comfort food with a vegan twist. You'll find an arepa stuffed with barbecued seitan, soy-free tempeh empanadas, Beyond Burgers on pretzel buns, barbacoa-style tempeh, mock chicken and rice, and more on this mouth-watering menu.

The dozen eateries at Raleigh's first food hall, **Morgan Street Food Hall** (411 W. Morgan St., 919/307-4481, www.morgan-foodhall.com, 9am-10pm Sun.-Thurs., 9am-midnight Fri.-Sat.), represent the range of the city's food scene all under one roof and carries with it a bit of nighttime college energy. **CowBar Burgers & Fries** ($4-16) serves some of the best burgers I've ever eaten, and with secret burgers adding to the selection, it's a can't miss. Get some french fries *con todo*—that's "with everything"—from **Buena Papa Fry Bar** ($12-15) where the menus is simple: baskets of fries heaped with delicious toppings. **Iyla's Southern Kitchen** (919/758-8369, $8-15) serves Southern food that's as interesting as it is tasty; the BBQ Sundae features mac-and-cheese with a pile of barbecue and slaw on top, and the chicken and waffle sandwich is a perfect combo. My favorite (it changes all the time) may be **Curry in a Hurry** ($7-14), an Indian food truck that's added this brick-and-mortar location; it's spicy, rich, delicious, and on point.

The second food hall in the city has a more relaxed vibe and a great slate of places to eat. ★ **Transfer Co. Food Hall** (500 E. Davie St., 984/232-8122, www.transfercofoodhall.com), on the other side of downtown, has an outpost from Asheville's **Burial Beer** (www.burialbeer.com, 2pm-10pm Mon.-Thurs., noon-10pm Fri.-Sat., noon-8pm Sun.) with two dozen taps full of Burial's flagship and experimental brews, along with 10 more options for places to grab a bite. Grab the best bagel in town from **Benchwarmer Bagels and Coffee** (www.benchwarmersbagels.com, 7am-2pm Tues.-Fri., 8am-2pm Sat.-Sun., 5pm-8pm Thurs.-Sat., $2-12). Seriously, their smoked fish spread on a bagel is unmatched. **Che Empanadas** (919/360-3356, www.cheempanadas.com, 10am-5pm Mon., 11am-5pm Tues.-Sat., 11am-7pm Sun., $3-3.50) brings a tasty bite of Argentina to Transfer, and **Chhote's** (919/390-1652, 11am-9pm Sun.-Thurs., 11am-10pm Fri.-Sat., $6-15) Indian street food delivers rich flavors from the streets of Mumbai to the streets of Raleigh. Satisfy your sweet tooth with a humongous cookie from **Captain Cookie & The Milkman** (919/909-6965, www.captaincookienc.com, 11am-9pm Wed.-Sat., 11am-8pm Sun., $1.50-15).

For fabulous Latin cuisine, **Centro** (106 S. Wilmington St., 919/835-3593, www.centroraleigh.com, 5pm-10pm Wed.-Sat., $13-20) delivers, and not with expected dishes. Fish tacos are made with fried salmon and sweet *pico de gallo*, the mole poblano turns a chicken breast into something luxurious, and the tacos del sur are loaded with fried chicken and spice.

Asian

One of Raleigh's culinary superstars, Chef Cheetie Kumar dishes up flavors of India and Asia at ★ **Garland** (14 W. Martin St., 919/833-6886, https://garlandraleigh.com, 5pm-9pm Wed.-Thurs., 5pm-9:30pm Fri.-Sat., $15-34), the downtown restaurant she co-owns with husband and bandmate Paul Siler. Chef Kumar isn't just a rock star in the kitchen, she's got chops on stage, but her passions led her to cook full time and perform when she can, which should make our stomachs happy but make our ears a little sad. The menu has sharing and large plates, and whether you're going for a Szechuan-glazed pork belly, the roasted brussels sprouts, a platter of braised biscuit, ghee-grilled lamb chops, or the vegetarian-friendly veggie sambar, you're in for a meal you'll write home about.

Waraji Japanese Restaurant (5910 Duraleigh Rd., 919/783-1883, www.warajijapaneserestaurant.com, 11:30am-2pm Tues.-Fri., noon-2pm Sun., 5pm-9:30pm Tues.-Sat., 5:30pm-10pm Fri.-Sat., 5pm-9pm Sun., $11-39) occupies a very spare storefront in a strip mall, belying the uniqueness of this very serious sushi restaurant. Dozens of traditional and imaginative specialty rolls are served, along with tempura, *udon,* and other Japanese entrées. **Sono** (319 Fayetteville St., Suite 101, 919/521-5328, www.sonoraleigh.com, 11am-2pm Mon.-Fri., 5pm-10pm Sun.-Thurs., 5pm-11pm Fri.-Sat., $10-70) makes many original

sushi rolls as well as bento and noodle dishes along with a seven-course meal.

French & Italian

In nearby Cary, **La Farm Bakery** (4248 NW Cary Pkwy., Cary, 919/657-0657, www.lafarm-bakery.com, 7am-6pm Mon.-Sat., 8am-4pm Sun., $7-14) makes the best bread I've ever eaten. Like any bakery, their baking schedule varies (check online), but standards include pain au chocolat, mini baguettes with white chocolate chips, and a several hearty loaves and boules (they have 15 loaves in the regular rotation, with another 20 making seasonal appearances, so eat up). On the café side, it's all traditional French—croque madame, eggs florentine with smoky mornay sauce, that sort of thing. La Farm is a boulangerie more than a bakery, and owner and master baker Lionel Vatinet is a member of the prestigious French artisans guild Les Compagnons du Devoir.

Chef Scott Crawford has brough the French bistro experience to downtown Raleigh with ★ **Jolie** (620 N. Person St., 919/803-7221, 5pm-10pm Tues.-Sat., $14-32), right around the corner from Crawford & Son. It's a French menu through and through, with steak frites, chicken confit, and trout amandine as always-on-the-menu main courses; and mussels, escargot, foie gras, chicken liver pâté, onion soup, and exceptional macarons rounding out the meal. Make a reservation, and if the weather's nice, make sure your space is on Le Rooftop, their rooftop patio.

The pastas at **Mulino Italian Kitchen & Bar** (309 N. Dawson St., 919/838-8595, www.mulinoraleigh.com, 5pm-10pm Tues.-Sat., 4pm-9pm Sun., bar open late, $18-28) are almost as good as the setting. This gorgeous restaurant has plenty of outdoor seating (if the weather's good, grab a table by the pool) where you can enjoy plates of fresh pasta, wood-fired pizza, and upscale spins on Italian dishes. The spaghetti carbonara is particularly good, as is the gnocchi *tartufo*.

Lilly's Pizza (1813 Glenwood Ave., 919/833-0226, www.lillyspizza.com, 11am-9pm Sun.-Thurs., 11am-10pm Fri.-Sat., $8-26) is a locally owned one-of-a-kind parlor that's been around for more than 15 years. They use lots of organic, local ingredients, even in the homemade crusts. You can choose favorite ingredients for a custom pie or have an equally tasty calzone, stromboli, or lasagna.

Middle Eastern

More than 30 years ago, **Neomonde Baking Company** (3817 Beryl Rd., 919/828-1628, www.neomonde.com, 11am-8pm daily, under $13) was founded in Raleigh by four brothers who had just emigrated from Lebanon. The superior quality of the baked-on-site bread is because the brothers grew up in a family that made bread from scratch—starting not with the flour but with planting a wheat field. Many favorite and less familiar Middle Eastern snacks and sandwiches are on the menu.

Sitti (137 S. Wilmington St., 919/239-4070, www.sitti-raleigh.com, 11am-9pm Sun.-Thurs., 11am-10pm Fri.-Sat., $12-25) derives its name from the affectionate Lebanese nickname for grandmothers, and its food also draws from Lebanese family traditions. Chef Ghassan Jarrouj prepares old family recipes as well as specialties he has developed during his 30-year career, which included jobs as chef for three U.S. ambassadors to Lebanon. The menu includes kebabs, hearty stews, and special chef's creations such as pan-seared sea bass.

Barbecue and Comfort Food

One of my favorite pit masters in all of North Carolina opened up an outpost of his popular barbecue joint here in Raleigh. ★ **Sam Jones BBQ** (502 W. Lenoir St., 984/206-2555, www.samjonesbbq.com, 11am-9pm Mon.-Sat., 11am-8:30pm Sun., $12-22) brings the legendary Jones family whole-hog barbecue to hungry diners here, giving them a sample of what true barbecue tastes like. Sandwiches, trays and platters of chopped barbecue, catfish bites and sandwiches, smoked chicken,

---

1: Morgan Street Food Hall **2:** a travel writer's working lunch at Transfer Co. Food Hall

and the 1947 Burger (made the way they originally were served at Skylight Inn, the family's legendary and James Beard Award-winning restaurant) make this place a hard one to stay away from.

It's not much to look at, and it's just hot dogs, but **Roast Grill** (7 S. West St., 919/832-8292, 11am-4pm Mon.-Sat., under $2.50), has been a Raleigh landmark since 1940. You can get a hot dog blackened to your specifications, chili, a glass-bottle Coke or beer, pound cake, and baklava, and that's all—unless the Christmas parade is going by outside, in which case you may also get hot chocolate or coffee. Don't ask for condiments; they admonish customers with "A word of warning: We do not serve French fries, potato chips, ketchup, cheese, kraut, pickles, relish, or mayonnaise. We feel them to be terribly unnecessary and truly demeaning to the passions of a great hot dog connoisseur."

When Ashley Christensen opened her first restaurant, ★ **Poole's Diner** (426 S. McDowell St., 919/832-4477, www.ac-restaurants.com, 5pm-9pm Sun.-Mon. and Thurs., 5pm-10pm Fri.-Sat., $12-30) in 2007, she gained the attention of the food community, appearing on TV's *Iron Chef America,* getting write-ups in major food magazines, and racking up several James Beard Award nominations for "Best Chef: Southeast." The menu at Poole's changes daily, but it's always loaded with fine North Carolina goods. ★ **Beasley's Chicken + Honey** (237 S. Wilmington St., 919/322-0127, www.ac-restaurants.com, dine-in 5pm-9pm Thurs.-Fri., 11:30am-9pm Sat., 110:30am-3pm Sun., takeout 11:30am-8pm Mon. and Thurs., 11:30am-5pm Fri., 3pm-9pm Sat., 3pm-8pm Sun., $8-17) makes some fabulous fried chicken. The biscuits are crazy good. Purists will want the quarter fried chicken, but those with a nose for unusual (but still classic) Southern dishes will want the fried chicken served over a waffle, smothered in honey.

Food Trucks

Augmenting all of Raleigh's fantastic restaurants is a fleet of food trucks. Events like the **Downtown Raleigh Food Truck Rodeo** (http://downtownraleighfoodtruckrodeo.com), held throughout the year on Fayetteville Street, bring as many as 50 food trucks from across the Triangle into one street-party smorgasbord. You'll find killer food trucks at the Rodeo, and at spots across town just about any time of day, and for a huge list of food trucks, go to **Triangle Food Trucks** (https://raleighfoodtrucks.org).

El Rey del Taco (901 Hodges St. 6pm-midnight Fri.-Sat. and 5pm-10pm Sun., 919/908-4665, http://elreydeltaconc.co, $2.50-10) serves Oaxacan-style tacos and tortas in an established spot on weekends. The Lithuanian food truck (they claim to the be the first in the nation, and who am I to doubt that?) **Baltic Bites** (919/413-6586, https://balticbites.net, $7-12) serves goulash, smoked sausage, chicken kebabs, and other flavors from Baltic Europe.

Can you guess what **Mr. Cheesesteak** (919/747-1730, https://mrcheesesteak.com, $6-10) sells? It's cheesesteak, and many say they're the best in the city. And **Safari Eatz** (919/332-7696, www.safarieatz.com, $4-17) is Afro-inspired Kenyan and East African street food and barbecue; beef and chicken kebabs, tacos topped with veggies or meat and plenty of Kenyan spices, and samosas make some unfamiliar ingredients welcoming and tempting.

Bakeries

Raleigh bakeries we love include **lucettegrace** (235 Salisbury St., 919/307-4950, www.lucettegrace.com, 8am-7pm Tues.-Fri., 9am-4pm Sat., $3-14), located downtown. The macarons are quite the treat, but their Dixie Cannonball—a drop biscuit imbued with smoked cheddar and breakfast sausage, then filled with sausage gravy—is a singular experience. The shortbread ducks at **Groovy Duck Bakery** (3434 Edwards Mill Rd., Suite 110, 919/787-9233, www.groovyduckbakeryllc.com, 8am-6pm Mon.-Sat., $2-10) are pretty groovy, but we like their muffins (with flavors like mojito, cinnabuf-fin, and gingerbread, how can you not?).

New to the Raleigh food scene, **Union Special** (919/200-3064, www.unionspecia-bread.com) has impressed me with the food and the social responsibility they exhibit as a company. Their loud and ever-present voice in supporting the Black Lives Matter movement, immigrant and LBGTQ+ rights, and other issues impacting the community makes me feel good about spending my money here. And when you consider that I have yet to eat a disappointing bite, it's the kind of place I'll patronize as often as possible. Their **Downtown Raleigh** (401 Fayetteville St., Suite 103, 7:30am-3pm Mon.-Fri., $3-12) location has breakfast, lunch, and baked goods (the hot ham sandwich and the classic club are great). And their **Gateway Plaza** (2409 Crabtree Blvd., Suite 102, 8am-3pm daily, $3-14) spot, just outside of downtown, adds brunch to the mix (try the seasonal salad and Grown Up Grilled Cheese—it's super cheesy and super delish).

ACCOMMODATIONS

Although many other cities in North Carolina have small nonchain and boutique hotels, Raleigh is still catching up. There are dozens of chain motels around the city, concentrated near the airport, downtown, and at various exits off I-40 and U.S. 70.

If you don't need to stay inside the city limits and are craving some pampering, ★ **Umstead Luxury Hotel and Spa** (100 Woodland Pond, Cary, 919/447-4000 or 866/877-4141, www.theumstead.com, from $369) in Cary has a 14,000-square-foot spa with a large menu of services: 10 different specialized massages; facial, man-icure, and pedicure choices; and a long list of body therapies and Asian body-care rit-uals. There's also a three-acre lake on the property, a 24-hour fitness center, and an outdoor heated pool. Guests have tee priv-ileges at the Prestonwood Country Club, about 10 minutes away. Don't overlook the on-site spa; it's one of the best in the state.

Dining at **Herons** (919/447-4200, 7am-10am and 11:30am-2pm Mon.-Fri., 7am-1pm Sat.-Sun., 5pm-9pm Tues.-Sat., reservations ad-vised, business casual dress code, $8-36) is an exquisite experience, especially at dinner. Dinner is a four-course ($130, wine pairing $90), affair that is simply spectacular, in-cluding desserts that are good enough to enjoy in a multicourse dessert bacchanal all on their own.

★ **Aloft Raleigh Hotel** (2100 Hillsborough St., 919/828-9900, www.thealoftraleigh.com, from $190) has a prime location right across from North Carolina State University, and it's a sleek, upscale spot with 135 rooms, the Aloft's signature WXYZ Bar, and a pool (open seasonally). Dine at the Aloft outpost of local favorite **Gonza Tacos y Tequila** (919/268-8965, www.gonsatacosytequila.com, 5pm-8:30pm Tues.-Sat., $8-20) on ceviche, *sopes*, fish or vegetarian or chicken *tinga* tacos, chiles rellenos, *chilaquiles verdes,* and more. It's one more thing making this a great home base while you're in town.

The Longleaf Hotel (300 N. Dawson St., 919/867-5770, www.thelongleafhotel.com, from $165), named for our state tree, is a yes-teryear motor lodge turned boutique hotel. Updated enough to give it a modern look, feel, and a bit of contemporary comfort, but not so much that it's unrecognizable as the gem it is, this hip spot is near Mulino, an awesome Italian restaurant, and all that downtown has to offer.

In Raleigh's Warehouse and Glenwood South Districts, just a couple of blocks from the Amtrak station, **Origin Hotel** (603 W. Morgan St., 984/275-2220, www.originho-tel.com, from $189) offers modern design in a spot walkable to downtown attractions. Brand-new in 2022, it's a gorgeous prop-erty and will be for years to come. Another newcomer on Raleigh's lodgings is the beau-tiful and bucolic boutique hotel **Heights House** (308 S. Boylan Ave., 919/594-1881, www.heightshousenc.com, from $254). This Italianate-style home was built in 1860, and the architectural charm—high ceilings, huge windows, the elegant parlor—remain, but modern luxurious showers, free-to-use bikes, a fitness center, Bluetooth speakers, and a European-style continental breakfast make it a must-stay in Raleigh.

Downtown chain choices tend to be more expensive than chain lodgings beyond the I-440 Beltline, many of which are near the airport on I-40. The **Sheraton Raleigh** (421 S. Salisbury St., 919/834-9900, www.sheratonraleigh.com, from $166) is in a good location to explore the city. The **Double Tree by Hilton Hotel Raleigh Brownstone-University** (1707 Hillsborough St., 919/828-0811, www.hilton.com, from $140) is convenient to both downtown and North Carolina State University.

INFORMATION AND SERVICES

The main hospital in Raleigh is **WakeMed** (3000 New Bern Ave., 919/350-8000), although Rex Healthcare and Duke Health also operate hospitals. If you have an emergency, call 911.

Visitor information can be found at the **Greater Raleigh Convention and Visitors Bureau** (Bank of America Plaza, 421 Fayetteville St., 800/849-8499, www.visitraleigh.com), the **Greater Raleigh Chamber of Commerce** (800 S. Salisbury St., 919/664-7000, www.raleighchamber.org), and the state's visitor's bureau, **Visit NC** (800/847-4862, www.visitnc.com). For international travelers who need to exchange currency, Raleigh-Durham Airport has **TRAVELEX outlets** (919/840-3366, Terminal 2 ticketing lobby 7am-8pm daily, Terminal 2 baggage claim 3pm-5pm daily).

GETTING THERE AND AROUND

I-40 and U.S. 70 are the main highways to and through town. The Raleigh Beltline, I-440, forms a ring around the city, with I-40, U.S. 70, and U.S. 64 radiating outward. I-40 is the quickest route west to Chapel Hill and east to I-95. I-40 and U.S. 70 are both good routes to Durham. U.S. 64 goes to Wilson, and on the other side of the city joins U.S. 1 headed southeast toward Sanford and the Sandhills.

Raleigh-Durham International Airport (RDU, 2400 John Brantley Blvd., Morrisville, 919/840-2123, www.rdu.com) is the primary airport in the Triangle and one of the main airports in the state. It's located 15 minutes northwest of Raleigh along I-40 and is a hub for major national airlines. **Amtrak** (800/872-7245, www.amtrak.com) has Raleigh's Union Station (510 W. Martin St.) and a station in neighboring Cary (211 N. Academy St., Cary) served by several trains daily on regional routes and long-haul trains between New York City and Miami.

Raleigh's **GoRaleigh** (919/485-7433, www.raleighnc.gov, fare $1.25 single ride, $2.50 day pass, $12 weekly pass, $40 monthly pass) system runs buses all over the city, both inside and outside the Beltline, and connects to major transportation hubs. Many taxi and car services are available, including **Taxi Taxi** (919/333-3333, www.taxitaxiofraleigh.com, around $48 to Raleigh or Durham). Rideshare services are easy and abundant.

Durham

Home of Duke University and North Carolina Central University, Durham hosts several major arts festivals, most notably the Full-Frame Documentary Festival, the American Dance Festival, and the North Carolina Gay and Lesbian Film Festival, that bring in tens of thousands of visitors every year. Duke University's famous Blue Devils are one of the nation's dominant college basketball teams, and Central's Eagles are a football powerhouse. There's a great deal of literary activity here too, with a wide variety of bookstores and many excellent writers at the city's universities publishing both academic and creative works.

Formerly abuzz with cigarette-rolling factories, Durham has met the demise of the tobacco industry, to which it owes its existence, gracefully. Many of the long brick warehouses, formerly factories for Lorillard, Winston, and American Tobacco, have been transformed into attractive restaurants and public venues. The American Tobacco Historic District ensures that the city's golden-leaved origins won't be forgotten.

Durham is also an important center of urban African American heritage. In the early 20th century it was called the capital of Black middle-class people. North Carolina Central University is a historically African American school, and although it's often overshadowed by nearby Duke, the University of North Carolina, and North Carolina State, it is one of the state's major educational institutions. Next to Central's campus is Hayti, a neighborhood where African Americans maintained a bustling commercial district during the era of segregation. Blind Boy Fuller, Reverend Gary Davis, and other Carolina blues legends did stints here as street performers, and a historical marker next to the Hayti Heritage Center commemorates their time in Durham.

★ DUKE UNIVERSITY

Duke University (www.duke.edu) is often considered a sort of Southern Ivy League school, and its students are among the academic elite in the country. The architecture of the Duke campus—much of it designed by turn-of-the-20th-century African American architect Julian Abele—is done up in dark Gothic stonework and feels like it could be in the Northeast. Originally called Trinity College and located in Randolph County, it came to Durham and became Duke University under the patronage of the Duke family, tobacco barons who were responsible for, among other things, the university's early policy of enrolling women. It continues to be a leading light in the world of academia.

Duke's **Center for Documentary Studies** (1317 W. Pettigrew St., 919/660-3663, http://documentarystudies.duke.edu, gallery 9am-7pm Mon.-Thurs., 9am-5pm Fri.-Sat.) is an invaluable resource for artists, documentarians, and educators throughout the region as well as a fascinating place to visit when you're in town. Occupying the Lyndhurst House, a handsome old home on Pettigrew Street within easy walking distance of the 9th Street shops and restaurants, CDS includes a gallery, teaching facilities, and extensive darkrooms and labs. The gallery showcases documentary screenings and cutting-edge photography and multimedia work and makes a fun stop for anyone intrigued by today's documentary renaissance.

The Nasher Museum of Art (2001 Campus Dr., 919/684-5135, www.nasher.duke.edu, 10am-5pm Tues.-Wed. and Fri.-Sat., 10am-9pm Thurs., noon-5pm Sun., free) is home to extensive collections of ancient and medieval art, including one of the largest collections of pre-Columbian Latin American art in the United States. The building is a stunningly modern creation by architect

Durham

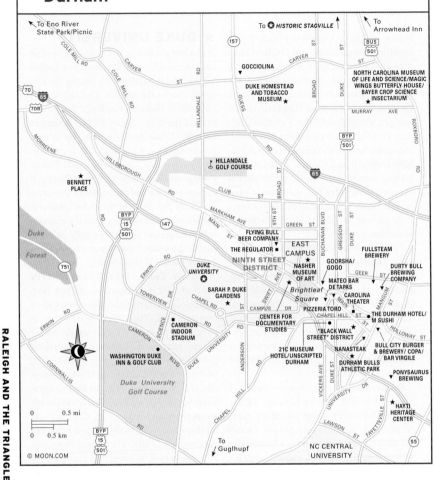

To Eno River State Park/Picnic

To ⊙ HISTORIC STAGVILLE

To Arrowhead Inn

COLE MILL RD

CARVER

ST

COLE MILL RD

70

85

70B

MORREENE RD

HILLSBOROUGH RD

BENNETT PLACE ★

Duke Forest

751

HILLANDALE DR

GUESS RD

GOCCIOLINA ▼

DUKE HOMESTEAD AND TOBACCO MUSEUM ★

157

CARVER ST

ST

BROAD RD

RD

DUKE ST

BUS 501

NORTH CAROLINA MUSEUM OF LIFE AND SCIENCE/MAGIC WINGS BUTTERFLY HOUSE/ BAYER CROP SCIENCE ★ INSECTARIUM

MURRAY AVE

ROXBORO RD

BYP 501

HILLANDALE GOLF COURSE ♦

CLUB ST

BROAD ST

85

RD

BYP 15 501

147

MARKHAM AVE

MAIN ST

RD

9TH ST

GREEN ST

FLYING BULL BEER COMPANY ■

THE REGULATOR ■

EAST CAMPUS

BUCHANAN BLVD

GREGSON ST

DUKE ST

FULLSTEAM BREWERY

ERWIN RD

DUKE UNIVERSITY ✪

NINTH STREET DISTRICT

NASHER MUSEUM OF ART ★

GOORSHA/ GOGO ●

GEER ST

DURTY BULL BREWING COMPANY

TOWERVIEW DR

CHAPEL RD

SARAH P. DUKE GARDENS ★

SWIFT AVE

Brightleaf Square ▼

MATEO BAR DE TAPAS ▼

CAROLINA THEATER

MANGUM ST

ERWIN RD

SCIENCE DR

CAMERON INDOOR STADIUM ■

CAMPUS DR

CAMERON BLVD

PIZZERIA TORO ▼

CHAPEL HILL ST

THE DURHAM HOTEL/ ● M SUSHI

CENTER FOR DOCUMENTARY STUDIES ●

UNIVERSITY RD

"BLACK WALL STREET" DISTRICT ★

HOLLOWAY ST

WASHINGTON DUKE INN & GOLF CLUB ●

Duke University Golf Course

CORNWALLIS

ANDERSON ST

21C MUSEUM HOTEL/UNSCRIPTED DURHAM ●

NANASTEAK ★

DURHAM BULLS ATHLETIC PARK

DUKE ST

VICKERS AVE

BULL CITY BURGER & BREWERY/ COPA/ BAR VIRGILE

PONYSAURUS ▼ BREWING

UNIVERSITY DR

CHAPEL HILL RD

LAWSON ST

FAYETTEVILLE ST

HAYTI ▼ HERITAGE CENTER

0   0.5 mi
0   0.5 km

BYP 15 501

To Guglhupf

NC CENTRAL UNIVERSITY

55

© MOON.COM

Rafael Viñoly. Adjoining the grounds of the Nasher are the **Sarah P. Duke Gardens** (420 Anderson St., 919/684-3698, http://gardens. duke.edu, 8am-dusk daily, free), 55 acres of some of the finest landscaping and horticultural arts to be seen in the Southeast.

NORTH CAROLINA CENTRAL UNIVERSITY

North Carolina Central University (www. nccu.edu) was founded in 1910, the first public liberal arts college for African Americans in

the United States. Central is one of the state's great universities, rivaling Duke, its much larger neighbor, in significance. The **North Carolina Central University Art Museum** (Lawson St., NCCU campus, between Fine Arts Bldg. and Music Bldg., 919/530-6211, www.nccu.edu, 9am-4:30pm Tues.-Fri., 2pm-4pm Sun., free) specializes in the work of 19th- and 20th-century African American artists. The collections include work by such prominent masters as Romare Bearden, Jacob Lawrence, Henry Ossawa Tanner, Minnie

Evans, and Nelson Mandela. Inside the William Jones Building on Central's campus is a display of Durham's **Woolworth Lunch Counter,** site of a 1960 sit-in attended by Martin Luther King Jr. that signaled a sea change in the civil rights movement.

AFRICAN AMERICAN HERITAGE SIGHTS

Sites of importance in African American history are found throughout Durham. **St. Joseph's Performance Hall** and the **Hayti Heritage Center** (804 Old Fayetteville St., 919/683-1709, www.hayti.org) celebrate the historic African American community of Hayti—pronounced "HAY-tye," to rhyme with "necktie." The former St. Joseph's AME Church sanctuary is a special venue for the performing arts in Durham, and the Heritage Center houses an art gallery, a dance studio, and a community meeting space. Also on Fayetteville Street is **White Rock Baptist Church** (3400 Fayetteville St., 919/688-8136, www.whiterockbaptistchurch.org), home of a congregation founded in 1866. Martin Luther King Jr. spoke here in 1960 after participating in the Woolworth sit-in.

The neoclassical revival-style **Mechanics and Farmers Bank Building** (116 W. Parrish St., 919/687-7803, 9am-5pm Mon.-Thurs., 9am-6pm Fri.) stands at the heart of a downtown district known in the early 20th century as **Black Wall Street.** Mechanics and Farmers Bank and "the Mutual" were the flagships of Durham's African American commercial establishment.

★ Historic Stagville

About 15 minutes' drive north of downtown Durham, **Historic Stagville** (5828 Old Oxford Hwy., 919/620-0120, www.stagville. org, 9am-5pm Tues.-Sat., tours 1pm Tues.-Fri., 11am, 1pm, and 3pm Sat.) preserves part of what was a staggeringly large plantation system. In 1860 the Cameron-Bennehan family's holdings totaled nearly 30,000 acres, and the 900 enslaved African Americans who worked the land were one of the South's largest enslaved communities. Historic Stagville includes 71 acres of the original plantations, with several notable vernacular structures, including a two-story timber-frame building as housing for the enslaved people on the property, a massive hipped-roof barn built in 1860, and the late-18th-century Bennehan plantation house. One of the main events on Stagville's calendar is its **Juneteenth Celebration,** an event celebrated in parts of the South for generations that marks the emancipation of enslaved African Americans at the end of the Civil War. Stagville's Juneteenth features music, food, crafts, and interpretation by costumed guides.

OTHER SIGHTS

A different side of 19th-century Durham life is presented at the **Duke Homestead and Tobacco Museum** (2828 Duke Homestead Rd., 919/627-6990, www.dukehomestead. org, usually 9am-5pm Tues.-Sat., free). Here the patriarch of Durham's tobacco industry, Washington Duke, began his career as a humble tobacco farmer. Discovering the popularity of bright-leaf tobacco among Union soldiers at the end of the Civil War, he began processing large quantities of it. This was the beginning of North Carolina's quick rise to the top of the world tobacco market, an economy that transformed the state and built the city of Durham. The Duke Homestead displays and demonstrates period techniques in tobacco culture throughout the year.

Celebrating Durham's tobacco past is the **American Tobacco Historic Campus** (Willard St. and Julian Carr St., https://americantobacco.co). This huge facility was once the home to a processing, manufacturing, and packaging plant for Lucky Strike Cigarettes, among other brands, but through some clever adaptive architectural reuse (a practice for which Durham is known), it was converted into a community hub. Now concerts and events are held on the lawn in the shadow of that Lucky Strike water tower and chimney. Where tobacco was once milled and rolled into cigarettes, offices, meeting spaces, restaurants, and businesses like Burt's Bees now make their headquarters. North Carolina Public Radio station WUNC broadcasts from here, Durham's Full Frame Documentary Film Festival has its headquarters in one of the buildings on campus, and several restaurants are open for business; there's even American Underground, an entrepreneurial incubator space, occupying the basement of one of the largest buildings here. Across the street, the Durham Bulls Athletic Park and Durham Performing Arts Center are part of the Historic Tobacco District, and as you walk around town, you'll spot relics of the city's tobacco past everywhere you look.

Bennett Place (4409 Bennett Memorial Rd., 919/383-4345, www.bennettplacehistoricsite.com, 9am-5pm Tues.-Sat., free) commemorates the meeting of Confederate General Joseph Johnston and Union General William Tecumseh Sherman in April 1865. In the last days of the Civil War, when Jefferson Davis was fleeing south to Georgia and Abraham Lincoln was dead, Johnston and Sherman held a series of negotiations here that led to the surrender of all the Confederate forces in the Carolinas, Georgia, and Florida; it was the largest surrender of Confederate forces in the war and effectively the end of the conflict.

The 84-acre **North Carolina Museum of Life and Science** (433 W. Murray Ave., 919/220-5429, http://lifeandscience.org, 10am-5pm Tues.-Sun., closed New Years Day, Presidents Day, Indigenous Peoples Day, Thanksgiving Day, Christmas Day, $23 adults, $21 over age 64 and military, $18 ages 3-12), home of the Magic Wings Butterfly House and the Bayer Crop Science Insectarium, is the perfect place for children who enjoy meeting strange bugs, climbing inside tornadoes, and taking a trip on a locomotive to see red wolves and more than 60 animal species. Grayson's Café, inside the museum, is open until 4pm daily.

One of the wildest sights in Durham is at the **Duke Lemur Center** (3705 Erwin Rd., 919/401-7240, www.lemur.duke.edu,

9:30am-4pm daily, self-guided tours $14). This is the largest, most diverse collection of lemurs outside of Madagascar, and the scientists here are making big steps to protect and understand the most threatened group of mammals on the planet. On tours, you'll see somewhere in the neighborhood of 10 species of lemurs. If you plan far enough in advance, you can get tickets to the summertime Friday Night Twilight Tours and take a look at these animals when their activity level is a bit higher, and if you really plan in advance you can get in to LemurPalooza, a fund-raiser and educational program where you can adopt a lemur (in name only; you don't get to take one home, as cute as they are and as much as you may want to).

SPORTS AND RECREATION

Hiking, Cycling, and Water Sports

Durham is loaded with choices for hikers, joggers, and bikers. The Eno River is surrounded by thousands of acres of parkland, much of which is marked for hiking. **Eno River State Park** (6101 Cole Mill. Rd., 919/383-1686, http://ncparks.gov, park office 8:30am-4:30pm Mon.-Fri., 9am-5pm Sat.-Sun. Nov.-Feb., 8:30am-4:30pm Mon.-Thurs., 8:30am-8pm Fri., 9am-5pm Sat.-Sun. Mar.-Oct., hours vary for river access points, call or check the website), northwest of Durham, offers hiking, canoeing through Class I-III rapids, and **camping** (877/722-6762, www.northcarolinastateparks.reserveamerica.com, $12-42) in the beautiful and wild river valley. The **Eno River Association** (www.enoriver.org) has more information on sites and ways to enjoy the river. **Frog Hollow Canoe and Kayak** (919/416-1200, www.froghollowoutdoors.com, 10am-4pm Tues.-Fri., by reservation, tours $35-85, most tours around $50) rents out boats and guides tours. Their guides

---

1: the Duke University campus **2:** sifaka lemur at the Duke Lemur Center **3:** the Durham Bull statue **4:** houses for enslaved people at Historic Stagville

can take you on moonlight paddles and other trips down various rivers in the area, with tours that include paddling and camping or even night paddles that end with a beer tasting at Fullsteam Brewery. They also offer rock guide services for experienced or learning climbers, as well as hiking excursions.

The **American Tobacco Trail** (www.triangletrails.org) is a 22-mile rails-to-trails project that has converted former railroad tracks into walking, hiking, and cycling trails through Durham, Cary, and Apex and across Durham, Chatham, and Wake Counties. Maps and routes are available online. The trail will eventually be 22 miles long. The **Carolina Tarwheels** (www.tarwheels.net), a weekend cycling club, welcomes newcomers and visitors and organizes rides of varying lengths around the region.

Golf

Golfers have several good public courses from which to choose. **Hillandale Golf Course** (1600 Hillandale Rd., 919/286-4211, www.hillandalegolf.com, 18 holes, par 71, greens fees Mon.-Fri. $22, cart $13, Sat.-Sun. $25, cart $16) has relatively few bunkers and almost no water hazards, making for a course where long drivers and aggressive players can score some eagles. The course record is 59, and with its player-friendly design, if you're on top of your game, you may be able to shave a stroke or two off that.

The **Duke University Golf Club** (3001 Cameron Blvd., 919/681-2288, http://golf.duke.edu, 18 holes, par 72, greens fees $45-100, cart $15-30, pull cart $13, same-day replay $25-55), the only Robert Trent Jones-designed course in the region. With numerous doglegs and narrowing fairways, this course can be a challenge for novice golfers. Number 13, a short par 4, demands proper ball placement or you'll end up in the pond in front of you or in one of two creeks, guarded by trees, on either side of the fairway.

Indoor Recreation

Play billiards, foosball, shuffleboard, and darts at **The Green Room** (1108 Broad St., 919/286-2359, www.greenroomdurham.com, 5pm-midnight Tues.-Sat.). They've got 100 brands of beer, including a decent selection of microbrews and craft brews, in bottles and cans. **XTreme Park Adventures** (7460 Wake Forest Rd./Hwy. 98, 919/596-6100, www.xtremeparkadventures.com, 10am-4pm Mon.-Fri., 10am-5pm Sat.-Sun., paintball from $27, Airsoft from $29, laser tag $270 for 6 players) is a paintball, Airsoft, laser tag, and combat-scenario extravaganza, but there's so much more to do here. This 50-acre facility has seven fields for paintball, laser tag, and shooting-sports enthusiasts, but there's tons of room for paintball, gem mining, zip lines, a ropes course, and more.

SkyZone (1720 Guess Rd., Suite 90, 919/425-0800, www.skyzone.com, 3pm-8pm Tues.-Thurs., 3pm-10pm Fri., 9am-10pm Sat., noon-7pm Sun., from $18 for 90 minutes) is one of those indoor trampoline parks that is packed with stuff to do. You can play dodgeball (with league play if you're a local), head to the foam zone and practice your moves as you dive into a pit, and use a trampoline launch pad that lets anyone dunk a basketball.

Spectator Sports

Thanks to the exploits of a demon and a smoke-snorting steer, Durham is probably even better known for its sports than its history as a tobacco dynamo. The NCAA Division 1 **Duke Blue Devils** embody the gold standard in college basketball and excel in many other sports. Their history is chronicled in the **Duke Sports Hall of Fame** (306 Towerview Rd., 919/613-7500, 9am-5pm Mon.-Fri., free), inside Cameron Indoor Stadium. Coach Mike Krzyzewski—that's pronounced "shuh-SHEV-skee," and don't mispronounce it, but you can call him Coach K.—has shepherded the men's basketball team since 1980, leading them to five national championships and more than 1,100 wins (plus he's earned six Olympic gold medals as coach of the U. S. Men's National Team). His resemblance to the Duke mascot, a blue-clad horned demon, is equally phenomenal. Duke has turned out some of the greatest basketball players of the last 20 years, including Grant Hill, Christian Laettner, and J. J. Reddick.

Not surprisingly, it is extremely difficult to come by Duke basketball tickets. Duke students are famous for living in tents for months on end outside Cameron Indoor Stadium, waiting to buy tickets and then to snag good standing-room spots in the courtside student section of the arena. If you're on campus in season, take a look at their tent city, known as Krzyzewskiville. If you're lucky enough to get into a game, you'll have the treat—or trauma, depending on your loyalties—of seeing the "Cameron Crazies" in the flesh.

The **Durham Bulls** (Durham Bulls Athletic Park, 409 Blackwell St., 919/956-2855, www.durhambulls.com)—of "Bull Durham" fame—are one of the nation's most recognizable minor-league baseball teams. They are the Triple-A farm team for the Tampa Bay Devil Rays, so you're likely to see big-league players here rehabbing from injury and rookies on the brink of making it big. The ballpark, designed by the architect who built Baltimore's Camden Yards, is comfortable and fun. A big wooden bull peers down from the end of the third-base line, and when a Bull hits a home run, the bull's eyes light up red, his tail flaps, and smoke billows from his nostrils.

ENTERTAINMENT AND EVENTS

I'm a big fan of comedy and a big fan of a city tour, so when you offer me an all-in-one package, I'm hooked. Asheville's got the La Zoom Tours (love it) and now Durham has **Bull City Laughs** (919/449-5237, https://bullcitylaughs.com, $28) and I couldn't be happier. Blending history, some city orientation, and sightseeing with some great jokes, these tours are R-rated and hilarious. The **Turn-up Tuesday Tour** departs from **Durty Bull Brewing Company** (206 Broadway St., Suite 104, 919/688-2337, www.durtybull.com, 2pm-10pm Mon.-Thurs., 2pm-midnight Fri., noon-midnight Sat., 1pm-9pm Sun.) on a 90-minute bus tour around the city. The **Rated-R History Tour** departs from **Beer Durham** (404 Hunt St., Suite 110, 919/680-0770, https://beerdurham.com, noon-8pm Mon.-Fri., 10am-8pm Sat., noon-6pm Sun.) for a frank and funny look at the sometimes not-so-nice history of Durham, the universities here, its tobacco-perfumed past, and more.

Nightlife

One of the best places to grab a beer in Durham is **Fullsteam Brewery** (726 Rigsbee Ave., 919/438-2337, www.fullsteam.ag, noon-10pm Mon.-Thurs., noon-11pm Fri.-Sat., noon-8pm Sun.). This fun and funky hangout celebrates two great things: Southern farmers and beer. The brews all incorporate Southern heirloom grains, botanicals, and locally foraged goods like persimmons for some creative and flavorful beers. They have a number of beers sold year-round, ranging from Carver Sweet Potato beer to the Working Man's Lunch (a rich beer that's malty and chocolaty, with notes of vanilla), and the namesake Fullsteam Southern Lager. Seasonal beers include a hickory-smoked porter, a basil saison, and an IPA laden with lemon thyme and bronze fennel. Many of the local food trucks stop by to feed the hungry crowds, and events like trivia, yoga, discussions on theology, chair massages, craft nights, belly dancers, music, and mystery movie night keep this place hopping.

Motorco Music Hall (723 Rigsbee Ave., 919/901-0875, www.motorcomusic.com), with concerts, comedy shows, and film screenings, and its companion restaurant and bar, **Parts & Labor** (5pm-midnight Mon., 3pm-midnight Tues.-Wed., 3pm-2am Thurs.-Fri., noon-2am Sat., noon-midnight Sun., $4-13), with cocktails, beer, and food, sit right across the street from Fullsteam Brewery. The food is a delicious mélange of styles you could call "all over the place," but taste the bean and cheese *pupusa,* the bratwurst, or the *poutine* and you'll be convinced the menu was a good idea.

Between the taproom, beer garden, and

pizza on offer at **Ponysaurus Brewing Co.** (219 Hood St., 844/369-7669, www.ponysaurusbrewing.com, 3pm-10pm Mon.-Thurs., 3pm-11pm Fri.-Sat., noon-8pm Sun., $9-16), you might not want to leave. The pizza pies are hot and fast, and with classics like the cheese pie or a margherita, and creations like the hot *soppressata* with Calabrian chilies, you'll find a bite that pleases. More than a dozen beers on draft give you plenty of options when it comes to quenching your thirst. Their Belgian single, *bière de garde,* and white IPA are favorites.

Bar Virgile (102 S. Mangum St., 919/973-3000, www.barvirgile.com, 5pm-midnight Mon.-Sat., $7-26) is all about the small plate and the carefully crafted cocktail. In this bar that's barely bigger than a garage, you'll find patrons elbow to elbow at tiny tables eating upscale plates of food and washing down each bite with a cocktail classic or nouveau. Order up some deviled eggs with smoked trout and caviar, roasted beets, or a charcuterie board to start, then tuck into the wild mushroom risotto, their excellent burger, or the delicious pappardelle bolognese.

Durty Bull Brewing Company (206 Broadway St., Suite 104, 919/688-2337, www.durtybull.com, 2pm-10pm Mon.-Thurs., 2pm-midnight Fri., noon-midnight Sat., 1pm-9pm Sun.) has a menu full of beers aged in *foeders,* bourbon barrels, and wine barrels for some exciting and funky flavors. Their sour beers are exciting, their canned Amateur Hour smoothie hard seltzers are delicious and aptly named, and you'll agree that the Extra Crispy Pilsner is a crispy boy indeed.

Dog-friendly and filled to the brim with great beer, **Flying Bull Beer Company** (752 9th St., 919/908-8180, https://flyingbullbeercompany.com, 3pm-11pm Mon.-Thurs., noon-11pm Fri.-Sun.) is a good spot to bring the pooch and hang for a bit. This is a nano brewery, so the house-brewed beers are in constant rotation (their saisons have been favorites), leaving a dozen or more guest taps open for great beer and cider from across the state. I love the selection here, love finding a herd of well-behaved dogs to hang out with, and love finding a new spot on 9th Street to check out.

Performing Arts

Downtown, the **Durham Performing Arts Center,** or **DPAC** (123 Vivian St., 919/680-2787, www.dpacnc.com), has 2,700 seats in a facility noted for its contemporary design and superb video and sound capabilities. Ranked the number four theater in the United States based on attendance, it's without a doubt the hub for performing arts in North Carolina. Everyone from Duran Duran to Jerry Seinfeld to Neil deGrasse Tyson to Yanni to Wanda Sykes plays here. They also host several Broadway plays each year—*Hamilton,* Monty Python's *Spamalot*—as well as ballets and other performances. Tickets vary by show, but if something or someone is playing that you would like to see, get your tickets fast; this place sells out quickly.

Duke has an ongoing series called **Duke Performances** (www.dukeperformances. duke.edu), which brings performers from a broad range of genres to venues on campus and across Durham for performances. In a given season, they may have acts like Kronos String Quartet, the Vienna Boys Choir, Buena Vista Social Club, the Royal Shakespeare Company, Los Lobos, Leo Kottke, dance troupes, and one-act plays by Samuel Beckett. On-campus venues are beautiful, and the level of the performers is magnificent.

Festivals

April brings the **Full Frame Documentary Festival** (919/687-4100, www.fullframefest. org, films $16, packages $100-325, some screenings and talks free), identified by the *New York Times* as the premier documentary film festival in the country before it was even in its 10th year. Venues around downtown host screenings, workshops, panels, and soirees where documentary fans and aspiring filmmakers can mingle with the glitterati of the genre.

For six weeks every summer, Durham is the site of the **American Dance Festival** (919/684-6402, www.americandancefestival. org), an internationally known event where the world's best choreographers often premiere new work. Durhamites and the visitors who come from around the world are one step ahead of audiences in New York. One of the region's most popular music festivals is the **Festival for the Eno** (www.enoriver.org), which takes place every 4th of July weekend. The festival is held on the banks of the Eno River, so you can listen to the performances from the comfort of your inner tube while floating in the river. In addition to showcasing dozens of excellent world, folk, and bluegrass bands, the Festival for the Eno is a great place for browsing the work of many of North Carolina's craftspeople.

August's **OutSouth Queer Film Festival** (919/560-3030, www.carolinatheatre.org, all access virtual pass $100) is the second-largest such event in the Southeast. Approximately 10,000 visitors attend the festival every year to watch new work by up-and-coming LGBTQIA+ filmmakers at Durham's Carolina Theater (309 W. Morgan St.), but in 2020-2021 it was an all-virtual event; stay tuned for a return to in-person events and in-person ticket pricing. In September, **Art of Cool Fest** (984/244-1033, www.aocfestival.org) brings three days of jazz to Durham. During those three days, there will be more than 20 concerts from world-class jazz musicians.

SHOPPING

Malls and Shopping Districts

Brightleaf Square District (905 W. Main St., 919/682-9229, www.historicbright-leaf.com) contains handsome circa-1900 American Tobacco Company warehouses that are no longer hives of cigarette rolling but have evolved into the flagship of Durham's post-tobacco industry revitalization. **Hamilton Hill Jewelry** (919/683-1474, www.hamiltonhilljewelry.com, noon-5pm Tues.-Sat.) has an outstanding selection of designer jewelry priced $100-10,000 and up.

Indio (919/797-0456, https://indiodurham. com, 11am-6pm daily) has design-forward gifts, jewelry, and home goods, with many Made in the USA products on hand.

The core of the **9th Street District** (www.discover9thstreet.com) of Durham, adjacent to the Duke campus, is the blocks between Main Street and Hillsborough Road-Markham Avenue. You'll find many small and very good eateries and an eclectic mix of shops that include several good bookstores and a pair of vintage boutiques worth exploring. The head shop and record store **Hunky Dory** (718 9th St., 919/286-1916, www.hunkydorydurham.com, noon-8pm Mon.-Thurs., noon-10pm Fri.-Sat., noon-6pm Sun.) is the quintessential college shop. Need a new piece of glass or some incense or a new mouthpiece for your vape pen? They have it, along with that Pink Floyd *Animals* shirt you've been looking for and a great selection of vinyl new and old. Just down the street, **Vaguely Reminiscent** (728 9th St., 919/286-3911, www.vaguelyreminiscent.com, 11am-6pm Mon.-Sat., noon-5pm Sun.) is a wacky little boutique stuffed with fun finds, including everything from clothing and jewelry to adult coloring books to cool backpacks and bags.

Away from downtown you'll find a cool collection of shipping containers that have been turned into restaurant and shop space at **Boxyard RTP** (900 Park Offices Dr., Research Triangle Park, 919/475-5321, www. boxyard.rtp.org, most shops 11am-8pm Tues.-Sat.). **PopBox** is a space dedicated to pop-up style shops, a new one every three months, so it's a place to see test concepts from area makers that can be quite cutting-edge. **Game On Escapes & More** (919/438-0798, www.gameonescapes.com) offers escape rooms in bite-size form, virtual reality logic and puzzle games, and other mental challenges. Fullsteam brewery has their outpost **Fullsteam RTP** (www.fullsteam.ag) here, so you can get a great pint and a square pizza (just like elementary school, except I probably had chocolate milk and pizza). Because it's North Carolina, you'll find barbecue, oysters, and sides galore at **Lawrence Barbecue** (www.lawrencebarbecue.squarespace.com, $11-27). Boxyard RTP is still growing, and more kitschy boutiques and cool concepts are on the way, so keep your eye on this space.

Books

The Regulator Bookshop (720 9th St., 919/286-2700, www.regulatorbookshop.com, 10am-6pm Tues.-Sun.) is one of the Triangle area's favorite bookshops. It hosts readings by important authors from around the world and carries an eccentric selection of literary journals and homemade zines. **Wentworth and Leggett Rare Books and Prints** (Brightleaf Square, 905 W. Main St., 919/688-5311, www. wentworthleggettbooks.com, 11am-6pm Mon.-Tues. and Fri.-Sat.) is an antiquarian book dealer also specializing in old prints, maps, postcards, and magazines.

FOOD
Eclectic Fusion

For barbecue (and you're in North Carolina, so there's no escaping barbecue), go to ★ **Picnic** (1647 Cole Mill Rd., 919/908-9128, www.picnicdurham.com, 11am-8pm Mon. and Thurs., 11am-9pm Fri.-Sun., $10-27). This is whole-hog barbecue, so it's flavorful even without sauce, but their brisket, ribs, fried chicken, deviled eggs, and fried green tomato BLT will do you right.

If you want a phenomenal burger and some great beer, **Bull City Burger and Brew** (107 E. Parrish St., 919/680-2333, www. bullcityburgerandbrewery.com, 11:11am-9:30pm Tues.-Thurs., 11:11am-10pm Fri.-Sat., 11:11am-9pm Sun., $8-15) is the place. Almost everything is made from scratch here; they grind the meat, bake the buns, and even make the hot dogs. Rumor has it there's a secret burger on the menu, topped with duck-fat fries and a fried egg.

Let's talk about pizza. ★ **Pizzeria Toro** (105 E. Chapel Hill St., 919/908-6936, www. pizzeriatoro.com, 4pm-11pm Mon.-Fri., 11am-11pm Sat.-Sun., $12-19) makes one of the tastiest pies in town. You won't find pepperoni and cheese on this menu, but you will find a pie topped with clams, hot pepper, and *grana padano;* another with soft eggs, oyster mushroom, and arugula; and even one with venison sausage. Antipasti are likewise unexpected, with crispy pigs ears and pickled shrimp on offer.

In 2022, Chef Ricky Moore was named Best Chef: Southeast by the James Beard Foundation for the exceptional fried seafood he serves at **Saltbox Seafood Joint** (2637 Durham Chapel Hill, Durham, 919/237-3499, www.ordersaltboxseafoodjoint.com, 11am-8pm Tues.-Sat., $11-23). Fried oysters, spicy mahi and catfish; soft shell crab or scallops or grouper on a roll; and sides that draw on Southern, Gullah, and Soul traditions make for a fine meal here.

There's no finer steak in Durham, some say the Triangle, than at ★ **NanaSteak** (345 Blackwell St., 919/282-1183, www.nanasteak. com, 5pm-9pm Tues.-Thurs. and Sun., 5pm-10pm Fri.-Sat., $18-42). Their wagyu New York strip is one of those steaks you use to measure other steaks against, and their cioppino is likewise outstanding. This place is a hot ticket, so do yourself a favor and make a reservation.

This is a pretty meat-heavy look at Durham's dining, but there's more to this town, and the vegetarian and vegan options on other menus don't replace a dedicated veggie-centric meal, so where to go? ★ **Pure Soul** (4125 Durham-Chapel Hill Blvd., Suite 1, 877/376-7685, www.puresoulff.com, 11am-7pm Mon.-Tues. and Thurs.-Sat., noon-4pm Sun., $9-17) is definitely one stop. This vegan soul food is legit. Fried "fish" and "shrimp" platters, a barvecue platter (the barvecue is made with soybeans grown in Asheville), soul rolls (think vegan soul food meets fried egg roll), plus drumsticks, "chkn" and barvecue sandwiches, and the always-awesome sides-only plate.

You'll find more vegan-only cuisine at **Earth to Us** (1720 Guess Rd., Suite 18, 919/908-1000, www.shopearthtous.com, 11am-8pm Thurs., 11am-9pm Fri.-Sat.,

11am-5pm Sun., $11-17), where you'll find American and Latin American comfort food. An arepa stuffed with barbecued seitan, soy-free tempeh empanadas, Beyond Burgers on pretzel buns, barbacoa-style tempeh, mock chicken and rice; it's a mouth-watering menu.

Durham's coffee culture keeps growing, and it's getting really interesting. Check out **Gojo** (823 W. Morgan St., 919/390-2338, www.gojobygoorsha.com, 8am-3pm Mon.-Sat., $2-12), an Ethiopian coffee shop, with a sister restaurant, **Goorsha,** to check out, serving café drinks and authentic Ethiopian coffee and food. Their vegan bowl with *gomen* (collard), *misir kik* (red lentil) and *metin shiro* (ground chickpea) is a great dish; and the egg *zilbo* (beef and collard) breakfast sandwich is a great meal first thing in the morning. **Cocoa Cinnamon** (420 W. Geer St., https://littlewaves.coffee, 7am-7:30pm Mon.-Fri., 8am-7:30pm Sat.-Sun., $2-8) makes a great cup and offers pour over, café drinks, and bakery items.

When you have a hankering for something sweet, **The Parlour** (117 Market St., 919/564-7999, www.theparlourdurham.com, 2pm-10pm Tues.-Fri., noon-10pm Sat.-Sun., $4-8) makes some excellent and exotic ice creams with flavors like Vietnamese coffee, rosewater, labneh, and malted cinnamon (it tastes like a cinnamon bun, but it's ice cream); they even have vegan flavors using a coconut milk base.

Japanese

Hands down the best sushi in the area is at ★ **M Sushi** (311 Holland St., 919/908-9266, www.m-restaurants.com, lunch 11:30am-2pm Tues.-Fri., dinner 5pm-9:30pm Tues.-Thurs., 5pm-10pm Fri.-Sat.). Here Seoul native chef Mike Lee rolls sushi, slices up sashimi, and produces a number of hot-kitchen Japanese dishes using high-end ingredients. Every time I've eaten *unagi* here, it was pulled from the sea the day before, and for many of the fish available on the East Coast, that time from hook to table is even shorter. It's spectacular, and grabbing a seat at the long counter gives you a good look at Lee and his kitchen in action.

Dashi (415 E. Chapel Hill St., 919/251-9335, www.dashiramen.com) is really three different Japanese food experiences under one roof. First, there's the **Ramen Shop** (11:30am-2:30pm Mon. and Wed.-Sat., 5pm-10pm Wed.-Mon., $12-14), then on the second floor there's **Izakaya** (5pm-10pm Wed.-Mon., $3-16). Their ramen is packed with fun ingredients; the *izakaya* (think Japanese tapas) has expected dishes like miso soup and sashimi, but surprises like bone marrow and stir-fried squid.

Spanish

If you want a meal you'll talk about for weeks after, look no further than ★ **Mateo Bar de Tapas** (109 W. Chapel Hill St., 919/530-8700, www.mateotapas.com, 5pm-10pm Tues.-Sat., $6-55). Mateo does Spanish tapas with what chef Matthew Kelly calls "a Southern inflection." By that he means they use Southern ingredients—like smoked trout and trout caviar, fresh local vegetables, and even locally raised and cured hams—to complement Spanish ingredients, flavors, and dish styles. Mateo was a James Beard Best New Restaurant semifinalist in 2013, and it's only gotten better since.

Italian

For top-notch Italian, **Gocciolina** (3314 Guess Rd., 919/973-4089, www.gocciolina.com, 6pm-10pm Tues.-Sat., $14-32) is the spot. This place keeps it simple but executes every dish perfectly. Six pastas and four meat options grace the menu, as well as a full antipasti list and a handful of fresh vegetables, plus a few specials each night. Go classic with the spaghetti carbonara or try something a little different with the baked gnocchi. But as good as their pasta is, give careful consideration to the lamb chops.

Cuban

Go for a taste of Cuba at **COPA** (107 W. Main St., 919/973-0111, www.copadurham.com, 6pm-9pm Tues.-Thurs., 6pm-10pm Fri.-Sat., takeout 5pm-8pm Tues.-Sat., $10-38), courtesy of chef Roberto Matos, who started his culinary journey with Old Havana Sandwich Shop, won a pack of fans, and expanded to this, a full-service restaurant dishing out lunch and dinner and flavors from his home. Must-order dishes include *fufu con picadillo* (green plantains with ground beef), the *ropa vieja a la americana* (his take on Cuba's signature dish), and, of course, the Havana, a Cuban sandwich to die for.

Ethiopian

If you've never eaten Ethiopian food, you're in for a treat when you go to Goorsha (910 W. Main St., 919/588-4660, www.goorsha-durham.com, 4pm-9pm Mon.-Fri., noon-9pm Sat.-Sun., $11-25) in Brightleaf Square. Most dishes are savory stews (a little thicker than a typical curry) that you eat with *injera* (a spongy, tangy flatbread), but the *sambusa* (a veggie-filled pastry like a samosa) and the *kashka* (a stack of collards, short ribs, and steamed corn bread) appetizers give you a look at other parts of the cuisine. Order the Doro Wot (chicken stewed in *berebere* sauce with garlic, onion, cardamom, and ginger), the peppery *awaze tibs* beef (beef in pepper sauce with tomato, garlic, onion, and jalapeño), or the *kitfo* (steak tartare with cardamom, *mitmita,* and seasoned butter).

Baked Goods

Best known as a bakery and patisserie, ★ Guglhupf Bakery, Patisserie, & Cafe (2706 Durham-Chapel Hill Blvd., 919/401-2600, www.guglhupf.com, 8am-6pm Tues.-Thurs., 8am-8pm Fri.-Sat., 9am-3pm Sun., $6.50-24) is also a wonderful café. Guglhupf's founder is from southern Germany, and the menu is based on that cuisine, with forays into other continental and American styles. Even if you don't have time for a full sit-down meal, stop in for dessert or to pick up a pastry or artisanal bread for the road.

Food Trucks

Durham has a lively food-truck scene, and the Food Truck Rodeo (www.durhamcentralpark.org) brings 60 or so food trucks to town five times a year, with Labor Day weekend being a big one, with bands and a lively scene. Popular food trucks at the Rodeo and around town include: Corner Boys BBQ (919/889-3882, www.cornerboysbbq.com, $10-19), a great barbecue truck with brisket, ribs, smoked chicken, pulled pork, and more (these guys know their way around a barbecue pit; they won the Whole Hog episode of *Smoke Ring,* a competition cooking show on Discovery+ TV); modern Mexican from Chef Orlando's La Republica (919/344-8390, www.larepublica.com, $2.50-9); killer dumplings from Chirba Chirba Dumpling (919/885-4328, www.chirbachirba.com, about $2 per dumpling); and Bulkogi Truck (847/530-6910, www.bulkogi.com, $7-10), serving Korean barbecue and Korean-inspired dishes like *bibimbap,* a Korean barbecue taco, and kimchi fried rice.

ACCOMMODATIONS

The most upscale place to stay in Durham is the Washington Duke Inn and Golf Club (3001 Cameron Blvd., 800/443-3853 or 919/490-0999, www.washingtondukeinn.com, from $200). It's on the Duke campus, and the guest rooms and suites are sunny and plush, with the option of bunk beds for families traveling with kids. Babysitting services can be arranged by the concierge. If you're staying here, or even if you're not, you'll want to make dinner reservations at the four-star AAA Four Diamond Fairview Dining Room (919/493-6699, 6:30am-11am, 11:30am-2pm, and 5:30pm-9:30pm daily, $8-50) where they have a pianist on Friday-Saturday nights; dishes like the lamb culotte, tobacco cured duck breast, and the tuna tataki never fail to please.

Durham's most celebrated bed-and-breakfast is the ★ Arrowhead Inn (106 Mason Rd., 919/477-8430, www.arrowhead-inn.com, $160-310), a AAA Four Diamond awardee on a Revolutionary-era estate about 15 minutes from downtown. All of the luxurious guest rooms have their own fireplaces, and several have two-person whirlpool tubs. On the inn's grounds are a garden cottage with a whirlpool tub and a two-person steam shower, along with a rather fabulous log cabin with a sleeping loft and spa-like bath appointments.

The chic **21c Museum Hotel** (111 N. Corcoran St., 919/956-6700, www.21cmuseumhotels.com, $190-830) opened in Durham in 2015, taking over the city's only proper skyscraper. 21c is known for rooms that are borderline elegant, but also their commitment to art of the 21st century; in the **21c Museum** (galleries 24 hours daily, guided tours 5pm most Wed. and Fri., free) you'll find commissioned work as well as the hotel's collection. Artists include Michael Combs, Yong ho Ji, Duke Riley, Astrid Krogh, and other emerging and established artists. In addition to the rooms and the museum, there's **Counting House** (919/956-6760, www.countinghousenc.com, 5pm-9pm Tues.-Thurs., 5pm-10pm Fri.-Sat., 1am-2pm Sat.-Sun., bar 4pm-10pm Tues.-Thurs. and 4pm-midnight Fri.-Sat., $14-45), a restaurant serving dishes reflective of the flavors and ingredients of the area.

★ **The Durham Hotel** (315 E. Chapel Hill St., 919/768-8830, www.thedurham.com, from $180) opened in 2015 and has become one of the most popular hotels downtown. The Durham's 53 rooms are big and stylish in a way that blends modern aesthetics with the hotel's retro architecture, and the designers carried it through from the rooms to the hotel's rooftop bar and restaurant. James Beard Award-winning chef Andrea Reusing (who owns Lantern in nearby Chapel Hill) opened **The Roof** (919/768-8831, 5pm-10:30pm Tues.-Thurs., 5pm-midnight Fri.-Sat., $5-24) and **The Restaurant** (919/768-8831, 8am-10:30am and 5pm-9:30pm Mon. and Thurs., 8am-10:30am Tues.-Wed., 8am-2pm and 5pm-10pm Fri.-Sat., 8am-10am, 10:30am-2pm, and 4:30pm-9pm Sun., $13-38, brunch $4-23). The Roof is a jewel in Durham's crown. The 3,000-square-foot space fills up fast and can

be difficult to get into, but the raw bar and small bites menu (beef tartare, picnic eggs, and other snacks) are excellent, and the cocktails are sublime. The Undeniable Truth—dry gin, dry vermouth, orange bitters, and olive oil—is a surprise, and the Airmail—rum, lime, honey, and prosecco—is a great warm-weather drink.

Downtown has developed a little cluster of boutique hotels. On the block between 21c and The Durham stands a motel with cool mid-century lines and a classic motel look. This is ★ **Unscripted Durham** (202 N. Corcoran St., 984/329-9500, www.unscriptedhotels.com, from $170), with 74 rooms and suites, a rooftop pool, a bar, and a restaurant. Guest rooms are bright, colorful, and funky, the pool area is throwback cute, and your room includes bike rentals if you want to pedal around Durham. Food options include a poolside bar and eatery, **The Patio** ($8-45), serving cocktails, sharable bites, and entrées; **The Studio,** a hangout serving cocktails, wine, and beer; and **allday** ($5-10), a coffee shop.

Aloft Durham Downtown (345 Blackwell St., 919/402-5656, www.aloftdurhamdowntown.com, from $175) has a great location: right beside DPAC, steps away from the Durham Bulls Athletic Park, across the street from American Tobacco Historic Campus, and three short blocks from downtown's busy restaurant and bar scene. With a prime location, the excellent in-house WXYZ Bar, and very competitive rates, it's worth a look.

There are many chain motels around the city, including **Durham Marriott City Center** (201 Foster St., 919/768-6000, www.marriott.com, around $150) and **Holiday Inn Express** (2516 Guess Rd., 919/313-3244, www.ihg.com, from $120). **Comfort Inn University Durham-Chapel Hill** (3508 Mt. Moriah Rd., 919/490-4949, www.choicehotels.com, from $95), **SureStay Plus** (3710 Hillsborough Rd., 919/382-3388, www.bestwestern.com, from $65), and **Comfort Suites Raleigh-Durham Airport** (5219 Paige Rd., 919/314-1200, www.choicehotels.com, from $77) are near the Raleigh-Durham

International Airport and I-40, making for easy travel access whether you're driving or flying.

INFORMATION AND SERVICES

Duke University Hospital (2301 Erwin Rd., 919/684-8111, www.dukehealth.org) is the main hospital in Durham. **Duke Regional Hospital** (3643 N. Roxboro Rd., 919/470-4000, www.dukehealth.org) is also operated by Duke Health Systems.

Information for travelers is available from the **Durham Convention and Visitors Bureau** (212 W. Main St., Suite 101, 919/687-0288, www.durham-nc.com). The *Durham Herald-Sun* is the primary Durham-specific newspaper, although many people also read the Raleigh *News & Observer. INDY Week* is a popular weekly cultural newspaper, available free throughout the region.

GETTING THERE AND AROUND

The Triangle's extensive network of buses and shuttles is run by **Triangle Transit** (www.gotriangle.org, regular routes $2.25-3, day pass $4.50, week pass $16.50). The Raleigh-Durham Airport is 10-20 minutes from Durham by cab or shuttle bus. **Amtrak** (800/872-7245, www.amtrak.com) runs the New York City-Charlotte *Carolinian* once daily in each direction and Raleigh-Charlotte *Piedmont* trains twice daily in each direction; both stop at Durham Station (601 W. Main St., 6:45am-9:45pm daily), in the heart of downtown. The New York City-Miami *Silver Star* stops at Raleigh's Amtrak station.

Chapel Hill, Carrboro, and Vicinity

The third corner of the Triangle is Chapel Hill and Carrboro, only 30 minutes from Raleigh. To many people in North Carolina this is hallowed ground because of the Dean Smith Center, where the University of North Carolina Tar Heels play basketball. Even for nonfans, Chapel Hill is a very cool college town. The University of North Carolina (UNC) is the heart of the town, and the 60,000 residents, many of whom are UNC alumni, maintain a stimulating community with fertile ground for arts and culture. Music is ubiquitous here. On a weekend tour of the clubs, you may well hear a future legend. Singer James Taylor, legendary blues guitarist Elizabeth Cotten, and the Squirrel Nut Zippers are among the many Chapel Hill-Carrboro natives who have gone on to wider fame.

SIGHTS

★ University of North Carolina

The UNC campus comprises a couple of beautiful quads surrounded by many outlying complexes; the quads date to 1789, making it the oldest state university in the country. Massive poplar trees on the quads make the campus an indulgent shady hideaway during the central Carolina summer. Elegantly unpretentious federal-style buildings were dorms and classrooms for 18th- and 19th-century students; today they're home to undergraduates. Guided tours of the historic sites on campus depart from the **UNC Visitors Center** (134 E. Franklin St., 919/962-1630, www.unc.edu, 10am-4pm Mon.-Fri.) throughout the day; call to check the schedule. You can also pick up a brochure and walk through campus at your own pace. It is a beautiful campus, especially when classes are in session, and it comes alive with the vibrancy unique to college campuses.

The 1851 **Old Playmakers Theater** (E. Cameron Ave., UNC campus, www.playmakersrep.org), was built by Alexander Jackson Davis and originally intended to be a library and a ballroom; in the 1920s, the university converted the building to a theater. The

Chapel Hill and Carrboro

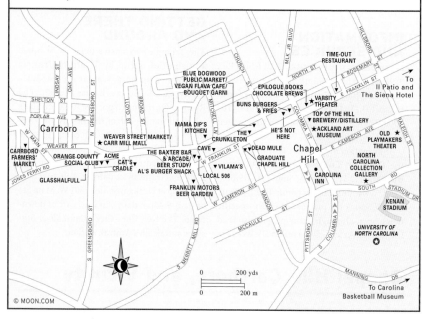

TIME-OUT RESTAURANT

To
Il Patio and
The Siena Hotel

BLUE DOGWOOD
PUBLIC MARKET/
VEGAN FLAVA CAFE/
BOUQUET GARNI

EPILOGUE BOOKS
CHOCOLATE BREWS

VARSITY
THEATER

BUNS BURGERS
& FRIES

TOP OF THE HILL
BREWERY/DISTILLERY

MAMA DIP'S
KITCHEN

HE'S NOT
HERE

ACKLAND ART
MUSEUM

OLD
PLAYMAKERS
THEATER

WEAVER STREET MARKET/
CARR MILL MALL

THE
CRUNKLETON

CAVE

Chapel
Hill

NORTH
CAROLINA
COLLECTION
GALLERY

Carrboro

CARRBORO
FARMERS'
MARKET

ORANGE COUNTY
SOCIAL CLUB

ACME

THE BAXTER BAR
& ARCADE/
BEER STUDY/
AL'S BURGER SHACK

CAT'S
CRADLE

DEAD MULE

GRADUATE
CHAPEL HILL

VILAMA'S

CAROLINA
INN

GLASSHALFULL

LOCAL 506

FRANKLIN MOTORS
BEER GARDEN

KENAN
STADIUM

UNIVERSITY OF
NORTH CAROLINA

SHELTON ST

POPLAR AVE

LINDSAY ST

OAK AVE

N GREENSBORO ST

BROAD ST

LLOYD ST

W MAIN ST

WEAVER ST

JONES FERRY RD

S GREENSBORO ST

S MERRITT MILL RD

MITCHELL LN

W FRANKLIN ST

W CAMERON AVE

MCCAULEY ST

RANSOM ST

CHURCH ST

MLK JR BLVD

NORTH ST

E ROSEMARY ST

E FRANKLIN ST

COLUMBIA ST

E CAMERON AVE

PITTSBORO ST

S COLUMBIA ST

RALEIGH ST

HILLSBORO ST

SOUTH RD

STADIUM DR

MANNING DR

To Carolina
Basketball Museum

0   200 yds
0   200 m

© MOON.COM

Playmakers Repertory Company is the professional theater company in residence, and they put on modern and classical works, ranging from Shakespeare to contemporary musicals.

UNC's **Ackland Art Museum** (101 S. Columbia St., 919/966-5736, www.ackland. org, 10am-5pm Wed.-Sat., 1pm-5pm Sun., 10am-9pm 2nd Fri. of the month, closed July 4, Thanksgiving, Dec. 24-25, and Jan. 1, free) has a collection of European sculpture and painting spanning centuries along with an acclaimed collection of Asian art, but the most amazing part of their collection is the works on paper—drawings, photos, prints, and the like. The **North Carolina Collection Gallery** (200 South Rd., 919/962-3765, www.lib.unc. edu, 9am-5pm Mon.-Fri., free), in the Wilson Library, is a cozy museum that will capture the fancy of any Southern history enthusiast; given the 50,000-plus items in the collection, you're sure to find some intriguing stuff here.

Carolina Basketball Museum

While on the UNC campus, visit the **Carolina Basketball Museum** (Ernie Williamson Athletic Center, 450 Skipper Bowles Dr., 919/962-6000, www.goheels.com, 10am-4pm Mon.-Fri., 9am-1pm Sat., free), a new addition to the roster of campus attractions. This multimillion-dollar 8,000-square-foot hagiological shrine holds mementos from a century of Carolina basketball. On a reproduction of the Heels' court, footprints and even players' actual shoes mark the spots from which some of the program's most memorable baskets were launched. There's a lot of video and interactive content, but the item most likely to please the Tar Heel faithful is a letter from Duke University basketball coach Mike Krzyzewski to a high school player from Wilmington, expressing his regret that the young man had chosen to attend UNC rather than Duke; the addressee was Michael Jordan.

Weaver Street Market

Weaver Street Market (101 E. Weaver St., Carrboro, 919/929-0010, www.weaverstreetmarket.coop, 8am-9pm daily) is the community hub of the politically liberal, artistically active, and often quite eccentric residents of Carrboro. Weaver Street Market is an organic foods co-op with a small dining area—it's too plain to be called a café—inside and on the front lawn. On nice days the lawn is jammed with families and college students eating food grown in nearby Pittsboro and Hillsborough, where there's an organic farm or creamery wherever there's an open patch of land. Diners listen to local bluegrass, old-time mountain music, punk, or perhaps Hare Krishna musicians. You'll probably see some tai chi or hula-hooping going on too. Weaver Street Market on a crowded day demonstrates what a peculiar and congenial community this is. If it seems too taxing to make the trip to Carrboro, they have locations in **Chapel Hill** (716 Market St., Chapel Hill, 919/929-2009, 8am-9pm daily) and in **Hillsborough** (228 S. Churton St., Hillsborough, 919/245-5050, 8am-9pm daily).

Botanical Gardens

UNC's **North Carolina Botanical Garden** (100 Old Mason Farm Rd., off U.S. 15/U.S. 501/Hwy. 54, 919/962-0522, http://ncbg.unc.edu, 9am-5pm Tues.-Sat., 1pm-5pm Sun., free) is the Southeast's largest botanical garden. The 800 acres contain beautiful hiking trails, an herb garden, an aquatic plant area, and a carnivorous plant garden. On the campus, **Coker Arboretum** (399 E. Cameron Ave., dawn-dusk daily, free) is much smaller, but it's also a beautiful retreat. The five landscaped acres are most beautiful in the spring, when students will make detours on their way to class just to pass through the amazing 300-foot-long arbor of purple wisteria.

SPORTS AND RECREATION

Golf

One of the finest courses in the area is the Tom Fazio-designed **UNC Finley Golf Course** (500 Finley Golf Course Rd., Chapel Hill, 919/962-2349, www.uncfinley.com, 18 holes, par 72, greens fees Mon.-Thurs. $60, Fri.-Sun. $70, discounts for students, alumni, and late play, carts $22, push carts $12). The first hole has a 240-yard carry over water and another 30 yards to the fairway. Few have the prowess to play from the back tees, which make this course considerably more difficult. For the most part, the fairways are wide and allow for some miscues, but if you keep the ball in play, you'll be rewarded with a number of birdie opportunities.

Spectator Sports

Tar Heel Athletics (www.goheels.com) are the beloved UNC sports teams. The most successful have been the men's basketball team, coached for many years by the legendary Dean Smith and now by fellow Hall of Famer Roy Williams, and college home court to all-time great basketball players Michael Jordan and James Worthy. The men play at the Dean E. Smith Center (300 Skipper Bowles Rd.), a glowing stadium that seats more than 20,000. UNC women's basketball is coached by Courtney Banghart, and they play at historic Carmichael Auditorium in the heart of campus, except when they play Duke University, when they move to the much larger Smith Center. Coach Mack Brown leads the football team, whose home field is the 1927 Kenan Stadium on the UNC campus. The baseball team plays at Boshamer Stadium, off Manning Drive in the southern part of campus. Other UNC sports achievers include soccer's Mia Hamm, golfer Davis Love III, and track star Marion Jones. Getting tickets to UNC men's basketball games is exceedingly difficult, but football and women's basketball games are somewhat easier to attend. Try the main **ticket office** (800/722-4335, www.goheels.com). If you're unsuccessful in getting basketball tickets—and you likely will have trouble especially against marquee opponents—there are innumerable sports bars, all tuned to the Tarheels game, around town.

ENTERTAINMENT AND EVENTS

Movies

Like any good college town, Chapel Hill has several movie theaters, including small theaters that show independent films. The **Varsity Theatre** (123 E. Franklin St., 919/967-8665, www.varsityonfranklin.com) is on the edge of campus, and the **Chelsea** (1129 Weaver Dairy Rd., 919/929-8428, www.thechelseatheater.org) is in the Timberlyne Shopping center north of downtown. The **Lumina Theater** (620 Market St., 919/969-8049, www.thelumina.com) is located in Southern Village, a development south of Chapel Hill on U.S. 15/501. The Lumina screens movies outdoors on summer evenings.

Nightlife

LIVE MUSIC

Chapel Hill-Carrboro is one of the best places in the Southeast to hear live music, and several small top-notch clubs are legendary venues where major artists get their start and return again and again. The best-known is the **Cat's Cradle** (300 E. Main St., Carrboro, 919/967-9053, www.catscradle.com), with lots of standing and dancing room and a small room in the back with a pool table and a beer counter. The artists who play the Cat's Cradle are leading lights in rock and roll, Americana, alt-country, and world music, and the audience comes to hear the music. Shows sell out quickly.

The **Cave** (452½ W. Franklin St., Chapel Hill, 9184/234-0293, http://caverntavern.com, no advance tickets) and **Local 506** (506 W. Franklin St., Chapel Hill, 919/942-5506, www.local506.com) are also important local venues, tending toward pop, rock, and punk. Note that to attend shows at Local 506, you must first join the club ($3), which you can do at the door.

PRIVATE CLUBS

Bars and pubs tend to be either beer-and-wine bars or private clubs. They're not being elitist; it has to do with obtaining a liquor license. To serve liquor, if a business doesn't make more than 30 percent of its revenue from food, it must be a members-only club that charges annual dues. The three-day advance-purchase rule applies to most such watering holes. Favorite members-only bars include the **Dead Mule** (303 W. Franklin St., Chapel Hill, 919/969-7659, www.deadmule.squarespace.com, 3pm-10pm Sun.-Thurs., 3pm-2am Fri.-Sat., $5-15), a hangout for grad students and literary types in a little house set back from the road on Franklin Street (they have snacks if you need a bite), and the **Orange County Social Club** (108 E. Main St., Carrboro, 919/933-0669, www.orangecountysocialclub.net, 4pm-2am daily, membership $5) in Carrboro, a hip and noisy bar frequented by students. New members must submit a written application and the fee before a membership card is issued.

Without a doubt, one of the coolest private clubs in Chapel Hill is **The Crunkleton** (320 W. Franklin St., 919/969-1125, http://thecrunkleton.com, 4pm-2am daily, membership $10), a serious bar with mission-style furniture in warm wood tones that makes it feel anachronistic, along with a classic menu filled with vintage and a few reimagined cocktails served by bow tie-wearing bartenders. There are more than 300 distilled spirits, with an impressive collection of bourbons, and a dozen beers on tap.

BEER AND WINE BARS

If you want to go out for a drink but haven't planned your barhopping three days in advance, you still have options. **He's Not Here** (112½ W. Franklin St., Chapel Hill, 919/942-7939, http://hesnotherenc.com, 4pm-2am Mon.-Fri., noon-2am Sat., 1pm-9pm Sun.) has been a hot spot since 1972. There's often live rock and roll with a low cover charge. **Caffe Driade** (1215-A E. Franklin St., Chapel Hill, 919/942-2333, www.caffedriade.com,

1: Morehead-Patterson Bell Tower at UNC, Chapel Hill **2:** Franklin Street in Chapel Hill **3:** The campus at UNC, Chapel Hill is quiet in the summer.

8am-2pm Mon.-Fri., 9am-3pm Sat.-Sun.), an elegant little coffee shop off East Franklin Street, serves wine and beer as well as coffee and pastries, and in the warm months they have live outdoor music on Wednesday and Friday-Saturday evening.

The Baxter Bar & Arcade (108 N. Graham St., Chapel Hill, 919/869-7486, www. baxterarcade.com, 2pm-2am Mon.-Fri., noon-2am Sat.-Sun.) is an unusual spot. It's a bar where you can grab a tasty brew, but it's also an arcade. In The Baxter, you'll find 50 or so vintage and contemporary arcade and pinball games; they post the high scores on a giant chalkboard for all to see. If you're game, try to get your name on the high score board.

Franklin Motors Beer Garden & Gastropub (601 W. Franklin St., Chapel Hill, 984/322-9023, www.franklinmotors. net, 11:30am-midnight Mon. and Wed.-Sat., 11:30am-10pm Sun.) has a sizable outdoor beer garden, a rooftop patio, plenty of beer and cocktails, and a permanent food truck parked in the middle of it all. **Roquette** (www.roquettechapelhill.com, 11:30am-11:30pm Mon. and Wed.-Sat., $4-15) uses lots of local providers to help out with their menu of fries, wings, sliders, and hand pies. You'll never go wrong with a couple of orders of fries and some nachos to share, but the short rib hand pie (with caramelized onions, mushrooms, and Dijon mustard) is an excellent call.

Top of the Hill Restaurant & Brewery (1000 E. Franklin St., Chapel Hill, 919/929-8676, wwwthetopofthehill.com, noon-midnight Sun.-Mon. and Wed., noon-2am Thurs.-Sat.) and **Top of the Hill Distillery** (505 W. Franklin St., 919/699-8703, www.topodistillery.com, tours 7pm Fri., by appointment Sat., $20) is a whole complex of alcoholic delights. Top of the Hill, called TOPO by everyone, is the eighth-oldest brewery in North Carolina, and they generally have six or so beers on tap, including a porter, at least one IPA, and a cask or two of ale. You can eat here ($9-27), and with a menu loaded with flatbreads, sandwiches, and a really good TOPO

whiskey-and-Coke-braised beef short rib, you'll want something to eat. TOPO Distillery makes gin, vodka, and whiskey available at ABC stores, restaurants and bars across the state, and in-house (bottles only).

The selection at **Beer Study** (106 N. Graham St., Chapel Hill, 919/240-5423, www. beerstudy.com, noon-8pm daily), Chapel Hill's first bottle shop, will keep beer fans intrigued and coming back. Eighteen taps on constant rotation, hundreds of bottles and cans to choose from, tap takeovers from North Carolina breweries and out-of-state operations (Jester Kings did a tap takeover and paired their beer with raw oysters), and space to sit down, share a pint, and hang for a bit, all make for a good time.

Carolina Brewery (460 W. Franklin St., Chapel Hill, 919/942-1800, www.carolinabrewery.com, 11am-11pm Mon.-Thurs., 11am-midnight Fri., 10:30am-midnight Sat., 10:30am-10pm Sun.), with a second location in nearby **Pittsboro** (120 Lowes Dr., Suite 100, Pittsboro, 919/545-2330, 11am-10pm Mon.-Thurs., 11am-11pm Fri., 10:30am-11pm Sat., 10:30am-10pm Sun.), founded in 1995, has the distinction of being the fifth-oldest brewery in the state. They regularly brew five beers in a range of styles, but they're known for their IPA and oatmeal porter; they also make four seasonal brews and have a list of nearly two dozen specialty and limited-release brews.

SHOPPING

Shopping in a town like Chapel Hill has lots of the usual: university-themed shops aimed at new students or alumni in town, the unofficial university bookstore, head shops full of incense and tie-dyes, a hip music store. But Chapel Hill, and adjoining Carrboro, has much more than that. The **North Carolina Crafts Gallery** (211 W. Main St., Carrboro, 919/942-4048, www.nccraftsgallery.com, 10am-6pm Tues.-Sat.) is chock-full of work by North Carolina artists, artisans, and craftspeople, and jewelry, pottery, artwork, and more found here might not be of much interest to your average undergrad, but it's the kind of place where parents on a visit might pick up a little something for themselves.

University Place (201 S. Estes Dr., Chapel Hill, 919/945-1900, www.universitymallnc. com, 10am-9pm Mon.-Sat., 1pm-6pm Sun.), on Estes Drive between Franklin Street and Fordham Boulevard (U.S. 15/501), is gradually changing from being a small 1970s-style mall to a collection of upscale boutiques and commercial art galleries. Stop in at **Wentworth & Sloan Jewelers** (919/942-2253, www.wentworthandsloan.com, 10am-5pm Tues.-Sat.) for an impressive and always changing collection of estate and heirloom jewelry. If you're there on Tuesday or Saturday, you can check out the **Chapel Hill Farmer's Market** (3pm-6pm Tues., 8am-noon Sat. Apr.-Oct., 9am-noon Tues. and Sat. Nov.-Mar.).

Behind Weaver Street Market, **Carr Mill Mall** (200 N. Greensboro St., Carrboro, 919/942-8669, http://carrmillmall.com) in Carrboro is an early example of what has become an important entrepreneurial movement in North Carolina: the transformation of obsolete but historic industrial buildings, particularly old textile mills, into stylish retail space. This 1898 cotton-mill building houses some small specialty shops. **Ali Cat Toys** (919/932-3954, www.alicattoysandbooks.com, 10am-6pm Mon.-Sat., 11am-4pm Sun.) has toys, books, and games for all ages, many of which are educational. **Mullberry Silks & Fine Fabrics** (919/942-7455, www. mullberrysilks.net, 10am-6pm Mon.-Sat.) carries sewing accessories, patterns, and fabric from functional to fine. Keep the creative juices flowing at **Firefly** (919/933-9439, www. firefly-carborro.myshopify.com, 10am-6pm Mon.-Sat.), where you'll find beads, jewelry-making tools and accessories, and pieces made in-house. If you're here and feel a little peckish or parched, **Weaver Street Market** (919/929-0010, www.weaverstreetmarket. coop, 8am-8pm daily) is a great co-op grocery store with great relationships with local farmers, ranchers, and suppliers; a food bar; and specialty items.

Books

Along Franklin Street, which becomes Carrboro's Main Street a few blocks west of campus, you'll find the usual college-town mix of textbook exchanges, all-night convenience stores, and purveyors of sustainably crafted fair-trade bongs (water pipes). There are also a handful of chichi women's clothing shops, trendy vintage-wear boutiques, and some great bookstores. Among the best is **Flyleaf Books** (752 Martin Luther King Jr. Blvd., Chapel Hill, 919/942-7373, www.flyleafbooks.com, 10am-5pm Tues.-Sat., 11am-5pm Sun.), a shop with a good mix of paperbacks, hardcovers, signed copies, and genres.

Epilogue: Books Chocolate Brews (109 E. Franklin St., 919/913-5055, www.epiloguebookcafe.com, 7am-11pm Mon.-Wed., 7am-9pm Thurs.-Fri., 8am-9pm Sat., 9am-7pm Sun., $2-11) is a bookstore, Spanish-style chocolate lounge, and coffee shop where you'll find the usual café drinks along with exciting stuff like churros and dipping chocolate; vegan empanadas and cupcakes; and a selection of Spanish pastries you don't often see in bakeries around here. It's a delightful spot.

FOOD

There's no better way to get to know a town's food scene than to take a food tour. In Chapel Hill and Carrboro, there are two walking food tours to choose from. **Taste Carolina Gourmet Food Tours** (919/237-2254, www. tastecarolina.net, 10:45am Sat. $60, 3pm Sat. $75) has an early tour that starts at the Carrboro Farmers Market and moves on to four different restaurants; the afternoon tour features dinner and drinks, with visits to four restaurants for slightly larger tastings and pairings of wine, beer, or even cocktails. **Triangle Food Tours** (919/623-4873, www.trianglefoodtour.com, 2pm and 2:30pm Fri.-Sat., $58 adults, $45 kids) visits five to six restaurants on your tour of Chapel Hill and Carrboro.

Soul

Folks around here will tell you that **Mama Dip's Kitchen** (408 W. Rosemary St.,

919/942-5837, www.mamadips.com, 11am-7pm Wed.-Sun., $13-23) is a legendary restaurant, and they are right. Perpetually named to the "Top Restaurants in Chapel Hill, The Triangle, or North Carolina" lists, it's a fantastic Southern, soul, and comfort food restaurant. Mildred Council, Mama Dip herself, started cooking when she was nine, and if you grew up in the South, you'll recognize at first bite the comfort-food recipes of a Southern matriarch. It's pure soul food, with fried chicken to die for and sides that are far from an afterthought—they're fabulous in their own right.

There's a debate on biscuits in Chapel Hill, with one camp firmly saying Time Out Restaurant has the best and the other camp swearing biscuit allegiance to Sunrise Biscuit Kitchen. Lucky for us it's a tasty debate to settle. **Time-Out Restaurant** (201 E. Franklin St., 919/929-2425, 24 hours daily, around $10) is known for being the only 24-hour restaurant in town as well as being a hangout for star athletes past and present. The highlight of the menu is the chicken cheddar biscuit, made fresh around the clock; the biscuit is split open, lined with fried chicken, and then topped with cheddar cheese. Honestly, it's one of the best things you'll ever eat. **Sunrise Biscuit Kitchen** (1305 E. Franklin St., 919/933-1324, www.sunrisebiscuits.com, 6am-2:30pm Mon.-Sat., 7am-2:30pm Sun., $1.29-12) makes an extra-large biscuit that's perfectly buttery, and whether you have yours as a BLT, an egg and cheese, with some honey or jam, or smothered in gravy, you're in for a bite that's going into your own biscuit hall of fame.

Eclectic Fusion

★ **Acme Food & Beverage Co.** (110 E. Main St., Carrboro, 919/929-2263, http://acmecarrboro.com, 5pm-9pm Wed.-Sun., $11-29) continues to be one of the top restaurants in town, garnering accolades from food writers and reviewers year after year. The menu is Southern but with international touches—coconut sticky rice served with the crab cakes, a BLT bento box, delicious chiles rellenos. Still, dishes like the fried green tomatoes, the cornbread, and the tomato pie are essential orders.

Carrboro's **Glasshalfull** (106 S. Greensboro St., Carrboro, 919/967-9784, http://glasshalfull.net, 11:30am-2:30pm and 5pm-9pm Tues.-Thurs., 11:30am-2:30pm and 5pm-9:30pm Fri., 5pm-9:30pm Sat., $10-34) is equal parts restaurant and wine bar. The menu of contemporary American fare makes use of local ingredients and offers vegetarians plenty of good choices.

A special treat for Triangle diners is **Sage Vegetarian Café** (Timberlyne Shopping Center, 1129 Weaver Dairy Rd., Chapel Hill, 919/968-9266, www.sagevegetariancafe.com, 4pm-8:30pm Wed.-Sat., $8-16), a vegetarian and vegan restaurant that draws at least as many omnivores as hard-core veggies. Sage's beautiful dishes are a fusion of classic Persian cooking and modern vegetarian cuisine.

Buns Burgers & Fries (107 N. Columbia St., 919/240-4746, www.bunsofchapelhill.com, 11am-9pm Sun.-Thurs., 11am-10pm Fri.-Sat., $9-17) serves "the best flippin' burgers in town": Walk in, choose your burger (Angus beef, fresh ground turkey, or homemade veggie), decide whether it's a single, double, or triple patty, and add your toppings. They also have a grilled salmon sandwich, french fries, sweet-potato fries, and a small selection of bottled beer.

In the **Blue Dogwood Public Market** (306 W. Franklin St., www.bluedogwood.com), a couple of dining treats await. **Vegan Flava Café** (919/960-1832, www.veganflavacafe.com, 2pm-7pm Wed.-Fri., 1pm-7pm Sat., noon-4pm Sun., $8-20) delivers vegan meals that don't skimp on flavor, with tacos; lettuce, seaweed, or collard wraps; smoothies; curry lentils with barbecued jackfruit; and even a Sunday brunch fit for a veggie-loving king or queen. At **Bouquet Garni Foods** (919/655-5000, www.bouquetgarnifoods.com, noon-8pm Wed.-Fri., 3pm-9pm Sat., $5-15) you'll find Senegalese cuisine, and that's something not a lot of diners here have been exposed to. Thanks to chef-owner Eric Ndiaye, it's delicious. He studied cooking in Lyon, France, and New York, and now find himself bringing dishes loaded with West African flavor and French techniques to diners in Chapel Hill. Chicken *yassa* (fried plantains go well with the tangy lemon sauce), Senegalese *maffe* (a savory peanut stew with beef, chicken or lamb), Lamb *jollof,* and Senegalese-style beignets make a great meal here.

Italian

★ **Osteria Georgi** (201 S. Elliot Rd., Suite 100, www.osteriageorgi.com, 5pm-9pm Mon.-Thurs., 5pm-10pm Fri.-Sat., $16-36) opened in 2021 and was a smash hit from the start. Within weeks, this was the most sought-after reservation in the area, so plan accordingly. It's Italian cuisine heart and soul, and chef Dan Jackson leads a kitchen that knows how to deliver flavor and authenticity. A New York strip with white beans; house-made pasta with a duck *ragù,* truffle cream, or an oh-so-fresh pomodoro; a half chicken served with polenta and roasted veggies that's transformative. And that's before you get to the wine list or selection of Italian amaro.

Il Palio (1505 E. Franklin St., 919/918-2545, www.ilpalio.com, 6:30am-10am Mon., 6:30am-10am and 5:30pm-8:30pm Tues.-Fri., 7am-11am and 5:30pm-8:30pm Sat.-Sun., dinner $21-84) has earned numerous AAA Four Diamond Awards for their beautiful take on Italian cuisine. Pasta is made fresh, and they use as many local ingredients as they can source—as they put it, "we cook as an Italian might in North Carolina." They import Italian cheeses, wines, oils, and vinegars. The grilled octopus is a personal favorite, as is the *maltagliati*—duck *ragù,* Taggiasca olives, and rosemary.

Indian

Small local farms provide much of the produce used in dishes at **Vimala's Curryblossom Café** (431 W. Franklin St., 919/929-3833, www.curryblossom.com, noon-7pm Mon.-Wed., noon-8pm Thurs.-Sat., $10-18). Deeply flavorful curries with salmon, chicken, eggplant and kofta; Nepali-style black-eyed pea and bamboo shoot curry; and many options for vegetarians have made this a popular spot for flavors from India and the region.

Asian Fusion

Offering a great take on contemporary and classic Asian dishes, including a number of Vietnamese dishes, **Elements** (2110 Environ Way, 919/537-8780, www.elementsofchapelhill.com, 5pm-9pm Tues.-Sat., $11-40) has established itself as one of the best restaurants in Chapel Hill. They use North Carolina products in every dish they can, which makes dishes like the Mekong Delta Hot Pot positively burst with flavor.

Local Fare

You can guess what's good from the name of **Al's Burger Shack** (516 W. Franklin St., 919/904-7659, www.alsburgershack.com, noon-8pm Mon.-Sat., $4-15), and if the name's not good enough, *Food & Wine* Magazine named Al's the Best Burger in America in 2018. You can get your burger bite-size (a regular burger) or Al Size (it's a big one) and in 10 variations with all sorts of toppings, including one vegetarian burger that's remarkably good.

At **The Pig** (630 Weaver Dairy Rd., 919/942-1133, www.thepigrestaurant.com, 11am-7pm Mon.-Sat., $7-18), chef-owner Sam Suchoff—a Lantern alumnus—makes whole hog barbecue, fried chicken and catfish, po' boys, fried bologna sandwiches (don't laugh—they're delicious, more so because he makes his own bologna) and even barbecue tempeh and country fried tofu. He uses pasture-raised, hormone-free hogs for his barbecue, marking a trend among the new generation of pit masters. It's a great updated version of the classic country restaurants and barbecue joints that used to dot the Carolina countryside.

The barbecue joint **Blue's on Franklin** (110 W. Franklin St., 919/240-5060, www.bluesonfranklin.com, 11:30am-3pm and 5pm-9pm Tues.-Wed., 11:30am-10pm Thurs.-Sat., noon-7pm Sun., $8-22) is something of a legacy restaurant: three generations of Tar Heels run the spot, and they're rabid fans and supporters of the university. From the burgers (one comes topped with a pile of barbecue, just to ensure you get a bite of 'cue today) to the barbecue to the chicken wings (oh, man, what wings), the menu is a crowd pleaser.

The **Carrboro Farmers Market** (301 W. Main St., 919/280-3326, http://carrborofarmersmarket.com, 7am-noon Sat. Apr.-Oct., 9am-noon Nov.-Mar., 3pm-6pm Wed. early Apr.-mid-Nov.) is a bustling, festive scene featuring local organic produce in abundance as well as gorgeous cut flowers, artisanal cheeses, and charmingly odd lawn art. They hold post-market food truck events throughout the spring and summer as well as specialty markets before Thanksgiving and on the winter solstice; check the website for hours for special events.

Merritt's Store & Grill (1009 S. Columbia St., 919/942-4897, www.merrittsblt.com, 7am-4pm Mon.-Fri., 8am-5pm Sat., $4-16) opened in 1929 as a gas station but is now one of the best places to grab a simple bite. Breakfast consists of breakfast sandwiches, and lunch includes burgers and a bunch of sandwiches, including their specialty, the BLT, which comes as a single, double, or even triple.

The Chapel Hill area is blessed with a local dairy that supplies residents with old-fashioned bottled milk and fantastic ice cream. To sample Mapleview Ice Cream, you have an option beyond the freezer aisle of the grocery store: At the Carrboro **Maple View Ice Cream and Country Store** (6900 Rocky Ridge Rd., 919/960-5535, www.mapleviewfarm.com, noon-7pm daily), you can pick up some ice cream and check out the farm while you eat it on the front porch.

ACCOMMODATIONS

A favorite inn for people in the entire state is ★ **The Carolina Inn** (211 Pittsboro St., 919/933-2001 or 800/962-8519, www.carolinainn.com, from $210), a landmark on the UNC campus since it first opened in 1924. It's the place where visiting dignitaries are hosted,

where the most important faculty functions take place, where lucky couples get married, and where old alumni couples celebrate their milestone anniversaries. It is at the center of campus, between the original quads and the modern medical school complexes, and not far from the Dean Smith Center. The inn will be completely booked far in advance for homecoming weekends, big basketball and football games, and other campus events. The inn's restaurant, **Crossroads** (919/918-2777, $8-45), serves three elegant meals a day by executive chef Jeremy Blankenship. Afternoon tea (2pm-4pm Sat.-Sun. except holidays, $25-50) at the Carolina Inn is a popular treat, but Sunday Brunch (9am-2pm Sun., $30) may be even more popular; reservations are advised for all meals.

The ★ **Graduate Chapel Hill** (311 W. Franklin St., 919/442-9000, www.graduatehotels.com, from $144) brings one of my favorite boutique hotel chains to Chapel Hill. These college-themed hotels are always decked out in the home-team colors, so it's Tar Heel blue through and through, and everything from the art to the wallpaper to the room keys says UNC. Rooms are well appointed, service is always good, and the food and drink from **Trophy Room** (919/442-9000, 5pm-10pm Tues.-Sat., $9-13)—the in-house restaurant and lounge—keeps it simple and tasty.

The Siena Hotel (1505 E. Franklin St., 919/929-4000, www.sienahotel.com, from $156), one of Marriott's Autograph Collection, is an Italian-inspired hotel where comfort is king. Rooms are plush and studios are spacious. There's a great Italian restaurant in the hotel, **Il Palio,** that's reason enough to visit, but if you go to eat, make an evening of it and enjoy more of the excellent wine list.

Chapel Hill also has a handful of motels where guest rooms usually run $100-170. The **Holiday Inn Express Chapel Hill** (6119 Farrington Rd., 919/489-7555, www.www.ihg.com); **Sheraton Chapel Hill Hotel** (1 Europa Dr., 919/968-4900 or 888/796-8235, www.marriott.com), recently renovated and a great deal; and **Hampton Inn & Suites**

(6121 Farrington Rd., 919/403-8700, www. hamptoninn.com) are all in convenient and safe neighborhoods a brief car ride or free bus trip from the campus.

GETTING THERE AND AROUND

Chapel Hill is accessed via I-40 and Highway 85; U.S. 15/501 runs through Chapel Hill from Durham to the northeast toward Pittsboro to the southwest.

Chapel Hill Transit (919/485-7433, www. townofchapelhill.org) runs 22 weekday routes and fewer, but still convenient, weekend routes. Check the website for route maps but know the bus system is convenient for more than just the student body, and during a visit here you can get to most places you want to visit for little cost. There are free local and express routes in Chapel Hill and Carrboro.

HILLSBOROUGH

The beautiful little town of Hillsborough, just 45 minutes west of Raleigh on I-40, is home to a large number of authors, artists, and overflow Chapel Hillians. Now on the National Register of Historic Places, Hillsborough was the site of an early trading path along the Eno River used by the indigenous Occaneechi people and later by European settlers. It was also the site of the Constitutional Convention of 1788, in which North Carolinians rejected the Constitution. And legend holds that Daniel Boone departed from here for Kentucky in 1776.

Historic Downtown

The **Orange County Historical Museum** (201 N. Churton St., 919/732-2201, www. orangechistory.org, 11am-4pm Tues.-Sat., 1pm-4pm Sun., free) is better than many small-town history museums. Of particular note is their exhibit on what they call North Carolina's Rip Van Winkle Period. In 1790-1850, the state stagnated while the other states grew. In this display, they look at the causes, the effects, and the methods used to pull the state out of stagnation and into relative prosperity until the Civil War took hold.

The **Alexander Dickson House** (150 E. King St.) was built in the 1790s, a Quaker-plan house that would be headquarters to General Joseph Johnston during the Civil War. Today it's the **Hillsborough Visitors Center** (919/732-7741, https://visithillsboroughnc. com, 10am-4pm Wed.-Sat.), where you can pick up local information before visiting the medicinal garden and beginning a self-guided walking tour of some of the historic sites.

The **Burwell School** (319 N. Churton St., 919/732-7451, www.burwellschool.org, 11am-4pm Wed.-Sat., 1pm-4pm Sun., free) has had several interesting lives. For its first 20 years, 1837-1857, the handsome old building was one of the state's earliest girls schools. During the Civil War, the Collins family, owners of Somerset Plantation in Creswell, sheltered here. A young enslaved woman named Elizabeth Hobbes Keckly grew up here, and she went on to become Mary Todd Lincoln's dressmaker and author of an insightful book about the first lady. Docent-led tours (1pm Wed.-Fri.) and self-guided tours are available.

The **Old Orange County Courthouse** (N. Churton St. and E. King St., https://visithillsboroughnc.com, 9am-5pm Mon.-Fri., free), now the county judicial building, is a pretty 1844 Greek Revival, just what one hopes for in a small Southern county seat. At the corner of Cameron and East King Streets, a historical marker identifies the spot where six regulators were hanged in 1771 after they refused Governor Tryon's order to declare loyalty to the crown.

Just east of downtown, **Ayr Mount Historic Site** (376 St. Mary's Rd., 919/629-0150, www.classicalamericanhomes.org, grounds open daily) preserves an important 1815 home built by a Scottish merchant. In the past, guided tours of this fine federal-style house would give visitors more context for this beautiful place; they hope to resume tours soon. A walking trail called the Poets Walk traverses scenic parts of the 265-acre property; it's free and open every day. Two other

trails not on Ayr Mount property, but across the Eno River, are the Historic Occoneechee Speedway Trail and the Johnston Nature Preserve. These two trails follow a former horse racetrack and later NASCAR Speedway and open up to some great river views.

Recreation

Occoneechee Mountain State Natural Area (625 Virginia Cates Rd., 919/383-1686, http://ncparks.gov, 8am-6pm daily Nov.-Feb., 8am-8pm daily Mar.-Apr. and Sept.-Oct., 8am-9pm daily May-Aug., closed Dec. 25) is located in Orange County, although it has a Durham address. It is a monadnock environment—an isolated rock knob—and one of the most diverse ecological areas in the Triangle. At 867 feet, Occoneechee Mountain hosts species of flora and fauna that are otherwise found only in the mountain ranges 100 miles west. The hiking trails are steep and rather strenuous, but the views and deep-mountain feeling of the knob make the effort worth every step.

The **Occoneechee Golf Club** (1500 Lawrence Rd., 919/732-3435, www.occoneechee.com, 18 holes, par 71, greens fees $40-47 for 18 holes, $29-33 for 9 holes, discounts for seniors, juniors, and walking) is a fun, playable course that's been called one of the great public courses in North Carolina. Well laid out with opportunities for big drives and nuanced play, it can present a challenge. Number 5 has a severe dogleg that requires some creative play; number 6 is a short par 4 that's well guarded by water; and number 17 has perfectly placed water hazards making for an interesting hole.

North Carolina's Mountains to Sea Trail stretches from Jockey's Ridge on the Outer Banks to the Smoky Mountains in the far west, and in doing so, it passes through urban areas like Hillsborough. Here, the Mountains to Sea Trail follows the **Riverwalk**, which runs 1.8 miles through town along the Eno River.

1: classroom inside the schoolhouse at the Burwell School **2:** the home of Quaker Alexander Dixon, now the Hillsborough Visitors Center

Events

Hillsborough's a small town, but lively, with an event calendar that touches every month of the year. Like many artsy communities, they hold an art walk and community-wide festival. The **Hillsborough Arts Council** (www.hillsboroughartscouncil.org) puts on Last Fridays (last Fri. Mar.-Nov.); it features an art walk, food trucks, and concerts. In September, the **Hog Day BBQ Festival** (www.hogday.org) brings barbecue enthusiasts together for two days of pulled pork, live music, and a street fair.

Food

★ **Panciuto** (110 S. Churton St., 919/732-6261, www.panciuto.com, 5pm-8pm Thurs.-Sat., $26-30) has the honor of being home to chef Aaron Vandemark, a multiple James Beard Award Best Chef semifinalist. The menu of fine Italian fare changes completely every month, and it goes through tweaks and evolutions daily as chef Vandemark and his crew are inspired by what's fresh. If you love Italian food, you won't be disappointed with Panciuto's high-end approach.

Hillsborough BBQ Company (236 S. Nash St., Hillsborough, 919/732-4647, http://hillsboroughbbq.com, 11:30am-9pm Wed.-Sat., 11:30am-8pm Sun., $8-20) cooks barbecue over live coals, the way it's meant to be done. You can order plates of brisket, turkey breast, ribs, chopped 'cue, a barbecue sandwich, and even a black-eyed pea po' boy; you can also order in bulk and pay for your barbecue by the pound.

El Restaurante Ixtapa (162 Exchange Park Lane, 919/644-6944, www.ixtapa.homestead.com, 9am-9pm Wed.-Mon., $6-14) makes Mexican food from scratch, and they go beyond expected dishes. You'll find flautas, chilaquiles, tortas, and huaraches, and a focus on seafood. They have shrimp and some fish throughout the week, but on weekends the specials often include dishes like tuna ceviche.

With an awesome craft beer selection, sizeable sidewalk dining spot, and some great pub grub, **The Wooden Nickle** (113 N. Churton

St., 919/643-2223, www.thewnp.com, 3pm-11pm Tues.-Thurs., 11am-11pm Fri.-Sun., $8-16) has been a hit since it opened in 2003. Skip the fried pickles and get the fried banana peppers with smoked onion ranch; they're crazy good. Wings are a staple here and they've got a dozen or so sauces that can deliver some heat. And for your main, it's something handheld: a burger (yes), some fish tacos (double yes), or the Nash-Fil-A (triple yes for this pickle-brined fried chicken breast slathered in hot sauce).

Saratoga Grill (108 S. Churton St., 919/732-2214, www.thesaratogagrill.com, 11:30am-2:30pm Mon.-Tues. and Thurs.-Sat., $9-16) continues to be recognized by area magazines as one of the top spots for casual dining. We couldn't agree more. The seafood—crab salad, shrimp, salmon, scallops, flounder, tuna—is great, the sandwiches and burgers are the perfect portion, and the service has never been anything short of excellent.

JORDAN LAKE

Just 23 miles west of Raleigh (via U.S. 64) is **Jordan Lake State Recreation Area** (280 State Park Rd., Apex, 919/362-0586, http://ncparks.gov, office 8am-4:30pm daily, park

8am-6pm daily Nov.-Feb., 8am-8pm daily Mar.-Apr., 8am-9pm daily May-Aug., 8am-8pm daily Sept.-Oct., closed Dec. 25). The 14,000-acre reservoir is surrounded by nine lake-access areas and includes more than 14 miles of trails and seven swimming beaches. It's a popular area for many kinds of boating, including sailing, windsurfing, and water-skiing. If you'd like to **camp** (877/722-6762, https://northcarolinastateparks.reserveamerica.com, $12-62) here—and many do—they have more than 1,000 campsites for tenting and RV camping, most with restrooms and running water nearby. Nearby **Crosswinds Marina** (565 Farrington Rd., Apex, 919/387-7011, www.crosswindsboating.com) rents out fishing and pontoon boats.

PITTSBORO

Pittsboro is 30 minutes' drive south of Chapel Hill on U.S. 15/501, an easy afternoon trip if you're staying in the Triangle. This small county seat is laid out like a wheel, with the 1881 courthouse at the hub and its antiques shops and cafés radiating out in all directions.

Carolina Tiger Rescue

Founded in 1981 by a geneticist from the University of North Carolina, the **Carolina**

waterfront campsite of Jordan Lake State Recreation Area

Tiger Rescue (1940 Hanks Chapel Rd., 919/542-4684, www.carolinatigerrescue.org, tours 10am Fri., 10am and 1pm Sat.-Sun., twilight Fri.-Sun. Apr.-Oct., $18 adults, $13 ages 4-12, free under age 3, twilight tours $28) had, as its original mission, the breeding of endangered wild cats. It soon became apparent that there was also an overwhelming need to create a safe haven for big cats that were abused or abandoned as illegal pets or in the entertainment industry, or that had lived at zoos that had closed. Among the dozens of cats living here today are a pair of tigers who were found as cubs walking along a highway near Charlotte; a tiger seized at a traffic stop (he was the passenger); a tiger rescued from an owner who tried to have him declawed and defanged; several other tigers; and many leopards, jaguars, serval cats, ocelots, kinkajous, caracals, and binturongs. Tours last approximately two hours and involve a lot of walking; paths are not equipped for strollers or wheelchairs. You'll see the greatest number of cats during the warm-weather sunset tours, when the animals are likely to be prowling around in the evening shade.

Food

The **Pittsboro Roadhouse and General Store** (39 West St., 919/542-2432, www.pittsbororoadhouse.com, 11am-9pm Mon.-Thurs., 11am-10pm Fri.-Sat., $11-21) is a casual and comfortable place to get a really good meal. Specialties include burgers, which come in ground beef, ground turkey, and "vegan veggie" versions. Dinner features pasta dishes, salmon, tilapia, shrimp, turkey meatloaf, and steaks. The Roadhouse is also a favorite live-music venue in the area with bands on Monday, Friday, and Saturday nights.

You'll get a great bite to eat at **Café Root Cellar** (35 Suttles Rd., 919/542-1062, https://caferootcellar.com, 4pm-8pm Fri.-Sat., $7-17). Great soups, comfort food like meatloaf, veggie and vegan options like a smoked beet burger and an Indian-inspired bowl, and a fried chicken sandwich give some flavorful options to every diner.

The Phoenix Bakery (664 West St., 919/542-4452, www.thephoenixbakerync.com, 8am-5pm Tues.-Fri., 8:30am-2:30pm Sat.-Sun., $1-8) has an assortment of cookies, cupcakes, brownies and bread, cinnamon rolls (from a family recipe), and beer-bread muffins (muffins packed with bacon, cream cheese, and even *pico de gallo*), making them a strong choice for breakfast or a snack.

FEARRINGTON VILLAGE

Located between Chapel Hill and Pittsboro, Fearrington Village offers up a swank place to spend some time. The "village" includes an outstanding inn and restaurant, a few shops, and a not-to-be-missed spa. The ★ **Fearrington House Inn** (2000 Fearrington Village Center, 919/542-2121, www.fearrington.com, $375-750), an extremely luxurious inn that earns awards and accolades from all quarters, is an experience you can't pass up even if it's for a one-night special-occasion stay. It's the only inn in North Carolina to receive both the AAA Five Diamond Award and Exxon Mobil's Five Star Award. Impossibly plush guest rooms feature canopied feather beds, restful colors and lighting, beautiful pine floorboards salvaged from an antique building in England, and vases of fresh flowers. Rates are steep, but the inn offers weekend package options that are good bargains, combining luxury guest rooms, three-course dinners, English teatime, and gift cards for the shops. **The Spa at Fearrington** (919/545-5723, 10am-5pm Wed.-Sun.) is a luxurious affair, recognized as a Forbes Four-Star establishment, where you can get all manner of treatments and pampering.

The **Fearrington House Restaurant** (919/542-2121, www.fearrington.com, 5pm-8pm Thurs.-Sun., 3-course prix fixe $99, 4-course $120, wine pairings $75-85, chef's tasting menu $165-135, vegetarian options available) is no less exceptional than the inn. The prix-fixe menu includes incredible seasonal use of the bounty of North Carolina's fields, pastures, woods, and waters.

Adding to the appeal of Fearrington Village are its activities and events: readings by prominent authors, concerts and square dances, antiques shows, and the popular annual **Folk Art Show** (919/542-2121, www. fearrington.com, $5) in February. The Folk Art Show runs more to outsider or visionary art, technically speaking, than folk art, but it's still an exciting event.

Sandy Lowlands

Between the Triangle and the beaches is a band of towns and cities that were once important in North Carolina's tobacco economy. Their roles have changed as that industry wanes, but towns like Wilson and its neighbors continue to be culturally vital, architecturally interesting, and full of good places to browse for antiques.

HENDERSON

Henderson is about 45 minutes northeast of Durham, near the Virginia state line. **Kerr Lake State Recreation Area** (6254 Satterwhite Point Rd., Henderson, 252/438-7791, http://ncparks.gov, office 8am-5pm daily, park 8am-6pm daily Nov.-Feb., 8am-8pm daily Mar.-Apr. and Sept.-Oct., 8am-9pm daily May-Aug., closed Dec. 25), outside Henderson, includes a 50,000-acre artificial lake and 800 miles of woods along the lakeshore straddling the state line.

Boating, including sailing, is the main activity. There are numerous public boat ramps, some available 24 hours daily, and two commercial marinas. It's also a great place to swim, but be aware that there are no lifeguards. The park offers many campsites, both drive-in and walk-in, some right along the shores of the lake. Visit the park's website to scout out the best camping locations and to read about the complicated fee schedule. To help you sound more like a native, in these parts, Kerr is pronounced "car."

HOLLISTER

About 80 minutes' drive northeast of Raleigh, the small town of Hollister is the site of

Medoc Mountain State Park (1541 Medoc State Park Rd., Hollister, 252/586-6588, http://ncparks.gov, office and visitors center 8am-5pm daily, closed Dec. 25, park 8am-6pm Nov.-Feb., 8am-8pm Mar.-May and Sept.-Oct., 8am-9pm June-Aug.), with more than 10 miles of hiking trails through loblolly pine and hardwood forests and alongside creeks and swamps. Should you happen to be traveling with your horse, you can enjoy 10 miles of bridle trails. There is also fine canoeing along Little Fishing Creek, ideal for beginning paddlers. Contact the park ahead of time to check on water levels; at times the creek can be swollen and less placid. There are 34 **campsites** (877/722-6762, https://northcarolinastateparks.reserveamerica.com, $12-28) for tents and trailers, 12 with electrical hookups.

WILSON

The town of **Wilson** (www.wilson-nc.com) sits 45 minutes east of Raleigh, just off I-95. A onetime cotton and tobacco town, Wilson, and the county of Wilson, is still agricultural, although other industries have moved in, and many residents treat the town as a distant bedroom community to jobs around Raleigh. Most people know Wilson from their travels on I-95, but folk art aficionados will know the town's most famous resident, Vollis Simpson. Simpson began making art at age 65 after a career of machinery repair and house moving. He started by building huge windmills in his yard, but not the *Don Quixote* kind—the kind of windmills more at home as a weathervane or a whirligig like you might find in your grandma's yard or atop her mailbox. Soon, he had a field full of giant brightly painted whirligigs. Something in his nature—he never called himself an artist, no matter where his works showed or how much they sold for—and something in the whirligigs caught people's attention, and his works have been displayed all over the world; you can see them today in downtown Wilson at the **Wilson Whirligig Park** (www.wilsonwhirligigpark.org, free). While you're here, stop in and grab a bite at a Wilson classic: **Burger Boy** (2012 Ward Blvd., 252/237-8365, 10:30am-8:30pm Mon.-Fri., 10:30am-9pm Sat., 1pm-8:30pm Sun., $2-12). They've been cooking up burgers and hot dogs at this cool little drive-in since 1969. I think it gets no finer than a Big Burger with cheese, an order of onion rings, and a shake, but this menu is loaded with classics, so have a little fun with your order (just don't forget the milk shake).

Lillington is almost an hour due south of Raleigh on U.S. 401. West of town you'll find **Raven Rock State Park** (3009 Raven Rock Rd., Lillington, 919/893-4888, www.ncparks.gov, visitors center 8am-5pm daily, park 7am-7pm Nov.-Feb., 7am-9pm Mar.-May and Sept.-Oct., 7am-10pm June-Aug., closed Christmas Day), named for a high rock outcropping that towers over this upper reach of the Cape Fear River. The **Cape Fear Canoe Trail** runs through the park, although there are no access points within the park. Contact the park to find out about the nearest put-ins. Beautiful hiking trails loop up and down and around the rock, making it easy to explore. **Camping** (877/722-6762, https://northcarolinastateparks.reserveamerica.com, $15-36) is available, both hike-in and, if you're traveling the Cape Fear Canoe Trail, canoe-in. Contact the park office for reservations.

Winston-Salem and Central Carolina

If you tell people "I'm going to North Carolina," they will probably picture a beach scene or a mountain sunset. Although neither of those apply to Winston-Salem and other Piedmont cities, they still make excellent getaway destinations.

The geography here is a lovely transition from the foothills of the Blue Ridge Mountains down into the true Piedmont and Sandhills. This is the heart of North Carolina's wine country, with great restaurants, art galleries, and lively arts communities. You'll also find engaging history, including religious and civil rights landmarks.

The two largest cities in this region—Winston-Salem and Greensboro—are close kin in both geographic terms and in their origins but different enough in their distinct flavors. Winston-Salem

Highlights

Look for ★ to find recommended sights, activities, dining, and lodging.

★ **Old Salem Pathways:** Expanding the way we understand Old Salem, this self-guided tour focuses on life in Salem for enslaved people, Indigenous people, and Moravians who lived, visited, and traded here (page 250).

★ **Yadkin Valley Wine Trail:** North Carolina's own little Napa Valley includes many wineries a short drive from Winston-Salem (page 255).

★ **International Civil Rights Center and Museum:** Hear the story of the fight for integration and justice in North Carolina, a lesser-known but crucial front in the Civil Rights Movement (page 267).

★ **North Carolina Zoo:** See elephants, alligators, and many more exciting creatures you wouldn't expect to encounter in the Carolina Piedmont (page 279).

★ **Seagrove:** The tiny town of Seagrove is home to a generations-old tradition of folk pottery. Start at the North Carolina Pottery Center, then move onto the 100-plus studios tucked along lovely country roads (page 280).

★ **Uwharrie National Forest:** Hiding under the hauntingly beautiful canopy of forest are miles of hiking trails and mysterious back roads (page 281).

Winston-Salem and Central Carolina

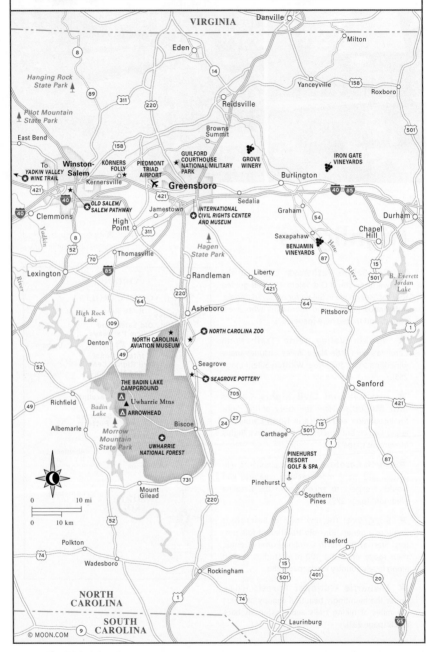

© MOON.COM

was once two towns. Salem traces its roots to the Moravians, a sect of Central European religious migrants who traveled down the Great Wagon Road in the 18th century from Pennsylvania. After traveling through the Shenandoah Valley and into these Carolina hills, they established a hard-working town known for the integrity, education, and skills of its residents. Greensboro has religious roots as well: a community of Quakers was integral in the town's early days. Known for their abolitionist and pacifist beliefs, the Quakers had a difficult time in the 18th- and 19th-century South as slavery and war raged around them. The struggles of racial equality continued through the civil rights movement of the 1960s, when the town played a key role in advancing equality for African Americans. Today, many Moravians and Quakers still practice their faith in this part of North Carolina.

Winston-Salem and Greensboro are also home to several distinguished universities and colleges, including Wake Forest University in Winston and the University of North Carolina at Greensboro. Both cities have active arts scenes with visual art, opera, ballet, and all kinds of music.

Located near the center of the state, the Uwharrie Mountains are one of North Carolina's biggest secrets. They rise out of the flatlands and rolling hills to form a beautiful and eerie cluster of high hills laden with hiking trails and campsites. At the edge of the Uwharrie Mountains is a tiny landlocked town called Seagrove, legendary for its pottery; it seems that everyone here throws clay and has at least a garage

ceramics studio. More than 100 studios turn out highly prized ceramic work, some using patterns and methods passed down for generations. As you move closer to Fayetteville, to the southeast, you'll find Sothern Pines and Pinehurst, the location of some of the world's best golf courses, some of which have hosted major professional golf events such as the U.S. Open.

PLANNING YOUR TIME

This is a large region with a lot to see, so plan on devoting more than just a day or two to exploring. The golf towns of the Sandhills are clustered in the southeast corner of the region and are an easy drive from Raleigh and Wilmington. The Seagrove potteries and Uwharrie Mountains are most easily accessed from U.S. 220, which also takes you past the North Carolina Zoo. Winston-Salem and Greensboro are less than 30 minutes apart by road, but it's easy to spend a weekend or more in each.

For the eastern and western regions of the state, summer is the busiest time and the high season for prices and traffic; not so here. The heat and humidity of July-August send many residents fleeing to the coast or retreating to the mountains. In the Southern Pines and Pinehurst area, the season for visitors peaks in the spring. March-May temperatures are in the 60-80°F range, beautiful and comfortable for golf. If you're planning to visit the Sandhills for golf, make your tee times and book your room and dinner reservations well in advance. In summer it's easier to book a tee time, but the heat makes it unpleasant or even dangerous on the links.

Previous: historic Moravian buildings in Old Salem; the oldest giant roadside coffee pot in North America, known as the Mickey Pot; grapevines in the Yadkin Valley.

Winston-Salem

In the mid-18th century, the Unitas Fratrum, better known as the Moravians, established the town of Salem. These Protestant migrants moved from Europe to Pennsylvania and eventually into the hills of North Carolina, bringing with them some of the sensibilities and folk traditions of the Pennsylvania Dutch. Known for excellent and unostentatious craftsmanship, strong religious faith, and community bonds, the Moravians were a unique cultural enclave in early North Carolina. Today, more than 20,000 North Carolinians belong to the Unitas Fratrum, keeping alive their religion and folk traditions, which include sacred brass bands and sought-after baked goods.

The Winston part of Winston-Salem was founded as Forsyth County's seat, and throughout the 19th and 20th centuries it boomed as an industrial and trading hub, powered by what appeared to be an endless stream of tobacco and textile money. Although the textile mills are mostly gone from North Carolina and the tobacco industry is dying a slow death, Winston-Salem thrives as a banking center and the home of Wake Forest University and Winston-Salem State University.

SIGHTS
★ Old Salem and Salem Pathways

Nestled in the center of a modern city, **Old Salem** (900 Old Salem Rd., 336/721-7300, www.oldsalem.org, museum and gardens 10am-2pm Wed.-Sun., Old Salem and MESDA $20 adults, $12 students, two-stop tickets $18 adults, $9 students) was once an independent town that was home to the industrious Moravians. Throughout the second half of the 18th century and the 19th century, the German-speaking Unitas Fratrum produced beautiful and functional ceramics, furniture, tools, and other goods for themselves and their neighbors. This era is recreated today in the streets and homes of the old village, where it's common to see costumed interpreters carrying on the Moravian ways and making expertly crafted goods as prized today as they were essential 150 years ago.

Old Salem is home to two museums that are both worth examining, along with a beautiful garden to tour. The **Museum of Early Southern Decorative Arts** (MESDA, 924 S. Main St., 336/721-7360, www.mesda.org, 9:10am-2pm Wed.-Sun., $10 adults and students, $5 ages 6-17) tells the story of the early South through the objects made by a diverse range of craftspeople: early Jamestown residents, African American decorative artists, and makers of furniture, ceramics, silver work, and textiles. Feel free to check out the galleries at your pace, or book a two-hour private tour (2:30pm Wed.-Sat., $50).

At each of the dozen or so gardens spread out around the village of Old Salem, you'll find the heirloom fruits, vegetables, and ornamental plants that the original Moravian inhabitants would have planted. One of the most impressive is the **Single Brothers Garden,** now only a fraction of its original 700 acres, laid out in squares on a series of terraces descending the slope behind the house, where a variety of vegetables and grains are grown, including corn, peas, winter wheat, lettuce, turnips, cabbage, and okra. Another garden of note is the **Miksch Garden,** a fine example of a household garden where crops like peas, leeks, garlic, lettuce, spinach, potatoes, and other commonly used crops are planted in raised beds. Many of the crops, as with other gardens around the village, are allowed to go to seed, meaning to grow beyond their culinary use, producing flowers and then the seeds that will be next year's crops. Costumed interpreters talk about the crops and gardening practices; inside the house,

Winston-Salem

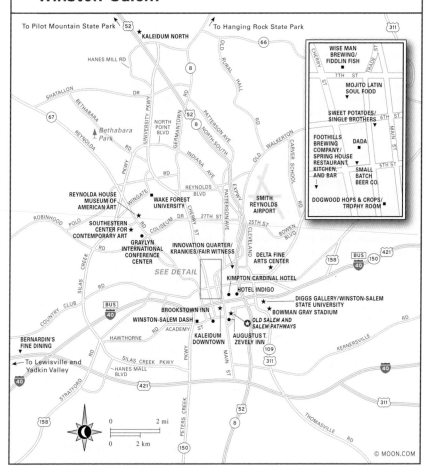

more interpreters demonstrate cooking and household chores.

Along the streets of the old village, you'll pass dozens of historic buildings that house artisans' workshops and that hold significance in the history of this religious community. Among these are the **Single Brothers' House** and **Single Sisters' House,** the 18th-century dormitories in which "choirs," groups of young unmarried Moravian men and women, lived and worked. The **Doctor's House** (463 Church St. SE, 9:30am-4:30pm Tues.-Sat., 1pm-4:30pm Sun.), home of the Berlin-trained doctor who came to be Salem's town physician in 1790, is a fascinating repository of early medical and pharmaceutical goods.

Winkler Bakery (521 S. Main St., 336/721-7302, 10am-2pm Wed.-Sun., $3-20) was run by Swiss-born Christian Winkler and his descendants for more than 120 years, and their wood-burning ovens are still turning out Moravian delicacies today (grab a tin of gingersnaps or Moravian cookies for the road).

Muddy Creek Café (137 West St., 336/201-5182, www.muddycreekcafeandmusichall.com, 10am-2pm Wed. and Fri.-Sat., 10am-2pm and 6pm-9pm Thurs., 10am-3pm Sun., $7-10) has sandwiches, panini, and salads.

While you're in Old Salem, visit one of the most important sites for African Americans and abolitionists in the state, St. Philips African Moravian Church (911 S. Church St.). Built in 1861, this the oldest African American church still standing in North Carolina and one of the oldest in the nation. In the church in 1865 a Union Cavalry chaplain announced emancipation to the enslaved people in and around Salem. The new Hidden Town Project is shedding light on the history and lives of enslaved people in Old Salem. Signage, tours (while the pandemic allowed researchers time to do their thing, it put a damper on the tour element), and enrichment projects are planned throughout Old Salem that will help sites like St. Phillips, the Doctor's House, and other locations tell these stories, creating a full and more honest look at history here.

Salem is a beautiful place for a morning or evening walk, when the light comes through the trees and dapples the cobblestone streets with sun and shadow, but it pales in comparison to the stark beauty of God's Acre (S. Church St. and Cemetery St.), the traditional name given to Moravian graveyards. Seeing this striking graveyard for the first time, you'll notice that all of the gravestones are the same—white marble of nearly uniform dimensions, all facing east—reflecting the emphasis Moravians place on the equality of the souls of the faithful after death.

You can take self-guided tours throughout Old Salem courtesy the Salem Pathways program. Using your mobile device, you'll scan a QR code at different sites and bits of signage throughout Old Salem and hear corresponding stories told about or from the point of view of Moravian, Indigenous, and enslaved residents of the town.

Museums

Winston-Salem earned the nickname "The City of Arts and Innovation" partly thanks to the 1949 establishment of the nation's first local arts council. Since then, the city has continued to be a hive of artists and art collectors, and there are a number of museums dedicated to the arts, exploring history, and for children.

Winston-Salem's many art museums represent various places and centuries. The Reynolda House Museum of American Art (2250 Reynolda Rd., 888/663-1149, www.reynoldahouse.org, 9:30am-4:30pm Tues.-Sat., 1:30pm-4:30pm Sun., $18 adults, free under age 18, students, and military) has a distinguished collection of American masterpieces from colonial times through the present day in the beautiful 1917 home of R. J. and Katharine Reynolds, of the R. J. Reynolds Tobacco Company.

The Southeastern Center for Contemporary Art (750 Marguerite Dr., 336/725-1904, www.secca.org, noon-5pm Wed., noon-8pm Thurs., 10am-5pm Fri.-Sat., 1pm-5pm Sun., donation) hosts changing exhibits of modern work in a variety of media. Exhibits rotate every few months; one gallery may show avant-garde short films one month and the next display photorealistic paintings or giant yarn sculptures.

The Diggs Gallery (601 S. Martin Luther King Dr., 336/750-2458, www.wssu.edu, 11am-5pm Tues.-Sat., free) at Winston-Salem State University has excellent permanent and changing exhibitions of work by African and African American artists from North Carolina and the Southeast, with some pieces from influential artists from outside the area. Delta Fine Arts Center (2611 New Walkertown Rd., 336/722-2625, www.deltaartscenter.org, 2pm-5pm Tues. and Fri., 3pm-6pm Wed.-Thurs., closed 3rd Sat. of the month, free) also promotes African American visual and performing artists.

Kaleideum North (400 W. Hanes Mill

1: the gardens at the Reynolda House Museum of American Art 2: Salem Pathways 3: Moravian church 4: God's Acre

Rd., 336/767-6730, www.north.kaleideum.org, 9am-5pm Tues.-Fri., 10am-5pm Sat., 1pm-5pm Sun., $9 adults and youth, $8 seniors, free under age 1 and educators) was named one of the top 25 science museums by *Parents* magazine. Children can pet horseshoe crabs, play a floor piano with their feet, brush giant teeth, and learn about physics and biology. There's 25,000 square feet of exhibits, a 17-acre science and environmental studies park with nature trails and picnic spaces, and a planetarium. Also fun for kids is the **Kaleideum Downtown** (390 S. Liberty St., 336/723-9111, www.downtown.kaleideum.org, 9am-5pm Mon.-Fri., 10am-5pm Sat., 1pm-5pm Sun. June 1-Labor Day, 9am-4pm Tues.-Fri., 10am-5pm Sat., 1pm-5pm Sun. Labor Day-May, until 8pm 3rd Thurs. of the month, $9 adults, $9 youth, $8 seniors, free under age 1, $3 EBT cardholders). Kids love to climb the giant beanstalk in the lobby, which ascends all the way to the second floor. Other exhibits include a space with oversize building blocks, an enchanted forest, an educational garden open in warm weather, and a gallery filled with giant alphabet sculptures and activities.

A very different kind of gallery is the **Winston Cup Museum** (1355 N. Martin Luther King Dr., 336/724-4557, www.winstoncupmuseum.com, 10am-5pm Thurs.-Sat., $8 adults, $4 ages 5-12, free under age 5), which chronicles R. J. Reynolds's 33-year sponsorship of NASCAR (there can be no more Carolinian combination than cigarettes and stock cars). Here you'll see cars driven by Dale Senior and Dale Junior (as the Earnhardts are known in these parts), drivers' helmets, winners' payout checks, and other great racing memorabilia. It's an interesting museum even for nonfans.

Historic Bethabara Park

In northern Winston-Salem, **Bethabara Park** (2147 Bethabara Rd., 336/924-8191, www.historicbethabara.org.org, 10:30am-4:30pm Tues.-Sat., 1:30pm-4:30pm Sun. Apr.-mid-Dec., $4 adults, $1 children) explores an even earlier period of Moravian settlement than at Salem. Bethabara was the first foothold of the Moravians in North Carolina: In the fall of 1753 a group of 15 Moravian men came down the Great Wagon Road from Pennsylvania, through the Shenandoah Valley of Virginia, and into the North Carolina Piedmont to begin construction of a village at the northwestern edge of the 100,000-acre tract of land that the church had bought and named Wachovia. The 15 original settlers and the other Moravians who would soon join them constructed a sturdy, attractive little village in just a few years.

During its first two decades of existence, Bethabara was a busy place. The Moravians' reputation as craftspeople drew settlers from the surrounding hills to buy their wares. The village's location on the Great Wagon Road was also an important factor in its growth. During the French and Indian Wars in the 1750s, Bethabara became a stockade, an enclosed safe haven not only for the Moravians, but for an even greater number of non-Moravian neighbors. It was touched by war again in 1771, when General Cornwallis and his troops ransacked the town and stole livestock.

By the late 1760s, construction of Salem was underway, and the population of Bethabara gradually began to decline. The village mill and distillery remained in operation for some decades, but by the early 19th century, Bethabara had become a small farming community, and Salem, to the south, became the Moravian metropolis.

Körner's Folly

One of the weirdest places you can visit in North Carolina is **Körner's Folly** (413 S. Main St., 336/996-7922, www.kornersfolly.org, 10am-4pm Tues.-Sat., $10 adults, $6 ages 6-18, free under age 6), located east of Winston-Salem in Kernersville. The seven-level house with 22 rooms of insanely ornate moldings and eccentric architectural contraptions fits all the requirements of a classic Victorian monstrosity. But it's no monstrosity; its peculiarities make it awkwardly beautiful.

Yadkin Valley Wine Trail

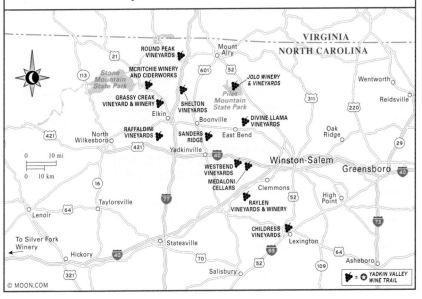

© MOON.COM

In its late-1870s infancy, Körner's Folly was intended not as a home but a display of designer Jule Körner's architectural innovations, a showroom for his clients to tour and experience the architectural elements he was proposing. Gradually it also became Körner's home. His wife created an exquisite children's theater in the high-ceilinged attic, well worth a visit on its own.

★ Yadkin Valley Wine Trail

The **Yadkin Valley** (www.yadkinvalleywine-country.com) is North Carolina's own little Napa Valley, a great place to spend a weekend touring and tasting some surprisingly good French- and Italian-style wines. There are close to 40 wineries in the 1.4-million-acre Yadkin Valley American Viticultural Area, most within a short drive of Winston-Salem, and every year one or two new vineyards are added to the roster. You'll find tasting rooms in barns, sleek modern buildings, and even Tuscan-style villas, along with winemakers who are still happy to take a minute or two to speak to visitors and explain the wine-making process. Yes, it's a little strange to hear the winemaker describe his grapes in a loving Southern accent, but you get used to it. Many towns in the northern Blue Ridge and the Blue Ridge Foothills are convenient to other ones in the Yadkin Valley.

Among the best vineyards in the Yadkin Valley is **Childress Vineyards** (1000 Childress Vineyard Rd., Lexington, 336/236-9463, www.childressvineyards.com, tasting room 10am-5pm daily, tours noon and 3pm Mon.-Fri., $10), owned by an unexpected wine fan, former NASCAR driver and NASCAR team owner Richard Childress. Childress Vineyards has more than 100 acres of grapes planted in a dozen varietals, including merlot and viognier, on land that resembles France's Burgundy region in many ways. In their 35,000-square-foot production facility, you'll have plenty of opportunities to taste their wines. The viognier, cabernet franc, and Meritage red blends are especially good, as is the Three; its name refers to the blend of three grapes used to make this crisp white as well as the legendary Dale Earnhardt, who drove a NASCAR race car painted with the number 3 for Richard Childress for many years. Here you'll also find **The Bistro** (10am-4pm daily, $10-28), serving the Childress family's favorite sandwiches as well as entrées that include flatbread pizza, shrimp and grits, and gnocchi.

Medaloni Cellars (9125 Shallowford Rd., Lewisville, 336/946-1490, 2pm-7pm Wed.-Thurs., noon-7pm Fri., 11am-6pm Sat., noon-6pm Sun., tastings $15) is a newcomer to the viticultural scene in the Yadkin Valley, established in 2011, but it's already getting noticed for the drinkable and accessible wines. This small winery produces only about 600 cases a year and is best known for its whites, including the Nude Chardonnay, an unoaked chardonnay that's great for sultry summer gatherings. They also have a pair of cabins and an Airstream ($150-249), for that "glamping" experience, to rent on the property, two of which are woodsy and very private; the third is adjacent to the tasting room but still has a good deal of private space.

The oldest winery in Yadkin County, **Westbend Winery and Brewery** (5394 Williams Rd., Lewisville, 336/945-9999, www.westbendwineryandbrewery.com, 2pm-9pm Thurs.-Fri., noon-8pm Sat., noon-7pm Sun.), still produces some great wine and now even brews some tasty beer. Wines include cabernet franc, sangiovese, and chambourcin, as well as syrah and chardonnay. Their brewery has a smaller selection, with four to six beers on tap.

Other vineyards worth a visit include **Divine Llama Vineyards** (4126 Divine Llama Lane, East Bend, 336/699-2525, www.divinellamavineyards.com, noon-6pm Thurs.-Sat.), where you'll find a couple of unusual varietals and a llama; **RayLen Vineyards & Winery** (3577 U.S. 158, Mocksville, 336/998-3100, www.raylenvineyards.com, 11am-6pm Mon.-Sat., noon-6pm Sun., tastings $8-15), home to a number of award-winning wines. **JOLO Winery & Vineyards** (219 JOLO Winery Lane, 336/614-0030, www.jolovineyards.com, 11am-8pm

Thurs.-Sun., tastings from $20) makes a really good red blend, Carolus, and an intriguing sweeter wine that's a great pre-dessert drink. **Grassy Creek Vineyard & Winery** (235 Chatham Cottage Circle, 336/835-2458, www.grassycreekvineyard.com, noon-6pm Thurs.-Sat., 1pm-5pm Sun., noon-6pm Mon.) has a 15-acre winery laced with hiking trails (including a trail dedicated to *shinrin-yoku,* or forest bathing), and they've got really good wine. Their chambourcin is a great option for red-lovers, and the dry riesling is a treat.

SPORTS AND RECREATION
Spectator Sports

Wake Forest University is the fourth school in the famous Tobacco Road athletic rivalry and a worthy competitor to its nemeses in the Triangle: Duke, the University of North Carolina, and North Carolina State. The jewels in the crown of **Demon Deacon Athletics** (499 Deacon Blvd., 366/758-3322, www.godeacs.com) are Wake's Atlantic Coast Conference Division I football and basketball teams. The basketball program has produced such notables as Billy Packer and the 5-foot-3 Muggsy Bogues, now both famous sports broadcasters, as well as Tim Duncan, Randolph Childress, and Chris Paul. The women's field hockey team is consistently among the nation's most successful, winning three consecutive NCAA championships in the early 2000s, and the golf program is the athletic alma mater of Arnold Palmer, Curtis Strange, and Lanny Wadkins. As is the case at its Tobacco Road counterparts, obtaining a ticket to see a Wake Forest football or basketball game can be quite difficult.

The Single-A farm team of the Chicago White Sox baseball team plays here in the Piedmont. The **Winston-Salem Dash** (926 Brookstown Ave., 336/714-2287, www.milb.com, $8-15) draw a fun, fervent fan

---

1: Many wineries feature outdoor areas to enjoy a bottle after a tasting. 2: Medaloni Cellars' tasting room

base, making this a great place to spend an afternoon or an evening—or both if it's a doubleheader.

NASCAR

NASCAR racing at **Bowman Gray Stadium** (1250 S. Martin Luther King Dr., 336/723-1819, www.bowmangrayracing.com, gates open 6pm, races at 8pm, $12 adults, $2 ages 6-11, free under age 5) is not only a classic Carolina experience—weekly races have been run here for 50 years—but also a less daunting experience than race events at the massive stadiums elsewhere in the state: Lowe's Speedway in Concord can accommodate more than 200,000 spectators, but Bowman Gray seats a cozy 17,000. It's also as inexpensive as a minor-league baseball game, making this an ideal place for your first NASCAR experience. Weekly races include modified, street stock, sportsman, and stadium stock car events.

ENTERTAINMENT AND EVENTS

Performing Arts

The **Piedmont Opera** (336/725-7101, www.piedmontopera.org, $22-168) has presented several operas each season since 1978; they emphasize classic Italian opera, so brush up on your Verdi. Now more than 60 years old, the **Winston-Salem Symphony's** (336/464-0145, www.wssymphony.org, $20-85) performance schedule includes a variety of baroque, pop, and other music.

The **University of North Carolina School of the Arts** (tickets and most performances at Stevens Center, 405 W. 4th St., 336/721-1945, www.uncsa.edu, box office 11am-5pm Mon.-Fri., $20 adults, $15 students) is one of the top performing arts schools in the world. In fact, their School of Drama was named by *The Hollywood Reporter* as the seventh-best in the world. The School of the Arts puts on a variety of performances throughout the year, including films, dance performances, plays, and concerts, but perhaps their most anticipated performance

of the year is December's brief run of *The Nutcracker*.

Nightlife

North Carolina is lousy with breweries, but one of the more interesting ones is **Small Batch Beer Co.** (241 W. 5th St., 336/893-6395, www.smallbatchws.com, 4pm-2am daily). These guys brew one small, experimental batch of beer at a time. They have cocktails in case you don't like the brew, and there's a small menu of sandwiches. **Fiddlin' Fish** (772 Trade St., 336/999-8945, www.fiddlinfish.com, 4pm-10pm Mon.-Wed., 4pm-11pm Thurs., 2pm-midnight Fri., noon-midnight Sat., noon-8pm Sun.) drew me in with the lilting strains of the Grateful Dead's 1972 European Tour but they kept me there with the beer. Pesca Pale Ale, the Dunkelweizen, and Amber Ale are all go-to brews, but I saw a lot of half-empty IPAs, a testament to the popularity of their take on this style.

Wise Man Brewing (826 Angelo Bros Ave., 336/725-0008, www.wisemanbrewing.com, 4pm-10pm Mon.-Wed., 4pm-11pm Thurs., 2pm-midnight Fri., noon-midnight Sat., noon-8pm Sun.) has taken over a 90-year-old warehouse and turned it into a brewing powerhouse. They make some of my favorite beers in North Carolina. Mountain Calling is a clean, citrusy IPA; Depths of My Mind is a flavor-packed wild ale; Tropical Shirts brings tart blackberries and raspberries to this sour brew; and big pints like Lasting Comfort (a barley wine; watch out) or a drinkable brew like Thousand Chords (a Grisette) are bound to be on your list of favorites too.

Foothills Brewing Company (638 W. 4th St., 336/777-3348, www.foothillsbrewing.com, 11am-midnight daily, $10-22) is a craft brewery, restaurant, and gathering place in the heart of downtown. They keep nine beers on tap at all times, with another two to four seasonal and special brews. A few menu items stand out, including the ale-battered fish-and-chips, bacon-wrapped trout stuffed with Granny Smith apples, and Paul's Spicy Ostrich Burger. A line starts to form each fall when they announce the release of their Sexual Chocolate Imperial Stout. It sells out quickly, and restaurants and bars are known to keep a keg or two in reserve for the middle of winter when supplies have seemingly been exhausted, much to the joy of Foothills fans. You can also visit the **Brewery and Tasting Room** (3800 Kimwell Dr., 336/977-9484, 4pm-9pm Mon.-Wed., 4pm-10pm Fri.-Sat., noon-8pm Sun., tours 3pm Sat.-Sun., free), where they have 28 taps and food trucks make regular visits.

Not content to stay in the brewhouse, Foothills has added **Footnote Coffee and Cocktails** (634 W. 4th St., 8am-10pm Mon.-Thurs., 8am-11pm Fri.-Sat., 11am-6pm Sun.) next door to the downtown brewery. As promised, there's coffee drinks and pastries, as well as a full bar, specialty cocktails, and more.

Incendiary Brewing Company (486 N. Patterson Ave., Suite 105, 336/893-6714, www.incendiarybrewing.com, 4pm-10pm Mon.-Thurs., noon-midnight Fri.-Sat., noon-10pm Sun.) serves a solid lineup of freshly brewed and barrel-aged beers from their location in Winston-Salem's **Innovation Quarter** (www.innovationquarter.com), where they occupy a building that was formerly a power plant. They hold concerts throughout the year (schedule varies, free) and are right next door to the best pizza in the state, so come on by, grab an IPA or a barrel-aged Baltic Porter, and enjoy.

Dogwood Hops & Crops (517 N. Liberty St., 336/955-1463, www.andrewsrestaurantsws.com, 3pm-10pm Mon., 3pm-midnight Tues.-Thurs., 1pm-1am Fri.-Sat., noon-8pm Sun.) has a large selection of beer from across North Carolina in coolers, but around two-dozen taps keeps fresh kegs in rotation. I was happy to find a hometown brewery—Flying Machine—on draft here, giving me an option I knew as I explored new breweries and beers from all around. Right next door is a sister speakeasy, **Trophy Room** (4pm-midnight Tues.-Thurs., 3pm-midnight Fri.-Sat.) serving Prohibition-era cocktails and an impressive bourbon selection. If fancy drinks and killer cocktails are what you're after, see what the bartenders are mixing up at **Fair Witness Fancy Drinks** (290 4th St. E., 336/607-4185, 4pm-11pm Tues. and Sun., 4pm-2am Wed.-Sat.). For craft cocktails in a surprising dive-bar setting, **Single Brothers** (627 N. Trade St., 336/602-2657, 4pm-2am Mon.-Sat., 2pm-2am Sun.) is the place to pull up a barstool. This is a hip, energetic bar with loyal local patrons and bartenders who know their way around a cocktail shaker.

Events

The **1st Friday Gallery Hop** (www.dadaws.org, 7pm-10pm 1st Fri. of the month) takes place on the first Friday evening of every month in the Downtown Arts District Association neighborhood along 6th, Trade, and Liberty Streets. Throughout the district, art galleries, craft studios, and shops are open well into the evening, with neighborhood restaurants and bars staying open even later for the event. Check the calendar for dates and additional events.

Starting at midnight and lasting into the early hours of Easter Sunday every year, **roving brass bands** play throughout the city in a tradition that the Moravians of Salem practiced 200 years ago and that remains an important part of Easter worship. The bands' rounds, as they're called, always begin with Bach's "Sleepers, Wake," a composition that was brand-new when the first Moravian band was organized in Saxony. Some bands play in Old Salem, but others get on buses and spread throughout the city, waking Winston-Salem to the news of Easter morning.

April brings the **RiverRun Film Festival** (336/724-1502, www.riverrunfilm.com, passes $50 for 6 films, $108 for 10 films), one of the largest film festivals in the Southeast. It is a great opportunity to see the work of both established and emerging filmmakers and to attend workshops and panels about the art and business of filmmaking. In June, at the **Spirits of Summer** (www.spiritsofsummer.com, $25 advance tickets, $30 at the gate), you'll have the chance to taste wine from the nearby Yadkin Valley as well as beer and spirits made across the region. The end of July and beginning of August is time for the **National Black Theater Festival** (336/723-2266, www.ncblackrep.org, prices vary). The six-day gathering includes classic and modern dramas as well as poetry slams and many other events. The *New York Times* reviewed 1989's inaugural festival, attended by 10,000 people, as "one of the most historic and culturally significant events in the history of Black theater and American theatre in general." It now draws 60,000 visitors annually.

November's **Piedmont Craftsmen's Fair** (Benton Convention Center, 336/725-1516, www.piedmontcraftsmen.org, $8 adults, $7 seniors and students, free under age 12, $12 weekend pass) has been held in Winston-Salem for more than 40 years. This large gathering of artists and art lovers celebrates craft in media such as fiber, clay, and metal and demonstrates how innovation and tradition interweave to make North Carolina one of the world's great craft centers. If you miss the fair, don't worry; the **Piedmont Craftsmen Gallery** (601 N. Trade St., 11am-3pm Tues.-Fri., 11am-4pm Sat.) is open year-round.

SHOPPING

The Downtown Arts District, referred to as DADA (www.dadaws.org), is a neighborhood of galleries and boutiques located downtown along 5th, 6th, and Trade Streets. There are more than a dozen commercial galleries, including the **Piedmont Craftsmen Gallery** (601 N. Trade St., 336/725-1516, www.piedmontcraftsmen.org, 11am-3pm Tues.-Fri., 11am-4pm Sat.), which has a beautiful showroom displaying the work of hundreds of North Carolina's finest studio potters, fiber artists, jewelry designers, and craftspeople in many other media. Several restaurants, bars, and coffee shops are located in DADA. The **Reynolda Village Shops** (2201 Reynolda Rd., 336/758-5584, www.reynoldavillage.com), near the historic Reynolda House and museum, is a cluster of specialty stores and boutiques full of unique jewelry, clothing, books, antiques, home goods, and gardening gifts.

For Americana, **Old Salem** (www.oldsalem.org, most shops 10am-5pm Tues.-Sat., 1pm-5pm Sun.) has fun shops as well as historical sites to visit. At the **Winkler Bakery** (521 S. Main St., 336/721-7302, 10am-5pm Mon.-Sat., 1pm-5pm Sun.), bread and the famous Moravian cookies are made in the old-time way. **Moravian Book & Gift Shop** (614 S. Main St., 10am-2pm Wed.-Sun.) has North Carolina pottery, food, books, and gifts along with Moravian items like candles and books. Inside you'll find **E. A. Vogler Coffee & Confections** (336/723-6262, $2-8) where you can grab a coffee and a snack. The **Horton Museum Center Store** (924 S. Main St., 336/721-7360, 9:30am-4:30pm Tues.-Sat., 1pm-4:30pm Sun.) is a great place to find Old Salem's wonderful in-house products or books about early Southern arts and crafts, including the work of master furniture makers from North Carolina.

FOOD
Traditional Moravian Food

When the Moravian people came to Salem, they brought their foodways with them. Many of the foods they cooked are old-fashioned now and belong in historical cookbooks; others—like their impossibly thin and crispy cookies, the delectable sugar cake, and other baked goods—have become staples in Winston-Salem and across North Carolina, and others—like the Moravian chicken pie—are beginning to disappear from menus, and it's a real shame; I'd love to see someone keep this tradition alive with a regular menu feature.

Salem Baking Company (at Reynolda Manor, 2876 Reynolda Rd., 336/724-0559, www.deweys.com, 11am-6pm Mon.-Sat., noon-6pm Sun.) and **Dewey's** (Thruway Shopping Center, 262 Stratford Rd., 336/725-8321, 9am-8pm Mon.-Sat., noon-7pm Sun.) keep the Moravian cookie tradition alive, and you'll find sleeves and boxes of these treats at their locations and at many gift shops and grocery stores around the area. Dewey's has been in business since 1930 and they make a ton of variations on the thin spicy Moravian cookie, plus treats like cheese straws, so you can balance sweet and savory if you like. **Wilkerson Moravian Bakery** (50 Miller St., Suite B, 336/830-8102, https://wilkerson-bakery.com, 10am-6pm Tues.-Sat.) and a few others bake these perfect little cookies as well. And if you need a Moravian sugar cake (and who doesn't?), look no farther than **Winkler Bakery** (521 S. Main St., Old Salem, 336/721-7302, 10am-5pm Mon.-Sat., 1pm-5pm Sun.), in Old Salem, where bread, sugar cakes, and Moravian cookies are made in the old-time way by bakers who do their thing in historic costume.

Barbecue and Comfort Food

Sweet Potatoes (607 N. Trade St., 336/727-4844, www.sweetpotatoes.ws, 4pm-8pm Wed.-Fri., noon-3pm and 5pm-8pm Sat., $9-21), a much-acclaimed Southern-style gourmet restaurant, is more formally known as "Sweet Potatoes (Well Shut My Mouth!)—a Restaurant." Everything here is an expertly crafted version of Southern favorites and regional delicacies, including fried green tomatoes, smothered yard bird (that's another way of saying chicken), house-fried pork rinds, and some of the best fried chicken you'll find anywhere.

Brothers Josh and Buddy Milner run the kitchen at **Milner's American Southern Restaurant** (630 S. Stratford Rd., 336/768-2221, https://gotomilners.com, 4pm-8pm Tues.-Sat., 11am-8pm Sun., $9-36), and while you may think that brothers in the kitchen would spell disaster, it spells success. The restaurant has been thriving since it opened in 2005 thanks to the dual vision of the Milner Brothers, their view on updating Southern classics, and their devotion to local flavors and ingredients. The Frogmore stew (a rich seafood soup in an ale-tomato broth), the Moravian cookie and pecan crusted salmon, the fried chicken with Carolina gold rice, and duck breast with jalapeño-lingonberry sauce

all speak to the creativity and technical skills in the kitchen here.

When you go to **Slappy's Chicken** (200 W. Acadia Ave., 336/761-0268, 11am-8pm Mon.-Sat., $9-14) expecting Nashville hot chicken, you're in for a surprise. The chicken here is close but it's not the same. At Slappy's, they take fried chicken and slather it with hot sauce—as Nashville style dictates—but the sauce is heavier and more sweet than spicy; still, it's delicious. So are the sides, which are country-style through and through: collards, mac-and-cheese topped with Cheez-Its, slaw, baked beans, and the like.

Eclectic

★ **Spring House Restaurant, Kitchen & Bar** (450 N. Spring St., 336/293-4797, http://springhousenc.com, 5pm-9pm Wed.-Sat., $15-42) is a farm-to-fork restaurant led by an exuberant and creative chef, Tim Grandinetti. The menu here is playful, with items like shrimp corn dogs, General Tso's crispy veal sweetbreads, chicken-fried foie gras, and slow-cooked Kobe beef cheeks. The cocktails are out of sight, and the bartender will pair your drink with your meal. The Tasting Menu, a four-course or more prix-fixe menu that serves omnivores and vegetarians, gives the chef a chance to show off and deliver a bevy of delicious small plates to your table.

Mozelle's Fresh Southern Bistro (878 W. 4th St., 336/703-5400, http://mozelles.com, 11am-9pm Tues.-Sun., $7-28) is a cozy place with fantastic food. Try the fried goat cheese salad or The Leaf, a salad with an okra-bourbon vinaigrette, for starters. Then move on to the shrimp and grits, scallops, or the pimento cheeseburger. When the weather is nice, sit at one of the tables outside.

Keep breakfast and lunch simple at **Young Cardinal** (424 W. 4th St., 336/448-5188, www.andrewsrestaurantsws.com, 8am-3pm Tues.-Sun., $1.50-12). Get a biscuit, biscuit sandwich, omelet, breakfast bowl, or plate of eggs and sides in the morning, then for lunch switch to one of their great sandwiches (like

the grilled cheese with bacon jam) or salads (the hot honey chicken salad is a top pick).

Jeffrey Adams Restaurant on 4th (321 W. 4th St., 336/448-1714, https://jeffreyadams-ws.com, 4pm-9pm Tues.-Thurs. and Sun., 4pm-10pm Fri.-Sat., $14-50) serves steaks, seafood, duck, and more cooked over a wood-fired grill. In true steakhouse fashion, they offer up classics like a wedge and caesar salad, an extensive wine list, and exceptional cuts of beef. You can also make a meal of a salad and the small plates—post roach nachos and the hanger steak with hot bourbon pickles are filling—if you'd rather keep it light.

Bernardin's Fine Dining (901 W. 4th St., 336/725-6666, www.bernardinsfinedining. com, 5pm-9pm Mon.-Sat., $19-40) is one of the most lauded restaurants in Winston. In fact, the *Greensboro News and Record* labeled it "the Triad's only five-star restaurant." Chef Freddy Lee honed his skills at several prominent New York City restaurants before moving south and opening Bernardin's with his brother Terry. Seafood and hearty cuts of beef and veal dominate the menu. The wine list is extensive, and the desserts alone are worth a visit. Bernardin's doesn't offer vegetarian options, but carnivores will be satisfied.

Forsyth Seafood Market & Café (108 N. Martin Luther King Jr. Dr., 336/748-0793, www.forsythseafood.com, café 11am-8pm Mon.-Thurs. and Sat., 11am-9pm Fri., $8-16) serves seriously good food. With the exception of chicken wings, sides (hushpuppies are great here), and dessert, it's all fried seafood—whiting fillets; croaker, flounder, and catfish; popcorn and jumbo shrimp, crabcakes, and oysters; sandwiches and trays.

Krankies Coffee (211 E. 3rd St., 336/722-3016, www.krankiescoffee.com, 8am-3pm daily) is a local roaster and café with a strong following that I knew first for roasting some great beans and making an excellent cup of coffee, but with the addition of an awesome breakfast-brunch menu, there's more to love. The Dirty Bird Biscuit has fried chicken, pimento cheese, and bacon, and it shows up on a lot of tables. A Krankies Classic brings Texas Pete (a Winston-Salem creation) together with fried chicken for a tasty bite. The Ham Jam is just that: a biscuit, ham, and jam. But you can keep it light with a pastry to go with your coffee if you like.

Italian

The owners of **Di Lisio's Italian Restaurant** (301 Brookstown Ave., 336/546-7202, www. delisiositalian.com, 4pm-9pm Tues.-Thurs., 4pm-10pm Fri.-Sat., $10-29) come to Winston-Salem from a little town called Naples, Italy, and they brought with them a stack of recipes and a desire to share home-cooked Italian food the way they grew up eating it. Expect gravy you'll crave for days, hearty dishes, and portions that please. The Seafood Di Lisio (shrimp, mussels, clams, lobster, and calamari in marinara sauce over linguini) is to die for, and the penne pesto (creamy or classic) has picture-perfect pesto.

I found the *pizza tradizionale di Napoli* at ★ **Cugino Forno** (486 N. Patterson Ave., Suite 115, 336/448-0102, www.cuginoforno. com, 11am-9pm Sun.-Thurs., 11am-10pm Fri.-Sat., $17-22) is easily my favorite in North Carolina. Not just of traditional Napoli-style pies, but out of all the pizza, period. The crust has the perfect chew, the right thickness, and durability to hold up to sauce and toppings and not fall apart. The cheese, meats, veggies, and herbs they use are flavor-packed and never out of proportion with the size of the pizza. They smell great and look even better. Go for the Calabrese—with spicy Calabrian peppers and a zesty salami—the exceptional Bianca or Pomodor, or the simple perfection of the Margherita; you'll leave happy.

Mission Pizza Napoletana (707 Trade St. NW, 336/893-8217, www.missionpizza-napoletana.com, 5pm-9pm Wed.-Thurs., 5pm-10pm Fri.-Sat., $12-15) sits on Trade Street near several breweries and bars, and as such delivers on one of the best things about

---

1: Mojito Latin Soul Food **2:** Winkler Bakery **3:** diners enjoying a brew from Incendiary Brewing while they wait for pizza from Cugino Forno

pizza: It's a great pregame snack or late-in-the-evening bite. The pies are hot and come out fast thanks to their 900-degree Italian oven, and if you're not in the mood for a pizza, they also have pasta, salads, and Italian-inspired entrées to choose from.

Asian Fusion

The Basil Leaf Thai and Sushi Restaurant (690 St. George Square Court, 336/283-9133, www.basilleafthai.com, 11am-2:30pm and 5pm-10pm Mon.-Fri., noon-10pm Sat.-Sun., lunch $6-19, dinner $6-30) bring the Thai deliciousness and a nice assortment of traditional and nouveau fresh sushi rolls. Personally, I love Thai soups like *tom yam* and *tom kar* and the Thai boat noodle soup, but every dish I've had off the Thai menu I'd gladly have again. The same goes for sushi, where I've enjoyed the *nigiri*, sashimi platters, and the rolls, whether they're straightforward or inventive.

Mediterranean

I was quite impressed with **Yamas Mediterranean Street Food** (624 W. 4th St., 336/842-5668, www.eatyamas.com, 11am-8pm daily, $10-15). This fast-casual spot gives Mediterranean food its time in the spotlight, and with tons of vegan and gluten-free options on the menu, it's drawing hungry diners from all corners. Pick a sandwich (in pita bread), a salad, or a grain bowl, then start adding dips, spreads, and toppings. Tahini-loaded hummus, a spicy feta mousse, baba ghanoush, falafel, dolmas, beef kofta, chicken souvlaki, slices of gyro meat, and more than two dozen toppings and sauces give you seemingly endless options. And it's reasonably priced and healthy, so what's not to love?

Soul Food

★ **Mojito Latin Soul Food** (723 N. Trade St., 336/723-7239, www.mojitolatinsoulfood.com, counter service noon-8pm Mon., noon-3pm Thurs.-Fri., table service 4pm-9pm Thurs., 3pm-10pm Fri., noon-10pm Sat., noon-4pm Sun., $11-24) didn't impress me;

they blew me away. I absolutely loved their ceviche (I owe my wife an apology for eating fully two-thirds of it) and couldn't decide between the *croqueta* or the empanada so we got them both (I'm still undecided; they're outstanding). And then we moved on to the mains. The deluxe Cuban sandwich (extra cheese plus a pair of *croquetas* thrown between the bread for good measure) is indulgent, the tacos damn near perfect, and the bowls are hearty and filling. Be warned: You'll eye every dish arriving at every table around you and wonder, "Why didn't I get that?" Which is a good sign you need to come back.

Bakeries

I have to admit, every time I'm in town, I turn to one of the two locations of **Camino Bakery** (www.caminobakery.com): **downtown** (310-B W. 4th St., 336/721-9990, 7am-5pm Mon.-Thurs., 7am-10pm Fri.-Sat., 7am-8pm Sun.) and in **Brookstown** (300 S. Marshall St., 8am-2pm daily) for breakfast. Which means I miss out on their lunch, and the look of their quiche is super tempting. Still, the selection of morning pastries (I can't resist a pain au chocolat, and their sticky bun is a thing of beauty) makes for an easy bite, and their all-day menu of café beverages means I can stop by for a pick-me-up and not miss much time on the road.

Black Mountain Chocolate Bar (450 N. Patterson Ave., Suite 110, 336/293-4698, www.blackmountainchocolate.com, noon-6pm Tues.-Thurs., 10am-10pm Fri.-Sat., noon-6pm Sun., $3-143) knows how to satisfy my sweet tooth, and if you're a chocoholic too, they've got your number. Tarts, cookies, brownies, bars (so many bars), and drinking chocolate (which they promise will cure you of using the powdered hot cocoa packets once you've tried theirs, and they're right) are loaded with chocolate and are, thankfully, big enough to share. They also have a little cocktail menu where everything is chocolate-centered, and the best (the Nib's Old Fashioned and Innovation Quarter) steer clear of being overly sweet.

ACCOMMODATIONS

The ★ **Graylyn International Conference Center** (1900 Reynolda Rd., 336/758-2600 or 800/472-9596, www.graylyn.com, $230-800) is a spectacular historic home and onetime residence of the Bowman Gray family. Gray was the son of a Wachovia Loan and Trust Company cofounder but left his banking job to become president of R. J. Reynolds Tobacco Company. The home was completed in 1932 and is the second-largest personal residence in North Carolina at around 45,000 square feet. It has been everything from a private residence to a mental hospital renowned for its "experimental treatments." Now owned by Wake Forest University, it's a stunning high-end hotel and conference center.

While visiting Graylyn, many guests choose the opulent Manor House for their stay, but I prefer The Mews, the estate's stable and working farmhouse (the honeymoon suite is a stunning room in the former chicken house). Beautiful stonework, a pair of turreted suites, a huge cobblestone courtyard, and a butler (yes, a tie-and-tails butler) at your service makes staying here the top option when you're in Winston-Salem.

Dining at Graylyn is an experience, and chef Gregory Rollins has never delivered anything short of excellence. This Barbadian honed his skills in his native Barbados before making his way to Graylyn. In 2021 the focus shifted from chef Rollins's impeccable plating and multicourse tasting menu in the **Graylyn Dining Room** (groups of less than 10, reservations required, 6pm-9pm daily) to the more casual fare served in the **Grille Room** ($7-29), where you'll find a great burger, a daily steak preparation, a vegetarian gnocchi, and a selection of appetizers.

★ **Kimpton Cardinal Hotel** (51 4th St. E., 336/724-1009, www.thecardinalhotel. com, $160-800) cuts a beautiful silhouette in the Winston-Salem skyline, and it's a shape you might recognize. This 1929 building that once housed the R. J. Reynolds Tobacco Company offices was the template and architectural muse for the Empire State Building. Touches of art deco opulence exist throughout from the entryway and check-in desk to adornments in the halls and elevators to the mailboxes and mail slots throughout the hotel. There are lots of surprises to find here, a trademark of the playful approach Kimpton Hotels takes to restoring properties like this. You can grab a bite here at the delightful French café, **The Katherine** (336/761-0203, breakfast 7am-10am Mon.-Fri., brunch 8am-2pm Sat.-Sun., lunch 11am-2pm Mon.-Fri., dinner 5pm-10pm daily, $9-38). Dinner is classic French—mussels, oysters on the half shell with champagne mignonette, chicken au poivre, seared duck, steak frites—and impeccably prepared, so be ready for a treat.

At **Hotel Indigo Winston-Salem** (104 W. 4th St., 336/722-0720, www.hotelindigo.com, $160-290) you'll have a fantastic location in downtown that's easily walkable to many of the restaurants, breweries, and venues in the city (you'll still need to dive out to Reynolda House and other more distant locations). The rooms are comfortable, stylish, and roomy enough to spread out in for a few days. There's an on-site restaurant, **Sir Winston Bar & Restaurant** (336/722-0795, https://sirwinstonrestaurant.com, 6:30am-10pm Mon.-Thurs., 6:30am-11pm Fri.-Sat., 6:30am-8pm Sun., $11-32) where you can get a full sit-down meal or pick up a grab-and-go bite as you head out the door.

A cotton mill built in the 1830s, the **Brookstown Inn** (200 Brookstown Ave., 336/701-3904, www.brookstowninn.com, $130-210) has been renovated and transformed into a luxurious hotel, with beautiful exposed brick walls, huge guest rooms, and Wi-Fi. Guests enjoy wine and cheese in the evenings and milk and cookies at night. The Brookstown Inn is within walking distance of Old Salem, and taking a stroll there and back in the morning is a great way to start your day.

Augustus T. Zevely Inn (803 S. Main St., Old Salem, 336/748-9299, www.zevleyinn. com, $169-279, children not allowed) is the only B&B in Old Salem. The beautiful 1830s house is furnished in original and reproduction

Moravian furniture, with special features peppered throughout, such as steam baths in some guest rooms, heated brick tile floors in others, and working cooking fireplaces. Each of the 12 guest rooms has a view of the old village or the house's period gardens. Add to this a quiet, beautiful neighborhood, an easy drive to great restaurants, and private baths.

Like all of North Carolina's major cities, Winston-Salem has a lot of chain motels. A pair of good bets are in the **Twin City Quarter** (425 N. Cherry St., 336/397-7777, www.twincityquarter.com) downtown: The **Marriott** (336/725-3500, http://marriot.com, from $155) and **Embassy Suites** (460 N. Cherry St., 336/724-2300, www.hilton.com, from $130) are adjacent to one another and to the Benton Convention Center. **Fairfield Inn & Suites Downtown** (125 S. Main St., 336/714-2800, http://marriott.com, from $114) is another good option. The downtown arts district is right around the corner, and many restaurants and bars are only steps away.

INFORMATION AND SERVICES

Winston-Salem's main emergency hospital is **Atrium Health Wake Forest Baptist** (Medical Center Blvd., 336/716-2011, www.

wakehealth.edu), located off Business I-40 between Cloverdale Avenue and Hawthorne Road.

The **Winston-Salem Journal** (www.journalnow.com) is the city's main newspaper. The **Winston-Salem Visitors Center** (200 Brookstown Ave., 336/728-4200, www.visitwinstonsalem.com, 10am-5pm Mon.-Fri., 10am-4pm Sat.) and its website provide extensive travel information.

GETTING THERE AND AROUND

Winston-Salem is on I-40, North Carolina's largest east-west highway. It is about 20 minutes' drive from Greensboro, about 2 hours from Raleigh, and about 1.5 hours from Charlotte.

Piedmont Triad International Airport (GSO, 1000 Ted Johnson Pkwy., Greensboro, 336/665-5666, www.flyfrompti.com), is nearby, on the northwest side of Greensboro, with many daily scheduled flights to U.S. cities. **Winston-Salem Transit Authority** (336/727-2648, www.wstransit.com), the city's bus system, is connected to that of Greensboro via Piedmont Area Regional Transit's **Express Bus** (336/662-0002, www.partnc.org).

Greensboro and Vicinity

Greensboro may be more densely packed with colleges and universities than any town in the state. It's home to the University of North Carolina Greensboro; North Carolina Agricultural and Technical State University (A&T); Guilford College, a small Quaker school; and Bennett College, a historically African American women's college often called "the Vassar of the South." As befits a college town, Greensboro has a lively arts and music scene and a creative, engaged population.

Greensboro has a surprisingly urban feel

for its size, partly due to its ethnic diversity. In the 1970s and 1980s a significant number of Southeast Asian refugees settled here, making this an important population center for the Hmong and Montagnard people. There is also a significant population of African immigrants and a growing population of Latin Americans. Mix in the long-established African American population, the Quaker traditions still carried on today, a handful of Native Americans, and college students of various backgrounds, and you have a culturally rich city.

Greensboro and Vicinity

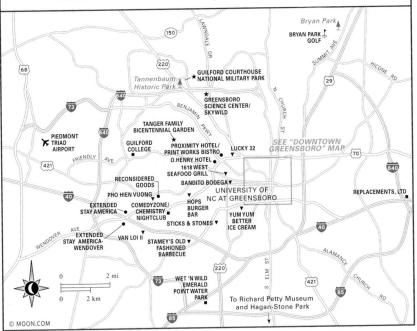

SIGHTS

★ International Civil Rights Center and Museum

Greensboro, the home of North Carolina A&T, a prominent historically Black university, has played an important role in African American history. The **International Civil Rights Center and Museum** (134 S. Elm St., 336/274-9199 or 800/748-7116, www. sitinmovement.org, 10am-6pm Mon.-Sat., $12 adults, $10 students and seniors, $8 ages 6-12) is housed in Greensboro's old downtown Woolworth's building, the site of the famous 1960 lunch-counter sit-in that galvanized North Carolina's civil rights movement. That whites-only counter is the touchstone for this museum's exploration of the civil rights movement. There are some fantastic tour options here, including filmed one-hour tours led by the museum's docents

($10), interactive virtual tours held over Zoom and led by a docent ($15 adults, $10 students), a two-hour seated tour and walk-through that combines a filmed tour and an in-person walkthrough of the gallery highlights ($15 adults, $10 students), and two-hour staff-guided tours through the museum ($25 adults, $15 students), all of which must be booked ahead to guarantee availability. The four men who staged the sit-in—David Richmond, Franklin McCain, Jibreel Khazan, and Joseph McNeil—are honored on the A&T campus with the **A&T Four Statue** (1601 E. Market St.).

In addition to the historic lunch counter, the museum has extensive exhibitions about life in the South in the Jim Crow era and about the struggles and successes of the civil rights movement. All tours are guided and begin every 30 minutes.

Downtown Greensboro

Guilford Courthouse National Military Park

When discussing the Revolutionary War, the battles that come to most people's minds are probably in the Mid-Atlantic region and New England. In truth, much of that war was fought in the South, and some of the major turning points occurred in North Carolina. The **Guilford Courthouse National Military Park** (2332 New Garden Rd., 336/288-1776, www.nps.gov/guco, 8:30am-5pm daily, free) commemorates the battle

of Guilford Courthouse, when 1,900 British troops led by General Cornwallis routed 4,500 Patriots under General Nathaniel Greene. It proved to be a Pyrrhic victory, however, as Cornwallis's army was severely hobbled by the action. A 2.5-mile self-guided tour, which can be driven, hiked, or biked, stops at the essential spots on the battlefield.

Greensboro Science Center

The **Greensboro Science Center** (4301 Lawndale Dr., 336/288-3769, www.

greensboroscience.org, 9am-5pm daily, closed Thanksgiving Day and Dec. 25, $19.50 over age 13, $18.50 seniors, $17.50 ages 3-13) is a great place for kids and adults. Outside, the **Zoo Trek** (10am-4pm daily fall-spring, 9am-5pm daily summer) displays live tigers, meerkats, alligators, crocodiles, and other wild animals. Inside are science exhibits and the **OmniSphere Theater** (hours vary by show, $3-5), showing 3-D digital shows on the domed planetarium ceiling. The **SciQuarium** (9am-5pm daily) is North Carolina's first inland aquarium, revealing the world under the waves to a new group of kids and adults.

Greensboro Children's Museum

For children under age 10, the **Greensboro Children's Museum** (220 N. Church St., 336/574-2898, www.gcmuseum.com, 9am-5pm Tues.-Thurs., 9am-8pm Fri., 10am-6pm Sat., and 1pm-5pm Sun., $10) features a pretend town with a Main Street where children can shop for groceries, bake and deliver pizza, put on a play with costumes and props, learn how houses are built, and scale a rock-climbing wall.

GreenHill Center for North Carolina Art

The **GreenHill Center for North Carolina Art** (200 N. Davie St., 336/333-7460, www.greenhillnc.org, noon-5pm Tues. and Thurs.-Fri., noon-7pm Wed., 10am-5pm Sat., free) presents exhibits of work by North Carolina artists. Much attention is given to folk art traditions, but the state is also rich with formal studio artists, and some of the best are represented here. A free Family Night (5pm-7pm Wed.) has art activities, art exploration, and a get-your-hands-dirty good time.

Weatherspoon Art Museum

The **Weatherspoon Art Museum** (500 Tate St., at Spring Garden St., 336/334-5770, www.weatherspoonart.org, 10am-5pm Tues.-Wed. and Fri., 10am-9pm Thurs., 1pm-5pm Sat.-Sun., free), on the campus of UNC-Greensboro, has been dedicated to modern art since the early 1940s and has assembled a collection that includes works by Willem de Kooning, Andy Warhol, Cindy Sherman, and many other well-known 20th-century artists. This is the best collection of modern art in North Carolina and one of the best in the Southeast.

Elsewhere Museum

Elsewhere Museum (606 S. Elm St., 336/907-3271, www.elsewheremuseum.org, call for hours, $5 donation) is a fascinating spot. Located in a three-story thrift store that closed in 1997 and packed with the findings and creations of a 58-year history of collecting and sorting, it's a living, growing museum; a collaborative art space dedicated to artistic experimentation, social action, and the integration of creativity and life. It's both cool and overwhelming. They've got tons of stuff here: 10,000-plus articles of military surplus from World War II and the Korean War; at least as many bolts of vintage fabric; 20,000 pieces of vintage clothing and books; thousands of pieces of dishware and assorted knick-knacks. All of it was left here after the thrift store closed, and now it's part and parcel to the international art colony that's cycled more than 500 artists through these doors.

Blandwood Mansion

Blandwood Mansion (447 W. Washington St., 336/272-5003, www.preservationgreensboro.org, 10am-5pm Tues.-Wed. and Fri.-Sat., 10am-8pm Thurs., $8 adults, $5 under age 12, $7 seniors) was built in 1790 as a farmhouse before the city appeared. In the 1840s its famous resident was Governor John Motley Morehead, the "Father of Modern North Carolina," whose efforts to institute humane treatment of the mentally ill, prisoners, and children with disabilities, as well as to modernize the state's schools and transportation infrastructure, made him an important historical figure. In 1844, Morehead engaged Alexander Jackson Davis, the architect largely responsible for the Gothic Revival style in U.S.

architecture, to redo Blandwood Mansion; the result is the Italianate villa you see today.

SPORTS AND RECREATION
Other Recreation

At the Greensboro Science Center you'll find SKYWILD (4301 Lawndale Dr., 336/288-3769, ext. 1402, www.skywild.org, 9am-5:30pm daily, courses hourly 9:30am-3:30pm, $46 adults, $43 seniors and children, ticket includes entry to Greensboro Science Center), one of the best rope courses or challenge courses I've done, combining elements like zip lines, rope bridges, Tarzan swings, cargo nets, and all sorts of obstacles to overcome while you're 10-30 feet in the air. It's an outstanding course, with options to suit many fitness and confidence levels.

Stroll the paths at Tanger Family Bicentennial Garden (1105 Hobbs Rd., 336/373-2199, www.greensborobeautiful.org, 8am-5pm daily Jan.-Feb. and Nov.-Dec., 8am-7pm daily Mar.-Apr. and Sept.-Oct., 8am-8pm daily May-Aug., free) any time of year and admire the permanent gardens and seasonal plantings. This 7.5-acre garden was started in 1976 when Greensboro Beautiful set out to turn an ignored piece of flood-prone land into a garden. Over four years they worked and created a garden with paths, benches, sculptures, and permanent and seasonal plantings. In 1995 they expanded, adding parking, restrooms, a sensory garden, and a wedding garden, and by 2017 those plans had grown to include the Old Mill, reminiscent of one that stood here in the 1780s.

Greensboro's Wet 'N' Wild Emerald Pointe Water Park (3910 S. Holden Rd., 336/852-9721, www.emeraldpointe.com, 10am-close daily May-Sept., $40 adults, $31 kids, discounts Tues.-Thurs.) offers more water rides than you could try in a full weekend. The central attraction is the two-million-gallon Thunder Bay wave pool, which features 84-foot-wide tsunami waves. There are also five-story slides and riptide pools for the most intrepid swimmers, lazy rivers and shallow pools for those who prefer to relax, and many other adventures.

ENTERTAINMENT AND EVENTS
Nightlife

Greensboro is a college town several times over, so there's a lot of late-night mischief to enjoy. At Natty Greene's Pub (345 S. Elm St., 336/274-1373, www.nattygreenes.com, bar 11am-11pm Mon.-Thurs., 11am-midnight Fri.-Sat., 11am-10pm Sun., kitchen closes 1 hour before the bar, $8-18) you'll find a tap list full of great beer (Guilford Golden Lager and the Buckshot Amber are my go-tos) and a kitchen serving plates for the table (the Cajun fries, the absolute mountain of nachos, and the *shishito* peppers are solid options), sandwiches and wraps (the Cohiba is a Cuban rolled up like a cigar, and Sir Charles brings ahi tuna together with wasabi sour cream and a brioche bun), burgers (Natty Melt—a patty melt—rules) and plates (barbecue, fish-and-chips, shrimp and grits). Bring plenty of quarters when you head out to Boxcar Bar + Arcade (120 W. Lewis St., 336/298-8386, 5pm-midnight Mon.-Thurs., 5pm-1am Fri., noon-1am Sat., noon-midnight Sun.) where you'll find more than 75 arcade and pinball games, several consoles and a pile of games to play, 24 local and craft beers on draft, and an outdoor wood-fired pizza kitchen ($9-11). The LGBTQ-friendly Chemistry Nightclub (2901 Spring Garden St., 336/617-8571, www.greensboro.chemistrynightclub.com, 8pm-2:30am Tues.-Sun.) has a strong local following. Between the go-go dancers, drag shows, karaoke contests, and college nights, there's plenty going on here.

If you're looking for a laugh, Greensboro has two comedy clubs. The Comedy Zone (1126 S. Holden Rd., 336/333-1034, http://thecomedyzone.com, doors open 6:30pm, shows 7pm and 9pm Fri.-Sat., from $25) is a

1: gearing up for a day on the SKYWILD challenge course 2: Guilford Courthouse National Military Park 3: aging sour beers at Natty Greene's Pub 4: Kayaking is a great way to enjoy local waterways.

2-YEAR
SOUR PROGRAM

traditional comedy club with the occasional major headliner. **The Idiot Box** (503 N. Greene St., 336/274-2699, www.idiotboxers. com, tickets vary) is the home of an improv, sketch, and stand-up comedy group that performs every weekend and even holds workshops in stand-up comedy.

Performing Arts

The **Greensboro Symphony Orchestra** (336/335-5456, ext. 224, www.greensborosymphony.org, $32-80, chamber performances $6 students) was created in the 1920s as a student orchestra at Greensboro Women's College, now the University of North Carolina at Greensboro. It grew to be a beloved institution in the wider community and a highly successful regional orchestra; performances are at various venues in town. The **Greensboro Opera** (336/273-9472, www.greensborooopera. org, $40-125) has been turning out wonderful performances of classical and modern opera for more than 30 years at various venues. Each season at various venues, the **Greensboro Ballet** (336/333-7480, www.greensborobal-let.org, call for prices) presents several major productions starring both longtime professional dancers and talented up-and-coming students. The School of the Greensboro Ballet, an affiliated institution, is one of only a handful of nonprofit ballet schools in the country and mints great dancers.

SHOPPING

Shopping in Greensboro always holds some surprises. You'll find big box stores, indoor and strip malls, and shops like REI here, but the real treat in shopping is the local spots. **Scuppernong Books** (304 S. Elm St., 336/763-1919, www.scuppernongbooks.com, 10am-5pm Mon.-Wed., 10am-8pm Thurs.-Sat., noon-6pm Sun.) has a great reputation among North Carolina writers, and they have a stock of signed copies by the state's most well-known to back that up. Writers like Jason Mott (the second North Carolinian to receive the National Book Award), David Joy, Wiley Cash, and others are among the local

writers you'll find here along with a selection of best-sellers, literary works, and local-interest books.

Reconsidered Goods (4118 Spring Garden St., 336/763-5041, www.reconsidered-goods.org, 10am-6pm Mon.-Sat., noon-6pm Sun.) is a super fun arts store. Technically they're a "creative reuse center" where they acquire, sort, and sell all kinds of stuff: art supplies, craft material, fabric, paper, boxes, bags, jars of buttons, test tubes, and the weirdest ever-shifting assortment of stuff makers and artists crave. Stop and have a look; you're guaranteed to find something weird. **Vintage to Vogue Boutique** (530 S. Elm St., 336/709-6181, www.vintgetovogue.net, noon-6pm Mon.-Thurs., noon-7pm Fri., 11am-7pm Sat., 11am-6pm Sun.) is a rarity among vintage places today: They have a great men's section. That rounds out their excellent women's selection and the impressive number of international and high-fashion labels they carry.

An unusual shopping experience can be had at Greensboro's **Fanta City International Shopping Center** (4925 W. Market St., between Market St. and Friendly Ave., 336/235-2300, 10am-9:30pm Mon.-Sat., noon-6pm Sun.), where you'll find four dozen shops offering international home goods, art, and food. It's a one-of-a-kind shopping day.

Greensboro Farmers Curb Market (501 Yanceyville St., 336/373-2402, http://gsofarmersmarket.org, 7:30am-noon Sat. year-round, 8am-noon late Apr.-early Oct.) is more than just a farmers market; it's a chance to make a connection with a farmer, craftsperson, or artisanal food maker. You can pick up steak, fresh eggs, cheese and assorted dairy products, seasonal produce, birdhouses, potted plants, fresh-cut flowers, and even soap, jewelry, and pottery. If you're hungry, just stop in for a bite; several food vendors are usually set up.

FOOD
Barbecue and Comfort Food
Lucky 32 (1421 Westover Terrace, 336/370-0707, www.lucky32.com, 11:15am-9pm Mon.,

11:15am-10pm Tues.-Thurs., 11:15am-11pm Fri.-Sat., 10am-9pm Sun., $10-29), just off Wendover Avenue, has been a Greensboro staple for 20 years. The menu features creative renditions of classic Southern fare. Standouts include chicken and dumplings, cornmeal-crusted catfish, and pulled pork on johnny cakes.

Stamey's Old Fashioned Barbecue (2206 W. Gate City Blvd., 336/299-9888, 11am-9pm Mon.-Sat.; 2812 Battleground Ave./U.S. 220, 336/288-9275, 11am-9pm Mon.-Sat., www.stameys.com, under $10) has been around in one form or another for almost 70 years. The Lexington-style barbecue is pit-fired over hickory wood for as much as 10 hours—old-time quality that's kept customers coming back for generations. I had my first taste of Lexington Dip here hours before a Bob Dylan concert, and even though the show was amazing, all I could think about was the 'cue.

I first had **Dame's Chicken and Waffles** (301 Martin Luther King Jr. Dr., 336/257-7333, www.dameschickenwaffles.com, 10am-3pm Mon., 11am-8pm Tues.-Thurs., 10am-9pm Fri.-Sat., 10am-4pm Sun., $12-22) in Durham and I've been craving it at least once a month ever since. I have to admit, I've seen the appetizers and salads and things on the menu, but I can't move past the waffle. I'll go for the sweet potato and classic waffle (done extra crispy, please) with an orange-honeycomb schmear, but the Barnyard Honcho (waffle, chicken cutlet, eggs) is a perfect breakfast any time of day, and the Quilted Buttercup (which uses a sweet potato waffle for the bread on a chicken cutlet sandwich) are so good they tempt me away every other time I'm in.

Eclectic

The **Liberty Oak Restaurant and Bar** (100-D W. Washington St., 336/273-7057, www.libertyoakrestaurant.com, 11:30am-9pm Tues.-Sat., $12-14) is credited with having started a culinary revolution in Greensboro, a fad for casual restaurants serving New American gourmet cuisine. Specialties include many seafood creations, duck confit, slow-roasted pork, and fried oysters. Originally a wine shop, Liberty Oak has a wine list a mile long, with some nice single-malt scotches and special-blend martinis thrown in for good measure.

Fisher's Grille (608 N. Elm St., 336/275-8300, www.fishersgrille.com, 11am-midnight Mon.-Sat., noon-10pm Sun., $6-10), the big sister to Corner Slice next door, has live blues on Tuesdays, but it's the awesome food and great people that will keep you coming back. The menus is simple: some salads, a lot of burgers, even more sandwiches, 15 draft and 25 bottled beers. But who doesn't love a good sandwich? The chicken club (with fried chicken) and the classic ham and swiss on rye are standouts, as are the patty melt, the mushroom and swiss burger, and the wings.

Corner Slice (600 N. Elm St., 336/333-3077, www.cornerslice.net, 11am-11pm Mon.-Sat., 11am-10pm Sun., $9-17) sits on the verge of Fisher Park, one of the oldest parks in Greensboro, and surrounded by the neighborhood of Fisher Park. That gives Corner Slice the perfect neighborhood feel. That and the pizzas named for streets nearby. In addition to The Magnolia (white pizza with mushroom, chicken, and spinach) and the Archer (roasted red pepper sauce, chicken, bacon, tomato), you'll find cheese pies, ones with mounds of meat, and an assortment of wraps, sandwiches, and appetizers.

Undercurrent Restaurant (327 Battleground Ave., 336/370-1266, http://undercurrentrestaurant.com, 11:30am-2pm and 5pm-9pm Tues.-Thurs., 11:30am-2pm and 5pm-9:30pm Fri., 5pm-9:30pm Sat., 10:30am-1:30pm Sun., $8-38) provides great food with a focus on supporting local and regional farms, fishers, and ranchers. The beer menu is somewhat limited, but the wine list is more extensive. The dinner menu is made up of small and large plates as well as main courses, with creative and flavorful dishes like crab cakes and duck breast.

★ **Hops Burger Bar** (2419 Spring Garden St., 336/235-2178; 2138 Lawndale Dr., 336/663-0537, 11am-10pm Sun.-Thurs.,

11am-11pm Fri.-Sat., $9-13) does an exceptional job maintaining their reputation for making one of the best burgers in the region. Burgers come in three sizes and topped with an array of items from goat cheese and bacon to grilled shrimp and wontons to onion rings and bourbon-marinated pickles. If awards and write-ups from local magazines and food bloggers aren't enough, how about accolades from national publications? The bottom line is this: for can't-find-a-better-bite-anywhere burger and fries, this is the place.

A second spot in the Crafted family, **Crafted—The Art of the Taco** (220 S. Elm St., 336/273-0030, www.eatcrafted. com, 11:30am-9pm Tues.-Thurs. and Sun., 11:30am-10pm Fri.-Sat., $9-14) tries to put a new spin on tacos and succeeds wildly. Fish tacos, Korean-inspired tacos, a breakfast taco with chorizo and eggs, mac-and-cheese and pulled pork tacos, and even spaghetti squash are just some of the delicious tortilla-wrapped bites you'll find.

★ **1618 West Seafood Grill** (1618 W. Friendly Ave., 336/235-0898, www.1618west. com, 5:30pm-9pm Mon., 5:30pm-10pm Tues.-Sat., 11am-2pm Sun., $10-44) draws from flavors the world over to create some remarkable seafood dishes. From appetizers like crispy oyster sliders to simple pan-seared fresh fish, they show a range of techniques and a playful side that keeps the food fresh and fun. They have a sister restaurant and wine bar, **1618 Midtown** (1724 Battleground Ave., Suite 105, 336/285-9410, www.1618midtown.com, 5pm-midnight Mon.-Sat., $7-33), serving small plates like flash-fried gochujang oysters, fish tacos, and truffle pommes frites, as well as entrées; everything dished up goes perfectly with the wine list and cocktails.

French

The award-winning ★ **Print Works Bistro** (702 Green Valley Rd., 336/379-0699, www. printworksbistro.com, 7am-2pm and 5pm-10pm Mon.-Thurs., 7am-11-pm Fri.-Sat., 7am-9:30pm Sun., $7-36) is located at the Proximity Hotel and shares its clean, green aesthetic. The menu here is French bistro through and through but with a touch of Southern character. Wednesday night is time for mussels, wine, and jazz, and the bar gets hopping; get here early, put in an order, and take a seat the bar. The people-watching is excellent.

Asian

Greensboro has a long-established Vietnamese community and a wealth of Vietnamese restaurants. A favorite of local diners is **Boba House Vegetarian Restaurant** (332 Tate St., 336/379-7444, http://bobahouse.com, 11:30am-3pm and 5pm-9pm Mon.-Fri., noon-9pm Sat., $8-16). Yes, it's vegetarian, but if you're a meat-eater, don't let it scare you away. The food here is great: noodles, stir-fry, and sauce-covered entrées that are delicious from the first to last bite. The spices and flavors on every dish are palate-pleasing.

Pho Hien Vuong (4109-A Spring Garden St., 336/294-5551, www.phohienvuong.com, 11am-3:30pm Tues.-Thurs., 11am-9:30pm Fri.-Sun., $7-16) has both Vietnamese and Thai food with several vegetarian options. **Van Loi II** (3829 W. Gate City Blvd., 336/855-5688, www.vanloirestaurant.com, 11am-3:30pm and 5pm-9pm Mon. and Wed.-Fri., 11am-9pm Sat.-Sun., around $12) serves good *phô* and Vietnamese sandwiches, but customers rave about the duck. Van Loi is popular with the local Vietnamese population.

Bandito Bodega (1609 W. Friendly Ave., 336/897-7878, www.banditobodega.com, 11:30am-9:30pm daily, $7-16) is the brick-and-mortar location of one of the city's most beloved food trucks (don't worry, they still have the truck). The food's a playful blend of Mexican and Korean cuisine, and you'll find fish tacos, Asian tacos (the protein gets a Korean soy glaze and there's Thai peanut sauce on there too), the fish taco's bigger burrito cousin, kimchi fried rice, a beef *birria* quesadilla, and more. It's fun; it's experimental; it's exceptional.

Snacks

Yum Yum Better Ice Cream (1219 Spring Garden St., 336/272-8284, 10am-5:30pm Mon. and Sat., 10am-10pm Tues.-Fri., under $10) began in 1906 as a pushcart operation, when a young man named Wisdom Aydelette, who had been working to support his family since he was in the third grade, started peddling ice cream. "W. B." gradually expanded his operations, first graduating from pushcart to mule and wagon and eventually becoming a full-fledged brick-and-mortar ice cream shop. He also began selling hot dogs, which quickly matched the ice cream in popularity. Today, the Aydelettes still runs Yum Yum, selling ice cream and hot dogs that draw crowds.

Cheesecakes by Alex (315 S. Elm St., 336/273-0970, www.cheesecakesbyalex. com, 7:30am-9pm Mon.-Wed., 7:30am-10pm Thurs.-Fri., 8am-10pm Sat., 10am-9pm Sun., slices from $4.50, whole cakes $16-36) might seem like an odd choice, but cheesecake is delicious, and this cheesecake is crazy delicious, and when you can get crazy delicious cheesecake by the slice, you should. Twenty flavors of homemade cheesecake with classics like New York-style and blueberry as well as some surprises like strawberry red velvet and peanut butter cup are going to complicate your choice, but trust me, there's nothing but good choices to make here.

ACCOMMODATIONS

The high-style luxury boutique ★ **Proximity Hotel** (704 Green Valley Rd., 336/379-8200, www.proximityhotel.com, from $289), opened in late 2007 with remarkable green architectural practices that have won awards and high praise. Solar panels on the roof, huge windows in each guest room that actually open, recycled building materials, and many other green features mean that the Proximity reduces energy and water use by almost half that of a comparable hotel. The interior is beautiful and chic, and guest rooms are comfortable, brightly lit with natural light, and full of modern amenities.

The ★ **O. Henry Hotel** (624 Green Valley Rd., 336/854-2000, www.ohenryhotel.com, from $269), named for the Greensboro-born author of "Gift of the Magi," is a 1920s-style luxury hotel. The more than 130 over-size guest rooms feature nine-foot ceilings, neighbor-silencing double walls, comfy beds, terrazzo showers, huge bathtubs, and, like the Proximity, windows that open. The O. Henry's own London taxi will carry you to and from the airport free of charge.

There's no shortage of recognizable chain hotels in and around Greensboro. **Hampton Inn & Suites Greensboro/Coliseum Area** (3033 W. Gate City Blvd., 333/553-1818, www.hilton.com, from $190) is a good option if you're in town for a concert or event, and both **Extended Stay America** (4317 Big Tree Way, 336/299-0200 www.extended-stayamerica.com, from $62) and **Extended Stay America Wendover** (1705 Stanley Rd., 336/547-0405) are conveniently located and budget-conscious.

Camping

Southeast of Greensboro in the town of Pleasant Garden, **Hagan-Stone Park** (5920 Hagan-Stone Park Rd., Pleasant Garden, 336/641-2090, www.guilfordcountync.gov, tent camping $15 up to 5 people, RV camping $25 up to 5 people, group camping $60 up to 40 people) offers pleasant individual campsites with tent pads, fire rings, lantern poles, and picnic tables. Restrooms and showers are nearby. RV sites, which can also be rented by tent campers who need an electric hookup, have a picnic table and 30-amp or 50-amp electricity and share water with the neighboring site. There are no sewer connections. Trails, a public pool, a pond, and a historic one-room schoolhouse are all within the park's boundaries. Reservations can be made online or by phone.

INFORMATION AND SERVICES

The **Greensboro Visitors Center** (2411 Gate City Blvd., 336/274-2282, www.visit-greensboronc.com, 9:30am-5:30pm daily), is

276

open seven days a week. Greensboro has several hospitals, the largest of which is **Moses H. Cone Memorial Hospital** (1121 N. Church St., 336/832-7000, www.conehealth. com).

GETTING THERE AND AROUND

Greensboro is connected to North Carolina's other cities by two of the state's major highways, I-40 and I-85. **Piedmont Triad International Airport** (GSO, 1000 Ted Johnson Pkwy., 336/665-5600, www.flyfrompti.com), commonly called "PTI," is on the northwest side of town, with many daily scheduled flights to U.S. cities. Once daily in each direction, Greensboro is a stop on the **Amtrak** (800/872-7245, www.amtrak.com) New York-New Orleans *Crescent* line and the New York City-Charlotte *Carolinian*. Regional Raleigh-Charlotte *Piedmont* trains stop twice daily in each direction. Trains stop at the **Greensboro Amtrak Station** (236 E. Washington St., 24 hours daily). **Greensboro Transit Authority** (336/335-6499, www. greensboro-nc.gov), the local bus system, is connected to its counterpart in Winston-Salem by Piedmont Area Regional Transit's **Express Bus** (336/662-0002, www.partnc. org).

BURLINGTON AND ALAMANCE COUNTY

One of North Carolina's early railroad towns, Burlington was an economic center in the Piedmont through much of the 19th and 20th centuries. The much smaller town of Graham, a short distance southeast of Burlington, is the seat of largely rural Alamance County. The county is crossed from east to west by I-85, but roughly north to south it is crossed by the lovely Haw River, a rocky channel that's an area favorite for canoeing, kayaking, and tubing.

Alamance Battleground

Alamance Battleground (5803 S. Hwy. 62, 336/227-4785, www.nchistoricsites.org,

9am-5pm Tues.-Sat., donation), south of Burlington, marks the spot where the War of the Regulation ended. On this battleground in 1771, Governor Tryon's colonial militia quashed an uprising by a band of backcountry settlers, the Regulators, who had banded together in protest of corruption in the colonial administration. On the grounds, a visitors center presents the history of the uprising, and a log house connected to the family of one of the Regulators is restored to period condition. Guided tours (11am, 1pm, and 3pm) are available and will help provide additional insights into the importance of what happened here.

Haw River Wine Trail

The **Haw River Wine Trail** (www.grovewinery.com/hrwt.htm) is a lovely day's excursion for the oenophile. Tracing 50 miles along the Haw River, the trail leads to four wineries in the graceful hills of the northern Piedmont. **Benjamin Vineyards and Winery** (6516 Whitney Rd., Graham, 336/525-2401, www. benjaminvineyards.com, noon-5pm Thurs.-Sun.) planted its first vines in 2002, so it's a young winery. They grow a range of grapes here but one of their big draws is the pick-your-own muscadine grapes. Muscadines are native to North Carolina, and plenty of old timers, new homesteaders, and foodies enjoy these sweet thick-skinned grapes for making their own wine, cooking, or just eating.

Grove Winery (7360 Brooks Bridge Rd., Gibsonville, 336/584-4060, http://grovewinery.com, noon-6pm daily) in Gibsonville produces more than a dozen award-winning wines, and they allow volunteers to help crush grapes on Saturday in season. **Iron Gate Vineyards** (2540 Lynch Store Rd., Mebane, 919/304-9463, irongatevineyards.com, noon-5pm Mon.-Sat., tasting $7) has won a great many awards, including gold medals in the Mid-Atlantic Southeastern Wine Competition for its chambourcin and Dixie Dawn wines.

Sports and Recreation

The Haw River, great for flat-water canoeing, rafting, wafting, and tubing, runs through

Alamance County. The **Haw River Trail** (www.thehaw.org) has designated access areas all along the river. Among the outfitters who run the Haw is the **Haw River Canoe and Kayak Company** (Saxapahaw, 336/260-6465, www.hawrivercanoe.com), with guided daytime and evening trips ($35-60), overnight paddle and camping trips ($175-235), and rental trips (from $30) in addition to providing lessons on stand-up paddleboards, kayaks, and canoes ($50-165). Some trips go through Class I and II rapids, which are large enough to be thrilling without putting you at too much risk. You'll find more information on the Haw River, the trail, and the river conservancy at www.thehaw.org.

HIGH POINT

High Point, 20 miles southwest of Greensboro, is on I-85 and roughly the same distance southeast of Winston-Salem.

North Carolina has contributed a surprising number of greats to the world of jazz—most famously John Coltrane from High Point, Thelonious Monk from Rocky Mount, and Maceo Parker from Kinston. A **Statue of John Coltrane** with his horn presides over the intersection of Commerce Avenue and Hamilton Street, near the home on Underhill Street where he grew up.

Also on Hamilton Street is the **World's Largest Chest of Drawers** (508 Hamilton St.). The 40-foot-tall Goddard block-front chest, a tribute to the city's furniture industry, has huge socks dangling out one of the drawers in recognition of the local hosiery mills. It was built in 1926 by the High Point Chamber of Commerce, which was unable to resist the temptation to designate the chest of drawers the High Point Bureau of Information.

Food

This part of North Carolina is barbecue country (what isn't, right?) but the best 'cue around is in the town of Lexington, just down the road, so while you're in High Point, why not try something else? Thanks in small part to the university here, there's a great assortment of international food in town. **Rice Paper Vietnamese Cuisine** (906 Greensboro Rd., High Point, 336/688-5779, www.ricepapernc.com, 11am-9:30pm Tues.-Sun., $6-20) has a menu with so much food I think every corner of Vietnam is represented on the plate. I can't resist a *bánh mì* (the bread is perfection), and theirs hits the spot, but you can venture beyond the sandwich and the *phô* and go for some hot and sour soup (seafood, beef, vegetable), or the delicious vegetarian Monk's Curry (tofu, potato, taro, and seasonal veggies in coconut red curry). At **Sumela Turkish & Mediterranean Restaurant** (805 N. Main St., Suite 101, High Point, 336/887-2645, www.sumelarestaurant.com, 10:30am-9pm Mon.-Sat.) they help introduce the beauty of Turkish cuisine through the broader and more familiar Mediterranean moniker, so you'll find Greek salad, spanakopita, dolmas, and hummus you expect, but also so much more. Shish kebab, lamb, beef, and shrimp skewers, fun sandwiches like the Turkish Kofte Burger (kofte is a type of meatball typically made from lamb), and the Durum Adana (a spicy beef and lamb patty served burger style) give you a flavor of Turkey. Dishes here are kosher, halal, and zabiha.

Accommodations

The **J. H. Adams Inn** (1108 N. Main St., 336/882-3267, www.jhadamsinn.com, $139-249), a 1918 Italianate villa listed on the National Register of Historic Places, operates as a small luxury hotel. Seven guest rooms are located in the house, while the rest of the bedrooms and suites are in a modern addition. The Adams Inn is a hotel rather than a bed-and-breakfast, but the attentive staff and special touches like an evening glass of wine combine the best of both lodging styles.

JAMESTOWN

There are many sites in this part of the state that are important to the history of Southern Quakers. **Mendenhall Homeplace** (603 W. Main St., 336/454-3819, www.mendenhallhomeplace.com, 11am-3pm Tues.-Fri.,

1pm-4pm Sat., $5 adults, $3 seniors and students, $2 children), built in 1811, is a beautiful plantation house located in what is now the center of Jamestown, southwest of Greensboro and about 10 minutes from High Point. The plantation is a significant example of the folk architecture of early German Americans, both in the simple Quaker aesthetic of the house and in its "bank barn," a traditional German livestock barn built into a hillside. The Mendenhalls were abolitionists, which was typical of Quakers but rarer in the South. On the estate is one of only a very few surviving false-bottomed wagons, in which enslaved people were hidden during their journey to freedom on the Underground Railroad.

LEXINGTON

Food

The Piedmont town of Lexington is a veritable mecca for Southern chowhounds, especially those following the religion of 'cue. Billing itself as the "Barbecue Capital of the World," Lexington is known as the epicenter of North Carolina's western barbecue tradition. Lexington barbecue comes from the pork shoulder rather than whole-hog meat, and unlike in the east, the sauce usually has a dose of ketchup in it. This is blasphemy to easterners, just as their vinegar-heavy sauce is regarded around these parts. If you want to see what it's all about, Lexington is just 30 minutes southwest of Greensboro along I-85 and 45 minutes northeast of Charlotte along the same route. It's just 21 minutes to Winston-Salem along U.S. 52, and Durham is only an hour away on I-40 and I-85.

Foodies will argue endlessly about which barbecue purveyor in the Lexington area is the best, but an oft-cited favorite is ★ **Lexington No. 1** (100 Smokehouse Lane, 10 U.S. 29/70 S., 336/249-9814, www.lexbbq.com, 10am-9pm Mon.-Sat., $4-11), called "Honey Monk's" or "The Monk" by locals. In this friendly homey eatery, the barbecue is slow-cooked over wood coals, the way it should be. The hush puppies, a category of food that can inspire nearly as much partisan

debate as barbecue, are also quite special. For some reason there's also a hamburger on the menu; skip it, get a chopped plate and a Cheerwine, and enjoy. If you want the best they have to offer, ask for "The Brown" when you order your plate: A bite of tender juicy 'cue with a bit of this smoky, almost crispy exterior meat on the outside is the kind of thing that will change your mind about barbecue.

Speedy's (1317 Winston Rd., 336/248-2410, http://speedysbbqinc.com, 10:30am-9pm Mon.-Sat., under $12) has plentiful good food along with waitstaff who will bring it right to the curb for you, old-time drive-in style. Curb-service barbecue? A reputation for extra-large portions? Get a car-seat cover and a bib and sign me up.

The Barbecue Center (900 N. Main St., 336/248-4633, www.barbecuecenter.net, 11am-9pm Mon.-Sat., $4-14) serves pit-cooked 'cue, barbecue chicken (Wed.-Sat.), and exclusively red slaw. If you want to feed an army, you can do it here with the Tailgate, a dozen or more plates of 'cue. The menu is priced so you can eat yourself into a barbecue coma if you want.

After a visit to one of Lexington's barbecue joints, make your way to **The Candy Factory** (15 N. Main St., 336/249-6770, www.lexingtoncandyfactory.com, 10am-5:30pm Mon.-Thurs., 10am-7:30pm Fri., 10am-4pm Sat.), a third-generation candy-making business housed in a 1907 old-time hardware store with beautiful creaky old floors. Lining the shop are barrels of candy—both the store's own Red Bird brand and hundreds of classic candies that you may not have thought of since childhood.

Barbecue Festival

October is officially Barbecue Month here in Davidson County, and late in the month every year, up to 100,000 people descend on Lexington for the **Barbecue Festival** (www.ncfestivals.com). Lexington No. 1, Speedy's, and a host of other local honeymonkeries provide the eats, while concerts, contests (lumberjacks, anyone?), and children's activities fill the city. It's your chance to sample the full array of Carolina 'cue in one place. Considering that more than 15,000 pounds of barbecue are served each day, there's plenty of each style to go around. Word of advice: consider keeping your favorite style a little close to the vest. There are some folks here who take their 'cue seriously.

The Sandhills

In the center of the state, far from the major highways, you'll find an area known as the Sandhills. This is a part of the state that's often forgotten by travelers and travel writers alike, aside from those with a penchant for golf. Here you'll find placid countryside and tiny towns where it seems that every inhabitant is an artist. You'll find savannas trampled by elephants and zebras; mysterious, hidden, and haunted mountains; and towns called Whynot and Climax. The centerpiece of the Sandhills and the geographic center of North Carolina is the town of Seagrove, population 250, where a distinctive style of folk pottery is nearing its third century of tradition and innovation. The Uwharrie Mountains, a strange upthrust of deep hills and dark forests, are nearby. Asheboro, the largest town in the Sandhills with a whopping 25,000 residents, is home of the North Carolina Zoo and one of the state's most important culinary contributions: Cheerwine. Let's not forget golf: Pinehurst is known the world over for its famed golf course, but this resort town offers more than just a day on the links; a number of great galleries and restaurants can be found here too.

U.S. 220, which runs from Greensboro almost to the South Carolina border, is the only major artery in this region, which has no major airports or rail lines. Charlotte, Greensboro, and Raleigh-Durham airports are all within one or two hours' drive.

ASHEBORO AND VICINITY
★ North Carolina Zoo
The **North Carolina Zoo** (4401 Zoo Pkwy., 800/488-0444, www.nczoo.org, 9am-4pm daily, $15 adults, $13 students and over age 62, $11 ages 2-12) sprawls over more than 500 acres of Purgatory Mountain at the edge of the Uwharries. Elephants, zebras, polar bears, alligators, and many more live on large expanses of land planted and landscaped to approximate their native habitats. There are also five miles of hiking trails, from parking lots at each end of the zoo, that provide a great way to see the animals from a different vantage point. Trails are wheelchair-accessible, and for those who don't want to walk long distances, buses and trams run from exhibit to exhibit within the park (but you still have to get out of the vehicle to see the animals).

North Carolina Aviation Museum
At the **North Carolina Aviation Museum** (2222-G Pilots View Rd., 336/625-0170, www.ncamhof.com, 11am-5pm Thurs.-Sun., $10 adults, $8 seniors and military, $5 under age 19), World War II through Vietnam-era fighter aircraft gleam in restored splendor. After touring the two hangars where the airplanes and other military memorabilia are housed, check out the gift shop, a model plane lover's dream. Be forewarned: This space isn't air-conditioned, so a summertime visit may be a little on the warm side.

Liberty Antiques Festival
Just outside Liberty, located between Asheboro and I-85, is a twice-yearly antiques fair that draws crowds from all over the Southeast. At the **Liberty Antiques Festival** (2855 Pike Farm Rd., Staley, 336/622-3041, www.liberty-antiquesfestival.com, $10 adults, free under age 13), held over a three-day weekend in late

April and again in late September, hundreds of vendors set up shop in a farm field, creating a huge outdoor antiques mall that offers many happy hours of browsing. Since it's in the open air, come prepared for bad weather and mud. There's huge variety among the dealers' wares, but overall the theme leans toward rustic Southern, including some fine early Southern furniture, museum-quality folk pottery, and other highly sought-after folk art collectibles, in a full range of prices.

INFORMATION AND SERVICES

Asheboro is the population center of Randolph County, where you'll find plenty of affordable chain motels and a fast-food jungle clustered along U.S. 64. This is also a center for area medical services. The **Asheboro/Randolph County Chamber of Commerce** (137 S. Fayetteville St., 336/626-2626, http://chamber. asheboro.com) will let you know a bit about the area, but **Asheboro—Heart of North Carolina Visitors Bureau** (145 Worth St., 336/626-0364, http://heartofnorthcarolina. com, 8:30am-4:30pm Mon.-Fri.) can fix you up with all the logistical information you need as you venture into the Sandhills.

★ SEAGROVE

The Carolina Sandhills are home to a generations-old pottery industry known as the Seagrove tradition, which still thrives today. The little crossroads town of Seagrove is built over beds of clay that were perfectly suited to the needs of 18th- and 19th-century Carolina potters. Several families of potters settled in this region and, drawing from the readily available excellent red and gray clays, were soon supplying much of the rest of the state with jugs, crocks, plates, and other utilitarian wares. The pottery that their descendants make today is much more decorative than the earlier style, combining beauty and function. Within just a few miles of Seagrove town and in little nearby communities such as Whynot and Westmoore are the shops and studios of over 100 potters.

Reaching Seagrove involves a pretty drive through the country. From Charlotte, a 90-minute drive east along I-85, U.S. 64, and U.S. 220 will get you here. Greensboro is only 35 minutes north on U.S. 220; Pinehurst and Southern Pines are within easy reach, a drive of about 35 minutes south and east along U.S. 220 and Highway 211. There are maps, along with more information on potters and the area, available at www.heartofnorthcarolina.com.

North Carolina Pottery Center

The **North Carolina Pottery Center** (233 East Ave., 336/873-8430, www.ncpotterycenter.org, 10am-4pm Tues.-Sat., $2.50 adults, $1 students, free ages 12 and under) is the ideal place to start your tour of Seagrove. The primary focus of the Pottery Center is to preserve and present the work of Seagrove-area potters, but you'll also see representative work from the state's several other distinctive pottery traditions. The permanent exhibit and rotating shows introduce visitors to such late master artists as M. L. Owens, A. R. Cole, and Dorothy and Walter Auman, all in a beautiful airy building designed to echo the lines of a barn. There's also a nice little gift shop. On your way out the door, pick up a map of area pottery studios.

Pottery Studios

Ben Owen Pottery (105 Ben's Place, 336/879-2262, www.benowenpottery.com, 11am-5pm Tues.-Sat., closed the week of July 4), three miles south of the Pottery Center on Highway 705, called "The Pottery Highway," is the studio and showroom of Ben Owen III, who learned the art from his grandfather. Incorporating elements of Asian ceramics into his native Seagrove tradition, Owen has made a name for himself in the fine-arts world. Much of his work is positively monumental: massive vases and jars, many glazed in the brilliant red for which the family is famous. A small museum attached to the shop shows some of his father's and grandfather's beautiful work.

Luck's Ware (1606 Adams Rd., Seagrove, 336/879-3261, www.lucksware.com, 9am-5pm Mon.-Sat.) is the workshop of Sid Luck and his sons Matt and Jason, today's representatives of a generations-old family tradition. Sid fires his pots in a groundhog kiln—an old-timey Carolina form with a long arched brick tunnel, part of which is usually subterranean.

David and Mary Farrell of **Westmoore Pottery** (4622 Busbee Rd., Westmoore, 910/464-3700, www.westmoorepottery.com, 9am-5pm Mon.-Tues. and Thurs.-Sat.) were attracted to Seagrove by its pottery tradition and are now part of the community. The Farrells specialize in recreating historical ceramics, primarily North Carolina styles. Their work is so accurate that it appears in historic houses throughout the United States, at Old Salem and Colonial Williamsburg, and has been featured in many movies, including *Amistad* and *Cold Mountain*.

Shopping

One other shop in Seagrove with wares that rival the gleaming pottery in beauty is **Seagrove Orchids** (3451 Brower Mill Rd., 336/879-6677, www.seagroveorchids.com, 10am-5pm Fri.-Sat. and by appointment, blooms $15-75) is a wonderful place to visit even if your hobbies don't include exotic horticulture. There are more than 220 kinds of orchids in the greenhouses here, from rare species to affordable plants for beginners. They're ready with tips and tricks that will help you set down roots in the orchid world. Seagrove Orchids even propagates new hybrid varieties of its own.

Accommodations

The **Duck Smith House** (465 N. Broad St., 336/872-4121 or 888/869-9018, www.ducksmithhouse.com, from $125), a farmhouse built in 1914, is a classic Southern bed-and-breakfast, with a large wraparound porch and a hearty country breakfast. The location is perfect for a weekend of pottery shopping, and the four beautiful guest rooms are large enough to accommodate you and the pottery you'll buy.

UWHARRIE MOUNTAINS

The Uwharrie Mountains are strange and beautiful, a range of hills covered in deep, rocky woods and dotted with quiet towns with names like Ether and Troy. Peaks of this range, one of the oldest in North America, once soared to 20,000 feet, but the millennia have worn them down until the highest mountain now stands at just over 1,000 feet. Lakes, hiking trails, and history are cached in these mountains.

★ Uwharrie National Forest

The trail system of the **Uwharrie National Forest** (www.fs.usda.gov) has been compared to the Appalachian Trail. Although the Uwharrie Mountains are significantly lower than the Blue Ridge Mountains and the Smokies, they do shelter delicate mountain ecosystems closely related to those of the Appalachians. There are nearly 67 miles of trails in the forest, but two major trails, the Uwharrie National Recreational Trail and the Dutchman's Creek Trail, run through the park. Both begin 10 miles west of Troy, with parking at Highway 24/27. The 10-mile Dutchman's Creek trail loops with the 20-mile Uwharrie Trail, which ends 2 miles east of Ophir at Highway 1306. The hikes are somewhat strenuous—these are mountains, after all—and travel through pretty and somewhat spooky terrain: rocky woods with old homesteads and graveyards, and even some abandoned gold mines nearby. The Denson's Creek Trail is short—a 2.3-mile loop or a 0.7-mile short loop—and easy. Pick up the trail two miles east of Troy on Highway 24/27 behind the District Office. There are more than just hiking trails here, though. Many folks come out to take their off-road vehicle (ORV) for a spin on the dirt and gravel roads crisscrossing the forest here. Add in mountain biking, equestrian opportunities, and even a shooting range and you've got a popular spot for the outdoors inclined.

Uwharrie National Forest is very easy to get to. From Rockingham and U.S. 73/74, the Forest is about 30 minutes north on U.S. 220;

1

2

3

4

it's an hour south of Greensboro along U.S. 220. From Charlotte, it's a 90-minute drive west along Highway 24/27.

Two large campgrounds are located near Badin Lake at the western edge of the park. **Arrowhead Campground** (Forest Rd. 597B, off Mullinix Rd./Forest Rd. 1154, 910/576-6391, www.fs.usda.gov, reservations 877/444-6777, www.recreation.gov, $20-54) has 48 sites with picnic tables and tent pads, 33 of which have electrical hookups. There are spigots for drinking water and a bathhouse with hot showers, flush toilets, and a laundry sink. The Arrowhead Campground is 0.5 miles from Badin Lake. **The Badin Lake Campground** (Forest Rd. 576, off Hwy. 109, 910/576-6391, reservations 877/444-6777, $20-40), which has 34 sites, is directly on the lake. Each site has a picnic table, a grill, and a tent pad. Water spigots and chemical toilets are nearby. Several smaller sites throughout the park are accessible for tent camping, and one, Canebrake Horse Camp near Badin Lake, is for equestrians.

Morrow Mountain State Park

Located catty-corner to Badin and Albemarle, **Morrow Mountain State Park** (49104 Morrow Mountain Rd., Albemarle, 704/982-4402, http://ncparks.gov, 7am-7pm daily Dec.-Feb., 7am-8pm daily Mar. and Nov., 7am-9pm daily Apr. and Oct., 7am-10pm daily May-Sept., office 8am-4:30pm daily) preserves one of the Uwharries' highest peaks, the 936-foot Morrow Mountain. Within the park, visitors can go boating on Lake Tillery or on the Pee Dee River, with rowboat and canoe rentals available in the spring and summer. More than 15 miles of trails snake up and down the mountains. There's plenty of **camping** (reservations 877/722-6762, www.northcarolinastateparks.reserveamerica.com) available. Cabins are available for rent ($538 weekly summer, $110

nightly with a 2-night minimum off-season). Over 100 campsites ($23-28) offer water, restrooms, and showers nearby, some with electricity. There's also a swimming pool ($5 over age 12, $4 ages 3-12) and boat rentals ($5 per hour) on the lake. Check out the exhibit hall (10am-5pm daily) to learn about the ecology and Native American heritage of the region and to visit the restored 1870s home and infirmary of the first physician to venture into these parts.

Denton

The second weekend in May brings countless bluegrass musicians and fans to the **Doyle Lawson and Quicksilver's Bluegrass Festival** (Denton Farm Park, 1072 Cranford Rd., Denton, 336/859-2755, www.dentonfarmpark.com, 3-day pass $80-90, 2-day pass $65-70, 1-day pass $35-40, half price ages 15-17, free under age 15). This three-day bluegrass jamboree has more than a dozen artists and groups descending on the park to celebrate the music they love.

The annual **Southeast Old Threshers' Reunion** (Denton Farm Park, 1072 Cranford Rd., Denton, 336/859-2755, www.dentonfarmpark.com, $18 adults, $6 ages 6-12, free under age 6) takes place in Denton, southwest of Asheboro and just to the north of the Uwharries. The gathering, usually held around the 4th of July, celebrates the old ways of farming that were replaced by tractors and other motorized equipment. Farmers who have kept the traditional methods alive gather to show off the strength of their draft horses in pulling competitions, horse-powered equipment demonstrations, and other feats of strength and skill. There's also plenty of music and food.

If you'd like a taste of Lexington-style barbecue, a good bet is **Troutman's BBQ** (18466 S. Hwy. 109, 336/859-2206, 8am-9pm Mon.-Sat., around $12), a local landmark for decades. On the weekend you can get barbecue chicken if you're not in the mood for pork, but nothing beats a chopped plate with a side of hush puppies and red slaw.

1: the North Carolina Zoo in Asheboro 2: the Holly Inn at Pinehurst Resort 3: the Horticultural Garden in Pinehurst 4: Badin Lake in Uwharrie National Forest

Mount Gilead

The **Town Creek Indian Mound** (509 Town Creek Mound Rd., Mount Gilead, 910/439-6802, www.nchistoricsites.org, 9am-5pm Tues.-Sat., free) is an extraordinary archaeological site, the remains and reconstruction of a center of ancient indigenous Pee Dee culture. The mound itself was the location of three successive structures, including an earthen lodge and a temple. More than 500 people were buried at this site, and the remains of a mortuary were excavated nearby. Today, in addition to the mound, visitors can see reconstructions of two temples and the mortuary. The visitors center includes displays of artifacts and interpretive exhibits about the site's history.

SOUTHERN PINES AND PINEHURST

Flip through the old postcards at any antiques shop in the Carolinas and you're likely to come across turn-of-the-century images of the Southern Pines region of the North Carolina Sandhills. The area's development kicked into high gear in the 1890s, when Bostonian James Tufts constructed the Pinehurst Resort with money made in the soda fountain industry. He commissioned Frederick Law Olmsted, the prolific landscape designer of New York's Central Park and Asheville's Biltmore Estate, to design a village, which he named Pinehurst. The first hotel opened in 1895, followed by the Pinehurst golf course (now called Pinehurst No. 1) in 1898 and the famed Pinehurst No. 2 course in 1907. The area quickly became a haven for Northern snowbirds. Postcards from that early era are clearly geared to a Northern audience, portraying the early spring blossoms that cover the Sandhills while New York, Chicago, and Milwaukee are still buried in snow, or showing rustic cabins and rural African Americans driving oxcarts or playing the banjo—holdovers from the stereotyped Victorian notions of the Old South, appealing to urbanites in search of a change of pace. The origins of the early visitors are also evident on street signs

in Southern Pines, where many of the roads are named for Northeastern and Midwestern states.

Today, this whole section of Moore County is a sea of golf courses and still a magnet for snowbirds and halfbacks (Northerners who retired to Florida, found it too hot, and came halfway back to North Carolina). Primarily known for golf, the Pinehurst area has hosted the U.S. Open, the U.S. Women's Open, and the USGA National Championship. The spring and fall are exceptionally pretty, and the weather is usually warm but not dangerously hot as it is in high summer, so in those seasons, hotels and restaurants fill completely and golf courses can be booked solid. Plan well in advance. Golf packages are key here; by bundling lodging and greens fees, you can save money and hassles.

Sights

Weymouth Woods-Sandhills Nature Preserve (1024 Fort Bragg Rd., Southern Pines, 910/692-2167, http://ncparks.gov, park 8am-6pm daily Nov.-Feb., 8am-8pm daily Mar.-Oct.) comprises nearly 900 acres that are home to red-cockaded woodpeckers, fox squirrels, and other natives of the longleaf pine barrens. Most of the preserve is a limited-use area subject to periodic prescribed burning, but several trails, most one mile or shorter, let visitors explore the woods and swamps without too much commitment.

At the **Horticultural Garden** (3395 Airport Rd., Pinehurst, 910/692-6185, www.sandhills.edu, dawn-dusk daily) at Sandhills Community College, a full acre of the property is dedicated to a formal English garden, while other areas show off plants of the woodlands and wetlands as well as collections of roses, holly, and conifers.

Shopping

Towns in this area may have been built around golf, but that's not all they offer; there is a surprising array of artists and a number of galleries displaying their wares. The **Artists League of the Sandhills** (129 Exchange St.,

Aberdeen, 910/944-3979, www.artistleague. org, noon-3pm Mon.-Sat.) is a group of some 200 Sandhills artists in various media. Not all have space in the studio-gallery, but more than three-dozen painters, jewelry makers, printmakers, and other artists do. On any given day you'll find several artists working on pieces alone or collaboratively. Most of the work is for sale.

The Country Bookshop (140 NW Broad St., Southern Pines, 910/692-3211, http://thecountrybookshop.biz, 10am-6pm Mon.-Sat., noon-4pm Sun.), one of our favorite bookstores in North Carolina, carries a great selection of books, including many about golf but more that are popular releases or were written by local and regional authors like Jason Mott (who became the second North Carolinian to win the National Book Award), Wiley Cash, and others. They also have well-stocked sections devoted to young-adult and children's literature.

Knitters and those with a flair for fiber arts will want to stop by **Bella Filati** (277 NE Broad St., 910/692-3528, www.bellafilati.com, 10am-5pm Mon.-Tues. and Thurs.-Sat., 10am-7pm Wed.), a premium yarn shop in Southern Pines. They carry everything a knitter would need, from books and patterns to wools and yarns of all sorts. **Gentlemen's Corner** (1 Chinquapin Rd., Village Square, Pinehurst, 910/295-2011, http://thegcorner.com, 10am-5pm Mon.-Sat., noon-5pm Sun.), a high-fashion men's boutique, carries all the resort wear you'll need to spend a week at Pinehurst. They carry some high-end brands like Peter Millar, Carrot & Gibbs, and Kroon.

River Jack Outdoor Trading Company (181 NE Broad St., Southern Pines, 910/692-5225, www.riverjack.com, 10am-6pm Mon.-Fri., 10am-5pm Sat.) carries everything you need for an outdoor adventure. Their selection of outdoor shoes, and fashionable shoes by outdoor companies like Teva and Merrill, is quite good. The staff can provide recommendations on gear or on nearby hiking, biking, or kayaking routes.

You can't come to the heart of golf in North Carolina without taking a piece of golf history home with you. **Old Sport & Gallery** (95 Market Square, Pinehurst, 910/295-9775, www.oldsportgallery.com, 10am-5pm Mon.-Sat.) was founded by a longtime golfer and golf writer to give lovers of the game the chance to celebrate their passion through books, art, and memorabilia. A number of original pieces by golf artists like Richard Chorley and Bill Williams hang on the walls here alongside rare books, celebrity-owned and hard-to-find clubs and sets, vintage signs, bits of tournament and course ephemera, and more. It's really a cool shop whether you're a golfer or collector or rare things.

Golf

The area around Southern Pines, Pinehurst, and Aberdeen is one of the most famous golf centers in the world, boasting more than 40 major courses. The **Pinehurst Resort** (80 Carolina Vista Dr., Pinehurst, 844/330-1669, www.pinehurst.com, call for greens fees) comprises eight major courses designed by some of the great golf course architects of the last century: Donald Ross, Ellis Maples, George and Tom Fazio, and Rees Jones. **Pine Needles** (1005 Midland Rd., Southern Pines, 910/692-7111, www.pineneedleslodge.com, greens fees $85-255) incorporates the Pine Needles (18 holes, par 71) course, a Donald Ross Design. **Mid-Pines Inn & Golf Club** (1010 Midland Rd., 910/692-2114, www.midpinesinn.com, 18 holes, par 72, greens fees $85-225) brings a Donald Ross designed course and an inn ($105-200) together for a great stay and play experience.

Other courses in the area were designed by Jack Nicklaus, Jack Nicklaus II, Dan Maples, Gary Player, and other leading lights of golf course architecture. Information about all of them can be found at the **Home of American Golf** (www.homeofgolf.com).

Food

Some of the best places to dine in the Pinehurst area are at the Pinehurst Resort (844/330-1669, www.pinehurst.com). The

Carolina Dining Room (Carolina Inn, Pinehurst, 6:30am-10am and 6pm-9pm daily, $22-50, resort wear required for breakfast, dinner jacket required for evening dining) is the resort's most formal dining room, serving fine chops and steak presented with the chef's suggestions for wine accompaniment. The breakfast buffet here is legendary.

At the 1895 Grille (Holly Inn, Pinehurst, 6:30am-10am and 6pm-9pm Wed.-Sat., $18-44), the menu changes with some regularity, but the signature cider-brined grilled pork chop is a constant; other entrées include some version of shrimp and grits, a play on a land-and-sea duo, lamb, and steaks. The Tavern (The Manor, Pinehurst, 11:30am-10pm daily, $13-30) serves lighter café fare, with entrée soups and sandwiches as well as an array of pasta dishes. Seven other restaurants, cafés, and tea shops are scattered throughout the Pinehurst Resort, offering everything from snacks to bar bites.

Southern Prime Steakhouse (270 SW Broad St., Southern Pines, 910/693-0123, www.southernprimesteakhouse.net, 5pm-9pm Mon.-Thurs., 5pm-10pm Fri.-Sat., 11:30am-2pm and 5pm-9pm Sun., $16-45) dry ages their steaks and chops in house for three to four weeks to achieve a depth of flavor you won't find in many places in the region. When you consider that they have a perfect filet and the perfect bottle of wine—from their 200-bottle list—to go with it, you have the makings of an exceptional dinner.

If you're looking for a good cup of coffee, The Roast Office (95 Cherokee Rd., 910/215-8861, www.roastofficecoffee.com, 6:30am-4pm Mon.-Sat., 8am-4pm Sun., $2-8) has an assortment of coffee drinks—using freshly roasted beans—as well as teas and specialty drinks. Perfect for a light breakfast, lunch, or snack, they serve muffins, quiche, sandwiches, and baked goods.

Serving British classics in a pub that feels like they picked it up in England and plopped it down in Southern Pines, The Sly Fox Gastropub (795 SW Broad St., Southern Pines, 910/725-1621, www.theslyfoxpub.com, 11:30am-9:30pm Mon.-Sat., $10-25) delivers on the Scotch egg, fish-and-chips, curry, and shepherd's pie. But they do more. Reuben Spring Rolls (a Reuben sandwich meets a spring roll to delicious results), shrimp and grits, beef cheeks with gnocchi, burgers, and a great brunch add some excitement to the menu.

Two excellent places to get a drink are Southern Pines Growler Company (160 W. New York Ave., Southern Pines, 910/693-7742, www.spgrowler.com, 1pm-8pm Mon., noon-8pm Tues.-Wed., noon-9pm Thurs., noon-10pm Fri., 10am-10pm Sat., noon-8pm Sun.), where you'll find 30-odd beers on tap and three times as many in bottles and six-packs, and The Wine Cellar & Tasting Room (241-A NE Broad St., Southern Pines, 910/692-3066, www.thewinecellarandtastingroom.com, 11am-10pm Mon.-Thurs., 11am-11pm Fri.-Sat. 3pm-6pm Sun.). The Wine Cellar has 15-20 wines available for sampling, a growing number of hard-to-find beers on tap and in the bottle, and a small menu of snacks and plates to keep your hunger at bay ($3-11). They host tasting events and live music (typically on weekends, but check the schedule to see what's happening).

Accommodations
RESORTS

A separate entity from the town of Pinehurst, the ★ Pinehurst Resort (80 Carolina Vista Dr., 844/330-1669, www.pinehurst.com), which opened in 1895, is the world's second-largest golf resort and also has three inns. The Carolina (from $550), built in 1901 and listed on the National Register of Historic Places, is a grand hotel in the Edwardian style, with long piazzas and lush lawns. The 1895 Holly Inn (from $450) was the first hotel built at the resort and is a smaller, cozier, more club-like spot. The third inn, the Manor (from $450), is the smallest and most laid-back of the accommodations, and recently underwent renovations to the guest rooms and public facilities.

The Pinehurst Golf Academy (from $2,330 weekly, $2,077 weekend) gives weekend and weeklong classes for beginners and experienced players taught on Pinehurst 1, 3, and 5, with a stay at the Carolina included in the fee. Also on the grounds is the four-star **Spa at Pinehurst** ($50-200), with a long menu of skin and body-care therapies and specials like the Spa Escape Package: accommodations, a 50-minute treatment, and full-day access to the spa facilities (rates vary by season and accommodations, $217-550 pp). The **Pinehurst Tennis Club** (courts 8am-9pm daily, $12-15 guests) is regarded as a top tennis resort nationally, with a high-quality pro shop and adult tennis camps. Golf, spa, and tennis packages can significantly reduce the overall cost of a stay at the Pinehurst, but surcharges for amenities might still apply.

INNS

The **Pine Crest Inn** (50 Dogwood Rd., Pinehurst, 910/295-6121, www.pinecrestinnpinehurst.com, $120-200) was owned for many years by Donald Ross, the golf course designer who helped make the Pinehurst Resort famous. Operated for the last 40 years by the Barrett family, the Pine Crest is a favorite for golfers and vacationers as well as for local diners who come to the Pine Crest Inn Restaurant and Mr. B.'s Lounge. The **Magnolia Inn** (65 Magnolia Rd., Pinehurst, 910/295-6900, www.themagnoliainn.com, $115-175), built in 1896, is in a great downtown location just steps from local shopping and restaurants and very close to the best area golfing.

Getting There and Around

Southern Pines and Pinehurst are most easily reached by U.S. 15/501 south from Chapel Hill and U.S. 1 south from Raleigh. The area can also easily be reached from Fayetteville, just a short drive to the east. **Moore County Airport** (SOP, 7825 Aviation Dr., Carthage, 910/692-3212, www.moorecountyairport. com) is open to private aircraft but currently has no scheduled passenger flights. Fayetteville is an hour east via Highway 690. Raleigh is 75 minutes northeast via U.S. 1 and U.S. 501. Wilmington is 2 hours and 20 minutes southeast via U.S. 74 and U.S. 501. Charlotte is 2 hours west via U.S. 74 and U.S. 501 (the most direct route, but others are available that avoid tolls).

Charlotte and Racing Country

Charlotte is one of the most diverse cities in the Southeast, and one of the most perplexing to old-school North Carolinians.

Charlotte's downtown is taller and more tightly filled with bankers than any other city in the state, but the countryside around the city is still filled with farmers. Two major sports franchises and the booming NASCAR scene have brought an influx of millionaires, but with them come the hordes of dreamers, up-and-comers, and wannabes. Besides that, the money NASCAR brings in has its roots in moonshining, and what's more of a surprise than a millionaire moonshiner?

There's a worldliness in Charlotte not found elsewhere in North Carolina. Immigrants from Africa, Latin America, Southeast Asia,

Highlights

Look for ★ to find recommended sights, activities, dining, and lodging.

★ **Mint Museum:** Two fantastic branches have galleries filled with art spanning the centuries and the world (page 294).

★ **NASCAR Hall of Fame:** Learn the history of the South's premier sport through its cars, tracks, and memorabilia (page 295).

★ **Levine Museum of the New South:** The complicated and sometimes painful story of the post-Civil War South, and Charlotte in particular, is told in ways that are both respectful and innovative (page 295).

★ **U.S. National Whitewater Center:** Home to the U.S. Olympic canoe and kayak teams, this facility is also designed for use by novice paddlers, hikers, and climbers (page 298).

★ **Charlotte Motor Speedway:** This Concord stadium seats well over 150,000 fans around a 1.5-mile track. It's a spectacular sight even when there's not a race (page 313).

VIRGINIA

NORTH CAROLINA

Mount Airy

Blowing Rock

Wilkesboro

Winston-Salem

Salisbury

Charlotte Motor Speedway

Kannapolis

U.S. National Whitewater Center

Concord

Gastonia

Charlotte

Mint Museum

NASCAR Hall of Fame

Rock Hill

Levine Museum of the New South

SOUTH CAROLINA

0   30 mi

0   30 km

© MOON.COM

Charlotte and Racing Country

© MOON.COM

Sanford

Aberdeen

Rockingham

Pageland

NORTH CAROLINA

SOUTH CAROLINA

Siler City

Asheboro

Greensboro

High Point

Winston-Salem

Lexington

Salisbury

Mocksville

THE BADIN LAKE CAMPGROUND

ARROWHEAD

Uwharrie National Forest

High Rock Lake

Badin Lake

Lake Tillery

Albemarle

REED GOLD MINE NATIONAL HISTORIC LANDMARK

Wadesboro

CHARLOTTE MOTOR SPEEDWAY

Concord

GREAT WOLF LODGE

Monroe

Mooresville

Kannapolis

Landis

Davidson

Huntersville

MINT MUSEUM

NASCAR HALL OF FAME

Charlotte

JAMES K. POLK HISTORIC PARK

Pineville

Fort Mill

Catawba R

Andrew Jackson Historical State Park

Lake Norman

Statesville

Catawba

LEVINE MUSEUM OF THE NEW SOUTH

CAROWINDS

Rock Hill

U.S. NATIONAL WHITEWATER CENTER

Gastonia

Lake Wylie

Clover

Taylorsville

Hickory

Claremont

Lincolnton

Crowders Mountain State Park

York

Kings Mountain

EARL SCRUGGS CENTER

Shelby

Gaffney

0 10 mi

0 10 km

and India have brought their food, religions, holidays, languages, and customs with them, adding to the flavor of the city. Some folks don't know what to make of this, but they accept it all the same; that's Southern hospitality showing through.

More than anything, Charlotte is still a Southern city. You may pay big-city prices for a meal, but on your way out the door your waitress will tell you, "Y'all come back and see us soon, OK, hon?" And even in the modern downtown banking neighborhood you'll still find men opening doors for women with a kindly "After you, ma'am."

The area just north and northeast of Charlotte is the epicenter for North Carolina's auto-racing industry and culture. Many NASCAR teams call the area around Mooresville, Concord, and Kannapolis home, with their shops and headquarters in old textile mills and state-of-the-art garages. The huge storied Charlotte Motor Speedway is here, and rarely a day goes by without the roar of race cars hurtling around the track. The sound is unmistakable and, around these parts, familiar.

PLANNING YOUR TIME

To get a good feel for Charlotte, spend at least a long weekend here. Lodging is plentiful, if expensive. Uptown hotels are within easy walking distance or a short cab ride from major museums, sports complexes, and performance venues. Lodging in the Myers Park, Dilworth, and Plaza-Milwood neighborhoods are a quick hop from Uptown but have a less urban pace. There's a great deal to do in the Plaza-Milwood area—good cafés, fun shopping, and easy access to NoDa (the North Davidson neighborhood). Motels along I-85 to the north of Charlotte, particularly in the Concord Mills area, are not far from the city and are also convenient to the destinations in Kannapolis, Mooresville, Salisbury, and Spencer.

Charlotte sprawls, but it's fairly easy to get from place to place in a short amount of time—if you're not on the road at rush hour. When traveling to the city, though, it's a good idea to check ahead to see if there will be any major sporting events during your visit. The Hornets (professional basketball) and Panthers (professional football) stadia are both downtown, so expect heavier traffic right before and right after games. The Charlotte Motor Speedway, a few miles north of the city in Concord, can hold more than 200,000 people, so you can imagine the state of traffic and hotel room availability during race weeks. Other events, like concerts by major acts and sports tournaments, can also sell out hotels in areas of the city and cause gridlock.

Charlotte

Charlotte has often been a boomtown. In the late 18th century it was a midsize county seat, not much bigger than Salisbury or Hillsborough, but the end of the century brought the first boom. A farm boy discovered a beautiful lumpy 17-pound rock in the creek in 1799. For years the family used his find as a doorstop until a visitor identified the mysterious rock as gold. The ensuing gold rush brought Charlotte and the frontier lands around it into the spotlight.

When railroad lines began to stretch across the Carolina backcountry, concerted efforts to court railroad decision-makers resulted in several important lines passing through Charlotte, and soon the town was a giant in the regional economy. Cotton farmers throughout the Piedmont brought their

Charlotte

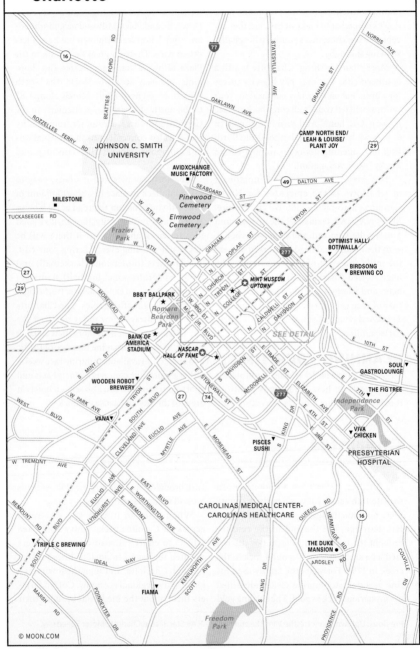

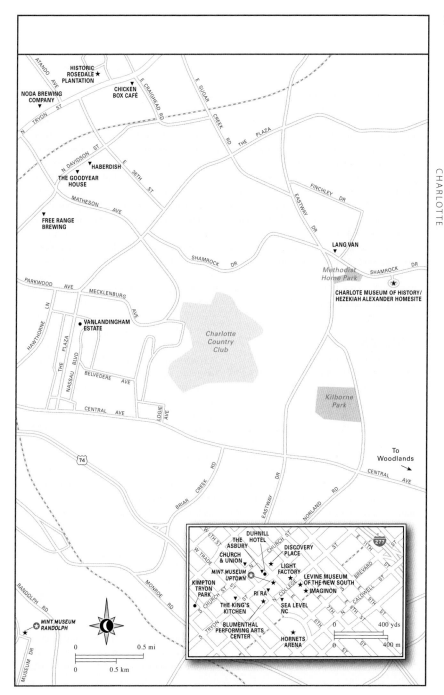

HISTORIC ROSEDALE PLANTATION ★

CHICKEN BOX CAFÉ ▼

NODA BREWING COMPANY ▼

ATANDO AVE

E CRAIGHEAD RD

E SUGAR CREEK RD

THE PLAZA

N TRYON ST

N DAVIDSON ST

HABERDISH ▼

THE GOODYEAR HOUSE

E 36TH ST

FINCHLEY DR

MATHESON AVE

EASTWAY DR

FREE RANGE BREWING ▼

LANG VAN ▼

SHAMROCK DR

SHAMROCK DR

Methodist Home Park

CHARLOTTE MUSEUM OF HISTORY/ HEZEKIAH ALEXANDER HOMESITE ★

PARKWOOD AVE

MECKLENBURG AVE

HAWTHORNE LN

THE PLAZA

NASSAU BLVD

VANLANDINGHAM ESTATE ●

Charlotte Country Club

BELVEDERE AVE

Kilborne Park

CENTRAL AVE

LOGIE AVE

74

To Woodlands

BRIAR CREEK RD

EASTWAY DR

NORLAND RD

CENTRAL AVE

MONROE RD

RANDOLPH RD

MINT MUSEUM RANDOLPH ☆

MUSEUM DR

0   0.5 mi

0   0.5 km

DUHNILL HOTEL

THE ASBURY

CHURCH & UNION ▼

MINT MUSEUM UPTOWN ✪

KIMPTON TRYON PARK ●

THE KING'S KITCHEN ▼

BLUMENTHAL PERFORMING ARTS CENTER

DISCOVERY PLACE

LIGHT FACTORY ★

RI RA ★

LEVINE MUSEUM OF THE NEW SOUTH ★

IMAGINON ★

SEA LEVEL NC ▼

HORNETS ARENA ★

277

W 5TH ST

W TRADE ST

W 4TH ST

CHURCH ST

S CHURCH ST

S TRYON ST

N COLLEGE ST

CHURCH ST

BREVARD ST

CALDWELL ST

11TH ST

9TH ST

8TH ST

7TH ST

6TH ST

0   400 yds

0   400 m

crops to Charlotte, and brokers funneled the raw cotton to Charleston. These early ties to South Carolina could be the origin of the subtle but pervasive sense that Charlotte is somehow part of South Carolina.

Economically adventurous, Charlotte rebounded quickly after the Civil War, encouraging Northern and foreign investment and business; this drew the disapprobation of people in other parts of North Carolina, but it laid the groundwork for greater prosperity. Textile mill money enriched the city through the early 20th century. In more recent years, Charlotte has become the second-largest banking center in the United States after New York City. Bank of America, Wachovia, and other locally based giants brought waves of newcomers to the Queen City. Today, North Carolina's booming film industry has found Charlotte, and television series that include *Homeland* as well as numerous commercials are filmed here.

SIGHTS
★ Mint Museum

The **Mint Museum** (704/337-2000, www. mintmuseum.org, $15 adults, $10 students, seniors, and educators, $6 ages 5-17, free under age 5, free to all 5pm-9pm Wed.), North Carolina's oldest art museum, comprises two spectacular museums with diverse collections. At the **Mint Museum Randolph** (2730 Randolph Rd., 1pm-5pm Sun., 11am-6pm Tues. and Thurs.-Sat., 11am-9pm Wed.), housed in an 1836 building originally home to a branch of the United States Mint, are galleries filled with art of the ancient Americas, European and African art, fashion, and decorative arts. The second location, the **Mint Museum Uptown** (at Levine Center for the Arts, 500 S. Tryon St., 1pm-5pm Sun., 11am-6pm Tues., Thurs., and Sat., 11am-9pm Wed. and Fri.), is home to the internationally recognized Craft + Design collection as well as wonderful collections of contemporary, American, and European art.

Other Art Museums

At the southern edge of Uptown Charlotte, the **Levine Center for the Arts** (www. levinecenterarts.org, 48-hour pass $20, www. carolinatix.org) is a bustling hive of artists, performers, and their patrons. Along with the Mint Museum, the Levine Center comprises three other institutions: The **Bechtler Museum of Modern Art** (420 S. Tryon St., 704/353-9200, www.bechtler.org, noon-6pm Sun. and Tues.-Fri., 10am-6pm Sat., $9 adults, $7 over age 64, students, and educators, $5 ages 11-18, free under age 11, military, and families) has more than 1,400 works by 20th-century artists in its collection, including works by Andy Warhol, Max Ernst, Alexander Calder, Pablo Picasso, and Alberto Giacometti. The building itself is a work of art, with a four-story glass atrium extending through the core of the museum. Housed in the **Harvey B. Gantt Center for African-American Arts + Culture** (551 S. Tryon St., 704/547-3700, www.ganttcenter.org, 10am-5pm Tues.-Sat., 1pm-5pm Sun., $9 adults, $7 over age 62, students, educators, and military, free under age 6) are fine examples of the arts, crafts, and cultural contributions African Americans have made to American culture, visual art, theater, literature, film, music, and dance. The **John S. and James L. Knight Theatre** (430 S. Tryon St., www.charlottecultureguide.com) is the home stage to the North Carolina Dance Theatre, and it often features performances by the Charlotte Symphony and Opera Carolina. Touring Broadway productions and other musicians also stop here regularly.

The **Light Factory** (1817 Central Ave., 704/333-9755, www.lightfactory.org, noon-6pm Wed.-Sat., free) is a gallery of modern photography and film. It hosts traveling exhibitions and offers classes and workshops. **Public art installations** are scattered throughout Uptown. A walking-tour brochure is available from the Arts and Science Council (www.artsandscience.org). Among the most notable North Carolinian artists whose work is on display are Charlotte-born Harlem Renaissance painter Romare Bearden, whose 1989 mural *Before Dawn* is at the main public library (310 N. Tryon St.), and Ben Long, whose celebrated frescoes include those at the Bank of America Corporate Center (100 N. Tryon St.) and the Charlotte-Mecklenburg Police Headquarters (601 E. Trade St.).

★ NASCAR Hall of Fame

The NASCAR Hall of Fame (400 E. Martin Luther King Jr. Blvd., 704/654-4400 or 888/902-6463, www.nascarhall.com, 10am-5pm Mon. and Wed.-Sun, groups only Thurs., $25 adults, $22 over age 59, $18 military and ages 4-12, free under age 4) is a 150,000-square-foot interactive attraction that explores the heroes, heritage, and history of NASCAR. One of the most interesting exhibits is the Glory Road, a huge hall where 18 cars from throughout NASCAR's history are displayed on a simulated track that shows the evolution of the sport from the dirt-track days to today's high-banked, sophisticated track surfaces. Other displays include garage and pit equipment, interactive activities that let you play Pit Crew member, and even a racing simulator. The Hall of Honor, where NASCAR Hall of Fame inductees are celebrated, also includes a number of race-driven cars and driver-worn helmets, suits, and other equipment.

History Museums and Sites

The Charlotte Museum of History (3500 Shamrock Dr., 704/568-1774, www.charlottemuseum.org, 11am-5pm Tues.-Sat., $10, $7 seniors and ages 6-17, $5 military) and the 1774 Hezekiah Alexander Homesite, the oldest structure in Mecklenburg County, tell the story of Charlotte's history.

On a busy block of North Tryon Street just outside Uptown is Historic Rosedale Plantation (3427 N. Tryon St., 704/335-0325, www.historicrosedale.org, grounds 10:30am-2pm Tues.-Fri., $5, guided house tours 11:30am and 1pm Fri. and last Sat. of the month $15 adults, $13 seniors and students,

free under age 6), a graceful 1830s house. Twenty enslaved African Americans worked the surrounding 911 acres, most of which are now under strip malls and parking lots. A farm of a similar era is recreated at the James K. Polk Historic Site (12031 Lancaster Hwy., Pineville, 704/889-7145, www.jameskpolk. net, 9am-5pm Tues.-Sat., free, tours 11am and 2pm Sat., $2 adults, $1 seniors and ages 5-12), where the 11th U.S. president was born. Visitors can tour log buildings that date to the era of his childhood (not original to the site); at the visitors center you can learn about Polk and the often overlooked significance of his presidency.

★ Levine Museum of the New South

The Levine Museum of the New South (200 E. 7th St., 704/333-1887, www.museumofthenewsouth.org, 10am-5pm Mon. and Fri., 10am-4pm Sat., noon-5pm Sun., $10 adults, $8 over age 61, students, educators, frontline workers, and military, $6 ages 6-18, free under age 6) tells the story in its permanent exhibit, *Cotton Fields to Skyscrapers,* of the South's emergence from the devastation of the Civil War and the rancor of Reconstruction. The exhibit includes the postwar reign of King Cotton and the lives of the tobacco and textile industries that for so long were the staples of North Carolina's economy. Interwoven are stories of segregation and the civil rights movement as well as the waves of globalization and immigration that are defining today's newer New South. Often in daring ways, changing exhibits address head-on issues of community, race, nationality, stereotyping, religion, and other fascinating and extremely complex aspects of Southern life past and present. Recent exhibits include Afrofuturism by a pair of local artists, signage and elements from the city's BLM protests, and plans for more artistic artifacts from our recent history.

If you are curious about Charlotte's culture, you'll enjoy the Levine Museum's New South for the New Southerner series (reservations required, $20). Led by retired museum historian Dr. Tom Hanchett, with guest speakers that include local politicians, writers, religious leaders, and other community experts, the evening salon will teach you the quirks and charms of Charlotte in a fun social setting while you sample a southern chicken dinner from Mert's Heart and Soul. Programs take place every other month, but take a break in summer; check the website for the current schedule.

Museums and Activities for Kids

Discovery Place (301 N. Tryon St., 704/372-6261, www.discoveryplace.org, 9:30am-4:30pm Fri.-Mon., $19-23 adults, $17-20 seniors, $15-18 children) is an interactive museum with an indoor rainforest, an IMAX theater ($10 adults, $9 seniors and children), and preserved human body parts. Discovery Place also operates Discovery Place Nature (1658 Sterling Rd., 704/372-6261, https://nature.discoveryplace.org, 9am-8pm Tues., 9am-5pm Wed.-Sat., noon-5pm Sun., $8) next to Freedom Park; it is home to live animals and a walk-through butterfly pavilion. ImaginOn (300 E. 7th St., 704/416-4600, www.imaginon.org, 9am-8pm Mon.-Thurs., 9am-5pm Fri.-Sat., 1pm-5pm Sun.) is a major Uptown arts complex for children and teens. It has theaters, libraries, a story lab, and a teen center.

Carowinds

The state's only big amusement park straddles the North Carolina-South Carolina state line just south of Charlotte. Carowinds (14523 Carowinds Blvd., 704/588-2600, www.carowinds.com, 10am-10pm daily summer, call for off-season hours, tickets $45-49 online, $47-67 at the gate, parking $16-20) has 14 coasters, including The Intimidator, the Dale Earnhardt-themed coaster. And they have the Fury 325, which, when it debuted in 2015, was the world's tallest and fastest Gigacoaster, reaching speeds around 95 miles per hour and dropping an amazing 81 degrees

for monster coaster thrills. They also have a wooden coaster called, unfortunately, the Hurler (don't eat a foot-long hot dog before hopping on this one), and another called the Carolina Goldrusher that's a little tamer (and presumably hot dog safe). On the Thunder Road coaster you'll cross over the state line, which runs through the park. There's also a water park called Boomerang Bay; it has some awesome slides, pools, and splash parks. The fascinating Dinosaurs Alive! exhibit brings dinosaurs to life with highly detailed animatronics. The exhibits are based on actual fossil evidence and were made with help from leading paleontologists to ensure their accuracy.

SPORTS AND RECREATION
City Parks

In Charlotte, a lot of emphasis is placed on community and on neighborhood pride. One of the reasons is the amazing city park system and green space in and among nearly every neighborhood and throughout Mecklenburg County. There are 210 parks in the county on more than 17,600 acres of land; in addition, there are 37 miles of developed greenway trails and 150 miles of undeveloped trails. Once you notice them, you'll start to find parks everywhere you look. Find more information on the parks, activity schedules, and detailed maps at the City of Charlotte (704/432-4280, http://charmeck.org).

There are many activities, classes, and sports in Charlotte's parks. Romare Bearden Park (300 S. Church St.), one of the newest parks, is home to a number of fitness programs, concerts, art and photography classes, and festivals small and large throughout the year. Its proximity to Bank of America Stadium, where the Carolina Panthers professional football team plays home games, ensures that this park has many visitors in addition to the regular neighborhood users.

1: NASCAR Hall of Fame 2: Mint Museum 3: Levine Museum of the New South 4: gardens outside Discovery Place Nature

Frazier Park (1201 W. 4th St.) has a soccer and flag football field, two full basketball courts, a pair of tennis courts, playgrounds, and a dog park and is on one of the many greenways that crisscross the city. There's also a community garden where neighbors can rent 150-square-foot plots and raise vegetables or flowers.

North of downtown but still in the Beltline, **Hornets Nest Park** (6301 Beatties Ford Rd., 980/314-1001), which has the best—or perhaps the scariest—name, is full of activities. In this 140-acre playground, you'll find four lighted softball fields, a disc golf course, a dozen tennis courts, shelters, a lake to fish in, playgrounds, horseshoe pits, and picnic shelters. The pièce de résistance is the **BMX bicycle track** (704/833-5183, www.ncbmx.com), the site of BMX competitions every Saturday. Open practice sessions and clinics will help you sharpen your skills and give you time to attack the course at your own pace.

Other parks, like **Druid Hills Park** (2801 Poinsett St.) and **Little People's Park** (1120 Harrill St.), with a playground for kids ages 12 and under, are less intense and have playgrounds, picnic areas, and open space where you can spread out to relax, play, and enjoy the outdoors.

Golf

It's no surprise that Charlotte, with professional athletes and big-business types, has some fabulous golf courses. What may surprise you is that not all of them are behind country club gates.

At the **Harry L. Jones, Sr. Golf Course** (1525 W. Tyvola Rd., 704/357-3373, www.charlottepublicgolf.com, 18 holes, par 72, greens fees Mon.-Thurs. $25.50 adults, $18.50 under age 17 and over age 55, Fri. $27.50 adults, $20.50 under age 17 and over age 55, Sat.-Sun., holidays, late play, and 9 holes $35.50, carts $9.50) the pace of play can be a little on the slow side, but the payoff is a day on a beautiful course. The back nine is more challenging, with a number of blind shots leading to the green.

The **"Old Course" at Sunset Hills** (800 Radio Rd., 704/399-0980, www.charlottepublicgolf.com, 18 holes, par 72, greens fees Mon.-Thurs. $32, Fri. $33, Sat.-Sun. and holidays $37, discounts for juniors, seniors, late play, and 9 holes, carts $9.50) is an enjoyable course where the fairways are wide and the hazards fairly placed. Novice golfers will find a number of confidence-building holes, and more seasoned players will find plenty of opportunities for aggressive shots.

TOP EXPERIENCE

★ White-Water Sports

The **U.S. National Whitewater Center** (5000 Whitewater Center Pkwy., 704/391-3900, www.usnwc.org, land activities $25-30, flat-water $30, passes $64 adults, $49 under age 10, canopy tours $89), which opened in 2007, features "the world's only multichannel recirculating white-water river"—that is, a complex of artificial rapids—designed for training athletes at the Olympic level; it is the home of the U.S. Olympic canoe and kayak team. Visitors can try white-water rafting, kayaking, stand-up paddleboarding, and white-water kayaking. The center's 300 acres also feature mountain biking trails, a climbing center, a concession area (with beer), and area for bands to perform.

Spectator Sports

The Carolinas' only professional basketball team, the NBA's **Charlotte Hornets** (704/467-6387, www.nba.com), play in Time Warner Cable Arena (333 E. Trade St.) in Uptown. The Hornets attract a statewide following by recruiting talent from the ranks of the University of North Carolina Tar Heel basketball alums. The roster perpetually includes one of the stars from the Heels teams, and Carolina legends Phil Ford and Buzz Peterson are part of the team's administration. Charlotte is also home to the Carolinas' only professional football team, the NFL's **Carolina Panthers** (704/358-7800, www.panthers.com), who play at the Bank of

Vicinity of Charlotte

Huntersville

To Davidson and Mooresville

To Kannapolis and Salisbury

Catawba River

MCCOY RD

Joplar

Concord

CHARLOTTE MOTOR SPEEDWAY

MOREHEAD RD

Latta Plantation Park

Hornet's Nest Park

24

N TRYON ST

Harrisburg

Westbourne

THE "OLD COURSE" AT SUNSET HILLS

Derita

★ UNIVERSITY OF NORTH CAROLINA AT CHARLOTTE

485

BROOKSHIRE BLVD

SUGAR CREEK RD

SEE "CHARLOTTE MAP"

U.S. NATIONAL WHITEWATER CENTER

GRAHAM ST

TRYON ST

THE PLAZA

SHAMROCK DR

24

To Reed Gold Mine

WOODSHED BAR

85

WILKINSON BLVD

77

CHARLOTTE

CENTRAL AVE

27

ALBEMARLE RD

CHARLOTTE/DOUGLAS INTERNATIONAL AIRPORT

WEST BLVD

WEST BLVD

Freedom Park

DIXIE RD

RANDOLPH RD

SARDIS RD

Mint Hill

INDEPENDENCE BLVD

SOUTH BLVD

PARK RD

OLDE MECKLENBURG BREWERY

SOUTH PARK MALL

FAIRVIEW RD

PROVIDENCE RD

485

160

YORK RD

QUAIL HOLLOW CLUB

Matthews

485

TAQUERIA MEXICO

CAROWINDS

Pineville

MALAY KITCHEN

74

JAMES K. POLK HISTORIC SITE

16

SOUTH CAROLINA

LANCASTER HWY

NORTH CAROLINA

77

521

0   2 mi

0   2 km

To Waxhaw

© MOON.COM

America Stadium (800 S. Mint St.) at the edge of Uptown. Fans twirling their growl-towels cheered them on to regional titles in 1996 and 2003.

The Chicago White Sox baseball team Triple-A affiliate is the **Charlotte Knights** (704/274-8300, www.charlotteknights.com), who play at the BB&B Ballpark (324 S. Mint St., 704/274-8300), a beautiful new stadium that opened just a couple of years ago. As with any AAA team, there's a good chance of seeing a major-leaguer rehabbing from injury or brushing up on his skills, or a young Turk about to break into a big-league career. A professional ice hockey team, the ECHL **Charlotte Checkers** (www.gocheckers.com, 704/342-4423), play at the Time Warner Cable Arena.

Each spring, the PGA Tour stops in Charlotte for some great golf at **The Wells Fargo Championship** (www.wellsfargo-championship.com) at the prestigious **Quail Hollow Club** (3700 Gleneagles Rd., 704/552-1800, www.quailhollowclub.com). The purse that comes with wining this tournament draws top-name talent from the PGA. Besides the opportunity to see golf idols swing a club, the event provides a rare look at this pristine course at one of the most exclusive clubs in Charlotte.

SHOPPING
Camp North End

Camp North End (300 Camp Rd., 980/337-4600, www.camp.nc) is a huge adaptive-reuse architecture project that's been years in the making and is still growing to maturity. This 76-acre campus has quite the industrial history. In 1924, Ford Motor Company built a factory and made 300,000 Model T and Model A cars here. In 1941, the U.S. Army used this as a quartermaster depot, building additional warehouses to help equip troops all across the South and East. In the 1950s a weird jeep-like vehicle called a Gamma Goat was built here for the French military, and the U.S. Military kept space here to pack munitions, calling it

the Charlotte Area Missile Plant, or CAMP for short. Now it's a hot spot for restaurants and home to offices and coworking suites, and there are galleries and tons of graffiti-style murals, offices for creatives, and it's still growing. It hosts events—I saw one of the traveling Van Gogh exhibitions here—and has become known as the place to be.

Restaurants here include Leah & Louise, Plant Joy, and La Caseta, but there's a dozen more. There's great shopping from places like **dupp & swat** (1824 Statesville Ave., Suite 109, 980/224-2128, www.duppandswat.com, noon-7pm Wed.-Fri. and by appointment) where you'll find wearable work by local designers, **That's Novel Books** (704/561-1793, www.thatsnovelbooks.com, 3pm-7pm Fri., 11am-4pm Sat.-Sun.) a used bookstore run by true bibliophiles, and **Prism Supply Co.** (1824 Statesville Ave., Suite 110, 980/819-6943, www.prismmotorcycles.com, 8am-5pm Mon.-Fri.), a shop for motorcycle culture and hand-crafted American-made goods.

Phillips Place

Phillips Place (Fairview Rd. and Cameron Valley Pkwy., www.phillipsplacecharlotte.com) is a premier outdoor shopping center in the South Park neighborhood. You'll find exclusive shops like **K-la** (704/643-7800, 10am-7pm Mon.-Sat., noon-6pm Sun.), a hot boutique carrying the most current men's and women's fashions; **Orvis** (704/571-6100, www.orvis.com, 11am-6pm Mon.-Thurs., 10am-6pm Fri.-Sat., noon-6pm Sun.), the famed fly-fishing and country lifestyle outfitter; **Granville** (704/999-6976, 10am-5pm Mon.-Sat.), an interesting collection of 18th- and 19th-century French and English antiques; and **Taylor Richards & Conger** (704/366-9092, www.trcstyle.com, 10am-6pm Mon.-Sat.), an exclusive boutique that was named to *Esquire* magazine's Gold Standard list as one of America's top retailers.

1: urban greenway near downtown Charlotte **2:** dining at Leah & Louise **3:** U.S. National Whitewater Center

Capitol

The chic clothing boutique **Capitol** (4010 Sharon Rd., 704/366-0388, www.capitolcharlotte.com, 10am-5pm Mon.-Sat.) was called "the finest boutique in America" by Isaac Mizrahi, and all of the press it has received in recent years backs him up. They've been covered in *Elle, Garden & Gun, Veranda,* and the *New York Times.* They carry some exclusive brands like Alexander McQueen and Proenza Schouler as well as a number of designers whose work is as elegant as it is cutting-edge.

Meyer's Park

In the Meyer's Park neighborhood are stores as diverse as the folks who live here. **Reid's Fine Foods** (2823 Selwyn Ave., 704/377-1312, www.reids.com, 8am-8pm Mon.-Sat., 11am-7pm Sun.) is more than a neighborhood grocery store; they're invested in providing their neighbors and customers with superior meats, wines, regional food, and service. They hold cooking classes and tasting programs, their butcher is top-notch, the wine selection is incredible, and they have a great deal of prepared foods you just need to heat to eat.

Circa Interiors & Antiques (2321 Crescent Ave., 704/332-1688, www.circainteriors.com, 9am-5pm Mon.-Fri., 10am-3pm Sat.) sells antiques and fabulous home furnishings. The owners are the authors of the book *The Welcoming House: The Art of Living Graciously,* and everything in their shop encourages gracious, stylish living. Taking a look around the welcoming shop will give you some ideas for your own place, even if you don't leave with anything more than inspiration.

ENTERTAINMENT AND EVENTS

Performing Arts

Among the city's excellent theater companies are **Theatre Charlotte** (501 Queens Rd., 704/376-3777, www.theatrecharlotte.org), which has been in business since the 1920s; the **Actor's Theatre of Charlotte** (1900 Selwyn Ave., Suite 1252, 704/342-2251, www.

atcharlotte.org), a company specializing in contemporary drama; and the **Children's Theatre of Charlotte** (704/973-2828, www.ctcharlotte.org), at the ImaginOn arts complex (300 E. 7th St.).

The **Blumenthal Performing Arts Center** (130 N. Tryon St., 704/372-1000, www.blumenthalarts.org) in Uptown is the home theater of the **Charlotte Symphony** (704/972-2000, www.charlottesymphony.org), which has been in existence for nearly 80 years. These days, under the direction of Christof Perick and conductor Alan Yamamoto, it puts together seasons of baroque, romantic, and modern classical music as well as a series of pops-style concerts with guest artists. Almost 40 years old, the **Charlotte Ballet** (704/372-1000, www.charlotteballet.org) is another venerable institution in Charlotte's arts scene. They perform full-length classical ballets and modern works and tour widely, and their *Nutcracker* has become a Charlotte holiday-season staple. **Opera Carolina** (704/332-7177, www.operacarolina.org), at 60 years old, is the leading opera company in the Carolinas. They produce four major operas each year as well as an annual run of *Amahl and the Night Visitors* at Christmastime.

Festivals

Each May, race fans take over several blocks of Uptown for **Speed Street** (704/455-8888, www.600festival.com). For three days entertainers, race drivers, and thousands of enthusiasts celebrate the area's auto racing industry. Autograph sessions throughout the festival bring participants in close contact with racing royalty. Summer's **Charlotte Pride Festival** (http://charlottepride.org) is the city's celebration of its LGBTQ+ residents and businesses. The two-day festival features a parade, comedy and dance performers, musicians, and all sorts of goings-on at local LGBTQ-owned and supportive businesses. Charlotte is an incredible city for foodies, and one way to learn the culinary ropes in a short time is to come to the early-June **Taste**

Beyond Banktown

Charlotteans and visitors alike often refer to the Queen City as Banktown, a name meant to conjure images of spotless sidewalks, shining office towers, and a nine-to-five corporate culture with little room for the arts or nonconformity. But there's more to Charlotte than the Bank of America tower, sometimes called the Taj McColl, for the bank's former CEO, Hugh McColl. I happen to think that Uptown, with its sparkly skyscrapers and stampede of suits, is kind of cool—a little bit like Washington DC's K Street in a more tropical clime. But we do a disservice to Charlotte and to ourselves as travelers if we overlook the beautiful variety of people who live here. In addition to the suggestions in this chapter, these websites along with publications you can pick up in Banktown will illustrate what's happening outside the tower's shadow.

- *Creative Loafing* (http://clclt.com): This free weekly paper, which you can find all over the city, does a good job covering the arts, food, politics, and everything else that makes Charlotte hum. The website is as good a resource as the print edition.

- *Charlotte Magazine* (www.charlottemagazine.com): A fantastic monthly arts and culture magazine with outstanding writing.

- *Thrillist* (www.thrillist.com): The popular and hip listicle publication gives you a good and concise rundown of all things going on in the Queen City.

of Charlotte (www.tasteofcharlotte.com). Dozens of area restaurants make samples of their art available, from haute European masterpieces to soul food favorites, plus plenty of international flavors from this wonderfully diverse community.

Charlotte's rapidly expanding population of immigrants has filled the city's entertainment calendar with dozens of festivals and holidays from around the world. Spring's annual **Asian Festival** (www.charlottedragononboat.com) features dragon-boat races on Ramsey Creek in Cornelius. Early September brings the **Yiasou Greek Festival** (Holy Trinity Greek Orthodox Cathedral, 600 East Blvd., 704/334-4771, www.yiasoufestival. org), which celebrates one of the South's long-established Greek communities. October's two-day **Latin American Festival** (www. latinamericancoalition.org, $25 Sat., free Sun.) celebrates the South's largest group of recent immigrants.

Nightlife

The **AvidXchange Music Factory** (1000 NC Music Factory Blvd., 704/916-8970, http:// avidxchangemusicfactory.com) is a huge complex of clubs and theaters on the northeast side of Uptown. Its venues range from the 5,000-seat Uptown Amphitheater to Butter, a new nightclub with top national DJs, and the **Comedy Zone,** where you'll see top stand-up. Visit the website to find out about upcoming acts and for a map of the factory; it helps to get your bearings before you go. The **Visulite** (1615 Elizabeth Ave., 704/358-9200, www.visulite.com) is another major venue hosting major rock-and-roll, reggae, and world bands.

The **Milestone** (3400 Tuckaseegee Rd., 704/398-0472, www.themilestone.club) has been hosting underground and up-and-coming bands since 1969; it was a major landmark for punk music in the South in the 1980s. Artists who've made appearances in the club's history run the gamut from R.E.M. to Hasil Adkins and Fugazi. Today's lineups are just as inspired. **Coyote Joe's** (4621 Wilkinson Blvd., 704/399-4946, www. coyote-joes.com, 7pm-2am Wed. and Fri.-Sat.) is a huge country dance hall and honky-tonk that hosts top Nashville artists.

There are several significant rock-and-roll clubs in Charlotte as well. The **Neighborhood Theatre** (511 E. 36th St., 704/942-7997, www.neighborhoodtheatre.

com, all ages) in the NoDa (North Davidson) neighborhood is a place where artists already high on the charts, or new artists starting to make the climb to stardom, appear when they're in Charlotte. Visitors of all ages are admitted to most shows. NoDa also has a folk club, **The Evening Muse** (3227 N. Davidson St., 704/376-3737, www.eveningmuse.com, 7pm-2am Mon.-Sat., 7pm-11pm Sun.). This is an intimate listening room with a penchant for booking great acts, and music fans of all ages are admitted. **Ri Ra** (208 N. Tryon St., 704/333-5554, www.rira.com) is an Uptown Irish pub, constructed from a Victorian Dublin pub that the owners disassembled and shipped to Charlotte. It serves traditional British Isles pub fare and hosts all sorts of music and pub games.

Charlotte has a number of gay bars, ranging from casual martini lounges to 180-beats-per-minute dance clubs. Two popular venues are **The Woodshed Bar** (3935 Queen City Dr., 704/394-1712, www.woodshedbar.com, 5pm-2am Mon.-Sat., 3pm-2am Sun.), a bar where members of Charlotte's bear and leather communities come together. Something's going on here every night, including free pool, a light dinner buffet, karaoke, and theme nights. Another popular bar is **The Scorpio** (2301 Freedom Dr., 704/373-9124, www.thescorpio.com, 10pm-3am Fri., 10pm-4am Sat.), Charlotte's longest-running nightclub that caters to the LGBTQ+ community; they've been around since 1968. Expect female impersonators, drag revues, dance parties, and drink specials.

BREWERIES

Charlotte's brewery scene is growing quickly, and to keep up with what's new, awesome, and worth the beer calories is daunting. I check in with the **NC Beer Guys** (www.ncbeerguys.com), a couple of beer lovers who check out all things brew related and put up videos, maps, and write-ups. There's a great—and constantly updated—list on **Charlotte's Got A Lot** (www.charlottesgotalot.com). With these resources at your disposal, you'll know the

best breweries and taprooms to visit; here are some of my favorites.

One Charlotte brewery that continues to excite me is **Triple C Brewing Company** (2900 Griffith St., 704/372-3212, www.triplecbrewing.com, 4pm-9pm Mon.-Wed., 4pm-10pm Thurs., noon-10pm Fri.-Sat., noon-8pm Sun.). They consistently produce outstanding brews on tap, in cans and in bottles—and have won a bronze medal at the 2018 Great American Beer Fest. I love their big barrel-aged beers, but their tart Zest-A-Peel ale and the Citra Acid Test sour session IPA are other favorites.

Birdsong Brewing Company (1016 N. Davidson, 704/332-1810, www.birdsongbrewing.com, 3pm-10pm Mon.-Thurs., noon-11pm Fri.-Sat., 11am-8pm Sun., tours by request) taps a new limited brew every Thursday, but you'll find their IPA-heavy offerings on tap year-round. Try their Jalapeño Pale Ale for a balance of hoppy bitterness and spicy peppers.

Wooden Robot Brewery (1440 S. Tryon St., Suite 110, 980/819-7875, www.woodenrobotbrewery.com, 4pm-10pm Tues.-Wed., 2pm-10pm Thurs., 2pm-midnight Fri., noon-midnight Sat., noon-9pm Sun.) makes beer that's right up my alley. Their list includes a berlinerweisse, a rye saison, a raspberry saison, and other Belgian brews. Toss in a food truck or two and these taproom seats start to look pretty comfy.

Olde Mecklenburg Brewery (4150 Yancey Rd., 704/525-5644, www.oldemeckbrew.com, 11am-10pm Sun.-Thurs., 11am-11pm Fri.-Sat., $4-20) is a brewery and eatery specializing in German-style food and drink. They stick to the Reinheitsgebot, the 1516 beer purity laws that say beer has just four ingredients: yeast, water, malt, and hops. Try a tasting flight to see just how much flavor they can coax out of these four elements.

NoDa Brewing Company (2921 N. Tryon St., 704/900-6851, www.nodabrewing.com, 4pm-9pm Mon.-Thurs., 3pm-10pm Fri., noon-10pm Sat., noon-8pm Sun.) has racked up more than a few awards, including a World Beer Cup Gold for their Hop, Drop 'n Roll IPA.

Personally, I like their darker winter beers, but IPA fans will find the rest of their menu quite tasty. This is one of Charlotte's largest breweries, and as of this writing, they're expanding around town with taprooms, commercial facilities, and more in the works.

Free Range Brewing (2320 N. Davidson St., 980/201-9096, www.freerangebrewing. com, 4pm-10pm Mon.-Thurs., noon-11pm Fri., 11am-11pm-Sat., 11am-8pm Sun.) is right across from Birdsong, adding another voice to this beer-crazy part of town. The taproom has great indoor and outdoor spaces, and their beer list changes frequently. Try the Jenny Set the Field on Fire, a smoked saison; Shellem's Mussel Beach, a Carolina mussel stout; All You Knead Is Love, a sourdough IPA with sea salt; or any of their creative and crushable brews.

FOOD

Charlotte is the eatingest place: There are so many good new restaurants opening every week that it's hard to keep up, but for reviews of the newest venues, with lots of interesting cultural observation, check out *Creative Loafing* (http://clclt.com), a free paper found at many area businesses; the food coverage in the *Charlotte Observer* (www.charlotteobserver.com); and Thrillist.com.

Soul

★ **Leah & Louise** (Camp North End, 301 Camp Rd., Suite 101, 980/309-0690, www. leahandlouise.com, 5pm-9:30pm Wed.-Sun., brunch 10:30am-1:45pm Fri.-Sun., $8-32) draws inspiration from the Deep South, following culinary traditions from Memphis, Jackson, Mississippi, and New Orleans. Think of it as a sort of modern juke joint, one that's opening folks' eyes to the depth and subtlety of often overlooked foods. Take the River Chips, seasoned and crispy-fried chicken skins with a tangy dipping sauce; or the Jive Turkey, a deboned, spicy-sorghum glazed, benne seed-rolled turkey wing on a bed of tender collard stems. Both of these dishes exalt what would otherwise be seen as kitchen waste, but both are absolutely exceptional. Smoked Rabbit Country Captain-style, blackened catfish, and exceptional cocktails are even more reasons to make a reservation (or two) when you're in town.

★ **The Goodyear House** (3032 N. Davidson St., 704/312-5894, www.thegoodyearhousecharlotte.com, 4pm-10pm Tues.-Thurs., 11am-11pm Fri.-Sat., 10am-9pm Sun., $7-31) is another great restaurant from chef-owner Chris Coleman, who split his time between Charlotte and Mississippi, where he'd spend summers with his grandparents. His menu reflects a broad inspiration from the South, and an inclusiveness (there are a couple of vegan and several gluten-free dishes on every seasonal menu) in his cuisine that's refreshing. Whether it's a smoked-cashew mac-and-cheese, the Maltagliati with oyster mushroom stroganoff, the current spin on fried chicken, or a pile of sharable plates (the shaken fry bag, butter bean spread, and marinated shrimp makes for a solid meal), every bite is exceptional.

Charlotte's not short on fried chicken. **Price's Chicken Coop** (1614 Camden Rd., 704/333-9866, www.priceschickencoop.com, 10am-6pm Tues.-Sat., under $13, cash only) is one of Charlotte's favorite chicken places, a take-out counter where you can buy a box of deep-fried chicken, perch, shrimp, or liver and gizzards. What can I say about this fried chicken that hasn't been said? It's nearly perfect: moist, crispy, just salty enough, and as Southern as sweet tea. You can also buy it by the gallon bucket. At the **Chicken Box Café** (1331 W. Sugar Creek Rd., 704/566-6000, 11am-7pm Wed.-Sun., $3-19), the food is undeniably rustic soul food. Since 1978 they've been serving Charlotte fried and barbecue chicken, neck bones (yes, chicken necks, where the meat is surprisingly tender and flavorful), turkey wings, trotters (pigs' feet), oxtail, and even chitterlings (if you have to ask, don't; they're an acquired taste).

Charlotte, like much of the region, was once dominated by mills making everything from flour sacks to fine fabrics, and the NoDa neighborhood is no exception. In NoDa, **Haberdish** (3106 N. Davidson St., 704/817-1084, www.haberdish.com, 5pm-10pm Tues.-Thurs., 5pm-11pm Fri., 11:30am-11pm Sat., 11:30am-10pm Sun., $5-30) celebrates the history and the foodways of the millworkers. Most of the furnishings and fixtures—tap handles, table tops, denim on the walls, and seat cushions—are salvaged from mills and warehouses nearby, but you come for the food and cocktails. Smoked and fried chicken are staples, as is the cast iron trout, all dishes similar to what the workers would have eaten at home and for lunch. Don't skip snacks like cheese straws, smokey boiled peanuts, or even the livermush toast, and definitely order sonker—a fruit-filled regional delicacy that falls somewhere between cake, pie, and cobbler—for dessert.

Anywhere you go in North Carolina, you're not far from fresh seafood. All you need to know is the right fisherman or fish market and you can dine on something tasty that was swimming just a few hours ago. **Sea Level NC** (129 E. 5th St., 704/412-2616, www.sealevelnc.com, 11am-10pm Mon.-Thurs., 11am-11pm Fri.-Sat., $5-135) brings their love for fresh catch, oysters, and more to Charlotte. Fish tacos, shrimp po' boys, oysters on the half shell, seafood towers complete with sturgeon caviar and lobster tails (that's the one coming in at $135, and worth every penny), and an intriguing cocktail list make for a fine dinner here.

Asian

Charlotte is a city of immigrants, with more arriving every year, and among the many benefits of such diversity is an amazingly rich culinary environment. Asian cuisines are especially prominent, with Vietnamese, Thai, Malaysian, and Japanese restaurants.

Pisces Sushi (1100 E. Metropolitan Ave., Suite 120, 704/334-0009, http://piscessushi.com, noon-9pm Tues.-Thurs., noon-10pm Fri.-Sat., noon-8:30pm Sun., $14-50) is the perpetual *Charlotte Magazine* winner for Best Sushi Restaurant, and given their reputation

for high-quality fish and a large menu of traditional and innovative rolls, it's no wonder. Lunch features by-the-piece or all-you-can-eat sushi; the remainder of the entrées are served hibachi-style.

For legit Thai, go to **Bahn Thai** (12206 Copper Way, Suite 122, 980/335-2313, www.bahnthaicharlotte.com, 11am-9pm Mon.-Fri., noon-9pm Sat., $7-20). The Thai side of the menu has some strong contenders for best in the city; the sushi side (why does everyone have sushi?) is good, though not quite at the same level.

Thai Taste (324 East Blvd., 704/332-0001, www.thaitastecharlotte.com, 11am-2:30pm and 5pm-9:30pm Mon.-Thurs., 11am-2:30pm and 5pm-10pm Fri., 5pm-10pm Sat., $11-18) has been a favorite for more than 20 years. The menu includes a variety of curries, noodle dishes, and stir-fries, including many vegetarian options. **Futo Buta** (222 E. Bland St., 704/376-8400, www.futobuta.com, 11am-9pm Sun.-Thurs., 11am-10pm Fri.-Sat., $7-18) has ramen, *bun, donburi,* and a few small plates. It's an intimate restaurant and the food is "why don't I have this in my hometown" good.

Charlotte has quite a few Vietnamese restaurants, which are great fun to sample. Perhaps the best known is **Lang Van** (3019 Shamrock Dr., 704/246-3401, 11am-10pm Tues.-Thurs., 11am-11pm Fri.-Sat., 11am-10pm Sun., under $10). Lang Van has an incredibly long menu, with many varieties of *phô,* noodle soup, and vermicelli dishes. Like many Vietnamese restaurants, this is an ideal eatery for vegetarians. *Charlotte Observer* readers have voted Lang Van the area's top Asian restaurant multiple times.

The reach of Charlotte's Asian food stretches all the way to Malaysia, and **Malaya Kitchen** (8200-400 Providence Rd., 704/541-6668, www.malayakitchen.com, 11am-9:30pm Tues.-Thurs. and Sun., 11am-10pm Fri.-Sat., $2.50-20) makes some of the best. Malaysian food resembles neighboring Thai, Indonesian, Chinese, and Indian fare, and the flavors are coherent and distinct and always good. For some authentic flavor, try the Hainan chicken, a poached chicken with rice; or the *sarang bu-rong*, a ring of fried taro filled with shrimp, chicken, and veggies, then topped with sauce.

Pizza

Among the many exotic foreigners arriving in Charlotte by the thousands every year, few have so difficult a time adjusting to the culture of the Southern United States as do Yankees. They have to become accustomed to a new language, a new climate, a new structure of social mores, and a new cuisine. Like so many immigrants, Northerners in Charlotte spend a lot of time trying to recreate aspects of their home culture in their new surroundings, often starting with native foodways—specifically, New York-style pizza.

At **Pure Pizza** (224 E. 7th St., 980/207-0037; 1911 Central Ave., 980/430-1701, www.purepizzaclt.com, 11am-10pm Mon.-Sat., noon-4pm Sun., $7-21) you'll find a pie that actually holds a candle to some New York pizzas. Toppings are creative without being too far out, and they offer something different—a sprouted ancient grains crust. For something really different, try the gluten-free sprouted ancient grains crust.

The loudly lauded **Hawthorne's Pizza** (1701 E. 7th St., 704/358-9339; 5814 Highland Shoppes Dr., 704/875-8502; 4100 Carmel Rd., 704/544-0299; 8410 Rea Rd., 980/272-9494, www.pizzacharlottenc.com, 4pm-9pm Tues.-Wed., 11am-9pm Thurs. and Sun., 11am-10pm Sat., $8-27) has pizzas, calzones, stromboli, baked and fresh pasta dishes, and a cannoli tray for dessert. There are other kinds of top-notch pizza around Charlotte; **Luisa's Brick Oven** (1730 Abbey Place, 704/522-8782, www.louisasbrickovenpizza.com, lunch 11am-2pm Mon.-Fri., dinner 5pm-9pm Sun.-Thurs. and 5pm-10pm Fri.-Sat., under $22) has, among other extremely tempting choices of topping, a muffuletta pie.

Latin American

Charlotte has a large Latino population, and their imprint on the culinary landscape adds a welcome dimension to the diversity of restaurants in the city. Many venues can be found along Central Avenue. Try **Taquería Mexico** (7001 South Blvd., 704/552-2461, 11am-8pm daily, under $10) and **Taquería Allende** (4801 N. Tryon St., 704/598-6666, 10pm-8pm daily, under $10) for an authentic Mexican taqueria experience.

Viva Chicken (1617 Elizabeth Ave., 980/335-0176, www.vivachicken.com, 11am-9pm daily, $4-26) serves that delicious *pollo a la brasa,* Peruvian rotisserie chicken. If you haven't had it, go now and pick up some of this lightly smoky, perfectly spiced, juicy chicken. The *hucacatay* sauce—made from Peruvian black mint—is addictive.

At Camp North End, **La Caseta** (108 N. Graham St., Suite 103, 980/226-5188, www.lacasetaclt.com, 11am-3pm Tues., 11am-8pm Wed.-Thurs. and Sun., 11am-9pm Fri.-Sat., $4-7) serves Latin street food from their corner spot. It's a simple menu—tacos two ways (al pastor and asada), a pair of pupusas (if you don't know these little cheese and protein-filled delicacies, now's the time), arepas, an empanada, and daily specials—and the prices won't break the bank. Most importantly, it's super good and in a location that might expose more folks to the flavors and dishes of Latin cuisine.

European

For French cuisine, many Charlotte diners turn to **The Fig Tree Restaurant** (1601 E. 7th St., 704/332-3322, www.charlottefigtree.com, 5:30pm-10pm Mon.-Fri., 5pm-10pm Sat., 5pm-9pm Sun., $14-62). The menu is nicely balanced between seafood, chops, and exotic proteins (ostrich and elk frequent the menu), with a decidedly French approach to preparation and plating. Add that to a nice wine list and you have an outstanding dinner spot.

Stagioni (715 Providence Rd., 704/372-8110, www.stagioniclt.com, 5pm-9pm Mon., 5pm-10pm Tues.-Sat., $10-40) is Italian done right. In an elegant setting, they offer superb service and pasta dishes that will make your head spin. All their dishes use fresh homemade pasta, including gnocchi with butter-poached lobster, smoked ricotta *plin* with wild chanterelle mushrooms, and tortelloni stuffed with braised lamb. They're hearty and flavor-packed, but the portions don't overwhelm you.

VANA (1440 S. Tryon St., Suite 100, www.vanarestaurant.com, 4pm-11pm Tues.-Thurs., 4pm-midnight Fri., 10:30am-midnight Sat., 10:30am-10pm Sun., $7-25) cooks just about everything over an open fire, and the highly refined dishes the kitchen puts out are earning this spot quite the reputation. When you come to this spot, be prepared to share, as it's almost exclusively small plates. The *burrata* is a must-order on any visit, as is the beef tartare. Their cabbage with red mole and the charred greens with trout roe are tantalizing dishes, but if you want to indulge, then it's an order of oysters on the half shell and some bone marrow and crispy sourdough.

Fiamma (2418 Park Rd., 704/333-3062, www.fiammacharlotte.com, 5pm-9pm Tues.-Thurs. and Sun., 5pm-10pm Fri.-Sat., $9-55), an Italian restaurant in the Dilworth neighborhood, was named one of "The Top 10 Restaurants in Charlotte" by Zagat a couple of years ago. For their spectacular menu, Fiamma has fresh fish flown in every day from Italy, and they make their pasta and pizza crust dough twice every day from scratch. Such dedication to quality can be tasted at first bite.

Indian

★ **Botiwalla** (in Optimist Hall, 1115 N. Brevard St., 980/296-3993, www.botiwalla.com, 11am-9pm Sun.-Thurs., 11am-10pm Fri.-Sat., $4-15) blew me away the first time I ate there. The decor transports you to India, which is exactly what Meherwan Irani intended when he was putting this place together. And if the decor doesn't do the trick, the food is a guaranteed ticket to the subcontinent. The Desi Salad topped with a veggie skewer, chicken or paneer tikka, or lamb boti, is an exceptional, every-time-I'm-there dish. But it keeps me from ordering the Chicken Tikka Roll and the delicious looking Crispy Masala Fish Roll (I've stared overlong at a neighboring table's food), and any of the curry. But when you find a dish you love and you feel torn because the other food looks and smells so good, that's a great problem to have.

Curry Gate (640 W. 24th St., 704/712-2968, www.currygates.com, 2pm-10pm Tues.-Sun., $9-17) is a new and welcome addition to Charlotte's Indian food scene, but it's not strictly Indian cuisine as there's a good bit of Nepali food showing on the menu too. Try the Manchurian, a sort of veggie meatball with a peppery kick; the Malai Kofta, a creamy potato curry; a veggie- or chicken-filled *momo*, a type of Nepali steamed dumpling; and the Nepali noodle and Shanghai fried rice.

Copper: Cuisine of India (311 East Blvd., 704/333-0063, www.copperrestaurant.com, lunch 11:30am-2:30pm Mon.-Sun., dinner 5pm-10pm Mon.-Thurs., 5pm-10:30pm Fri.-Sat., 5pm-9:30pm Sun., $5-27) is upscale Indian at its best. Vegetarians flock to this place because the food is rich, filling, and flavor-packed, but dishes like chili lamb and tandoori duck leg confit guarantee that everyone can find a plate they'll love.

Eclectic Fusion

Few restaurants excite me the way ★ **Heirloom Restaurant** (33 Glenway St., Belmont, 704/829-8232, www.heirloomrestaurantnc.com, 5pm-10pm Tues.-Sat., $16-38) does. Chef Clark Barlow has committed his restaurant to North Carolina so fully, not a single product he uses is sourced from outside the state. He has beehives on the roof, he forages for mushrooms, he has relationships with fishermen on the Outer Banks who drive the day's catch right to his door. And despite the limitation, his food has the potential to leave you speechless based on flavor, technique, and creativity. Dishes change with regularity, but what he does with hen of the woods mushrooms, the way he fries a chicken, and his duck confit (with sumac jus) are exemplary dishes. While you can order à la carte, I recommend doing the six-course tasting menu

($70, $100 with drink pairings) as it shows the full range of chef Barlow's culinary genius.

Plant Joy (1801 N. Graham St., 980/237-4855, http://plantjoyclt.com, 11am-8pm Wed.-Thurs., 11am-9pm Fri.-Sat., 11am-3pm Sun., $3-15) is one of the best of the vegetable-forward restaurants in town, with a menu full that's vegan top to bottom. Omnivores and the culinarily curious take note: if you want to see the potential in vegan cuisine, check this place out. It's Mediterranean, so dishes you know—like falafel, kebabs (made with shiitake mushrooms), socca, hummus, gyros—are all here. And if you need to feed a crowd, you can: their Rainbow Platter ($30) has a little of everything on the menu, and Falafel Mountain ($28) is a pile of falafel so high, the menu compares it to "a land mass." They also have a pay-what-you-can meal, ensuring that folks who are food insecure can still get a healthy meal. You'll find this spot in Camp North End near some other excellent eats.

Sorghum-sesame-glazed pork belly. That's the first thing you should know about **Dogwood Southern Table & Bar** (4905 Ashley Park Lane, 704/910-4919, www.dogwoodsoutherntable.com, 5pm-9pm Mon.-Sat., $10-50). Every menu item is a reflection of the season's best ingredients and the creative—but restrained—flair the kitchen brings. Any lamb dish, the seasonal duck preparations, and the daily pastas are stellar options for dinner, and at lunch it's hard to order something other than the crab cake BLT.

The food at **Church and Union** (127 N. Tryon St., 704/919-1322, www.churchandunioncharlotte.com, 5pm-close daily, brunch 10am-4pm Sat.-Sun., $10-115, brunch $11-20) is upscale and recognizable but prepared impeccably. Chef-owner Jamie Lynch has appeared on TV's *Top Chef,* has been named in numerous lists and rankings as one of the best chefs in Charlotte, and continues to prove why he's earned the talk. Whether it's a croque madame for brunch, a lobster roll for lunch, or the dry-aged tomahawk steak for two at dinner, each dish is as near to perfect as it can be.

At **Haymaker** (225 S. Poplar St.,

704/626-6116, www.haymakerclt.com, 5pm-10pm Wed.-Sat., brunch 10am-2:30pm Sat., 10am-4pm Sun., $10-42) it's all about local flavors, in-season veggies and proteins, and the freshest of the fresh hitting your plate. NC Blue Crab Fritters with a ramp-kimchi aioli, crispy pork belly over rice middlings (they're like grits), a legitimately great cauliflower steak, and a some of the best housemade pickles I've ever had are just a few of the treats waiting for you on this menu.

★ **The King's Kitchen** (129 W. Trade St., 704-375-1990, www.kingskitchen.org, 5pm-10pm Tues.-Thurs., 11am-2:30pm and 5pm-10pm Fri., noon-10pm Sat., $6-21) operates on an interesting concept: They're a not-for-profit establishment. The King's Kitchen provides employment opportunities to Charlotteans in need of a hand and returns 100 percent of profits to hungry people in the area, all the while serving upscale Southern comfort food in an elegant setting.

Soul Gastrolounge (1500-B Central Ave., 704-348-1848, http://soulgastrolounge.com, 5pm-midnight daily, $7-40) also blends global cuisines, with a dinner menu of traditional and original sushi dishes as well as Mediterranean tapas. On Sunday the menu features classic brunch fare, with special items like *loukoumades* (Greek deep-fried doughnuts) and Southern-fried chicken with waffles.

ACCOMMODATIONS

When it comes to the languid elegance of the Old South, ★ **The Duke Mansion** (400 Hermitage Rd., 704/714-4400, www.dukemansion.com, $219-379) is close to heaven. The circa-1915 mansion in Charlotte's lovely Myers Park neighborhood was home to North Carolina royalty, the Duke family, including the young Doris Duke. The downstairs foyer and gallery were clearly designed for entertaining high society, but the bedrooms—most restored to reflect the Duke family's tastes around 1930—are simple and comfortable, and some of the en suite baths still have their original tubs and tiles. In a wonderful

Southern tradition, most guest rooms open onto sleeping porches, which are worth more than the room rates. You'll receive first-rate service, and the culinary team will present you with a splendid breakfast. If you visit while the magnolias are blooming, you'll never want to leave.

The ★ **VanLandingham Estate** (2010 The Plaza, 704/334-8909 or 888/524-2020, www.vanlandinghamestate.com, from $139), built in 1913, provides a glimpse of the affluent infancy of the neighborhood known as Plaza-Midwood. A streetcar ran down the middle of The Plaza, and wealthy families established five- and six-acre estates in what was then a bucolic suburb. Plaza-Midwood now feels very close to the center of the city, and the lots have long since been subdivided, but it is still a charming enclave of early 20th-century craftsman-style bungalows. The staff take good care of guests, the grounds are beautiful, and Uptown is only a few minutes away.

★ **Kimpton Tryon Park Hotel** (303 S. Church St., 704/445-2626, www.tryonparkhotel.com, from $199) sits in the center of Uptown only a few blocks from the football stadium, baseball field, basketball arena, and art museums. With 217 rooms; the rooftop bar **Merchant & Trade** (704/445-2550, 5pm-midnight Tues.-Sun.), where the only thing better than the cocktail list is the view; and **Angeline's** (7am-10am, 11am-2pm, and 5pm-10pm Mon.-Fri., 8am-2pm and 5pm-10pm Sat., 8am-2pm Sun., $15-42, brunch $10-24), an Italian-inspired restaurant where they serve three meals a day and brunch on weekends (try the house pasta bolognese and that sausage pizza).

Dunhill Hotel (237 N. Tryon St., 704/332-4141, www.dunhillhotel.com, $249-379) has been a luxurious stopover for visitors since 1929. Although the 10-story hotel opened early in the 20th century, renovations have brought it up to modern standards. With cozy upscale rooms inside and one of the city's best restaurants next door, this hotel is the ideal culmination of location and comfort.

About 20 minutes from downtown Charlotte, the **Davidson Village Inn** (117 Depot St., Davidson, 704/892-8044, www.davidsoninn.com, $175-260) is tucked away on a cozy side street in this tiny college town. The guest rooms are nicely appointed, the staff are helpful, and the breakfast is bountiful. This is a pleasant alternative to staying in the city.

By North Carolina standards, lodging is expensive in Charlotte. It's pretty hard to find a good place to stay for under $100 and extremely difficult to find a decent low-cost room near Uptown. However, there are more choices as you head out of town. The **Microtel Inn and Suites** (6309 Banner Elk Dr., 704/227-3377, www.microtelinn.com, from $84) is located on the north side of the city. On the opposite side of town, the **Best Western Sterling Hotel and Suites** (242 E. Woodlawn Rd., 704/525-5454, http://book.bestwestern.com, from $89) is not too far from the airport.

INFORMATION AND SERVICES

Two Uptown (Charlotte's name for its downtown) locations serve as **visitors centers** (501 S. College St., 800/231-4636, www.charlottesgotalot.com, 11am-2pm Thurs.-Mon.; lobby of the Levine Museum of the New South, 200 E. 7th St., 704/333-1887, ext. 235, www.museumofthenewsouth.org, 10am-5pm Mon. and Fri., 10am-4pm Sat., noon-5pm Sun.). There is also a visitors center at the Charlotte Douglas International Airport (5501 Josh Birmingham Pkwy., 704/359-4027, www.cltairport, 7:45am-11pm daily), and another Uptown (329 S. Tryon St., 800/231-4636, 9am-5pm Mon.-Sat., noon-5pm Sun.). The *Charlotte Observer* (www.charlotteobserver.com) publishes an excellent annual guide to the region called *Living Here*. Pick up a print copy at many major destinations, or read it on the website. Be on the lookout for any of the free local magazines, from the quirky and independent newsprint pieces to the glossy magazines; they're packed with great information on the best new places to dine and drink as well as events and happenings in town.

Carolinas Medical Center (1000 Blythe Blvd., 704/355-2000, www.atriumhealth.org) is one of the largest hospitals in the Carolinas.

GETTING THERE AND AROUND

Charlotte Douglas International Airport (CLT, 5501 Josh Birmingham Pkwy., 704/359-4013, www.cltairport.com) is the 10th-largest hub in the United States, with nonstop flights to more than 120 destinations worldwide and nearly 30 million passengers each year. A short cab ride from major Uptown hotels and attractions, Charlotte's Amtrak Station (1914 N. Tryon St., 704/376-4416, www.amtrak.com) is served by the New York-New Orleans *Crescent,* the *Carolinian* to New York City, and the *Piedmont* line to Raleigh.

Charlotte's extensive and ever-expanding public transportation system provides routes around the city. The LYNX Blue Line Light Rail operates 5:30am-2am daily with 15 stations; fares are $2.20 each way. There's also the free LYNX Gold Line, which has a shorter route and shortened hours of operation. If you fly into town, hybrid electric Sprinter buses connect the city center to the airport ($2.20, info at www.charlottenc.gov), and the Charlotte Area Transit System (CATS) bus service has 40 routes that traverse the county. Check with the city (704/336-7433, www.charlottenc.gov) for route maps and fares.

Racing Country

There are far too many NASCAR-related attractions and racing sites of interest to name, but you'll find a selection of the best listed below. This region's love of stock cars is part of a general devotion to things with wheels. Within an easy drive of Charlotte are a museum honoring a fleet of red trucks, an old roundhouse that shelters beautiful restored locomotives, and even a paddle-wheel steamboat.

Several of the state's special food traditions intersect in this region. The fumes of Lexington barbecue waft over the entire Piedmont, and serious aficionados of fried fish scout out inland fish camps on the back roads of Gaston and neighboring counties. Folks in country kitchens radiating out from Shelby and the foothills know that the best thing to do with those spare pig heads and organs is to mash them up with cornmeal and serve them as livermush. You'll see livermush sandwiches on the menus of many little cafés in this region.

The rocky rivers that cross what is now the I-85 corridor once powered hundreds of textile mills, brick fortresses around which sprouted little towns with a culture all their own. As international trade becomes more globalized, the ramifications are still being felt as the last generation of these mill villages is vanishing, scattering residents to the wind, and leaving unwieldy (but sometimes beautiful) structures to puzzle the developers tasked with demolishing or repurposing them.

MOORESVILLE AND LAKE NORMAN AREA

Downtown Mooresville is an attractive historic area filled with appealing turn-of-the-20th-century small-town commercial architecture. Mooresville is also home to some of the nation's most important racing facilities and attractions as well as more than 60 individual teams.

Racing Sights

There are several racing museums in the area, including the North Carolina Auto Racing Hall of Fame (Mooresville Visitor Center, 119 Knob Hill Rd., 704/663-5331, www.ncarhof.com, 10am-5pm Mon.-Fri., 10am-3pm Sat., $6 adults, $4 ages 6-12 and over age 54).

Some of the major teams and racing companies based here operate public facilities and gift shops. Dale Earnhardt Jr.'s **JR Motorsports** (349 Cayuga Dr., 704/799-4800, www.jrmracing.com, 8:30am-4:30pm Mon.-Fri., 10am-3pm Sat., reservations required for guided tours, see website for details), and **Penske Racing** (200 Penske Way, www.penskeracing.com, gift shop 704/799-7178, 10am-4pm Mon.-Fri.) are among the teams you'll find.

Racing Schools

Not to be missed are the **NASCAR Technical Institute** (220 Byers Creek Rd., 704/658-1950, www.uti.edu), a formal training school for motorsports automotive technology, and **PIT Instruction and Training** (156 Byers Creek Rd., 704/799-3869, www.visitpit.com), a pit-crew training school.

Sports and Recreation

If it's too hot to be around all that asphalt, there's plenty to do on the water. **Lake Norman State Park** (759 State Park Rd., Troutman, 704/528-6350, http://ncparks.gov, 7am-6pm daily Nov.-Feb., 7am-8pm daily Mar.-Apr. and Sept.-Oct., 7am-9pm daily May-Aug., office 8am-5pm daily, swimming area $6 over age 12, $4 under age 13) is home to the state's largest artificial lake, with boating, swimming, camping, and more than six miles of cycling and hiking trails. Fishing is good for striped and largemouth bass, perch, and crappie. On the five-mile Lake Shore Trail you'll pass several spots to fish from the shore, dip your toes in the water, or just take in the scenery. They have several camping (reservations at 877/772-6762, www.northcarolina-stateparks.reserveamerica.com) options from nonelectric campsites ($23) to electric sites ($33) and a primitive group campsite ($62).

If you want to get out onto the lake and into the coves and spots where the big ones congregate, **Pro-Am Guide Service** (704/491-8719, www.proamguideservice.com, half-day $165 for 2 people, full-day $200) can get you there. Guide Drew Montgomery meets you at the boat ramp with all the rods, reels, and tackle you need, but you have to get your own fishing license. He has a no-fish, no-pay policy, so even if you don't catch anything, you will have spent a nice day on the lake.

Entertainment

Queens Landing (1459 River Hwy., Mooresville, 704/663-2628, www.queenslanding.com, 10am-7pm Mon.-Wed., 10am-11pm Thurs.-Sat., 11am-6pm Sun.) is a huge lakeside entertainment complex that offers sightseeing and dinner cruises on the paddleboat *Catawba Queen* (sightseeing $20, $18 seniors, $15 ages 5-12, $8 ages 2-4; dinner cruises $65, $59 seniors, $32 ages 5-12, $18 ages 2-4) and the yacht *The Lady of the Lake* (dinner cruises $75, $69 seniors, $34 ages 5-12, $18 ages 2-4).

Food

DeLuxe Ice Cream (168 N. Broad St., 704/746-9371, www.deluxe1924.com, 11am-8pm Mon.-Thurs., 11am-9pm Fri.-Sat., 1pm-7pm Sun.) has been in operation since 1924. Today, they have many more flavors than when they started, with around four dozen from which to choose.

Three of the best restaurants in North Carolina are in Davidson and the neighboring town of Cornelius. ★ **Kindred,** (131 N. Main St., Davidson, 980/231-5000, www.kindreddavidson.com, 5pm-10pm Tues.-Sat., $10-45) comes from the minds of chef Joe Kindred and his wife and Sommelier, Katy, and if it were legal for a person to marry food, I would marry every bite of food I've had here. From the milk bread—warm, sweet, pillowy, with an exceptional texture—to a wagyu beef tartare I dream about (it's embarrassing to admit, but it's that good) to the squid ink conchiglie with sea urchin butter, the food is exquisite.

Also from the Kindreds is ★ **Hello, Sailor** (20210 Henderson Rd., Cornelius, 704/997-5365, www.hellosailornc.com, 11am-9pm Wed.-Sun., $8-67). Hello, Sailor is a more casual place, with fried fish (done Calabash-style), chicken and fish sandwiches (ooh, that crispy triggerfish sandwich is really something), and French fries cooked up in beef fat. But they also give the menu—and everything on it—a culinary kick with dishes like a citrus crab Louie salad, baby back ribs, and an unbelievably good (and priced accordingly) strip steak.

Barrel and Fork (20517 N. Main St., Cornelius, 704/655-7465, www.barrelandfork.com, 5pm-9pm Tues.-Thurs., 5pm-10pm Fri.-Sat., $22-48) in an old house on Main Street, serves an upscale dinner and fantastic specialty cocktails. The menu is split into Whites and Reds, with Reds being the place to find a bone-in rib-eye, roasted elk rack, and wagyu meatloaf; and the Whites featuring the fresh catch served over risotto, grilled sea bass, sautéed scallops, a roasted chicken, and some of the best gnocchi you'll ever eat.

CONCORD AND KANNAPOLIS

Cabarrus County, which wraps around the northeastern corner of Charlotte, is one of the linguistic zones that tends to cause stress among newcomers and longtime North Carolinians alike. The place-names tend not to be pronounced as the standard rules of Carolinian speech would dictate. The county's name is stressed on the middle syllable, breaking one of the cardinal Carolinian rules of front-loading multisyllabic words: It's "cuh-BAH-russ," with the "a" pronounced as in "hat." Similarly, Kannapolis is stressed on the second syllable to rhyme with Annapolis. Even more vexing are the two-syllable place-names. The stress in the words Concord and Midland falls equally on the two syllables—"con-cord" and "mid-land." Even so, these towns are well known to NASCAR fans and North Carolina history buffs, and if you're interested in either, they're worth the hour-long drive from uptown Charlotte.

★ Charlotte Motor Speedway

Charlotte Motor Speedway (704/455-3200 or 800/455-3267, www.charlottemotorspeedway.com, tours 10am-3pm Mon.-Sat., group tours only Sun., call to reserve), on Highway 29, is Concord's best-known attraction. The 167,000-seat arena with a 1.5-mile track hosts the NASCAR Sprint Cup as well as other NASCAR, Busch, and Craftsman Truck Series events. Tours give you a look at much of the speedway but they focus on what matters: the infield and track. On the Infield Experience Tour (10am, noon, and 2pm, $15) you'll ride around the track, cruise through the NASCAR garages, stop at the Winer's Circle for a picture, then tour the media center. The **Fast Pass Tour** (10am, noon, and 2pm, $30 per vehicle) puts you on the track in your own vehicle (easy now, not for racing) for a tour where your guide leads the tour via radio. And their **STEAM Program** (prices and times vary by activity, call for rates and times) delivers an educational experience at the track that's perfect for relating STEAM (that's science, technology, engineering, arts, mathematics) to motorsports.

The speedway is also home to the **Richard Petty Driving Experience,** where you can ride—or even drive—a 600-hp stock car at speeds up to 165 mph, as well as the **Rusty Wallace Racing Experience** (www.racewithrusty.com, $299-3,299) and **Seat Time American Racing School** (www.seattimeracingschool.com, $75-2,498).

Racing Sights and Racing Schools

Not to be outdone by its neighbor Concord, Kannapolis honors racing and the life of its hometown star Dale Earnhardt Sr. with the **Dale Trail.** Dale Sr. died at the age of 50 in a famous last-lap crash at the Daytona 500 race in 2001, one of the tragedies in racing history that have most starkly illustrated the great danger to which drivers subject themselves. Dale Sr. is honored by a nine-foot bronze statue, a fan-financed granite monument, and huge murals at the **Dale Earnhardt Tribute** (Main St. and B St.) in the middle of Cannon Village, a historic shopping district in Kannapolis. The Dale Trail also goes by **Mike Curb's Motorsports Museum** (600 Dale Earnhardt Blvd., 704/938-6121, www.mikecurb.com), which displays more than 20 race cars driven by Curb Motorsports drivers,

a star roster that includes Richard Petty, Dale Jarrett, and many others. The **Backing Up Classics Museum** (4545 Concord Pkwy., 704/788-9500, www.morrisonmotorco.com, 10am-4pm Mon.-Tues. and Thurs.-Sat., $6, $5 seniors, students, and military) is just north of the Speedway and houses more than 50 classic cars, muscle cars, and rides from the 1950s and 1960s.

The **NASCAR Racing Experience** (5555 Concord Pkwy., Concord, 704/886-2400, www.nascarracingexperience.com, $130-4,500) gives you a track-level view of the Charlotte Motor Speedway and provides some perspective on what your favorite drivers face on Sundays. Ride along at top speed with a pro driver, or see if you can hit those top speeds yourself as you take on the track for nearly an hour of solo driving. Not enough? Try a racing session against other drivers.

Garage Pass Shop Tours (704/455-2819, www.garagepassshoptours.com, $60-135) offers several tour packages that include race shops and the NASCAR Hall of Fame.

Historic Sights

In all the racing excitement, don't miss the sights of downtown Concord. The **Union Street Historic District** preserves some of the area's most spectacular homes, built with turn-of-the-20th-century textile dollars. Also along Union Street is the **Cabarrus Creamery** (21 Union St. S., 704/784-1923, www.cabarruscreamery.com, 3pm-8pm Thurs.-Sun., $2-7), an old-time ice cream shop.

Bost Grist Mill (4701 Hwy. 200, 704/782-1600, www.bostgristmill.com, free) is a beautiful and interesting building, home to a working gristmill where, in the 1800s, a water wheel created 15 hp and allowed the mill to produce around 150 bushels of meal per day. Today it's still in operation and still uses the same French Buhr millstones as it

did two centuries ago. In addition to a number of varying events (check the calendar on the website), you can arrange in advance for a group tour.

While in Cabarrus County, pay a visit to the **Reed Gold Mine National Historic Landmark** (9621 Reed Mine Rd., 704/721-4653, www.nchistoricsites.org, 9am-5pm Tues.-Sat., free, gold panning $3) in Midland to find out about a bonanza that hit this area long before the heyday of the textile mills and before stock cars were even imagined. In 1799, a local 12-year-old discovered—but didn't recognize the value of—a 17-pound gold nugget. Three years later, a sharp-eyed visitor noticed the huge lump of gold that the family was using as a doorstop and bought it for $3.50. This was the beginning of the first gold rush in the United States.

Great Wolf Lodge

Great Wolf Lodge (10175 Weddington Rd., 866/925-9653, www.greatwolf.com, from $279) is a resort that is filled with children and families frolicking in the 80,000-square-foot, 84°F indoor water park. There are slides, splash areas, and a giant bucket that dumps an unbelievable amount of water on the people below. There are racing water slides, tube slides, and a waterslide called the Howlin' Tornado that shoots you and three others into a six-story funnel where you swirl and twist and splash your way up and down the 30-foot walls until you're spit out the bottom. You can go bowling at a kid-size bowling alley, play mini golf, and take part in dozens of daily activities. There's a restaurant on-site, and the guest rooms are sizable.

Food

The beer impressed me at **Southern Strain Brewing Company** (165 Brumley Ave. NE, Suite 3001, Concord, 704/218-9106, www.southernstrainbrewing.com, 4pm-10pm Tues.-Thurs., 3pm-11pm Fri., noon-11pm Sat., 11am-9pm Sun.) but the food from **Hot Box Next Level Kitchen** (704/218-9823, www.hotboxnc.com, 4pm-10pm Tues.-Thurs.,

1: Lake Norman in Mooresville 2: the shrimp roll from Hello, Sailor 3: the NASCAR Bank of America 500 at Charlotte Motor Speedway in Concord 4: King's Pinnacle, Crowders Mountain State Park

3pm-11pm Fri., noon-11pm Sat., 11am-9pm Sun., $9-14) lived up to its name and is indeed next level. The beer is wide-ranging in terms of style, but I like their O.K. Lager, a crisp and clear pilsner, and Hot Box Lager, which brings peach wood-smoked malts to the brew for a great result. Hot Box serves great accompaniments to any beer, including their HBX fries and pimento cheese, fish-and-chips, rice and beans, and a Cuban sandwich; it's a hit in every bite.

Speaking of Cuban sandwiches, there's an outstanding one at Havana Carolina Restaurant & Bar (11 Union St. S., Suite 108, Concord, 704/793-4233, www.havana-carolina.com, 11am-9pm Mon. and Fri.-Sat., 11am-8pm Wed.-Thurs., 11am-6pm Sun., $11-25). Start with the Cubanitas sampler, an assortment of five Cuban-style *croquetas,* a bite of food I find myself craving, or go for the *croquetas'* better-known cousin, the empanada. *Lechón asado*—slow roasted pork, shredded and served in *mojo* sauce—and the *vaca frita*—shredded brisket seared crispy—are go-to entrées if you're not drawn to that Cuban sandwich.

SALISBURY AND POINTS NORTH

Well north of Charlotte and well worth a day trip are the Salisbury and Mocksville areas (each about an hour north). This is another area where place-names have unusual pronunciations. Salisbury is easy enough as "SAWLS-bree," with the first syllable rhyming with Paul. More unusual is Rowan, the county of which Salisbury is the seat. In the Carolinas, Rowan, both as a place-name or a person's name, is pronounced with stress on the second syllable, "row-ANN," which makes it sound like a girl's name. Oddest of all is Cooleemee, a tiny mill village in Davie County, pronounced "COOL-uh-mee."

Sights

Salisbury has a very pretty downtown, girded all around by attractive historic residential and commercial neighborhoods. There are many historically significant buildings downtown, including Kluttz Drug Store (101 Main St.), which was the tallest commercial building in North Carolina at the time of its construction in 1858; The Plaza, directly across the street, an early seven-story "skyscraper"; the 1819 Utzman-Chambers House (116 S. Jackson St.); the 1820 Josephus Hall House; and hundreds more. Many of these places are open to the public, and a walking tour brochure can be found at the local Visitors Bureau (204 E. Innes St., 704/638-3100 or 800/332-2343, www.visit-salisburync.com, 9am-5pm Mon.-Sat.).

In Spencer, just north of Salisbury, the North Carolina Transportation Museum (Spencer Shops, 411 S. Salisbury Ave., 704/636-2889, http://nctrans.org, 9am-5pm Tues.-Sat., $6, $5 seniors and military, $4 ages 3-12, free under age 3, with train ride $12, $10 seniors and military, $8 ages 3-12, free under age 3) occupies the old Spencer Shops, a 100-year-old Southern Railroad complex. The museum includes a restored 1890s passenger station, a mechanics office, a boiler flue repair shop, and a 37-bay roundhouse where more than 25 restored locomotives and train cars are on display. Extensive exhibits about railroad history and a gift shop full of transportation books and ephemera are great fun for any train spotter. Train rides are available hourly 10:30am-1:30pm Thurs.-Fri., 10:30am-2:30pm Sat., 1:30pm-3:30pm Sun.

Shopping

Downtown Salisbury is home to many restaurants, antiques shops, and boutiques. Stop in at the South Main Book Company (110 S. Main St., 704/630-9788, www.southmain-bookcompany.com, 10am-6pm Mon.-Sat., 1pm-5pm Sun.), a small bookshop with a good array of titles in many genres, including a well-chosen selection of books about North Carolina. Be warned: The more than 40,000 titles on their shelves are guarded by a gang of black cats.

In nearby Gold Hill, a former mining town, you'll find the E. H. Montgomery General

Store (770 St. Stephens Church Rd., Gold Hill, 704/267-9439, www.historicgoldhill. com, 11am-5pm Thurs. and Sat., 11am-9pm Fri., noon-5pm Sun.), an 1840s general store that once supplied the town with just about everything it needed. Today, you'll find a little gift shop that sells old-fashioned candies, hand-dipped ice cream, glass-bottled sodas, jams, jellies, and other canned goods from nearby Amish communities, and coffee. Starting at 7pm on Friday evening, there's an open bluegrass jam session.

Food

City Tavern (113 E. Fisher St., Salisbury, 704/603-4656, www.citytavernsalisbury.com, 11am-10pm Sun.-Tues., 11am-11pm Wed.-Thurs., 11am-midnight Fri.-Sat., $7-16) keeps it simple and tasty with soup, sandwiches, salads, and a bar list befitting a tavern. Hard to beat a burger (especially that chorizo blend burger), but the Buffalo chicken sandwich and the tavern cheese steak give the burgers a run for their money.

Go Burrito! (115 W. Fisher St., Salisbury, 704/754-4755, www.goburrito.com, 11am-11pm daily, bar until 2am daily, $7-10) makes monster California-style burritos in a fast-casual restaurant that's fun and inviting. These burritos are stuffed with rice and beans, tons of grilled veggies, even french fries (do it and you'll never go back), and there's an assortment of proteins to pick from. This is a new regional chain and they have two other locations in North Carolina, one in Tennessee, and locations planned in Florida. From what I can tell, they're onto a good thing and soon we might see them everywhere.

Sabaidee Thai & Sushi Bar (2204 S. Main St., Salisbury, 704/637-0111, www. sabaideethaisushi.com, 11:30am-3pm and 5pm-9pm Tues.-Thurs., 11:30am-3pm and 5pm-9:30pm Fri.-Sat., noon-3pm and 5pm-8pm Sun., $5-27) always has great service and delivers on the food too. Thai dishes and curries are flavorful and spiced just right, and the sushi and Japanese dishes are surprisingly good. You'll spot many families here but also

a number of business types (and even some blue-collar guys) grabbing a bite on the way home.

Accommodations

The Turn of the Century Victorian Bed and Breakfast (529 S. Fulton St., 704/642-1660, www.turnofthecenturybb.com, $130-165) has four lovely guest rooms and is only a short walk to historic downtown Salisbury. The home dates to 1905, and the delicate preservation efforts undertaken to turn it around in the mid-1990s garnered attention and official recognition from the state and the town of Salisbury.

Across the Pond Bed & Breakfast (324 N. Fulton St., 866/296-7965, www.across-thepondbandb.com, $140-160) offers a love place to stay, with big comfortable beds, sitting areas in each room, and charming spaces throughout the house. There are only a trio of rooms here, each taking their names from the artwork—photos and prints—on the wall. Rooms are airy and modern, and the service is impeccable.

WEST OF CHARLOTTE
Sights

Bluegrass has always been a hot ticket in North Carolina, and with the rise in popularity of bluegrass, old time, and Appalachian music, the Earl Scruggs Center (103 S. Lafayette St., Shelby, 704/487-6233, www. earlscruggscenter.com, 10am-4pm Tues., 10am-6pm Wed., 10am-4pm Thurs.-Sat., $12 adults, $8 seniors and students, $5 ages 6-17, free military and under age 6) has become an even more important place to visit. Earl Scruggs, the five-string-banjo-picking half of legendary bluegrass duo Flat and Scruggs, was raised and learned to play not far from here, and you'll find a series of galleries and exhibits that tell his story and the story of the rise of bluegrass.

Sports and Recreation

Crowders Mountain State Park (522 Park Office Lane, 704/853-5375, http://ncparks.gov,

8am-7pm daily Nov., 8am-6pm daily Dec.-Feb., 8am-8pm daily Mar.-Apr. and Oct., 8am-9pm daily May-Sept., office 8am-5pm daily) embraces a small mountain range where Crowders Mountain and King's Pinnacle tower dramatically over the upper Piedmont landscape. Ten trails, ranging from short and easy to long, steep, and extremely strenuous, scale the ridges and explore the woods below. The high sheer cliffs are frequented by experienced rock climbers (who must obtain permits and observe strict rules, laid out on the website). Primitive **campsites** (reservations 877/772-6762, www.northcarolinastateparks.reserveamerica.com, $12) are located about one mile from the visitors center.

Food

One might not expect to find a generations-old seafood tradition here in the Piedmont, but in fact this region is dotted with old-time eating places called fish camps. Today's fish camps evolved from riverside and lakeside shacks, where a day's catch would be fried up and served to local mill workers and neighbors. While most of the fish served nowadays is not locally caught, the tradition of waterfront fried-fish eateries persists. Presentation is often plain—a heap of fried stuff on a paper plate—but folks don't come to these places for aperitifs and tapas. Some favorite area fish camps include **Love's Fish Box** (1104 Shelby Rd., Kings Mountain, 704/739-4036, www.lovesfishbox.net, 11am-9pm Tues.-Sat., under $15), **Twin Tops Fish Camp** (4574 S. New Hope Rd., Gastonia, 704/825-2490 or 704/825-3604, http://twintopsfishcamp.com, 4pm-8pm Tues.-Thurs., 4pm-9pm Fri., 3pm-9pm Sat., $7-20), and **Kelly's Seafood** (1204 E. Dixon Blvd., Shelby, 704/482-9941, under $15). Fish camp hours are unpredictable, so call ahead.

For beers in Shelby, stop in **Newgrass Brewing Co.** (213 S. Lafayette St., Shelby, 704/937-1280, www.newgrassbrewing.com, 4pm-10pm Tues.-Thurs., 4pm-midnight Fri., 11am-midnight Sat., noon-6pm Sun., $4-15). There's a steady rotation of live music—much of it newgrass, a sort of jam-rock-bluegrass hybrid—in the taproom, but there's always a slate of IPAs (New England, double, traditional), stouts, and even a few bottled sours. And you can grab a burger, grilled cheese, and assortment of snacks here if you're hungry; I recommend the deviled eggs, a grilled cheese sandwich, and, for dessert, grilled pound cake with ice cream.

Red Bridges Barbecue Lodge (2000 E. Dixon Rd., Shelby, 704/482-8567, www.bridgesbbq.com, 11am-7pm Wed.-Sat., 11am-3pm Sun., under $15) opened in 1946 and has been cooking with the same traditions ever since. You're not limited to barbecue here, but why would you order a burger or deviled egg sandwich? Trust me, the 'cue is the way to go, and Bridges has the accolades to prove it. They've won *Garden & Gun* magazine's "Ultimate Barbecue Bracket 2015," and they've been named on too many Top 10 lists to mention.

There is a second Bridges barbecue in Shelby, and though the names are the same and they both cook barbecue, there's no relation. **Alston Bridges Barbecue** (620 Grover St., 704/482-1998, 10:45am-7pm Mon.-Fri., $5-10) serves sandwiches, plates, and trays of chopped barbecue, ribs, and chicken, and they even sell "Q for" packs serving four ($25) and six ($35) and come with plenty of sides. When you're in Lexington barbecue country (as a refresher, North Carolina has two styles of barbecue: Eastern is whole hog and splashed with a tangy vinegar sauce, and Lexington uses shoulders or butts and a slightly sweeter sauce) the only order is coarse chop brown. Coarse chop means bigger pieces, and brown is the outside of the shoulder where the rub, smoke, and fat conspire to make the most delicious bite.

The Shelby Cafe (220 S. Lafayette St., Shelby, 704/487-8461, 7am-8:30pm Mon.-Fri., 7am-3pm Sat.-Sun., breakfast $2.50-10, lunch $2-11) is a no-frills diner: burgers, hot dogs, sandwiches for lunch; eggs, biscuits, pancakes, even livermush (a North Carolina delicacy that I steer clear of) for breakfast. No frills is not a judgment on the food—as with most diners, the grub here is good and simple—rather, it's to say that if you somehow went back in time 60 years, not much would change other than the prices.

If you've got a sweet tooth or just cannot take one more minute without a milk shake, get to **Uptown Sweets & Treats** (221 S. Lafayette St., Shelby, 980/404-0167, 11:30am-8:30pm Mon.-Thurs., 11:30am-9pm Fri.-Sat., $3-10) as fast as you can. With 28 flavors of hand-dipped ice cream (they actually use scoops), 30 flavors of gourmet popcorn (my friends at NC Tripping swear by the dill pickle popcorn), plus fudge and cupcakes, you'll find something that delights your tastebuds.

GETTING THERE AND AROUND

Charlotte sits at the intersection of two major arteries, I-77 and I-85, as well as Highway 74. As the center of the region, most roads lead to, through, or around the city. Winston-Salem sits 90 minutes north via I-85 or I-77 and I-40. A major east-west route, I-40 is 45 miles north of Charlotte via I-77 and gives easy access to Asheville (2.3 hours west) and Raleigh (2.75 hours east). To the south, you'll reach Columbia, South Carolina, in 90 minutes if you take I-77; Atlanta is four hours southwest on I-85. Charlotte itself is nearly ringed by I-485, but one section needs to be finished before the Beltline is complete.

The small cities surrounding Charlotte are easy to get to. Gastonia is 26 miles west along I-85, and Shelby is 30 minutes beyond that. Salisbury is 50 minutes northeast on I-85 and Lexington only 15 minutes more along the same route. Statesville and I-40 are 45 miles north of the city, and Mooresville is less than 30 miles away on I-77. Concord and Kannapolis are 40 miles distant, just off I-85 to the east-northeast. The Charlotte Motor Speedway is 25 minutes from downtown Charlotte on I-85.

Northern Blue Ridge and Foothills

There was a time when this region of rolling

mountains and foothills was the wild west of Colonial America, calling to the brave and foolhardy to carve out a place among the hollows and hills.

In 1752 one of the first written impressions of the area was recorded by Bishop Augustus Spangenberg, traveling from Pennsylvania on the Great Wagon Road (which followed a long, essentially continuous valley from Philadelphia to Alabama) looking for a suitable tract of land for his Moravian Church and community. He eventually found a welcoming spot in the city of Salem, but his first sight of the Blue Ridge filled him with dread. Cresting a ridge, Spangenberg, who had crossed the Atlantic and braved thousands of miles of the frontier, wrote, "We

Highlights

Look for ★ to find recommended sights, activities, dining, and lodging.

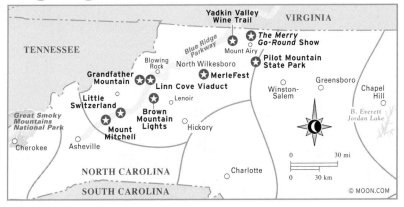

★ **Pilot Mountain State Park:** One of the state's most beautiful parks has plenty of recreation opportunities—not to mention the namesake mesa-like monolith itself (page 332).

★ **Yadkin Valley Wine Trail:** The wine country stretches all the way into the foothills of the Blue Ridge (page 332).

★ **MerleFest:** For one long weekend in April, the best artists in American roots music are in North Wilkesboro (page 336).

★ **Grandfather Mountain:** It's smaller than Mount Mitchell but still fully a mile high and no less beautiful (page 363).

★ **Linn Cove Viaduct:** One of the most photographed sections of the Blue Ridge Parkway, this elevated section of road seems to float in space (page 363).

★ **Brown Mountain Lights:** Mysterious lights have appeared over Brown Mountain, near Morganton, for centuries and you can watch the skies in hopes of catching a glimpse (page 364).

★ **Little Switzerland:** Mine for gems, hike to a nearby waterfall, or just admire the scenery, which, as its name suggests, is reminiscent of the Swiss Alps (page 366).

★ **Mount Mitchell:** The East's tallest peak was the subject of a scholarly feud in the mid-1800s, and one of the feuders, Mitchell himself, is buried at the summit (page 368).

Northern Blue Ridge and Foothills

© MOON.COM

VIRGINIA

NORTH CAROLINA

TENNESSEE

Mount Airy

PILOT MOUNTAIN STATE PARK and Divine Llama Vineyards

SHELTON VINEYARDS

WESTBEND VINEYARDS

To Winston-Salem

To Charlotte

ROUND PEAK VINEYARDS

YADKIN VALLEY WINE TRAIL

MCRITCHIE WINERY AND CIDERWORKS

Elkin

RAFFALDINI VINEYARDS

Statesville

Lake Norman

Cumberland Knob Recreation Area

Stone Mountain State Park

North Wilkesboro

Conover

Hickory

Lake Hickory

Wilkesboro

MERLEFEST

Blue Ridge Parkway

Blue Ridge Mountains

Blue Ridge

West Jefferson

Morganton

Lake Rhodhiss

South Mountains State Park

Boone

Valle Crucis

Blowing Rock

TRADITIONS POTTERY

FORT DEFIANCE

Lenoir

Pisgah National Forest

BROWN MOUNTAIN LIGHTS

LINN COVE VIADUCT

BEECH MOUNTAIN

Beech Mountain

GRANDFATHER MOUNTAIN

Crossnore

Spruce Pine

SILVER FORK WINERY

Lake James

Marion

Cherokee National Forest

Watauga Lake

Bristol

ORCHARD AT ALTAPASS

LITTLE SWITZERLAND

Linville Gorge

Penland

Burnsville

Erwin

Pisgah National Forest

MOUNT MITCHELL

Mt Mitchell State Park

Old Fort

Black Mountain

Swannanoa

To Asheville

10 mi

10 km

have reached here after a hard journey over very high, terrible mountains and cliffs. . . . When we reached the top we saw mountains to the right, to the left, before and behind us, rising like great waves in a storm."

This corner of the state wasn't just the frontier in Spangenberg's time; until the 20th century the farthest northwestern counties of North Carolina were known as the "Lost Provinces" because they were so remote and difficult to reach. As automobiles and improved roads, including the Blue Ridge Parkway, found their way to this area, so too did the flatlanders. Since then, the region has evolved into a popular destination for vacationers throughout the year. The mountains around Boone, a town named for the famed frontiersman and his kin, feel subtly different from the ranges closer to Asheville and the Smokies farther south and west; they're more spread out and softened. The northern Blue Ridge is no less beautiful, and the valleys become even wider and the peaks less craggy.

Although the wilderness is a little less wild now, it's still isolated. Stands of virgin forest, or at least forest that hasn't been logged in more than a century, still stand in remote coves, and spots like Linville Gorge challenge the most intrepid outdoor enthusiasts. Getting lost in the tangle of winding mountain roads is easy, especially as you move closer to the Tennessee state line, where the mountains get taller and the valleys narrower. Here you'll find back roads and hollows (pronounced "hollers" in much of these parts) where only the noonday sun reaches the valley floor, and in winter, some are lucky to see a few hours of true daylight. The trees are gnarled and mossy and cling to the edge of windy ridges and cliffs. You'll find waterfalls and wide rivers perfect for wading, floating, or fishing.

Much of the Appalachian folklore collected and popularized in the last 100 to 150 years has come out of this section of North Carolina. It was here that the young Confederate Army veteran known as Tom Dooley—who was a real person, and whose actual identity is still debated around these parts—killed his girlfriend, Laurie Foster, a ghastly crime immortalized in legend and song. In Wilkesboro, you can see the jail cell where he waited to go to the gallows in Statesville. Another crime immortalized in legend is the 1831 murder of Charlie Silver, apparently in self-defense, by his young wife, Frankie. She too was carried down the mountain to hang and was executed in Morganton. It's not all ghost stories, though. Many of the "Jack Tales," which became a sort of signature of Appalachian storytelling, were recorded around Beech Mountain and have been told by families here for generations. Head into Mount Airy or any other mountain town on any weekend and you'll find old-time musicians singing traditional songs the way their daddy (and their daddy's daddy) taught them, or old-timers telling Jack Tales old and new on some front porch or park bench.

When you visit, leave room in your luggage for some cheese; Ashe County is known for it, along with homemade jam or preserves. Take home a piece by area potters or weavers, eat dinner at a barbecue joint and get a feel for western North Carolina style 'cue, and visit a winery. Go skiing, rafting, caving, and gallery hopping; just remember to leave time to explore the back roads at your own pace, windows down, soaking it all in.

PLANNING YOUR TIME

Be aware of the weather when traveling in the region. Thick mountain fog in spring, fall, and even summer can form out of nowhere, making driving on twisting, unfamiliar roads dangerous. Pop-up thunderstorms in summer can put a damper on hiking, especially in high or exposed places, and can slow your drive to a crawl as your windshield wipers struggle to keep up. Snow squalls and even

Previous: Drive or climb to the top of Grandfather Mountain; sunset view at Pilot Mountain State Park; Grassy Creek Falls in Little Switzerland.

black ice in winter and cold days in spring and fall will slow you down too. When unexpected weather descends, slow to a comfortable safe pace or find a good spot to pull over and wait it out; most of the time, you won't be there long. With a little foresight, seasonal planning, and weather updates, you'll have no trouble discovering the beauty of this part of North Carolina. Know too that the mountain roads can be confusing, so bring a good paper map, gazetteer, or road atlas with you.

Three days will give you a general overview of the area and let you experience parts of what these mountain towns have to offer, but five days will provide ample time to explore by car, on foot, and by raft. If you're planning on spending most of your time in the deep mountains near Tennessee or around Mount Mitchell and Grandfather Mountain, Linville Gorge, Banner Elk, or Beech Mountain, Boone offers the convenience of bigger-town amenities including a wider selection of restaurants and shopping for day-trip supplies, but Blowing Rock offers picturesque mountain-town digs. Both towns are not far from the Blue Ridge Parkway (recorded information 828/271-4779, park headquarters 828/348-3400, www.blueridgeparkway.org), and most destinations are 30-60 minutes' drive from either one. Mount Airy and Wilkesboro are both at the edge of the mountains and easily accessible to the junction of I-77 and U.S. 421, a jumping-off point for most foothills locations.

GETTING THERE AND AROUND

There are no major airports in this region, but two are reasonably close: Asheville Regional Airport (AVL, 61 Terminal Dr., Fletcher, 828/684-2226, www.flyavl.com), with regularly scheduled domestic flights, and the larger Piedmont Triad International Airport (GSO, 1000 Ted Johnson Pkwy., 336/665-5600, www.flyfrompti.com) in Greensboro. The major

highway I-77 runs north-south along the edge of the mountains west of Mount Airy. Two other major interstate highways run just beyond the boundaries of the northern mountains: I-40, to the east and south, runs from Winston-Salem to Asheville, and I-26, to the south and west, runs from Asheville to Johnson City, Tennessee. U.S. 321 and U.S. 421 are the main roads, and U.S. 19 winds through the southwest edge of the area covered in this chapter.

The Blue Ridge Parkway follows some of its most beautiful miles in the northern mountains and connects several important towns. While it's probably the most fun and scenic route, it is not the most efficient if you're trying to cover a lot of ground quickly. The maximum speed limit is 45 mph, and because of weather, traffic, and twists and turns, you can count on driving slower than that most of the time.

Watauga County, which includes the towns of Blowing Rock, Boone, and Deep Gap, is covered by AppalCart Bus Routes (828/297-1300, www.appalcart.com). Riders must make reservations to ride, and the service is only available Monday-Friday, but the fares, which vary by route, are much cheaper than driving. AppalCart also runs routes to Charlotte, Winston-Salem, Hickory, Lenoir, and Wilkesboro, with fares ranging $10-50 round-trip.

INFORMATION AND SERVICES

The state Department of Transportation operates a real-time Road Conditions Map (www.drivenc.gov). For current conditions along the Blue Ridge Parkway, you can check the recorded message at 828/298-0398. Hospitals are located in most of the major towns in this region, but in case of an emergency, help might be delayed by weather, road conditions, or distance. In many areas—not just deep in the woods, but in populated areas as well—there may be no cell phone signal.

Driving the Blue Ridge Parkway

The Blue Ridge Parkway rides the crest of the mountains here as it follows its course from Waynesboro, Virginia, to Cherokee, North Carolina. Known as America's Byway, the Blue Ridge Parkway is a 469-mile two-lane road that traverses some of the most rugged, most picturesque mountains in the East. Somewhere around 15 million visitors will drive some or all of the parkway in a given year, making it the most-visited property of the National Park Service. It's easy to get on the parkway in North Carolina's High Country. You can pick up the Blue Ridge Parkway in Virginia, just eight miles from the North Carolina state line at a town called Fancy Gap, and then follow it south to Boone, Asheville, or even Cherokee. You can get on the parkway near Stone Mountain State Park and U.S. 21. Near Boone and Blowing Rock, U.S. 421 and U.S. 321 meet the parkway. A number of other roads—U.S. 221, Highway 80, Highway 181, and I-26—intersect the Blue Ridge Parkway between here and Asheville.

the Brinegar Cabin

Along this section of the parkway you'll encounter twice as many awe-inspiring vistas as there are overlooks (and there are a lot of overlooks). And you'll pass a number of sights that are as close to mandatory as you'll find along any route. If you stopped to take in the landscape at every view or paused to investigate every sight of note, it would take you four days to drive from Boone to Asheville. So to save you some time, we've made a list of a few places where you should stop and smell the mountain laurel. Since the Blue Ridge Parkway measures everything in mileposts, we did too.

- **Milepost 238.5: Brinegar Cabin in Doughton Park.** A typical mountain cabin dating to the 1870s. Great short trails are nearby.

- **Milepost 294: Moses Cone Manor.** Home of the Southern Highland Craft Guild Shop, a lovely walk around a bass-filled lake, and some challenging trails.

- **Milepost 304.4: Linn Cove Viaduct.** One of the most photographed sections of the Blue Ridge Parkway, this elevated section of road seems to float in space.

- **Milepost 305: Grandfather Mountain.** An impressive peak. Visit one of the subpeaks and cross the Mile High Swinging Bridge to a pinnacle where you'll have one of the best views along the whole of the parkway.

- **Milepost 316: Linville Falls.** These falls are in Linville Gorge, a spot often called the Grand Canyon of the East. They're impressive, especially in autumn.

- **Milepost 355: Mount Mitchell.** The highest peak east of the Mississippi, Mount Mitchell has an observation deck that gives you unobstructed views in every direction.

- **Milepost 364: Craggy Gardens.** Rocky crags, rhododendron thickets, and piles of mountain laurel give this spot an eerie beauty.

Mount Airy and Vicinity

In downtown Mount Airy you'll notice 1960s police squad cars, business names that may seem oddly familiar, and cardboard cutouts of Barney Fife peering out from shop windows. Mount Airy is the hometown of Andy Griffith and a mecca for fans of *The Andy Griffith Show*. People who grew up in small towns in the Carolinas and probably in small towns elsewhere recognize their families and neighbors in the fictional residents of Mayberry. The show's inspired writing and acting are a deep well of nostalgia, and its fans are legion. **TAGSRWC** (www.imayberry. com) is an intentionally obtuse acronym for *The Andy Griffith Show* Rerun Watchers Club, the show's international fan club, which has hundreds of chapters that have names referencing the series, such as "Her First Husband Got Runned Over by a Team of Hogs" (Texas) and "Anxiety Magnifies Fearsome Objects" (Alabama). The Surry Arts Council hosts the citywide **Mayberry Days** (www.mayberry-days.org), an annual fall festival entering its second decade in which TAGSRWC members, other fans, some of the remaining cast members, and impersonators of Mayberry characters come to town and have a big-eyed time getting haircuts at Floyd's Barbershop, riding in squad cars, and arresting each other.

ANDY GRIFFITH SIGHTS

You can't leave Mount Airy without paying a visit to the sites that honor favorite son Andy Griffith. It isn't open for tours, but you can rent **Andy's boyhood home** (711 E. Haymore St., 336/789-5999, $179-200) on Haymore Street if you care to spend the night. The **Andy Griffith Museum** (218 Rockford St., 336/786-1604, www.andygriffithmuseum.com, 9am-5pm Mon.-Sat., 1pm-5pm Sun., $8 adults, $6 under age 13, audio guide $2) features hundreds of pieces of memorabilia from Griffith's long career in television, movies, and music, including scripts and props

from his still-running eponymous TV show. Outside the museum and the attached **Andy Griffith Playhouse** (336/786-7998, www.surryarts.org, show times and ticket prices vary) stands a lifelike statue of Andy and Opie with fishing poles in tow that looks like it was grabbed right out of *The Andy Griffith Show*'s opening credits.

If you can't get enough of Andy and Barney, hop into a Mayberry squad car to tour all the major sights in town. **Mayberry Squad Car Tours** (625 S. Main St., 336/789-6743, www.tourmayberry.com) leave from "Wally's Service Station" and cost "$40 for a carload." And if that's not enough, stop by **Floyd's City Barber Shop** (129 N. Main St., 336/755-8637, 9:30am-3pm Tues.-Sat.) for a haircut. You won't find Floyd the barber in there, but you will find some friendly folks in an old-fashioned barbershop. If you're in the mood for a trim, you may just sit in the same seat as Andy Griffith, who received many a haircut here during his Mount Airy days.

THE MERRY-GO-ROUND SHOW

Teamed up with WPAQ 740 AM, the Surry Arts Council hosts *The Merry-Go-Round Show* (Earle Theater, 142 N. Main St., Mount Airy, 336/786-7998, www.surryarts.org, 11am-1:30pm Sat., $8, includes admission to the Andy Griffith Museum), the country's third-longest-running live bluegrass and old-time music radio show. Come to the Earle Theater for the show, or show up as early as 9am toting an instrument if you'd like to join in the pre-show jam session. It's one of the state's great small-town treats.

OTHER SIGHTS

A little more than 20 miles away in Pinnacle is **Horne Creek Living Historical Farm** (308 Horne Creek Farm Rd., Pinnacle, 336/325-2298, www.nchistoricsites.org, 9am-5pm

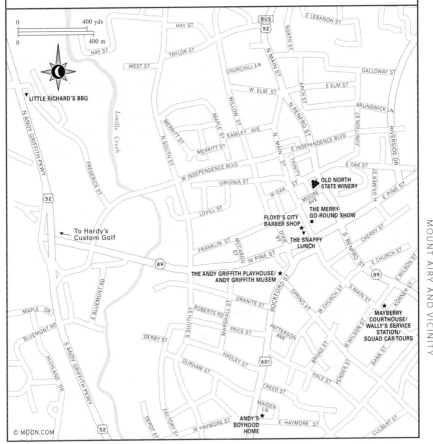

Mount Airy

LITTLE RICHARD'S BBQ

OLD NORTH STATE WINERY

THE MERRY-GO-ROUND SHOW

FLOYD'S CITY BARBER SHOP

THE SNAPPY LUNCH

THE ANDY GRIFFITH PLAYHOUSE/ ANDY GRIFFITH MUSEM

To Hardy's Custom Golf

MAYBERRY COURTHOUSE/ WALLY'S SERVICE STATION/ SQUAD CAR TOURS

ANDY'S BOYHOOD HOME

© MOON.COM

Tues.-Sat., free). The farm life of the Hauser family—an ancient clan in this area—is recreated as Thomas and Charlotte Hauser, and their lone daughter and 11 sons, would have experienced it around 1900. Costumed interpreters demonstrate the old ways of farm work while livestock of historic breeds go about their own work, probably not realizing that they're museum docents. The Hausers had an orchard, of which only a single superannuated pear tree remains, but today a new orchard has taken its place. The Southern Heritage Apple Orchard preserves old Southern heirloom species, trees grown from seeds that have been passed down in families for generations.

RECREATION
Golf

A rare golf course among the pastures and hay fields is the beautiful **Cross Creek Country Club** (1129 Greenhill Rd., 336/789-5131, www. crosscreekcc.com, 18 holes, par 72, greens fees $33-45 for 18 holes, $20-25 for 9 holes, includes cart) in Mount Airy. Course conditions are always fantastic, and the course presents quandaries to golfers of all levels.

Welcome to Mayberry RFD

"People started saying that Mayberry was based on Mount Airy. It sure sounds like it, doesn't it?"

—Andy Griffith

Surely the bucolic town of Mount Airy was the inspiration for Mayberry. Comedian and actor Andy Griffith grew up here, drawing inspiration for his stand-up comedy, hit television show, and just about every character he ever played during his long career from its landscape and people. Like its fictional counterpart, Mount Airy is filled with friendly folks, and something in the air here just feels like yesteryear. It's calmer, easier, slower.

Griffith got his break in 1953 when a recording of one of his stand-up routines, a story called "What It Was, Was Football," sold more than 800,000 copies and landed him a spot on *The Ed Sullivan Show* the next year. The premise was pretty simple: a country preacher, naive to all but his little world, happens upon a college football game. You owe it to yourself to hear Griffith deliver it in his charming drawl.

If you want a fun little par-3 course, head to **Hardy's Custom Golf** (2003 W. Pine St., 336/789-7888, www.hardrockgolf.net, 18 holes, par 54, greens fees $8, with cart $10, 9 holes $5, with cart $8). The course is lighted for play day or night. You can also try something a little different here: **FootGolf** (walking: $5 for 9 holes, $8 for 18, $10 day pass, riding: $8 for nine holes, $10 for 18, $20 day pass). Think golf meets soccer and you're on it: You kick a soccer ball from a tee to a green and attempt to get it in the hole using a scoring system like golf.

Hiking

A series of 400-foot rock faces extending for two miles are the most striking feature of **Hanging Rock State Park** (1790 Hanging Rock Park Rd., 336/593-8480, http://ncparks. gov, 7am-7pm daily Dec.-Feb., 7am-9pm daily Mar.-Apr. and Oct., 7am-10pm daily May-Sept., 7am-8pm daily Nov.), four miles northwest of Danbury. It's a great place for rock climbing and rappelling (which requires a permit and registration with park staff). You can also hike to waterfalls and beautiful overlooks, and swim in a nearby lake. Hanging Rock State Park has great **camping** (877/722-6762, www.northcarolinastateparks.reserveamerica.com), with 73 tent and trailer campsites ($22-26), one of which

is wheelchair-accessible, and five primitive group campsites (6-12 campers, $32). Each site has a tent pad, a picnic table, a grill, access to drinking water, and access to a washhouse (mid-Mar.-Nov.) with hot showers and laundry sinks. There are also two-bedroom, four-bed vacation cabins (around $517 weekly summer, from $95 daily off-season) for rent.

Rafting

Yadkin River Adventures (104 Old Rockford Rd., Dobson, 336/374-5318, www.yadkinriveradventures.com, canoe trips $65 for 2 hours, $75 for 4 hours, and $85 for 6 hours, kayak trips $40 for 2 hours, $50 for 4 hours, $60 for 6 hours) offers rentals of canoes, kayaks, and sit-on-tops, along with shuttle service for full- and half-day paddling adventures. The Class I Yadkin River is great for paddlers of all ages and experience levels, and it has some beautiful views of Pilot Mountain.

ENTERTAINMENT
WPAQ Radio

When you're in the area, tune in to **WPAQ** (AM 740, www.wpaq740.com), which has

---

1: Floyd's City Barber Shop **2:** a statue of Andy and Opie by sculptor Stuart Williamson **3:** the Mayberry Squad Car in front of Wally's Service Station

provided a venue for live local talent to perform old-time, bluegrass, and gospel music for more than 60 years. To get a really good idea of this community's life, tune in for the live Saturday-morning *The Merry-Go-Round Show* (11am-1:30pm Sat.), or any other day of the week when you'll hear local call-in shows, old-style country preaching, and more music.

Across the Virginia state line at Blue Ridge Parkway Milepost 213 is the **Blue Ridge Music Center** (Music Center information 276/236-5309, concert information 866/308-2773, ext. 212, www.blueridgemusiccenter.org, museum 10am-5pm Thurs.-Sun. early-Nov.-late-Apr., 10am-5pm daily May-Oct., free, concerts $15-40), a museum dedicated to the roots music of the hills in this part of North Carolina and Virginia. Midday Mountain Music concerts (noon-4pm daily, free) give area musicians opportunities to play for a crowd, and regular evening concerts by more established acts draw crowds from all over.

FESTIVALS AND EVENTS

A local institution that has a great deal to do with the vitality of Mount Airy's musical traditions is the **Bluegrass and Old-Time Fiddlers Convention** (691 W. Lebanon St., 336/345-7388, www.mountairyfiddlersconvention.com, $10, camping $35) held for almost 40 years during the first full weekend in June at Veterans Memorial Park. Thousands of people come to the festival from around the world to play old-time and bluegrass music with their friends and compete in what is a very prestigious competition in this genre. The heart of the action takes place at the hundreds of individual campsites that spring up all over the park in informal jam sessions among old and new friends. It's some of the best old-time music to be heard anywhere.

The Surry Arts Council is a hub of artistic activity in the Mount Airy-Surry County area. They sponsor and host many events throughout the year that showcase local talent in drama, visual arts, and especially music. Local and regional old-time and bluegrass

bands perform in the **Voice of the Blue Ridge Series** (7:30pm selected Sat., check calendar for upcoming shows, $7 adults, free under age 12) at the Earle Theater (142 N. Main St., Mount Airy, 336/786-2222).

FOOD

While you're in Mount Airy, you have to eat at **The Snappy Lunch** (125 N. Main St., 336/786-4931, www.thesnappylunch.com, 5:45am-1:45pm Tues.-Wed. and Fri., 5:45am-1:15pm Thurs. and Sat., $1-5), a diner which has a claim to fame that includes mentions on *The Andy Griffith Show*. They also have a "World Famous Pork Chop Sandwich," which is notoriously sloppy, delicious, and cheap. Eating here is like stepping back in time. The Snappy Lunch has been in the community since 1923.

In North Carolina you cannot escape barbecue. Lucky for you, Mt. Airy's **Little Richard's Barbecue** (455 Fredrick St., 336/783-0227, www.littlerichardsbarbeque.com, 11am-9pm Mon.-Sat., 11am-2:30pm Sun., $3-29) serves everything from smoked chicken to chopped pork to beef brisket and sausages, and they have a good lineup of sauces to match. If you want a little more refinement with your meal, make your way to **Old North State Winery** (308 N. Main St., 336/789-9463, www.oldnorthstatewinery.com, 11am-3pm Tues.-Wed., 11am-9pm Thurs.-Sat., $9-26). Here, chef Wishart makes sandwiches, burgers, salads, and flatbreads for lunch, and phenomenal dinner entrées that are familiar—shrimp and grits, a great steak—as well as unexpected dishes like pork belly ramen and seared tuna tacos, each paired with one of their wines.

ACCOMMODATIONS

In Mount Airy, **Quality Inn** (2136 Rockford St., 336/789-2000, www.qualityinnmountairy.com, from $72), **Holiday Inn Express** (1320 Ems Dr., 336/719-1731, www.ihg.com, from $109), and **Hampton Inn** (2029 Rockford St., 336/789-5999, www.hamptoninn.com, from $123) are good options.

Pilot Knob Inn Bed and Breakfast (361 New Pilot Knob Lane, Pinnacle, 336/325-2502, www.pilotknobinn.com, $129-249) in Pinnacle is an unusual B&B in that guests can stay in suites in the main lodge or in one of several restored century-old tobacco barns on the property. Each one-bedroom barn-turned-cabin is well equipped with modern conveniences, including two-person hot tubs and stone wood-burning fireplaces. Children are not allowed but you can bring two well-behaved dogs under 25 pounds ($30 per night) and horses can occupy a stall on the property ($50 per night).

INFORMATION AND SERVICES

Find out more of what Mount Airy has to offer by stopping by the **Mount Airy Visitors Center** (200 N. Main St., 800/948-0949 or 336/786-6116, www.visitmayberry.com, 8:30am-5pm Mon.-Fri., 10am-5pm Sat., 1pm-4pm Sun.).

There is a hospital in town, **Northern Hospital of Surry County** (830 Rockford St., 336/719-7000, www.northernhospital.com). If you require the police, contact the **Mount Airy Police Department** (150 Rockford St., 336/786-3535, www.mountairy.org).

GETTING THERE AND AROUND

You can reach Mount Airy from the Blue Ridge Parkway by turning south on U.S. 52 at Fancy Gap (Milepost 199.5), a 14-mile journey; by taking I-77/74 south to Highway 89 west, a trip of 24 mostly interstate miles; or by taking a curvy backroad that will let you catch a glimpse of life on the slopes of the Blue Ridge Mountains. To take the backroad, Highway 679/1717, turn onto Orchard Gap Road at Milepost 194, then stay straight on Wards Gap Road, which will lead you into town over the course of a 14-mile, 30-minute journey.

Blue Ridge Foothills

The foothills of the Blue Ridge are among the most beautiful stretches of countryside in North Carolina. You'll find the iconic Pilot Mountain, a mesa-like monolith standing alone in a wide valley, drawing the eye as soon as you come down off the mountain from Virginia. The Yadkin Valley Wine Trail, an American Viticultural Area, comprises 1.4 million acres of land and includes three-dozen local vineyards and wineries.

The land is incredibly rich: Just as the mountain streams bring nutrient-laden water to the valley floors, the valley fosters what we think of today as "mountain music." Several major festivals are held here in the spring and summer, most famously North Wilkesboro's annual MerleFest, which has become one the country's most important music festivals, drawing major bluegrass,

country, old-time, and Americana artists for a weekend of outdoor performances. Aficionados of the genre who can recognize the cadences of string-band and bluegrass music can pick out a fiddler or banjo player from this region almost immediately, and the best can tell you which side of the Blue Ridge—Virginia or North Carolina—they're from. From Mount Airy west to Wilkesboro, north to Galax, Virginia, and east to Floyd, Virginia, you'll find that 20-something old-time and bluegrass musicians number almost as many as musicians in their 70s. In the world of folk and traditional music, this is something of an anomaly, but it speaks to the genre's deep and strong roots.

For outdoor adventurers, the foothills conceal environments as wild and challenging as any you'll find in the deep mountains.

★ PILOT MOUNTAIN STATE PARK

Pilot Mountain State Park (1792 Pilot Knob Park Rd., Pinnacle, 336/444-5100, http://ncparks.gov, mountain section 8am-6pm daily Dec.-Feb., 8am-8pm daily Mar. 1-Mar. 15, 7am-8pm daily Mar. 15-Apr., 7am-9pm daily May-Sept., 7am-8pm daily Oct., 7am-6pm daily Nov., Yadkin River section 8:30am-5pm daily Nov.-Feb., 8:30am-7pm daily Mar.-Apr. and Oct., 8:30am-8pm daily May-Sept.) is a beautiful place for **hiking, swimming, rock climbing, rappelling** (in designated areas), **canoeing** on the Yadkin River, and **camping** (877/722-6762, www.northcarolinastateparks.reserveamerica.com, Mar. 15-Nov., $12-23) at one of the 42 designated tent and trailer sites. Each site has a tent pad, a picnic table, and a grill as well as access to drinking water and hot showers. There are a dozen trails here, ranging in length from 0.1 miles (from parking lot to overlook) to 4.3 miles (circling the mountain) and 6.6 miles (connecting the two sections of the park). Pilot Mountain, the park's namesake 1,400-foot-high rocky protrusion, is a startling sight that reminds some of a UHF knob on an old television set but others say it's a giant, earthen nipple; I guess that just like looking for patterns in clouds, it's up to the imagination of the viewer.

Camping

At Pilot Mountain, there are three distinct areas for **camping** (877/722-6762, www.northcarolinastateparks.reserveamerica.com, $15-23), each catering to a different type of camper. On the lower slopes of the mountain, there are 42 campsites for tents and trailers in their family camping area. This campsite has tent pads, tables, and grills as well as drinking water and washhouses with hot showers. Finally, there are two canoe campsites on the south bank of the Yadkin River. These two sites are available by permit only and are totally primitive, meaning no water and you pack out all waste. To camp here, you must have advance reservations.

★ YADKIN VALLEY WINE TRAIL

The Yadkin Valley stretches from the Virginia state line down past Winston-Salem and includes stretches of both the Blue Ridge foothills and the Piedmont. The terrain, climates, and microclimates are remarkably similar to that of France's Burgundy and Italy's Piedmont, two areas where viticulture has thrived for centuries. Winemakers discovered that North Carolina's soil was ideal for a number of familiar varietals, including the sweeter native muscadine and scuppernong grapes. There are three-dozen vineyards in this 1.4-million-acre American Viticultural Area, most within an easy drive of Elkin, Mount Airy, and Winston-Salem.

Raffaldini Vineyards and Winery (450 Groce Rd., Ronda, 336/835-9463, www.raffaldini.com, tours 1pm and 4pm Wed.-Sun., tasting room 11am-5pm Mon. and Wed.-Sat., noon-5pm Sun.) has a stunning Tuscan villa-style tasting room that overlooks 27 acres of vines. There are 10 wines to sample and purchase in the tasting room. The 2019 Vermentino Superiore is particularly good, as are the 2020 Girasole and their Montepulciano, which sells out quickly. After a tasting and tour, grab your favorite bottle and a bite to eat—they have a nice selection of antipasti on hand—and enjoy it on the terrace overlooking the vines and the valley.

McRitchie Winery and Ciderworks (315 Thurmond Post Office Rd., Thurmond, 336/874-3003, www.mcritchiewine.com, 10am-5pm Wed.-Sat., 1pm-5pm Sun.) has nine wines, including one blackberry wine that's sweet but interesting, and a pair of ciders. Their wines are fair, but their cider, which comes in semisweet and dry, is intriguing because it's sparkling, and they use heirloom apples that have been grown in the area for many years. The vineyard and kitchen garden are operated as sustainably as possible

1: Pilot Mountain State Park 2: Raffaldini Vineyards and Winery's tasting room

using low-impact methods that other wineries have yet to adopt.

Shelton Vineyards (286 Cabernet Lane, Dobson, 336/366-4724, www.sheltonvineyards.com, tasting room 11am-6pm Mon.-Sat., noon-6pm Sun. year-round) is a perennial North Carolina favorite, available at most grocery stores across the state. They offer tours and standard tastings ($12 pp) every two hours noon-4pm daily and 3pm Sunday. You can also move up to the **Reserve Tasting** (reservation required, $35 pp), which includes a tasting of Shelton's Reserve wines and a souvenir crystal wine glass, or even go for the **Gazebo Tasting** (reservation required, $55 pp, minimum 4 people). Be sure to try their dry riesling and port, unusual for the area. They are also home to **Harvest Grill** (336/366-3590, 11am-9pm Mon.-Thurs., 11am-10pm Fri.-Sat., 11am-5pm Sun. year-round, $14-35), a bistro that serves "sophisticated comfort food."

One of the most fun wineries to visit is **Divine Llama Vineyards** (4126 Divine Llama Lane, East Bend, 336/699-2525, www.divinellamavineyards.com, noon-6pm Thurs.-Sat., 1pm-5pm Sun.), with five acres of grapes and 20 acres of pasture for miniature horses and regular-size llamas on the llama farm ($10, free under age 5). The cabernet franc is tasty, and they have several wines named for (but not tasting like) their llamas. Throughout the year they host concerts at the vineyard, often running into October. You can arrange for a creek-side picnic and have the llamas pack your chairs, food, and wine in for you; call in advance to set up your llama picnic (from $50 pp).

RayLen Vineyards & Winery (3577 U.S. 158, Mocksville, 336/276-2687, www.raylenvineyards.com, 11am-6pm Mon.-Sat., noon-6pm Sun.) makes a number of good varietals, but one of their more popular wines is their Category 5 Red Blend, a wine that took home gold in the 2022 San Francisco Chronicle International Wine Competition. Cat 5 is one of my favorites and I've served and gifted at least a case worth, but try their cabernet franc (in a pure red or rosé form) and the 2020 reserve petit verdot if you're into reds; for whites, I'm all about their sauvignon blanc and viognier.

Round Peak Vineyards (765 Round Peak Church Rd., Mount Airy, 336/352-5595, www.roundpeak.com, noon-5pm Sun.-Thurs., noon-8pm Fri., noon-6pm Sun. Apr.-Dec., noon-8pm Fri., noon-6pm Sun. and by appointment Jan.-Mar.) has 13 acres of vineyards producing 10 French and Italian varietals. Unlike some of the larger vineyards in the Yadkin Valley, Round Peak makes wine using only grapes grown in its own vineyards. On Saturday during summer there are concerts and tastings, lawn games, and a number of special events. Round Peak is dog-friendly, and they have an area set aside for your four-legged traveling companion to play while you taste wine.

Food and Accommodations

In downtown Elkin, **Angry Troll Brewing** (222 E. Main St., 336/258-2251, www.angrytrollbrewing.com, 4pm-11pm Mon. and Thurs., 11:30am-midnight Fri.-Sat., 11:30am-11pm Sun., $6-17) is a brewery and restaurant serving wood-fired pretzels and pizza, wings (need to feed a crowd? get 100 wings for $125), sandwiches, and a bevy of fried appetizers that are perfect matches with the beer. On tap you'll find a hoppy IPA, a chocolate milk stout, and a hibiscus-flavored witbier. Just a block away you'll come to **Southern on Main** (102 E. Main St., 336/258-2144, www.southernonmain.com, 11am-9pm Tues.-Thurs., 11am-9:30pm Fri.-Sat., 11am-3pm Sun., $6-24, brunch $3-11), a tasty and adorable spot where they serve country comfort food that's a couple of steps above what your granny would serve. The meatloaf gets rave reviews, as does the blackened catfish and fried green tomatoes at lunch. For dinner, the braised short ribs and mountain trout are favorites.

At **Frog Holler Cabins** (564 E. Walker Rd., Elkin, 336/526-2661, www.froghollercabins.com, $145) you can stay in a well-appointed cabin with a fireplace and a hot tub overlooking Big Elkin Creek. Three cabins, The Cottage, Hawks Nest, and Mill House, are around 400 square feet and suitable for a couple; Deer Run is a bit bigger and sleeps four. There's plenty of peace and quiet, and they're within 30 minutes of more than two-dozen vineyards and wineries. On the property are miles of hiking trails and a fishing pond, but one of the big draws is the fact that you can park and take a tour ($60) of wineries, letting Frog Holler be your guide so that everyone can enjoy tasting.

CUMBERLAND KNOB RECREATION AREA

Much like the rest of the Blue Ridge Parkway, the section between Boone and the Virginia state line is stunning in any season. In addition to the scenic overlooks with photo opportunities of panoramic views of the valleys and mountains, there are a number of trails and sights. At Milepost 238.5, the **Cedar Ridge Trail** includes 4.2 miles that are part of a larger trail complex at Doughton Park. Here you can wander trails one to five miles in length, or string together several trails for a challenging 14-mile day hike. Farther north, at Milepost 217.5, the **Cumberland Knob Trail** is an easy 0.5 miles that's the perfect way to stretch your legs after a couple of hours in the car. Also at Milepost 217.5, the 2-mile **Gully Creek Trail** leads across a stream to a small picturesque waterfall. Cumberland Knob itself is of particular note because this is the place where construction began on the Blue Ridge Parkway on September 11, 1935. The 1,000-acre recreation area is a great place to stop and stretch your legs or picnic, even if you don't hike either trail.

STONE MOUNTAIN STATE PARK

You can't see the namesake Stone Mountain upon entering **Stone Mountain State Park** (3042 Frank Pkwy., Roaring Gap, 336/957-8185, www.ncparks.gov, 7am-6pm daily Nov.-Feb., 7am-8pm daily Mar.-Apr. and Sept.-Oct., 7am-9pm daily May-Aug., closed Dec. 25), but when you do, you'll remember it. Just a few miles south of the Blue Ridge Parkway along U.S. 21, this 14,000-acre park's most prominent feature is the 600-foot granite dome that is Stone Mountain. The 25-square-mile pluton (an upthrust of igneous rock) is fun to hike but difficult to see from the park. For the best views, get back on the Blue Ridge Parkway

Stone Mountain State Park

and head to the **Stone Mountain Overlook** (Milepost 232.5).

Stone Mountain State Park was established in 1969 and named a National Natural Landmark in 1975. In the years before it was a park, the lands around were settled by the typical mix of Europeans who make up much of the Appalachian ancestry—English, Irish, Scots-Irish, and German, with a few French families thrown in for good measure. They shaped churches, farms, log homes, and all they needed to create a community out of these woods, and three sites around the park show different aspects of life for the early European inhabitants here. The **Mountain Culture Exhibit** in the park office provides some historical context to these bold families who settled here. The **Hutchison Homestead** was built in the mid-1800s and is representative of a typical homestead for the region; it includes a log cabin, a barn, outbuildings, and even a blacksmith shop. Finally, the **Garden Creek Baptist Church,** built in 1897, is one of the few churches in the county that stand in nearly original form, having undergone no remodeling or major repairs during its long life.

Hiking

There are a number of hiking trails in the park, ranging from easy forest strolls to the challenging Stone Mountain Loop Trail that takes you to the top of the impressive granite dome. Visit www.hikingthecarolinas.com for information on Stone Mountain's trails as well as other trails across the state.

Camping

The 94 **campsites** (877/722-6762, www.northcarolinastateparks.reserveamerica.com) in Stone Mountain State Park are divided into three types: nonelectric sites ($23), sites with electricity ($30), and group campsites ($62). They have a two-night minimum stay on holiday weekends, and they lock the gates when the park closes. So if you have to leave, it had better be an emergency, as you'll be dialing 911 in order to get out. If you're a backpacker, they do have six backpack camping sites along Widow's Creek, and these sites are by permit only, no more than six campers per permit for a site.

WILKESBORO
★ **MerleFest**

It began as a small folk festival more than 20 years ago, but **MerleFest** (800/343-7857, www.merlefest.org, late Apr., $70-90 per day, multiday packages $185-500) has grown into one of the premier roots-music events in the country. It was founded in honor of Merle Watson, the son of legendary guitarist Doc Watson. Merle, also a guitarist, died unexpectedly in 1985 in a tractor accident, cutting short an influential career. Doc Watson, who grew up in the nearby community of Deep Gap, was the festival's ceremonial host until his death in 2012. Though his absence is deeply felt by musicians and fans alike, MerleFest is as strong and successful as ever, speaking to his lasting legacy in bluegrass, roots, and Appalachian music. MerleFest draws thousands of visitors every year for many of the top-name performers in folk, country, and bluegrass music. Recent headliners have included Steep Canyon Rangers, Chatham County Line, Sam Bush, Jim Avett, The Avett Brothers (Jim's sons), and Tift Merritt. With multiple stages and dozens of artists, there's a great deal of musical variety to sample.

Springtime in the mountains can be changeful; some years it's boiling hot and sunny at MerleFest, other times as damp and raw as winter, and sometimes both by turns. If you're traveling through the northern mountains during MerleFest, keep in mind that all the motels within an hour's drive of North Wilkesboro, and probably farther, will be booked solid, so be sure to reserve a room well in advance. Tenting and RV camping are available on the festival grounds. Before you pack a cooler full of adult refreshments that may be common at other music festivals, note that tobacco, alcohol, and pets are not allowed at MerleFest.

Moonshine

You can't talk about Wilkesboro or Wilkes County without mentioning moonshine, the illegal white-hot corn liquor that's achieved both legendary status and legal production (whether a legal "moonshine" is actually moonshine is a debate you can settle after you do a tasting). This area was a hotbed of moonshine production for decades, probably more like a century. Moonshine runners—daring young men with hot-rod cars, a penchant for fast driving, and a distaste for local law enforcement—would haul loads down to the cities and mill towns in the Piedmont, outrunning the police and eventually racing one another to see who's got the fastest car and the most nerve, inadvertently giving birth to the sport of stock car racing. In fact, several early NASCAR drivers got their start in these parts running 'shine and racing on dirt ovals. Novelist Taylor Brown gets into the history of moonshine in his book *Gods of Howl Mountain*, but you can go get a taste at a pair of distilleries in town.

Call Family Distillers (1611 Industrial Dr., 336/990-0708, www.callfamilydistillers.com, noon-5pm Tues.-Wed., 10am-10pm Thurs., 10am-midnight Fri.-Sat.) is one of the original moonshiners in North Carolina: their family's been in the business since the 1860s and have a great story. Reverend Daniel Call was the first distiller in the family, cooking up batches of whiskey in Lynchburg, Tennessee, with the help of his assistant, Jack Daniels. They opened the legal distillery, Daniel & Call Distillery No. 7, and operated it for a while until the Reverend was forced to choose between his congregation and his still. He kept preaching, sold the recipes and still to Jack, and the rest is history. But fast forward a few years and you get to "The Uncatchable" Willie Clay Call, who ran at least one still secreted away in the woods here and hauled his moonshine across the state in a fleet of souped-up cars. Today they make five varieties of moonshine, one pure "white lightning" and the others flavored. Belly up to the bar, sample to find your favorite, and ask a few questions about the history of the place.

Copper Barrel Distillery (508 Main St. N., 336/260-6500, www.copperbarrel. com, 5pm-11pm Fri.-Sat., call for hours Sun.-Thurs.) worked with local moonshine legend Buck Nance to get their recipes and process down right. They take pride in using a grain bill from North Carolina mills and farms in their five moonshines. Their unflavored White Lightning is the classic stuff and surprisingly smooth, and the other flavors—which includes black cherry and strawberry—bring the harsh edge down with a little residual sweetness. They offer tastings and tours ($10-50) if you're so inclined.

Food

North Wilkesboro's **Brushy Mountain Smokehouse and Creamery** (201 Wilkesboro Blvd., 336/667-9464, www.brushymtnsmokehouse.com, 11am-9pm Mon.-Sat., around $12) is famous for its pulled pork barbecue (it's legit and even made an appearance on TV's *BBQ with Bobby Flay*) and country sides (biscuits, fried okra, baked apples), but it's also a great ice cream shop. The ice cream is made here, and they bake their own waffle cones, so it's as fresh as can be. Fried apple pie, cobbler, and ice cream pie are all available by the slice.

Chow down at **The Dispensary Restaurant & Pub** (833 Main St. N., 336/818-1152, 11am-11pm Wed.-Thurs., 11am-12:30am Fri.-Sat., $6.50-17) on cheesesteak sandwiches, pulled pork, crabcakes, prime rib, burgers, and pizzas. They run specials—like the Hoosier Sandwich, that massive fried pork tenderloin sandwich, and dishes like fish-and-chips and chicken and dumplings.

GETTING THERE AND AROUND

The towns in this chapter are all an easy drive from Winston-Salem, Boone, and, slightly farther away, Charlotte. Wilkesboro is on U.S. 421, between Winston-Salem and Boone. U.S. 321, a pretty road, winds through Happy Valley to Lenoir and Hickory. I-77 runs from Charlotte to the Virginia state line, passing just west of Mount Airy.

West Jefferson and Vicinity

Just 11 miles from the Blue Ridge Parkway at Milepost 261 on Highway 163 west is the charming small town of West Jefferson, a good launching point to explore this corner of the North Carolina High Country. New River State Park is only 12 miles away, and the quaint little community of Todd is only 16 miles to the southwest.

West Jefferson, Jefferson, and Todd are in Ashe County, which is where the North and South Forks of the New River join to create the second-oldest river in the world, the New. The New flows through North Carolina, Virginia, and then West Virginia, where it joins other rivers on the way to the Ohio. In West Virginia, the New River is known for white-water rafting and an impressive single-span arch bridge. Here, though, the river is wide, gentle, and slow, and you're more likely to wade in it while casting a fly rod or float it in an inner tube than brave rapids in a raft or kayak.

Ashe County is also the center of two of North Carolina's more interesting industries: Christmas trees (Fraser firs, mostly) and cheese. North Carolina is the second-largest producer of Christmas trees in the United States; the industry brings in more than $100 million annually. The cheese here is also quite good.

West Jefferson is a surprisingly artsy town. There are 15 (at my last count) murals adorning buildings downtown, creating a lovely walking tour that gives you a look at how local artists have interpreted their history and surroundings. You'll also spot strange concrete squares, once utilitarian (they were the bases of long-gone streetlights) and now painted in whimsical forest scenes.

Highway 194, which runs through West Jefferson and is connected to Jefferson by U.S. 221, roughly parallels the parkway. It's a beautiful drive in and of itself, leading by red barns and countless tree farms with orderly rows of Fraser firs. Many of these barns are decorated with vivid color-block paintings that resemble old-fashioned quilts. They're part of the **Quilt Trails of Western North Carolina** (www.haywoodarts.org), an ongoing art project. There are two dozen in the vicinity of West Jefferson and even more in other parts of North Carolina.

RECREATION

There are two undeniable natural features in West Jefferson that beg to be explored: Mount Jefferson (visible from the Mount Jefferson Overlook at Milepost 267, Blue Ridge Pkwy.) and the New River.

Mount Jefferson State Natural Area

Just outside of town is the **Mount Jefferson State Natural Area** (1481 Mt. Jefferson State Park Rd., 336/246-9653, www.ncparks. gov, park 8am-sunset daily, office 8am-5pm Mon.-Fri.). The two main activities here are **picnicking** and **hiking.** A winding road dotted with scenic overlooks takes you close to the summit of the 4,683-foot Mount Jefferson, and from there you can reach the summit after a short 0.3-mile hike. From the **Summit Trail,** you can join up with the strenuous **Rhododendron Trail** (1.1 miles), which circles the summit ridge and passes through innumerable rhododendron thickets. From Rhododendron Trail you can hike out to Luther Rock, an odd exposed piece of the black volcanic rock that makes up this massif. There's also **Lost Province Trail,** a 0.75-mile loop off Rhododendron Trail that passes through a lovely hardwood forest. These trails are accessible from the Summit Trailhead in the parking lot and are well marked, making it quite easy to do a little hiking. Be sure to at least hit the summit; from here you can see a number of the Christmas tree farms in the county and the New River (on a clear day).

New River State Park

New River State Park (358 New River State Park Rd., Laurel Springs, 336/982-2587, www.ncparks.gov, 7am-7pm daily Dec.-Feb., 7am-9pm daily Mar.-Apr. and Oct., 7am-10pm daily May-Sept., 7am-8pm daily Nov.), 12 miles from West Jefferson, encompasses 2,200 acres of hills, meadows, and river just northeast of West Jefferson. This is a great park for canoeing and kayaking; there are no rentals available in the park, so bring your own or contact the park office for a current list of outfitters. Bass fishing is quite good on the North and South Forks of the New River, while trout fishing is best along the feeder streams and smaller, faster tributaries. You'll need a North Carolina fishing license (available at the Walmart in West Jefferson or online at www.ncwildlife.org/licensing, $20-36), and be sure to heed fishing regulations as established by the North Carolina Wildlife Resources Commission (www.ncwildlife.org/fishing). In addition to fishing, there are six miles of trails spread throughout the park. The best hikes are canoe-access only, so hop in a boat and head to the Alleghany Access for the Farm House Loop Trail and Riverview Trail; they're both filled with beautiful views of the river and park environs. This is home to some of the best camping (reservations 877/722-6762, www.northcarolinastateparks.reserveamerica.com) in the area; they have canoe-access-only campsites ($12), two-dozen canoe-in or walk-in sites ($12-23), a pair of improved group campsites (maximum 35 people, $62), a primitive group site ($32-52), and 20 drive-to campsites for tents and RVs ($23-33).

Elk Knob State Park

The small scenic New River town of Todd is a slow winding 12 miles north of Boone. Elk Knob State Park (5564 Meat Camp Rd., Todd, 828/297-7261, www.ncparks.gov, park 7am-6pm daily Nov.-Feb., 7am-8pm daily Mar.-May and Sept.-Oct., 7am-9pm daily June-Aug., office 8am-5pm daily Mon.-Fri.) is one of the newest parks in the North Carolina State Park system, and some areas are still under development. Elk Knob is the second-highest peak in Watauga County at 5,520 feet; a 1.9-mile hike takes you to the summit. Photographers love it here as wildflowers carpet the forest floor in spring and summer, providing breathtaking photo opportunities. Backcountry campers love it too, as a handful of primitive campsites (first-come, first-served, free), including a nice backcountry spot, accommodate only a few campers. The sites are a short hike in: The closest is about one mile away and the farthest about two miles.

Outfitters

In Todd, 13 miles to the southwest, RiverGirl Outfitters (4041 Todd Railroad Grade Rd., Todd, 336/877-3099, www.rivergirlfishing.com, 9am-5pm daily Apr.-Nov., by reservation only Dec.-Apr., call for availability, from $20) offers fishing lessons, fly-fishing guided trips, kayak and canoe rentals, and tubing trips on the New River. Kelly, the RiverGirl herself, changed careers from being a fisheries biologist to a river guide and angler and has ingrained herself into the community of Todd, drawing in thousands of visitors every year for fishing, tubing, and other river activities. Before you leave, take your picture with Petunia, a huge potbellied pig.

New River Outfitters (10725 U.S. 221 N., Scottville, 336/982-9192, www.canoethenew.com, 9am-3pm daily, call for off-season availability, from $10) gets you on the water for a short, 3.5-mile paddle or an overnight adventure. It also offers tubing trips, a popular way to pass an afternoon here. Located just nine miles north of Jefferson, the outfitters are close enough to the parkway for an impulse tubing session.

ENTERTAINMENT AND EVENTS

The center of the arts community is the Ashe County Arts Council (303 School Ave., Jefferson, 336/846-2787, www.ashecountyarts.org, 10am-5pm Mon.-Fri. and 10am-3pm Sat.). It has a gallery that features a rotating series of exhibitions by local artists and art collectives working in a variety of media, and helps put on musical events and plays in the community. The Arts Council is also heavily involved in the **West Jefferson Arts District Gallery Crawl** (5pm-7:30pm 2nd Fri. of the month June-Oct.), with a final event, the **Christmas Crawl**, taking place in late November or early December.

On Friday nights May-August, the **Backstreet Park Concert Series** (5:30pm-7pm Fri. June-Labor Day, free) brings in family-friendly musical entertainment in the form of traditional, old-time, and bluegrass musicians. A **Christmas in July Festival** (www.christmasinjuly.info) is held every July 3-4, with music, a street fair, a farmers market, Civil War reenactors, activities for kids, and a pretty sizable crowd. September brings the **On The Same Page Literary Festival** (www.onthesamepagefestival.org), **Olde Time Antiques Fair** (336-846-1231, www.wjantiquesfair.com), and **Art on the Mountain** (www.ashecountyarts.org).

SHOPPING

Originals Only Gallery (3-B N. Jefferson Ave., 336/846-1636, www.originalsonlygallery.com, 10am-5pm Wed.-Sat. and by appointment) carries works by a select few Ashe County artists and the pieces—paintings, pottery, and furniture—are excellent. Offering a mix of new and vintage clothing, home goods, and regional foodstuffs that make great gifts, **The Vintage Farmhouse General Store** (424 E. 2nd St., 336/846-4777, 9am-5pm Mon.-Sat.) will send you home with a few souvenirs to remember your trip. If you find yourself here in need of outdoor gear, **Mountain Outfitters** (102 S. Jefferson Ave., 336/246-9133, 9:30am-5pm Mon.-Sat.) can help. Boots, vests and jackets, water bottles, backpacks, and just about anything you need, you'll find here.

FOOD

Breakfast at **Hillbilly Grill** (601 S. Jefferson Ave., 336/846-4745, 6am-2pm Mon.-Fri., 6am-4pm Sat., 6am-8pm Sun., $3-13) is of the down-home variety, and you can get a full-on stack of pancakes for just a few bucks. The eatery has fun with those pancakes too, offering up bunny, snowman, and heart-shaped flapjacks on the appropriate holiday, and even writing your name (okay, your kid's name, but if you ask nicely, you never know) in pancake batter for a birthday treat. The burgers are hand-pattied and dripping with greasy-spoon goodness.

West Jefferson's brewpub, **Boondocks Brewing Tap Room & Restaurant** (108 S. Jefferson Ave., 336/246-5222, www.boondocksbeer.com, 11:30am-3pm Sun.-Thurs., 11:30am-8:30pm Fri.-Mon., $5-21), does a brisk business. Boondocks serves its own beer—a kölsch, IPAs, a stout, a saison, and other seasonal creations—and a number of other North Carolina brews, in addition to a handful of domestics and imports. On the menu you'll also find a full slate of pub fare, with steak, quiche, flatbread pizza, and burgers. You can also head to their **Brew Haus** (302 S. Jefferson Ave., 336/846-7572, 4pm-10pm Thurs.-Sat.) where they brew all the beer. Grab a seat, order a pint, and enjoy the music, get a trivia team together, or just hang out.

Black Jack's Pub & Grill (18 N. Jefferson Ave., 336/246-3295, www.blackjackspubandgrill.com, 12:30pm-8:30pm Mon.-Thurs., 11:30am-9:30pm Fri.-Sun., $5-15) is known for two things: burgers and wings galore (seriously, you can get an order of 30). If you're not in the mood for either of those, try the Philly Jack, a tasty take on the Philly cheesesteak. If you're really hungry, consider Black Jack's Hamburger Challenge—a timed race to eat a three-pound burger and giant order of fries. This is a sports bar, so expect larger crowds on game days and fight nights.

Mountain Aire Seafood & Steaks (9930 Hwy. 16, 336/982-3060, www.mountainaireseafoodnc.com, 4:30pm-8pm Thurs.-Fri., 4pm-8pm Sat., noon-8pm Sun., $7-29) serves Calabash-style seafood—a preparation that was developed on the North Carolina coast that involves a light batter and flash frying—shrimp cocktails, and fresh oysters, along with steaks and burgers.

Ashe County Cheese (106 E. Main St., 336/246-2501 or 800/445-1378, www.ashecountycheese.com, 8:30am-5pm Mon.-Sat.) has been making cheese here since 1930, and you can watch the process or just pick up some cheese, butter, fudge, or other homespun food goods in this store.

ACCOMMODATIONS

There are a few B&Bs and cabin rentals in and around West Jefferson, as well as options for camping.

Doughton Hall Bed & Breakfast (12668 Hwy. 18, Laurel Springs, 336/596-2468, $95), 17 miles from West Jefferson, is a solid option. It was named in part for an important but often forgotten member of the U.S. House of Representatives, Robert Doughton, who was responsible for ensuring the Blue Ridge Parkway ran through North Carolina rather than an alternate route through Tennessee. The Queen Anne-style home dates to the 1890s, and it has been a bed-and-breakfast since the early 1990s. Guest rooms are filled with antiques, but don't be afraid to make use of what you find.

Buffalo Tavern Bed-and-Breakfast (958 W. Buffalo Rd., 828/278-7394, www.buffalotavern.com, $109-175) is a four-bedroom B&B built in 1872. This beautiful home is situated just outside of West Jefferson, surrounded by Bluff, Buck, and Three Top Mountains. Though it was a tavern in its early days, now it's a tastefully decorated, comfortable spot to rest your head for a night or two.

★ **River House Country Inn and Restaurant** (1896 Old Field Creek Rd., Grassy Creek, 336/982-2109, www.riverhousenc.com, $135-225) has close to a dozen rooms and cabins spread out across a farm along the banks of the North Fork of the New River. The property and rooms are stunning. Whether you go for a cozy room in The Caretaker's Cottage, The Chicken House (which is much more romantic than it sounds), or The Carriage House, your accommodations will be outstanding. They also have a great restaurant on-site, serving prix fixe ($50) and à la carte menus ($20-36) filled with fine dining delights. If you're looking for a luxurious stopover in this area, River House is it.

In Deep Creek, south of West Jefferson, is **Fall Creek Cabins** (1105 Fall Creek Rd., Purlear, 336/877-3131, www.fallcreekcabins.com, $210-235), a 78-acre private retreat with eight two-story cabins and a trout stream running right through the property. It's beautiful, private, and close to the Blue Ridge Parkway. From the parkway, exit at Milepost 276 and you're just a few minutes away.

CAMPING

The best camping in the area is at **New River State Park** (358 New River State Park Rd., Laurel Springs, 336/982-2587, www.ncparks.gov, camping reservations 877/722-6762, www.northcarolinastateparks.reserveamerica.com), 12 miles from West Jefferson, where you'll find canoe-access-only campsites ($12), two-dozen canoe-in or walk-in sites ($12-23), a pair of improved group campsites (maximum of 35 people, $62), a primitive group site ($32-52), and 20 drive-to campsites for tents and RVs ($23-33). The improved campsites, especially the tent and RV sites, are very nice, with water, restrooms, and shower facilities available, plus picnic tables and grills.

INFORMATION AND SERVICES

Find information on cheese and more at www.ashechamber.com, and head over to www.visitwestjefferson.org for more on the town and what's going on here. If you need a hospital, the nearest is **Ashe Memorial Hospital** (200 Hospital Ave., Jefferson, 336/846-7101, www.ashememorial.org).

Boone and Other Mountain Towns

Boone is a fun mountain town, with its own countercultural flair based at Appalachian State University and its 15,000 students. There are good organic markets, plenty of restaurants, good antiques shops, and outdoor activities in every season. From Boone, you can access the beautiful mountain towns of Valle Crucis and Banner Elk as well as Beech Mountain.

BOONE

Boone is the quintessential western North Carolina city, a blend of old and new where proponents of homesteading and holistic living find a congenial habitat in the culture of rural Appalachia. It's also a college town, home to Appalachian State University and some 18,000 students, lending the city an invigorating youthful verve. Boone continues to grow as more people discover how amenable this part of the state is for year-round living. In recent years, the town has received a number of accolades, including being named one of the 10 Best Places to Retire by *U.S. News.* Located only 1 hour and 45 minutes west of Winston-Salem and 2 hours northeast from Asheville, it sits in a rugged and beautiful part of the state.

Daniel Boone and his family inspired the name for the town. Local legend, and historical evidence, says Boone camped here several times on trips to explore the region and blaze his trail west into Tennessee and Kentucky. His nephews, Jesse and Jonathan Boone, were founders of the first church in town, Three Forks Baptist, which still stands today. *Horn in the West,* an outdoor drama running since 1952, tells the story of Daniel Boone and an interesting slice of the region's history.

Sights

The mountains of North Carolina are loaded with artists and art lovers. At Appalachian State University, the **Turchin Center for the Visual Arts** (432 W. King St., 828/262-3017, www.tcva.org, 10am-6pm Tues.-Thurs. and Sat., noon-8pm Fri., free) provides access to the arts for the community and visitors of Boone. The Kay Borowski Sculpture Garden displays contemporary sculpture outdoors, while six indoor galleries exhibit the Turchin's permanent collection as well as traveling exhibitions. Throughout the year, photography and drawing competitions grace gallery walls.

In the heart of downtown Boone, the **Jones House Community and Cultural Center** (604 W. King St., 828/268-6280, www.joneshouse.org, 10am-5pm Mon.-Fri., 11am-4pm Sat.-Sun., concert and event prices vary), a beautiful home built in 1908, serves as a gallery for community artists, a meeting place for area groups, and a center for Independence Day and Christmas celebrations. Outdoor summer concerts and indoor fall concerts bring in string bands, bluegrass and roots country musicians, and other mountain music acts.

Sports and Recreation
ROCK CLIMBING

Rock Dimensions (131-B Depot St., 828/265-3544, www.rockdimensions.com, from $70) is a guide service that leads rock climbs at gorgeous locations throughout western North Carolina and parts of Tennessee and Virginia. Guides teach proper multi-pitch, top-rope anchoring, and rappelling techniques and lead caving expeditions ($360 for 4 people). Rock Dimensions also has a Discovery Course ($70-95), comprising a series of towers that make up a sort of vertical playground; think balance beams, tightropes, and cargo nets to traverse high above the ground. It's fun, safe, and an interesting challenge.

If you're an experienced climber, take a look at the **Boone Adventure Guide** (http://advguides.com/boone), a website that will lead you to some nice pitches.

Deep Mountains

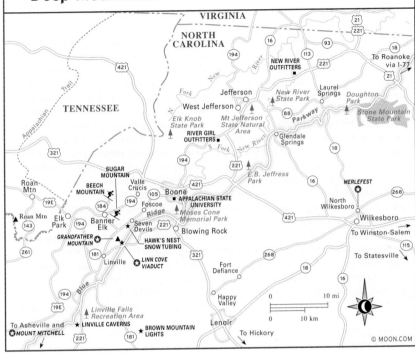

WINTER SPORTS

The Banner Elk area, just 15 miles west of Boone, has some of the state's best ski slopes. **Sugar Mountain** (1009 Sugar Mountain Dr., Sugar Mountain, 828/898-4521, www.skisugar.com, lift tickets $33-80 adults, $27-57 children, rentals $23-38 adults, $16-28 children) is North Carolina's largest winter resort, with 115 acres of ski slopes and 20 trails. In addition to skiing, activities on the 5,300-foot-high mountain include snowtubing, skating, and snowshoeing. Skiing and snowboarding lessons are available for adults and children. In summer, the slopes are open to hikers, chairlift riders, and mountain bikers. Advanced bikers can go from summit to base in five exhilarating minutes.

Beech Mountain Resort (1007 Beech Mountain Pkwy., Beech Mountain, 828/387-2011 or 800/438-2093, www. beechmountainresort.com, lift tickets $33-80 adults, $27-57 ages 5-12, free under ages 5, rentals $23-38 adults, $16-28 children and seniors) peaks 300 feet higher than Sugar Mountain and has 15 slopes and 10 lifts, as well as snowboarding and ice-skating areas. In summer, focus shifts to mountain biking and disc golf, with challenging downhill biking trails that range from beginner-friendly to advanced, plus a beautiful disc course. Be sure to check out the 5506⊠ Sky Bar, a snack and beverage spot with killer views at the summit. The resort also has a brewery on-site, Beech Mountain Brewing Company, which makes a half-dozen beers that are quite good, especially after a day on the slopes.

Between Boone and Blowing Rock is one of the best places to learn to ski: **Appalachian Ski Mountain** (940 Ski Mountain Rd., Blowing Rock, 828/295-7828, www.

appskimtn.com, lift tickets $29-77 adults, $22-56 children and seniors, $24-77 students, rentals $15-38). Home of the French-Swiss Ski College, they've been teaching since 1969 and designing ski instructional programs (for the Special Olympics and for elite military units) ever since, so they know how to get you on your feet on the slopes. Slopes here are very beginner-friendly for both skiers and snowboarders.

Hawksnest Snow Tubing (2058 Skyland Dr., Seven Devils, 828/963-6561, www.hawksnesttubing.com, snow-tubing $35-45, ziplining $70-80) is on a 4,800-foot mountain in Seven Devils, 11 miles southeast of Boone. It has 12 slopes dedicated to the family-friendly art of tubing—making it one of the largest snow-tubing parks on the East Coast. For the cost of admission, you'll get to ride the tubes for 1.75 hours. Throughout the year you can experience the thrill of zip-lining on more than four miles of zip lines (including two longer than 2,000 feet) that can get you to speeds up to 50 mph.

HIKING, RAFTING, AND CAVE TRIPS

Down the road from the Mast General Store in Valle Crucis, **River and Earth Adventures** (1655 Hwy. 105, 828/355-9797 or 866/411-7238, www.raftcavehike.com) leads all sorts of exciting trips on the water, in the woods, and in the area's deep caves. Rafting expeditions ($45-85) ride the French Broad River (Class III-IV) and Watauga River (Class II-III). Cave trips ($45-75) are offered on a daily basis year-round and meet at the company's outpost in Elizabethton, Tennessee, about an hour away, for a day's spelunking in Worley's Cave. Guided hiking trips are available, including an all-day kids-only hikes with adult guides—to free up parents who'd like a day on their own. Guide services are available for rock climbing and bouldering as well; inquire about routes and rates.

High Mountain Expeditions (3149 Tynecastle Hwy., Banner Elk, 828/202-7296, www.highmountainexpeditions.com) leads rafting trips ($65-249) on the Watauga River (Class I-III) and the much more challenging Nolichucky River (Class III-IV). It also leads caving expeditions ($55) and guided hikes ($40-50), up to 10 miles long for adults and children.

GEM MINING

Many people don't know that North Carolina is rich in gems and gold. Around Boone and

snowshoeing around the ski resorts

the more heavily visited places in the mountains, you'll find businesses that offer gem "mining." You don't need a pick and a shovel, just a keen eye and a few bucks. To "mine," you buy a bucket of material, graded and priced according to the likelihood of it having a valuable gem in it, and then sort, sift, and pan it yourself. You get to keep what you find, and you really can come across some beautiful specimens, some even worthy of jewelry. **River and Earth Adventures** (1655 Hwy. 105, 828/355-9797 or 866/411-7238, www. raftcavehike.com, $15-100) offers gem mining, as does **Foggy Mountain Gem Mine** (4416 Hwy. 105, 828/963-4367, www.foggy-mountaingems.com, $30-325), where you can get gemstones cut and polished in-house, and **The Greater Foscoe Gem Mining Co.** (8998 Hwy. 105, Boone, 828/963-5928, www.foscoeminingco.com, $16-212), where 24 kinds of gemstones can be found and the owner, a master goldsmith and stonecutter, will cut and polish the larger gems you find.

Entertainment
NIGHTLIFE

This is a college town, and as such there are several college bars around. You know the kind: the band starts tuning up at 11pm, the drinks are of the beginner variety, and there's a cover to get in. If that's your scene, find a kid with a black-and-gold "A" on their shirt and have that Appalachian State student point you in a direction. Otherwise you're looking at the bars in the restaurants around town. You can also check out Lost Province Brewing and **Appalachian Mountain Brewery** (163 Boone Creek Dr., 828/263-1111, www. amb.beer, noon-10pm daily), a microbrewery that's become popular with beer connoisseurs and more erudite members of the college crowd. It brews about three dozen beers and a cider, some of which are seasonal. Though many love the IPAs, the brewery's dark beers are also quite good. On any given night, some college band will set up in the corner of the main room and play for the evening. Outside there's a giant set of Jenga blocks. And if you're hungry, the brewery also owns **Farm to Flame** (www.f2flame.com, 1pm-9pm Sun.-Mon., 1pm-10pm Tues.-Thurs., noon-10pm Fri., 3pm-10pm Sat., $7-13), a food truck that has a sizable wood-fired pizza oven—which takes about 90 seconds to cook a pie.

THEATER

Boone's outdoor drama *Horn in the West* (591 Horn in the West Dr., 828/264-2120, www.horninthewest.com, $35 adults, $27 students, $24 under age 13) runs every summer and is the nation's oldest Revolutionary War drama. It tells the story of early settlers in these mountains, using Daniel Boone as both character and narrator. The amphitheater is adjacent to the **Hickory Ridge Living History Museum** (828/264-2120, www. horninthewest.com, 10am-4pm Tues.-Fri., 10am-2pm Sat., $8-10 adults, $5-7 ages 5-12), a collection of cabins and structures that reveal life here in the late 1700s.

Shopping

Several antiques shops in Boone make downtown a great place for browsing. **Appalachian Antique Mall** (631 W. King St., 828/268-9988, 10am-5pm Mon.-Fri., 10am-6pm Sat., 11am-5pm Sun.) is one of the best and biggest in the area. You'll find everything from farm implements to paintings and furniture from far and wide. **Footsloggers** (139 S. Depot St., 828/355-9984, www.footsloggersnc.com, 10am-6pm Mon.-Sat., 11am-5pm Sun.), which has another store in Blowing Rock, has been selling gear for climbing, hiking, and camping since the early 1970s. It also has a 40-foot climbing tower that simulates conditions you may find climbing the real rock faces that attract so many climbers and outdoor enthusiasts to this area.

There are several branches of the **Mast General Store** (www.mastgeneralstore. com) in the Carolina High Country, including one in Boone (630 W. King St., 828/262-0000, 10am-6pm Mon.-Sat., 11am-6pm Sun.), but the original is in Valle Crucis (Hwy. 194, 828/963-6511, 10am-6pm Mon.-Sat.,

11am-6pm Sun.), about 20 minutes west of Boone. It has been a visitor attraction for about 30 years, but its history as a community institution goes back to before the 1880s. When the Mast family owned it, the store had the reputation of carrying everything "from cradles to caskets," and today it still has a varied inventory, with specialties in outdoor wear, camping gear, and more penny candy than a modern-day store should have.

Food

Boone is a college town and has dining that suits both students and their visiting parents. That means three things must be done well: pizza, breakfast, and moderately priced bistro or steakhouse fare. This town delivers on all counts.

★ **Sunrise Grill** (1675 Hwy. 105, 828/262-5400, www.sunrisegrillboone.com, 7am-1pm daily, $4-12) is widely considered the best breakfast place in Boone. It's a regular bacon-and-eggs sort of place, with some interesting omelets, tasty grits, hot coffee, and excellent specials. Those specials range from red velvet pancakes to the Lonestar Benedict, which uses biscuits and gravy in lieu of English muffins and hollandaise.

Support good work by dining at **F.A.R.M. Café** (617 W. King St., 828/386-1000, www.farmcafe.org, 11am-2pm Mon.-Fri., pay what you want). The volunteer-run, pay-what-you-can restaurant has an awesome mission, expressed in its acronym: Feed All Regardless of Means. The café serves lunch only, and the healthy menu includes a daily sandwich special, vegetarian options, great soups, and salads. Price listed on the menu are suggestions only, but those who can afford to pay are encouraged to do so to help the café support those who can't.

★ **CoBo Sushi Bistro and Bar** (161 Howard St., 828/386-1201, www.cobosushi.com, 4pm-9pm Tues.-Thurs., 4pm-10pm Fri., 5pm-1am Sat., $4-24), a hip spot for drinks and excellent sushi, both traditional and inventive, consistently draws crowds. Unless you're like me—traveling solo and much easier to seat when it's crowded—you'll want to call and make a reservation or be ready to wait. It's great sushi, and the rest of the menu is no laughing matter, so a little wait is par for the course.

The menu at ★ **Wild Craft** (506 W. King St., 825/262-5000, www.wildcraftboone.com, 4pm-9pm Sun.-Thurs., 4pm-10pm Fri.-Sat., 11am-3:30pm Sat.-Sun.) has delicious options for vegans, vegetarians, and omnivores, a rare and welcome sight in the mountains. I've not done the math, but the menu feels balanced: for every dish with meat, there's one loaded with veggies (and sometimes cheese or another nonvegan item). Lots of Latin-inspired dishes from Cuban beans and rice (vegan) to a veggie tamale (vegetarian or vegan) to tacos with mahimahi or tempeh to a burger that comes in an all-beef or Beyond variety.

Melanie's Food Fantasy (664 W. King St., 828/263-0300, www.melaniesfoodfantasy.com, 8am-2pm Thurs.-Mon., $6-18) has a breakfast menu that is nothing short of spectacular, with enough options to keep both carnivores and vegetarians full: a variety of whole-grain waffles, pancakes, french toast, and fancy omelets (try the one with spinach, garlic, provolone, and swiss). Lunch at Melanie's—featuring sandwiches, burgers, soups, and salads—is every bit as good.

Proper (142 S. Water St., 828/865-5000, www.propermeal.com, 4pm-9pm Thurs.-Sun., reservations required, $12-35) serves a refined Southern menu based on what's in season, with fried chicken that isn't too heavy and tomato pie that's not too sloppy (and you won't find tomato pie here out of season). The pulled pork can be very good, and the buffalo chicken sandwich is a playful take on the Nashville-style hot chicken craze.

People in Boone love them some **Stick Boy Bread Co.** (www.stickboybread.com). The **bakery** (345 Hardin St., 828/268-9000, 7am-6:30pm Mon.-Fri., 7am-5:30pm Sat., $2-18) is right across from the Appalachian State campus, but this is the spot to pick up bread, a grab-and-go quiche, cakes, and larger orders. If you want a bite, head to the **kitchen**

(211 Boone Heights Dr., 828/265-4141, 7am-6:30pm Mon.-Fri., 7am-5:30pm Sat., $2.50-12) where they serve smoothies, breakfast sandwiches, bagels, and breakfast plates. If you go late in the week, you're likely to spot a few bleary-eyed college students there looking for something to help ease their entry into the day.

At ★ **Lost Province Brewing Company** (130 N. Depot St., 828/265-3506, www.lost-province.com, 11:30am-9pm Mon.-Wed. and Fri.-Sun., 11:30am-11pm Thurs., $6-20), expect to find fine wood-fired pizza—and wood-fired everything else, for that matter: mac and cheese, veggies, and pretzels all spend time in the giant copper-topped oven. Pizzas range from the expected to creative in terms of toppings. Don't forget to order a tasting flight, as the beer is also excellent. Fun fact: The brewer and owner is a former toxicologist for the state of North Carolina, and all that lab experience made him meticulous in his recipes. In 2021, Lost Province opened a second location, **Lost Province at Hardin Creek** (289 Daniel Boone Dr., 828/386-1328, 3pm-10pm Fri., noon-10pm Sat., noon-9pm Sun.), where they serve beer, wine, some snacks. You'll have to go to the downtown spot if you want a pizza, though I suppose you could order one to-go and bring it here; it's a family- and pet-friendly spot.

Accommodations

★ **The Horton Hotel** (611 W. King St., 828/832-8060, www.thehorton.com, from $239) provides a posh stay in a gorgeous space. Boone's first boutique hotel and the only hotel downtown has a prime downtown location and pays admirable attention to detail: Everything from the linens to the bathrobes to the shower products are top-notch. Add on a rooftop lounge serving delicious drinks and bites, and you may hear The Horton calling your name.

Parkway Cabins (599 Bamboo Heights, 828/262-5024 or 828/964-3560, www.parkwaycabins.com, $170-185) is just 5 minutes from downtown Boone and 10 minutes from Blowing Rock; it sits at 4,000 feet in elevation, providing a panoramic view of Grandfather Mountain, Beech Mountain, Seven Devils, and other peaks. Most of the cabins sleep four or more, making them perfect for mountain excursions with a group. They have pet-friendly accommodations ($50 per pet), so you can bring your four-legged friend along for the adventure.

The **Yonahlossee Racquet Club** (120 Honey Bear Campground Rd., 828/963-2393, www.yonahlosseeclub.com, from $125), between Boone and Blowing Rock, is a former girls camp built in the 1920s. The resort has a big stone inn and studio cottages, a fitness center and sauna, tennis courts with a pro shop, and a 75-foot indoor heated pool. **Parkway Cabins** (599 Bamboo Heights, 828/262-3560 or 828/262-5024, www.parkwaycabins.com, $170-185, 2-night minimum) is just a short convenient drive from downtown Boone or Blowing Rock—but sits at an elevation of 4,000 feet, providing panoramic views of Grandfather Mountain, Beech Mountain, Seven Devils, and other peaks. Most of the cabins sleep four or more, making them perfect for mountain excursions with a group.

Among area chain motels, some good bets are **Fairfield Inn and Suites** (2060 Blowing Rock Rd., 828/268-0677, www.marriott.com, from $152), **Courtyard by Marriott** (1050 Hwy. 105, Boone, 828/265-7676, www.marriott.com, from $204), and **Hampton Inn & Suites** (1252 U.S. 421 S., Boone, 828/386-6464, www.hilton.com, from $153).

Information and Services

You can find all sorts of visitor information at the official site of the **Watauga County Tourism Development Authority** (www.ExploreBooneArea.com). You can also stop by the **High Country Host Visitor Center** (1700 Blowing Rock Rd./U.S. 321, 828/264-1299, www.highcountryhost.com, 9am-5pm Mon.-Sat., 9am-3pm Sun.). The **Blue Ridge National Heritage Area** (www.blueridge-heritage.com) has a great deal of traveler resources available online, covering not just Boone and the High Country but the extent of North Carolina's Blue Ridge Mountains.

Radio stations include **WASU** (90.5 FM) and **WQUT** (101.5 FM). **Watauga Medical Center** (336 Deerfield Rd., 828/262-4100, www.apprhs.org) is a 117-bed complex with primary and specialty care.

Getting There and Around

Boone sits at the junction of U.S. 421 and U.S. 321. To the east, Winston-Salem is 90 minutes away (via U.S. 421) and Raleigh is 3 hours away (via U.S. 421 and I-40). Charlotte is 2 hours south (via U.S. 421 and I-77), and Asheville is 2 hours west (via U.S. 321 and I-40). Blowing Rock is only 15 minutes away (south on U.S. 321), and the Blue Ridge Parkway is a few miles closer.

AppalCart (828/297-1300, www.appal-cart.com) operates a dozen free bus routes in Boone, with maps and schedules available online.

VALLE CRUCIS

Valle Crucis, nine miles west of Boone, traces its first recorded land sale back to the 1700s, and since then, it doesn't appear that much has changed. There's a two-lane blacktop road winding through the valley now, but the shape of the hills and the sweet mountain air is much the same. This small community is known far and wide for four things: the stunning beauty of the place; the Mast Farm Inn and its restaurant, Simplicity; and the original Mast General Store.

The Original Mast General Store (Hwy. 194, 828/963-6511, www.mastgeneralstore. com, 10am-6pm Mon.-Sat., 11am-6pm Sun.) is the mother to the other iterations of this fine country store and community gathering place. Though the locations in Asheville, Boone, and several other mountain towns don't lack for charm, the original has a certain something that's hard to pin down. The building dates back to 1883; the floor has a rich patina that speaks of hundreds of thousands of boots and shoes crossing its surface;

you'll find marks from axes, adzes, and saws on floor and wall boards; and you'll see more than a few crooked door frames. It's dim in parts of the store, and it feels like a time machine slowly catching up to the present. Still, it's a working country store that's every bit as important to the community as it was when it opened. You can get various sundries and foodstuffs here that will hold you over for a couple of days until you decide to make the arduous (read: 15-minute) trek to a full-fledged grocery store. You can also pick up your mail here, grab a cup of coffee, and jaw with the clerk, the shopkeeper, or any other mail-getter or shopper who'll listen. All this in addition to a selection of outdoor gear, toys, candy, and a few tourist tchotchkes.

Just across the street is ★ **Over Yonder** (3608 Hwy. 194, 828/963-6301, www.overyon-dernc.com, 11am-3pm and 5pm-8pm Thurs.-Sun. $10-29), a restaurant in the "Hard" Taylor house, a home built in 1861 with lumber milled and bricks fired on-site. Over Yonder was opened by the folks who run the Mast Farm Inn down the road, and it serves a menu of updated Appalachian cuisine that "Hard" Taylor himself would find familiar, comforting, and delicious. Menus are seasonal, so the tomato pie and tomato cobbler are strictly for summer (unless they lay aside a few cans of tomatoes), but dishes like mountain trout and pork chops are ever present; it's their sides that change.

The Mast Farm Inn (2543 Broadstone Rd., 828/963-5857, www.themastfarminn. com, $199-399) is perfectly at home in Valley Crucis. The inn has seven guest rooms, each with tastefully rustic decorations and big comfortable beds. There are also eight cabins on the property, several of which date to the mid-1790s to 1820s. Everything here is warm wood, antiques, rustic contemporary pieces, and luxe country comfort. Mast Farm Inn has received a number of awards and nominations as a historic hotel—it's on the National Register of Historic Places—and it lives up to the hype. Charming, comfortable, and adorable, it's an excellent stay.

Craft Brews in High Country

North Carolina has a craft brewery scene that impresses even the most jaded of beer fans. While our cities—Asheville in particular—tend to get most of the attention, in small towns and hamlets across the state brewers take their craft seriously. In this corner of the state the breweries tend to be smaller, which means styles and flavors that really reflect local palates and, for the bold, allows for more experimentation. While you're here, check out one of the breweries below or find a new one where you can plan your next adventure over a cold pint. Oh, and by no means is this a list of every brewery in this pocket of North Carolina, you'll find some of my favorites (including one of my top five in the state) as you read on.

sampling craft beer

- **Fonta Flora Brewery** (317 N. Green St., Morganton, 828/475-7501, www.fontaflora.com) impressed me from the first sip I had. They experiment with flavors and styles in a way few other breweries do, and their use of local ingredients—black raspberries, native grapes, foraged fruits and herbs—and wild yeasts give everything a flavor that's North Carolina to the core.

- **Skull Camp Brewing** (2000 N. Bridge St., Elkin, 336/258-8124, www.skullcampbrewing. com) doesn't stick to one style or tradition, instead they draw on anything and everything they love in beer and have brewed more than 75 beers. This type of volume and experimentation means you should be ready to try something unusual like a lychee passionfruit IPA.

- **Boondocks Brewing** (302 S. Jefferson Ave., West Jefferson, 336/846-7525, www.boondocksbeer.com) makes an outstanding honey-orange kölsch and a Scottish ale that's got just the right amount of peaty, smoky goodness to live up to its name: Backwoods Campfire Scottish Ale.

- **Blowing Rock Brewing Company** (152 Sunset Dr., Blowing Rock, 828/414-9600, www.blowingrockbrewing.com) has a strong selection of regular brews and a great array of seasonal and limited-release draughts. The pilsner is excellent and their stone-fruit saison is a great choice when it's available.

- **Kettell Beerworks** (567 Main St. E., Banner Elk, 828/898-8677, www.kettellbeerworks.com) sits at 3,715 feet above sea level and here they brew German, Belgian, and American styles. They make a tasty marzen, a German-style lager called wunderbier that's malty and floral, and a great Imperial Oatmeal Cherry Stout.

- **Mica Town Brewing** (25 Brown Dr., Marion, 828/559-8300, www.micatownbrewing.com) serves up an easy-drinking kölsch and a great farmhouse ale, but their Ginger Beerd—an alcohol-laced ginger beer—is a real surprise.

- **Sidetracked Brewery** (609 S. Green St., Morganton, 828/544-5840, www.sidetrackedbrew. com) offers up a range of styles from a great hefeweizen to a light and quaffable American blond ale to the Whistleblower, a sour American pale wheat ale.

- **Olde Hickory Brewery** (2 3rd St. SW, Hickory, 828/322-1422, www.oldehickorybrewery. com) has been around since 1994, so their beer game is tight. One of my favorites of theirs is The Event Horizon, an imperial stout brewed with honey and then aged in bourbon barrels. It's a big beer and is a limited release, so it's worth the try if you find it.

BANNER ELK

Banner Elk (www.townofbannerelk.org), 16 miles and only 30 minutes southwest of Boone, is one of the highest towns in the eastern United States, and as such, summers here are blissfully cool, with only the rarest of days creeping into the 80s Fahrenheit. This mountaintop town is small, tightly knit, and, thanks to the weather and Sugar Mountain, on the radar of more than just a few folks. Small and beautiful, it's worth the visit in any season.

Sugar Mountain (1009 Sugar Mountain Dr., 828/898-4521, www.skisugar.com, lift tickets $32-80 adults, $27-57 children, rentals $23-38 adults, $16-28 children) is a big winter resort with skiing and snowboarding, ice-skating, tubing, and snowshoeing. Ski runs vary from beginner to low-level advanced, so it's good for a day of mixed-skill snow sports folks.

High Mountain Expeditions (3149 Tynecastle Hwy., Banner Elk, 828/202-7296, www.highmountainexpeditions.com) has an outpost here as well as in Boone. They guide white-water trips ($65-249) with Class I-V rapids, caving ($85), and hiking tips up to 10-miles long ($50 adults, $40 children), as well as river tubing trips on the New River ($20).

Banner Elk Winery & Villa (60 Deer Run Lane, 828/898-9090 or 828/260-1790, www.bannerelkwinery.com, noon-6pm daily) was the first winery built in Avery and Watuga Counties, and they've won a few awards for their wines. Tastings (daily noon-6pm, $10) are held daily year-round, and tours (12:30pm and 2:30pm Sun. May-Sept. by appointment, $12) are Sundays only May-September. Their wines include a seyval blanc, an ice wine, and a very fruity blueberry wine. You can stay here at their **Villa** (828/260-1790, from $199), where eight rooms, each with awesome mountain views and private hot tubs, book up fast.

Another place to stay is the **Little Main Street Inn & Suites** (607 Main St., 828/898-6109, www.thelittlemainstreetinn.com, $98-209). This quaint little inn has one- and two-bedroom condo-style rooms that are an excellent place to return after a day on the slopes. The **Smoketree Lodge** (11914 Hwy. 105 S., 828/963-6506 or 800/422-1880, www.smoketree-lodge.com, from $94 summer, from $74 off-season) is another good choice; it's a large hotel with basic but comfortable guest rooms and efficiencies, a large rustic lobby, a nice indoor pool, and saunas.

For dinner, make a reservation at **Artisanal** (1200 Dobbins Rd., 828/898-5395, www.artisanalnc.com, 5:30pm-10pm May-Oct., prix fixe around $95). It's a chic spot where reservations are recommended and business attire is acceptable, but a jacket is preferred. The menu is killer: charred octopus, tuna sashimi, crab beignets, Korean-style lamb belly, and braised beef cheeks are among the seasonal offerings.

My good friend David introduced me to a Banner Elk favorite: **The Ham Shoppe** (32 High Country Square, 828/898-6313, 8am-5pm Mon.-Fri., 9am-5pm Sat.-Sun., $1-9). Since he told me about it, The Ham Shoppe has become one of those restaurants I think about as soon as I get close to the foothills. From the most basic bites—like that $1 plain biscuit—to the most extravagant—a $9 whole honey ham sandwich on a sourdough with a little sriracha mayo, sprouts, and cheese (or however you like it)—it's delicious. And if you stop in and pick up a couple of sandwiches and some sweet tea, that makes for a great excuse for a picnic on the Blue Ridge Parkway.

If you want to do something unusual in Banner Elk, visit the town on the third weekend in October for the **Woolly Worm Festival** (www.woollyworm.com, $6 adults, $4 ages 6-12, free under age 6). For those of you who don't know, the woolly worm is a black and brown fuzzy caterpillar whose stripes foretell the winter weather with *Farmer's Almanac*-like accuracy. Festivalgoers dress as woolly worms, check the weather against several woolly worms, have woolly worm races, and generally make merry at this street fair that attracts close to 20,000 every year.

1: Banner Elk 2: Beech Mountain's Land of Oz

BEECH MOUNTAIN

An hour's drive southwest of Boone will take you to one of the state's best ski areas. Holding the distinction of being the highest town in the eastern United States, Beech Mountain (www.beechmtn.com) stands at 5,506 feet (that's 226 feet higher than Denver, if you're counting). Thanks to that elevation, fall comes early here, and some years the leaves begin to change in mid-September. The elevation also means **Beech Mountain Resort** (1007 Beech Mountain Pkwy., 828/387-2011 or 800/438-2093, www.beechmountainresort. com, lift tickets $33-87 adults, $26-46 seniors and ages 5-12, rentals $10-34) can get snow on the slopes early and keep it later in the season.

Most folks come here for skiing, but Beech Mountain Resort offers more than just snowy fun. In summer, the slopes are green and home to some outstanding mountain biking through **Magic Cycles** (800/438-2093, lift tickets $12 per trip, $45 all day, mountain bike lessons from $200, tours $65, rentals $135-185, helmet and armor $30-50). There are bike runs for beginners and expert downhill bombers, so don't be shy when it comes to riding; just know your abilities and limits and stay safe. Emerald Outback at Beech Mountain (www.emeraldoutback.com) is a town park with more than eight miles of single- and double-track trails and gravel paths that traverse the mountain. The Oz Forest Run is an easy one-mile trail that will give you a sense of the place.

The Oz Forest Run Trail is so named because of a nearby amusement park oddity that's only open once a year: **The Land of Oz** (2669 Beech Mountain Pkwy., 828/222-0770, rentals www.emeraldmtn.com, events www.landofoznc.com). The second weekend in September, they open the door for Autumn at Oz ($55) and you can walk the Yellow Brick Road (made with 44,000 yellow bricks), interact with characters, explore the Munchkin Village, and even Dorothy's house. Speaking of Dorothy's house, you can rent it for a minimum of three nights ($575-630) or for a week ($1,100). The house sleeps four, and it's a really weird place to stay, not because it isn't comfy but because it's surrounded by an odd half-abandoned amusement park. The area has a creepy Ray Bradbury-esque vibe, which also makes it incredibly fun.

Popular with skiers and mountain bikers is **The Pinnacle Inn Resort** (301 Pinnacle Inn Rd., 828/387-2231, www.beechmountainvacationrentals.com, from $225, 2-night minimum). It's on a peak opposite the ski resort, so getting there involves a short drive or shuttle ride. Guest rooms are nice, it's affordable, and they have an indoor pool, dry sauna, steam room, and free weekend shuttle to Ski Beech.

Frazier's Tavern (1003 Beech Mountain Pkwy., 828/387-4171, www.themilehightavern. com, 4pm-midnight Mon.-Thurs., 11am-8pm Sun.-Wed., 11am-9pm Thurs.-Sat., $11-30) has 18 North Carolina beers on draft and an even bigger selection of bottles. Throw in pizzas, wings, burgers, tacos, and sandwiches and you've got a winner. In winter, grab a drink and have it outside by the fire bar or stay inside for the band, the game, or the grub.

The best pizza in Beech Mountain is at **Famous Brick Oven Pizzeria** (402 Beech Mountain Pkwy., 828/387-4000 or 828/387-4209, www.famousbrickoven.com, 11am-late daily, $9-28), a place where you can also pick up something from their ice cream and espresso bar, drop a few quarters into an arcade game, browse a staggering selection of craft beer, and get a hot sandwich if you're all pizzaed out. But who is ever sick of pizza? The white pizza is good enough to make you order a second one to go (you know, for later), the margherita is excellent when tomatoes are in season, and it's hard to beat the tried-and-true cheese pizza.

Fred's General Mercantile (501 Beech Mountain Pkwy., 828/387-4838, www.fredsgeneral.com, 7:30am-10pm daily) has all sorts of food, snacks, and outdoor gear (think gloves and hats, not parkas), but, most importantly, it serves breakfast. **Fred's Backside Deli** (7:30am-3pm Thurs.-Mon., $2-10) dishes up a hot, cheap, hearty plateful. Their biscuits are awesome and will fill you up for a day of skiing.

Blowing Rock

Blowing Rock, named for a nearby geological oddity, is an old resort town filled with beautiful homes that once belonged to wealthy early-20th-century industrialists. It's a small town, but the surprising array of restaurants, cafés, and galleries makes it pleasant to stroll, window-shop, and sit to enjoy an ice cream. Blowing Rock also provides easy access to Moses Cone Manor and other notable landmarks.

Aside from the Blowing Rock itself, the best thing to see in Blowing Rock is downtown. Main Street is lined with shops, galleries, and restaurants, and it's a good spot for people-watching most of the year (winter excluded). The vibe here is very relaxed, so you won't find much by way of active entertainment; for that you'll need to venture out onto the parkway or into nearby Boone.

Blowing Rock is 15 minutes away from Boone, south along U.S. 321. You can also access Blowing Rock from U.S. 221 and the Blue Ridge Parkway at Milepost 291.9. Just south of Blowing Rock along U.S. 321 are a few places showcasing Piedmont and Appalachian folk tradition, especially pottery.

SIGHTS
Blowing Rock

Many of western North Carolina's best-known attractions are geological: Chimney Rock, Linville Caverns, Mount Mitchell, and stately Grandfather Mountain. The **Blowing Rock** (432 The Rock Rd., 828/295-7111, www.theblowingrock.com, hours vary, $7-9 adults, $2-8 students, $6-7 seniors and military, $2-3 ages 5-12, free under age 5) is a strange rock outcropping purported by *Ripley's Believe It or Not* to be the only place in the world where snow falls upward. Indeed, light objects (think handkerchiefs, leaves, and hats) thrown off Blowing Rock—not allowed, by the way, to prevent the valley from filling up with litter—do tend to come floating back up. Adding

to its otherworldly draw, there's a Native American legend associated with Blowing Rock. The story goes that a Chickasaw chieftain, fearful of the admiration his beautiful daughter was receiving, journeyed far to Blowing Rock, where he hoped to hide her away in the woods and keep her safe and pure. One day, the maiden spied a Cherokee warrior wandering in the valley below. Smitten by his looks, she shot an arrow in his direction, hoping he would seek her out. Soon he appeared at her home, courting her with songs of his land. They became lovers, and one day, a strange reddening sky brought the pair to the Blowing Rock. He took it as a sign that he was to return to his people in their coming time of trouble; to her it spelled the end of their love. Torn between staying loyal to his duties and following his heart, in his desperation he leapt from their perch into the gorge below. The young maiden prayed for him to be spared death, but it didn't work. She remained at the site, and one day the sky reddened and the now famous winds of the John's River Gorge shifted, blowing her lover back into her arms. Since that day, a perpetual wind has blown up onto the Blowing Rock from the valley below.

Moses Cone Manor

The **Moses Cone Manor** (Milepost 294, 828/295-7938, 10am-5pm daily Jun.-Oct., 10am-4pm Wed.-Sun. Nov., 10am-4pm Thurs.-Sun. Apr. 15-30, 10am-4pm Wed.-Sun. May, free), more commonly called Flat Top Manor, is a wonderfully crafted house, a huge white and ornate mountain palace built in 1901 that was the country home of North Carolina textile baron Moses Cone. He became a leading philanthropist, and as you drive around the state, especially in the northern Piedmont, you'll notice his name on quite a few institutions. Today, the manor is the centerpiece of the Moses H. Cone Memorial Park. Appropriately, it is home to

Blowing Rock

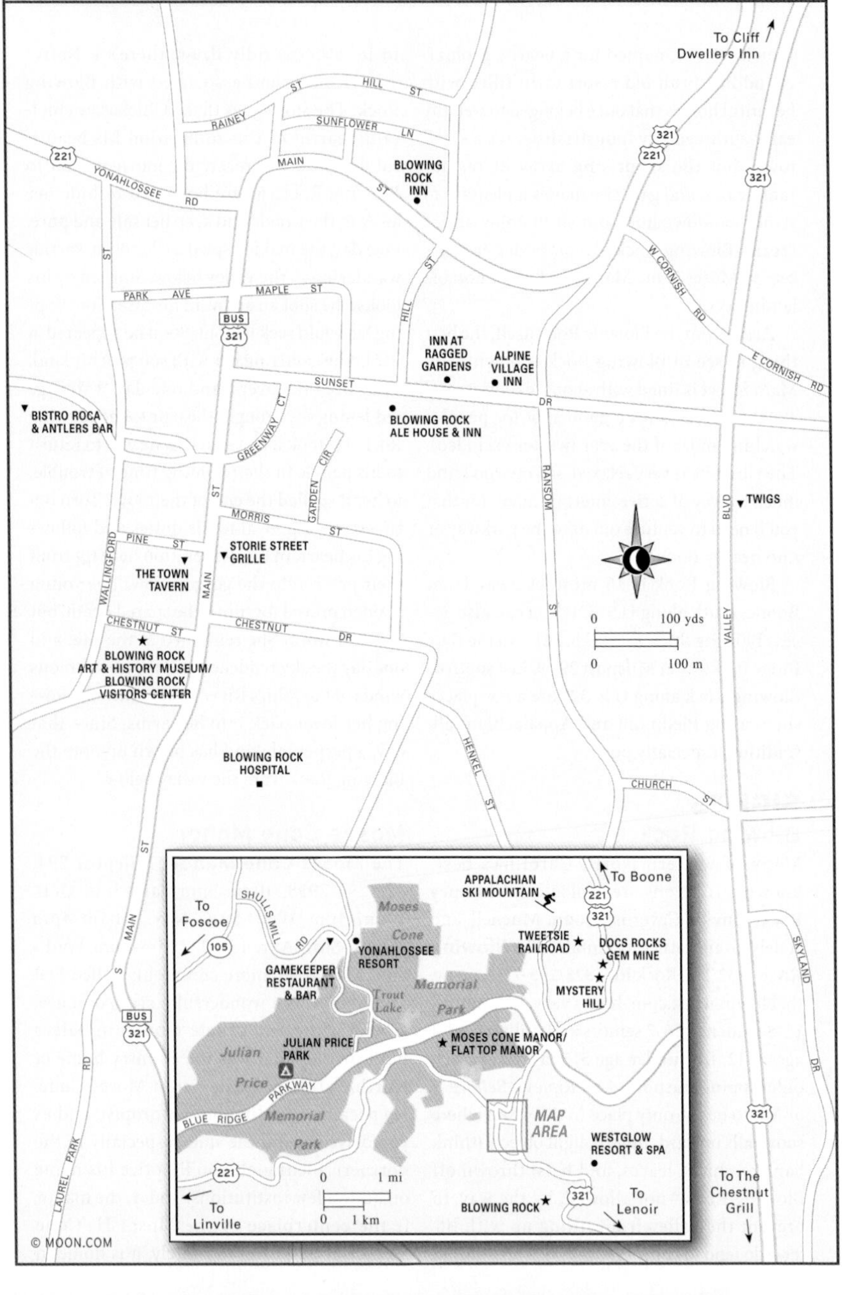

To Cliff Dwellers Inn
HILL ST
RAINEY ST
SUNFLOWER LN
221
321
YONAHLOSSEE RD
MAIN ST
BLOWING ROCK INN
W CORNISH RD
PARK AVE
MAPLE ST
HILL ST
BUS 321
INN AT RAGGED GARDENS
ALPINE VILLAGE INN
E CORNISH RD
SUNSET DR
BLOWING ROCK ALE HOUSE & INN
BISTRO ROCA & ANTLERS BAR
GREENWAY CT
GARDEN CIR
RANSOM ST
VALLEY BLVD
TWIGS
MORRIS ST
PINE ST
STORIE STREET GRILLE
THE TOWN TAVERN
WALLINGFORD ST
MAIN ST
CHESTNUT ST
CHESTNUT DR
BLOWING ROCK ART & HISTORY MUSEUM/ BLOWING ROCK VISITORS CENTER
0 100 yds
0 100 m
HENKEL ST
BLOWING ROCK HOSPITAL
CHURCH ST
S MAIN ST
LAUREL PARK RD
SKYLAND DR
To The Chestnut Grill
To Foscoe
105
SHULLS MILL RD
Moses Cone Memorial Park
GAMEKEEPER RESTAURANT & BAR
YONAHLOSSEE RESORT
Trout Lake
APPALACHIAN SKI MOUNTAIN
To Boone
TWEETSIE RAILROAD
DOCS ROCKS GEM MINE
MYSTERY HILL
JULIAN PRICE PARK
Julian Price Memorial Park
MOSES CONE MANOR/ FLAT TOP MANOR
BLUE RIDGE PARKWAY
MAP AREA
WESTGLOW RESORT & SPA
0 1 mi
0 1 km
To Linville
BLOWING ROCK
To Lenoir
© MOON.COM

NORTHERN BLUE RIDGE AND FOOTHILLS
BLOWING ROCK

one of the **Southern Highland Craft Guild** (828/295-7938, www.southernhighlandguild. org, 9am-5pm daily Mar. 30.-Nov.) stores, a place to buy beautiful textiles, pottery, jewelry, furniture, and dolls handmade by some of the best craftspeople of the Appalachian Mountains. I have several pieces—turned wooden bowls, cutting boards, rustic art pieces—in my house and often pick up something that catches my eye because everything here makes for a great gift.

The 3,500-acre Moses H. Cone Memorial Park is one of the parkway's largest developed areas set up for public recreation. There are 25 miles of trails for hiking and horseback riding, a 16-acre trout lake, and a 22-acre bass lake on the property. You can pick up a map of the trails at the Manor House and Bass Lake Entrance (on U.S. 221). The trails here are largely old carriage roads, so they're wide, well maintained, and pretty gentle.

Blowing Rock Art and History Museum

The **Blowing Rock Art and History Museum** (159 Ginny Stevens Lane, 828/259-9099, www.blowingrockmuseum.org, 11am-5pm Tues.-Sat., free) features rotating exhibits of fine art from private collections, gallery shows by local and regional artists, and traveling exhibitions. BRAHM also has galleries with rotating exhibits displaying artifacts of historical value to the area. It's small, but the art displayed is carefully curated and excellent. It's easy to spend a couple of hours admiring the collections. Tours ($7) are available and must be arranged up to two weeks ahead.

Tweetsie Railroad

Between Blowing Rock and Boone, **Tweetsie Railroad** (300 Tweetsie Railroad Rd., 828/264-9061, http://tweetsie.com, 10am-6pm Sat.-Sun. Apr.-May and late Aug.-mid Sept., 10am-6pm Thurs.-Mon. Jun.-mid Aug., Halloween Ghost Train 7:30pm Fri.-Sat. late Sept.-late Oct., Tweetsie Christmas 5pm-10pm Fri.-Sat. late Nov.-Dec., $45 ages over 12, $30 ages 3-12, free under age 3) is a veritable gold mine for kids who are into trains. There are opportunities to pan for gold and gems in one section of the park; a Country Fair-themed area and a Western store and Cowboy Cantina in another; and the Tweetsie Junction area, where you'll find a saloon, a blacksmith, and an antique photo parlor. And, of course, the train: The Tweetsie Railroad's steam engines, number 12 *(Tweetsie)* and number 190 *(Yukon Queen),* encircle the amusement park on a narrow-gauge track as part of a Wild West show featuring a frontier outpost. The railroad isn't all fun and games; it's also partly a history lesson, as the *Tweetsie* was an actual working train in the early part of the 20th century, until washed-out tracks and the advent of reliable automobiles and roads rendered it obsolete. In the weeks building up to Halloween, Tweetsie's Ghost Train sees everything in the park dolled up in "scary" costumes (well, scary-ish), and kids are welcome to come in costume for trick or treating along Main Street, to take in the black light puppet show, and to play the games and rides at the Creepy Carnival they stage. Christmas sees a similar theme, but it's all Santa and elves, not ghosts and cobwebs. Tweetsie Christmas sees the park transformed into a light-filled holiday celebration with complex displays, elegant arrangements, visits with Santa in the gingerbread house, and plenty of places to make s'mores.

Mystery Hill

One little oddity in Blowing Rock is **Mystery Hill** (129 Mystery Hill Lane, 828/264-2792, www.mysteryhill-nc.com, 9am-8pm daily June-Aug., 9am-6pm daily Sept.-May, $13, free under age 4). Like Mystery Hills in other states featuring some "gravitational anomaly," this one is best for kids, which is fine, because it's fun to watch them try to figure out the mystery of Mystery Hill.

Doc's Rocks Gem Mines

Adjacent to Mystery Hill is **Doc's Rocks Gem Mines** (100 Shoppes on the Parkway

Rd., 828/295-2034, www.docksrocks.org, 9:30am-5pm Thurs.-Mon., buckets of ore $8-75). As at other gem mines, here you'll buy a bucket of ore that they source from a variety of mines across the Blue Ridge, and then you pan and sift through it for gems and fossils. As you make your way through your bucket, they will help you identify the stones you find. You can find all sorts of things, from a variety of fossils to gems like rubies and emeralds. They also have a **Fossil Museum** ($15 adults, $5 ages 4-12, free under age 4) that's the state's largest private collection on public display, and an indoor mini golf course called **Paleo Putt-Putt** ($8).

RECREATION

VX3 Trail Rides (828/963-0260, www.vx-3trailrides.com, ages 12 and up, 10am and 2pm daily, $120) offers horseback riding outings with Tim Vines, a trail guide with decades in the saddle. Groups are small, typically a maximum of five riders, unless it's one family or group, and you need reservations at least a day in advance.

As you drive by Tweetsie, you can't help but catch sight of **High Gravity Adventures** (215 Tweetsie Railroad Rd., 828/266-0176, www.highgravityadventures.com, check website for hours and reservations), an aerial adventure park featuring a wooden tower. There are a trio of obstacle courses that start on solid ground and get higher—and harder—as you go. The **Ninja Ground Course** (no entry fee) has four obstacles that every ticket holder can warm up on. The **Foothills Course** (over age 3, $39) is one level up; from 15 feet in the air you'll face 13 challenges, including wild rope bridges and precarious floating steps. The toughest and highest course, the **Blue Ridge Course** ($59 over age 10, $49 ages 7-10), delivers 65 challenges on a high-ropes course that includes ladders, swinging logs, and platforms.

1: Moses Cone Manor 2: Blowing Rock

ENTERTAINMENT
Festivals and Events

Blowing Rock may be a small town, but you won't want for things to do. You won't find a free concert or wine tasting every night of the week, but the events and activities that go on here are put on well and are well attended.

Late May-late September, the **Blowing Rock Farmers Market** (3pm-6pm Thurs.) takes over Park Avenue, brining all sorts of baked goods, artisanal cheeses, and the usual bounty of fruits and veggies. The **Music on the Lawn** (5:30pm-8:30pm Fri. June-early-Oct.) series has made **The Inn at Ragged Gardens** (203 Sunset Dr., 828/295-9703, www.ragged-gardens.com) a hot spot every Friday night. They have a cash bar and serve a limited menu, so get here early, find a place for your blanket, and order a bite to eat.

SHOPPING

Along Blowing Rock's Main Street, you'll have your pick of galleries. Park at the Blowing Rock Art and History Museum (159 Ginny Stevens Lane), which also happens to be the location of the visitors center, and gallery-hop your way down Main Street.

Martin House Gallery (1098-12 Main St., 336/508-2828, www.martinhousegallery.com, 9am-5pm Thurs.-Sun. and by appointment) has paintings, photography, sculpture, and more from artists working here in Blowing Rock and from across the country. Whether you're looking for a contemporary-expressionist painting, a photorealistic scene, or just something that catches your eye, you'll find it hanging here.

Morning Star Gallery (1151 S. Main St., 828/263-7692, www.morningstargalleryusa.com, 10am-5pm Mon., Wed., and Fri., 11am-5pm Tues., Thurs., and Sat.) showcases fine arts and crafts by contemporary U.S. artists, including a good number of local and regional artists. Works include blown glass, pottery and ceramics, paintings, prints, photography, and fiber arts.

There's more than a fair share of antiques stores, boutiques, and gift shops on and around Main Street. If you're in the market for antiques, it's hard to beat **Windwood Antiques** (1157 Main St., 828/295-9260, 10am-5pm Mon.-Sat., 11am-5pm Sun.) and **Carriage Trade Antiques** (1079 Main St., 828/295-3110, 10am-5:30pm Mon.-Thurs., 10am-6:30pm Fri.-Sat., 10am-5pm Sun.). **Blowing Rock Estate Jewelry & Antiques** (167 Sunset Dr., 828/295-4500, call for hours) has a large and constantly changing selection of fine estate jewelry; with an eye for precious gems and heirloom pieces, this is the spot to look for a piece of stunning jewelry from past ages.

At **Gaines Kiker Silversmith** (132 Morris St., 828/295-3992, www.gaineskikersilver-smith.com, 11am-5pm Tues.-Sat.), the silver jewelry is exquisite. Gaines Kiker finds inspiration for the shapes and curves of his jewelry in the mountains around him, and his work displays a simplicity and elegance that's difficult to master.

Pick up a new pair of hiking poles, maps to area hiking, and some fresh duds at **Footsloggers** (921 Main St., 828/295-4453, www.footsloggersnc.com, 10am-5pm Mon.-Thurs., 10am-6pm Fri.-Sat., 11am-5pm Sun.). They've been outfitting the High Country since 1971 and the folks here know about the trails, peaks, rock faces, mountain biking routes, fly fishing spots, and they'll gladly set you up with the right gear, point you in the right direction, and generally help you have a good getaway to their beautiful slice of North Carolina.

If it's a souvenir T-shirt you're looking for, try **Sunset Tee's & Hattery** (1117 Main St., 828/295-9326, 9am-6pm Sun.-Thurs., 9am-8pm Fri.-Sat.). They have loads of gift items from tacky to fridge-worthy, and the selection of hats is huge. In the back of the store, hats from poker visors to baseball caps to leather stovepipe hats to bowlers and derbys are for purchase.

FOOD

★ **The Chestnut Grille** (9239 Valley Blvd., 828/414-9230, www.greenparkinn.com,

6pm-9pm Fri.-Sat., call for additional availability, $13-28) is in the Green Park Inn on the edge of town. The food draws inspiration from across the globe: Cuban spice-rubbed scallops, seared tuna with wasabi and soy-ginger sauce, rigatoni with chicken, lamb, steaks, pulled pork, and even tempeh grace the menu. The **Divide Tavern** (9239 Valley Blvd., 828/414-9230, www.greenparkinn.com, 5pm-9pm daily, $5-18), also in the Green Park Inn, serves a smaller menu of pub food.

★ **The Best Cellar** (203 Sunset Dr., 828/295-3466, www.ragged-gardens.com, 5pm-late Thurs.-Mon., $19-44), located inside The Inn at Ragged Gardens, is a longtime Blowing Rock occasion place. The seafood-heavy menu shows a good range of flavors, techniques, and influences, with dishes like North Carolina black grouper, locally sourced mountain trout, sea scallops over shiitake mushrooms and spinach, and crab cakes. There's also steak, lamb, and a roasted half duckling. On the wine list, you'll find more than a dozen excellent by-the-glass options and pages of bottles that span the globe.

You can probably tell from the name of **Sunny Rock Eggs and Things** (8146 Valley Blvd., 828/414-9636, www.sunnyrockeggs.com, 7:30am-1:30pm Mon.-Sat., $2-12) that breakfast is the priority here. If the name's not enough of a giveaway, the breakfast sandwiches, stacks of pancakes, and biscuits flying out of the kitchen should clue you in. Though breakfast draws in many a hungry diner, lunch can be quite good, especially their simple Meat and Three weekday menu: pick your meat (country fried steak, meatloaf, tuna salad, and the like) and three sides (collards, fried green tomatoes, watermelon, pickled beets, and more) and chow down.

Foggy Rock Eatery & Pub (8180 Valley Blvd., 828/295-7262, www.foggy-rock.com, 11:30am-8:30pm Tues.-Thurs., 11:30am-9pm Fri.-Sat., 11am-8:30pm Sun., around $15) is a sports bar with upgraded food. Seafood graces their menu, with dishes like Appalachian fish-and-chips (fried catfish and waffle fries) and Trout Trout Trout (a trio of trout); they also have a good selection of sandwiches, burgers, and Philly cheesesteaks. The Notorious P.I.G.—with house-smoked pork, pulled ham, diced bacon, pepper jack cheese, and sriracha aioli—is a fine and filling sandwich.

★ **The Speckled Trout Restaurant & Bottle Shop** (922 Main St., 828/295-9819, www.thespeckledtrout.com, 11am-3pm Thurs.-Mon., 5pm-9pm Sun.-Mon. and Thurs., 5pm-10pm Fri.-Sat., $10-25) is one of those rare restaurants where the past and present intersect. Most of their dishes are of the rootsy Appalachian sort—chicken and dumplings (almost as good as my granny's), fresh mountain trout, fried chicken, soup, beans, and pickled watermelon rinds—but nearly all of them have been updated. Sometimes it's in terms of ingredients—like the Cheerwine aioli and mountain apple chowchow served with the fried chicken—other times it's in the plating, which can leave rustic behind and be quite lovely. They also have an excellent bottle shop where you'll find a wide variety of drinks, from sour beers and wild ales to delicate rosés and bottles of bubbly.

Six Pence Pub (1121 Main St., 828/295-3155, www.sixpencepub.com, 11:30am-midnight Sun.-Thurs., 11:30am-2am Fri.-Sat., $10-22) brings a different menu and atmosphere to Blowing Rock dining: a proper British pub. Fish-and-chips, grilled cheese (which for some reason they don't call a toastie), bangers and mash, shepherd's pie, all the best food from Britain plus a small, but lovely, selection of scotch whisky. When you're looking for it, don't bother with the address: It's the restaurant flying the U.S. flag alongside the flags of Scotland, Wales, England, and the Union Jack.

In downtown Blowing Rock, there's not much going on after 10pm, so if you're looking to grab a beer and a bite to eat a little later in the evening, your options are limited. At the north end of Main Street you'll find **The Town Tavern** (1182 Main St., 828/295-7500, www.towntavernbr.com, 1am-midnight Sun.-Tues. and Thurs., 4pm-midnight Wed., 11am-2am Fri.-Sat., around $10). This is a sports bar, with all the wings, fried appetizers, burgers, and nachos you'd expect to find. With more than 30 bottled beers and about a dozen local brews on draft, they have a good beer selection too.

ACCOMMODATIONS

There's a reason *Southern Living* magazine called ★ **Chetola Resort** (185 Chetola Lake Dr., 800/243-8652, www.chetola.com) "one of the best stays in the Blue Ridge," and it's because this place is exceptional from start to finish. On the 78-acre property there's the Chetola Lodge ($199-349 summer, $129-329 winter), luxury condos ($199-449 summer, $149-399 winter) with 1-4 bedrooms, the **Bob Timberlake Inn** ($229-399 summer, $199-349 winter), the Spa at Chetola Resort ($70-320) to help you get rid of the stiff muscles from all the hiking and driving. There are lots of on-property activities—including the only Orvis-certified fly-fishing instructor in the area—to keep you busy if you decide to plant yourself here for a day or two (which isn't a bad idea at all).

★ **Blowing Rock Inn** (788 Main St., 828/295-3380, www.blowingrockinn.com, Apr.-early Dec., rooms $109-239, villas $169-329) has the feel of an old motor court, with rooms wrapped around a lawn and parking area, but it has been upgraded to modern standards. Just a short walk or an even shorter drive to downtown, Blowing Rock Inn is both quiet and conveniently located. The inn provides free Wi-Fi, and you can add all sorts of packages to your room or villa, including a wine basket, cake, and flowers.

The lavish 1916 Greek Revival mansion of painter Elliot Daingerfield is now home to the **Westglow Resort and Spa** (224 Westglow Circle, 828/295-4463 or 800/562-0807, www.westglow.com, rooms $300-1,600), where you can get a room or rent the whole place as part of the Westglow Estate Package ($3,200, spa and private chef incur additional costs). In addition to the cushy guest rooms, many of which have whirlpool tubs, private decks, and views of Grandfather Mountain, the menu of spa treatments and health services befits the elegance of the surroundings. Taking advantage of the spa's wonderful location, visitors can also sign up for hiking, cycling, snowshoeing, and camping trips.

★ **Hellbender Bed & Beverage** (239 Sunset Dr., 828/295-3487, www.hellbender. bar, $175-220) has seven luxurious rooms and a cottage, all with roomy showers, fantastic linens, and breakfast at the delicious restaurant included. That **restaurant** (smoothies 8am-11am daily, food noon-8pm Tues.-Sat., $9-18) serves an excellent smashburger and great trout, and they have many seating options (the porch and yard are choice spots in good weather). So you know, a hellbender is a ginormous salamander found high in the Smoky Mountains.

Alpine Village Inn (297 Sunset Dr., 828/295-7206, www.alpine-village-inn.com, from $100), in downtown Blowing Rock, has comfortable accommodations at good rates. The guest rooms are located in the main inn and in a motel-style wing. It's a convenient location for checking out the shops and restaurants in town. Another good value is the **Cliff Dwellers Inn** (116 Lakeview Terrace, 828/414-9596, www.cliffdwellers.com, from $89), with clean, simple guest rooms and a beautiful lakefront view.

Camping

Julian Price Memorial Park (828/963-5911, www.recreation.gov) abuts Moses H. Cone Memorial Park, but unlike Cone, which was a family home and estate, Price was set aside as a retreat for the employees of Julian Price's insurance company. Price's death in 1946 put those plans on hold, and the land was deeded to his company. His company, with the approval of his family, turned the land over to the National Park Service for inclusion in the Blue Ridge Parkway. So, in a roundabout way, Price's wish that this beautiful mountain land be used and enjoyed by his employees came to be. Today, there's a 47-acre pond, created by the damming of Boone Fork, as well as a large amphitheater, more than 100 picnic sites,

camping, and the 13.5-mile Tanawha Trail, which parallels the parkway and skirts the lower edges of Grandfather Mountain.

There are 193 **campsites** (campground info 828/963-5911, reservations 877/444-6777, www.recreation.gov, mid-May-late Oct., $20) at Julian Price Memorial Park, with spaces for tents and RVs. Canoeing on the lake is also a possible activity here.

INFORMATION AND SERVICES

You'll find all the information you need about Blowing Rock at the **Visitor Center** (132 Park Ave., 828/295-4636, www.blowingrock.com).

The nearest hospital is the **Watauga Medical Center** (336 Deerfield Rd., Boone, 828/262-4100, www.apprhs.org), a 10-minute drive north on U.S. 321.

SOUTH ALONG U.S. 321
Sights

Three miles south of Blowing Rock, **Traditions Pottery** (1155 Main St., 828/295-5099, www.traditionspottery.com, 10am-6pm Mon.-Sat., 12:30pm-6pm Sun.) is a hotbed of Piedmont and Appalachian folk traditions. The Owen-Bolick-Calhoun families trace their roots as potters back through six generations in the Sandhills community of Seagrove and here in Caldwell County. They have also become renowned old-time musicians and storytellers. In addition to ceramics with an impeccable folk pedigree, Traditions Pottery is the location of numerous music jams and kiln openings throughout the year as well as the Jack Tales Festival in August; Glenn Bolick learned storytelling from the great Ray Hicks of Beech Mountain, a National Heritage Award winner. They hold kiln openings twice a year, in June and November, at 4443 Bolick Road, three miles south of Blowing Rock.

The seat of Caldwell County, Lenoir (pronounced "luh-NORE"), was named for General William Lenoir, a Revolutionary War hero and chronicler of the Battle of King's Mountain. **Fort Defiance** (1792 Fort Defiance Dr./Hwy. 268, Happy Valley,

828/758-1671, www.historicfortdefiance.org, 10am-4pm Thurs.-Sat., 1pm-4pm Sun. Apr.-Oct., 10am-4pm Sat.-Sun. Nov.-Mar., $7 adults, $5 under age 14), his 1792 plantation house in Happy Valley, is beautifully restored and open to visitors. Among its unusual charms are a 200-year-old oriental chestnut tree, an English boxwood garden of the same vintage, and the largest beech tree in the state.

The **Hickory Museum of Art** (243 3rd Ave. NE, Hickory, 828/327-8576, www.hickoryart.org, 10am-4pm Wed. and Fri.-Sat., 10am-8pm Thurs., 1pm-4pm Sun., free) was established in the early 1950s and was the first major museum of American art in the Southeast. Its early partnership with the National Academy of Design in New York gained it the nickname of the "Southern Outpost of the National Academy." The museum has an impressive permanent collection, with special emphases on American painting, outsider and folk art, North Carolina folk pottery, and American studio pottery and glass.

One part spectacle, one part shopping experience, one part North Carolina heritage, the **Hickory Furniture Mart** (2220 U.S. 70 SE, Hickory, 828/322-3510 or 800/462-6278, www.hickoryfurniture.com, 9am-6pm Mon.-Sat.) houses more than 100 factory outlets, stores, and galleries representing more than 1,000 furniture and home accessories manufacturers. It's a draw for designers, shop owners, and those looking for a serious redecoration project; the spectacle of the four-level showroom is amazing.

Sports and Recreation

Between Hickory and Morganton, outside the town of Connelly Springs, is one of the state's most rugged recreational areas, **South Mountains State Park** (3001 South Mountain Park Ave., Connelly Springs, 828/433-4772, http://ncparks.gov, office 8am-5pm daily, park 7am-7pm daily Dec.-Feb., 7am-9pm daily Mar.-Apr. and Oct., 7am-10pm daily May-Sept., 7am-8pm daily Nov.), rising to elevations of 3,000 feet. One trail follows the Jacob Fork River to the top

of 80-foot-tall High Shoals Falls. Another 0.75-mile trail travels along the lower reaches of Jacob Fork and is wheelchair-accessible. There are 17 miles of strenuous mountain-biking trails. Hike-in campsites (reservations 877/722-6762, www.northcarolinastateparks.reserveamerica.com, $12) are located in various spots throughout the park, from 0.5 miles to 5.5 miles away from the Jacob Fork parking area, and there are campsites in the South Mountains Family Campground (nonelectric $23, electric $28) that are pet-friendly and RV-ready (size limits vary; check when reserving sites). Pit toilets are located near campsites, but all supplies and water must be packed in.

Festivals

Every year on Labor Day weekend in early September, Caldwell County is home to the **Historic Happy Valley Old-Time Fiddlers Convention** (828/758-9448, www.happyvalleyfiddlers.org), a laid-back event in a gorgeous location, the Jones Farm. The festival includes music competitions and concerts, drawing some great traditional artists from all over the hills. Other events include a rubber duck race, demonstrations by instrument makers, tours of Fort Defiance, and visits to the grave of Laura Foster, the 1867 victim of North Carolina's most famous murderer, Tom Dooley. The crime is a common theme in bluegrass and roots music death ballads. Participants and visitors can camp ($10-25) along the Yadkin River on the Jones Farm during the festival. No alcohol is allowed; pets are permitted as long as they're leashed.

The Catawba Valley is an important place for North Carolina folk pottery, with a tradition all its own dating back to the early-19th-century potter Daniel Seagle and exemplified in modern times by the late Burlon Craig, one of the giants of Southern folk art, and contemporary master Kim Ellington. Hickory's annual **Catawba Valley Pottery and Antiques Festival** (Hickory Convention Center, 828/324-7294, www.catawbavalleypotteryfestival.org, late Mar., $10 adults, $5 ages 3-12) brings together more than 100 potters and dealers in pottery and antiques. It's a great introduction to Southern folk pottery, and the covetable wares are dangerous if you're on a budget.

Food

Fourk (1410 4th St. Dr. NW, Hickory, 282/855-3437, www.fourkrestaurant.com, 5pm-9pm Mon.-Wed., 5pm-10pm Thurs.-Sat., $10-38) serves food with a twist—expected dishes with some extra touch. The mahimahi sandwich gets some spicy tomato aioli, ahi tuna gets hit with a miso-peanut crust and a bit of spicy Thai peanut sauce, and the Korean pork and rice brings the depth of spicy-sweet Korean barbecue sauce to a bowl.

In the center of downtown Hickory you can dine in a historic train station at **The Olde Hickory Station Restaurant and Market** (232 Government Ave. SW, Hickory, 828/322-2356, 7am-10pm Sun.-Thurs., 7am-midnight Fri.-Sat., $9-29). For dinner you've got pizza, burgers, more apps and salads than you can shake a pepper grinder at, and then there are entrées—crab cakes, a rib-eye, shrimp and grits. Lunch drops the entrées, but that's fine, you want the chicken sandwich or a giant salad anyway, unless you came for breakfast, in which case you're probably still full from the biscuits and eggs.

If you're traveling between Lenoir and Hickory on a weekend, take a detour to the little community of Dudley Shoals, where you'll find **Sims Country BBQ** (6160 Petra Mill Rd., Granite Falls, 828/396-5811, www.simscountrybbq.com, 5pm-9pm Fri.-Sat., all-you-can-eat buffet $16 adults, $7 ages 4-11, free under age 4). Sims is known not only for its all-you-can-eat Texas-style barbecue (we're mighty far from Texas, but I can forgive that because good 'cue is good 'cue), which they pit-cook all day, but also for live bluegrass music and clogging (starts at 7pm). It hosts the annual Molasses Festival on the second Saturday in October, with bluegrass, dancing, and harvest-time activities.

Along the Blue Ridge Parkway

The Blue Ridge Parkway is a stunning bit of road, especially south of Boone. There are a number of sights on and near this stretch of the parkway, including plenty of places to pull off for pictures or exploration, and marked trails meandering up and down the mountain and into thick woods, rocky coves, and waterfalls. Stop at the wide spots in the road to photograph a tree in a field, a herd of cows grazing, a trail wandering into the shadows of the trees, or the mountains marching off into the distance.

Venturing off the parkway and into the mountains, artistic communities like Penland, Crossnore, and other towns in the Toe River Valley await your visit. Many artists came to the area to be part of the folk school in Penland, which has exerted a great deal of influence on the modern American craft movement; there is a dense concentration of artists working in folk and studio pottery and glasswork, hand-wrought ironwork, delicately crafted jewelry, and unusual textile arts.

BEACON HEIGHTS

Beacon Heights (Milepost 305.2, Blue Ridge Pkwy.) sits on the edge of Grandfather Mountain, affording a fabulous view of the slope and one of the peaks of Grandfather as the parkway sweeps around the massif. The Grandfather Mountain view is from the parking area, but a spectacular view of the lands south of the parkway can be had at the actual Beacon Heights—a rocky escarpment up a short strenuous trail that departs from the parking lot.

★ GRANDFATHER MOUNTAIN

Grandfather Mountain (U.S. 221, 2 miles north of Linville, 828/733-4337, www.grandfather.com, 8am-7pm daily summer, 9am-6pm daily spring and fall, 9am-5pm daily winter, weather permitting, $22 adults, $20 over age 60, $9 ages 4-12, free under age 5), at a lofty 5,964 feet, is not the highest mountain in North Carolina, but it is one of the most beautiful. The highest peak in the Blue Ridge Mountains (the only peak higher, Mount Mitchell, is in the Black Mountains), Grandfather is a United Nations-designated biosphere reserve. Privately owned for decades though open to the public, Grandfather Mountain has remained a great expanse of deep forests and wildlife with many hiking trails. The main attraction is the summit and the **Mile High Swinging Bridge.** It is indeed a mile high, and it swings a little in the breeze, but it should be called the "Singing Bridge" because of the somewhat unnerving sound of the constant wind moving through the steel cables holding it in place. The view from Grandfather Mountain is stunning, and the peak is easily accessible via the scenic road that traces the skyward mile. From the parking lot just below the summit, you can access a number of trails (open during park hours only) that lead to nearby peaks, under the crest of Grandfather, and along nearby ridgelines.

Although the Mile High Swinging Bridge has a fearsome name, don't be too intimidated; that mile is a mile above sea level. Even so, with the giant views all around and the dizzying distance to the valley floor below, some visitors find themselves more than a little nervous when it comes time to cross the bridge. If you find that the bridge is a little much for you, don't sweat it; just take in the impressive view from the parking lot and spend some time at the other attractions on Grandfather Mountain. The **Wildlife Habitats** are always popular. Here, large enclosures provide a place for white-tailed deer, eagles, river otters, black bear, and cougars to live. Daily feedings draw the animals out of their secret places in each enclosure and bring them into view. Grandfather Mountain opened the **Wilson Center for Nature Discovery,** the focal point of a new Conservation Campus, in June 2022. The center adds a dozen interactive exhibits that connect to the mountain's 16 natural communities, weather, climate, and natural history; an ADA-accessible auditorium; classrooms; an event space; and new outdoor learning spaces.

Aside from the view, many come to Grandfather Mountain for the hiking. There are a few short hikes along the drive to the top and more hikes that will test your stamina and mettle as you climb to the true summit of Grandfather Mountain. At the Grandfather Mountain Picnic Area, the 0.4-mile **Woods Walk** trail leads you on an easy stroll through the forest on the lower flanks of the mountain; it's gentle on the youngest and oldest visitors. Near the Swinging Bridge, park in the Trails parking area and hike the **Bridge Trail,** another 0.4-mile winding trail that takes you under the Swinging Bridge. There's one more easy hike of note, but the rest are significantly tougher.

★ LINN COVE VIADUCT

One of the most iconic spots along the Blue Ridge Parkway, the Linn Cove Viaduct (Milepost 304.4, Blue Ridge Pkwy.) is a bridge-like structure hanging from the side of the mountain in a dizzying S-curve. At nearly 1,300 feet long, this amazing feat of engineering makes you feel like you might just fly off into space if you lose focus. A pair of viewing areas about 0.25 miles from either end of the viaduct give you the chance to stretch your legs and snap a few pictures of this amazing part of the road.

Grandfather Mountain looming above offers great photo opportunities, as does the road itself when it ducks back into one deep cove and emerges on the side of the mountain opposite, snaking away into the trees. The sight of this concrete and asphalt structure peeking out from the trees and following the contours of the mountains is enough to take your breath away.

The story of the viaduct is a long one, but it is well told at the **Linn Cove Viaduct Visitors Center** (828/348-3400, 10am-5pm daily May-Oct.). It was the last piece of the parkway to be completed, and on September 11, 1987, on its completion 52 years after construction began on this jewel of a road, the route from the Shenandoah Valley to the Great Smoky Mountains was whole. What caused the delay? One reason was the route. Hugh Morton, the owner of Grandfather Mountain, wasn't fond of the proposed site of the parkway, which would have climbed much higher up the side of Grandfather Mountain. After the parkway route was settled at a lower elevation, Morton donated land to the National Park Service, and all that was left was the engineering.

Nearby Accommodations

Linville's **Eseeola Lodge** (175 Linville Ave., 800/742-6717, www.eseeola.com, from $325) has been in the business of luxury mountain vacations for more than 100 years. The first lodge was built in the 1890s, along with a nine-hole golf course. The original lodge burned down and was replaced by the present lodge; in 1924, Donald Ross was engaged to build the championship golf course now known as the Linville Golf Club. Eseeola Lodge offers a complex but splendid array of lodging packages, with breakfast and dinner at the Lodge's restaurant included and, depending on your predilections, tee times at the Linville Golf Club, spa services, and even croquet lessons.

CROSSNORE WEAVING ROOM

Since the early 1920s, the master weavers of the **Crossnore Weaving Room** (Crossnore School, 100 DAR Dr., Crossnore, 828/733-4305, www.crossnore.org, gallery hours 9am-5pm Mon.-Fri., 10am-5pm Sat.) have produced beautiful textiles—afghans, rugs

and runners, baby blankets, and scarves—that they've sold to benefit the Crossnore School. Founded in the 1910s for orphaned and disadvantaged children, the Crossnore School is today an actively operating children's home for western North Carolina kids who have no guardians, and for some local children who live with their families but whose educational needs are best served by the structure that the school offers. The fame of the weaving room is much more than a fund-raising program. The skills of the Crossnore Weavers are highly regarded, and the sales gallery is an essential stop for anyone interested in North Carolina's fine crafts.

★ BROWN MOUNTAIN LIGHTS

One of North Carolina's most enduring mysteries is the **Brown Mountain Lights.** These mysterious orbs are seen floating in the air on some evenings around Brown Mountain, along the Burke County-Caldwell County line. A number of official agencies have studied the phenomenon, and the U.S. Geological Survey determined the orbs may be the reflection of the headlights of cars and trains in the valley below, completely ignoring the fact that the lights have been seen since at least 1833. The Brown Mountain Lights are believed by many to be supernatural. One legend, related in the song "Brown Mountain Lights," says the lights are the lanterns of a hunter lost in these woods and the enslaved person who died searching for his enslaver. Ghost fanciers will be delighted to know that the Brown Mountain Lights can be observed by visitors from the Lost Cove overlook on the southeast side of the Blue Ridge Parkway near Milepost 310. An even better place to see them is along Highway 181, about 20 miles north of Morganton. There, a marked turnout and parking area give you plenty of space to set up a chair and a tripod for your camera. If you want to look for them, try a clear evening in the summer, right around dusk.

LINVILLE GORGE

The deepest gorge in the United States, Linville Gorge is located near Blue Ridge Parkway Milepost 316 in a 12,000-acre federally designated Wilderness Area. It's genuine wilderness, and some of the hollers in this preserve are so remote that they still shelter virgin forests—a rarity even in these wild mountains. Linville Falls (Blue Ridge Pkwy. Milepost 316) is one of the most photographed places in North Carolina, a spectacular series of cataracts that fall crashing into the gorge. It can be seen from several short trails that depart from the Linville Falls Visitors Center (Milepost 316.3, 828/298-0398, 10am-5pm daily late Apr.-Nov.). The National Park Service operates the Linville Falls Campground (Blue Ridge Pkwy. Milepost 316.3, campground 828/765-7818, reservations 877/444-6777, www.recreation. gov, $20, group camping $35) near the falls. Tent and RV sites are interspersed, and water and flush toilets are available May-October.

Not to be confused with the National Park Service campground, the Linville Falls Campground, RV Park & Log Cabin Rentals (717 Gurney Franklin Rd., 828/765-2681, www.linvillefalls.com, primitive tent sites $25, tent sites with water and electricity $30-55, RV sites $55-75, cabins $75-198) has plenty of options available for camping, or you can stay in a cabin. With full hookups, a camp store, fire rings, grills, a laundry facility, and a nice bathhouse (with accessible facilities), this is a solid option in this area.

Linville Gorge has some great climbing spots, including Table Rock, parts of which are popular with beginning climbers, and other parts which should only be attempted by experts. Other extremely strenuous options are the Hawksbill cliff face and Sitting Bear rock pillar. Speak to the folks at the visitors center or at Fox Mountain Guides (234-A S. Broad St., Brevard, 888/284-8433, www.fox-mountainguides.com), a Brevard-area service that leads climbs in the gorge, to determine which of Linville Gorge's many climbing faces would be best suited to your skill level.

Nearby Food

Famous Louise's Rockhouse Restaurant (23175 Rockhouse Lane, Linville Falls, near Blue Ridge Pkwy. Milepost 321, 828/765-2702, 7am-7:30pm Wed.-Thurs., 7am-8pm Fri.-Sat., 7am-3pm Sun.), built in 1936 with stones taken from the Linville River, is not a large restaurant, but the dining room is spread out over three counties: The lines of Burke, McDowell, and Avery Counties meet on this exact spot, and customers, for reasons of loyalty or legality, often have preferences about where to take their repast. Famous Louise's is owned by a mother and daughter, and Louise, the mom, is a cook of some renown. The fare is traditional and homemade—the pimento cheese is mixed here, the cornbread and biscuits are whipped up from scratch, and the pot roast stews at a leisurely simmer. On your way out, pick up a jar or two of Louise's homemade berry jams, probably the best $3 souvenirs to be found in the mountains. You'll find them in the Avery County part of the restaurant.

ORCHARD AT ALTAPASS

At Milepost 328 on the Blue Ridge Parkway, the Orchard at Altapass (1025 Orchard Rd., Spruce Pine, 828/765-9531, www.altapassorchard.org, 10am-5pm daily May-Oct.) is much more than an orchard, although it does produce apples in abundance. The land on which the orchard grows has been settled since the 1790s, when Charlie "Cove" McKinney and his large family lived here. McKinney had four wives—at the same time—who bore him 30 sons and a dozen daughters. An early chronicler of local history wrote that the four wives "never had no words bout his havin so many womin. If it ware these times thar would be har pulled." Many of the McKinneys are buried on the mountain. Around the turn of the 20th century, the land became an orchard, and in its best years produced 125,000 bushels of apples. To get a sense of how many apples that would have been, consider that today's standard for a bushel of apples is 48 pounds.

Today, the Orchard at Altapass continues to turn out wonderful apples. It is also a favorite music venue in this region. Country, bluegrass, old-time, and gospel musicians as well as artists in a variety of other styles perform at the orchard on the weekend. There is a staggering amount of musical talent in these mountains, and the Orchard at Altapass is a showcase of local treasures.

PENLAND SCHOOL OF CRAFTS

In the 1920s, Lucy Morgan, a teacher at a local Episcopal school, and her brother embarked on a mission to help the women of the North Carolina mountains gain some hand in their own economic well-being. Equipping several households in the Penland area with looms, they touched off a local cottage industry in weaving, which quickly centralized and grew into the Penland School, a center for craft instruction and production. Several "folk schools" sprouted in the southern Appalachians in that era, most of them the projects of idealistic Northerners wanting to aid the benighted mountaineers. The Penland School, however, has the distinction of being one of the few such institutions that was truly homegrown, as Miss Lucy was herself a child of the rural Carolina highlands.

Today, the **Penland School of Craft** (67 Doras Trail, Penland, 828/765-2359, www. penland.org) is an arts instruction center of international renown. More than 1,000 people, from beginners to professionals, enroll in Penland's one-, two-, and eight-week courses every year to learn about crafts in many different media. Tours of the campus (1:30pm Wed. Apr.-Dec., reservations required) are available, and the school operates a beautiful shop, the **Penland Gallery** (3135 Conley Ridge Rd., 828/765-6211, www.penland.org, 11am-5pm Wed.-Sat.), where the work of many of the school's instructors and students can be purchased.

★ LITTLE SWITZERLAND

Little Switzerland, 90 minutes southwest of Boone via the Blue Ridge Parkway, earned its name thanks to the views of the surrounding mountains and deep valleys, which are reminiscent, many say, of the foothills of the Swiss Alps. The mountains around here have been mined for years, and possibly millennia, if some archaeological findings are correct. Mica, that shiny stone, is found here in abundance, and there's evidence to suggest that Native Americans mined for it here some 2,000 years ago. Desoto is thought to have visited the area around 1540, searching for gold and silver but finding mica instead. Mica was mined here during the Civil War and Reconstruction. In 1895, emerald mining began. Soon Tiffany's and the American Gem & Pear Company had a large mine here. That mine is abandoned today, but gem hunters and rock hounds still make their way inside to see what they can find. And for good reason: In addition to mica and emeralds, mines nearby have produced aquamarine, beryl, garnet, kyanite, and smoky quartz.

Emerald Village

Emerald Village (331 McKinney Mine Rd., Spruce Pine, 828/765-6463, www.emerald-village.com, 10am-4pm daily Apr., 9am-5pm daily May 1-Memorial Day and Labor Day-Oct., 9am-6pm daily Memorial Day-Labor Day, $10 adults, $8 ages 5-12, free under age 5), a can't-miss collection of gem mines and historical attractions, shows the story of Little Switzerland's long mining history. Emerald Village has seven mines to explore, the **North Carolina Mining Museum** (self-guided underground mine tour $8 adults, $7 seniors, $6 students), and gem mining, gold panning, and dig-your-own emeralds. The very unusual Black Light Mine Tour is held on selected Saturdays. This tour is wild, as the minerals shine with otherworldly light under the black light.

Grassy Creek Waterfall

An easy hike leads to the pretty **Grassy Creek Falls** (trailhead on Grassy Creek Falls

---

1: the Mile High Swinging Bridge 2: Linville Falls
3: Linn Cove Viaduct 4: the Orchard at Altapass

Rd., off Chestnut Grove Church Rd. after it passes under the parkway). Park before the "No Parking Beyond This Point" sign and follow the road about 0.6 miles, then turn at the sign and hike another 0.3 miles to the 30-foot falls. It's mossy and lush, and when there's been rain, the thin sheets of water flowing over the falls are quite lovely.

Food and Accommodations

The **Switzerland Café** (9440 Hwy. 226A, 828/765-5289, www.switzerlandcafe.com, 10:30am-4pm daily mid-Apr.-Oct., under $12) is a combination restaurant and general store, so you can pick up everything from a barbecue sandwich to a souvenir T-shirt. Most of the food is smokehouse inspired, and the trout is surprisingly good.

The ★ **Switzerland Inn** (86 High Ridge Rd., 828/765-2153, www.switzerlandinn.com, $189-279) opened in 1910 and continues to serve travelers today with accommodations ranging from the Diamondback Motorcycle Lodge (a collection of eight rooms and a central living area catering to motorcyclists) to the luxurious Heidi and Alpine Suites. This inn is simply stunning, with fabulous views. Two restaurants are on-site: the **Fowl Play Pub** (hours vary, $12) and the **Chalet Restaurant** (hours vary, $15-18), which serves breakfast, lunch, and dinner year-round. Make reservations early to stay here.

Big Lynn Lodge (10860 Hwy. 226A, 828/765-4257, www.biglynnlodge.com, $105-169) is another fixture in the Little Switzerland lodging community that began 75 years ago with a collection of cabins on a dahlia farm and has grown into a 42-room lodge. It's a charming little spot to stay, and includes breakfast and dinner.

★ MOUNT MITCHELL

At 6,684 feet, **Mount Mitchell** (accessible from Milepost 355.3, near Burnsville, 828/675-4611, http://ncparks.gov) is the highest mountain east of South Dakota. It is the pinnacle of the Black Mountain range, a 15-mile-long J-shaped ridge that was formerly considered one mountain. Now that the various peaks are designated as separate mountains, 6 of them are among the 10 highest in the eastern United States. Elisha Mitchell, for whom the mountain is named, is buried at the summit. He was one of North Carolina's first great scholars, a geologist and botanist who taught at the University of North Carolina in Chapel Hill. His skill as a scientist is demonstrated by his 1830s calculation of the height

the summit of Mount Mitchell, the highest peak in the East

of the peak that now bears his name; amazingly, he estimated the height within 12 feet of today's measurement. In the 1850s, he became embroiled in a controversy when Senator Thomas Clingman, one of his former students, disputed the calculation. On a return trip to remeasure Mount Mitchell, Elisha Mitchell fell from the top of a waterfall (now Mitchell Falls) and drowned in the water below.

From the Blue Ridge Parkway, the best view of the mountain is at Milepost 350. **Mount Mitchell State Park** (Milepost 355.3, 2388 Hwy. 128, 828/675-4611, http://ncparks.gov, 7am-6pm daily Nov.-Feb., 7am-8pm daily Mar.-Apr., 7am-10pm daily May-Aug., 7am-9pm daily Sept.-Oct.) is not only a place to get an amazing panoramic view—up to 85 miles in clear weather—it also has an education center, a gift shop, and nine **campsites** (www.northcarolinastateparks.reserveamerica.com, May-late Oct., $23). There is also a restaurant (828/675-1888, 11am-7pm daily May-Oct., $15, reopening for 2023 season), which is unremarkable to all but hungry hikers.

CRAGGY GARDENS

Craggy Gardens is one of the most appropriately named spots on the parkway. The principal features here are the rocky crags studded with rhododendrons, mountain ash, wildflowers, and other rare plants. As with much of Appalachia, this area was settled by Scots and Scots-Irish, and the rugged rocks along the peak reminded them of the craggy mountains back home.

The **Craggy Gardens Visitor Center** (Milepost 364.6, Blue Ridge Pkwy., 10am-5pm daily Memorial Day-Oct.) has information on the flora and fauna of this part of the park, and the folks here can answer just about any question you throw at them. There's a picnic area here as well as a pair of worthwhile hikes.

Morganton

Morganton, a charming but often overlooked town on I-40 an hour east of Asheville, is actually a vibrant little community with an active arts scene, a handful of good restaurants, and a budding wine and brewery scene.

ART GALLERIES

The **Hamilton Williams Gallery** (403 E. Union St., 828/438-1595, www.hamiltonwilliams.com, 10am-6pm Mon.-Fri., 10am-5pm Sat.) started as a studio and gallery for potter Hamilton Williams, but he realized the space he was renovating—a 100-year-old warehouse and storefront—had enough room for a big gallery where he could sell his work and display works by dozens of other artists. You'll find pottery, jewelry, sculpture, and textile in this bright, inviting gallery. At **West Union Art Studios** (113 W. Union St., 828/403-4148, www.westunionartstudiosllc.com, 10am-6pm Wed.-Sat.), more than a dozen working artists and musicians have set up a space for music lessons, artists studios, and a gallery with pottery, paintings, photography, and more.

WINERIES AND BREWERIES

Along a 30-mile stretch of I-40 east and west of Morganton is the **Catawba Valley Wine Trail** (information www.discoverburkecounty.com). A recent and growing addition to North Carolina's vineyard and winery population, there are five wineries to visit, each making wine in different styles and geared toward different palates. I found **Silver Fork Winery** (5000 Patton Rd., off I-40 exit 94, 828/391-8783, www.silverforkwinery.com, noon-6pm Wed.-Sun. Mar.-Dec., noon-5pm Fri.-Sat. Jan.-Feb.) to have a beautiful tasting room. The cabernet sauvignon is especially nice, as is their rosé. Taste a few, pick your favorite bottle, and enjoy it on their shaded patio or stick around for a movie or some live music in the summer months. To go along with the Wine Trail, there's also the **Catawba Valley Ale Trail** (information www.discoverburkecounty.com) that visits 14 different breweries that follow the Catawba River as it meanders across four counties.

Morganton's **Fonta Flora Brewery** (317 N. Green St., 828/475-7501, www.fontaflora.com, 5pm-9pm Mon.-Wed., 4pm-10pm Thurs.-Fri., noon-10pm Sat., noon-8pm Sun.) has been one of my favorite breweries since they opened their doors. They create some outstanding beers from their little brewery in downtown Morganton, and though I love their bottled and canned beers, nothing beats a cold pint straight from the tap. Fonta Flora brews a number of saisons, and they get pretty creative with the ingredients they use; don't be surprised if you find miso, beets, pine needles, or rye giving your pint a flavor boost. IPA fans will want to try their Hop Beard Mountain Man IPA, while porter lovers should try whatever iteration is on tap. In early June, Fonta Flora organizes **State of Origin** (www.fontaflora.com/stateoforigin), a beer festival that celebrates the flora and fauna of each brewery's state of origin, hence the name. Some 30 breweries show up and serve outstanding brews. It's a one-day event, so plan to be in Morganton for this festival next year.

Sidetracked Brewery (609 S. Green St., Suite 100, 828/544-5840, www.sidetrackedbrew.com, 3pm-10pm Mon.-Thurs., 1pm-11pm Fri., noon-11pm Sat., 1pm-8pm Sun.) sits, appropriately, by the railroad tracks in downtown Morganton. The cozy taproom has a stack of board games (from backgammon to *Cards Against Humanity*—try to remember you're in public when you play this one), table tennis and darts, and TVs. The brewhouse spread the love across several styles, and you'll find IPAs and DIPAs (those are double IPAs), blonde and brown ales, and even kettle sours, plus odd spinoffs and riffs on these styles, ready to pour every day.

Catawba Brewing Co. (212 S. Green St., 828/430-6883, www.catawbabrewing.

com, 5pm-9pm Mon.-Thurs., 1pm-11pm Fri., noon-11pm Sat., 1pm-7pm Sun.) originated in Morganton and has since expanded to a pair of Asheville locations and one in Charlotte; opening a shop in those two beer towns says volumes about what they're doing here. Here in Morganton, they keep 10 beers on tap and the rest in cans. Their White Zombie white ale is a personal favorite, though Astral Bootie (session IPA) and Brown Bear (brown ale) never disappoint.

If you didn't find what you were looking for at these breweries, maybe it's waiting in a bottle or can over at **Brown Mountain Bottleworks** (115 E. Union St., 828/413-2678, www.brownmountainbottleworks.com, noon-10pm Mon.-Sat., 2pm-7pm Sun.). There are hundreds of breweries, styles, and variations on the shelves and in the coolers here, and the folks who staff this joint are happy to help guide you to an ideal beer; just order up a pint from their dozen taps and strike up a conversation.

RECREATION

Lake James State Park (7321 Hwy. 126, 828/584-7728, http://ncparks.gov), five miles northeast of Marion, comprises 6,500-acre Lake James and its 150 miles of shoreline. Created around 1920, the artificial lake is in a graceful mountain setting among hemlocks and rhododendrons. Canoes and kayaks ($10 per hour) are available to rent, and there are campsites (reservations www.northcarolinastateparks.reserveamerica.com, Mar. 15-Nov. 30, $12-23) with restrooms, showers, and drinking water nearby. There's a great swimming beach (day-use $6 adults, $4 ages 3-12, 10am-6pm daily May 1-Sept. 30) and the park features 15 miles of multiuse hiking and biking trails as well as many miles of hiking-only trails. The 2.25-mile Fox Den Loop is a good option; the 1.5-mile Lake Channel Overlook gives you a peek at Lake James and Linville Gorge; Mill's Creek Trail leads you 3.6 miles through forest ridges and opens up to a few lovely vistas along the way; and the 2-mile Overmountain Victory Trail follows the route taken by colonial rebels on their way to battle British Loyalists at King's Mountain.

FOOD

★ **Root and Vine** (139 W. Union St., 828/433-1540, http://rootandvinerestaurant.com, 11:30am-2:30pm and 5pm-9:30pm Mon.-Sat., $12-36) is a hip, slightly more upscale place than other venues in Morganton. The menu changes with some frequency, but entrées are grilled on a wood fire and draw on all sorts of culinary inspiration: vindaloo curry with shrimp, scallops, mussels, or organic tofu; grilled North Carolina mountain trout served with tasso ham gravy and collard greens; and the seared duck breast with pork belly and an orange-raspberry coulis. The cocktails are good, and their wine list is well done for a restaurant this size. When the weather is mild, take your dinner on the patio and dine alfresco.

Mountain Burrito (408 W. Fleming Dr., 828/438-5008, www.mountainburritonc.com, 10:30am-9pm daily, $10) is an interesting spot as it blends Appalachian flavors with Mexican-inspired quick service. Pick your protein (chicken, steak, slow roasted pork, veggie blend) and decide if it's a burrito, a pair of tacos, or a bowl or nacho situation, and then pick your rice, beans, and other toppings. It's perfect for a quick stop lunch or dinner, or for something you can take up to the Brown Mountain Overlook and eat while you look for the lights.

For many, myself included, no trip to or in North Carolina is complete without stopping for barbecue at least once, and in towns like Morganton you'll always find some good hometown 'cue. **Butch's BBQ & Breakfast** (1234 Burkemont Ave., 828/432-5040, www.butchsmorganton.com, 6am-10pm Mon.-Sat., 7am-10pm Sun., $3-19) brings two of my favorite food together under one roof and does both very well. Breakfast is simple, with six breakfast sandwiches or biscuits on offer (the country ham is great, livermush is a regional "delicacy" that I've never developed a taste for, but if you're feeling adventurous, order one, but get a backup biscuit just in case). They pull several tasty bites off the barbecue pit, including smoked chicken, chicken wings, and pulled pork, all served in sandwiches and plates and platters. You'll also find chicken tenders and sandwiches (pulled pork, smoked chicken, chicken tenders) if you're in the mood.

Asheville and the Southern Blue Ridge

There's an energy in the mountain town of

Asheville that you don't find in many other places in North Carolina. For more than a century Asheville has been a hive of progressive thinking and a surprisingly cosmopolitan level of living.

With all the writers, artists, musicians, dancers, wealthy industrialists, and eclectic personalities that have inhabited this town, it's easy to understand how it earned the nickname "Paris of the South." Built on a series of hills around the confluence of the Swannanoa ("swan-uh-NO-uh") and French Broad Rivers, commerce found its way here in the 18th and 19th centuries via water routes and a mountain stagecoach road. In the late 1800s the town experienced a boom as railroad lines began to bring vacationers by the tens of thousands. It was around

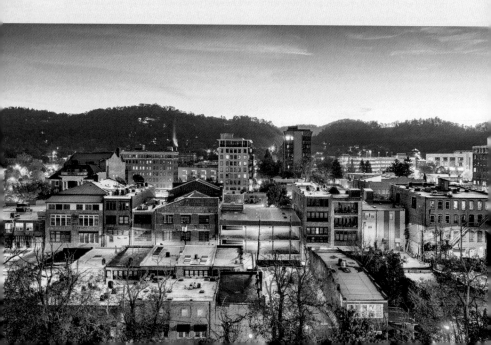

Highlights

Look for ★ to find recommended sights, activities, dining, and lodging.

★ **Downtown Architecture:** In the early 20th century, wealthy visitors left their mark on Asheville's downtown, a district packed with art deco and beaux arts masterpieces (page 376).

★ **North Carolina Arboretum:** One of the most beautiful garden spaces in the country, this enormous collection is worth a visit. Don't miss the special Bonsai Collection (page 377).

★ **Biltmore Estate:** Asheville's most popular attraction is not only an awe-inspiring palace and symbol of the Gilded Age; it's also a collection of great little restaurants, shops, and a popular winery, all in a beautiful riverside setting (page 380).

★ **Folk Art Center:** Learn about the master craftspeople of the southern Appalachians and purchase gorgeous handmade items such as traditional weaving, woodcarving, and fine-art furniture (page 384).

★ **Hiking:** Hit the trail at the North Carolina Arboretum, Biltmore Estate, or Blue Ridge Parkway; there are plenty of trails to choose from (page 385).

★ **Live Music:** You'll hear great music everywhere here, from buskers on street corners to the nation's premier live music hall (page 389).

★ **River Arts District:** Asheville's repurposed warehouses have become a lively collection of art galleries and studios, restaurants, and breweries (page 398).

★ **Waterfall Touring:** Head to Brevard and Transylvania County to see how many of the 250 waterfalls here you can visit (page 424).

Asheville

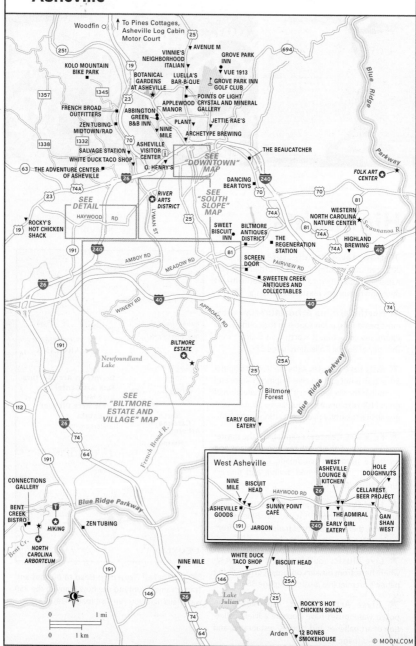

Woodfin

To Pines Cottages,
Asheville Log Cabin
Motor Court

251

19

KOLO MOUNTAIN
BIKE PARK

1357

1345

1338 1332

BOTANICAL
GARDENS
AT ASHEVILLE

23

FRENCH BROAD
OUTFITTERS

ZEN TUBING
MIDTOWN/RAD

70

SALVAGE STATION
WHITE DUCK TACO SHOP

63

THE ADVENTURE CENTER
OF ASHEVILLE

26

23

74A

19

ROCKY'S
HOT CHICKEN
SHACK

191

26

AVENUE M

25

VINNIE'S
NEIGHBORHOOD
ITALIAN

GROVE PARK
INN

VUE 1913

LUELLA'S
BAR-B-QUE

GROVE PARK INN
GOLF CLUB

POINTS OF LIGHT
CRYSTAL AND MINERAL
GALLERY

ABBINGTON
GREEN
B&B INN

APPLEWOOD
MANOR

PLANT

NINE
MILE

JETTIE RAE'S

ARCHETYPE BREWING

ASHEVILLE
VISITOR
CENTER

O. HENRY'S

SEE
"DOWNTOWN"
MAP

THE BEAUCATCHER

240

694

Blue Ridge Parkway

FOLK ART
CENTER

DANCING
BEAR TOYS

70

70

240

74A

81

WESTERN
NORTH CAROLINA
NATURE CENTER

SEE
DETAIL

HAYWOOD RD

RIVER
ARTS
DISTRICT

LYMAN ST

SEE
"SOUTH
SLOPE"
MAP

25

SWEET
BISCUIT
INN

BILTMORE
ANTIQUES
DISTRICT

81

THE
REGENERATION
STATION

SCREEN
DOOR

Swannanoa R.

81

74A

HIGHLAND
BREWING

40

74

AMBOY RD

MEADOW RD

40

WINERY RD

APPROACH RD

FAIRVIEW RD

SWEETEN CREEK
ANTIQUES AND
COLLECTABLES

40

191

26

74

64

191

BILTMORE
ESTATE

Newfoundland
Lake

French Broad R.

SEE
"BILTMORE
ESTATE AND
VILLAGE" MAP

25A

25

Biltmore
Forest

Blue Ridge Parkway

EARLY GIRL
EATERY

112

CONNECTIONS
GALLERY

BENT
CREEK
BISTRO

HIKING

NORTH
CAROLINA
ARBORTEUM

Bent Cr.

ZEN TUBING

Blue Ridge Parkway

191

NINE MILE

146

26

WHITE DUCK
TACO SHOP

BISCUIT HEAD

146

74

64

25A

25

Lake
Julian

ROCKY'S HOT
CHICKEN SHACK

Arden

12 BONES
SMOKEHOUSE

0   1 mi

0   1 km

West Asheville

NINE
MILE

BISCUIT
HEAD

HAYWOOD RD

WEST
ASHEVILLE
LOUNGE &
KITCHEN

26

HOLE
DOUGHNUTS

CELLAREST
BEER PROJECT

ASHEVILLE
GOODS

SUNNY POINT
CAFÉ

THE ADMIRAL

191

JARGON

240

EARLY GIRL
EATERY

GAN
SHAN
WEST

© MOON.COM

that time that George Vanderbilt, scion of the massively wealthy Vanderbilt dynasty, began building his mountain home, the Biltmore, just south of downtown. From the 1880s to the 1930s the mountain town underwent a long and rapid expansion, eventually becoming a small city in its own right.

Surrounding Asheville are mountains and hundreds of years of folk traditions, with folk art, music, dancing, and customs that survive today. Old-time Appalachian string-band music (not to be confused with bluegrass, although bluegrass is alive and well here too) thrives in the hills and hollows among the descendants of the region's early settlers, whose songs, instruments, and techniques have been passed down over many generations. Four- and five-string banjo pickers, guitarists, fiddlers, and other musicians have migrated here from all across the globe to be part of the music traditions and the thriving music scene. Asheville is one of the best places in the world to hear old-time and bluegrass music as well as a sidetrack genre known as mountain swing.

One of the epicenters for visual arts in the Southeast, Asheville draws from centuries-old Appalachian folkways and traditions like woodcarving, weaving, and other arts and merges them with elements of the modern craft and fine arts movement. The results from these seemingly disparate elements being put in Asheville's pressure cooker together is a vibrant set of studios and galleries where art and craft of all sorts have a home. Arts organizations such as the Southern Highland Craft Guild (www.southernhighlandguild.org) help preserve the traditional arts, while places like the River Arts District and a number of small guilds, groups, and galleries support contemporary artists.

All of this makes Asheville feel like a countercultural center. Elements of Haight-Ashbury circa 1968 mix with Woodstock, the Grand Ole Opry, Andy Warhol's Factory, and a beatnik vibe, but with better food, to create an electric atmosphere.

PLANNING YOUR TIME

Once the last leaf drops from autumn trees, many mountain towns close until spring. Asheville is vibrant year-round (although the pace does ease quite a bit when the snow falls). In winter, Asheville is less expensive; rooms at hotels, inns, and B&Bs are plentiful; and reservations at the hot-ticket restaurants are easier to score. Fortunately, the breweries and cocktail lounges don't slow down, and some of the best bands roll through town in winter months. The city will see snow several times throughout the season, but it's not generally a problem, despite the fact that it does occasionally shut down the Blue Ridge Parkway, and some of those higher mountain roads can be impassable.

Once spring breaks and bunches of wildflowers start to show up in earnest, so do the warmer-weather visitors. This is a prime time for wildflower hikes and visits to waterfalls (which can be quite impressive with snowmelt and spring rains), plus there's an energy to the city as everyone and everything begins to wake up after the dark of winter. Spring at the Biltmore Estate is marvelous thanks to their outstanding gardens that are thick with tulips.

Summer, of course, is a great time to be in Asheville, as the elevation brings cooler air on the same day it will be sweltering across the Piedmont and Sandhills. Summer also brings a number of festivals and special events, and it's the time when the greens and blues of the Blue Ridge are most vivid. Fall colors arrive at slightly different times each year, so you'll want to keep an eye on leaf forecasts for ideal getaway times. Generally speaking, however, you can plan to see leaves start to turn in mid-September, peak in mid-October, and finish by the second week of November. Fall is prime season to visit Asheville, so make

ASHEVILLE

Previous: Asheville; a bonsai on display at the North Carolina Arboretum; the River Arts District is a must-see for artists and art lovers.

lodging reservations early and expect some delays on scenic routes like the Blue Ridge Parkway.

Asheville's proximity to Great Smoky Mountains National Park (GSMNP) makes it a natural launch point for trips into the park. Visiting the Smoky Mountains brings the same seasonal concerns as visiting Asheville. Fall is peak season and crowded with leaf-peeping visitors; things slow down in winter and pick up in spring as the wildflowers begin to bloom. Then summer brings the hikers and national park enthusiasts back in full force. The elevation of Newfound Gap Road, the only road across GSMNP, is such that it can have weather-related delays or closures, so keep this in mind when planning a visit.

The **Blue Ridge National Heritage Area** (www.blueridgeheritage.com) has a number of valuable trip-planning resources, but a preferred resource is **Explore Asheville** (www.exploreasheville.com), the Asheville Convention and Visitors Bureau's website. The site's creators and the people at the **Asheville Visitors Center** (36 Montford Ave., 828/258-6129, www.exploreasheville. com, 8:30am-5:30pm Mon.-Fri., 9am-5pm Sat.-Sun.) take a lot of pride in their town and can help steer you toward new and old favorites in the area. For planning a trip to the Smoky Mountains, you'll find many resources through **Great Smoky Mountains National Park** (GSMNP, 865/436-1200, www.nps.gov/grsm); of course, you'll also find a number of resources through Asheville's local visitor services.

Asheville

SIGHTS

Getting around Asheville isn't much of a problem once you get oriented, and getting yourself oriented is no problem. Downtown Asheville sits at the center, on the crest of a couple of hills, and it's here we find the largest concentration of hotels, restaurants, and bars. Just south of downtown is the South Slope and an assortment of places to eat and drink. The French Broad River flows to the west of Downtown, and the River Arts District sits here, between downtown and the river. In the warehouses and industrial facilities are hundreds of art galleries. Across the river is West Asheville, a destination with its own vibe and set of restaurants and breweries. The Biltmore Estate, and Biltmore Village (an actual miniature village built to support the workers on the estate, gardens, and house), sit at the foot of South Slope. South of here is I-40 and the rough dividing line between South Asheville and the rest of the area. To the north of downtown you'll find the University of North Carolina Asheville and residential neighborhoods. The Blue Ridge Parkway wraps around the eastern and southern sides of the city.

Downtown

In Downtown Asheville, pick a parking garage, or park at your hotel, and stow the car, then head out by foot. From Pack Square at the heart of Downtown, you're only a few blocks or a few minutes away from galleries, boutiques, breweries, restaurants, and places to stay.

★ DOWNTOWN ARCHITECTURE

As beautiful as Asheville's natural environment may be, the striking architecture is just as attractive. The Montford neighborhood, a contemporary of the Biltmore, is a mixture of ornate Queen Anne houses and craftsman-style bungalows. The Grove Park Inn, a huge luxury hotel, was built in 1913 and is decked out with rustic architectural devices intended to make vacationing New Yorkers and wealthy people feel like they were roughing it. In downtown Asheville is a large concentration of art deco buildings on the scale of Miami Beach. Significant structures dating to the boom before the Great Depression include the **Buncombe County Courthouse** (60 Court Plaza, built 1927-1929), the **First Baptist Church** (Oak St. and Woodfin St., 1925), the **S&W Cafeteria** (56 Patton Ave., 1929), the **Public Service Building** (89-93 Patton Ave., 1929), and the **Grove Arcade** (1 Page Ave., 1926-1929).

The **Jackson Building** (22 S. Pack Square, built 1923-1924) is a fine example of neo-Gothic architecture with a disturbing backstory. According to legend, on the day of the stock market crash in 1929 that started the Great Depression, one of the wealthiest men in Asheville lost it all and leaped to his death from the building. Three or four (depending on who's telling the story) more of Asheville's wealthiest followed suit. What is known to be true is that there's a bull's-eye built into the sidewalk in front of the building as a morbid monument to the story.

ASHEVILLE ART MUSEUM

The **Asheville Art Museum** (2 S. Pack Square, 828/253-3227, www.ashevilleart.org, 11am-6pm Tues.-Wed. and Fri.-Sun., 11am-9pm Thurs., $15 adults, $13 over age 60, $10 students, free under age 6) recently underwent two years of renovations to add new exhibition space and a fresh approach to their collection. They've been around since 1948, and in the intervening decades have enriched the art community of Asheville by displaying works by some of the most important, influential, and up-and-coming artists of the 20th century. The permanent collection includes a wide array of media and styles, including photo portraits, ceramics, statuary, and beautiful modern pieces. A large collection from the nearby experimental school, Black Mountain College, shows the highlights of works created by faculty and students.

South Slope and River Arts District

Restaurants, breweries, and nightlife make the South Slope a distinct destination. The former warehouses and industrial spaces turned art galleries make the River Arts District a great spot to spend a few hours, but the breweries and restaurants here make it easy to spend the day.

West Asheville

In West Asheville you might have trouble parking as this once entirely residential neighborhood continues to evolve. Popular restaurants and breweries, a number of boutiques and shops, and some vibrant murals make this a great place to grab a bite or spend the bulk of your weekend away.

★ NORTH CAROLINA ARBORETUM

The enormous **North Carolina Arboretum** (100 Frederick Law Olmsted Way, 828/665-2492, www.ncarboretum.org, 8am-9pm daily Apr.-Oct., 8am-7pm daily Nov.-Mar., Bonsai Collection 9am-5pm daily, admission free, parking $16 cars, $50 RVs) is considered by many to be one of the most beautiful in the country. The 434 natural and landscaped acres back into the Pisgah National Forest, just off the Blue Ridge Parkway. Major collections include the National Native Azalea Repository, featuring nearly every species of azalea native to the United States as well as several hybrids, and the special Bonsai Collection, comprising more than 200 bonsai plants, many of the staff horticulturists' own creation.

Bicycles and leashed dogs are permitted on many of the arboretum's trails. Walking areas range from easy to fairly rugged, but with 10 miles of trails, you will find one that suits your skill level. To learn more about the history of the arboretum and its plants, as well as the natural history of the region, join one of the guided tours (1pm Tues. and Sat.). These two-mile walk-and-talk tours happen rain or shine, so dress for the weather. The arboretum also has a nice café, the **Bent Creek Bistro** (828/412-8584, 10am-4pm Tues.-Sun., $4-9), and gift shop, the **Connections Gallery** (10am-4pm daily).

Downtown Asheville

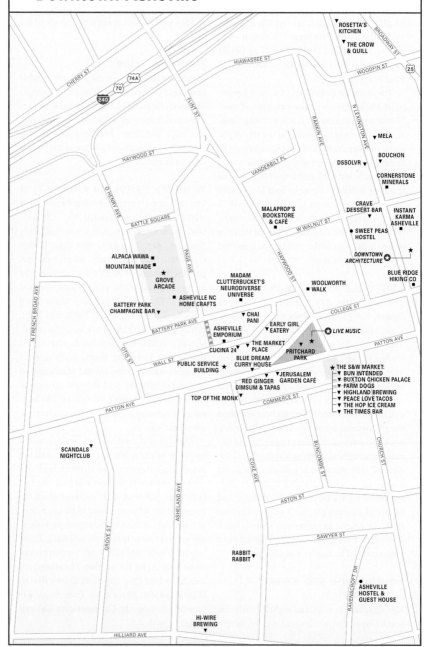

ROSETTA'S KITCHEN

THE CROW & QUILL

HIAWASSEE ST

WOODFIN ST

CHERRY ST

74A
70
240

FLINT ST

RANKIN AVE

N LEXINGTON AVE

BROADWAY ST

25

MELA

BOUCHON

DSSOLVR

CORNERSTONE MINERALS

HAYWOOD ST

VANDERBILT PL

W WALNUT ST

CRAVE DESSERT BAR

INSTANT KARMA ASHEVILLE

O HENRY AVE

BATTLE SQUARE

MALAPROP'S BOOKSTORE & CAFÉ

PAGE AVE

SWEET PEAS HOSTEL

DOWNTOWN ARCHITECTURE

BLUE RIDGE HIKING CO

N FRENCH BROAD AVE

ALPACA WAWA
MOUNTAIN MADE

GROVE ARCADE

ASHEVILLE NC HOME CRAFTS

MADAM CLUTTERBUCKET'S NEURODIVERSE UNIVERSE

HAYWOOD ST

WOOLWORTH WALK

COLLEGE ST

BATTERY PARK CHAMPAGNE BAR

BATTERY PARK AVE

CHAI PANI

EARLY GIRL EATERY

LIVE MUSIC

PATTON AVE

ASHEVILLE EMPORIUM

OTIS ST

CUCINA 24

WALL ST

PUBLIC SERVICE BUILDING

THE MARKET PLACE

BLUE DREAM CURRY HOUSE

PRITCHARD PARK

THE S&W MARKET:
BUN INTENDED
BUXTON CHICKEN PALACE
FARM DOGS
HIGHLAND BREWING
PEACE LOVE TACOS
THE HOP ICE CREAM
THE TIMES BAR

RED GINGER DIMSUM & TAPAS

JERUSALEM GARDEN CAFÉ

TOP OF THE MONK

COMMERCE ST

PATTON AVE

SCANDALS NIGHTCLUB

ASHELAND AVE

COXE AVE

BUNCOMBE ST

CHURCH ST

ASTON ST

GROVE ST

SAWYER ST

RABBIT RABBIT

RAVENSCROFT DR

ASHEVILLE HOSTEL & GUEST HOUSE

HI-WIRE BREWING

HILLIARD AVE

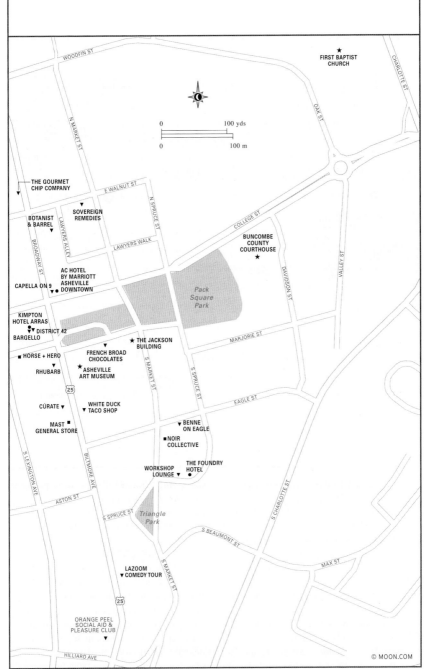

ASHEVILLE
ASHEVILLE

Biltmore Estate and Village

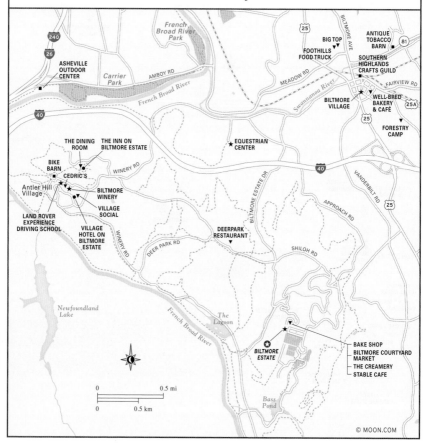

Biltmore Estate and Village

The area around the Biltmore Estate includes the estate itself but also Biltmore Village, where workers on the estate, grounds, and home lived during and after construction. The estate is a kingdom unto itself, with a winery (it's the most-visited wine tasting room in the United States, incidentally) and brewery in Antler Hill, amazing gardens and that stunning house at the center, a vineyard (it's on the other side of the estate, the working side), nearly a dozen places to eat, a pair of inns, a whole slew of outdoor activities to get into, and so much space. It's a beautiful place to explore. And Biltmore Village is no exception. This lovely little grid of brick and stone cottages is charming as can be and full of boutiques, galleries, restaurants, and more.

★ BILTMORE ESTATE

Much of downtown Asheville dates to the 1920s, but the architectural crown jewel, the **Biltmore Estate** (1 Lodge St., 800/411-3812, www.biltmore.com, ticket office 8:30am-4pm daily, house 10am-5pm daily, gardens 9am-7:30pm daily, admission $66-86, additional fees for activities), predates that by decades. It was built in the late 1800s for owner

One Day in Asheville

Only have one day to devote to Asheville? Here are the city's must-see, must-do, and must-eat attractions:

MORNING

Start the day with some great breakfast grub from Sunny Point in West Asheville. Spend the morning exploring boutiques and galleries like those in the Grove Arcade and Woolworth Walk, taking time to stroll by examples of Asheville's notable downtown architecture, including the First Baptist Church, the Jackson Building, and the Buncombe County Courthouse before joining a Hood Huggers Tour.

AFTERNOON

At lunchtime, make your way over to the S&W Market for chicken sandwiches, bao, tacos, and a beer from Highland Brewing. Buxton Hall Barbecue, a few blocks off downtown on the South Slope, is another good lunch option. After lunch, get a new perspective on the city by boarding the LaZoom Comedy Tour bus, floating down the French Broad River with Zen Tubing, or by heading out for a hike or woodsy walk at the North Carolina Arboretum or at any of a number of trailheads along the Blue Ridge Parkway.

You could spend the afternoon at the Biltmore Estate, a three-mile drive from downtown. Enjoy the first part of your afternoon at Antler Hill Village for a wine tasting at the Winery, and then lunch at the Bistro, making sure to leave at least three hours to tour the house and gardens before they close at 4:30pm (3:30pm in winter).

EVENING

Head back downtown for the evening, kicking the night off with a pint at Hi-Wire or DSSOLVR, or cocktails from Sovereign Remedies. When you're ready for dinner, try Cucina 24 for Italian, Benne on Eagle for a splendid meal of African diaspora-inspired cuisine, or Mediterranean at Jerusalem Café. Walk dinner off with a stroll—a number of buskers will entertain you. Grab a nightcap at Crave Dessert Bar or a chocolate at French Broad Chocolates. If you're in town on a Friday, check out the drum circle at Pritchard Park.

George Vanderbilt, grandson of Gilded Age elite Cornelius Vanderbilt. Like many of his wealthy Northern contemporaries, George Vanderbilt was first introduced to North Carolina when he traveled to Asheville for the mountain air and nearby hot springs. He found himself so awestruck by the land that he amassed a 125,000-acre tract south of Asheville where he would build his "country home" and enjoy the area's restive and healthful benefits. He engaged celebrity architect Richard Morris Hunt to build the home, and because the land and the views reminded them of the Loire Valley, they planned to build the home in the style of a 16th-century French château. The Biltmore Estate was once the largest privately owned

home in the country. Vanderbilt also hired the esteemed Frederick Law Olmsted, creator of New York City's Central Park, to design the landscape for the grounds, gardens, and surrounding forest, a project nine times the size of the New York park for which he is famous.

A three-mile-long approach road leads through manicured forests, revealing bits of the landscape and hiding the house until you are upon it, creating a sense of drama and wonder for arriving visitors. While the Biltmore Estate's original 125,000 acres are now greatly diminished—the estate comprises a little more than 8,000 acres today—it's easy to see just how big it was; standing on the South Terrace and looking south and west, everything in view was once part of the estate. A large tract of the land was sold to the federal government and has become part of the Pisgah National Forest; what remains is immaculately manicured.

Construction of the home was done primarily between 1888 and 1895, although there were a number of projects that continued up through World War II (when part of the home was turned into a bunker to store part of the National Gallery of Art's collection). Many are astounded at how long it took to complete the home, but think of the house this way: Approximately 5,000 tons of stone were used to build it, there are 65 fireplaces and more than 250 rooms, the square footage is nearly four acres, and they put up a 35-foot Christmas tree in the banquet hall. The numbers don't lie; this is a house unlike any you've been in. Most of the house is open to visitors on self-guided tours, and other parts—like the roof and some servants' areas—are accessible on behind-the-scenes tours. As astounding as this may be, it's nothing compared to the art collected here. There are paintings by Renoir, James Abbott Whistler, and John Singer Sargent; a collection of European antiques including Napoleon's chess set; and room upon room of masterwork in tiling, woodworking and carving, masonry, and stone carving. For its time, the Biltmore was a technological marvel, with electricity, elevators, central heat, and hot water. And we haven't even talked about the basement, where there's a heated pool, a gymnasium, and a bowling alley.

BILTMORE VILLAGE

George Vanderbilt found the concept of a self-sustaining estate appealing, and he included a working farm with crops, herds of cattle, a dairy, and all the farmers and workers required for such an operation. The Asheville neighborhood known as **Biltmore Village** was part of this mountain empire.

If George Vanderbilt stepped onto his estate today, he'd be happy to find that one million people every year come to visit and that his vision of a self-sustaining estate endures. A vineyard (not open to the public) produces grapes that are processed at the estate's winery; a livestock breeding program produces fine stock; and their farm supplies more than 70 percent of seasonal and specialty vegetables to the estate's restaurants. Visitors can eat, shop, tour, explore, relax, and unwind without leaving the grounds, and there's easily enough here to fill a weekend.

The **Biltmore Winery** in **Antler Hill Village,** part of the estate, operates in what was formerly the dairy; check out the industrial-farm rafters in the tasting room. Daily tours and tastings allow visitors to sample some award-winning wines and see how they're made. More than 500,000 people visit the tasting room annually, so expect a wait if you're here in high season.

Antler Hill Village is also home to **Cedric's,** a brewery named after a beloved family dog, as well as a small museum, a souvenir shop, and a green where you can relax. **River Bend Farm** is a beautiful compound that was once the hub of the estate's farming operation but now stands as a showpiece for traditional period crafts like woodworking and blacksmithing.

The **Equestrian Center** gives lessons and the opportunity to ride more than 80 miles of equestrian trails, many with sweeping views of the estate and glimpses of the main house that will take your breath away. Other ways to tour the estate include carriage rides, paved bike trails and mountain bike trails, canoes, kayaks, and rafts (the French Broad River bisects the estate), and on foot. You can even challenge your driving skills at the **Land Rover Experience Driving School.**

Admission cost for the Biltmore Estate varies by season and includes the house, gardens, and winery; activities such as horseback riding, rafting, and behind-the-scenes tours

---

1: architecture in Pack Square Park **2:** the Quilt Garden at the North Carolina Arboretum **3:** view from the Biltmore Estate

cost extra. Special events, like the Christmas Candlelight Tour (Nov.-early-Jan.) also have additional fees. Parking is free, and a complimentary shuttle runs to the house.

Outside Downtown

Outside Downtown is a big area, and I suppose that, technically, everything from the Outer Banks to Paris is Outside Downtown, but we're keeping the focus tight and looking at this as greater Asheville. Pockets of restaurants, boutiques, and breweries have sprung up in different places around town, from the area near the university to the extreme western part of West Asheville to the area between Asheville and Black Mountain. The Blue Ridge Parkway, Botanical Gardens, and Western North Carolina Nature Center are three highlights in this part of town.

BOTANICAL GARDENS

Adjacent to the UNC-Asheville campus, **The Botanical Gardens at Asheville** (151 W. T. Weaver Blvd., 828/252-5190, www.ashevillebotanicalgardens.org, dawn-dusk daily year-round, donation) is a 10-acre preserve for the region's increasingly threatened native plant species. Laid out in 1960 by landscape architect Doan Ogden, the gardens are an ecological haven. The many "rooms" are planted to reflect different environments of the mountains, including the Wildflower Trail, the Heath Cove, and the Fern and Moss Trail. Spring blooms peak in mid-April, but the Gardens are an absolutely lovely and visually rich place to visit any time of year. Because of its serious mission of plant preservation, neither pets nor bicycles are allowed. Admission is free, but as the gardens are entirely supported by donations, your contribution will have a real impact. On the first Saturday in May, the **Day in the Gardens** brings food and music to this normally placid park, and garden and nature enthusiasts from all around come to tour and to buy native plants for their home gardens. There is also a visitors center and gift shop (11am-3pm daily).

WESTERN NORTH CAROLINA NATURE CENTER

Asheville, and western North Carolina generally, tend to be very ecologically conscious, as reflected in the **Western North Carolina Nature Center** (75 Gashes Creek Rd., 828/259-8080, www.wildwnc.org, 10am-4:30pm daily, closed Thanksgiving Day, Dec. 24-25, and Jan. 1, $14 adults, $13 over age 64, $14 ages 13-15, $10 ages 3-12, free under age 3, discounts for locals). On the grounds of an old zoo—don't worry, it's not depressing—wild animals that are unable to survive in the wild due to injury or having been raised as pets live in wooded habitats on public display. This is the place to see some of the mountains' rarest species—those that even most lifelong mountain residents have never seen: cougars, wolves, coyotes, bobcats, and even the elusive hellbender. What's a hellbender, you ask? Come to the Nature Center to find out.

★ FOLK ART CENTER

Anyone with an interest in Appalachian handicrafts and folk or fine art should stop by the **Folk Art Center** (382 Blue Ridge Parkway, Milepost 382, 828/298-7928, www.southernhighlandguild.org, 10am-5pm daily, free). Home to the Southern Highland Craft Guild, the Folk Art Center has around 30,000 square feet of space that includes three galleries, an auditorium, a research library, a tiny Blue Ridge Parkway info booth, and the **Allanstand Craft Shop,** oldest continuously operated craft shop in the United States. It was started in 1897 by a Presbyterian missionary and carries out the same vision it had the year it was born: to help preserve traditional art forms and raise the visibility of the arts and crafts of the Appalachian Mountains. Although the folk arts are well represented in beautiful pottery, baskets, weaving, and quilts, you'll also find the work of contemporary studio artists in an array of media, including gorgeous handcrafted furniture, clothing, jewelry, and toys. Bring your holiday shopping list even if it's April. Every day, one or more members of the Southern Highlands

Craft Guild is on hand to demonstrate their craft at the entrance to the Folk Art Center. They may be whittling away at a chunk of wood with their pocketknife, spinning wool into yarn, weaving, or tying brooms. No matter what they're doing, they're happy to talk to you and explain their process and the history of their craft.

SPORTS AND RECREATION

Asheville's a very active town and it's not unusual to see cars loaded with kayaks, mountain bikes, platform tents, or hauling little camper trailers as folks head off for adventures. With the Blue Ridge Parkway ringing the city to the south and east, with Great Smoky Mountains National Park a short drive away, and with the huge Pisgah National Forest and all its waterfalls and hiking-biking trails, it's no wonder folks use Asheville as a basecamp. But there's plenty to do in town too. The French Broad River is home to kayakers and packs of people floating on tubes. On the Biltmore Estate there are more than 40 miles of hiking and biking trails. And there are tours to take that will lead you to an afternoon of superb food and beer, get you out into lovely parts of town, and give you a better perspective on Asheville and on yourself.

For visitors to Asheville, this city looks like a perfect mountain playground: plenty of hiking and waterfalls and scenery to take in, too many restaurants to visit in a week, art galleries and boutiques and something wonderful to discover everywhere you look. But things haven't always been so rosy, especially not for all of Asheville. One of the most eye-opening and impactful looks I've had at Asheville and its history came courtesy of DeWayne Barton and his **Hood Huggers Tour** (828/275-5305, www.hoodhuggers.com, $25 adults, $15 ages 4-15). Hood Huggers tells the unvarnished story of Black Asheville, from the triumphs and points of pride to the darkest moments and ongoing moves toward equality and Black opportunity. Barton leads three tours, one starting on the Block, the former heart of Black entrepreneurship and enterprise in Asheville (meet at the Foundry Hotel); another on Burton Street, the center of one of the city's oldest Black communities; and the Southside Walking tour focused on Black Commerce. Tours take a couple of hours and lead you to locations where Barton, through stories and photographs, makes the place come alive, tying contemporary issues (like the Black Lives Matter movement) to historic ones (like redlining) to environmental issues (the ways bad policies impact minority communities) and what we can do today to ensure lasting change comes on our watch.

★ Hiking

Ready for mountain air? Join **Blue Ridge Hiking Co.** (70 College St., 828/713-5451, http://blueridgehikingco.com) for a hike. Founder Jennifer Pharr Davis has hiked more than 11,000 miles of long-distance trails and was the first woman to become the overall record holder for fastest through-hike of the Appalachian Trail, hiking all 2,181 miles in 46.5 days. You're not expected to have this kind of trail mobility or backpacking savvy, but Blue Ridge Hiking Co. is there to help you learn to love a hike, long or short. Join them on a private day hike or sunset hike ($190 for 1-3 hikers, $35 per additional hiker), a group half-day hike ($80), a private full-day hike ($290 for 1-3 hikers, $50 per additional hiker), the Brew + Brew hike ($400 for 1-3 hikers, $60 per additional hiker), led by Jennifer's husband, Brew, and ending at some Asheville breweries, or an overnight hike ($300-930). The overnight hikes are often themed—women only, 50- or 60-plus, low intensity, orienteering workshops, high peaks—so pick one from their current calendar or work with the team to create a private overnight trip perfect for you and your group. One of the places the team at Blue Ridge Hiking Co. goes is the little town of Hot Springs north of Asheville. It's easy to access the Appalachian Trail here and to find hikes good for beginners or to challenge trail pros, so they've set up the **Appalachian Trail-er Bunkhouse,** a mobile home turned bunkhouse serving AT hikers, and they have a hiking shuttle (828/622-3319).

Asheville Hiking Tours (828/818-9103, www.ashevillehikingtours.com, $55-119) leads waterfall and Blue Ridge Parkway tours and wildflower and birding walks along trails in the Roan Highlands and other wild places nearby, as well as private guided hikes. In typical years, backpacking trips are also available (starting around $350) and are built around themes like fall color and destination-specific hikes. Their guides are experts in a number of fields—zoology, forest ecology, primitive skills—and are naturalists, storytellers, and experienced backpackers.

Hiking on the **Biltmore Estate** can mean anything from walking the 2.5 miles of mulched paths in the manicured gardens to exploring the hills, meadows, streams, and riverbank on more than 22 miles of trails. None are rugged, so you don't need any special equipment: just water, your camera, and maybe a walking stick. The Outdoor Adventure Center in Antler Hill Village has maps and can help you identify the right hike, or you can join a guided hike ($20 over age 8, free under age 9) along the French Broad River or through Westover Woods.

Zip-Lining

For a different perspective on the Asheville area, head north for 30 minutes along I-26 west and spend the day at **Navitat** (242 Poverty Branch Rd., Barnardsville, 855/628-4828 or 828/626-3700, www.navitat.com, 8am-6pm daily). You can streak through the forest canopy on a pair of zip-line courses like an overgrown flying squirrel. The **Mountaintop Tour** ($110) has the tallest zip line here; it's an incredible 350 feet high—they say "Don't look down," but do; it's amazing. The longest is more than 3,600 feet. Two rappels, a pair of sky bridges, and three short hikes provide interludes from all the zipping and flying, and there are plenty of opportunities for photos and action-camera videos. A smaller course, the **Treetop Tour** ($99) has

six ziplines, rope descents, sky bridges, and timber stair climbs. Or you can **combine the two courses** ($190) into one giant day of adventure. Not down with strapping yourself to a steel cable and hurtling through space? The **Guided RTV Shadow Tour** (from $50) lets you take in the scenery and follow the zippers from the ground, safe and secure in your RTV.

If you're tempted to zip-line but want something a little less heart-pounding, consider **The Adventure Center of Asheville** (85 Expo Dr., 877/247-5539, www.ashevilletreetopsadventurepark.com, check for times). The Adventure Center has a number of high-flying adventures to try. The **Treetops Adventure Park** ($55-76) has 60 challenges (read: rope swings, sky bridges, cargo nets, short zip lines, leaps from tall platforms) spread over five different adventure trails, allowing you to face the trail that presents you with the best challenges. The **Zip Line Canopy Tours** ($69-89) has 11 zips, three sky bridges, and so many great views you'll forget about the zip lines. **Kid Zip** ($55) is a zip-line course designed for children ages 4-10. There's also the **KOLO Mountain Bike Park** ($5-21 if you bring the bike, $20-69 with rental bike and gear), where you can build up your skills before you head out on some of the single-track trails south of town.

Biking

Take a tour of Asheville by bicycle. If you're thinking: "It's too hilly; I'll never be able to climb that," **The Flying Bike** (meeting point 225 Coxe Ave., 828/338-8484, www.flyingbiketours.com, from $59) can provide you with pedal-assisted electric bikes that make the hills easier and the flats seem like nothing at all. You'll still have to work, but not as hard as these ingenious bikes use their power to make pedaling easier. You'll start with the hill to the Grove Park Inn (which will demonstrate how well the pedal-assist system works), the first stop on a three-hour tour around Asheville's historic and cultural sites.

There are more than 20 miles of **bicycle trails** on the Biltmore Estate, and you can bring your bike or rent one in Antler Hill Village from the **Bike Barn** (828/225-1425, 2-hour rentals $20 regular bike, $30 electronic bike, half-day rentals $30 regular bike, $50 electronic bike adults, $20 regular bike under age 13) and lead your own trip. You can also join Biltmore guides for a guided ride on the **Farm Trail** ($35 over age 9, $10 under age 10), on the **West Range Loop** ($100 over age 15), or an **Intro to Mountain Biking** ($75, over age 11 only).

Water Sports

Wai Mauna Asheville SUP Tours (192 Riverside Dr., 828/808-9038, www.waimaunaashevillesuptours.com, rentals from $49, tours $85-99) is a natural fit for Asheville (*wai mauna* is Hawaiian for "mountain waters"). While most SUP outfitters ignore the two most beautiful parts of the day—dawn and dusk—these folks embrace it, with four tours daily at sunrise and sunset, as well as mid-morning and midday. As rave-worthy as sunsets are, there's something about the Dawn Patrol tour. At that time of day, the river is often shrouded in fog, the birds are waking up, and the river is as still as it will ever be; it's a perfect time to paddle. Most tours go through the River Arts District, but you can do a seven-mile trip through the Biltmore Estate, an interesting way to see the estate from a different angle.

Tubing isn't a sport, inasmuch as you simply recline in an inner tube and float from point A to point B, but it's a lot of fun. If you want to go tubing in Asheville, do it with **Zen Tubing** (855/936-8823, www.zentubing.com, trips 10am-3pm, $30). The French Broad is a calm river, especially on the sections where Zen sends their tubers (what else would you call one who rides a tube?). If you pick up a six-pack of your favorite canned (or plastic-bottled) beverage, you'll want the cooler carrier tube so you can keep any snacks and beverages close at hand. Tube trips take a while, but you'll have plenty of company, as the river is mobbed by tube enthusiasts. If you've got a crowd, check out their private

three-hour tour (don't worry, it won't end up like *Gilligan's Island*) aboard the Rasta Turtle (groups of 6-12, $55 pp), a river raft-picnic table hybrid that comes with snacks and a river guide who'll paddle you toward your destination. They have two locations, one in the **River Arts District** (608 Riverside Dr.) and one in **South Asheville** (1648 Brevard Rd.), so check the website or call ahead to see which one will be the best to visit.

French Broad Outfitters (704 Riverside Dr., 828/505-7371, www.frenchbroadoutfitters.com, 10am-6pm daily) rents gear and leads trips along the French Broad River. You can get active and go for a paddle on a 6-mile ($45) or 12-mile ($65) trip that can take you past the Biltmore Estate or the Biltmore and River Arts District (on the longer version); stand-up paddleboards available on some trips. You can paddle all manner of craft ($45-175) through the River Arts District on a 6-mile trip. Or you can just get lazy and float down the river in a tube ($25 over age 12, $12.50 ages 6-12); just don't forget the tube for the beer cooler ($5). You can also rent tubes (from $20), kayaks (from $35), paddleboards (from $45), and canoes (from $50), arrange for storage for you watercraft if you're in town for a while ($1 per day), rent bikes and pedal the greenway (from $30 adults, from $15 children), or rent the camping equipment you need for day trip into the woods or an overnighter (from $10).

Asheville Outdoor Center (521 Amboy Rd., 828/232-1970, www.ashevilleoutdoorcenter.com) rents kayaks ($50 over age 12, $40 ages 8-12, $45 military), tandem kayaks ($100), canoes ($100 for 2 paddlers), rafts ($180 for 4 paddlers, $45 per additional paddler), stand-up paddleboards ($70) and tubes ($20 half-day, $425 full day) to get you out on the water for a seven-mile self-guided tour. They also offer shuttle services ($20 per boat) and parking ($5, river access $5 per boat) if you plan on heading out for a long paddle.

Golf

Play a round at the 18-hole par-70 **Grove Park**

Inn Golf Club (828/252-2711 or 800/438-5800, reserve tee times at www.groveparkinn.com, greens fees $70-140 Mon.-Thurs., $70-155 Fri.-Sun. Apr.-Nov. 15, $77-87 Nov. 16-Mar., discounted rates for junior golfers, rental clubs $55 for 9 holes, $80 for 18 holes), where President Obama played during his 2010 stay. *Golf Digest* named this course one of the top 10 courses that are at least 100 years old, and it plays beautifully. This is a must-play course for serious golfers, not just because the views are spectacular but also because the course contains so much history.

Other Outdoor Activities

The Biltmore is an Orvis-endorsed **fly-fishing school,** and it's an excellent place to learn or hone your technique. Outings include introductory lessons ($125), half-day lessons ($225), kid's fishing outings ($125), a fly-tying class ($100), and full-day guided fishing trips on the French Broad River ($500); no fishing license is required.

For a loud, blood-pumping good time, try **clay target shooting** ($100-750). If you've never handled a shotgun before or have never shot clay targets, the introductory sporting clays lesson will have you on target in no time. For more experienced shooters, two-hour advanced lessons, a sporting clay course, and even full-day shotgun sports clinics will challenge your skills and help you refine them. If you'd still like to shoot at some targets but would rather not shoot a firearm, try archery ($45) and get a little coaching on your stance, pull, and release to see how you do with a bow in your hands. All equipment is provided for your activities on the Biltmore Estate, except your hiking shoes. Stop in at the **Outdoor Adventure Center** (828/225-1425) in Antler Hill Village for the full scoop.

1: zipping on the heart-pounding Blue Ridge Experience at Navitat **2:** floating down the French Broad River with Zen Tubing

ENTERTAINMENT AND EVENTS

Nightlife

★ LIVE MUSIC

Great live music is the rule rather than the exception in Asheville, in the form of national touring acts as well as regional and local bands that give them stiff competition for audiences on any given night. It seems that everywhere you turn in this town, you'll find live musicians—buskers playing on street corners, solo guitarists in cafés, or a bluegrass trio set up on a restaurant deck. Follow the sound of drums to **Pritchard Park** (Patton Ave. at Haywood St. and College St.), where a huge drum circle forms every Friday night. There are also formal music venues where you can hear rock, jam bands, bluegrass, funk, blues, country, rockabilly, alt-country, mountain swing, old-time music, and electronica.

A favorite spot for live music is the **Orange Peel Social Aid and Pleasure Club** (101 Biltmore Ave., 828/398-1837, www.theorangepeel.net, noon-midnight or later daily). The Orange Peel is a cool concert hall with a big dance floor, great sound, and great history. It's billed as "the nation's premier live music hall and concert venue," and can back that up with some powerful acts taking the stage, including Bob Dylan, Smashing Pumpkins, Shovels and Rope, Ministry, Lettuce, The Wood Brothers, Girl in Red, Joe Russo's Almost Dead, Beach House, Bon Iver, and My Morning Jacket.

Asheville has another super cool music venue: **Rabbit Rabbit** (75 Coxe Ave., 828/255-4077, www.rabbitrabbitavl.com) Acts like Trey Anastasio Band, King Gizzard & the Lizard Wizard, Band of Horses, Bright Eyes, Sylvan Esso, and stand-up comedy shows frequent this spot, as do food trucks. On nights when there's not a big act in town, you'll find trivia, silent cinema, and silent discos (where attendees wear headphones), and of course the house kitchen dishing up tacos, burritos, and the like ($3-9).

Because you can't have too many places to see live music, there's also the **Salvage Station** (468 Riverside Dr., 828/707-8902,

ASHEVILLE

www.salvagestation.com), a salvage yard turned music venue. A big outdoor stage and lawn and a smaller indoor stage and setup give you plenty of space to spread out for a show. They've got a restaurant on-site, **Root Down Kitchen** (www.salvagestation.com, open during shows, $3-13), selling New Orleans-inspired food-truck grub with vegetarian, vegan, and gluten free options; several full bars, featuring loads of Asheville beers, keep the libations flowing. Acts include The String Cheese Incident, Doom Flamingo, and Goose as well as the **Brewgrass Music Festival** (www.brewgrassfestival.com) in fall.

WINE AND COCKTAILS

Asheville has a growing reputation as a craft-cocktail destination to match its food renown, and one big contributor to that movement is **Sovereign Remedies** (29 N. Market St., 828/919-9518, www.sovereignremedies.com, 5pm-10pm Wed.-Sun.). The minute it opened its doors, it became a go-to for Asheville's cocktail lovers and those hankering for de-licious food ($9-35). It serves dinner most nights, brunch on weekends, and light bites in between. Between the bartenders and some local foragers, Sovereign Remedies stays stocked with wild herbs, berries, fruits, and roots, used to infuse or macerate various li-quors and craft bitters and to create drink-ing vinegars. If it's not busy, have a seat and chat with the bartenders, and challenge them to create tasty drinks for you based around a certain spirit.

Taste natural wines and ciders at **Botanist & Barrel** (32 Broadway St., Suite 110, 828/338-9516, www.botanistandbarrelasheville.com, 1pm-8pm Mon.-Fri., 11am-8pm Sat.-Sun., $2-50) where they keep more than two dozen on hand to taste and another 300 or so bottles from across the state and the South. Natural wine or cider, which you'll sometimes see marked *pét-nat*, is a light sparkling drink that gets the fizz from the bottling process (they bottle it before the first fermentation is finished, so the natural carbon dioxide re-leased as fermentation is trapped in the bottle,

giving it the bubbles), and here they have a great selection if you're already keen on this type of wine or if you need or order a flight and learn the ropes. So order up a flight and some snacks to go with it—bowls of olives or chips, platters of dairy or vegan cheese, sand-wiches, even tinned seafood or a tinned sea-food tower, and you can add caviar ($75) if you're feeling fancy.

Over at **The Barksdale** (42 Banks Ave., 828/424-7449, 3:30pm-2am daily, $3-6), Asheville's, well, Asheville side, is on display. Quirky, friendly, weird, and certainly in full grasp of its own personality, The Barksdale is one of those places you were going to end up anyway, so why not start the evening here? They serve hot dogs named after former pro wrestlers and topped with odd toppings (fried pickle and ranch seasoned popcorn, kimchi chowchow and white Korean barbecue sauce, a dusting of blue and red Takis tortilla chips) and that, if anything, is a good indication of what's happening here.

Grab a cocktail—classic or modern—at **Top of the Monk** (92 Patton Ave., 828/254-5470, www.thirsty-monk-brewery.square.site, 4pm-10pm Sun.-Mon., 4pm-11pm Wed.-Sat.), where they've got a massive library of whis-key (this may be the biggest whiskey library in Asheville, and if it's not the biggest, it's in the top three) and some amazing views of downtown and the mountains in the distance. Cocktails are great, the view is excellent, and the people have always been awesome. This place is trying to keep it small and intimate, so if you're in a big group—more than seven people—know they discourage large parties after 7pm on weekends; oh, and as they say on the website, "no hootin' 'n' hollerin'!" If you're more in the mood for beer, head downstairs to the original **Thirsty Monk & Delirium Bar** (4pm-10pm Thurs., noon-midnight Fri.-Sat., 2pm-9pm Sun.), a two-story bar where the first floor focuses on domestic and local beers, and the downstairs Delirium Bar that has a Belgian focus.

Asheville has North Carolina's old-est gay bar, **o.henry's** (237 Haywood St.,

828/254-1891, www.ohenrysofasheville.com, 4pm-2am daily). A landmark unto itself, o.henry's hosts drag shows on Saturday, throws a potluck on the first Sunday of the month, and does Karaoke on Wednesday. They also have **The Underground,** an industrial dance bar known for its "Total Gold Dance Your Ass Off" parties held the first Friday of the month. If you want more drag shows to attend, **Scandals Nightclub** (11 Grove St., 828/505-1612, www.scandals-nightclub.com, 10pm-2:30am Fri.-Sat.) has your back. Drag shows with known queens and up-and-comers plus DJ-led dance parties make it a raucous spot all weekend.

Travel writers get all sorts of tips from friends and readers, and I found **The Crow & Quill** (106 N. Lexington Ave., 828/505-2866, www.thecrowandquill.com, 5pm-midnight Tues.-Sun.) through just such a recommendation—and am I ever glad I listened. It stocks nearly 1,000 spirits, and the wizards behind the bar know how to use every one of them. The cocktails are superb, the space is lively (you might catch some live music here), and everywhere you look there's some interesting bit of art. Note that at least one member of your party will have to become a member of The Crow & Quill, and pay a small membership fee ($10)—North Carolina has some rigid laws regarding spirits, and technically only private clubs are permitted serve them. Buy a drink for whoever ponies up.

BREWERIES

Asheville earned the title Beer City USA for several years running and has been a contender for the title in subsequent years. It seems there's a brewery on every corner, or one planning to open there next month, and brewers are getting experimental, introducing new styles, funky ingredients, and any little twist they can to get people talking. And they do; loyal locals and pint hounds from all over frequent the bars, breweries, and pubs here.

Hi-Wire Brewing (www.hiwirebrewing.com) came into Asheville with one location on the **South Slope** (197 Hilliard Ave.,

828/738-2452, 3pm-10pm Mon.-Thurs., 3pm-midnight Fri., noon-midnight Sat., noon-10pm Sun.), called the **Big Top** (2 Huntsman Place, 3pm-10pm Mon.-Fri., noon-midnight Sat., noon-9pm Sun.) near Biltmore Village, and a third, the **RAD Beer Garden** (284 Lyman St., 828/738-2454, 3pm-10pm Mon.-Fri., noon-10pm Sat., noon-9pm Sun.), in the River Arts District. They focus on lagers, pale ales, and IPAs, and I quite like their American Lager, the Bed of Nails brown ale, and the Lo-Pitch IPA.

Burial Beer Co. (40 Collier Ave., 828/475-2739, www.burialbeer.com, noon-11pm daily) is a favorite biergarten spaces in Asheville, and they have an Instagram-worthy mural of Sloth from *The Goonies* and Magnum P.I. on one wall of the brewery. And then their beers. Start with the names—The Fortress of Immaculate Thought, A Portal Into Infinite Nonexistence, Mythologies of Realism—they're improbably weird but perfectly fit the brews. Now, for what's in the glass; Burial isn't afraid of any style or flavor, so you'll find s'mores-inspired barrel aged imperial stouts; rich double IPAs infused with wine grapes or peaches and mangoes; IPAs with orange or pineapple sage; and coffee saisons.

Colorado's **New Belgium Brewing Company** (21 Craven St., 828/333-6900, www.newbelgium.com, noon-8pm Thurs.-Mon., tours every hour on the half hour11:30am-4:30pm Thurs.-Mon.) found an East Coast home in Asheville. It sits across the French Broad from the River Arts District and has great views. It is bikeable and very bike-friendly, and their brews on offer go beyond Fat Tire and the other cans you find in stores. They show off their top-notch barrel-aging program with a slate of ever-changing and always-delicious brews like their Carnie Blood Golden Sour, Transalantique Kriek, and La Folie Sour Flanders Ale.

DSSOLVR (63 N. Lexington Ave., Asheville, 4pm-10pm Mon.-Thurs., 1pm-11pm Fri., 11am-11pm Sat., 11am-9pm Sun.) says they're more than just a brewery, they're a beverage company, and given what you find on their tap list, they're making good on that promise. A kölsch and schwarzbier share menu space with a foraged fruit-laden wild cider, a double dry-hopped hazy IPA, funky aged IPAs, fruited sours, and more. They've got a cellar dedicated to funky and wild brews, a tiny brewhouse where they can experiment, and their regular production brewhouse. It all makes for a wildly delicious stop on your beer tour. With a heated patio, they're a great visit anytime you're in town.

In West Asheville (conveniently across the street from one of my favorite restaurants, The Admiral), **Cellarest Beer Project** (395 Haywood Rd., www.cellarestbeer.com, 5pm-9pm Mon.-Thurs., noon-10pm Fri.-Sat., noon-8pm Sun.) serves barrel-rested beer imbued with and inspired by local ingredients. They capture wild yeast to pitch into their farmhouse-inspired beers and serve everything from tart and tasty wild ales to Vienna lagers to golden farmhouse ales, IPAs, and some delightful blended farmhouse brews. Their outdoor space is spacious and hip, and if you're hungry, **West Asheville Lounge and Kitchen** (401 Haywood Rd., 828/505-7929, 11:30am-10pm Mon.-Thurs., 11:30am-11pm Fri.-Sat., 10:30am-10pm Sun., $3-15) is right next door and serves plenty of food to Cellarest customers, so you can pick up some chips and salsa, wings, chicken tendies, *queso* fries, or a big sandwich and wash it down with a beer or two.

Also in Mills River is **Burning Blush Brewery** (4891 Boylston Hwy., Mills River, 828/595-9859, www.burningblush.com, noon-9pm Mon.-Thurs., noon-10pm Fri.-Sat., noon-8pm Sun.), a spot recommended to me by a brewer friend and one I've come to love. Their beers are on point in terms of style and flavor, so whether you're going for their Helles, a rice and corn American lager, their Belgian Amber Strong, or something like a juicy or double IPA, you'll find an exemplary beer in your glass.

Asheville's oldest brewery, **Highland Brewing** (12 Old Charlotte Hwy., Suite 200, 828/299-3370, www.highlandbrewing.com,

2pm-9pm Mon.-Thurs., noon-10pm Fri.-Sat., noon-7pm Sun.) poured their first pint back in 1994, beginning to build a reputation that's made them one of the best and most consistent breweries in North Carolina in addition to being one of the first crop of breweries to spring up in the state. Visiting their taproom is an experience. They have a large meadow with a stage and bar where you can catch a show or have a picnic (or both), and there are volleyball courts, a hiking trail, and a disc golf course. The taproom pours all the flagship (the Gaelic Ale was Asheville's first beer, but I'm partial to the pilsner and High Pines Imperial IPA) and seasonal brews (October's Clawhammer Marzen is a favorite) as well as a frequently rotating list of experimental brews. They have an additional taproom downtown in **S&W Market** (56 Patton Ave., 3pm-8:30pm Tues.-Thurs., 11:30am-9pm Fri.-Sat., 3pm-7pm Sun.), with a small bar downstairs and a larger, showier bar upstairs where you'll find more taps and more room to spread out and enjoy yourself.

One of my favorite ways to get to know a city's food or beer scene is to join a tour. Asheville, naturally, has several to choose from, the best being **Asheville Brewery Tours** (828/233-5006, www.ashevillebrewerytours.com, Wed.-Sun.). Asheville Brewery Tours offers three ways to see the city: their Downtown "Brew & Chew" Walking tour ($89, $49 nondrinker) to eight places, including four breweries; the Downtown 3-Brewery Walking Tour ($69, $29 nondrinker), which is exactly what it sounds like; and the Mobile Brewery Tour (inquire for prices), where they drive you around for an afternoon of beer tasting. They also book private three-brewery ($79 pp) and four-brewery ($89 pp) tours. They visit a lot of the breweries I've already mentioned on their tours, along with **Archetype Brewing** (www.archetypebrewing.com, 174 Broadway St., 828/505-8305, 5pm-9pm Mon.-Wed., 5pm-10pm Thurs., 4pm-8pm Sun; 265 Haywood Rd., West Asheville, 828/505-4177, 3pm-9pm Mon.-Thurs., 1pm-10pm Fri., 11am-10pm Sat., 11am-8pm Sun.), **Oyster House**

Brewing Company (625 Haywood Rd., West Asheville, 828/575-9370, www.oysterhouse-beers.com, 3pm-11pm Mon.-Fri., 11am-11pm Sat.-Sun.), and others.

Beer lovers should absolutely pick up some bottles and cans while they're at the brewery, but the bottle shop to check out is **Appalachian Vintner** (745 Biltmore Ave., 828/505-7500, www.appalachianvintner.com, 11am-7pm Mon.-Sat.). Their selection of beer ranges from hard-to-find European bottles (like Vichtenaar, my favorite beer ever) to the best of craft beer from across the United States, and that means plenty of representation from Asheville and from North Carolina. Not sure what you want? Strike up a conversation with the folks in the shop and let them lead you to a tasty discovery or two.

Comedy

Around Asheville you may notice a giant purple bus zipping through the streets, laughter and bubbles (yes, bubbles) coming from the windows. That's the **LaZoom Comedy Tour** (76 Biltmore Ave., 828/225-6932, www.lazoomtours.com, $39, minimum age 13), delivering tours big in history and hilarity. The tour guides are outrageous—they're some of Asheville's weirdest (in a good way) people—and I guarantee you'll learn a thing or two: some history, a joke you may or may not want to tell your mom. They also offer Ghosted: Haunted Comedy Tour ($37), which adds in a supernatural note and tales of some of Asheville's spectral denizens, and the Fender Bender: Band & Beer Bus Tour ($49) visits a trio of area breweries for samples and some live music from local performers. In 2022 they added the Li'l Boogers: Kids Comedy Tour ($27) a hilarious all-ages tour, perfect for the funny kids, the ones who get caught in a fit of giggles, the performers, and the silly.

Performing Arts

As an artsy town, Asheville has a lively theater and dance community. **Terpsicorps Theatre of Dance** (www.terpsicorps.org), a professional dance company and school, puts on a number of shows a year, as does **Asheville Ballet** (www.ashevilleballet.com), which puts on *The Nutcracker* every year. **NC Stage Company** (828/239-0263, www.ncstage.org) performs many times throughout the year, staging contemporary, classic, and holiday performances, and **Asheville Community Theatre** (www.ashevilletheatre.org) draws on the deep well of talent in town to put on performances like *Avenue Q, Footloose, Alice in Wonderland,* and other surprising shows.

Festivals

In mid-October, the Southern Highland Craft Guild hosts the **Craft Fair of the Southern Highlands** (Harrah's Cherokee Center, 87 Haywood St., 828/298-7928, www.southern-highlandguild.org, 10am-6pm Thurs.-Sat., 10am-5pm Sun., $10 adults, free under age 12). Since 1948 this event has brought much-deserved attention to the guild's more than 900 members, who live and work throughout the Appalachian Mountains. Hundreds of craftspeople participate in the event, selling all sorts of handmade items. This event used to happen twice a year, with an additional in-person event in late July, but with pandemic-related precautions in place, it has been scaled back, and the July event has moved online, though there are plans to return to the pair of in-person events soon.

Probably the biggest of Asheville's festivals and fairs, or at least the most anticipated, is the annual **Warren Haynes Christmas Jam** (www.xmasjam.com). Warren Haynes, long-time guitarist for the Allman Brothers Band, founding member of Government Mule, and Asheville native, invites a who's who of musical acts to come perform a benefit concert for Habitat for Humanity. The acts are generally biggies in the rock-jam world and bands on the rise.

Asheville's **Restaurant Week** (www.ashevillerestaurantweek.com) generally takes place in late January. Given the city's food scene, it's a great opportunity to score some delicious meals at a bit of a discount; usually restaurants offer a prix fixe menu for $15-30.

George Vanderbilt's Great Outdoors

The thing that drew George Vanderbilt to Asheville was the mountain air and glories of nature that surround this place. The **Biltmore Estate** was once a huge estate of some 125,000 acres, almost every bit of it untamed. Frederick Law Olmsted worked to groom the forest around the house, the same forest you see when you drive onto the estate, but the rest was left to be a sort of natural playground. Today visitors can play in the forests, fields, trails, and waters of the Biltmore Estate and try their hand at sports and activities from the familiar (bicycling) to the exotic (the Land Rover Experience Driving School). **The Adventure Center** (828/225-1425) in **Antler Hill Village** can make reservations and point you in the right direction for any number of outdoor activities.

The 22 miles of hiking and biking trails take you all across the estate, from Antler Hill Village to the house and gardens and back. Paved and wooded trails allow all experience levels to get out and ride, run, or hike. You're free to explore the hiking trails at no cost, but you can join guided hikes ($20 over age 8, free under age 9) of the Westover Woods and a stroll along the French Broad River. Rent a bike (from $10 per hour) or bring your own and explore the 20-plus miles of bike trails on the estate. Guided rides along the Farm Trail ($35 over age 9, $10 under age 10) and the West Range Loop ($100 over age 15), and an Intro to Mountain Biking class ($75 over age 11) are great ways to spend some time in the saddle and see a new side of the Biltmore.

Equine enthusiasts can saddle up for an hour-long guided ride ($75), a two-hour private trail ride ($195), or a private trail ride and picnic lunch ($230). If you'd rather sit back and ride, there are carriage rides ($350 up to 4 people) and wagon rides (from $35) too.

If you'd rather spend the day on the water, you can. Guided raft trips ($30) and self-guided kayak trips ($30) on the French Broad give you a rare view of the estate, while a day on the water fly-fishing gives you a different experience altogether. Novice anglers may want a lesson (from $125, children's lessons available), but experienced anglers will opt for a day-long wade trip or drift boat trip ($500).

For something really adventurous, try learning to shoot sporting clays. If you've never handled a firearm, don't worry; they've got lessons ($100-247), and they'll have you knocking clay pigeons out of the sky in no time. There's also a Sporting Clay course ($100) and a full-day shotgun sports clinic ($750). Then there's the Land Rover Driving Experience. Get behind the wheel of a Land Rover and get a lesson ($275 for 1 hour, $425 for 2 hours) on off-road driving. After your lessons, go out for a full day ($1,200) and master those off-road skills while exploring a seldom-seen side of the estate property.

The one-day **Beer City Festival** (www.beercityfestival.com) in late-May or early-June makes for a great way to celebrate the start of summer and hear some live music while sampling some brews from across the region.

See the gardens and grounds at Biltmore when they're in truly show-stopping form at **Biltmore Blooms** (www.biltmore.com, Apr.-May). One look at the gardens and you'll think there are billions of bulbs and bushes blooming, and you're probably not far off. Tulips, orchids, azaleas, and hundreds of roses, vines, locals, and exotics are at their showiest, making it a perfect time to visit the estate. Biltmore has events throughout the year, the biggest of which is **Christmas at Biltmore** and the **Candlelight Christmas Evenings** (early-Nov.-early-Jan.), which sees the home decorated for an 1895 Christmas complete with carolers and performers, candlelight tours, and more.

Asheville's home to **Chow Chow** (www.chowchowasheville.com, tickets $15-150), a food festival celebrating the flavors of Southern Appalachia. The city's biggest chefs and culinary personalities were joined by noted guest chefs Jose Andreas, Vivian Howard, Ashley Christensen and others for demos, tastings, charity dinners, and swank soirees. It's a great opportunity to taste outstanding dishes and meet some culinary legends. The festival takes place June-September with a calendar chock-full of events small and large. Check them out, pick a time packed with things to do, get your tickets, and go.

Hi-Wire Brewing's **NC Small Batch Festival** (www.hiwirebrewing.com, $10) brings a couple dozen North Carolina breweries to Hi-Wire's Big Top location in mid-March for a delightfully odd one-day beer fest. Breweries can only bring a small one-off batch to sample—no flagships, nothing you can get in the taproom, nothing folks outside the brewhouse have tasted. You'll be in for some interesting samples from some of the state's most progressive breweries.

In June, **GRINDfest** (www.blackwallstreetavl.com), a three-day festival celebrating Juneteenth, brings Black entrepreneurs and artists together for a community-wide event featuring a poetry slam, a lip-synch battle, food vendors, artists and craftspeople, and folks there to get the folks excited about and engaged. September sees some 20,000 people celebrating at the **Blue Ridge Pride Festival** (www.blueridgepride.org), where there's a parade, a street fair, a gender identity-inclusive pageant, and all sorts of mixers, storytelling events, gatherings, and performances built around championing the diversity and accomplishments of western North Carolina's LGBTQ+ community.

Combine your love for beer and bluegrass music at the Salvage Station's **Brewgrass Music Festival** (www.brewgrassfestival.com) in early October, when Asheville is stunning thanks to the autumn leaf show. It's a full day of music with indoor and outdoor stages and plenty of room to spread out, sample some suds, and start tapping your toes to that high, lonesome sound of banjos, fiddles, and flat-picked guitars.

The **Mountain Dance and Folk Festival** (828/258-6101, ext. 345, www.folkheritage. org, $25 adults, $5 students and under age 12) is the nation's longest-running folk festival, an event founded in the 1920s by musician and folklorist Bascom Lamar Lunsford to celebrate the heritage of his native Carolina mountains. Musicians and dancers from western North Carolina perform at the UNC Asheville Lipinsky Hall for three nights each August. Also downtown, many of the same artists can be heard on Saturday evening at the city's **Shindig on the Green** concert series (Pack Square Park, 80 Court Plaza), a music bonanza that's been going on since 1967.

SHOPPING
Antiques

For lovers of vintage, retro and aged things, the **Antique Tobacco Barn** (75 Swannanoa River Rd., 828/252-7291, www.atbarn.com, 10am-6pm daily) has more than 77,000 square feet of goodies to plunder. This perpetual winner of the *Mountain XPress* "Best Antiques Store in Western North Carolina" category has toys, art, tools, furniture, radios, sporting equipment, folk art, farm relics, oddball bric-a-brac, mid-century furniture, and all those great weird things you can only find in a collection this large. It takes a while to explore this humongous shop, so carve out some time.

Sweeten Creek Antiques and Collectables (115 Sweeten Creek Rd., 828/277-6100, 10:30am-5:30pm Mon.-Sat., noon-5:30pm Sun.) and **Screen Door** (115 Fairview Rd., 828/277-3667, www.screendoorasheville.com, 10am-5pm Mon.-Sat., noon-5pm Sun.) offer a wide selection as their vendors and pickers number in the hundreds. Somewhere in the 36,000 square feet of re-purposed and rediscovered treasures in **The Regeneration Station** (26 Glendale Ave., 828/505-1108, www.regenerationstation.com, 10am-6pm Mon.-Sat., 10am-5pm Sun.), you'll find the thing you're looking for whether it's a hip light fixture, a cool industrial relic that'll be perfect on your bookshelf, signage, or some piece of esoterica. The Regeneration Station was born from the useful excess one of the owners found in their other business, a junk removal company; storing up the best of his finds, it wasn't long before crafty and like-minded folks joined in and began to breathe new life into these old pieces and this excellent spot was born.

Along Swannanoa River Rd., you'll find yourself in the **Biltmore Antiques District** (120 Swannanoa Rd.), a small shopping district that's packed with an intriguing group of antiques shops. Some specialize in imports, others in lamps, European furniture, or fine jewelry. Exploring here is always a good time because you never know what you'll find or where you'll find it.

Galleries

One of Asheville's shopping highlights is the 1929 **Grove Arcade** (1 Page Ave., 828/252-7799, www.grovearcade.com), a beautiful and storied piece of architecture that is now a chic shopping and dining destination in the heart of downtown. The expansive Tudor Revival building, ornately filigreed inside and out in ivory-glazed terra-cotta, was initially planned as the base of a 14-story building, a skyscraper by that day's standard. There are some fantastic galleries and boutiques, including **Mountain Made** (828/350-0307, www. mtnmade.com, 10am-6pm Mon.-Sat., noon-5pm Sun.), a gallery celebrating contemporary art created in and inspired by the mountains around Asheville. Another favorite is **Alpaca Wawa** (828/505-0048, www.alpacawawa.com, 11am-6pm daily), a shop loaded with beautiful alpaca wool and pima cotton goods. Pick up some alpaca, llama, angora, or other yarn (most from local fiber-bearing animals) at **Asheville NC Home Crafts** (828/350-7556, www.ashevillehomecrafts.com, 10am-6pm Mon.-Sat., noon-5pm Sun.). There are more stores and restaurants to discover in Grove Arcade, so grab a little shop directory and sit down at **Battery Park Champagne Bar** (828/252-0020, 11am-9pm Mon.-Thurs., 11am-10pm Fri.-Sat., $3-25) to figure out your next move. Battery Park has two things that go great together: wine and books. And they serve food to share as well as sandwiches and salads, all in a really relaxed atmosphere. Outside the Grove Arcade is a row of shaded stalls, and it's here that you'll find many of

the best sell-it-on-the-street artisans selling things like soap, miniature topiaries you can wear as a necklace, and fine-art prints.

I own and have gifted several prints from **Horse and Hero** (14 Patton Ave., 828/505-2133, www.horseandhero.com, 11am-7pm Sun.-Thurs., 11am-9pm Fri.-Sat.), a gallery that's developed a niche in Neo-Appalachian art and crafts. Woodblock prints, lithographs, digital prints, stickers, cards, shirts, and even sculptural pieces that can only be described as contemporary riffs on traditional Appalachian art make it an intriguing place to browse and buy.

There are a number of galleries in downtown Asheville, and while most of them exhibit works from multiple artists, none can match the size of the **Woolworth Walk** (25 Haywood St., 828/254-9234, www.woolworth-walk.com, 11am-6pm Mon.-Sat., 11am-5pm Sun.), a two-story 20,000-square-foot gallery featuring more than 160 local artists. Nearly every conceivable medium is represented, including digitally designed graphic prints, oil paintings, watercolors, jewelry, and woodworking. This gallery is a favorite not just because it has a soda fountain but because the work on display is affordable and tasteful.

Working to keep the folkways, crafts, and artistic traditions of the Southern Appalachians relevant and thriving, the **Southern Highlands Crafts Guild** (www. southernhighlandguild.org) operates several galleries in the Asheville region, the most well-known of which is the **Allanstand Gift Shop** (382 Blue Ridge Pkwy., 828/298-7928, 10am-5pm daily), at the Folk Art Center on the Blue Ridge Parkway, but the gallery in **Biltmore Village** (26 Lodge St., 828/277-6222, 10am-5pm Mon.-Sat., noon-5pm Sun.) is outstanding. Housed in an old bank building, the gallery is almost as pleasing as the art and crafts inside. For sale here are quilts in traditional and new patterns; hand-woven baskets and brooms made in the traditional fashion; pens, bowls, boxes, sculptures, and vessels whittled, carved, and turned by woodworkers; plus pottery, paintings, and other works of art. Whether you're looking for a gift or a new piece for your home, you'll find gorgeous work in every case and on every wall.

Just off Pack Square, **Noir Collective** (39 S. Market St., Suite C, 828/484-2323, www. noircollectiveavlllc.business.site, 11am-4pm Wed.-Sat.) celebrates black artists and makers in their small boutique and gallery space. Asheville artists like Jenny Pickens have paintings and prints hanging here and at other galleries around town, and you'll find a selection of Afro-centric shirts, masks, jewelry, art, and goods on the walls and shelves. The space is a significant one as it sits on the Block, the onetime center for Black entrepreneurism and culture in Asheville, and it's good to see this and other Black-owned businesses returning.

Books, Toys, and Crafts

One of the social hubs of this city is **Malaprop's Bookstore and Café** (55 Haywood St., 800/441-9829, www.malaprops. com, 10am-6pm Mon.-Sat., 11am-4pm Sun.). This fun and progressive bookstore carries a deep selection of books that includes tomes by North Carolina authors and a particularly fine collection of regional authors. You'll find the requisite coffee bar and café with wireless internet access, making it a particularly good spot to hang out. It's bright and comfortable, and the staff are well versed in all sorts of literature, so they can help you find a local author you'll enjoy reading. People in all walks of Asheville life come to Malaprop's, so expect to see creative dressers, the tattooed, business types, artists, students, and grannies. They always keep signed copies on hand, and when authors like Wiley Cash, Taylor Brown, David Joy, and other North Carolina writers stop in for a reading, they leave behind a stack of autographed copies (I've been known to swoop in and sign a shelf full of books too), so look for those special signed books and check out their schedule to see if a writer you love is in town for a talk or reading while you're in Asheville.

Given that Asheville is in the middle of some mountains loaded with semiprecious and precious gems, and that the town has a general hippie, crunchy, recharge-your-crystals-at-the-full-moon vibe, there are some excellent gem and crystal shops in town. The crystals are cool, but I'm drawn to the fossils—of fish, sea stars, plants, even teeth and claws and shells—on display and on sale. A favorite that my wife and I visit every time we're in town is **Cornerstone Minerals** (52 N. Lexington Ave., 828/225-3888, www. cornerstoneminerals.com, 11am-7pm Sun.-Mon., 11am-9pm Tues.-Thurs., 11am-9pm Fri.-Sat.) because I like to stare at their sheets of fossil-imbued stone, and my wife always finds some cool bauble here. There are huge, and breathtakingly beautiful crystals and geodes to admire and take home (if you don't mind an overweight carry-on bag) at **Points of Light Crystal and Mineral Gallery** (391 Merrimon Ave., 828/257-2626, www.point-soflight.net, 10:30am-6pm Mon.-Sat.), just a few minutes north of downtown. The selection here is very well curated, meaning everything from their orbs, balls, bowls, and huge decorative crystals to their sculpted pieces and mineral specimens to their jewelry and crystal clusters are of the utmost quality.

The **Mast General Store** (15 Biltmore Ave., 828/232-1883, www.mastgeneralstore. com, 10am-6pm Mon.-Thurs., 10am-7pm Fri.-Sat., 11am-6pm Sun.) is an institution in western North Carolina and beyond. They call themselves a general store, but they mean it in a very contemporary way. Cast-iron cookware, penny candies, and Mast logo shirts and jackets sit alongside baskets and handmade crafts. A good selection of outdoor clothing and equipment can get you outfitted for some time in the woods, or you can fill up a bag with candy and eat it while you drive the Blue Ridge Parkway—your call.

Dancing Bear Toys (518 Kenilworth Rd., 800/659-8697, www.dancingbeartoys.com, 10am-6pm Mon.-Sat.) is located among the motels and chain restaurants out on U.S. 70 (Tunnel Rd.), but inside it has the ambience of a cozy village toy shop. Dancing Bear has toys for everyone from babies to silly grown-ups: a fabulous selection of Playmobil figures and accessories, Lego, Brio, and other favorite lines of European toys; beautiful stuffed animals of all sizes; all sorts of educational kits and games; and comical doodads.

Asheville's creative streak doesn't stop with the visual and performing arts. The culinary arts scene is the envy of the state, and that includes the sort of packaged foodstuffs made by passionate locals that allow you to take a bite of Asheville home with you. You'll find a handpicked selection of tasty culinary treats at Asheville Goods (7 Brevard Rd., 828/252-9175, www.ashevillegoods. com, 10:30am-2:20pm Tues.-Thurs., by appointment Mon.-Fri.), in West Asheville near Biscuit Head (it's convenient: eat a giant biscuit, then do a little shopping after). They also do gift baskets and boxes with preassembled options and some custom options.

Several gift shops are of the "I went there and got this cool T-shirt" variety, but being Asheville, most of the shirts and Asheville-emblazoned gear is actually good. At Instant Karma Asheville (36 N. Lexington Ave., 828/301-8187, www.instantkarmaasheville. com, 9am-7pm Sun.-Thurs., 9am-8pm Fri.-Sat.) it's a combo kitsch, hippie, college-kid souvenir shop where you can pick up a fridge magnet proclaiming some witty barb, a Grateful Dead shirt, a vegan-leather bag, and some incense. On Wall Street, Asheville Emporium (35 Wall St., 828/785-5722, www. asheville-emporium.com, 9:30am-6pm Mon.-Thurs., 10am-8:30pm Fri.-Sat., 9am-5:30pm Sun.) they have the touristy T-shirts plus handmade gifts, gourmet treats, and home goods made by local artisans. And at Madam Clutterbucket's Neurodiverse Universe (21 Battery Park Ave., Suite 101, 828/552-3013, www.madamclutterbuckets.com, 11am-7pm Sun.-Mon. and Wed.-Thurs., 11am-8pm Fri.-Sat.) you'll find some vintage goods (quirky glassware, weird ashtrays, and little decorative pieces) and weird items in a store that prides itself in employing neurodivergent individuals.

★ River Arts District

You can get your hands dirty, so to speak, in the River Arts District as some places offer hands-on art experiences. The North Carolina Glass Center (140 Roberts St., Suite C, 828/505-3552, www.ncglasscenter. org, 10am-5pm Sun.-Mon. and Wed.-Thurs., 10am-6pm Fri.-Sat.), a hot shop (that's a glass studio, so called because the place is full of furnaces and kilns) open to budding artists and the folks curious about making art out of glass. Classes range from 30-minute "make it and take it" classes ($65-80), where you might make a glass or paperweight, to half-day workshops ($200) to multi-week courses ($835) where you learn the ins and outs of the art. They also have a gallery stocked with objects made by the artists here. Odyssey Center for Ceramic Arts (236 Clingman Ave., www.odysseyclayworks.com, 10am-6pm daily, co-op gallery 11am-5pm Fri.-Sun.) is full of sculptors and teachers. Part of their mission is to promote artistic appreciation and the advancement of ceramic arts; they hold regular classes, workshops, and talks led by master ceramic artists.

Marquee (36 Foundry St., 828/989-1069, www.marqueeasheville.com, 10am-5pm Mon.-Sat., 11am-5pm Sun.) seeks to blend Asheville's vibrant creative spirit and the feel of a European street market, and though they're in a big warehouse, they manage to pull it off. Great home decor, eclectic vendors, and 50,000 square feet of booths and studios to explore make this a natural stop in the River Arts District. At the 1910 Cotton Mill Studios (122 Riverside Dr., www.cottonmillasheville.com, hours vary), several painters work alongside potters and jewelers. Riverview Station (191 Lyman St., www. riverviewstation.com, hours vary) is a circa-1896 building that houses the studios of a wonderful array of jewelers, ceramicists, furniture designers, painters, and photographers. Another favorite gallery is CURVE Studios & Gardens (3 River Arts Place, 828/388-3526, www.curvestudiosnc.com, most studios 11am-4pm Mon.-Sat.). A fun funky studio

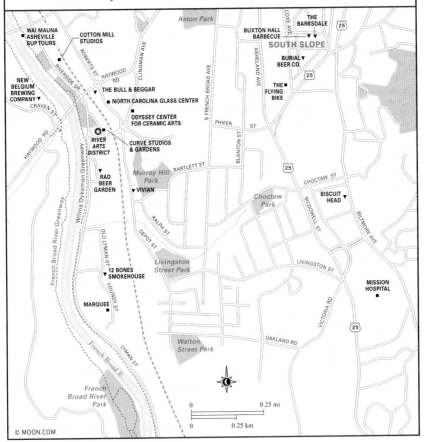

South Slope and River Arts District

that has been around since before the River Arts District was a thing, and once a punk-rock club called Squashpile—you can't make up stuff like that—CURVE is home to encaustic painters, ceramic workers, jewelry designers, glass artists, fiber artists, and more. This is just a sampling of what's happening in the River Arts District; visit the website for detailed listings of the artists and their studios.

FOOD

No matter what you're craving, from Mediterranean to vegetarian, four-star to down-home, Asheville has eateries that both embrace the Southern traditions of its mountain home and explore well beyond its borders. This is a town that clearly loves its food, with more than 17 local tailgate farmers markets, more than 250 independent restaurants, and more breweries per capita than any other city in the United States (26 in town, 60 in the region as of this writing). Farmers work with restaurants to provide the highest-quality produce and meats, and artisanal bakers and cheese-makers supply their tasty foodstuffs to restaurants high and low.

With such a robust food scene, it can be hard to pick out where you want to go. For a sampling of the best of what Asheville has to offer the gastronome, take a walking tour with **Eating Asheville** (828/489-3266, http://eatingasheville.com, classic tour $69, high-roller tour $79, food and brewery tour $69). Tours stop in at six of Asheville's best farm-to-table restaurants for a taste of what they're cooking. Restaurants provide two drink pairings as well as a talk about their food philosophy and sometimes a chance to meet the chef. Their new Cold One tour makes five stops where you'll pair food and beer, two things Asheville's known for.

Downtown

★ **Cúrate** (13 Biltmore Ave., 828/239-2946, www.curatetapasbar.com, 4pm-10:30pm Sun. and Tues.-Thurs., 4pm-11pm Fri., 11am-11pm Sat., $5-28) is led by Chef Katie Button, a James Beard Award semifinalist who previously cooked at the legendary El Bulli restaurant in Spain. At Cúrate she serves a Spanish tapas menu, so you'll get to try a variety of flavors and textures. One of the best meals in the place is the Spanish Experience ($55, wine pairing $30), a multicourse feast that highlights the best of the menu. A number of vegan and gluten-free selections are also on the menu. The lively restaurant features a long bar that faces the kitchen, so you can watch Chef Button and her expert kitchen brigade work.

The Foundry Hotel sits in the center of Asheville's once-thriving Black neighborhood, the Block, and one restaurant pays homage to foods and flavors from Afrolachian (the portmanteau adopted by many Black Appalachians) cuisine and dishes from across the African diaspora: ★ **Benne on Eagle** (35 Eagle St., 828/552-8833, www.benneoneagle.com, $10-32). Chef John Fleer, of nearby Rhubarb, owns this spot, but he leans on his *chef de cuisine* and a team of legends in Asheville's Black culinary world to develop and execute the menu. And they do a phenomenal job. The menu changes constantly, but expect high-end execution of dishes like Haitian *griot* (pork shoulder), an East-African veggie platter, pepper-pot stew, *fufu gnudi* and *maafe* sauce (casava-flour *gnudi* in a spicy peanut stew). The menu will be full of unfamiliar spices, ingredients, and phrases, but it's a delicious cultural and culinary exploration, and one I'm happy to tuck into any time I'm in Asheville.

Italian restaurant ★ **Cucina 24** (24 Wall St., 828/254-6170, www.cucina24restaurant.com, 5:30pm-9pm Sun.-Thurs., 5pm-10pm Fri.-Sat., $10-35), headed by Chef Brian Canipelli, is dedicated to sourcing as much as possible from local farms, ranches, and fisheries, and these ingredients are enticingly crafted into the restaurant's curated menu offerings. You can't go wrong no matter what you order, so go wild. Pizzas and veggies are roasted in a wood-fired oven, and pastas are made in-house and come with sauces to die for. Or let the chef decide for you and get the five-course chef's dinner ($60).

One of Asheville's most amazing restaurants—and that's quite the qualification given the food scene here—is **Rhubarb** (7 N. Pack Square, 828/785-1503, http://rhubarbasheville.com, 5pm-9:30pm Mon. and Thurs., 5pm-10pm Fri., 10:30am-2pm and 5pm-10pm Sat., 10:30am-2pm and 5pm-9:30pm Sun., $9-36). Chef John Fleer is a culinary magician with a kitchen full of talented cooks. The best farmed, foraged, and pasture-raised ingredients are used to create dishes like pork belly with daylily-walnut slaw, peanut-braised collard greens, and wood-roasted whole trout.

Friends first told me about **The Market Place** (20 Wall St., 828/252-4162, www.marketplace-restaurant.com, 5pm-9:30pm Mon.-Thurs., 5pm-10:30pm Fri., 10:30am-2:30pm and 5pm-10:30pm Sat., 10:30am-2:30pm and 5pm-9:30pm Sun., $6-55), but it was Chef-Owner William Dissen's appearance on National Geographic's *Gordon Ramsay: Uncharted*—when Chef Ramsay visited the Smoky Mountains near Asheville to talk traditional foods and culinary heritage—that sealed the deal. Dissen impressed Ramsay, who called him "one of the best chefs in the country," and I agree. Seasonal farm-driven dishes that aren't afraid to put a local protein, exotic spice, and foraged fruit, nut, or veggie on the plate together. It's an intriguing and delicious menu. Whether you want to share some truffle fries, kale fritters, or another small plate and pair it with a wood-grilled slab of steak or bit of yellowfin tuna, or if you just want to dive in and go for the lamb pappardelle and the wild mushroom ravioli, every bite you take will be bliss.

Early Girl Eatery (8 Wall St., 828/259-9292, ext. 1, www.earlygirleatery.com, 8am-8pm daily, $10-15) has caused a stir among area locavores and is gaining a following among visitors. More than half of the vegetables, meat, and fish used at Early Girl were raised or caught within 20 miles of the restaurant. The menu accommodates Asheville's large vegetarian and vegan contingent, but nonveg diners can feast on pan-fried trout with pecan butter, free-range chicken, or cheeseburgers made from hormone-free beef and topped with farmstead cheese, basil mayo, and all the fixings. Their breakfast, served all day, is among the best in Asheville. Their multigrain pancakes are out of this world. Wherever you are in town, you'll find an Early Girl, as they have locations in West Asheville (444 Haywood Rd., Suite 101, 828/259-9898, ext. 2) and South Asheville (1378 Hendersonville Rd., Suite A, 828/259-9292, ext. 3), as well as Downtown.

Take a good long look at the gorgeous art deco S&W Building when you stop by ★ **The S&W Market** (56 Patton Ave., 828/575-1500, www.swmarketavl.com, 11:30am-9pm Sun.-Mon. and Wed.-Thurs., 11:30am-10pm Fri.-Sat.) for a bite and a drink. Originally built to house the S&W Cafeteria, it is back to its original intentions. Several vendors occupy the space. **Highland Brewing** (www.highlandbrewing.com) has an outpost here. **Bun Intended** (www.bunintendedavl.com, $5-12) added this brick and mortar to their food truck and serves up *bao* and noodles, curry, and fried rice bowls. **Buxton Chicken Palace** (www.buxtonchickenpalace.com, $7-13), from chef and pit master Elliott Moss,

dishes up the best damn fried chicken sandwich you'll ever eat, plus a bourbon and Cheerwine slushie. **Peace Love Tacos** (www.mountainmadreavl.com, $4-6) serves up tacos with a side of positivity. **Farm Dogs** (www.farmdogsavl.com, $5-8) is a concept from the folks at Farmburger (around the corner) and has sausages and hot dogs made from local grass-fed beef. **The Hop Ice Cream** (www.hopicecreamnc.com, $3-6) has traditional and vegan ice cream options available, as well as coffee and other treats. And **The Times Bar** (828/774-5028, www.thetimesbarasheville.com, 4:30am-11pm Mon.-Tues., 10am-11pm Wed. and Sun., 10am-midnight Thurs., 10am-1am Fri.-Sat.) shakes up classic and inventive cocktails for your sipping enjoyment and offers a full coffee bar (Wed.-Sun.) to help wake you up or clear your foggy head.

Bouchon (62 N. Lexington Ave., 828/350-1140, www.ashevillebouchon.com, 5pm-9pm Sun.-Thurs., 5pm-10pm Fri.-Sat., $3.50-35) is a green restaurant. I don't mean they're cannabis-friendly (you'll have to wait a few years on that; North Carolina is still in the dark ages with respect to cannabis), I mean they're eco-friendly and they recycle or compost everything they can, so you can dine on some decadent French cuisine guilt-free. They serve small plates and entrée-size dishes, so whether you're there to share some fries and steak tartare, or if you're hungry for *moules frites,* or if boeuf bourguignon is the only thing that'll satisfy, make this hometown favorite your stop for dinner.

Local favorite **Chai Pani** (22 Battery Park Ave., 828/254-4003, www.chaipaniasheville.com, 11:30am-3:30pm Tues.-Sun., 5pm-9pm Tues.-Thurs., 5:30pm-9:30pm Fri.-Sun., $8-14) continues to win fans with its great food and cool atmosphere. Don't go expecting your typical Indian fare; it's inspired by Indian street food vendors and serves casual and affordable specialties from all over India, including lamb burgers, paneer and chicken and fish rolls, and more. The restaurant's name means "tea and water," a phrase that refers to a snack or a small gift, and, honestly, everything is so well

put together and so tastefully made, every bite is like a gift.

Mela (70 Lexington Ave., 828/225-8880, www.melaasheville.com, 11:30am-2:30pm and 5:30pm-9:30pm daily, $10-19) is one of the best Indian restaurants in North Carolina. The elaborate menu offers dozens of choices, combining cuisines of both northern and southern India with great meat, seafood, and vegetable dishes. The restaurant is dark and elegant, but the prices are surprisingly low; you can put together a great patchwork meal of appetizers, which start at $3, along with soup and roti. Don't miss the samosas.

A longtime late-night spot, Rosetta's Kitchen (116 N. Lexington Ave., 828/232-0738, www.rosettaskitchen.com, noon-9pm Tues.-Sun., $6-12) has been satisfying the hungry since 2002. There's so much to recommend about this place: The food is very good, it's all vegetarian and mostly vegan, and it's made with local produce in season. They compost everything that makes its way back to the kitchen, recycle all their trash, and make sure their used vegetable oil goes to power biodiesel cars—it's Asheville's signature countercultural reinterpretation of the South, and it's one of the best vegetarian places in town. Downstairs is The Buchi Bar, where they serve Buchi *kombucha* and *kombucha*-based cocktails, as well as beer, wine, cocktails, and all-natural sodas.

White Duck Taco Shop (12 Biltmore Ave., 828/232-9191, www.whiteducktacoshop.com, 11:30am-9pm Thurs.-Tues., $4-6) serves tacos that intrigue and delight. I know that sounds trite or overhyped, but White Duck lives up to every word. You can get jerk chicken, fried chicken, Korean beef *bulgogi* with kimchi, duck confit with mole and cranberry salsa, even a *bánh mì* tofu taco that tastes like the awesome Vietnamese sandwich. Priced so you can scarf down two or three without breaking the bank, they're just about perfect, but if you're a taco fan (who isn't?) and someone who

likes to try things that are a little left of center, this is your place. You'll find White Duck in a couple of other cities across the state, and at two other places in Asheville: the River Arts District (388 Riverside Dr., 828/254-1398) and south of Asheville in Arden (16 Miami Circle, Arden, 828/676-1859).

The vegetarian platter at Jerusalem Garden Café (78 Patton Ave., 828/254-0255, www.jerusalemgardencafe.com, 11am-8pm Tues.-Thurs., 11am-9pm Fri., 10am-9pm Sat., 10am-8pm Sun., $8-24) has become a favorite when my wife and I visit Asheville. Loaded with hummus, baba ghanoush, dolmas, tahini salad, and tabbouleh, it's a filling, sharable meal (as long as we add an order of pita), and honestly it's so good I've barely ventured beyond it on the menu. The falafel wrap is a great one, as is the chicken gyro, and every time I see the lamb shawarma or Jordanian chicken arrive on a neighboring table, I have a moment of regret, but that's quickly wiped away by another delicious bite.

Blue Dream Curry House (81 Patton Ave., 828/258-2500, www.bluedreamcurry. com, 11:30am-9pm Mon.-Thurs., 11:30am-10pm Fri., noon-10pm Sat., $7-12) is one I hope becomes an Asheville staple. They have a taco served on naan; they serve pickled peanuts in a spicy, curried, briny sauce; their curries are Japanese, Indian, Thai, and Peruvian; and they aren't afraid to offer up a couple of meat options on a veggie- and vegan-centered menu.

Just across the way from Blue Dream is Red Ginger Dimsum & Tapas (82 Patton Ave., 828/505-8688, www.redgingerasheville.com, 11:30am-3pm and 5pm-9pm Mon.-Thurs., 11:30am-3pm and 5pm-9:30pm Fri., 11:30am-9:30pm Sat., 11:30am-9pm Sun., $6-26), and if you're a fan of dumplings, it's a must-dine. The crystal shrimp dumplings, *gua bao* (Chinese pancake with pork belly), scallion pancake, and pan-fried vegetable dumplings are spectacular dishes to share.

You might think Crave Dessert Bar (41 N. Lexington Ave., Suite 100, 828/254-1974, www.cravedessertbar.com, 5pm-midnight

1: S&W Cafeteria 2: Buxton Hall Barbecue 3: Wall Street in downtown Asheville 4: West Asheville's Cellarest Beer Project

Wed.-Sun., $2-32) is all sweets, all the time, but that's not the case; they just happen to have an absolute smorgasbord of sweets—boozy tiramisu, decadent chocolate mousse, a s'mores platter, churros, hot doughnuts, cheesecakes galore, a caramel pineapple upside-down cake with gold leaf, and cupcakes—to go with a menu of savory dishes—empanadas, poutine, barbecued jackfruit sliders, sharable flatbreads—so you can have a well-rounded meal. Their selection of dessert wines and *digestivos,* as well as reds, whites, bubbles, and beer, makes for the perfect compliment.

French Broad Chocolates (10 S. Pack Square, 828/252-4181, http://frenchbroadchocolates.com, 11am-10pm daily) describes itself as "a sacred space for chocophiles," and with its prominent location in Pack Square, hordes of chocophiles are getting in line to find out why this particular chocolatier has been the talk of the town for a decade. French Broad offers chocolate truffles, brownies, pastries, sipping chocolates, floats, bars, beans, and a laundry list of chocolate products nearly as long as the line here on a Friday night (and trust me, it's long). This is a true "bean-to-bar" chocolatier, as they roast their own cacao in a rooftop solar roaster at their nearby factory (821 Riverside Dr., 828/504-4996, tours noon and 2pm Mon.-Tues., noon, 2pm, and 4pm Wed.-Sat., chocolate tasting noon and 2pm Sun.), and it's getting closer to being a "farm-to-bar" chocolatier, as the owners also happen to own a cacao farm in Costa Rica that they hope to harvest any season now.

The Gourmet Chip Company (43½ Broadway St., 828/254-3335, www.gourmetchipcompany.com, 11am-5pm Thurs.-Tues., $7-12) has made me love potato chips again. They make chips fresh all day (and have a huge stack of potato sacks to prove it) and top them with some lovely and intriguing ingredients: goat cheese and sea salt, dehydrated apple cider vinegar and a balsamic reduction, dark chocolate and applewood smoked bacon, buffalo sauce and bleu cheese, honey and lavender. Served up in a paper cone, they're attractive and fun to eat. The only downside is that they're so good you'll want to eat them fast, and that means using both hands, which means you can't walk down the street gobbling these delicious chips. But you should sit over them for a while and savor them anyway.

South Slope and River Arts District

What's a trip to North Carolina without barbecue? ★ **Buxton Hall Barbecue** (32 Banks Ave., 828/232-7216, www.buxtonhall.com, 11:30am-3pm and 5:30pm-9pm Sun.-Thurs., 11:30am-3pm and 5:30pm-10pm Fri.-Sat., $15-20) is old-school barbecue at its best but with some modern takes on classic sides. In researching the menu, the Buxton crew crossed the Carolinas, dining in dozens of barbecue joints and testing countless recipes to create barbecue nirvana. Chicken bog (chicken, rice, sausage) from the South Carolina Lowcountry is on the menu along with South Carolina barbecue hash and eastern North Carolina whole-hog barbecue. Also on the menu are smoked sausages, fried catfish, and smoked chicken. Meals are accompanied by an excellent selection of classic barbecue sides. I used to rave about their fried chicken sandwich, a truly exceptional meal, an I'd alternate between it and barbecue when I'd visit, but the opening of a sister restaurant, **Buxton Chicken Palace** (inside S&W Market, 56 Patton Ave., www.buxtonchickenpalace.com, 11:30am-9:30pm Tues.-Thurs., 11:30am-9pm Fri.-Sat., 11:30am-7pm Sun., $7-13), a spot dedicated to chicken sammies and chicken tendies as well as those bourbon and Cheerwine slushies, I can tuck into a plate of barbecue on every visit and save my chicken fix for another meal. Whatever you do, don't leave Asheville without eating at one of these places.

If you're in the mood for a killer hot dog, burger like no other, or a Cuban sandwich that will make you think about proposing marriage to the guy or gal operating the grill, or even a bologna sandwich (seriously), head to **Foothills Food Truck** (2 Huntsman Place, at Hi-Wire's Big Top, 828/606-9372, www.foothillslocalmeats.com, 4pm-8pm Mon.-Thurs.,

Craft Brews in Beer City

Asheville is regarded as the epicenter of North Carolina's beer and culinary scenes, and it's well deserved. Asheville itself is packed with award winning restaurants and breweries, and every time a new one opens, it makes the news. Winner of the title "Beer City USA" and perpetually at the top of any beer geek's list of cities to visit, Asheville's brewery scene is exemplary in terms of variety, innovation, and sheer volume. When you're in town you'll have no problem finding a brewery to visit, but this list will give you a head start on your search for the perfect brew.

- **Hi-Wire Brewing** (www.hiwirebrewing.com) has a trio of locations: on the **South Slope** (197 Hilliard Ave., 828/738-2452), where you'll find experimental quaffs to try; the **Big Top** (2A Huntsman Place, 828/738-2451), with their flagship brews and a great food truck; and the **River Arts District Beer Garden** (284 Lyman St., 828/738-2454), a fantastic beer garden.

- **Zillicoah Beer Company** (870 Riverside Dr., Woodfin, 828/424-7929, www.zillicoahbeer. com) is new to the scene but strong with beer aged in French oak, collaboration brews with local breweries, and an exceptional kölsch.

- **Bhramari Brewing Co.** (101 S. Lexington Ave., 828/214-7981, www.bhramaribrewing. com) delivers the unexpected: black gose with orange blossom, sour pale ales, dry hopped berlinerweisse, a sour beer that tastes like fruit punch, even a *foeder*-aged honey-infused beer.

- **Burial Beer Co.** (40 Collier Ave., 828/475-2739, www.burialbeer.com) makes intriguing brews with intriguing names. Their taproom, with its indoor and outdoor spaces, excellent food truck, and funky mural, make it a great place to stop and enjoy one of the double IPAs.

- **Highland Brewing Company** (12 Old Charlotte Hwy., Suite 200, 828/299-3370, www. highlandbrewing.com) has the honor of being the first microbrewery in Asheville, and it's a fine one. They continue to keep their flagship brews relevant by tweaking the recipes, but they also continue to innovate, releasing an impressive set of single-hop brews.

- **New Belgium Brewing Company** (21 Craven St., 828/333-6900, www.newbelgium. com) is one of the biggest in the area, and their tour is exceptional. Most craft beer fans know Fat Tire and their other brews, but the taproom here carries specialties and barrel-aged beers not available elsewhere.

- **Archetype Brewing** (www.archetypebrewing.com) has locations downtown (174 Broadway St., 828/505-8305) and in West Asheville (265 Haywood Rd., 828/505-4177) where you'll find their interpretations of Belgian beers like a saison, witbier, strong ale, and more.

- **Green Man Brewery** (27 Buxton Ave., 828/252-5502, www.greenmanbrewery.com) has lagers, fruity IPAs, even tart berlinerweisses, but their monster Rainmaker Double IPA is a hit, as are their barrel-aged and sour beers like Bootsy and Snozzberry.

- **DSSOLVR** (63 N. Lexington Ave., 828/515-4473, www.dssolvr.com) serves familiar styles with surprising twists from bourbon barrel aging to foraged ingredients to blending fermented grapes into old-world brews.

- **Black Mountain Brewing** (131 Broadway Ave., Black Mountain, 828/357-5010, www.blackmountainbrewing.com) pairs their spins on familiar styles with a tasty barbecue food truck.

- **Sierra Nevada Brewery** (100 Sierra Nevada Way, Mills River, 828/708-6176, www.sierranevada.com) was described to me as "the Taj Mahal of Beer" and "like Willy Wonka's factory, but with beer," and it lives up to that hype. There's a good restaurant on-site, a great tour, an impressive facility, and a *long* tap list that goes beyond what you expect from Sierra Nevada.

- **Oskar Blues Brewery** (342 Mountain Industrial Dr., Brevard, 828/883-2337, www.oskarblues.com) is the East Coast outpost for this Colorado staple. Old Chub Scotch Ale, Mama's Little Yella Pils, and their Pinner IPA are made fresh here.

4pm-9pm Fri., noon-9pm Sat., noon-8pm Sun., $8-14). I love this place and it has become one of my go-tos in Asheville. We meet friends at Hi-Wire's Big Top, grab a couple of orders of poutine and a sandwich (their cheeseburger is crave-worthy), then enjoy the beer and food and company.

In the River Arts District, **The Bull and Beggar** (37 Paynes Way, 828/575-9443, www. thebullandbeggar.com, 5pm-9pm Sun.-Mon. and Thurs., 5pm-10pm Fri.-Sat., $10-80) has become the dinner spot of choice for those in the know. With a menu that runs from the raw bar to the $80 bone-in rib-eye for two, they serve rich, filling, French-inspired entrées along with a killer charcuterie platter and a list of sides ($4-8) that are meal-worthy in themselves. On Monday night they offer a $9.99 burger. When I once asked a friend if we should go, she was rendered temporarily speechless by her memory of the previous week's burger.

When President Obama was in Asheville (he stayed at the Grove Park, incidentally), he and the First Lady wanted barbecue, and the ribs from **12 Bones Smokehouse** (5 Foundry St., Suite 10, 828/253-4499, www.12bones.com, 11:30am-4:30pm Mon.-Fri., $8-32) were the only thing to satisfy their craving for 'cue (the Secret Service, I'm told, feasted on Luella's). You can get a full rack (that's 12 bones, hence the name), a half rack, or even a little baby-size three-bone sampler that'll whet your appetite for more. More includes pulled pork, smoked turkey, and smoked BLT sandwiches, plus platters and all those excellent sides. Another location is in Arden, south of Asheville (2350 Hendersonville Rd., Arden, 828/687-1395, 11:30am-4pm Tues.-Sat., takeout 11:30am-7:30pm Tues.-Sat.), where, like most things in Asheville, they have a **brewery** (828/214-9827, www.12bonesbrewing.com, noon-9pm Tues.-Sat., noon-7pm Sun.); the Stay Golden Light Lager is an ideal accompaniment to a rack of ribs, by the way.

In the River Arts District, **Vivian** (348 Depot St., 828/225-3497, www.vivianavl.

com, 5pm-9pm Thurs.-Sat., 10:30am-1:30pm Sun., $14-42) delights diners with impeccable French techniques and exceptional local ingredients. Think of seared duck, pork terrine, and scallop quenelle as well as venison osso buco, smoked oysters, and fried chicken. Stop by for brunch and you'll be delighted by their fried-chicken biscuit, the smoked lamb benedict, and the usual run of eggs, quiche, and smoked fish.

West Asheville

★ **The Admiral** (400 Haywood Rd., 828/252-2541, www.theadmiralasheville.com, 5pm-10pm Thurs.-Mon., $16-45) has been West Asheville's prime food destination since it opened in a humble cinderblock building in 2007. The kitchen is driven by talent and culinary curiosity. On the menu you'll find an ever-evolving collection of New American dishes, like a rib-eye with roasted potato and cabbage or half-chicken with Carolina Gold rice and pole beans. The Admiral also has a great cocktail program. The cozy spot is divey yet chic.

West Asheville's ★ **Jargon** (715 Haywood Rd., 828/785-1761, www.jargonrestaurant. com, 5pm-9pm Sun.-Thurs., 5pm-10pm Fri.-Sat., $12-45) is out to do one thing, and it does it very well: delight diners with technique, ingredients, and the final dish. Strong relationships with farmers and food folk make the kitchen's job a little easier, as everything they serve is perfection or right next door. Grilled peaches take center stage in a summer salad, yuca gets a salt and vinegar treatment, and whether you get a vegetarian or meat-centered main, it's going to look and smell so good, you'll forget to take a picture before you dig in.

Nearby is **Hole Doughnuts** (168 Haywood Rd., 828/774-5667, www.hole-doughnuts.com, 8am-1pm Wed.-Sun., $2-3) one of my worldwide top-three doughnuts (I eat a lot of doughnuts; don't judge). Yeasted dough cooked to order, they're always hot, always fresh, and always interesting. My favorite from here had a sugared sumac glaze, making that yeasty little doughnut that much more tart.

Sunny Point Café (626 Haywood Rd., 828/252-0055, www.sunnypointcafe.com, 8:30am-2pm Sun.-Mon., 8:30am-8:30pm Tues.-Sat., $10-17) serves three meals most days but is so famous for its brunch that a line sometimes forms out the door. The breakfast menu is popular and served any time of day, although the lunch and dinner menus are also well worth a trip. This is a great bet for vegetarians—the meatless options are imaginative and beautifully created. Whatever you get, you must order one of their angel biscuits; those things are tall, airy, and so good.

Another excellent breakfast option, if you don't mind a little wait, is **Biscuit Head** (733 Haywood Rd., 828/333-5145, 8am-2pm daily, $3-12) in West Asheville, near Mission Hospital (417 Biltmore Ave., Suite 4F, 828/505-3449), and in South Asheville (1994 Hendersonville Rd., 828/585-2055). They specialize in an Appalachian delicacy: cathead biscuits. These things are huge, and as the name implies, as big as a tomcat's head. And they're so good. Get one plain and go load it up at the topping bar (where things like nut butters, fresh jams and jellies, and concoctions like sriracha-laced honey await you and your biscuit); go for a pulled pork, fried green tomato, or country ham biscuit; or go sweet with something like the biscuit french toast or the Nutella Elvis: banana, bacon, and Nutella on a monster biscuit.

★ **Gan Shan West** (285 Haywood Rd., Suite 20, 828/417-7402, www.ganshangroup.com, 4pm-9pm Mon.-Sat., $9-16) takes a broad look at Asian cuisine and serves up rice dishes, ramen, and an assortment of Asian-inspired plates in a small menu that's as intriguing as it is tasty. *Gai lon,* a broccoli-like Chinese green, gets a spicy treatment; steam buns come served in a pair and are filled with your choice of a meat or veggie filling; and dishes like ramen and *mapo doufu* will help some diners push into new territory with this cuisine.

Biltmore Estate and Village

There are no fewer than nine places to eat (plus snacks, ice cream, and coffee) on the

Biltmore Estate (1 Lodge St., 800/411-3812, www.biltmore.com, estate admission required to visit restaurants). For Biltmore lodging guests only, **The Dining Room** (7am-11am, 11:30am-4pm, and 5pm-9pm daily, reservations required, breakfast $56-20, buffet $13-22, 3-course tasting menu $65, 5-course tasting menu $95) is an elegant restaurant featuring estate-raised Angus beef, mountain trout, Biltmore wines, and vegetables grown on estate gardens. The food is spectacular, and tables with a mountain view make the meal all that much better. Evening dress and reservations are recommended.

The **Biltmore Bistro** (noon-9pm Sun.-Fri., 11:30am-9pm Sat., lunch $8-21, prix-fixe lunch $29, dinner $19-44, prix-fixe dinner $52) in Antler Hill Village, adjacent to the winery, has a well-rounded gourmet menu sourced from the Biltmore's own kitchen garden, locally raised heirloom crops, meat and seafood delicacies, and artisanal cheeses and breads. Lunch and dinner are dramatically different (pizza at lunch, braised veal cheeks at dinner), but each menu features something from the wood-fired oven.

The dining room of the **Deerpark Restaurant** (11am-2pm Fri.-Sat., 10am-2pm Sun., Fri.-Sat. buffet $20, free under age 10, Sun. buffet $35, free under age 10) is a former barn designed by architect Richard Morris Hunt, now renovated to airy splendor with walls of windows. Expect hearty and homey meals based on Appalachian cuisine. Like the Deerpark, the **Stable Café** (lunch 11am-4pm and 5pm-9pm daily, $14-35) was once livestock housing, and guests can sit in booths that were once horse stalls. This is a meat eater's paradise, where you can order estate-raised Angus beef and pork barbecue with the house special sauce, among others.

In the stable area near the house, both the **Bake Shop** (9:30am-10pm daily) and the **Biltmore Dairy Bar** (11am-6pm Mon.-Wed., 11am-10pm Thurs.-Sun.) serve fresh treats, and **The Courtyard Market** (11am-4pm daily, weather dependent) has hot dogs, salads, and snacks. The **Creamery** (11am-9pm daily) is the place for sandwiches and hand-dipped ice cream in Antler Hill Village, and **The Conservatory Café** (from 11:30am daily), adjacent to the gardens, will keep you fed after a day admiring the roses. If you have a hankering for barbecue, a quick sandwich, some snacks, or a cold drink, the **Smokehouse Food Truck** (noon-8pm daily) in Antler Hill Village serves just what you need.

While you're in Antler Hill Village, check out **Cedric's Tavern** (11:30am-4pm Sun.-Mon., 11:30am-9pm Tues.-Sat., $13-46). Named for George Vanderbilt's beloved Saint Bernard (you can see his huge collar on display at the entrance), Cedric's pays homage to pubs and taverns found in Britain, with a Southern twist. The fish-and-chips and scotch egg are both delicious. You can also grab a pint of Cedric's Pale or Brown Ale, both brewed by the Biltmore Brewing Company. Also in Antler Hill Village is the new Village Hotel on the Biltmore Estate and its restaurant, **Village Social** (828/257-5968, 7am-11am and noon-9pm Fri.-Mon., 7am-11am and noon-4pm Tues.-Thurs., $6-36). With a menu focused on small plates and tasting menus—all of which are seafood-centric—this is a place to make a meal as light or as filling as you'd like.

Burial Beer has their business offices in Biltmore Village at a former Civilian Conservation Corps location called **Forestry Camp** (10 Shady Oak Dr., 828/505-4452, www.burialbeer.com, 5pm-10pm Mon. and Wed.-Fri., noon-10pm Sat.-Sun.). This is where workers lived during the early stages of construction on the Blue Ridge Parkway, so it's got history tied to Asheville. And it's a really cool spot. They serve the whole of Burial's beer lineup here, but the kitchen puts our food that's far beyond what you'd expect to find in a brewery, which is to say this ain't your run-of-the-mill pub grub; it's real, good food.

Well-Bred Bakery & Café (6 Boston Way, 825/774-5307, www.wellbredbakery.com, 9am-4pm Sun.-Thurs., 9am-5pm Fri.-Sat., $3-15), which started north of Asheville in Weaverville, has a location in Biltmore Village. Sandwiches, salads, quiche, and breakfast burritos share menu space with pastries, ice cream sandwiches, coffee, and specialty drinks. Stop in for a bite before wandering around Biltmore Village—which was constructed as a village for workers on the massive Biltmore Estate project—for a little sightseeing or window shopping.

Outside Downtown

There are several notable vegetarian and vegan restaurants in Asheville, and among the best is the vegan spot, **Plant** (165 Merrimon Ave., 828/258-7500, www.plantisfood.com, 5pm-9pm Wed.-Thurs. and Sun., 5pm-10pm Fri.-Sat., $10-22), where they make "vegan fare without borders." I'm an admitted omnivore, but Plant is exceptional. From the applewood smoked mushroom (served with their V2 black currant steak sauce), their seasonal spin on ramen (you won't be able to tell the difference in the broth), tempeh chili con queso, and the raw "lasagna" crudo, every bite is a delight, and you won't leave with that heavy, "I'm too full" feeling even if you stuff yourself.

One restaurant folks have been clamoring about is the Caribbean-inspired **Nine Mile** (233 Montford Ave., 828/505-3121, www.ninemileasheville.com, 4pm-9pm daily, $8-23). With its Caribbean inspiration and heavily Jamaican bent, you'll find bold flavors and a selection of seafood, vegetarian, and vegan options here. Jerk tofu with mushrooms, green onions and cavatappi; dairy-free basil pesto with garden veggies, and mahimahi with mango salsa in a ginger-coconut sauce are just a few of the dishes on offer. They have two other locations, one in West Asheville (751 Haywood Rd., 828/575-9903, 4pm-9pm daily), and one on the south side of town (33 Town Square Blvd., 828/676-1807, 4pm-9pm daily), so if you're hungry, they've got you covered no matter what part of town you're in.

It makes sense that in a food city this close to Tennessee (Great Smoky Mountains National Park and the Tennessee border are 90 minutes away) we'd get some great flavors from the Volunteer State, and **Rocky's Hot Chicken Shack** (1455 Patton Ave.,

828/575-2260, www.rockyshotchickenshack. com, 11am-9pm Sun.-Thurs., 11am-10pm Fri.-Sat., $9-23) in West Asheville delivers. Their fried chicken starts out plain, then you tell them how hot you want it, or how much you'd like to suffer with each bite, depends on how you view hot food. Seriously, though, the hot is real hot, and the mild is delicious even if you think ice water is spicy. And if you're out here needing to feed a crowd (or just have a nostalgia for a cold fried-chicken picnic), they have platters that'll feed a family (8-16 people), with wings, dark and white meat platters, and an order that's a little bit of everything ($38-90). There's a second location just south of Asheville in Arden (3749 Sweeten Creek Rd., Arden, 828/676-3222, 11am-9pm Sun.-Thurs., 11am-10pm Fri.-Sat.).

You'll feel at home in **Avenue M** (791 Merrimon Ave., 828/350-8181, www.avenue-mavl.com, 5pm-9pm Tues.-Sat., $15-30), a place that offers free Wi-Fi for the kids' devices and some fresh water for your faithful furry friend alongside a menu of creative dishes and excellent wines. A half-dozen pastas, a great mix of veggie-friendly and omnivorous entrées, a burger and its Impossible cousin, and a legion of sharable, snackable appetizers ensure you're well fed, but also make it easy to linger here for a while.

Seafood lovers take note: **Jettie Rae's** (143 Charlotte St., 828/505-4499, www.jettieraes. com, 4:30pm-9pm Wed.-Thurs., 4:30pm-10pm Fri.-Sun., $8-60) has what you want for dinner, whether it's a pile of clam strips, caviar service, or something between. A raw bar and a menu packed with oysters, crabs, clams, fish-and-chips, and a lobster roll will have your stomach growling before you even get to the restaurant.

At **Luella's Bar-B-Que** (501 Merrimon Ave., 828/505-7427, www.luellasbbq.com, 11am-8pm Sun.-Thurs., 11am-9pm Fri.-Sat., $7-15) you can try the range of styles and sauces that make North Carolina 'cue distinct. Ribs, chopped pork, brisket, smoked wings, and sides like mac-and-cheese, fried okra, collard greens, and hush puppies are staples here, but there's a surprising item on the menu: barbecued tempeh. I'm a barbecue judge (really, I'm certified!), so trust me when I say it's good. As is everything here, from the grub to the vibe to the impressive array of local beer on draft. Pay a visit to their spot in South Asheville (33 Town Square Blvd., Biltmore Park, 828/676-3855) if you're hungry and down that way.

Vinnie's Neighborhood Italian (641 Merrimon Ave., 828/253-1077, www.vinniesitalian.com, 5pm-9:30pm Sun.-Thurs., 5pm-10:30pm Fri.-Sat., $11-26), is an Italian eatery they say is "reminiscent of Brooklyn, the Bronx and the North End of Boston." That means pasta, pizza, heroes, and calzones are offered in abundance, along with heartier veal and chicken dishes, lasagna, and eggplant parmigiana. It also means big portions that could feed a family (incidentally, they do serve family-style portions of lasagna, and eggplant or chicken parmigiana that'll feed three for $45-49), which is exactly what this style of Italian is all about.

ACCOMMODATIONS

There are a lot of places and ways to stay in Asheville at all sorts of price points. With B&Bs and inns tucked away in the neighborhoods and hills surrounding downtown, grand resorts like the Grove Park Inn and luxe stays on the Biltmore Estate, glamping, tiny cottages, boutique hotels, and, of course, the chain hotels ubiquitous to any city, you'll find a place to rest your head that's convenient to the concert you're headed to, those dinner reservations you made, to the Blue Ridge Parkway, downtown, or whatever's brought you to the mountains. The Explore Asheville website (www.exploreasheville.com) has an exhaustive list of hotels and accommodations in the area, and at the **Asheville Bed & Breakfast Association** (www.ashevillebba.com), inns and B&Bs in the area band together to promote getaways, tours, and seasonal packages.

Downtown

Built in a former foundry in what was once the heart of Asheville's Black neighborhood, ★ **The Foundry Hotel** (51 S. Market St., 828/552-8545, www.foundryasheville.com, $260-1,712) pays homage to the building's past, while the restaurant attached to the hotel, **Benne on Eagle** (35 Eagle St., 828/552-8833, www.benneoneagle.com, $10-32), offers a hat-tip to Black and Appalachian cuisine. Only a block off Biltmore Avenue, the Foundry is walkable but still gives you separation from Asheville's bustling downtown. Exposed brick on the walls and quirky art—wallpaper and framed pieces with details, newspaper clippings, and photos from the foundry's operating years—give the hotel a bohemian touch. The bedding, lounge, gym, and other hotel amenities are decidedly upscale. Relax and grab a drink in the **Workshop Lounge** before you head out for the evening.

In recent years the face of downtown Asheville has changed with the arrival of several hotels. AC Hotel (a Marriott chain) made a splash when it arrived, as did **Kimpton Hotel Arras** (7 Patton Ave., 828/255-0303, www.hotelarras.com, $280-595). Asheville's tallest building, on Pack Square, was reduced to a skeleton and rebuilt, and the result is this stunning Kimpton that hosts works by local artists. Grab drinks and dinner at **District 42** (828/774-5564, www.district42avl.com, 5pm-10pm Sun.-Wed., 5pm-11pm Thurs., 5pm-midnight Fri.-Sat., pizza bar 4pm-10pm Mon.-Wed., 4pm-11pm Thurs., 4pm-midnight Fri., 2pm-midnight Sat., 2pm-10pm Sun., $10-37) or sit for a more upscale dinner or brunch at **Bargello** (828/774-5564, www.bargelloavl.com, breakfast 7am-11am Mon.-Fri., 7am-10am Sat.-Sun., dinner 5pm-10pm Sun. and Wed.-Thurs., 5pm-11pm Fri.-Sat., brunch 10am-3pm Sat.-Sun., $9-64), plating up Mediterranean-inspired dishes using local ingredients.

AC Hotel by Marriott Downtown Asheville (10 Broadway St., 828/258-2522, www.marriott.com, from $340, winter rates as low as $175) is one of my favorites for the spacious rooms, generally excellent views, and a great rooftop bar, **Capella on 9** (828/771-5156, 7am-11am and 3pm-11pm Mon.-Thurs., 7am-11am and 3pm-midnight Fri.-Sat., 7am-11am and 3pm-10pm Sun., $11-30), with cocktails, wine, beer, and a tasty tapas menu—olives, charcuterie and cheese boards, *patatas bravas*, even pan-fried trout—while you take in the views.

In keeping with Asheville's mountain hippie vibe, there's a hostel in downtown. **Sweet Pea's Hostel** (23 Rankin Ave., 828/285-8488, www.sweetpeashostel.com) has loads of ways to stay. They've got a 16 coed bunks ($32), each with a power outlet and reading light; 24 pods ($40), reminiscent of a train-car sleeper with a locker, shelves, outlets, and an acoustic curtain; a pair of small private rooms ($75) with sinks and locking doors; and a studio room ($105) with a private bath. There's free Wi-Fi throughout the property. Feel free to cook up a meal in the kitchen (just clean up after yourself), hang out for some TV or a movie in the living room, or venture out into town to see what's happening. Stay here and you're on the same block as a coffee shop, brewery, a couple of restaurants, and a cocktail lounge, and you're only a short walk from everything downtown.

South Slope and River Arts District

With so many neo-hippie types, college kids, dirtbags (it's not an insult; it's what rock climbers often call themselves), kayakers, hikers, and bikers coming through, it's no surprise to find a nice hostel nestled in among the hotels and bed-and-breakfasts. At the **Asheville Hostel & Guest House** (16 Ravenscroft Dr., 828/423-0256, www.avl-hostel.com, $100-112, tiny house with private bath $175) you'll find only private guest rooms and even a private tiny house. Reservations are available up to a year in advance, so it's easy to get a room if you know when you're traveling. At the hostel you'll find free waffles, coffee, and tea at make-your-own stations; free Wi-Fi; free parking; and, since you're on the South Slope, there's a lot to eat and drink nearby, and downtown is within walking distance.

Biltmore Estate and Village

If you've spent the day touring the Biltmore Estate, viewing the incredible splendor in which a robber baron of the Gilded Age basked, it may be jarring to return to real life (unless you're a billionaire). You can soften the transition with a stay at **The Inn on Biltmore Estate** (866/336-1245, www.biltmore.com, $379-2,700). It's everything you'd wish for from a hotel in this location. The rooms and suites are beautifully furnished and luxurious, the views are magnificent, and the lobby, dining room, and library have the deluxe coziness of a turn-of-the-20th-century lodge. In the off-season, it's possible to find rooms from around $200. **Village Hotel on Biltmore Estate** (from $288) in Antler Hill Village has 209 rooms and is a testament to the ongoing and growing popularity of the Biltmore. You can find specials for as low as $144.

Outside Downtown

The **Grove Park Inn** (290 Macon Ave., 828/252-2711 or 800/438-5800, www.omni-hotels.com, $439-1,999, spa and golf packages available) is the sort of place Asheville residents bring their out-of-town houseguests when giving them a grand tour of the city, simply to walk into the lobby to ooh and aah. The massive stone building—constructed by a crew of 400 who had only mule teams and a single steam shovel to aid them—was erected in 1912-1913. Eight U.S. presidents have stayed here, as has a glittering parade of early-20th-century big shots, among them Henry Ford, Thomas Edison, Eleanor Roosevelt, Harry Houdini, and F. Scott Fitzgerald.

Even if you're not staying here, it's worth a visit just to see the lobby and enormous fireplaces, and take in the atmosphere while having a cocktail or dinner at one of the many on-site establishments: **Vue 1913** (5pm-10pm Wed.-Sun., $34-60) has French and American dishes and a few premium options like a

Wagyu filet ($98) and an elk tenderloin ($75) if you're treating yourself; **Edison Craft Ales + Kitchen** (11am-10pm Sun.-Thurs.,11am-11pm Fri.-Sat., brunch noon-2:30pm Sun., $12-48) serves some high-quality bar food and craft beer; and **Blue Ridge** (7am-10:30am daily, 5pm-9pm Fri.-Sat., noon-2:30pm Sun., $29-48 adults, $17-23 ages 6-12) is a farm-to-table artisanal buffet. The hotel's **Sunset Terrace** (11am-3pm and 4:30pm-10pm daily, reservations required, $13-50) has phenomenal views, allowing you to enjoy dinner and the sunset.

Being a guest at the Grove Park Inn is quite an experience. In addition to the spectacle of the lodge and its multiple restaurants, cafés, bars, and shops, for an additional charge guests have access to its world-famous **spa** (daily, day pass $244). The pass gives access to the lounges, pools, steam room, inhalation room, and outdoor whirlpool tub. The indoor pool is a fantastic place, a subterranean stone room with vaulted skylights and tropical plants. For extra fees ($180-540, most $200-300), guests can choose from a long menu of spa treatments: massages, facials, manicures, aromatherapy, and body wraps.

There's also an exceptional Donald Ross-designed 18-hole par-70 **golf course** (828/252-2711 or 800/438-5800, reserve tee times online at www.groveparkinn.com, greens fees $70-140 Mon.-Thurs., $70-155 Fri.-Sun. Apr.-mid-Nov., $77-87 mid-Nov.-Mar., 9 holes $55 Apr.-mid-Nov., $45 mid-Nov.-Mar., rental clubs $55 for 9 holes, $80 for 18 holes). The 6,400-yard course is where President Obama played when he stayed at the Grove Park Inn; one look around at the mountains and views from the elevated tee boxes and you know he was impressed.

Asheville has a history in hospitality, and one of the longest continuously operated bed-and-breakfasts in town is a real charmer. ★ **Applewood Manor** (62 Cumberland Circle, 828/254-2244, www.applewoodmanor.com, $275-310) has six gorgeous rooms (each named for a type of apple) and a great farm-to-table breakfast. The owners—a husband-and-wife team—share their interests with guests via road cycling and culinary programs. They'll set you up with a bike rental and point you toward a place to ride, or you can join them for a guided ride with a former national road race champion. If that's not your speed, you can get in the kitchen for some baking or a cooking class. If you're headed to Asheville or the Smokies with a group, look into renting the whole place ($1,900) and making it your home away from home.

Just a mile from downtown in the lovely and walkable Montford Historic District, ★ **Abbington Green Bed & Breakfast Inn and Spa** (46 Cumberland Circle, 828/251-2454 or 822/251-2454, www.abbingtongreen. com, $239-469) will charm you from the moment you lay eyes on this Colonial Revival-style home. Completed in 1908, this home was designed by Biltmore Estate's on-site supervising architect, Robert Sharpe Smith, and has received a number of accolades, including one from the Preservation Society, for excellence in historic preservation, so it retains every bit of the magic it was imbued with more than a century ago. It's a AAA Four Diamond property, a rating that doesn't come easily, but with king beds, a gourmet breakfast, a cozy but well-appointed spa (services from $100), and gorgeous English-style gardens, AAA might need to make this one a six-star property. Eight rooms, including three suites in the Carriage House, give guests plenty of privacy without sacrificing the intimate homey feel of the property. There are dog-friendly rooms available if you're traveling with your four-legged friend.

Nestled in the Kenilworth neighborhood, a truly lovely bed-and-breakfast is **Sweet Biscuit Inn** (77 Kenilworth Rd., 828/250-0170, www.sweetbiscuitinn.com, $160-275). I have to admit, I was drawn here by the name, but the place, the host, and the three-course breakfast conspired to make me like it even more. The seven bedrooms and carriage house are accented by tiger-oak wood floors and high ceilings. Queen or king beds are comfy, and breakfast is excellent, especially the biscuits.

In the days before budget hotels became the norm, the motor court or cottage court was the stay-over of choice for middle-class travelers. Today these motor courts and cottage courts are relics of the past, and few remain, but the mountains of North Carolina contain a handful of fine examples. In the Asheville area, at least two are still operating, providing travelers with throwback accommodations. **Asheville Log Cabin Motor Court** (330 Weaverville Hwy., 828/645-6546, www. theashevillecabins.com, $95-305, 2-night minimum stay weekends, pets allowed for a fee), 6.2 miles north of downtown Asheville, has cable TV and Wi-Fi but no phones. Some rooms are air-conditioned, but that's not usually a necessity at this elevation. Another great cabin court is the **Pines Cottages** (346 Weaverville Hwy., 828/645-9661, www. thepinescottages.com, $109-330, up to 2 pets allowed, $15 per pet), only 6.3 miles north of Asheville. How could you resist staying at a place billed as "A nice place for nice people"?

Want to stay in a tree house? How about a retro camper with a hot tub? Or a dome with skylight windows so you can watch the stars? Or a yurt? If this sounds good, you need **Asheville Glamping** (address provided on booking, 828/450-9745, www.ashevilleglamping.com, $140-600). They have a trio of properties with a host of quirky but refined places and ways to stay, from safari-style tents to tree houses to yurts and more. When you book they'll send you the address of the property; it's a slight inconvenience but a way to keep their immensely Instagrammable campgrounds and properties a haven to their guests and free of lookers and lurkers.

At **The Beaucatcher** (60 Tunnel Rd., 825/254-0805, www.thebeaucatcher.com, $75-155), you're only a three-minute drive to downtown, and just a little longer to I-240 or the Blue Ridge Parkway. New owners took over this property back in 2016 and they've been steadily making improvements since. The rooms are comfortable, and there's plenty of space to spread out your gear if you're here for a hiking or outdoorsy adventure. In summer, the courtyard can get lively with a pair of fire pits and a beer from the stock of local brews in the lobby.

INFORMATION AND SERVICES

The Asheville Visitors Center (36 Montford Ave., near I-240 exit 4C, 828/258-6129, www.exploreasheville.com, 8:30am-5pm Mon.-Fri., 9am-5pm Sat.-Sun.) can set you up with all the maps, brochures, and recommendations you could need. Other sources are Explore Asheville (www.exploreasheville.com) and the Asheville Area Chamber of Commerce (www.ashevillechamber.org). Mission Hospital (509 Biltmore Ave.; 428 Biltmore Ave., 828/213-1111, www.mission-health.org) in Asheville has two campuses and two emergency departments.

Listen to public radio at WCQS (88.1 FM) and WNCW (88.7 FM); music stations are WTMT (105.9 FM) and WOXL (96.5 FM).

As Asheville is the best gateway city when venturing into the Smoky Mountains, know you'll find some information on planning a trip to the Smokies at Explore Asheville (www.exploreasheville.com). The website of Great Smoky Mountain National Park (www.nps.gov/gsmnp) has trip planning tools useful for day trips or overnight excursions into the park.

GETTING THERE AND AROUND

Asheville is spread around the junction of I-40, North Carolina's primary east-west highway, and I-26, a roughly north-south artery through the southern highlands. U.S. 19 runs at a diagonal, deep into the Smokies in one direction and into the northern Blue Ridge in the other. Asheville has an extensive public bus system called ART (www.ashevillenc.gov, 5:55am-midnight Mon.-Sat., 7:55am-6:30pm Sun., limited hours holidays, hours

vary by route, $1, $0.50 seniors), connecting most major points in the metropolitan area, including the airport, with downtown. See the website for routes and schedules. Asheville Regional Airport (AVL, 61 Terminal Dr., Fletcher, 828/684-2226, www.flyavl.com) is a 20-minute drive on I-26 south of the city in Fletcher. Several airlines run flights to Atlanta, Charlotte, and other U.S. cities.

From Asheville it's easy to get to Great Smoky Mountains National Park (GSMNP). In just over an hour you can be in Cataloochee, at the north end of the park, to camp, hike, and watch for elk in a serene mountain cove; to get here, take I-40 west to exit 20 and follow the signs. You can also take I-40 west into Tennessee, follow the Foothills Parkway to U.S. 321, and skirt the edge of GSMNP to Gatlinburg, Tennessee, and the entrance to the park, a trip of about 90 minutes. From Gatlinburg, you can make a loop back to Asheville by taking Newfound Gap Road across GSMNP to Cherokee, North Carolina (about 2.5 hours), and then back to Asheville via U.S. 441 to U.S. 19 to I-40, a total loop of about 3.5 hours and some 175 miles.

You can also head straight to Cherokee from Asheville and enter GSMNP via Newfound Gap Road. It's an hour's drive following I-40 west to exit 27, then taking U.S. 19 south to U.S. 441, which runs right into Cherokee. Alternately you can take the more scenic, but much longer, route and get to Cherokee via the Blue Ridge Parkway. This route is only 83 miles, but it takes 2-2.5 hours. If you want to go this way, head south out of Asheville along U.S. 25 and pick up the Blue Ridge Parkway about 5.5 miles out of town; turn south on the parkway and drive until you reach Cherokee and GSMNP. And, of course, you can reverse the course if you're making that grand loop and return to Asheville via the Blue Ridge Parkway by picking it up in Cherokee and driving north.

Around Asheville

Throughout the mountains around Asheville you'll come across towns official and unincorporated—some collections of houses at a wide spot on a mountain road, others established towns with deep histories and more than a little creative juice flowing in their collective blood. Whatever the reason for visiting, these towns have personalities, histories, cultures, and environments distinct enough to allow the truly curious to discover a small town (or two) full of surprises.

BLACK MOUNTAIN

Named for a onetime train depot, the town of Black Mountain sits 15 miles west of Asheville and is one of several bedroom communities for the city. At one time, Black Mountain's claim to fame was the experimental Black Mountain College and its intellectual and artistic legacy. The school is long gone, and the Black Mountain College Museum and Arts Center is located in Asheville, but some of the artistic residue is still around in the form of the Lake Eden Arts Festival, or LEAF, which takes place on the former college campus.

Sights

Step into the Swannanoa Valley Museum (223 W. State St., 828/669-9566, www.swannanoavalleymuseum.org, 10am-5pm Thurs.-Sat. Mar.-Dec., 10am-5pm Sat. Feb., $5, free students and under age 18) to learn about the history of this area, including settlement by the Cherokee people, early industrialization, and the shutdown of the Beacon Blanket Factory. The museum offers something a little different: hikes, and not just short ones. The current iterations of the Swannanoa Rim Explorer Series (series of 11 hikes, $500 members) and Valley History Explorer Hiking Series (series of 8 hikes, $280 members) take museum members on a series of hikes that reveal the history, geography, and rugged beauty of the Swannanoa Valley; in the recent past these hikes were open to guests and sold as packages and individual guided hikes, and there's hope to renew that program in 2023 (prices were around $50 for nonmembers; expect a little increase). Some of these hikes are difficult—steep, long, exposed in places—and others are geared toward beginners; check with the museum to register and for questions on difficulty and schedules.

The Black Mountain Center for the Arts (225 W. State St., 828/669-0930, http://blackmountainarts.org, 10am-5pm Mon.-Fri.) is a gallery and performance space in the heart of town. Once the town hall, the Center for the Arts now houses art classes and summer camps for kids and adults, workshops and talks, performances of all sorts (concerts, dance, poetry, storytelling, live theater), and gallery openings.

Shopping

If I said Sassafras on Sutton (108 Sutton Ave., 828/419-0677, www.sassafrasonsutton.com, 10am-6pm Mon.-Sat.) has it all, you might think I was exaggerating, but this bookstore, gift shop, and espresso café delivers. Well, as long as you're looking for a curated selection of fiction and local books, hand-poured candles, and a gift for yourself or someone else, they've got it all.

There are several galleries in Black Mountain, so you'll have your choice of where to browse and where to buy. Stop in at Mountain Nest (133 Cherry St., 828/669-0314, www.mtnnest.com, 10am-6pm Mon.-Sat., 11am-5pm Sun.), a gallery of art and handcrafted pieces; you'll find work from many North Carolinians for sale here, as well as pieces from fine artists from around the world. Styles and skill levels vary from artist to artist, but there's solid and reasonably priced work. Seven Sisters Craft Gallery (119 Broadway Ave., 828/669-5107, www.sevensistersgallery.com, 10am-6pm Mon.-Sat., noon-5pm Sun.) has been around for more than 30 years and carries large-scale photos, oil paintings by local and regional artists, and other art in a host of styles, media, and price points.

Entertainment and Events

In May and October, Black Mountain is the scene of the **Lake Eden Arts Festival** (377 Lake Eden Rd., 828/686-8742, www.theleaf. org), better known as LEAF. Based around roots music, LEAF is also a festival of visual arts, poetry, food, and even the healing arts. It's an amazing scene, and it takes place, appropriately, at Camp Rockmont, once the campus of Black Mountain College, the short-lived but historically important avant-garde institution that was home to a number of influential American artists and writers.

NIGHTLIFE

Pisgah Brewing Company (2948 U.S. 70, 828/669-0190, www.pisgahbrewing.com, 4pm-9pm Mon.-Wed., 2pm-11pm Thurs.-Fri., noon-11pm Sat., 1pm-10pm Sun., open late for concerts, cash only) is both a brewpub and a music venue, featuring an eclectic mix of bands from roots music to rock. Pisgah was the Southeast's first certified organic brewery, and several beers are on tap all year, including their pale ale, porter, and stout; a long list of seasonal brews rotates through the year, and a growing list of specialty brews, like their sour brown ale, is gaining a loyal following. Tour the brewery (2pm and 3pm Sat.), but stop in a try a beer anytime they're open.

You'll find a stellar mural of Roberta Flack and a tap list of great beer at **Black Mountain Brewing** (131 Broadway Ave., 828/357-5010, www.blackmountainbrewing.com, 3pm-9pm Mon.-Thurs., noon-10pm Fri.-Sat., noon-9pm Sun.). Creative spins on sour beer, some big double dry-hopped IPAs, and seasonal styles appear on the draft list, but they also carry hard cider and ginger beer from friendly fermentation specialists nearby. Their food truck, **Smoke Black Mountain** (4pm-7:30 Mon.-Thurs., noon-8pm Fri.-Sat., noon-7pm

Sun., $12-24), serves pulled pork poutine, smoked lobster rolls, brisket sandwiches, and a few other delectable bites on-site.

Black Mountain Cider + Mead (104 Eastside Dr., Suite 307, 828/419-0089, www. blackmountainciderworks.com, 2pm-7pm Thurs.-Fri., 1pm-7pm Sat.-Sun.) is one of several spots across the state making cider and one of only a select few to make mead (a fermented honey beverage that should make you think of Vikings and Beowulf). Their ciders aren't cloyingly sweet or closer to carbonated apple juice than an alcoholic beverage; rather, they're on the dry side and tend to be complex in flavor. At any time they're pouring a half-dozen of their ciders and meads, and many are blended to make some interesting concoctions. In summer, they'll throw basil into a mix of mead and cider, or blend apple cider and cherry mead, or try something completely different by adding blueberry and cardamom, fresh ginger, lavender, quince, or rose.

Food

You'll enjoy munching breakfast at **Blue Ridge Biscuit Company** (601 W. State St., 828/357-8501, www.blueridgebiscuitcompany.com, 8am-2pm Wed.-Sun., $3-12), where they serve up cathead biscuits (if you're not familiar, they contain no felines, but are big biscuits, the size of a tomcat's head) plain, buttered, sweet, with egg and cheese, and with sausage or shiitake gravy. Their twisted biscuits are quirky biscuit sandwiches and benedicts; the Grey Beard (fried chicken, fried green tomatoes, honey mustard, arugula) might just have you dancin' in the streets, but if it doesn't, the Smoky Mountain Brook (smoked trout spread, poached egg, tomato jam) will definitely have you bouncing around the room with joy.

Stop in at **Dripolator Coffeehouse** (221 W. State St., 828/699-0999, 6:45am-6pm daily, $2-6) for coffee, pastries, and the like. This cute little shop keeps winning "Best of WNC" (western North Carolina) from *Mountain Xpress* (a free magazine found nearby), and folks keep coming, not because of the awards but for the best coffee in the North Carolina mountains.

Berliner Kindl German Restaurant (121 Broadway St., 828/669-5255, http://berlinerkindl.homestead.com, 11am-8pm Mon.-Sat., $9-28) serves traditional German food like schnitzel, a variety of sausages, and the sides you'd expect: fried potatoes, German potato salad, sauerkraut, and red cabbage. They make their own sauerkraut in-house.

When you're ready for dinner, try **Black Mountain Bistro** (203 E. State Rd., 828/669-5041, www.blackmountainbistro.com, 11am-8pm Mon.-Thurs., 11am-9pm Fri.-Sat., $12-28). They keep a couple of tasty steaks on the menu, and their work with salmon and local trout is awesome, but check out the pork chop with blackberry barbecue sauce, the backyard garden pasta (loaded with seasonal veggies), and their lunchtime sandwich menu (the Up North Reuben is excellent).

Accommodations

The 45-room **Monte Vista Hotel** (308 W. State St., Black Mountain, 828/669-8870, www.mvhotel.com, $169-269) has been serving visitors to the North Carolina mountains since 1937 when the original portion of the hotel was built, but it's the second Monte Vista here; the first was a school building turned hotel back in 1919, giving this place a long history of hospitality. Rooms are more spacious than you'd think a place built in 1937 would offer, but the styling blends a modern and turn-of-the-20th-century feel. The on-site restaurant, **Milton's** (5pm-9pm Wed.-Sun., $18-32), has a good assortment of cocktails and a menu of dishes that are as comforting as they are delicious. Honey roasted pork tenderloin, chicken and dumplings with a bit of fried sage, shrimp and grits, locally raised trout, and a great hanger steak with chimichurri are some of what you'll find here.

The **Inn around the Corner** (109 Church St., 828/669-6005, www.innaroundthecorner.com, $155-245) is a classic bed-and-breakfast in a lovely 1915 home with a huge front porch.

Just about every room has a great view, but the best is from the porch bed, where you'll fall asleep under the gaze of the mountains and wake when the birds start their day.

Arbor House of Black Mountain (207 Rhododendron Ave., 828/357-8525, www.arborhousenc.com, $175-290), a four-room bed-and-breakfast, hosts travelers year-round, but like at most places in the area, peak season coincides with the turning of the leaves every fall. Views from the inn are wide and beautiful, especially when the leaves are out, but book early for leaf season.

Information and Services

The **Black Mountain and Swannanoa Chamber of Commerce** (www.explore-blackmountain.com) maintains a list of member businesses and has a small bit of visitor information on its site, but the best visitor information for Black Mountain is going to be at **Explore Asheville** (www.exploreasheville.com).

Getting There and around

On I-40, take exit 70 or exit 64 to get to Black Mountain. From Asheville, Black Mountain is about 15 minutes east.

WEAVERVILLE

Weaverville, just 10 minutes north of Asheville, served as a vacation town for wealthy city and Piedmont dwellers in the late 1800s, though it had been settled by a handful of families since the 1780s. At one time, a pair of grand hotels—the Dula Springs Hotel and Blackberry Lodge—welcomed well-heeled and notable visitors like author O. Henry when they escaped to the mountains. The town never grew to be much more than a bucolic getaway, and today, with a population hovering around 2,500, Weaverville holds onto its former identity even as it grows into a bedroom community for Asheville. The **Weaverville Business Association** (www.visitweaverville.com) lists all the town's amenities.

Sights

At the **Dry Ridge Museum** (41 N. Main St., 828/407-3701, www.dryridgemuseum.org, 11am-5pm Wed.-Sat. Apr.-Oct., 11am-5pm Thurs.-Sat. Dec.-Mar., free) you'll find a collection of artifacts, letters, and photos telling the history of Weaverville. It's small and has odd hours but may be of interest to local history buffs.

A few miles down the road is the birthplace of North Carolina's Civil War governor, Zebulon T. Vance (if ever there was a Civil War governor's name, that's it). The **Vance Birthplace** (911 Reems Creek Rd., 828/645-6706, www.nchistoricsites.org, 9am-5pm Tues.-Sat.) has a reconstructed log house as well as a tool house, smokehouse, spring house, cabin where enslaved people lived, and a few more recreated structures. Tours of the home are available at the bottom of the hour. Vance and his legacy are notably tarnished due to his speech and actions supporting the traitorous Confederate States of America, but his support for the attempted turncoat nation and the despicable institution of slavery aren't reasons to erase him or this place from our collective history. Instead it's an opportunity to learn about the times, people, and conditions of that stain on the history of the United States. As with many other historic sites across North Carolina and the South, the Vance Birthplace is slowly rolling out the stories and biographies of enslaved people here and in the whole of Reems Creek, helping to paint a more accurate and factual portrait of this place and its people.

Recreation

Curtis Wright Outfitters (24 N. Main St., 828/645-8700, www.curtiswrightoutfitters.com, 9am-6pm Mon.-Sat.) keeps a store stocked with fly-fishing gear, clothing, tackle, and supplies. They offer a range of guided fishing trips (1 angler $200 halfday wading, $300 full-day wading, $350 halfday float trip, $75 per additional person) on area streams and rivers. You can also shoot some sporting clays (shooting $125, beginner instruction $195, advanced instruction $250), or take part in one of their fly fishing schools ($175) or classes ($75) to hone your technique or learn to tie flies. They also offer falconry ($125, $50 to observe) where you'll be able to handle the birds after some instruction and under careful guidance.

Shopping

There are a lot of great potters in western North Carolina, but Rob and Beth Mangum of **Mangum Pottery** (16 N. Main St., 828/645-4929, www.mangumpottery.com, 9am-5pm Mon.-Fri., 10am-4pm Sat.) are two of the most innovative. They make beautiful earthy-colored dinnerware and mugs to satisfy the practical side of life, and they also build the most unexpected things out of pottery—ceramic clocks, ceramic furniture, ceramic musical instruments that really play—all in Seussian shapes and colors.

Maggie B's Wine & Specialty Store (10-C S. Main St., 828/645-1111, www.maggiebswine.com, 11am-6pm Tues.-Sat.) is Weaverville's first wine and specialty food shop opened by a husband and wife who know what tastes good. Maggie B's has an excellent selection of wine and beer and an assortment of meats, cheeses, and snacks to make for a perfect picnic. If you're here and you're hungry, they do have a menu of sandwiches and salads ($5-11), and they sell wine and beer by the glass.

The artwork at **MIYA Gallery** (20 N. Main St., 828/658-9655, www.miyagallery.com, 10am-5pm Mon.-Sat.) includes fine art, jewelry, furniture, and sculpture. More than 90 area artists and craftspeople have their work on display here. Pick something up, or just admire the leather books, exquisite and experimental wooden vessels, and fine photo prints of mountain scenes.

Food

If you're in Weaverville and you have a hankering for pizza, **Blue Mountain Pizza** (55 N. Main St., 828/658-8778, www.bluemountainpizza.com, 11am-9pm Wed.-Sun., $9-25) is your spot. Blue Mountain Pizza serves specialty pizzas, calzones, stromboli, subs, and salads. Their Henny Penny Pizza is a barbecued chicken pizza with red onion and bacon, and the Marge is simply olive oil, Roma tomatoes, fresh mozzarella, and basil. Grab a specialty pie, make your personal favorite, or even pick up a take-and-bake pizza or just the dough and play pizza parlor back at your place.

A few doors down from Mangum Pottery you'll find **Well-Bred Bakery & Café** (26 N. Main St., 828/645-9300, www.wellbredbakery. com, 9am-4pm daily, $2-8), which sells soups, sandwiches, quiche, and salads as well as a dazzling array of artisanal breads and elaborate desserts. They promise "karma-free coffee" (I think that means fair-trade) and even sell the *New York Times,* so you don't have to go into crossword-puzzle withdrawal on your trip.

Mediterranean fare is the go-to at **Twisted Laurel Weaverville** (10-A S. Main St., 828/645-2700, www.twistedlaurel.com, 11am-9pm Sun.-Thurs., 11am-10pm Fri.-Sat., $9-17) and that means plenty of Greek- and Italian-inspired dishes to choose from. An Italian sub or a gyro, Greek-style meatballs, the classic chicken parm, even pizza pies that play on house favorites (like the Fat Jake's, with chicken, bacon, onions, and ranch) and veggie- or meat-loaded options. Their draft beer selection is great, and considering they have a sister restaurant in Asheville, it'd better be.

At the moment there's one brewery in Weaverville, **Eluvium Brewing Company** (11 Florida Ave., 828/484-1799, www.eluviumbrewing.com, 2pm-9pm Mon.-Thurs., 11:30am-10pm Fri.-Sat., noon-9pm Sun.), and since downtown Weaverville is so small, it's easy to find. They keep more than a dozen beers on draft, with a few guest taps mingling with the house brews. For house brews, they take a broad approach to style, making hazy IPAs, farmhouse ales, cream ales, a sour lager, porters, stouts, and more.

Also in Weaverville, **Glass Onion** (18 N. Main St., 828/645-8866, www.glassonionasheville.com, 5pm-8pm Wed.-Sun., $22-38) serves a fantastic dinner. Dishes are mostly Italian, but a few French influences sneak in, and everything on the menu uses foraged and locally sourced ingredients. House-made ravioli are stuffed with wild mushrooms. Rigatoni comes served with wild-boar bolognese (you must try it). The black Angus rib-eye au poivre (see, told you some French slipped in) comes from Brasstown, a spot in the far southwestern corner of the state, but not too far from Weaverville.

Accommodations

Dry Ridge Inn Bed and Breakfast (26 Brown St., 828/658-3899, www.dryridgeinn. com, $159-199) has eight guest rooms in a former parsonage built in 1849. Rooms feature king or queen beds, a gas fireplace, and reliable Wi-Fi. A fridge stocked with complimentary beverages is on the main floor. Breakfast is served either in the dining room or on the patio. Weather permitting, have breakfast outside and feel that fresh mountain air that made this town a vacation spot for generations.

The Inn on Main (88 S. Main St., 828/645-4935 or 877/873-6074, www.innonmain.com, $119-219) offers an eco-friendly place to rest your head. They use no cleaning chemicals or deodorizers in the inn, all bath products are natural, and they cook their vegetarian meals using as many organic ingredients as possible. There are three rooms, a pair of one-bedroom mini suites, and a two-bedroom apartment that can sleep five. Each of the accommodations is comfy and cozy; on top of that, the owners, who still live on-site, know the area and are quick with a recommendation.

Information and Services

The **Weaverville Business Association** (www.visitweaverville.com) provides visitor information. You can also find visitor information at **Explore Asheville** (www. exploreasheville.com).

Getting There

Weaverville is just 10 minutes north of Asheville along a very easy drive. Simply follow U.S. 70 west, U.S. 19 north, and U.S. 23 north, then turn right on Weaver Boulevard.

MADISON COUNTY

North of Asheville, Madison County is a world unto itself. Just 30 minutes north of Asheville, the wild mountain terrain is spotted with hot springs and towns no bigger than ink blots on a map, but still this county, which shares a border with an equally wild corner of Tennessee, draws visitors. Some come for the solitude, others the hot springs, others the rafting and to explore the great outdoors; still others come for the music. As is true all along the Appalachian Range and especially in the Blue Ridge Mountains, music plays an important role in the identity of the place. In most towns you'll find a stage, porch, coffee shop, or gas station where bluegrass musicians will gather to play, carrying on the long-held traditions of the people here.

Sports and Recreation

On a 4,700-foot mountaintop above Mars Hill, the **Wolf Ridge Ski Resort** (578 Valley View Circle, 828/689-4111 or 800/817-4111, www.skiwolfridgenc.com, 9am-4:30pm and 6pm-10pm Mon.-Sat., 9am-4:30pm Sun. Dec.-Mar., $28-82 adults, $23-66 students and ages 5-18, free over age 64 and under age 4, rentals $28-36) has more than 80 acres of prime skiing and snowboarding slopes. It is also the home of the Snow Sports School, which offers private and group lessons for all ages of beginning and intermediate winter sports enthusiasts. There are multiple lifts, two lodges to relax in, and multiple hearty dining options. The attached **Scenic Wolf Resort** offers year-round cabin accommodations ($300-550 in season), a huge indoor heated pool, and numerous recreational activities.

    Sandy Bottom Trail Rides (1459 Caney Fork Rd., Marshall, 828/649-3464 or 800/959-3513, www.sandybottomtrailrides.net, 8am-5pm daily, 1 hour $65, 2 hours $95, 3 hours $130, $10 discount for cash), based at a 100-year-old family farm, leads horseback treks deep into the forest to an early-19th-century garnet mine. You can take private riding lessons (additional $20 per hour) with an experience guide, and there's a gem mine ($50 pp full day, $25 pp half day, one gallon limit) on the property you can visit. The mine itself is closed, but you can root through the tailings (that's the stuff that's left over from the commercial mining) and find some gorgeous and possibly precious stones. Bring your own tools and buckets, and feel free to ride here as part of your equestrian experience, or drive: the road will get you close, but you'll have a short hike in, so be prepared.

    There are plenty of white-water rafting opportunities in the area, with several guide companies to choose from. **Hot Springs Rafting Co.** (81 Bridge St., 843/319-4586, www.hotspringsraftingco.com, rafting $50-85, funyak $50 per day, river tubing float trips $30) keeps you on the river right around Hot Springs. Their guided rafting trips are quite the thrill, but the unguided trips and "funyaks" (think white-water raft meets inflatable kayak) can give you a satisfying day on the water. **French Broad Adventures** (12 Good Adventures Lane, Marshall, 828/649-0486 or 800/570-7238, www.frenchbroadrafting.com, white-water rafting $55-88, flat-water rafting $40-53, zip-lining $95, canyoneering $130) can get you equipped and ready for a guided or unguided rafting trip on the French Broad River, which has both white-water and calm sections. Or get your adrenaline rush in the trees on a course that mixes zip lines, rappels, and short hikes to make a unique mountain experience.

Entertainment and Events

Mars Hill, a tiny college town, is a center of mountain culture thanks to Mars Hill College. The **Bascom Lamar Lunsford "Minstrel of the Appalachians" Festival** (828/689-1115, www.blueridgemusicnc.com, early fall, free) is a nearly 50-year-old annual gathering of some of the best mountain musicians, dancers, and craftspeople from this hot bed of folk traditions. Mars Hill College is also the home of the **Southern Appalachian Repertory Theatre** (Owen Theater, 44 College St., 828/689-1232, http://sartplays.com), a highly regarded ensemble presenting a range of contemporary drama, musicals, and family productions. SART's stage is in the Owen Theater, a great-looking old Baptist Church on the Mars Hill College campus.

Many other venues in Madison County towns feature live bluegrass and old-time music. **Zuma Coffee** (7 N. Main St., Marshall, 828/649-1617, www.zumascoffee. com, 8am-4pm Mon.-Fri., 8am-3pm Sat., under $10) has a free weekly bluegrass jam session (7pm Thurs.) and serves up a good cup of coffee. **The Depot** (282 S. Main St., Marshall, 828/206-2332), a former railroad depot building, has free concerts (6:30pm Fri.). And the **Madison County Arts Council** (90 S. Main St., Marshall, 828/649-1301, www.madison-countyarts.com) wouldn't be worth their salt if they didn't host a few concerts, but lucky for you, they have plenty. The Arts Council puts on shows at their headquarters on Main Street and at the **Ebbs Chapel Performing Arts Center** (271 Laurel Valley Rd., Mars Hill, 828/689-3465, www.ebbschapelaudi-torium.com); check the schedule for shows, times, and prices.

Food

The **Smoky Mountain Diner** (70 Lance Ave., Hot Springs, 828/622-7571, www. hotspringsnc.org, 6am-2pm Mon.-Wed., 6am-7pm Thurs.-Sat., $2-17) is one part diner, one part your granny's kitchen table. Country staples like cornbread, pinto beans, chicken livers, and pork chops are on the menu, as are biscuits, pancakes, French toast, omelets, and even pizza. If you're so inclined, they have all-you-can-eat pinto beans for $5.

Big Pillow Brewing (26 Andrews Ave. N., Hot Springs, 828/539-1939, www.bigpillow-brewing.com, noon-8pm Tues.-Thurs., noon-9pm Fri.-Sat.), Hot Spring's first brewery, has arrived, and it brought with it the **Grey Eagle Taqueria** ($5-15). They have a very cool space with a biergarten feel and a stage where there's live music every Wednesday night. Their beer—they keep 9 or 10 on draft—runs the gamut from IPAs to kettle sours to porters and pale ales, and to go with that, the Grey Eagle Taqueria serves up tacos, burritos, bowls and more, so grab a light lager and some tacos and chow down.

You can grab a bite to eat or pick up some gourmet groceries (anyone fancy a fancy picnic?) at **Vast Rivière Provisions** (158 Bridge St., Hot Springs, 828/777-9379, www.vasteriv-iere.com, 11am-7pm daily, $10-24). Options are on the healthy side, so go with a quiche and mixed greens, a ramen or rice bowl, or a salad; or you can head to the store for grab-and-go and ready-to-eat meals along with goods for a charcuterie tray or stocking up a pantry.

When you head over to **Dave's 209** (13075 Hwy. 209, Hot Springs, 828/622-0001, www. daves209.com, 11:30am-7:30pm Mon.-Tues. and Thurs.-Sat., 11:30am-5pm Sun., $2-11.50), be ready for a craveable burger and a milk shake you'll adore. This motorcycle-friendly spot is frequented by visitors on two wheels, four wheels, and more, and it's because of those burgers and the secret seasoning—Mountain Dust—they put on their fries. One taste and you'll get it.

Accommodations

Defying that worn-out stereotype of mountain isolation, Madison County has for centuries been a destination for vacationers because of its natural hot springs. Going back at least to the mid-18th century—and, according to tradition, long before the first European settlers arrived—the springs have had a reputation for curative powers. A succession of grand hotels operated at Hot Springs, all long since burned down. In one of the area's odder historical moments, the resort served as an internment camp for German prisoners during World War I, mainly commercial sailors and members of an orchestra who had the misfortune of being in the United States when the war broke out.

Modern visitors can still take a dip in the mineral springs. **Hot Springs Resort and Spa** (315 Bridge St., Hot Springs, 828/622-7676, www.nchotsprings.com, suites $120-225, cabins $75-250, camping $45-60, RV sites $65-75) is a much simpler affair than the old hotels; it's not a luxury destination but a place where you can lodge or camp for the night and soak in the famous 100°F water. Spa services run $50-130, and there's a series of outdoor mineral baths (1:30pm-9:45pm Mon.-Thurs., 9am-9:45pm Fri.-Sun., premium mineral bath $25-55 pp); come early as rates increase after 6pm.

There's an abundance of **rental homes** in Hot Springs, many of which you'll find under the Lodgings tab at www.hotspringsnc.org, but if you want to keep it simple, go with **Springbrook Cottages** (94 Andrews Ave. S., Hot Springs, 828/622-7385, www.springbrookcottages.com, $85-100). They have seven one-bedroom cottages overlooking Spring Creek and each cottage has a balcony where you can soak up that view in private. Three of the cottages have kitchens, so if you're planning on using Hot Springs as a base camp and you want to make a meal or two, be sure to request a cottage with something more than a microwave and a fridge.

Appalachian Trail hikers, and those who like to play hard and live cheap, should take notice of **Laughing Heart Lodge** (289 NW U.S. 25/70, Hot Springs, 828/622-0165, www.laughingheartlodge.com). Here you'll find several types of accommodations. First, the hostel ($30 bunk room, $40 single private room, $55 double private room, tent with full hostel facilities use $15), which was built in 1974 but still offers a modicum of comfort and privacy; then the lodge ($100-170), which has seven rooms, each with a private bath.

Information and Services

You'll find visitor information through the **Madison County Tourism Administration** at www.visitmadison-county.com. This site covers all the towns in the county and is therefore comprehensive. If you'd like to get more specific, try www.hotspringsnc.org from the **Hot Springs Tourism Association** for details on the town of Hot Springs and www.townofmarshall.org, for information that's more municipal than touristy on the town of Marshall. **Mars Hill**'s website—www.townofmarshill.org—is also geared more toward municipal information than tourist interests, but there is some that visitors may find of interest.

Getting There

To get to Madison County and the towns of Marshall and Hot Springs, you'll want to head north out of Asheville along U.S. 25/70. Take exit 19A for Weaverville-Woodfin, but continue on U.S. 25/70. You'll reach Marshall first, a 20-mile drive from Asheville; Hot Springs is another 16 miles north. Mars Hill is a 20-minute drive north from Asheville via U.S. 23/19. Follow U.S. 25/70 out of Asheville and stay on this route past Weaverville, where it will turn into U.S. 23/19; take exit 11 onto Highway 213 to get to Mars Hill.

Southern Blue Ridge and Foothills

The mountains of Polk, Rutherford, and Henderson Counties, south of Asheville, have an air of enchantment to them—meaning that the area gives the impalpable sense of having had a spell cast on it. No doubt a parapsychologist could assign a name to this atmosphere; it has a weird energy where it seems as likely that you'll encounter a fairy or an alien as a postal worker. There are some quantifiable symptoms of this peculiarity. For one, Polk County has its own climate; called the Thermal Belt, the meteorological pocket formed on this sheltered slope of the Blue Ridge has distinctly milder summers and winters than the surrounding areas. In the 19th century it became a favorite summering spot for the Southern elite. Some old houses and inns remain as vestiges of this genteel past.

In early 1874, Bald Mountain, north of Chimney Rock, began to rumble; it grew louder until, by the spring of that year, the mountain shook with such force that windows and crockery in valley homes shattered. A smoking, hissing crack opened in the side of the mountain, causing residents to fear a volcanic eruption. Many moved away or found religion. The shaking and rumbling eventually settled down. A crew of spelunkers a generation later concluded that the mountain was hollow and that enormous boulders sometimes became dislodged inside, showering into the caves below and causing the enormous booms. At least that's one theory.

Chimney Rock itself was the scene of bizarre phenomena in the first decade of the 1800s. Locals and visitors began to report witnessing spectral gatherings, crowds of people gathered on top of the rock and rising together into the sky. In the fall of 1811 multiple witnesses saw, on different occasions, two armed cavalries mounted on winged horses battling in the air over Chimney Rock, their gleaming swords clashing audibly. Whichever phantom cavalry triumphed in that battle, the rock is now maintained by the state of North Carolina and climbed daily by hundreds of visitors, none of whom have reported sightings of any spectral cavalry, horse droppings, or flashing sabers.

BREVARD

Brevard is the pleasant seat of the improbably named Transylvania County (unlike in vampire stories, it's not creepy, but beautiful in a Gothic forest way) only 48 minutes southwest of Asheville. As you might expect, Halloween is a big deal in this town. Brevard is also known for sheltering a population of rather startling and odd-looking white squirrels. The local legend about their origins is that their ancestors escaped from an overturned circus truck in Florida in 1940 and made their way to Brevard as pets. More likely, say researchers, they came from an exotic pet breeder in Florida and were acquired by a Brevard area family. In any case, the white squirrels escaped into the wild of Transylvania County, and you'll probably see their descendants in the area when you visit.

Sports and Recreation

About 10 miles south of Brevard, **DuPont State Recreational Forest** (U.S. 276, 828/877-6527, www.dupontstaterecreationalforest.com) has more than 90 miles of hiking trails on 10,000 acres. Some of Transylvania County's beautiful waterfalls are located within the forest and accessible on foot via moderate or strenuous forest trails, or, for people with disabilities only, with special permits and advance reservation, by vehicle. Visitors should use caution, wear brightly colored clothing, and leave that bearskin cape at home September-December, when hikers share the woods with hunters. The **Aleen Steinberg Visitor Center** (89 Buck Forest Rd., Cedar Mountain, 9am-5pm daily mid-Mar.-Dec., 10am-4pm Sat.-Sun.

Southern Blue Ridge and Foothills

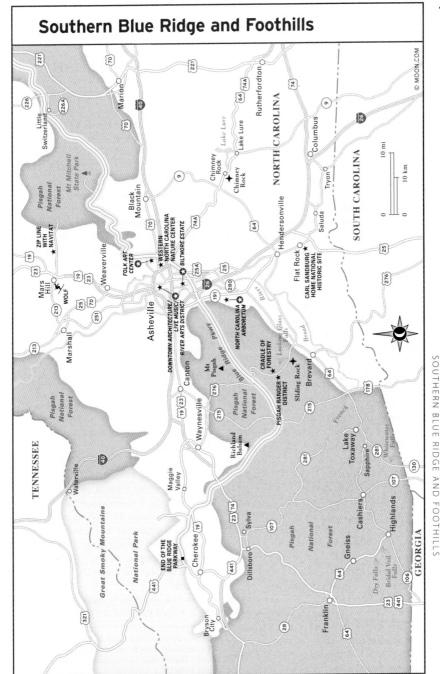

© MOON.COM

Jan.-mid-Mar.) has restrooms and trash cans and is staffed by volunteers who are happy to help with trail recommendations. The visitors center is near the trailhead to Hooker Falls.

Many of the hiking and mountain biking trails are true rugged forest paths; others, like those that lead to a trio of waterfalls—Hooker, Triple, and High Falls—are wide maintained avenues through the woods. The hike, or hikes, as you'll follow several trails, to Triple and High Falls can be hot, sweaty affairs in spring and summer, so bring water. But the views are more than worth it, and in fall it's a phenomenal hike. After you make this longer hike, make the shorter one to the lower Hooker Falls and go for a swim in the crisp mountain water. Already cool, it will feel downright cold—and quite refreshing—on a hot day. If you hike the three falls, you're looking at a 2-mile loop for High Falls, a 0.4-mile trail to Triple Falls, and another 0.4-mile trail to Hooker, for a total of 2.8 miles. Downloadable maps and more information are available through **Friends of DuPont Forest** (www.dupontforest.com).

★ **WATERFALL TOURING**
Local Guide Craig Miller helps visitors discover some of the more beautiful and remote waterfalls in Transylvania County through his **Land of Waterfalls Tours** (828/884-8982, www.tourwaterfalls.com, $75 for 2 people, $10 per additional person). When you're ready to chase some waterfalls, Miller will meet you at your hotel, B&B, or another convenient spot to start your tour. Most tours hit 6-7 waterfalls, and all within an easy walk of the parking area (which makes this great for kids or folks with mobility difficulties), but you can customize your tour to fit your ability level and interests (as you can imagine, Craig leads a lot of photographers to the falls around here).

You'll find maps for sale—and possibly some for free—showing the area's waterfalls in the outdoor shops and visitors center. And there are specific books—full sized guides like this, as well as little pocket-size trail-friendly write-ups and maps. I've used all of these and

then some, but I always end up looking at the waterfalls page on www.explorebrevard.com, so save yourself a few minutes and start there.

Entertainment and Events

The **Brevard Music Center** (349 Andante Lane, 828/862-2100, www.brevardmusic.org) has attracted the highest-caliber young musicians for more than 70 years for intensive summer-long classical music instruction. Throughout the summer, Brevard Music Center students, as well as visiting soloists of international fame, put on world-class concerts, performing works that have included Tchaikovsky as well as Gilbert and Sullivan.

Brevard Brewing Company (63 E. Main St., 282/885-2101, www.brevard-brewing.com, 2pm-10pm daily) was the first brewery in the county, and it always keeps six taps flowing with its own brews, including a Bohemian pilsner, a Munich-style dunkel, a lager, an IPA, and an American red ale. **Ecusta Brewing** (43 Pisgah Hwy., Suite 3, Pisgah Forest, 828/966-2337, www.ecustabrewing.com, 1pm-9pm Mon.-Thurs., noon-9pm Fri.-Sat., noon-8pm Sun.) is a few miles north of town but worth the short drive. Its range of styles will please everyone from hop-heads (IPAs, pale ales) to sour fans (sours incorporating ginger and mint, blood orange, and wild yeasts).

An import from Colorado but no less welcome is **Oskar Blues Brewery** (342 Mountain Industrial Dr., 828/883-2337, www.oskarblues.com, noon-8pm Sun.-Thurs., noon-9pm Fri.-Sat.), which serves popular beers that include Mama's Little Yella Pils (a Czech pilsner) and Old Chub Scotch Ale as well as hard seltzer and the thirst-quenching Margarita Gose. If you're hungry, the **Oskar Blues Chubwagon** ($4.50-12) serves burgers, fries, hot dogs, and a mean chicken-tender sandwich.

The Hub and Pisgah Tavern (11 Mama's Place, Pisgah Forest, 828/884-8670, www.

1: Brevard's small-town charm **2:** waterfall in Transylvania County **3:** covered bridge above High Falls in Dupont State Recreational Forest **4:** Sliding Rock waterfall

thehubpisgah.com, 10am-6pm Mon.-Fri., 9am-6pm Sat., 10am-5pm Sun.) is a kind of all-in-one taproom, bike shop, gear depot, and food-truck stop that sits right at the edge of the Pisgah National Forest. The tavern serves cold brews on tap as well as in cans and bottles. Beer choices span the country, but you'll always find a good selection of local beers. While you work on your pint, shop for a new bike or some new gear, or step outside and see which food truck is serving; if there's a line of locals waiting to order, that's a good sign.

Brevard's new **Lumber Arts District** (100-300 blocks of King St., Brevard) has a number of things going on in an area once home to Brevard Lumber and other building-supply houses. Live music at **185 King Street** (185 King St., Brevard, 828/877-1850, www.185kingst.com, 4pm-9pm Tues., 4pm-11pm Wed.-Fri., noon-11pm Sat., noon-10pm Sun.), where you'll also find a **kitchen** (4pm-8pm Tues., 4pm-9pm Wed.-Fri., noon-9pm Sat., noon-8pm Sun., $4-14) serving snacks, along with **Noblebräu Brewing** (4pm-9pm Tues., 4pm-11pm Wed.-Fri., noon-11pm Sat., noon-10pm Sun.) with a half-dozen brews on draft. Nearby **UpCountry Brewing Company** (212 King St., Suite B, Brevard, 828/885-7538, www.upcountrybrewing.com, 4pm-9pm Mon., 2pm-9pm Wed.-Thurs., 2pm-10pm Fri.-Sat., 2pm-9pm Sun.) has spirits from their distillery in Asheville as well as beers in cans and on draft; style-wise they're wide-ranging, and you'll find sours, stouts, several spins on IPAs, and a great maibock.

Shopping

Brevard calls to a number of fine and folk artists, and some of the best local work is represented at **Number 7 Fine Arts and Crafts Cooperative** (2 W. Main St., 828/883-2294, www.number7arts.org, 11am-5pm Mon.-Sat., noon-4pm Sun.). This gallery has featured works by a diverse group of around 25 Transylvania County artists for more than 15 years. Ask about the photography, textiles, oils and watercolors, sculptures, and pottery on display—the artists themselves work the

register and can help you find a piece you love.

Named for Brevard's famed creatures, the **White Squirrel Shoppe** (6 W. Main St., 828/877-3530, www.whitesquirrelshoppe. com, 10:30am-5:30pm Mon.-Thurs., 10am-6pm Fri.-Sat., 11:30am-5pm Sun.) is where to go for souvenirs. The shop's got a bit of everything, so drop in and pick up a memento or two.

Over in the Lumber Arts District, **The Underground Salvage Co.** (22 W. French Broad St., Brevard, 828/885-2744, 10am-5pm Thurs.-Sat.) is a wonderland for the curious and crafty. These folks salvage old barns, houses, and buildings of all sorts and have a warehouse full of stuff to show for it. Live-edge wood slabs and reclaimed lumber, antique doors, fireplace fixtures, tin ceilings, and all sorts of stuff is on hand for you to buy, or you can take home something they made in the shop around back. They also have furniture and fixtures (door knobs, hinges, and the like) and all sorts of stuff to dig through.

Outdoor gear and a solid selection of T-shirts, plus some North Carolina beer on tap—which you can sip while you shop—makes **D. D. Bullwinkel's Outdoors** (60 E. Main St., 828/862-4700, www.ddbullwinkels. com, 10am-6pm Mon.-Thurs., 10am-7pm Fri.-Sat., noon-6pm Sun.) a must-stop. You'll find whatever you forgot or just realized you need on a trip along the parkway, including backpacks, hiking poles, boots and socks, water bottles, and technical clothing. The staff are outdoors devotees, so ask any of your gear questions or for suggestions on where to hike, picnic, or skinny dip.

Food

Located in Brevard's Lumber Arts District, ★ **Vescovo** (175 King St., Brevard, 828/885-7630, www.vescovobrevard.com, 5pm-9pm Tues.-Sat., $17-45) has become a favorite spot in town. Everything here—the dry-aged steaks, the crazy-fresh seafood, and the Italian dishes—is beautiful on the plate and terrific on the fork. Start off with the Filet Meatballs or the Beets by Trey (he's the chef-owner), move on to the Cacio e Pepe or the veggie-loaded Spaghettini Verdura, then your choice of mains—scallops, sea bass, steak, a monster pork chop—and cap it off with an after-dinner espresso or drink.

★ **Marco Trattoria** (204 W. Main St., 828/883-4841, www.marcotrattoria.com, 11am-3pm daily, 5pm-9pm Mon.-Sat., $9-24) is from the former owners of Hobnob, one of Brevard's top restaurants for years. Following a little break to find some inspiration, chef Marc Dambax is back with an Italian-inspired restaurant that's quickly become known as one of the best restaurants in town. Pizzas fly out of the wood-fired oven, and the menu is full of Italian classics and Dambax's Italianate spin on things through dishes like North Carolina mountain trout *piccata* and pancetta-wrapped monkfish served over seasonal veggies.

The Blind Mule at Toxaway Station (14 S. Gaston St., 828/553-8978, www.blindmulerestaurant.com, 5pm-9pm Wed.-Sun., reservations required, $10-35) serves a menu rich in tapas and small sharable plates, but they don't forget the entrées, with 3-4 on offer at any given time. Fresh seasonal ingredients inspire the menu, which changes weekly, and whether you're ordering a salad, some poutine, a burger, an Indian-spiced lamb pot pie, or an entrée (their treatment of trout—often served with some great grits—is a winner), you'll leave happy you stopped by for a meal.

For an old-school shake or a quick bite, head to **Rocky's Grill & Soda Shop** (50 S. Broad St., 828/877-5375, 11am-6pm Thurs.-Mon., $5-12). This must-stop has been around since 1942, and the nostalgic counter with its line of chrome stools will transport you back to the heyday of soda fountains. Grab a malt, a milk shake, an ice cream soda, a root beer float, or an egg cream, which are especially rewarding after a morning hike or bike ride.

When the weather's right, dining on the patio at **Jordan Street Café** (48 W. Jordan St., 828/883-2558, www.thejordanstreetcafe.com, 4pm-9pm Thurs., 4pm-10pm Fri.-Sat.,

11am-2pm and 4pm-9pm Sun., dinner $10-28, brunch $14-20) is the way to go. They serve a little bit of everything—fish-and-chips, blackened chicken sandwiches, burgers, salads, daily flatbread pizza and quesadilla specials—but the menu is simple enough to keep it focused.

If you want a picnic lunch you can always head to the store and pick up a few things for your meal alfresco, or you can pay a visit to **Smoke On Drive-Thru BBQ** (585 S. Caldwell St., Brevard, 828/552-4584, www.eatsmokeonbbq.com, 11am-8pm Mon.-Sat., $12-25). Pick up a pulled pork, pimento cheese, brisket or jackfruit sandwich or taco plate; grab a hearty platter piled with ribs, smoked chicken, pulled pork, or brisket; and don't forget the sides, then head out to a park downtown, a picnic table in the Pisgah National Forest, or an overlook on the Blue Ridge Parkway for a memorable meal.

PISGAH RANGER DISTRICT

Just north of Brevard in the town of Pisgah Forest is the main entrance to the **Pisgah Ranger District** (1600 Pisgah Hwy., Pisgah Forest, 828/877-3265, www.fs.usda.gov, 9am-4:30pm daily Nov.-Mar., 9am-5pm daily Apr.-Oct.) of the Pisgah National Forest. The forest covers 500,000 acres, which is a large swath of western North Carolina, but this 157,000-acre ranger district has many of the forest's favorite attractions. A good topographic map is available from National Geographic (www.natgeomaps.com). You'll find miles of U.S. Forest Service roads to explore, plenty of backcountry camping, and some amazing mountain bike riding, including some excellent single-track runs. In the ranger district are more than 275 miles of hiking trails and several campgrounds; the most easily accessible is **Davidson River Campground** (1 Davidson River Circle, Pisgah Forest, campground 828/384-6666, reservations 800/444-6777, www.recreation.gov, year-round, $28-56), which is 1.5 miles from the Brevard entrance. It has showers and toilets.

The **Shining Rock Wilderness** and the **Middle Prong Wilderness,** which adjoins Shining Rock to the southwest, are a rugged terrain that rises from 3,200 feet at its lowest point, along the West Pigeon River, to a towering 6,400 feet at Richmond Balsam. **Cold Mountain,** made famous by the book and movie of the same name, is a real peak located within the Shining Rock Wilderness, and seeing it helps make the struggles of the fictional characters more real. These mountains are steep and the forests dense, and what trails there are have no signage. This is a popular area among experienced backwoods trekkers, but it is not recommended for casual visitors because it is exceedingly easy to get lost. At a minimum, hikers should be adept at using both a compass and a topographic map before venturing into these wilderness areas.

Not to be confused with Shining Rock, **Sliding Rock** is an easily accessible waterfall and swimming spot with a parking lot ($4), bathhouse, and lifeguards (10am-6pm daily late May-early Sept.). You can actually ride down the 60-foot waterfall, a smooth rock face (not so smooth that you shouldn't wear sturdy britches), over which 11,000 gallons of water rush every minute into the chilly swimming hole below.

If you have kids with you, make sure you stop at the **Cradle of Forestry** (11250 Pisgah Hwy., Pisgah Forest, 828/877-3130, www.cradleofforestry.com, 10am-5pm Wed.-Mon. mid-Apr.-early Nov., $6 adults, $3 ages 5-12). This museum and activity complex commemorates the rise of the forestry profession in the United States, which originated here at a turn-of-the-20th-century training school in the forests once owned by George Washington Vanderbilt, master of the Biltmore Estate. Plow days and living history days throughout the year give an interesting glimpse into this region's old-time methods of farming and frontier living. Self-guided trails lead through the woods to many interesting locations of this campus of America's first school of forestry. Most of what's here is geared toward little ones.

Accommodations

Slip back in time at the ★ **Sunset Motel** (523 S. Broad St., 828/884-9106, www.thesunsetmotel.com, $115-160), a kitschy throwback to the days of the classic roadside motel: It's cheap, comfortable, and has chairs right outside your door so you can visit with your neighbors. It also has the best modern convenience—free Wi-Fi. The staff is super friendly and ready to help with suggestions for places to eat and things to do. You can add on tickets to the Brevard Music Center, waterfall tours, and more when you book your room.

Built in 1885 and listed on the National Register of Historic Places, **The Inn at Brevard** (315 E. Main St., 828/884-2105, www.theinnatbrevard.com, $195-300) is spacious, beautiful, and kid-friendly. The stately 14-room B&B was built in 1885 and makes a good picture; the rooms are well appointed, and there's a full breakfast every day. Throughout the Inn you'll find photography showing the inn through history and the owners' incredible art collection of paintings from the Renaissance to today.

One of the most lauded places to stay in North Carolina is the nearby ★ **Greystone Inn** (220 Greystone Lane, Lake Toxaway, 21 miles west of Brevard, 828/966-4700, www.greystoneinn.com, $309-429). Perched on the banks of Lake Toxaway, Greystone Inn has 30 rooms, many with balconies overlooking the lake; a spa (treatments from $90) that's the picture of tranquility; and a gorgeous lakeside restaurant serving breakfast (8am-11am daily, $12-15), lunch (noon-3pm daily, $16-20), and dinner (5pm-9pm daily, $20-51). The concierge can help you arrange activities like falconry, horseback riding, mountain biking, road cycling, fishing, and recreation on Lake Toxaway. The elite have been playing on Lake Toxaway for quite some time, and back in 1910, Lucy Armstrong, a socialite from Savannah, and her husband were vacationing here, joining the Rockefellers, Vanderbilts, Firestones, and other Gilded Age barons on their getaway, when she fell in love with the place. By 1913 she decided to build a vacation home here, and by 1915, what we know as the Greystone Inn was built. After years of use, Armstrong died and the property fell into disrepair until the mid-1980s, when the current owners discovered the place and began the long process of restoring it to its former glory and beyond.

CAMPING

Davidson River Campground (1 Davidson River Circle, Pisgah Forest, campground 828/384-6666, reservations 800/444-6777, www.recreation.gov, year-round, $28-56) is just outside Brevard in the Shining Rock Wilderness Area. There are around 160 sites here, some with river access. Each site comes equipped with a picnic table, fire ring, and grill. Hot showers and flush toilets are available. It's the most convenient campground for exploring the hiking and fishing in the area as well as checking out the waterfalls.

Just a 10-minute drive south of Brevard, on 14 mountaintop acres, is **Ash Grove Mountain Cabins and Camping** (29 Ash Grove Way, 828/885-7216, www.ash-grove. com, tent and RV sites $33-55, cabins $130-150, $10 per night for 2 pets), with some pet-friendly facilities available. This retreat is open year-round, unlike others in the area, so you can experience all four seasons in this lovely spot. The cabins are quaint and cozy, and the campsites are well maintained. Common areas feature a bonfire pit, a few lawn games, and a tiny waterfall.

The Adventure Village & Lodgings (129 Israel Rd., 828/862-5411, www.theadventure-village.com) has loads of places to stay. Across the property are 19 cabins ($89-155), 50 RV sites ($44) with 50 more expected to open by late 2022, and a whole heap of primitive tent camping sites ($22). The property is 90 acres all set up to help you have a good visit. There's a catfish pond, biking and hiking trails, a playground, and a swimming and wading pool. Add in the super-friendly folks who run the place and you've got an excellent spot to stay.

HENDERSONVILLE

An easy drive of 30 minutes south from Asheville, Hendersonville is a comfortable small city with a walkable downtown filled with boutiques and cafés. It's also the heart of North Carolina's apple industry. Hundreds of orchards cover the hillsides of Henderson County, and all along the highway, long packinghouses bustle in late summer as they process more than three million tons of apples. There are also many shops and produce stands run by members of old orchard-owning families, where you can buy apples singly or by the bushel, along with cider, preserves, and many other apple products.

Sights

One of North Carolina's cool small transportation museums is located at the Hendersonville Airport. The **Western North Carolina Air Museum** (1340 Gilbert St., 828/698-2482, www.westernnorthcaroli-naairmuseum.com, noon-5pm Sat.-Sun., free) houses a collection of more than a dozen historic small aircraft, both originals and reproductions. Most are from the 1930s and 1940s, though some are even older; all are wonderfully fun contraptions to visit.

Sierra Nevada Brewery (100 Sierra Nevada Way, Mills River, information 828/681-5300, taproom 828/708-6242, www. sierranevada.com, 11am-9pm Sun.-Thurs., 11am-10pm Fri.-Sat.) is about 20 minutes from Hendersonville, midway between Hendersonville and Asheville, and it's a beer lover's playground. They have tours of the brewery (on the hour 11am-3pm Mon.-Thurs., 11am-4pm Fri.-Sat., noon-4pm Sun., free), tours showing off their sustainable practices (2:30pm Fri.-Sat., free), and a three-hour Beer Geek Tour (their name, not mine; 2:30pm Thurs., $30), as well as plenty of beer to sample. There's a fantastic little restaurant ($9-28) on-site and an indoor and outdoor space for concerts and special events.

Shopping

Hendersonville's downtown **Curb Market** (221 N. Church St., at 2nd Ave., 828/692-8012, www.curbmarket.com, 8am-2pm Thurs. and Sat. year-round, 8am-2pm Tues. Apr.-Dec.) has been in operation since 1924. Here you can buy fresh locally grown fruits, vegetables, and flowers; fresh-baked cakes, pies, and breads; jams, jellies, and pickles made in local home kitchens; and the work of local woodcarvers, weavers, and other craftspeople.

Along the curved main street cutting through downtown are plenty of shops and some adorable man-sized bear statues that shop owners and community members have painted, bedazzled, and displayed, but one shop that stands out is **Dancing Bear Toys** (418 N. Main St., 828/693-4500, www.dancingbeartoys.com, 10am-5:30pm Mon. and Wed.-Sat.). This place is lousy with games, toys, kits, models, gadgets, and accessories for kids and lighthearted adults.

Food

★ **Umi Japanese Fine Dining** (633 N. Main St., 828/698-8048, www.umisushinc.com, 11am-3pm and 4:30pm-9pm Mon.-Thurs., 11am-3pm and 4:30pm-9:30pm Fri., noon-9:30pm Sat., noon-9pm Sun., $8-28) surprised me. For starters, I didn't expect to find good sushi anywhere in the mountains except maybe Asheville, but this is some of the best I've eaten in the state. Every roll is as close to perfect as you'll get because their sushi chef and his crew of maki rollers take fish deliveries 3-4 times a week. Sure, you can get beef teriyaki or miso salmon, but why would you when the rolls are so good? They also have a nice sake menu, and they serve their own wine here.

Asheville's **White Duck Taco Shop** (500 7th Ave. E., Hendersonville, 828/595-9871, 11:30am-9pm Tues.-Sun., www.whiteducktacoshop.com, $4-7) has slowly spread across the region and now has locations here in Hendersonville as well as Charlotte and Matthews, North Carolina; Greenville, South Carolina; and two locations in Tennessee. At every spot they serve an eclectic and delicious blend of tacos like Korean beef bulgogi, duck with mole, Thai peanut chicken, buffalo chicken, a tofu *bánh mì*, and more.

There are a good many gastropub-type restaurants in Hendersonville, so a restaurant like **Postero** (401 N. Main St., Hendersonville, 828/595-9676, www.posterohvl.com, 11:30am-2:30pm Thurs.-Sat., 5pm-8:30pm Tues.-Thurs., 5pm-9:30pm Fri.-Sat., $12-30) really stands out, but let me say this place would stand out anywhere. Whether you're getting a table full of starters to share (their duck liver mousse and their locally sourced cheese and charcuterie boards are top-notch) or an entrée to fall in love with (and you will fall in love with monkfish that gets a Tuscan treatment, a massive pork chop with a comforting set of sides, or whatever's special today), pair it with a couple of crafty cocktails or local libations, and you're in for a great meal.

I find local trails are a good way to familiarize myself with an area, and the **Hendersonville Cheers! Trail** ($10) is no exception. This craft beverage trail features beer, wine, cider, and mead (an ancient wine-beer hybrid made with fermented honey) across 23 possible stops in the region. Maps are available at the **Visitor Center** (201 S. Main St., 828/693-9708, www.visithendersonvillenc.org, 9am-5pm Mon.-Fri., 10am-5pm Sat.-Sun.), and after you collect a dozen stamps, you can redeem your passport for some Cheers! Trail swag.

You can dine on some tasty grub and benefit a program devoted to aiding the survivors of violence at **Dandelion, a Local Eatery** (127 5th Ave. W., 828/595-9365, www.safelightfamily.org, 11am-2:30pm Mon.-Fri., $10). The menu stays simple, but you'll leave full and happy after a sandwich—there's a dozen on the menu—or a Southern dish like grits or Tomato Pie (it's exactly what it sounds like, and you should totally try it) or a filling salad. Their Halfski is a classic half sandwich, half soup combo, and the chicken salad sandwich is one of the best in the area.

Accommodations

At **Melange Bed & Breakfast Inn and Gardens** (1230 5th Ave. W., 828/697-5253, www.melangebb.com, from $225) is just a short walk from downtown and is the sort of place you don't want to leave. The six rooms are comfy and tastefully decorated (not overdone with thematic decorations or antiques, like too many B&Bs), and you just feel at home here. If you have special dietary needs—vegan, paleo, gluten-free—they're happy to accommodate.

Pinebrook Manor (2701 Kanuga Rd., 828/698-2707, www.pinebrookmanor.com, $195-265) has four rooms named for literary figures, and I think their pricing reveals something about the owners' literary tastes. The hosts are top-notch, the whole place is lovely, and the breakfast is much better than the typical B&B quiche.

There are a number of recognizable chain hotels in and around Hendersonville and nearby Flat Rock, and if you need to boost your loyalty points, any of those will do for a night or two, but I always like local options even if it's not a B&B. In Hendersonville, the **Echo Mountain Inn** (2849 Laurel Park Hwy., Hendersonville, 828/693-9626, www. echomountaininn.com, $99-205) consists of two facilities, the 17-room Main Inn, built in 1896, and the Little Echo, a motel-style stay with 8 rooms; each facility has a distinct look and feel, but the Main Inn is the more elegant of the two. And near Flat Rock, but still only a few minutes from Hendersonville, **The Lodge at Flat Rock** (42 McMurray Rd., Flat Rock, 828/693-9910, www.mountainlodgeflat-rock.com, $99-205) has more of a traditional hotel feel in an all-suites configuration.

FLAT ROCK
Sights

Just south of Hendersonville is the historic village of Flat Rock. Founded in the early 19th century as a vacation spot for the Charleston plantation gentry, Flat Rock retains a delicate, cultured ambience created many years ago. Many artists and writers have lived in this area, most famously Carl Sandburg, whose house, Connemara, is preserved as the **Carl Sandburg Home National Historic Site** (1800 Little River Rd., Flat Rock, 828/693-4178, www.nps.gov/carl, grounds sunrise-sunset daily, house tour $8 adults, $5 over age 61, free under age 16). Sandburg and his family lived here for more than 20 years, and during that time he wrote and won the Pulitzer Prize for *Complete Poems,* no doubt observed bemusedly as his wife and daughters raised champion dairy goats (a herd of goats lives on the grounds today). Half-hour tours take visitors through the house to see many of the Sandburgs' belongings. There is a bookstore in the house and more than five miles of trails through the property. As a poet whose first steps were in the mountain clay, I have a soft spot for this place, and it's easy for me to see what Sandburg found so inspiring and appealing about the quiet, the air, and the space; take a moment to sit and reflect while you're here, and try writing a couple of lines of your own.

Throughout the mountains you're in apple country. **Sky Top Orchards** (1193 Pinnacle Mountain Rd., 828/692-7930, www.skyto-porchard.com, 9am-6pm daily Aug.-Nov.) is a pick-your-own orchard with 22 varieties of apples as well as fresh cider, jams, jellies, and awesome apple cider doughnuts. Be sure to bring cash when you visit, as their card reader doesn't always work.

Entertainment and Events

Another literary landmark in the village is the **Flat Rock Playhouse** (2661 Greenville Hwy., Flat Rock, 828/693-0731, www.flat-rockplayhouse.org). Now the state theater of North Carolina, the Flat Rock Playhouse's history dates to 1940, when a roving theater company called the Vagabonds wandered down from New York and converted an old gristmill in the village into a stage. They returned every summer for the next few years, entertaining the locals with plays held in a succession of locations, from the old mill to a circus tent, eventually constructing a permanent theater.

They now have a 10-month season, drawing more than 90,000 patrons each year.

Shopping

You'll find quite a few nice galleries and studios in Flat Rock along a strip called Little Rainbow Row. One place that jumps out is the anchor of Little Rainbow Row, **The Wrinkled Egg** (2710 Greenville Hwy., 828/696-3998, www.thewrinkledegg.com, 10am-5pm Mon.-Sat., noon-5pm Sun.). This weird little store sells custom care packages for kids heading off to summer camp: scout camp, equestrian camp, religious camp, and whatever other summer camps kids go to these days. It's a fun place to stop to get a little something for the kids in your life.

Firefly Craft Gallery (2689-D Greenville Hwy., Flat Rock, 828/231-0764, www.firefly-craftgallery.com, 11am-5pm Tues.-Sat.) carries the work of dozens of artisans, artists, and craftspeople from western North Carolina in a wide range of media. You'll find jewelry, oil paintings, watercolors, pottery, sculpture, photography, and more in this charming spot. Just up the road a piece, **The Gallery at Flat Rock** (2702-A Greenville Hwy., Flat Rock, 828/698-7000, www.galleryflatrock.com, 11am-4pm Tues.-Sat., noon-4pm Sun., and by appointment) presents a well-curated selection of fine art from 60 or so regionally and nationally acclaimed artists as well as artist talks and workshops.

Food

Flat Rock's a pretty small town but there are a few good places to eat if you know where to look. I feel like I have to recommend a place for barbecue, and the folks at **Hubba Hubba Smokehouse** (2724 Greenville Hwy., Flat Rock, 828/694-3551, www.hubbahub-basmokehouse.com, 11am-3pm Thurs.-Sun. mid-Apr.-Oct., $10-20) make it easy because the 'cue and sauces—which encompass styles from North and South Carolina as well as Texas—deliver. Locals say you can eat any of the barbecue naked (meaning without sauce, not without pants), but I'm a sauce lover,

so you're going to have to decide for yourself. Their sister restaurant, **Campfire Grill** (2770 Greenville Hwy., Flat Rock, 828/595-9849, www.campfiregrillnc.com, 11am-3pm Tues.-Wed., 11am-8pm Thurs.-Sat., $15-32), serves smoked wings, some awesome salads (the harvest salad will do you right), burgers, sandwiches, and entrées like chicken pot pie and crab cakes for lunch and dinner; the menu lets you have a substantial meal or split a salad and sandwich for a lighter lunch. **Honey and Salt** (2730 Greenville Hwy., Flat Rock, 828/676-8322, www.honeyandsaltnc.com, 8am-2pm Wed.-Sun., $6-12) keeps breakfast and lunch simple with grit and granola bowls, egg sandwiches, biscuits, and an assortment of bakery goods.

SALUDA AND VICINITY

Just 10 minutes east and south of Hendersonville, bordering South Carolina, Polk County is home to several interesting little towns, most notably Tryon and Saluda, along with a lot of beautiful mountain countryside. In Saluda you'll find a tiny downtown laid out along the old Norfolk Southern Railway tracks. The tracks at Saluda are the top of the steepest standard-gauge mainline railroad grade in the United States. This county's history abounds with exciting stories of runaway trains that derailed at spots like Slaughterhouse Curve; more than two dozen railroad workers have been killed on this grade. Visitor information on Polk County is available through **First Peak of the Blue Ridge** (www.firstpeaknc.com).

Sports and Recreation

Equestrian life plays a growing role in Polk and the surrounding counties of North Carolina's southern mountains. The **Foothills Equestrian Nature Center** (3381 Hunting Country Rd., Tryon, 828/859-9021, www.fence.org), known as FENCE, occupies 380 beautiful acres along the border with South Carolina. The equestrian center has stables for 200 horses and two lighted show rings. FENCE hosts cross-country, three-day,

A-rated hunter and jumper, dressage, and many other equestrian events throughout the year, along with offering regular hikes and bird-watching excursions on its beautiful property.

The Gorge (166 Honey Bee Dr., Saluda, 828/373-2312, www.thegorgezipline.com, $125) gives you a treetop view of the mountains and Green River Gorge as you zip-line from tree to tree. There are 11 zips, three rappels, and a heart-pounding sky bridge on this course that descends 1,100 feet in total. The zip lines total well over a mile, and this is one of the best in the state; if adrenaline is your thing, you have to check it out.

Entertainment and Events

Saluda's got a lot going on throughout the year. The **Saluda Arts Festival** happens on the third Saturday in May and features 80-plus artists from the Carolinas and Tennessee in this all-day art fair. The **Saluda Tailgate Market** (4:30pm-6:30pm Fri. May-Oct.), an agriculture-only market, brings growers and ranchers into town to sell what's fresh. The **Top of the Grade Concert Series** runs June-September and brings in musicians and bands for free monthly concerts. In July, Saluda celebrates **Coon Dog Day** with a festival devoted to these baying and barking hounds that includes a parade, skills tests, a street fair, and music.

Food

We love to eat in North Carolina, and even in a tiny town like Saluda, you'll find some great bites. With a menu that's packed with flavorful dishes, **The Purple Onion** (16 E. Main St., Saluda, 828/749-1179, www.purpleonionsaluda.com, 11am-8:30pm Mon. and Thurs.-Sat., 11am-3pm Sun., $6-34) is a favorite. Pizzas—including a great wild mushroom and arugula pie—and salads take inspiration from the Mediterranean coastlines of Spain, Italy, and Greece. Entrées like the Sunburst mountain trout and the Brasstown farm rib-eye keep other inspirations and flavors local.

Wildflour Bakery (173 E. Main St., 828/749-3356, http://wildflourbakerync.com, 9am-2pm Sat.-Mon., 9am-8pm Wed., 11am-8pm Fri., $8-13, pizza night $8-26) stone-grinds wheat every morning to make absolutely delicious breads. Breakfast and lunch are served, making this a great place to fill up before a day of kayaking or hiking. Don't miss Pizza Night (Wed. and Fri.), where they serve up regular or thin-crust (and even gluten-free) pies with your choice of toppings, along with 10 specialty pizzas. You can bring your own wine or beer on pizza night, so order a pie or two, crack open a local brew, and settle in for a little while.

CHIMNEY ROCK AND LAKE LURE

Just one of the many geological beauties you'll find along the Blue Ridge Parkway corridor, **Chimney Rock State Park** (Main St., Chimney Rock, 828/625-9611, www.chimneyrockpark.com, ticket plaza 8:30am-5:30pm daily, park 10am-4:30pm daily Jan.-mid-Mar., 8:30am-5:30pm daily mid-Mar.-early-Nov., 8:30am-4:30pm daily early-Nov.-Dec., $17 adults, $8 ages 5-15, free under age 5) is about 45 minutes from Asheville, at Milepost 384.7 on U.S. 74 Alt east. The 315-foot tower of stone that is Chimney Rock stands on the side of the mountain. To get to the top of the chimney, you can take a 26-story elevator ride, or hike the **Outcroppings Trail,** a 0.25-mile trail nicknamed "The Ultimate Stairmaster." No matter how you get here, the view is spectacular.

There are number of additional dizzying views to take in and mountain-hugging trails to hike in Chimney Rock State Park. The **Needle's Eye** and **Opera Box** are two such formations. The **Hickory Nut Falls Trail** takes you to the top of the 400-foot Hickory Nut Falls via a moderately difficult 0.75-mile trail. One of the most recognizable views is on the **Skyline-Cliff Trail** loop, a strenuous two-hour hike that will take you to some places you may recognize from the 1992 film *The Last of the Mohicans.* There are also kid-friendly trails. Bring your little ones along on the 0.6-mile Woodland Walk, where animal sculptures and "journal entries" from Grady the Groundhog wait to be discovered. A trail map covering the entire park is available at the park's website (www.chimneyrockpark.com).

Chimney Rock is more than just hiking trails. In November, Santa rappels down the tower in a pre-Christmas display of his chimney-navigating prowess, but year-round you'll find rock climbers in the park for bouldering, top-rope, and multi-pitch climbs. Want to try but don't know the terms? Fox Mountain Guides (888/284-8433, www.foxmountainguides.com, 2-hour lesson $110 for 1 climber, $160 for 2 climbers, $180 for 3 climbers) will gear you up and show you the ropes.

Nearby Rumbling Bald Mountain (112 Mountain Blvd., Lake Lure) is part of Chimney Rock State Park, and climbers couldn't be happier. Here you'll find more than 1,500 bouldering "problems" to solve (solving it means traversing it successfully). Currently, only the south face is open to climbing, and commercial climbing guides are not allowed to operate here.

Sports and Recreation

Lake Lure, a 720-acre artificial highland lake, was created in the 1920s. Several local outfitters will set you up for a day on the lake or on area rivers. Try Lake Lure Adventure Company (470 Memorial Hwy., 828/625-8066, www.lakelureadventurecompany.com, 9am-8pm daily Memorial Day-Labor Day, call Sept.-Apr.) for water-ski and wakeboard trips ($205 per hour), fishing (half-day $300), or kayak and stand-up paddleboard rentals (from $20 per hour). Rent a boat (2-hour minimum, from $95 per hour) to ride around and sightsee, go fishing, or have a picnic. For a relaxed sightseeing tour on the lake, Lake Lure Tours (next to Lake Lure Town Marina, 877/386-4255, www.lakeluretours.com, 9am-5pm daily, tours hourly from 11am, $18 adults, $16 seniors, $8 under age 12) offers dinner and sunset cruises as well as daytime jaunts.

In nearby Mill Springs, about 15 minutes south on Highway 9, a huge equestrian center hosts competitions, horse shows, lessons, and rides year-round. Tryon International Equestrian Center (TIEC, 25 International Blvd., Mill Spring, 828/863-1000, www.tryon.coth.com) puts on free hunter-jumper shows and competitions, hosts concerts and events, and has everything riders, spectators, and equine enthusiasts could want. Choose from eight on-site restaurants including Legends Grille (828/863-1122, 5pm-9pm Tues.-Thurs., 11am-10pm Fri.-Sat., 11am-9pm Sun., $14-47), an upscale eatery serving steaks and seafood; Roger's Diner (828/863-1113, 7am-3pm Mon., 7am-9pm Tues.-Thurs. and Sun., 7am-10pm Fri.-Sat., $8-13), serving breakfast and traditional diner fare; and Blue Ginger Sushi (828/863-1121, 11am-9pm Wed.-Sun., $6-16). There's also a coffee shop, a snack bar, a pizza oven, and a sandwich-centric café.

Since riders and show enthusiasts travel from far and wide, TIEC has lodging for horses and riders. The Stable House Inn (828/863-1015, $125) has 50 rooms, each with two queen beds; the Tryon River Cabins have one- ($185), three- ($750), and five-bedroom cabins ($1,000) available, each with weekly rental discounts, along with several RV pads ($43).

There are two golf courses at Rumbling Bald Resort (112 Mountains Blvd., Lake Lure, www.rumblingbald.com). Bald Mountain Golf Course (828/694-3042, 18 holes, par 72, greens fees $56 Mon.-Fri., $61 Sat.-Sun.) makes the most of the bald rock faces that gave the course its name and gives you some beautiful views of them as they tower overhead. You may recognize the 16th hole, a picturesque par-3 where a couple of scenes from Dirty Dancing were shot. At Apple Valley Golf Course (828/694-3043, 18 holes, par 72, greens fees $63 Mon.-Fri., $68 Sat.-Sun.) you'll find a set of links that's been called one of the most beautiful mountain courses. This is especially true in fall when the hillsides surrounding the course are in full blaze.

1: Chimney Rock State Park 2: Lake Lure

Food

In addition to the dining options at Rumbling Bald, the Lodge on Lake Lure, and TIEC, there are a few other spots worth checking out.

When you're in Lake Lure and you need a bite to eat, picnic supplies, or something to snack on back at your getaway house, stop by **Lured Market and Grill** (2655 Memorial Hwy., Lake Lure, 828/625-9192, 11am-3pm Sun.-Mon., 11am-7pm Wed.-Thurs., 11am-9pm Fri.-Sat., $5-13). Chock-full of local and regional flavors—craft beer, wine, snacks, and cheese—and stocked with everything from pantry sundries to lake-life necessities, Lured carries what you're looking for or something close, and their little grill serves a bevy of sandwiches, salads, burgers and handheld eats. Try the Trout Bites or the Not Your Routine Poutine starters, then go for a big salad and a burger or their Quirky Turkey Sandwich topped with peach habanero jam for extra quirky points.

Dining at **La Strada at Lake Lure** (2693 Memorial Hwy., Lake Lure, 828/625-1118, www.lastradaatlakelure.com, 11:30am-late daily, $13-28) is Italian American through and through, and you're bound to see plenty of rock climbers in there carbing up as they prepare for a day on the rock face. The menu is packed with pizza and pasta, with many of the classics—chicken parm, lasagna, chicken alfredo—appearing alongside daily specials that use ingredients that are a little closer to home.

I am a fool for french toast, and at **Victory Kitchen & Restaurant** (961 Buffalo Creek Rd., Lake Lure, 828/436-5023, 8am-2pm Tues.-Sat., 8am-noon Sun., 5pm-8pm Wed.-Fri., $5-15) I've found a version I look forward to getting, if I don't order the shrimp and grits, that is. This place has great breakfast; sleepyheads take note that it's served until 11am, as well as a great lunch, including a killer cheeseburger topped with a fried egg, just in case you like a little breakfast with lunch.

Accommodations

The 1927 **Lake Lure Inn and Spa** (2771 Memorial Hwy., 828/625-2525, www.lakelure.com, from $135) is a grand old hotel that was one of the fashionable Southern resorts of its day. Franklin Roosevelt and Calvin Coolidge stayed here, as did F. Scott Fitzgerald. The lobby is full of strange antiques that are the picture of obsolete opulence—a Baccarat chandelier much older than the hotel and a collection of upright disc music boxes, up to eight feet tall, that were all the rage before the invention of the phonograph. The Lake Lure Inn has been restored beautifully and equipped with two restaurants, a bar, and a spa.

Rumbling Bald Resort on Lake Lure (112 Mountains Blvd., Lake Lure, 828/694-3000 or 800/260-1040, www.rumblingbald.com) has studios ($125-165), condos ($235-415), RV facilities ($80-95), and vacation homes ($285-650) in a quiet mountain cove. On the resort's property there a few miles of hiking and biking trails as well as a variety of water activities: pontoon boats ($200 for 2 hours, $350 for 4 hours, $650 for 8 hours); kayaks, canoes, paddleboats, and stand-up paddleboards (from $22-27 per hour); and scenic cruises ($22 adults, $5 under age 4). There's also a fitness center, golf, tennis, and a spa (828/694-3017, treatments from $55).

At Rumbling Bald there's one restaurant where you can grab a bite: **Legends on the Lake** (828/694-3032, 11am-9pm Wed.-Sun., $10-25), serving pizza, salads and sandwiches, and a small selection of entrées.

HIGHLANDS AND VICINITY
Waterfalls

This part of the country is blessed with some beautiful waterfalls, some of which are easily visited. **Whitewater Falls** (Hwy. 281, at the Georgia state line, south of Highlands), at over 400 feet, is reported to be the highest waterfall east of the Rockies. An upper-level viewing spot is located at the end of a wheelchair-accessible paved trail, while a flight of more than 150 steps leads to the base of the falls. The falls are a fabulous sight, but remember to stay on the trails; several visitors have fallen to their deaths when they left the trail to get a different perspective.

A much smaller but still very beautiful waterfall is **Silver Run Falls** (Hwy. 107, 4 miles south of Cashiers), reached by a short trail from a roadside pullout. **Bridal Veil Falls** (U.S. 64, 2.5 miles west of Highlands) flows over a little track of road right off U.S. 64. You'll see a sign from the main road where you can turn off and actually drive behind the waterfall, or park and walk behind it. Another waterfall that you can walk through is **Dry Falls** (U.S. 64, between Highlands and Franklin, $3 per vehicle), reached by a small trail off the highway, curving right into and behind the 75-foot waterfall.

Sports and Recreation

North Carolina's newest, **Gorges State Park** (Hwy. 281, Sapphire, 828/966-9099, http:// ncparks.gov, park 7am-7pm daily Dec.-Feb., 7am-9pm daily Mar.-Apr. and Oct., 7am-10pm daily May-Sept., 7pm-8pm daily Nov., picnic areas 8am-7:30pm daily, visitors center 9am-5pm daily) is a lush mountain rainforest that receives 80 inches of precipitation annually. The steep terrain rises 2,000 vertical feet in four miles, creating a series of rocky waterfalls and challenging trails. This 7,500-acre park is the only state park west of Asheville, and it's a sight, with a collection of waterfalls and a fantastic concentration of rare and unique plant and animal species; explore on a number of rugged trails for hiking, mountain biking, and horseback riding, or fish for rainbow and brown trout as well as smallmouth bass. Primitive camping (free) is allowed in designated areas.

Food and Accommodations

The 3,500-foot-high town of Cashiers ("CASH-ers") is home to the **High Hampton Resort** (124 Hwy. 107, Cashiers, 800/648-4252 or 828/547-0662, www.highhampton.com, 2-night minimum, from $250), a popular resort for generations of North Carolinians. This was originally the home of Confederate General Wade Hampton,

the dashing Charlestonian cavalryman. The lodge, a big old 1930s wooden chalet with huge cozy fireplaces in the lobby, is surrounded by 1,400 acres of lakeside woodlands, with an 18-hole golf course, a good buffet-style restaurant (dinner jacket requested in the evening), clay tennis courts, and a fitness center that features a climbing tower.

INFORMATION AND SERVICES

In addition to Asheville's **Mission Hospital** (509 Biltmore Ave., Asheville, 828/213-1111, www.missionhealth.org), there are several regional hospitals with emergency or urgent care departments. In Hendersonville, the primary hospital is **Pardee Hospital** (800 N. Justice St., Hendersonville, 828/696-1000, www.pardeehospital.org). In Brevard, the main hospital is **Transylvania Regional Hospital** (90 Hospital Dr., Brevard, 828/884-9111, www.missionhealth.org), and in Rutherfordton it is **Rutherford Regional Medical Center** (288 S. Ridgecrest St., Rutherfordton, 828/286-5000, www.myrutherfordregional.com).

Maps and guides are available at the **Hendersonville and Flat Rock Visitors Information Center** (201 S. Main St., Hendersonville, 800/828-4244 or 828/693-9708, www.visithendersonvillenc.org) and at the **Transylvania County Tourism Development Authority** (175 E. Main St., Brevard, 800/648-4523 or 828/884-8900, www.visitwaterfalls.com).

GETTING THERE AND AROUND

The Brevard-Hendersonville area is an easy drive from Asheville, with Hendersonville less than 30 minutes down I-26 and Brevard a short jog west from it on U.S. 64. To reach Tryon and Rutherfordton, follow U.S. 74 south and east from Hendersonville. **Asheville Regional Airport** (AVL, 61 Terminal Dr., 828/684-2226, www.flyavl.com), south of Asheville, is very convenient to this region; several airlines have flights to Atlanta, Charlotte, and other U.S. cities.

Great Smoky Mountains

The Smokies draw more than 12 million visitors

annually. It's easy to see why: These mountains are laced with hiking trails, rivers, and waterfalls and populated with diverse wildlife—from rare salamanders to huge elk.

The diversity is second only to the sublime mystery of the area. The wild forests of the Great Smoky Mountains have historically been home to outlaws and rebels hoping to hide from the world under the cover of the fertile landscape. In fact, in 1996, the Atlanta Olympic Park bomber fled to the Smokies to evade capture. While people watching the news were scratching their heads, wondering how one man could vanish in such a relatively small geographical area, folks in these parts had their doubts he'd ever be found. After driving a little ways in the

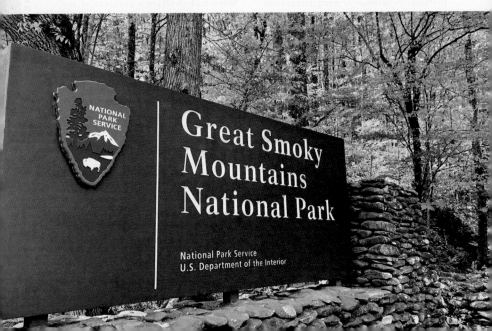

Highlights

Look for ★ to find recommended sights, activities, dining, and lodging.

★ **Cades Cove:** The most visited spot in Great Smoky Mountains National Park is a formerly bustling mountain village that is witness to the depth of history in the Southern highlands (page 447).

★ **Clingmans Dome:** From this third-highest peak in the eastern United States, set in a dramatic alpine environment, you'll find an astounding view up to 100 miles on a clear day (page 450).

★ **Newfound Gap Road:** Bisecting the park, the 33-mile route offers plenty of long views, short hikes, and streamside driving (page 451).

★ **Museum of the Cherokee Indian:** The Cherokee people have lived in the Smoky Mountains for thousands of years. This excellent museum tells unforgettable tales of their history (page 464).

★ **Qualla Arts and Crafts Mutual:** Ancient craft traditions still thrive among Cherokee artists in western North Carolina. At the Qualla Mutual, visitors can learn about and purchase the work of today's masters (page 465).

★ **Oconaluftee Indian Village:** Demonstrations in traditional cooking, flint knapping for arrowheads and spear points, and ritual dance give visitors a glimpse into 18th-century life at this recreated Cherokee Indian Village (page 466).

★ **Great Smoky Mountains Railroad:** Depart Bryson City on a rail tour along mountain

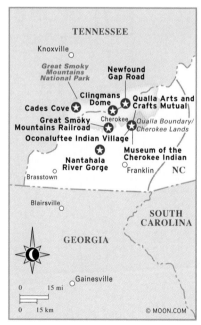

rivers and lakes; enjoy kid-centric tours or tours focused on fall color, moonshine, and craft beer (page 470).

★ **Nantahala River Gorge:** So steep that in some places the water is only brushed by sunlight at high noon, this gorge is an unbeatable place for white-water rafting (page 470).

Great Smoky Mountains

© MOON.COM

NORTH CAROLINA

SOUTH CAROLINA

TENNESSEE

GEORGIA

Pisgah National Forest

Cherokee National Forest

Pisgah National Forest

Nantahala National Forest

Nantahala National Forest

Cherokee National Forest

Great Smoky Mountains National Park

Qualla Boundary/ Cherokee Lands

Qualla Boundary/ Cherokee Lands

Blue Ridge Parkway

Canton
Clyde
Waynesville
BALSAM MOUNTAIN INN
Sapphire
Lake Jocassee
Highlands
Cashiers
Cullowhee
Sylva
Dillsboro
Franklin
Maggie Valley
CATALOOCHE
CATALOOCHE SKI AREA
END OF THE BLUE RIDGE PARKWAY
MUSEUM OF THE CHEROKEE INDIAN
NEWFOUND GAP ROAD
QUALLA ARTS AND CRAFTS MUTUAL
Cherokee
OCONALUFTEE INDIAN VILLAGE
CLINGMANS DOME
Bryson City
GREAT SMOKY MOUNTAINS RAILROAD
Crowe Mountain
Tuckasegee River
Nantahala River
Appalachian Trail
Appalachian Trail
Gatlinburg
Pigeon Forge
CADES COVE
FONTANA DAM
Fontana Lake
NANTAHALA RIVER GORGE
Stecoah
Fontana Village
Santeetlah Lake
Robbinsville
Andrews
Hayesville
Chatuge Lake
Brasstown
Murphy
Hiwassee Lake
Maryville
To Knoxville
Tennessee River
Little River
Cherokee National Forest
Nantahala National Forest

Blue Ridge

Great Smoky Mountains

Appalachian Trail

276
178
74
276
276
64
107
28
107
64
23
441
23
74
19
23
74
28
64
28
129
74
19
76
19
129
64
74
68
411
75
321
129
66
331
40
40
441

5 mi
5 km
0
0

High Country southwest of Asheville, among the rugged terrain and the lush vegetation, it isn't difficult to imagine how someone could hide here unnoticed.

The 521,085-acre Great Smoky National Park straddles the North Carolina-Tennessee state line and is just about equally split between the states. The slightly larger North Carolina side of the park is wilder and less developed than the Tennessee side, and in both places you can find spots so remote they have stood undisturbed by humans for untold lengths of time. You'll also find places like Cades Cove, a wide, secluded valley that welcomed some of the first pioneers to push west into Tennessee.

In addition to pioneers traveling westward, the Smokies were also home to the Cherokee people, who have roots here going back centuries, from the early days described in their mythology, when the Ani-gituhwa-gi shared these mountains with witches, fairies, and birds the size of bears. The early 19th century and the Trail of Tears were the darkest hour for them, when they were split into two groups—those forced into exile and those forced into hiding and resistance. Today, the Cherokee Nation is still split, but the Eastern Band's seat of government is here in the land known as the Qualla Boundary.

PLANNING YOUR TIME

Many people plan visits to the Smokies around what's blooming or turning color on the mountainsides, but it's a wonderful area to visit any time of year. Spring wildflowers begin to appear in late March, peaking in late April. Azaleas, mountain laurels, and rhododendrons put on the best show during summer, blooming first at lower elevations and then creeping up the mountains. Flame azalea is an unusual plant, peaking in different areas as the microclimates dictate; they're ablaze with color April-July. Mountain laurel overlaps with blooms in May-June, and rhododendron shows its color in June-July. Fall colors appear in the opposite order, with the mountaintops the first to show autumn's arrival in early October. Colors then bleed down until late October-early November, when trees from the foot to the crest of the mountains are aflame with color. Summer heat can throw off the schedule for blooms and fall colors, as can rainfall levels. If you call the Great Smoky Mountains National Park or check with regional websites, you can find out how the season is progressing.

Bisecting the park is the Newfound Gap Road, striking northwest from Cherokee, where it meets with the southern end of the Blue Ridge Parkway, to Gatlinburg and Pigeon Forge, Tennessee. On the Tennessee side of the park, the valleys spread out a little and mountain coves form, making that the area to visit for side-road exploration and short loop roads. Cherokee is a great place to stay, as it's not as touristy as Gatlinburg, which is good to visit for a day. There are campsites available on both sides of the park if you're roughing it, or find a rustic cozy cabin for a taste of country living. While you can certainly get from Cherokee to Gatlinburg in an hour and see a sight or two in a day, the more time you can spend here, the better. This is the nation's most visited national park for a reason, so spend at least three days; a week provides enough time for a touristy day in Tennessee, a couple of days for trail and side-road exploration, a day learning about Cherokee culture in Cherokee, and time in the casino. Many campgrounds here limit stays to one week mid-May-October and two weeks November-mid-May, so plan accordingly if you're packing your tent.

Previous: the iconic Great Smoky Mountains National Park sign; elk along the Oconaluftee River; Mingus Mill.

Great Smoky Mountains National Park

Great Smoky Mountains National Park (GSMNP, 865/436-1200, www.nps.gov/grsm) is like no other, and it's very close to my heart. My family would vacation here for weekend and weeklong getaways, and I remember taking my first bite of trout here, riding my first roller coaster at Silver Dollar City in Pigeon Forge (now Dollywood), and seeing R2-D2 outside of Ripley's Believe It or Not in Gatlinburg. GSMNP comprises more than 800 square miles of cloud-ringed high peaks and rainforest. There are tens of thousands of species of plants and animals that call the park home, with 80 species of reptiles and amphibians alone, which is why the park is sometimes called the Salamander Capital of the World. More than 200 species of birds nest here, and 50-plus mammal species, from mice to mountain lions, roam these hills. The nonprofit organization Discover Life in America (www.dlia.org) has been conducting an All-Taxa Biodiversity Inventory, a census of all nonmicrobial life forms in the GSMNP; as of 2012 they had discovered over 900 species of plants and animals previously unknown to science. The deep wilderness is an awesome refuge for today's outdoor enthusiasts, and the accessibility of absolutely ravishing scenery makes it ideal for visitors of all ability levels and nearly all interests.

VISITING THE PARK
Weather Considerations

To get a sense of the variability of the weather in the GSMNP, keep in mind that the elevation ranges from below 1,000 to over 6,600 feet. Low-lying areas like the one around Gatlinburg, Tennessee, are not much cooler than Raleigh in the summer, with an average high of 88°F in July. Gatlinburg's average lows drop just a few degrees below freezing during only three months of the year (Dec.-Feb.). The opposite extreme is illustrated by Clingmans Dome, the highest elevation in the park, where the average high temperature is only 65°F in July, and only in June-August can you be sure that it won't snow. If ever there were a place for wearing layers of clothing, this is it. No matter what season the calendar tells you it is, be on the safe side and

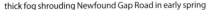

thick fog shrouding Newfound Gap Road in early spring

Great Smoky Mountains National Park

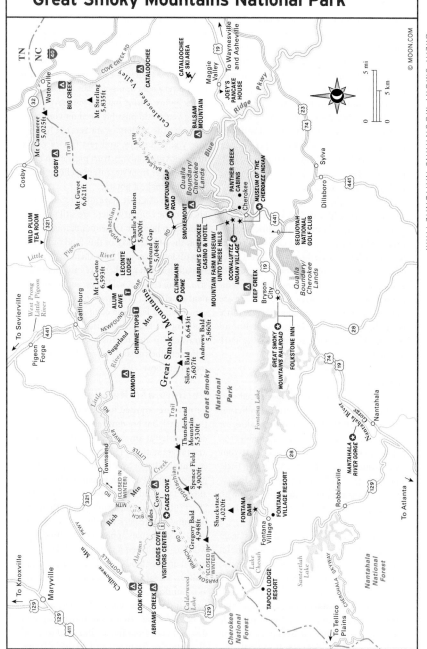

© MOON.COM

pack clothing for the other three as well. Keep these extremes in mind in terms of safety as well; a snowstorm can bring two feet of snow at high elevations, and it's not at all unusual for the weather to be balmy at the foot of the mountain and icy at the top. At times the temperature has fallen to -20°F. Roads can be closed in the winter or restricted to 4WD vehicles and those with snow chains. Drive very slowly when it's icy. Leave plenty of room between you and the next car, and shift to a lower gear when going down slippery slopes. You can find out current conditions by calling the park's weather information line (865/436-1200, ext. 630).

Seasonal Considerations

The most crowded times in the park are mid-June–mid-August and all of October. Traffic is most likely to be heavy on the Cades Cove Loop Road and Newfound Gap Road. Several roads in the park are closed in winter, but closing dates vary. Among these are Balsam Mountain, Clingmans Dome, Little Greenbrier, Rich Mountain, and Round Bottom Roads as well as the Roaring Fork Motor Nature Trail.

Safety

Sometimes even the most experienced outdoorspeople have emergencies. Whether you're going into the backcountry alone or with others, make sure that someone you trust knows where you're going, what your likely route is, and when to expect you back. The National Park Service recommends leaving their phone number (865/436-1230) with someone at home to call if you're not back when expected.

Some of the basic safety rules may seem obvious, but it's good to review them. Climbing on rocks and waterfalls is always dangerous, and crossing a deep or flooded stream can be treacherous as well. If you have to cross a stream that's more than ankle deep, it's recommended that you unbuckle the waist strap on your backpack (so you don't get pinned underwater if you fall), use

a hiking stick to steady yourself, and wear nonslippery shoes.

Cold is a concern, even in summer. Wear layers, pack additional warm duds (warmer than you think you'll need), and try to stay dry. It may be shorts-and-T-shirt weather when you set out, but even in the summer it can be very cold at night. Plan well, double-check before setting out that you have everything you could possibly need on your trek, and, says the National Park Service, "eat before you're hungry, and rest before you're tired" (it's good advice; trust me, I'm an Eagle Scout). Water from streams must be boiled or filtered to make it potable.

Wildlife can pose hazards. Despite assurances to the contrary, there are still panthers (mountain lions) in these mountains. Ignore what the officials say in this (and only this) regard; locals see and hear them throughout Appalachia. But panthers are rare and reclusive, as are coyotes, wild hogs, and other resident tough guys. It's always better to hike or camp with at least one companion. A sturdy walking stick can be a lifesaver, and bear spray, cheap and readily available in many different kinds of stores, is good for deterring more than bears.

Permits and Regulations

Permits are required for camping in the national park but are quite easy to obtain. You can register at any of the 12 visitors centers and ranger stations. This must be done in person, not online or over the phone. Fishing requires a permit as well, which can be bought at outfitters and bait shops in nearby towns. Strict rules governing fishing apply; these can be found on the park website (www.nps.gov/grsm). Other rules apply to interacting with wildlife. Don't feed animals, and make sure to seal up your foodstuffs to discourage night visitors. Firearms are forbidden in the park, as is hunting.

Your dog is welcome in the park, but only in certain areas. To prevent transmission of diseases to or from the wildlife, and to avoid disrupting or frightening the resident fauna,

One Day in GSMNP

Great Smoky Mountains National Park (GSMNP, 865/436-1200, www.nps.gov/grsm) was the first—and the largest—of three National Park Service units established in the southern Appalachians. The park was founded in 1934, followed in 1935 by the Blue Ridge Parkway and in 1936 by Shenandoah National Park. These sister facilities include some 600 miles of contiguous road and close to 800,000 acres of land, all of it acquired from private landholders and all of it standing today as a testament to the wild rugged beauty of the Appalachian Mountains and the people who helped tame these places.

MORNING

Enjoy breakfast at the **Pancake Pantry** (628 Parkway, 865/436-4724, www.pancakepantry. com, 7am-4pm daily June-Oct., 7am-3pm daily Nov.-May, $6-10) in Gatlinburg, the first pancake house in Tennessee. Head out of town toward GSMNP and stop off at the **Sugarlands Visitor Center** (1420 Old Hwy. 73 Scenic, Gatlinburg, 865/436-1200, www.nps.gov/grsm, daily, closed Christmas Day) to pick up maps, then continue on down Little River Road to **Cades Cove**. Easily the most popular auto tour in the park, Cades Cove has amazing scenery but even more amazing wildlife-watching. Get here at the right time of day (early morning or near dusk) and you'll see herds of deer grazing the fields and black bears playing, eating, and napping in the remnants of former apple orchards.

If you're in an SUV, truck, or high-clearance off-road-appropriate vehicle, leave Cades Cove via **Rich Mountain Road,** a beautiful eight-mile road that takes you up and over the mountains to Townsend (not far to the east of Gatlinburg). The views of Cades Cove are unparalleled, so have your camera ready.

AFTERNOON

Leave the park for lunch in Gatlinburg, then hit the **Roaring Fork Motor Nature Trail,** from which you can hike to four falls with relative ease. For a 2.6-mile round-trip hike, try **Grotto Falls Trail,** which leads through a lovely forest to the 25-foot Grotto Falls. You can hike behind the falls, and if you're lucky, you may see pack llamas hauling supplies to the LeConte Lodge. As you're leaving the Motor Nature Trail, stop at the **Thousand Drips Falls,** sometimes called Place of a Thousand Drips. It's just a few steps off the road and is an excellent cascade as it falls down the mossy rock face.

---

dogs are not permitted on hiking trails. They are allowed to accompany you at campgrounds and picnic sites.

WILDLIFE IN THE PARK

The largest animals in the park are also the most recent arrivals. In the spring of 2001, the National Park Service reintroduced **elk** to the Great Smoky Mountains, a species that used to live here but was hunted to regional extinction in the 18th century. In the years since their reintroduction, the herd has reproduced steadily, boding well for a successful future. If you hear a strange bellowing in the early autumn, it may be a male elk showing off for his beloved. One of the best places to see the elk is in the Cataloochee Valley, particularly in fields at dawn and dusk. Be sure to keep your distance; these animals can weigh up to 700 pounds, and the males have some formidable headgear.

An estimated 1,600 **black bears** live in the GSMNP—two per square mile—so it's quite possible that you'll encounter one. They are a wonder to see, but the 100-400-pound creatures pose a real risk to humans, so it's important to be aware of how we interact with them. It is illegal to come within 150 feet of a bear or elk, and those who knowingly get closer can be arrested. If you see a bear, the recommended procedure is to back away slowly. The National Park Service recommends that if the bear follows you, you should stand your ground. If it keeps coming toward you persistently and looks menacing, make yourself big and scary. Stand on a rock to look taller, or get close to anyone else present, to show the bear that it's outnumbered. Make a lot of noise (bear bells or bear whistles are handy for this) and throw rocks or sticks. Should a bear actually attack you, the National Park Service recommends that you "fight back aggressively with any available object." Don't try to run, because they're much faster than you, and don't climb a tree, as black bears are avid climbers.

The best course of action is simply to avoid them and hope that any sightings you have will be from a safe distance. When camping, lock your food in the trunk of your car, or hoist it into a tree too high off the ground for a bear to reach it and suspended far enough from the nearest branch that it can't be reached by climbing the tree. Bears may approach picnic areas. Don't feed them, no matter how sweet they look. "Habitual panhandler bears" (this is a real term, Scout's honor) die younger than those afraid of humans, as they are more likely to be hit by cars, swallow indigestible food packaging, become easy targets for hunters, or, if they are too problematic, be captured and euthanized.

Bears are not the only huge ferocious animals in the park. Believe it or not, there are hundreds of snorting tusky **wild hogs** here, descendants of a herd that escaped from a hunting preserve in Murphy in the 1910s. There are also **coyotes, wolves, bobcats,** and extremely rare **mountain lions,** often called panthers or painters in this region.

Of the many natural miracles in this park, one of the most astonishing is the light show put on for a couple of weeks each year by synchronous **fireflies.** Of the park's 14 species, only one, *Photinus carolinus,* flashes in this manner. While the average backyard's worth of fireflies twinkles like Christmas lights, synchronous fireflies, as their name implies, are capable of flashing in unison, by the hundreds or thousands. The sight is so amazing that,

during the peak flashing period in June, the park organizes nighttime expeditions to the best viewing spots.

If you go hiking in the backcountry, you may see a **snake.** It's unlikely that you'll encounter a poisonous one, as there are only two kinds of vipers here—rattlesnakes and copperheads—that pose a danger to humans. There has never been a death from snakebite in the park, and snakes are shy. But to be on the safe side, watch where you step or put your hands; you don't want to be the first on that list.

SIGHTS

Oconaluftee Visitor Center and Mountain Farm Museum

As you begin your trip along Newfound Gap Road through the park from the North Carolina side, your first stop will probably be the "Welcome to Great Smoky Mountains National Park" sign, but the second stop you'll likely make is the **Oconaluftee Visitor Center and Mountain Farm Museum** (1194 Newfound Gap Rd., Cherokee, 828/497-1904, www.nps.gov/grsm, 9am-4:30pm daily Dec.-Feb., 9am-5pm daily Mar. and Nov., 9am-6pm daily Apr.-May and Sept.-Oct., 9am-7pm daily June-Aug., closed Dec. 25, Mountain Farm dawn-dusk daily), just two miles north of Cherokee on U.S. 441 (Newfound Gap Rd.). You can pick up a park map, grab the schedule of ranger-led programs, and see exhibits on the people who called these hills home long before the park was in existence. The visitors center and adjacent comfort station are LEED Gold certified.

Next to the visitors center is **Mountain Farm Museum** (sunrise-sunset daily year-round, free), which showcases some of the finest farm buildings in the park. Most date to the early 1900s, and among them are a barn, an apple house, and the Davis House, a log home built from chestnut wood and constructed before the American chestnut blight decimated the species. This collection of structures is original to the area and dates to the turn of the 20th century. Though the

The Appalachian Trail

The 2,184-mile Appalachian Trail runs from Georgia to Maine, with 95.5 miles within North Carolina and another 200 straddling the border of North Carolina and Tennessee. It's a high climb, with many peaks over 5,000 feet and gaps brushing 4,000 feet, but the fantastic balds (natural and agricultural areas devoid of trees) along the trail here—like Cheoa Bald and Max Patch—are big draws for day hikers and segment hikers, and having vistas this beautiful this early on in the long journey helps through-hikers retain their focus and determination to reach their goal.

The Appalachian Trail cuts a path through the Nantahala Forest, regarded by many as one of the best sections of the southern portion of the trail, before crossing the rills of the southern Blue Ridge and following the crest of the Smokies along the Tennessee border. This section of the trail is rated between a 3 and a 6 on the AT's 10-point scale, which means the trail ranges from moderate elevation changes on well-graded trails to strenuous and short but steep, extended climbs that last hours, and short sections with difficult footing. For through-hikers, who often have years of trail experience, the path here isn't as difficult as it may be for some day hikers or even overnight hikers.

Finding a day hike isn't hard west of Asheville, especially in the deeper mountains along Great Smoky Mountain National Park. Driving the Newfound Gap Road from the town of Cherokee into Tennessee, go about 16 miles from the Oconaluftee Visitors Center to the Newfound Gap parking lot. The trailhead is to the left of the overlook. Take the moderate four-mile hike to Charlies Bunion, a peak along the trail with a very odd name. You'll gradually gain around 1,600 feet in elevation, but if you bring a picnic lunch, you'll have a lovely dining spot.

barn is the only structure original to this site, the other buildings were moved here from inside and adjacent to the park and arranged much like a typical farm of the era. If you visit during peak times, you'll see living-history interpreters in costume, demonstrating the day-to-day chores on this farm: preparing meals, sewing, maintaining and harvesting the garden, taking care of the hogs, and the like.

★ Cades Cove

On the Tennessee side of the park, the 11-mile one-way **Cades Cove Loop Road** traverses Cades Cove, a historic settlement dating to the late 18th century. Originally part of the Cherokee Nation, the land was ceded to the United States in 1819. The population grew throughout the 19th century until it was a busy town of several hundred. The village is preserved today as it appeared around 1900, with homes, churches, barns, and a working gristmill, but without the people—a mountain counterpart to Cape Lookout National Seashore's Portsmouth Village. Because of the cove's scenic beauty and abundance of wildlife, this is the most popular part of the nation's most visited national park. The loop road through Cades Cove takes about an hour to drive when visitors are sparse; on crowded days—peak summer and fall seasons and most weekends—it can take several hours to cover the 11 miles.

To take this lovely-in-any-season drive, follow Little River Road west from the Sugarlands Visitor Center for 17.2 miles. The road becomes Laurel Creek Road and leads to Cades Cove in another 7.4 miles. You can also access Cades Cove by entering the park at Townsend on Highway 73, then turning right on Laurel Creek Road, following it for 16 miles to the entrance to the cove. Cades Cove is closed to vehicle traffic every Wednesday May-September, when the loop is open exclusively to bicycle and foot traffic. The rest of the year, the road is open to motor vehicles sunrise-sunset daily, as long as the weather allows.

The **Cades Cove Campground** (10042 Campground Dr., Townsend, TN, campground 865/448-4103, reservations 877/444-6777, www.recreation.gov, $25) is a popular spot where you'll definitely want to reserve a campsite. This campground is open year-round, and although the occupancy is a little lower in the dead of winter, you'll still find a few intrepid visitors taking refuge from the cold in one of the 159 campsites. Hikers take note: There are several backcountry campsites off the trails in Cades Cove, making it a good base for overnight trips.

Today, several historic structures remain standing along the valley floor. Among them is the most photographed structure in the park, the **Methodist Church.** From time to time, a wedding is held here, though it's more common for visitors to leave handwritten prayers on scraps of paper large and small at the altar.

The **Cable Mill Area** is the busiest section of the loop, even if the Methodist Church is the most photographed. At the Cable Mill, you can see an actual mill in operation and even buy cornmeal and flour ground on-site. In addition to the mill and Methodist church, there are two other churches, a few barns and log houses, and a number of smaller structures.

Halfway around the loop, you'll find the **Cades Cove Visitor Center** (Cades Cove Loop Rd., Townsend, Tennessee, 865/436-7318, 9am-4:30pm daily Dec.-Feb., 9am-5pm daily Mar. and Nov., 9am-6pm daily Apr.-May and Sept.-Oct., 9am-7pm daily June-Aug., closed Dec. 25), which has a good bookstore and gift shop, and, most important, one of two public restrooms you'll find on the tour (the other is at the Cades Cove Campground Store at the entrance).

Cataloochee

Nestled in the folds of the mountains and encircled by 6,000-foot peaks, the Cataloochee Valley was settled in the early 1830s. This isolated valley on the northeastern edge of GSMNP was home to two communities—Big

and Little Cataloochee—and more than 1,200 people in 1910. By the 1940s, all but a few were gone, leaving the valley, and its new status as one of the more beautiful spots in the new national park, for hills and hollows nearby. Today, the few historic structures that stand in Cataloochee Valley are all that remains of the communities, save a few memories and written stories.

Cataloochee Valley is not far from I-40, but poor signage makes it a little difficult to find. On I-40, take exit 20 onto U.S. 276. Take an immediate right onto Cove Creek Road. The condition of the road—it's alternately gravel and paved—and the narrow winding route will make you doubt you made the right turn, but you did. Zigzag up this road for about 12 miles. Suddenly it will open into the wide grassy expanse that is Cataloochee Valley. Before you begin your descent into the valley, stop at the overlook just past the intersection with Big Creek Road. From here, you can marvel at the valley sweeping away before you and the mountains rising up all around.

The valley is open to vehicle traffic 8am-sunset. Though less visited than other areas, like Cades Cove on the western side of the park, Cataloochee sees its fair share of visitors. Most arrive in the evenings shortly before sunset to see the elk grazing in the fields. If you don't plan on camping and you'd rather avoid the crowds, as small as they may be, visit in midday, take a hike, and see if you can find the elk in the woods; it's where they go to escape the heat.

The ★ **Cataloochee Campground** (campground 828/497-9270, reservations 877/444-6777, www.recreation.gov, reservations required, mid-Apr.-Oct., $25) has 27 tent and RV sites. There is a horse camp with seven sites not far up the valley; down the valley there's a group campground with three sites and room for much larger parties. This highly recommended campsite is one of the most secluded you'll find in the front country.

1: Cades Cove 2: Clingmans Dome 3: Palmer Chapel in Cataloochee 4: a hiking trail along a river

SIGHTS

There are four prominent structures still standing in Cataloochee Valley: two homes, a school, and a church. A few other structures and ruins, cemeteries, fences, and walls remain throughout the valley. The most prominent building is the **Palmer Chapel and Cemetery.** The chapel was built in 1898, but it's been some time since there's been a regular service here. Now it stands empty, its doors open to the forest, the view from its windows nothing but trees. Throughout the year there are some great opportunities to capture the chapel in all sorts of lighting, weather, and seasonal conditions. Today the chapel sees sporadic use, the most regular being the annual reunion of the descendants of some of the oldest Cataloochee families. Descendants of the Barnes, Bennett, Caldwell, Noland, and Palmer families gather here to eat, hold a short church service, and maintain the cemetery.

Across the road is the **Beech Grove School,** the last of three schools to serve the children of the valley. It's empty too, save a few artifacts. Beech Grove School operated on a very different school schedule than most were familiar with: The only regular school sessions were held November-January, sometimes February, and rarely into March.

Just up the road is the **Caldwell House.** We know from records that the owner, Hiram Caldwell, was prosperous, but you could tell that by looking at the 1906 home and comparing it to the other historic homes in the park, which are mostly log cabins. The Caldwell House is frame-built, similar to modern houses, with paneling on the interior walls.

The final structure is the **Palmer House,** located off Big Creek Road, not far from the Cataloochee Ranger Station. Once this was a log home—two, actually—connected by a covered walkway called a dog trot, but as the owners came into money in the early 1900s, they began making improvements and remodeling the home. They covered the exterior and interior with weatherboarding and began using fancy wallpaper in some rooms (scraps of the wallpaper are there today). When the son

inherited the property, he began to remodel, adding rooms to the home and operating it as a boarding house. Renters were primarily anglers, there to fish in the three miles of stocked trout stream the family owned.

★ Clingmans Dome

At 6,643 feet, Clingmans Dome is the third-highest mountain in the eastern United States and the highest in the Great Smoky Mountains. A flying saucer-like observation tower at the end of a long steep walkway gives 360-degree views of the surrounding mountains, and on a clear day, the view can be as far as 100 miles. More often, though, it's misty up here in the clouds, and Clingmans Dome receives so much precipitation that its woods are actually a coniferous rainforest. The road to the summit is closed December-March, but the observation tower remains open for those willing to make the hike. To get to Clingmans Dome, turn off Newfound Gap Road 0.1 miles south of Newfound Gap, and then take Clingmans Dome Road (closed in winter), which leads seven miles to the parking lot. The peak is near the center of the park, due north from Bryson City.

Fontana Dam

At the southern edge of GSMNP lies Fontana Lake, a 10,230-acre reservoir created in the 1940s as part of the efforts of the Tennessee Valley Authority (TVA) to supply electricity to communities and industrial facilities in the region. The 480-foot-tall, 2,365-foot-wide Fontana Dam, complete with three hydroelectric generators, was completed in 1944, providing electricity to the factories churning out materials for World War II, including in Oak Ridge, Tennessee, where research leading to the atomic bomb was conducted.

To build Fontana Dam, the TVA purchased more than 1,000 tracts of land and relocated around 600 families in five communities. Those folks left behind homes, schools, churches, and barns, all of which were covered by the lake. This displacement of so many families and elimination of these small communities was part of the tradeoff that resulted in the modernization of the region, when electric power became cheap and readily available, and many jobs were required to complete the project. The dam also provides much-needed flood control to a region that receives 55-82 inches of rainfall each year. Today, the TVA can regulate the depth of the lake by releasing water as they anticipate flood events, and the water level of Fontana Lake can vary by as much as 50 feet.

Fontana Dam is the highest concrete dam east of the Mississippi, and it provides great recreational opportunities. The Appalachian Trail crosses the dam itself, and thousands of boaters and anglers take to the lake each year. There are more than 238 miles of shoreline along Fontana Lake and over 10,000 acres of water surface. If you have your own boat, you can launch it from the **Fontana Marina** (40 Fontana Dam Rd., 828/498-2017, www.fontanavillage.com), or you can rent a kayak, canoe, or paddleboard ($15-20 per hour, $60 per day) as well as a pontoon boat ($75-85 per hour, $350-400 per day) or fishing boat ($70 per hour, $300 per day); if you need a slip, rent one ($5-40 per day). Fishing guide services, shuttles to backcountry sites ($30-95 one-way, $50-190 round-trip), and seasonal tours of the lake ($30 adults, $15 ages 3-12) are also available.

The exhibits at the **Fontana Dam Visitor Center** (Fontana Dam Rd., www.tva.com, 9am-7pm daily Apr.-Aug., 9am-6pm daily Sept.-Oct., free), off Highway 28 near the state line, about 45 minutes from Bryson City, tell the story of the region and the construction of the dam. There's also a small gift shop and a viewing platform overlooking the dam. Hikers take note: They sell backcountry camping permits and have showers in the back.

★ Newfound Gap Road

While many visitors use this 32-mile road that bisects Great Smoky Mountains National Park as a mere throughway, it's actually one of the prettiest drives you'll find anywhere. This curvy road alternates between exposed and tree-enclosed, and a number of scenic overlooks provide spectacular views of the Smokies. Stop at one that has a trail (more than half of them do) and take a short walk into the woods or eat a picnic lunch on one of the mountainside overlooks. Whatever you do on this road between Cherokee and Gatlinburg, take your time and enjoy the ride.

SPORTS AND RECREATION

The Great Smoky Mountains National Park covers over 500,000 acres, and within that expanse are more than 800 miles of hiking trails, ranging from easy walks around major attractions to strenuous wilderness paths suited to the most experienced backpackers. A section of the Appalachian Trail goes through the park, crossing the Fontana Dam. There are dozens of books available about hiking in the Smokies, available at bookstores and outfitters throughout the region as well as online. The park's **Backcountry Information Office** (865/436-1297, 8am-5pm daily) has knowledgeable staff who are a good first resource when planning a hiking trip. The park website (www.nps.gov/grsm) has some downloadable maps to give you a general sense of the lay of the land. The Great Smoky Mountains Association website (www.smokiesinformation.org) has a good online bookstore.

Hiking

The Great Smoky Mountains National Park contains hundreds of miles of hiking trails, ranging from family-friendly loop trails to strenuous wilderness treks. Below are a sampling of hikes in the park. Before embarking on any of these trails, obtain a park map, and talk to a park ranger to ascertain trail conditions and gauge whether it's suited to your hiking skills.

SPRUCE-FIR TRAIL

A quick and easy foray into the woods is the **Spruce-Fir Trail,** off Clingmans Dome Road, a walk of just over 0.3 miles. Almost flat, and mostly following a wooden boardwalk, this

Best Hikes

This is a beautiful country to tour by car, but you're not doing the landscape justice if you only experience it through your windshield. Here are some fantastic chances to get out and be surrounded by nature.

ANDREWS BALD

At Clingmans Dome, a few miles off Newfound Gap Road, this **3.5-mile round-trip** trail is one of the loveliest and most rewarding hikes you'll find.

KEPHART PRONG

A perfect trail if you're new to the Smokies, this **4-mile round-trip** hike passes through a Civilian Conservation Corps camp, crosses the Oconaluftee River and Kephart Prong, and is loaded with wildflowers in spring.

DEEP CREEK LOOP TRAIL

This wide, mostly flat and easy trail takes you past Tom Branch, Indian Creek, and Juney Whank Falls in the span of **4.9-miles round-trip** on this hike near Bryson City.

HEN WALLOW FALLS TRAIL

In Cosby, a few miles northeast of Gatlinburg, you'll find this **4.4-mile round-trip** hike to a delicate waterfall some 90 feet high.

MOUNT CAMMERER TRAIL

It's a tough **11.2-mile round-trip** hike to the summit, but you're rewarded with some of the best views in the park, courtesy of a stone fire tower built in the 1930s.

LITTLE RIVER TRAIL

Keep this trail short and sweet as you follow an old logging road alongside the Little River and through the home of the synchronous fireflies, or follow all **12.3 miles** for an out-and-back day hike.

ABRAMS FALLS TRAIL

A hike suited to just about anyone that leads to a great waterfall, this **5-mile round-trip** hike is in Cades Cove, and you'll drive right by the trailhead.

RICH MOUNTAIN LOOP

This **8.5-mile round-trip** loop in Cades Cove is one of the most fabulous hikes in the park.

is an ideal trail if you simply want to stretch your legs and experience a bit of easily accessible forest atmosphere.

OCONALUFTEE RIVER TRAIL

A longer but also fairly easy walk is the **Oconaluftee River Trail,** which begins behind the Oconaluftee Visitors Center. This path, which is gravel-covered, follows the river and goes through part of the Mountain Farm Museum grounds. Unlike all the other trails in the GSMNP, dogs and bicycles are allowed. It's about three miles round-trip, popular with families, and absolutely littered with wildflowers in the spring. An added bonus is that one end is adjacent to the GSMNP "Welcome" sign, and the National Park Service has conveniently installed a post and platform to hold your camera for selfies in front of it.

QUIET WALKWAYS

At many of the pullouts deeper in the park, you'll find **Quiet Walkways.** These short, easy trails pull you into the woods just far enough off the road that the road noise is drowned out by birdsong, rustling leaves, flowing streams, and mountain breezes that build a cocoon around you. Signs at the trailhead encourage you to take your time and lose yourself in the sounds of nature, the aroma of the leaves, water, flowers, and mountain air, and the textures of the wild woodlands.

ALUM CAVE AND ARCH ROCK

At the **Alum Cave Trail** trailhead, off Newfound Gap Road, you'll find a trio of hikes ranging from easy to rugged. Hiking to **Arch Rock** is an easy 2.8-mile round-trip. Arch Rock has eroded into a giant arch. A moist, winding set of stairs goes under, up, and through the arch, and the trail continues to **Alum Cave,** another mile in, making for a 4.6-mile round-trip. Just before you get to Alum Cave is Inspiration Point, with a commanding view of the valley below, including the interesting Eye of the Needle rock formation on an adjacent ridge. Shortly after Inspiration Point you'll come to Alum Cave, where Epsom salts and saltpeter (used in the manufacture of gunpowder) were mined starting in the 1830s. To get to Alum Cave the path transitions from easy to moderate, but if you want to push on another 3.7 miles to the peak of Mount LeConte, for a hike that's a little over 10 miles round-trip, you'll be in for a much more difficult trail. For around 2 miles you'll encounter many exposed ledges, some with waterfalls to negotiate, all with a cable handhold for when the rocky path is slick. When you get to the top, you'll find yourself at the LeConte Lodge, but not at the actual summit. To reach the highest point, the summit of Mount LeConte, follow a short trail to High Top. The views from High Top are nice but not fantastic; for the best views, try Myrtle Point, a great spot to photograph the sunrise, or Cliff Top, near the lodge.

BOOGERMAN TRAIL

The **Boogerman Trail** is a loop trail off Cove Creek Road in the Cataloochee section of the park. This is a moderate 7.5-mile round-trip that takes 2-3 hours to complete. You'll pass old-growth trees, streams and cascades, and several old homesites, including that of "Boogerman" himself, an early resident named Robert Palmer.

CHIMNEY TOPS TRAIL

Another popular hike on the Newfound Gap Road is the **Chimney Tops Trail.** This four-mile round-trip starts out easy enough, but the last mile gains more than 830 vertical feet. Severe weather in 2012 turned parts of the trail into an obstacle course of rocks, roots, and mud, and at times the trail may be closed for ongoing rehabilitation. If the trail is open, the effort is worth the reward, as the views of Mount LeConte and Mount Kephart to the east and Sugarland Mountain to the west are amazing. This is one of the few mountains in the Smokies with a bare-rock top, and although the trail here is steep, it doesn't require any technical gear, just caution and the ability to scramble up steep rocks.

WATERFALLS

As if the mountains and valleys, flora and fauna, and close-enough-to-touch clouds weren't wonder enough, the GSMNP has literally hundreds of waterfalls. Several of the most popular and most beautiful are accessible from major trails. Close to Bryson City, 25-foot **Indian Creek Falls** is a moderate hike of less than two miles round-trip; it's a two-for-one deal, as the path also goes by Tom Branch Falls. Crossing Deep Creek on bridges and logs and going by old homesites, this is an especially interesting hike. The Deep Creek-Indian Creek Trailhead is at the end of Deep Creek Road in Bryson City. It gets very crowded in nice weather, particularly because this is a popular area for tubing, which makes parking quite difficult. Restrooms are available at the picnic area. Also accessible from the Indian Creek Trailhead is the path to 90-foot **Juney Whank Falls.** This hike is shorter but more difficult than to Indian Creek Falls. Since it shares the same trailhead, you can expect to find the same crowds and parking difficulties.

Mingo Falls, a beautiful 120-foot plume, is just outside the park, on the Qualla Boundary (Cherokee land). It can be seen from the Pigeon Creek Trail, which begins in the Mingo Falls Campground, off Big Cove Road south of Cherokee. The hike is very short, less than 0.5 miles round-trip, but it is fairly strenuous.

Some longer hikes on the Tennessee side of the park lead to equally beautiful falls. **Rainbow Falls** is 80 feet high and produces such a cloud of mist that when the sun hits it right, you can see a rainbow. In winter it sometimes freezes solid, which is an amazing sight. The Rainbow Falls Trail, near Gatlinburg, is a difficult 5.5 miles round-trip. It ascends about 1,500 vertical feet and is rocky most of the way, but it provides some great views of the falls and of Gatlinburg. Parking is available on Cherokee Orchard Road in Gatlinburg, but it fills up quickly, and you may need to pay to park a little farther from the trailhead.

The tallest waterfall, 100-foot **Ramsey Cascades,** is also the most difficult to reach. Those able to make a strenuous eight-mile round-trip hike are richly rewarded with a journey through old-growth hardwood forests and along fast-moving rivers. The pool at the bottom of the falls is a great place to glimpse some of the creatures that make GSMNP the Salamander Capital of the World. The parking area for the Ramsey Cascades Trail is off Greenbrier Road, a few miles southeast of Gatlinburg. The nearest portable toilets are at the picnic area on Greenbrier Road.

As tempting as it may be, don't try to climb the waterfalls; it's never a good idea. Because of its height, Ramsey Cascades is particularly dangerous. Maps and guides to the waterfalls are available at many locations in the park and at bookstores and outdoors shops nearby.

Horseback Riding

Three commercial stables in the national park offer rental horses. **Smokemont Riding Stable** (135 Smokemont Riding Stable Rd., 828/497-2373, www.smokemontridingstable.com, $40 per hour, 2.5-hour waterfall ride $100, 4-hour ride $160, wagon ride $20) is located in North Carolina near Cherokee. Two are in Tennessee: **Smoky Mountain Riding Stable** (865/436-5634, www.smokymountainridingstables.com, $27 per hour) and **Cades Cove Riding Stable** (10018 Campground Dr., Townsend, TN, 865/448-9009, http://cadescovestables.com, $40 adults, $35 ages 6-12).

In North Carolina, near Cherokee, an equestrian-friendly campground at **Round Bottom Horse Camp** (Straight Fork-Round Bottom Rd., campground 865/436-1261, reservations 877/444-6777, www.recreation.gov, mid-Apr.-late-Oct., $23) has five campsites, stalls, and bedding for horses. Its location, just inside the park and far up a narrow riverside road, makes it perfect for long rides with larger groups.

Bicycle Rentals

The **Cades Cove Store** (near Cades Cove Campground, 865/448-9034, www.cadescovetrading.com, 9am-6pm daily) rents bicycles in summer and fall ($15 per hour adults, $10 per hour under age 16, 24-hour rental $50). May-September, the park closes off the loop road through Cades Cove for the full day on Wednesday so that cyclists and hikers can enjoy the cove without having to worry about automobile traffic. It's an awesome program, and whether you get here early and rent a bike, bring your own, or just decide to hoof it around the loop, there's no better way to experience this part of the park.

Field Schools

Two Tennessee-based organizations affiliated with the GSMNP offer ways to get to know the park even better. The **Smoky Mountain**

1: bridge on the Kephart Prong trail 2: Ramsey Cascades 3: Juney Whank Falls in the Deep Creek area

Field School (865/974-0150, www.smfs.utk. edu) teaches workshops and leads excursions to educate participants in a wide array of fields related to the Smokies. One-day classes focus on the history and cultural heritage of the park, the lives of some of the park's most interesting animals, folk medicine, and cooking of the southern Appalachians. Instructors also lead one-day and overnight hikes into the heart of the park. This is a great way to discover the park far beyond what you would be able to do on your own, so check their schedule and sign up for a class that interests you.

The **Great Smoky Mountains Institute at Tremont** (9275 Tremont Rd., Townsend, TN, 865/448-6709, www.gsmit.org) teaches students of all ages about the ecology of the region, wilderness rescue and survival skills, and even nature photography. Many of the classes and guided trips are part of Road Scholar, kids camps, or teacher-training institutes; however, there are also rich opportunities for unaffiliated learners.

FOOD

Unless you're staying at the LeConte Lodge, you'll have to leave the park for meals. The easiest way is simply to drive into Bryson City or Cherokee, or in Tennessee, Gatlinburg or Pigeon Forge, which are all right on the edge of the park. In Gatlinburg, try the **Smoky Mountain Brewery** (1004 Parkway, Suite 501, Gatlinburg, 865/436-4200, www.smoky-mtn-brewery.com, 11am-midnight daily, $11-28), a popular brewpub and restaurant. The menu is about what you'd expect—burgers, wings, and cheesesteaks—but they also have some pretty good pizzas and even barbecue ribs. Their beer selection includes porters, wheat beers, red ales, and hoppy pale ales.

If there's one thing Gatlinburg has, it's pancake houses. But frankly, they all fall short of the original pancake house, the very first one to open in Tennessee: **Pancake Pantry** (628 Parkway, 865/436-4724, www.pancakepantry. com, 7am-3pm daily, $6-10). They griddle up 24 varieties of pancakes and crepes as well as waffles, omelets, and french toast. Breakfast is served all day, but if you feel like a burger or sandwich for lunch, there are a few of those too. If you're going for a hike, go easy on the pancakes—they sit a little heavy—but you can get a to-go boxed lunch made just for hikers and day-trippers into the park.

Delauder's Smoky Mountain BBQ (1875 E. Parkway, 865/325-8682, 4pm-8pm Thurs., 12:30pm-8pm Fri.-Sat., noon-8pm Sun., $5-25) will draw you in through smell alone, and once you taste the pulled pork or ribs, you won't want to leave. Other options are a Smoky Mountain Potato (a baked potato heaped with barbecue and fixings), nachos piled with barbecue goodness, and a number of sandwiches, including the Holy Bologna Sandwich, a grilled bologna behemoth topped with pulled pork, onions, pickles, sweet jalapeño mustard, barbecue sauce, and cheese.

Smith & Son Corner Kitchen (traffic light no. 8, 812 Parkway, 865/430-1978 or 865/436-8878, www.smithandsoncornerkitchen.com, 11am-9pm Sun.-Thurs., 11am-10pm Fri.-Sat., $10-25) has a prime location, loads of space, and a sizable menu that remains navigable. The salads are whoppers, and when paired with an appetizer, there's more than a meal for one. Burgers and sandwiches are fresh and filling, and the entrées—ranging from smoked chicken to meatloaf to fajitas to fried catfish—are so generous you won't mind sharing a bite or two.

While you're here, you may as well sample some 'shine. **Sugarlands Distilling Company** (805 Parkway, 865/325-1355, www. sugarlands.com, 10am-10:30pm daily, tours free) has an excellent distillery where you can see the whole operation in action, do a little sampling, and grab a quart or two to take home. With eight moonshines ranging from flavored to high-test and a pair of whiskeys to try, you'll have to pace yourself.

ACCOMMODATIONS

There is only one inn in the entire 500,000-acre park, and it's an unusual one: the ★ **LeConte Lodge** (865/429-5704, www. lecontelodge.com, late Mar.-mid-Nov., $162 adults, $89 ages 4-12, includes lodging, breakfast, and dinner). Like the summit, the Lodge is accessible only via the network of hiking trails that crisscross the park. And if the accessibility limitation isn't rustic enough for you, this collection of cabins has no running water or electricity. What the lodge does have is views for days and the seclusion of the Smoky Mountains backcountry. Oh, and a hearty breakfast and dinner come with each room.

LeConte Lodge has no hot showers, but in every cabin there is a bucket for a sponge bath (which can be surprisingly refreshing after a hot day on the trail), which you can fill with warm water from the kitchen, though you need to supply your own washcloth and towel. There are a few flush toilets in a separate building. The only lights, aside from headlamps and flashlights, are kerosene lanterns. For the most part, it's a rustic spot, harking back to the lodge's 1934 origins on the slopes of Mount LeConte. Dinner and breakfast are served at the same time every day, 6pm for dinner and 8am for breakfast, and the meals are substantial enough to fuel you for another day on the trail.

The Lodge doesn't lack for charm, but it does for comfort, so if you're the five-star-hotel breakfast-in-bed type, this may not be the place for you. Catering to hikers who are happier to have a dry place to sleep and a bed that's comfier than their sleeping bag, it's short on the luxury amenities, and guest rooms are bunk beds in small drafty cabins. But if you're a hiker or if you just love to have a completely different experience when you travel, this is a one-of-a-kind place to stay. Rooms book quickly—up to a year in advance.

For those who don't want to camp or hike to a rustic lodge, there are countless motels just outside the GSMNP. Reservations are always a good idea, especially in summer and in leaf season. There are many choices in Cherokee, Maggie Valley, Bryson City, Pigeon Forge, Gatlinburg, Sevierville, and other neighboring communities. In addition to the many chain motels, affordable mom-and-pop

motels also dot this landscape in abundance. Two good choices in Gatlinburg are **Westgate Smoky Mountain Resort & Water Park** (915 Westgate Resorts Rd., Gatlinburg, 865/430-4800, www.westgateresorts.com, from $179) and the **Riverhouse at the Park** (904 River Rd., Gatlinburg, 865/436-7821, www.riverhousemotels.com, $102-220). In Cherokee, on the North Carolina side of the park, go with a hotel like **Cherokee Grand Hotel** (196 Painttown Rd., 828/497-0050, www.cherokeegrandhotel.com, $179-219), only five minutes from the park entrance, or cabin accommodations with **Panther Creek Cabins** (Wrights Creek Rd., Cherokee, 828/497-2461, www.panthercreekresort.com, cabins $75-325, pets $49 for 1 dog, $39 2nd dog), a quiet, quaint, comfortable set of cabins just outside downtown Cherokee.

Camping

The GSMNP has many locations for camping. Campers can stay up to 14 consecutive nights at car-accessible campsites, but no more than three consecutive nights at backcountry campsites, and only nonconsecutive nights in shelters and at campsite 113. There are 10 car-accessible campgrounds, each of which has cold running water and flush toilets but no showers, power, or water hookups. Most of these sites are first come, first served, but May 15-October 15, sites at the Elkmont, Smokemont, Cades Cove, Cataloochee, and Cosby campgrounds can be reserved (877/444-6777, www.nps.gov/grsm).

The **Cataloochee Campground** (campground 865/436-1200, reservations 877/444-6777, www.recreation.gov, mid-Apr.-Oct., reservations required, $25) has 27 tent and RV sites. There is a horse camp with seven sites not far up the valley; down the valley is a group campground with three sites and room for much larger parties. This highly recommended campsite is one of the most secluded you'll find in the front country.

Cosby Campground (127 Cosby Park Rd., Cosby, TN, campground info 423/487-2683, reservations 877/444-6777, www.

recreation.gov, mid-Apr.-Oct., $17.50) has 157 sites for tents and RVs. Despite being home to the park's third-largest campground, Cosby is known as the quietest of the park's gateways. There are a number of trails that originate from the campground.

The **Elkmont Campground** (434 Elkmont Rd., Gatlinburg, 865/430-5560, reservations 877/444-6777, www.recreation.gov, $25-27, mid-Mar.-late-Nov.) has 220 campsites, 55 of them along the Little River, with front-row seats to the firefly light show, provided you're here at the right time. This is the largest of the campgrounds in GSMNP, and one of the most used. In addition to the firefly show and the attraction of Little River, this site also serves as a good base for exploring the area.

The **Cades Cove Campground** (10042 Campground Dr., Townsend, TN, information 865/448-4103, reservations 877/444-6777, www.recreation.gov, year-round, $25) is a popular spot where you'll definitely want to reserve in advance. Occupancy is a little lower in the dead of winter, but you'll still find a few intrepid visitors taking refuge from the cold at one of the 159 campsites. Hikers take note: There are several backcountry campsites off the trails in Cades Cove, making it a good base for overnight trips.

Just outside the park, **Fontana Village Resort** (300 Woods Rd., Fontana Dam, 828/498-2211 or 800/849-2258, www.fontanavillage.com, lodge $119-179, cabins $159-339, camping $15-40) offers a place to lay your head in your choice of accommodations: tent or RV camping, one- to three-bedroom cabins, and lodge rooms. There are 100 lodge rooms, 110 cabins, and 20 campsites.

Another car-accessible camping option is the **Mile High Campground** (828/269-2945, www.campmilehigh.com, mid-May-mid-Oct., tent or RV $25, primitive cabin $35) located on the Cherokee Reservation and owned by a member of the Eastern Band of the Cherokee. It is near Blue Ridge Parkway's Milepost 458; turn onto Wolf Laurel Gap, and

the campground entrance is one mile along, on the left, after the "Molly's Gap Road" sign. This campground is indeed a little over a mile high in elevation and has around 50 sites in tent and RV areas along with primitive cabins. A beautiful campground near a number of hikes, the Blue Ridge Parkway, Cherokee, and the Great Smoky Mountains National Park, it's a great spot to set up for a few days. All campsites have fire rings and are fairly private. Bears and elk are common sights, so take pictures, but use caution.

Backcountry camping is abundant. It is only permitted at designated sites and shelters, and a permit is required, but the permits are free and can be obtained at any of 15 different visitors centers and campground offices throughout the park or online (https://smokiespermits.nps.gov). The Appalachian Trail runs through, hugging the ridgeline and the border between North Carolina and Tennessee, and shelters on the trail fill up fast with through-hikers and day hikers, but other shelters and campsites on side trails are ideal for out-and-back camping trips. The Kephart shelter and the shelter at Laurel Gap are on two beautiful trails, and a number of campsites—numbers 52-57—are on the Mountains-to-Sea Trail that traverses North Carolina. There are also five drive-in horse camps ($20-25) and seven group campgrounds ($35-65). A map of the available campsites can be found on the park's website (www.nps.gov/grsm). Before camping at the GSMNP, be sure to familiarize yourself with the park's backcountry regulations and etiquette, available online and at locations in the park.

INFORMATION AND SERVICES

The official website of **Great Smoky Mountains National Park** (www.nps.gov/grsm) has a good deal of the information you'll need to plan a trip. At the visitors centers in Sugarlands, Oconaluftee, Cades Cove, and Clingmans Dome you'll find additional information from helpful rangers and fellow travelers. The websites of **Smoky Mountain Host**

1: Cosby Campground 2: LeConte Lodge

(www.visitsmokies.org) and the **Blue Ridge National Heritage Area** (www.blueridge-heritage.com) provide additional information. Detailed touring suggestions for sites associated with Cherokee history and heritage can be found at the website on the **North Carolina Folklife Institute** (www.ncfolk.org) website, and in the book *Cherokee Heritage Trails.*

The nearest hospitals are **LeConte Medical Center** (742 Middle Creek Rd., Sevierville, TN, 865/446-7000, www.lecontemedicalcenter.com), about 25 minutes from the west park entrance; **Blount Memorial Hospital** (907 E. Lamar Alexander Pkwy., Maryville, TN, 865/983-7211 or 800/448-0219, www.blountmemorial.org), an hour from the west park entrance; **Cherokee Indian Hospital** (1 Hospital Rd., Cherokee, NC, www.cherokeehospital.org, 828/497-9163), minutes away from the Oconaluftee Visitors Center in Cherokee; and **Swain Community Hospital** (45 Plateau St., Bryson City, NC, 828/488-2155, www.myswaincommunity.com), a little less than 30 minutes from the eastern park entrance in Cherokee.

GETTING THERE AND AROUND

From Asheville it's easy to get to GSMNP. In just over an hour you can be in Cataloochee, at the north end of the park, to camp, hike, and watch for elk in a serene mountain cove; to get here, take I-40 west to exit 20 and follow the signs. You can also take I-40 west into Tennessee, then follow the Foothills Parkway to U.S. 321 and skirt the edge of GSMNP to Gatlinburg, Tennessee, and the entrance to the park, a trip of about 90 minutes. From Gatlinburg, you can make a loop back to Asheville by taking Newfound Gap Road across GSMNP to Cherokee (about 2.5 hours) and then back to Asheville via U.S. 441 to U.S. 19 to I-40, a total loop of about 3.5 hours and some 175 miles.

You can also head straight to Cherokee from Asheville and enter GSMNP via Newfound Gap Road. It's an hour's drive on I-40 west to exit 27, then take U.S. 19 south to U.S. 441, which leads into Cherokee. Alternately you can take the more scenic, but much longer, route and get to Cherokee via the Blue Ridge Parkway. This route is only 83 miles, but it takes 2-2.5 hours. If you want to go this way, head south out of Asheville along U.S. 25 and pick up the Blue Ridge Parkway about 5.5 miles out of town; turn south on the parkway and drive it until you reach Cherokee and GSMNP. And, of course, you can reverse the route if you're making that grand loop and return to Asheville via the Blue Ridge Parkway by picking it up in Cherokee and driving north.

Maggie Valley

Maggie Valley is a vacation town from the bygone era of long family road trips in wood-paneled station wagons. Coming down the mountain toward Maggie Valley you'll pass an overlook that, on a morning when the mountains around Soco Gap are looped with fog, is surely one of the most beautiful vistas in the state.

SIGHTS AND ENTERTAINMENT

In a state with countless attractions for automotive enthusiasts, Maggie Valley's **Wheels Through Time Museum** (62 Vintage Lane, 828/926-6266, www.wheelsthroughtime.com, 10am-5pm Thurs.-Mon. Apr.-late Nov., $15 adults, $12 ages over 65, $7 ages 6-14, free under age 6) stands out as one of the most fun (and it's the only one, to my knowledge, to have Jason Momoa stop by on a tour through the Smokies and Mike Wolfe from TV's *American Pickers* pay them a visit). A dazzling collection of nearly 300 vintage motorcycles and a fair number of cars are on display, including rarities like a 1908 Indian, a 1914 Harley-Davidson, military motorcycles from both world wars, and some gorgeous postwar bikes. This collection, which dates mostly to before 1950, is maintained in working order—almost every one of the bikes is revved up from time to time.

Elevated Mountain Distilling Co. (3732 Soco Rd., 828/944-0766, 10am-5pm Mon.-Wed., 10am-11pm Thurs., 10am-midnight Fri.-Sat.) is right on the main drag in Maggie Valley, but if you decide to go for more than a quick sample or two, bring a designated driver, because the moonshine—flavored or straight—is fiery. Tastings include a sample of five of the distilling company's spirits. On the fourth Saturday of each month, Elevated Mountain hosts a bluegrass jam and, in September, a small music festival.

SHOPPING

As you might expect, Maggie Valley has its fair share of touristy T-shirt shops and places where you can pick up some fudge and a refrigerator magnet. **Maggie Mountaineer Crafts** (2394 Soco Rd., 828/926-3129, www. maggiemountaineercrafts.com, 10am-5pm Sat.-Sun. Jan.-Mar., 9am-5pm daily Apr. and Nov.-Dec., 8am-6pm daily May-Oct.) and its attached sister store, **A Day in the Valley,** have all that and more. They've got plenty of fudge (and they ship; seriously, it's that good) and shirts to choose from, but they also have a pretty large selection of quilts and home decor items; knives, moccasins, and toys; and a great section of local foodstuffs like apple butter, sorghum molasses, and some seasonal treats. Throw in the deck overlooking the creek and you have yourself a charming little souvenir store.

Antiques shopping at **Sutton and Son's Antiques** (3156 Dellwood Rd., Waynesville, 828/944-1212, www.suttonandsonsantiques. com, 10am-5pm Mon.-Sat., 1pm-5pm Sun.) is an experience best summed up by their tagline: "Treasure hunting in the Smokies." The store is large and loaded with a nicely curated selection of antiques such as mountain crafts, automotive memorabilia, kitchen goods, and records.

RECREATION
Skiing and Winter Sports

Maggie Valley's **Cataloochee Ski Area** (1080 Ski Lodge Rd., off U.S. 19, 800/768-0285, snow conditions 800/768-3588, www.cataloochee. com, late Nov.-mid-Mar., lift tickets $26-76, rentals $28-33) has slopes geared to every level of skier and snowboarder. Classes and private lessons are available for all ages. At Cataloochee's sister snow-sports area, **Tube World** (4721 Soco Rd., 828/926-0285, www. cataloochee.com, late Nov.-mid-Mar., minimum 42 inches tall, $30-35), you can zip down the mountain on inner tubes.

Hiking

Near Maggie Valley, the mountains become rough. Located on the valley floor, Maggie Valley is surprisingly short on trails, and those that exist are quite strenuous. There's the 2.6-mile stroll around **Lake Junaluska,** but the majority of the trails are found at the crest of the mountains, along the Blue Ridge Parkway. To the east of Maggie Valley, the mountains are a little more forgiving. There are many trails of various intensities and lengths, but in the immediate area, you'll have to take the Heintooga Spur Road, a connector road between the parkway and Great Smoky Mountains National Park, to a mile-high campground, a picnic area with unparalleled views, and the **Flat Creek Trail.** On Heintooga Spur Road, you'll pass into Great Smoky Mountains National Park proper and be treated to no fewer than five stunning overlooks, the best of which is the Mile High Overlook, offering a glimpse of Clingmans Dome, Mount LeConte, Mount Kephart, and Mount Guyot.

The Blue Ridge Parkway is not far from Maggie Valley, which means there are a number of hiking trails to explore. Easy trails include the **Buck Springs Trail** (Milepost 407.6, Blue Ridge Pkwy.), just over 1 mile long, and the 0.25-mile **Bear Pen Gap Trail** (Milepost 427.6, Blue Ridge Pkwy.) that connects to the Mountains-to-Sea Trail; additionally, you can go for a stroll around **Lake Junaluska** in the

Maggie Valley

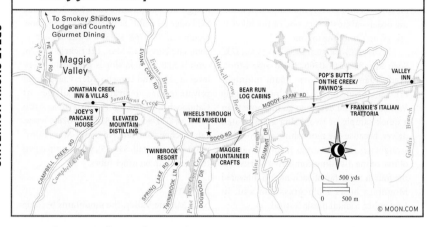

town of Maggie Valley. Moderate trails are longer and usually involve some elevation gain and loss; a couple of the best are **Graveyard Fields Loop Trail** (Milepost 418.8, Blue Ridge Pkwy.), a 3.2-mile loop through alpine-like meadows. Extend your hike here by following one of the spur trails that lead to some fantastic waterfalls. Another moderate option is the **Richland Balsam Trail** (Milepost 431, Blue Ridge Pkwy.), a loop through a spruce and fir forest. Tougher trails often pay off with the best views, and **Waterrock Knob Trail** (Milepost 451.2, Blue Ridge Pkwy.) does that on a 1.2-mile trail that's steep and a little rocky but manageable. It leads to a summit where views await. Another option is the **Devil's Courthouse Trail** (Milepost 422.4, Blue Ridge Pkwy.), a short but strenuous hike of just under 0.5 miles leading to another panoramic summit view.

FOOD

★ **Joey's Pancake House** (4309 Soco Rd., 828/926-0212, www.joeyspancake.com, 7am-noon Mon.-Tues. and Fri.-Sun., $2-9) has been flipping flapjacks for travelers and locals alike since 1966, and it's exactly what you picture: paper menu placemats, hot coffee, a little kitschy, and packed with regulars. Lines form on weekends for the pancakes, waffles, and

country ham—get here early. If you're taken by the pancakes, pick up some of Joey's mix to take home with you.

My favorite restaurant in Maggie Valley is **Frankie's Italian Trattoria** (1037 Soco Rd., 828/926-6216, www.frankiestrattoria.com, 2pm-9pm Tues.-Sat., $10-24). Service is great, the wine list more than adequate, and the food—pizza, linguine with clams, eggplant parm—puts it over the top.

If you're looking for a late lunch or early dinner that includes a piping hot pizza pie or a burger, then **Pavino's** (1560 Soco Rd., 828/944-0007, https://pavinos.com, 3pm-9pm Wed.-Sat., 3pm-7pm Sun., $9-23) is it. Thin crust and hand-tossed pies from personal to family-size, burgers, grinders, calzones, all piping hot and ready to put your hunger to bed.

Try the local spin on barbecue at **Pop's Butts on the Creek BBQ** (1584 Soco Rd., 828/926-7885, www.popsbuttsonthecreeknc. com, 11am-8pm Tues.-Sun., $10-29). Like a lot of places in western North Carolina, Pop's doesn't adhere to our state's unspoken rule that barbecue is pork only, and no ribs. I'm glad because they have a killer rib game, and their brisket and burnt ends are a welcome and beefy relief from all the pork. That said, the chopped pork is great (thanks to their butts-only approach), their spare rib dinner could feed two people, and those burnt ends are especially good on a sandwich.

ACCOMMODATIONS

Along Maggie Valley's main drag (Soco Rd./ U.S. 19) you'll see a lot of creek-side motels and mom-and-pop mountain inns. Among the pleasant independent motels are The Valley Inn (236 Soco Rd., 800/948-6880, www.thevalleyinn.com, from $79) and Jonathan Creek Inn and Villas (4324 Soco Rd., 800/577-7812, www.jonathancreekinn. com, from $100), which has creek-side rooms with screened porches.

High in the mountains—at 4,500 feet elevation—Smokey Shadows Lodge & Country Gourmet Dining (323 Smoky Shadows Lane, 828/926-0001, www.smokeyshadows.com) offers up lodge rooms (from $110) and a pair of cabins (from $150) in a converted grist mill that once served the Cataloochee Valley. With a long covered porch affording some spectacular views, and a yard frequented by elk, it's a special kind of place. They also have a dining room where they serve family-style country dishes ($35)— think tomato pie, pot roast, meatloaf, and other homey dishes—or you can take your meal on the porch (call and reserve a seat on the porch; there may not be one if you wait until you get there to ask for it).

If you want to get a feel for the mountains, try one of the cabin rentals. Bear Run Log Cabins (1604 Moody Farm Rd., 828/926-7566, www.bearrunlogcabins.com, $150-180 June-Dec., $130-150 Jan.-May) has a quartet of cabins that sleep five and have Wi-Fi, a fireplace, and a small kitchen. Their decks overlook Jonathan Creek, one of the area trout streams. Cozy, comfy, and cabin-y, they're exactly what you picture when you think of a mountain cabin getaway.

Stay in a cabin at Twinbrook Resort (20 Twinbrook Lane, 828/962-1388, www.

twinbrookresort.com, cabins $249-499, RV site $59) or bring your RV; either way, you're staying in a beautiful place. Here you're within easy striking distance of the park and the parkway, only 30 minutes' drive to the Oconaluftee Visitors Center, a little longer if you take the scenic route on the Blue Ridge Parkway. On-site you'll find an indoor pool and hot tub, decks with grills, a playground, and one of the namesake brooks. If your travel plans are flexible, keep an eye on the website, as they're constantly running specials on lodging.

There is one fantastic campground in the area: the ★ Balsam Mountain Campground (Milepost 458.2, Heintooga Spur Rd., 828/497-9270, www.nps.gov/grsm, reservations www.recreation.gov, mid-May-mid-Oct., $18), the highest campground in Great Smoky Mountains National Park at 5,310 feet. This primitive campground has 43 sites for tents and RVs, with a dedicated tent-only section. It's a beautiful isolated campground that's often overlooked as it's slightly off the beaten path. Because it's also a primitive campground (pit toilets, no showers), most of the year you won't have many neighbors here. If you're driving a vehicle you feel comfortable taking on forest roads, Balsam Mountain Road, sometimes called Round Bottom Road, continues on from the campground, making a nice trip through the forest down to Cherokee. It's about two hours but worth the drive.

GETTING THERE AND AROUND

U.S. 19 is the main thoroughfare in these parts, leading from Asheville to the Great Smoky Mountains National Park. If you're taking your time between Asheville, Boone, or parts north, the Blue Ridge Parkway is a beautiful, but slow, drive to this part of the state. Maggie Valley is also a reasonably short jog off I-40 via exits 20, 24, and 27.

Cherokee and the Qualla Boundary

The town of Cherokee is a study in juxtapositions: the cultural traditions of the Cherokee people, the region's natural beauty, a 24-hour casino, and community-wide preparation for the future. Cherokee is the seat of government of the Eastern Band of the Cherokee, who have lived in these mountains for centuries. Today, their traditional arts and crafts, government, and cultural heritage are very much alive, although their language seems to be disappearing. The Qualla ("KWA-lah") Boundary is not a reservation but a large tract of land owned and governed by the Cherokee people. Institutions like the Museum of the Cherokee Indian and the Qualla Arts and Crafts Mutual provide a solid base for the Eastern Band's cultural life. As you drive around, take a look at the road signs: Below each English road name is that same name in Cherokee, a beautiful script created by Sequoyah, a 19th-century Cherokee silversmith. This language, once nearly extinct, is being taught to the community's youth now, and there is a Cherokee language immersion school on the Qualla Boundary. This doesn't mean the language is not in danger; few Cherokee people speak it fluently.

The main street in Cherokee is a classic cheesy tourist district where you'll find "Indian" souvenirs—factory-made moccasins, plastic tomahawks, peace pipes, faux bearskins, the works. In a retro way, this part of Cherokee, with its predictable trinket shops and fudgeries, is charming.

Aside from its proximity to the Great Smoky Mountains National Park and the Blue Ridge Parkway, the biggest draw in town is Harrah's Cherokee Casino, one of the largest casino hotels in the state and home to a world-class spa. The 24-hour entertainment opportunities attract visitors from far and wide, some of whom stay on the property the whole time, while others take a break from the slap of cards and the flash of slot machines to experience the natural and cultural wonders of Cherokee.

Take all of this that you see—the casino, the tacky tourist shops, and the stereotyping signs—with a grain of salt, as they don't represent the true nature of the Cherokee people and their long history.

SIGHTS

Harrah's Cherokee Casino

The Eastern Band of the Cherokee operates **Harrah's Cherokee Casino and Hotel** (777 Casino Dr., 828/497-7777, www.harrahscherokee.com, 24 hours daily). This full-bore Vegas-style casino has more than 3,800 digital games and slot machines along with around 150 table games, such as baccarat, blackjack, roulette, and a poker-only room. Inside the casino complex is a 3,000-seat concert venue where acts like Alicia Keys and the Black Crows have performed, a huge buffet, and a grab-and-go food court next to the casino floor. Unlike in the rest of the state, smoking is allowed on the casino floor, though certain areas have been designated as nonsmoking. Inside the hotel portion of the casino are a restaurant, a Starbucks, and the **Mandara Spa,** which offers salon and spa services like massages and facials.

★ Museum of the Cherokee Indian

The **Museum of the Cherokee Indian** (589 Tsali Blvd., 828/497-3481, www.mci.org, 9am-5pm daily, $12 adults, $7 ages 6-12, free under age 6) was founded in 1948 and was originally housed in a log cabin. Today it is a well-regarded modern museum and locus of community culture. In the exhibits that trace the long history of the Cherokee people, you may notice the disconcertingly realistic mannequins. Local community members volunteered to be models for these mannequins, allowing casts to be made of their faces and

Cherokee

To River's Edge Outfitting, Smoky Mountain Tube & Raft, Wize Guyz Grille, and Native Brews

PETER'S PANCAKES & WAFFLES

LAMBERT BRANCH RD

RIVER'S EDGE MOTEL

TSALI BLVD

BJ'S DINER

OCONALUFTEE INDIAN VILLAGE

FIRE MOUNTAIN TRAILS

JOSEPH WASHINGTON DR

UNTO THESE HILLS

QUALLA ARTS AND CRAFTS MUTUAL

ACQUONI RD

Cherokee

1361

MUSEUM OF THE CHEROKEE INDIAN

Fair Grounds

FIRE MOUNTAIN OUTFITTERS

441

B'IA HWY 1390

B'IA HWY 316

B'IA HWY

Oconaluftee River

0   200 yds
0   200 m

441 19

TSALAGI RD

To Harrah's Cherokee Casino and Hotel

19

© MOON.COM

bodies so that the figures would not reflect an outsider's notion of what Native Americans should look like. The Museum of the Cherokee Indian traces their history from the Paleo-Indian people of the Pleistocene, when the ancestral Cherokees were hunter-gatherers, through the ancient days of Cherokee civilization, and into contact with the European settlers.

A great deal of this exhibit focuses on the 18th-19th centuries, when a series of tragedies befell the Cherokee as a result of the invasion of their homeland. It was also a time of great cultural advancement, including Sequoyah's development of the script to write the Cherokee language. The forced relocation of Native Americans called the Trail of Tears began near here, along the North Carolina-Georgia border, in the early 19th century. A small contingent of Cherokees remained in the Smokies at the time of the Trail of Tears, successfully eluding, and then negotiating with, the U.S. military, who were trying to force most of the Native Americans in the Southeast to move to Oklahoma. Those who stayed out in the woods, along with a few others who were able to return from Oklahoma, are the ancestors of today's Eastern Band, and their history is truly remarkable.

A favorite part of the museum are the stories, legends, and myths described on placards throughout the building. There's the story of a boy who became a bear and convinced his entire clan to become bears also. There's one about Spearfinger, a frightening creature that some say still lives in these woods today. And there are tales about Selu, the corn mother, and Kanati, the lucky hunter. Cherokee member and contemporary writer Marilou Awiakta has written widely about Selu, tying the past and present together with taut lines of thought that challenge our views on culture and technology.

★ Qualla Arts and Crafts Mutual

Across the street from the museum is the **Qualla Arts and Crafts Mutual** (645 Tsali Blvd., 828/497-3103, http://quallaartsandcrafts.com, 8am-5pm Mon.-Sat., 8am-4:30pm Sun.), a community arts co-op where local artists sell their work. The gallery's high standards and the community's thousands of years of artistry make for a collection of very special pottery, baskets, masks, and other traditional art. The Qualla co-op does a great service to this community by providing a year-round market for the work of traditional Cherokee artists, whose stewardship of and innovation in the arts are so important. The double-woven baskets are especially beautiful, as are the carvings of the masks representing each of the seven clans of the Cherokee people (the Bird, Deer, Longhair, Blue, Wolf, Paint, and Wild Potato).

★ Oconaluftee Indian Village

Oconaluftee Indian Village (778 Drama Rd., 828/497-2111, www.cherokeehistorical. org, 9:30am-4:30pm Mon.-Sat. Apr.-Nov., $25 adults, $15 ages 6-11, free under age 6) is a recreated Cherokee Indian Village tucked into the hills above the town. Here, you'll see how the tribe lived in the 18th century. Tour guides in period costumes lead groups on walking lectures with stops at stations where you can see Cherokee cultural, artistic, and daily-life activities performed as authentically as possible. From cooking demos to flint knapping (for arrowheads and spear points) to wood carving and clay work, you'll get a look at how the Cherokee lived centuries ago. The highlight of the tour is the ritual dance demonstration showing a half-dozen dances and explaining their cultural significance.

RECREATION
Fishing

Cherokee has more than 30 miles of streams, rivers, and creeks ideal for fishing. The Eastern Band owns and operates a fish hatchery that releases around 250,000 trout into these waters every year, creating the perfect mix for fantastic fishing. Unlike in the rest of North Carolina, you don't need a North Carolina fishing license; you need a **tribal fishing permit** (www.fishcherokee.com, 1 day $10, 2 days $17, 3 days $27, 5 days $47, season permit $250, trophy waters permit $25 1-3 days, $75 annually), sold at a number of outlets in Cherokee. You'll find brook, brown, golden, and rainbow trout, and it's fly-rod only, so you need to have your cast down pat if you want to bring in a big one. There are both catch-and-release and catch-and-keep waters in the Qualla Boundary, but if you want to fish outside the boundary, you need a North Carolina or Tennessee fishing

permit. Tennessee permits are only valid inside the Great Smoky Mountains National Park boundaries in North Carolina.

If you're unsure of your fly-fishing skills or want a guide to take you to a hot fishing hole, talk to the folks at **Rivers Edge Outfitters** (61 Big Cove Rd., 828/497-9300, www.wnc-fishing.com, 8am-5pm Sun.-Thurs., 7am-6pm Fri.-Sat., $25-500). Their shop is fully stocked with all the gear and tackle you need for a day on the water, and they offer lessons in casting and fly tying as well as guided trips. You can go for a two-hour, half-day, or full-day wading trip on local waters; other options are half- and full-day float trips or wading trips on private waters nearby.

Mountain Biking

Fire Mountain Trails (778 Drama Rd., https://visitcherokeenc.com, free) has 10.5 miles of trails suitable for mountain bikers, as well as hikers and trail runners. Riders of all skill levels can get in a good session here, with beginner-friendly runs that will boost your confidence and some rip-roaring single-track runs that will have expert riders catching air and finessing their way through rock gardens. The trailhead is adjacent to the Oconaluftee Indian Village.

Just across the street from where you head up to Fire Mountain Trails is **Fire Mountain Outfitters** (516 Tsali Blvd., 828/750-4196, www.firemountainoutpost.com, 10am-5pm Sun.-Mon., 10am-6pm Wed.-Sat.), an outdoor gear shop with plenty of stuff to outfit you for a hiking, camping, or biking adventure. They've partnered with **Motion Makers Bicycle Shop** (www.motionmakers.com, 828/586-6925) for mountain bike sales, repairs, and rentals ($45-150 per day). If you're staying in Bryson City (it's only 15 minutes away), **Tsali Cycles** (35 Slope St., Bryson City, 828/499-9010, www.tsalicycles.com, 10am-5pm Mon.-Fri., 9am-4pm Sat., $30-50 adults,

1: the Museum of the Cherokee Indian entrance with *Sequoyah* sculpture by Peter Wolf Toth **2:** musical instruments on display in Cherokee **3:** street sign in Cherokee and English **4:** fishing on the Oconaluftee River

$20-25 children) can get you set up with a mountain bike rental to use here or on the Tsali Trails closer to their home base.

Water Sports

For fun on the water, try **Smoky Mountain Tube and Raft** (1847 Tsali Blvd., 828/497-4545, http://cherokeetubeandraft.com, 10am-5pm daily Memorial Day-Labor Day weekend, weather permitting, $14, cooler tubes $10). It has mountains of tubes, so rent one and float down the Oconaluftee River for 2-3 hours. It also has a fleet of shuttle buses to pick you up a few miles downstream.

ENTERTAINMENT AND EVENTS

Of the several outdoor dramas for which North Carolina is known, among the longest running is Cherokee's *Unto These Hills* (Mountainside Theater, 688 Drama Rd., adjacent to Oconaluftee Indian Village, 866/554-4557, https://visitcherokeenc.com, 8pm Mon.-Sat. June-Aug. 15, $35-60 adults, $25-60 ages 6-12, free under age 6). Since 1950, Cherokee actors have told the story of their nation's history, from ancient times through the Trail of Tears. Every seat in the house is a good seat at the Mountainside Theater, and the play is enlightening. Be warned: There is some cannon fire and gunfire in the play.

Hear stories, learn dances, and interact with Cherokee storytellers at the **Cherokee Bonfire** (Oconaluftee Islands Park, Tsalagi Rd. and Tsali Blvd., 800/438-1601, https://visitcherokeenc.com, 7pm-8pm Sun., Mon., Wed., and Sat. May-Oct., free), at the intersection of U.S. 19 and U.S. 441. Bring your bathing suit and some water shoes; afterward, you may want to go for a wade or a quick dip in the Oconaluftee River, which is wide, rocky, and fun.

FOOD

Harrah's Cherokee Casino is home to one of the best restaurants in town, **Brio Tuscan Grille** (777 Casino Dr., 828/497-8233, www.brioitalian.com, 11am-10pm Sun.-Thurs., 11am-11pm Fri.-Sat., $10-36), which specializes in dishes from northern Italy. The food is great, the wine list is excellent, and the ambience makes you forget you're in a casino. There are other options in Harrah's, from the expected casino buffet to the grab-and-go back-to-gaming food court, even **Guy Fieri's Cherokee Kitchen + Bar** (4pm-10pm Sun.-Thurs., 4pm-11pm Fri.-Sat., $13-35), whose burgers, wings, steaks, and ribs don't hide from bold flavor. **Wicked Weed Brewpub** (4pm-11pm Wed.-Fri., 11am-11pm Sat.-Sun., $8-34) has set up an outpost here where they pour their Asheville-brewed beers and serve smashburgers, hot chicken sandwiches, and even steaks and beef tartare.

With a focus on wings, pizza, and burgers, **Wize Guyz Grille** (68 Big Cove Rd., 828/497-2838, https://wizeguyzgrille.com, 11am-7pm Mon.-Thurs., 11am-8pm Fri.-Sat., $6-50) gives diners a good option away from the casino. Dozens of iterations of chicken sandwiches and burgers, a bevy of appetizers (pickle fries, anyone? Get two baskets), and 15 pizzas to choose from means you have options aplenty.

I'd be remiss if I didn't mention the best burger in town, which comes from a roadside trailer. **BJ's Diner** (840 Tsali Blvd., 828/497-4303, https://bjs-diner.business.site, 11am-6pm Mon.-Thurs., 11am-8pm Fri.-Sat., 11am-4pm Sun., $2-9) keeps it simple: burgers with or without cheese, hot dogs, chicken tenders, and a few sandwiches. They do have a bacon cheeseburger served on a grilled cheese (which you should definitely get), but that's about as far afield as they go. If there's room at the picnic tables, grab a seat as the Oconaluftee River flows by just a few feet away. You might just see a few elk wading by.

At **Sassy Sunflowers Bakery & Café** (1655 Aquoni Rd., 828/497-2539, 9am-4pm Mon.-Fri. Mar.-Dec., $3-10), you can get the usual coffee and pastry treats but also excellent soups and sandwiches. The chicken salad is especially good—and quite portable if you're hoping to picnic in the park later in the day. Just remember to bring a cooler.

Up early to hit the trail? Grab breakfast in town at **Peter's Pancakes & Waffles** (1384

Tsali Blvd., 828/497-5116, 6:30am-2pm daily, $2-11), where you can order flapjacks (the blueberry pancakes are a sure bet), eggs with bacon, or a biscuit sandwich. Offerings are cheap, filling, and tasty.

Native Brews Tap and Grill (1897 Tsali Blvd., 828/497-2739, www.native-brews.com, noon-9pm Mon.-Thurs., noon-10pm Fri.-Sat., 11am-9pm Sun., $9-30) has a quartet of their own beers—an IPA, pale ale, golden lager, and blond—as well as spiced ales (think hard root beer, cream soda, and lemonade) and hard seltzers on offer alongside their own label of vodka, gin, and whiskey. As you taste your way through the liquid offerings, you're going to need a snack or a meal. The Colossal Pretzel is a whopper of an appetizer (not quite a wagon wheel, but still huge), the sandwiches hit the spot, and there are full-size entrées if you are feeling more than peckish.

ACCOMMODATIONS

Cherokee has many motels, including the family-owned and aptly named Rivers Edge Motel (1026 Tsalil Blvd., 828/497-7995, www.riversedgecherokee.com, from $179), and an Econo Lodge (20 River Rd./U.S. 19, 828/497-4575, www.choicehotels.com, from $120).

★ Harrah's Cherokee Casino Resort (777 Casino Dr., 828/497-7777, www.harrahscherokee.com, $125-510) is, without a doubt, the best place to stay in Cherokee. The hotel's 1,800 rooms are spacious, comfortable, and well kept; the casino and a number of dining options are an elevator ride away; and the spa provides an added layer of amenities you don't find at other hotels in town.

There's something about visiting a place and living where the residents live, and ★ Panther Creek Cabins (Wrights Creek Rd., 828/497-2461, www.panthercreekresort.com, $75-325, 2-night minimum seasonally) gives you that chance. The 13 cabins range from private two-person affairs to larger lodges that could easily sleep eight. Just outside downtown Cherokee, the quaint cabins are quiet and comfortable. Pets are welcome in most cabins for a flat fee ($49 for the first dog, $39 for the second).

On the outskirts of Cherokee are a couple of RV parks. Happy Holiday RV Park and Campground (1553 Wolfetown Rd., 828/497-9204, www.happyholidayrv.com, tents $25-46, RVs $48-70, cabins $90-180) sits just to the east of town on 40 acres. They have more than 375 sites and a half-dozen cabins. There's a pool, an ice-cream parlor, and a little spot where you can grab a quick snack, and if you're a bluegrass lover, they have a small bluegrass festival here in the early June and early September. Just south of town is Fort Wilderness Campground & RV Park (284 Fort Wilderness Rd., Whittier, 828/497-9331, www.fortwilderness.net, tent sites $35-45, RV sites $40-60), with 130 sites on 11 acres. Even though it's technically in the town of Whittier, it's only 1.5 miles to Harrah's Casino and 7 miles from the entrance to Great Smoky Mountains National Park and the Blue Ridge Parkway.

INFORMATION AND SERVICES

The Cherokee Welcome Center (498 Tsali Blvd., 800/438-1601, www.visitcherokeenc.com, 8am-5pm daily) can help you with tickets, directions, and things to do and see. There's one radio station in Cherokee, WNCC (101.3), a country station, although you can pick up distant stations with a wider selection.

GETTING THERE

Cherokee is on a particularly pretty and winding section of U.S. 19 between Maggie Valley and Bryson City, 2.5 miles south of the southern terminus of the Blue Ridge Parkway. From the Blue Ridge Parkway, a six-minute drive south along U.S. 441 will take you to the center of Cherokee. Asheville is 1 hour and 10 minutes to the west via I-40 and U.S. 19. If you're coming from the Tennessee side of the Smoky Mountains, Gatlinburg is 1 hour west via Newfound Gap Road (U.S. 441), and Knoxville is 2 hours west via U.S. 441 and I-40. If you're coming up from the south, Atlanta is 2 hours and 45 minutes away via I-85, I-985, and U.S. 19.

Bryson City and the Nantahala Forest

To look at the mountains here, you'd think that the defining feature in this part of North Carolina would be the surrounding peaks, but you're only partly right. This is a land dominated by water: Smoke-thick fog crowds valleys in the predawn hours. The peaks stand ringed in clouds. Moss, ferns, and dense forests crowd the edge of rivers and streams. When you're in the Nantahala Gorge, it feels like you've stepped into a fairy tale. According to Cherokee legends, a formidable monster called Spearfinger lived here, as did a monstrous snake and even an inchworm so large it could span the gorge. Spearfinger and her cohorts haven't been seen in years, and the Nantahala River, which runs through the narrow gorge, attracts white-water enthusiasts.

Nearby Bryson City is a river town whose proximity to white water makes it a favorite haunt for rafters, kayakers, and other white-water thrill seekers. If you approach Bryson City from the north on U.S. 19, you're in for a strange sight: The banks of the Tuckasegee River are shored up with crushed cars.

SIGHTS
★ Great Smoky Mountains Railroad
The **Great Smoky Mountains Railroad** (GSMR, depots in Bryson City and Dillsboro, 800/872-4681, www.gsmr.com, from $45 adults, $34 children) is one of the best and most fun ways to see the Smokies. Using historic trains, the GSMR carries sightseers on excursions that average 4.5 hours and take passengers through some of the region's most beautiful scenery. Trips between Dillsboro and Bryson City, with a layover at each end for shopping and dining, follow the banks of the Tuckasegee River; round-trips from Bryson City follow the Little Tennessee and Nantahala Rivers deep into the Nantahala Gorge. Many other excursions are offered, including gourmet dining; wine-, beer-, and

moonshine-tasting trips; rides on a steam locomotive; autumn leaf-peeping trips; and more. There are *Thomas the Tank Engine* and the *Little Engine That Could* trips for kids, and runs to and from river-rafting outfitters.

Museums
Inside Great Smoky Mountains Railroad's gift shop is the **Smoky Mountain Trains Museum** (100 Greenlee St., 800/872-4681, www.gsmr.com, generally 9am-4pm daily late May-Dec., 9:30am-4:30pm daily Jan.-late May, call ahead, $9 adults, $5 children, free with train ticket).

The **Fly Fishing Museum of the Southern Appalachians** (210 Main St., 828/488-3681, www.flyfishingmuseum.org, 9am-5pm Tues.-Fri., 10am-4pm Sat., free) tells the story of fly-fishing on the 14,000 miles of trout waters in North Carolina and across the southern Appalachians. Displays of hand-tied flies, antique rods and reels, drift boats, and even live fly-tying demos round out this free museum.

Across the street is the **Swain County Heritage Museum** (2 Everett St., 828/488-7857, www.swainheritagemuseum.com, 9am-5pm Mon.-Sat., 10am-4pm Sun. Apr.-Dec., 10am-5pm Mon.-Sat., 10am-4pm Sun. Jan.-Mar., free); downstairs is a Great Smoky Mountain Association Bookstore, and upstairs is a small but thorough museum telling the history of Bryson City and Swain County.

SPORTS AND RECREATION
★ Nantahala River Gorge
The stunningly beautiful Nantahala River Gorge, just outside Bryson City in the Nantahala National Forest, supports scores of river guide companies, many clustered along U.S. 19 west. Nantahala is said to mean "land of the noonday sun," and there are indeed parts of this gorge where the sheer rock

walls above the river are so steep that sunlight only hits the water at the noon hour. Eight miles of the Nantahala River flow through the gorge over Class II-III rapids. The nearby Ocoee River is also a favorite of rafters, and the Cheoah River, when there are controlled water releases, has some of the South's most famous and difficult Class III-IV runs.

Outfitters and Tours

There's a lot to do in and around Bryson City beyond the borders of Great Smoky Mountains National Park. White-water rafting, kayaking, and tubing are popular ways to spend a day. Many river guide companies are located along U.S. 19. Other popular options are zip-lining, hiking, and mountain biking. Fortunately, several outfitters can help you arrange for guided tours, rentals, and just about anything else you need to make your time here memorable.

You can explore the mountains around Bryson City with the **Nantahala Outdoor Center** (13077 U.S. 19 W., 828/785-4846, www.noc.com, 8am-8pm daily, from $30), which offers a variety of adventure options that include white-water rafting, stand-up paddleboarding on the flat-water sections of the river, hiking, mountain biking, and zip-lining. Half-day, full-day, and overnight trips are possible, and excursions like the Rapid Transit combine a relaxing morning train ride with an afternoon rafting trip.

Carolina Bound Adventures (35 Slope St., 828/788-6885, www.carolinabound-adventures.com, from $39) has guide and concierge services for a variety of outings, including hikes, mountain bike rides, overnight camping trips, waterfall tours, and brewery and winery tours. The company can assist in planning just about any aspect of your getaway, even pet-sitting if you're planning on a long day.

River Adventures

In addition to river guide services on the nearby Nantahala and Little Pigeon Rivers and farther afield on the Chattooga (where the 1972 movie *Deliverance* was filmed) and Ocoee Rivers, **Wildwater Rafting** (10345 U.S. 19 W., 12 miles west of Bryson City, 866/319-8870, www.wildwaterrafting.com, $50-110) leads half- and full-day **Wildwater Jeep Tours,** excursions on back roads and through wilderness to waterfalls and old mountain settlements.

Endless River Adventures (14157 U.S. 19 W., Bryson City, 828/488-6199, www.endlessriveradventures.com, $45-159) guides trips on the Nantahala River, the tamest of the rivers around with Class II-III rapids; the Ocoee River, with bigger rapids and more technical challenges; and the Cheoah River, where big rapids—Class IV and above—await.

Fly-Fishing

The Smoky Mountains, especially the eastern grade of the Smokies, are laced with streams perfect for fly-fishing. Anglers from all over come to float, wade, camp, fish, hone their fly-tying craft, and learn the finer points of fly-fishing. The Tuckasegee River flows through downtown Bryson City, and many of its feeder streams and creeks are ideal spots to throw a line. At **Great Smokies Fishing** (www.greatsmokiesfishing.com) you'll find resources that include license and permit information; regulations; seasonal information; maps; write-ups on lakes, streams, and rivers; and an exhaustive list of guides. We've put a few of the best right here.

Fly Fishing the Smokies (Bryson City, 828/488-7665, www.flyfishingthesmokies.net, $200-850) has a number of guides and options for a day or more of fly-fishing the streams on the north shore of the lake and other trout waters. Go bass fishing on Fontana for a half day, wade the streams with them for a half-day or full-day outing, try a float trip, go fly-fishing in Great Smoky Mountains National Park, or up the ante with some backcountry camping and fly-fishing in the park.

The name says it all: **Mac Brown Fly Fish** (779 W. Deep Creek Rd., 828/736-1469, www.

macbrownflyfish.com). Mac's been an outfitter, guide, instructor, and casting maestro since 1987, and he knows where to find the fish and exactly how to get them on his side of the water. He offers **float trips** ($625 pp) and **wading trips** ($575) on nearby waters.

Nantahala Fly Fishing Co. (Robbinsville, 828/557-1409, www.flyfishnorthcarolina.com, $200-350) provides guided fly-rod fishing trips and private half- and full-day lessons. If you've never held one of these odd fishing rods in your hands before, there's also a fly-fishing school (2 days, $600) and private instruction. Best of all, the company has a "No Fish, No Pay" guarantee.

Fly fishers who don't need a guide can check out a number of streams that are packed with fish, but be sure to inquire about regulations for individual streams. Some are catch-and-release, while a neighboring stream might be catch-and-keep, and some have regulations about the types of hooks you can use. Once you're ready to put your line in the water, try **Hazel Creek** on the north shore of Fontana Lake, where you'll find pristine waters and a good number of fish. Other nearby creeks, like **Eagle Creek** and any of the feeder creeks that empty into the lake, are prime spots as well.

Hiking and Mountain Biking

Great Smoky Mountains National Park has more than 800 miles of wilderness trails, and with around 40 percent of the park located in Swain County, more trails than you could hike in a week are within striking distance of Bryson City. **Deep Creek Loop** is a 4.9-mile loop that passes two waterfalls on its easy, mostly flat, track. You can also take the strenuous **Deep Creek Trail** to Newfound Gap Road, a 14.2-mile one-way hike that will require a return ride. The **Noland Creek Trail** is a fairly easy 6-mile trail near the end of the Road to Nowhere (a failed road-building project from the 1930s and 1940s). At the end of the Road to Nowhere, just past the tunnel, is the **Goldmine Loop Trail,** a 3.1-mile track that's beautiful and enjoyable. The nature and

lake views are especially welcome after trekking through the dark 0.5-mile tunnel on the way in (bring a flashlight; you won't regret it).

With all these mountains, you'd think mountain biking would be a big deal around here, and you'd be right. The **Tsali Recreation Area Trail System** (Tsali Rd./Hwy. 28, Robbinsville, www.fs.usda.gov, $2) is only 15 miles from Bryson City and draws riders throughout the year. Named for Tsali (SAH-lee), a Cherokee martyr who led the resistance to removal at the start of the Trail of Tears, the area has four loops constituting 42 miles of trails that trace courses across the mountains. These multiuse trails are rated as moderate, and if you're up for the challenge, give these fun flowy single-tracks a try. You'll share the road with hikers and equestrians, but there's a schedule: two trails for bikes, two for horses each day. More information on area mountain biking, including an overview map showing 15 more places to ride, is available at www.greatsmokies.com.

SHOPPING

Bryson City Outdoors (169 Main St., 828/341-6444, www.brysoncityoutdoors.com, 10am-6pm Mon.-Thurs., 10am-7pm Fri.-Sat., 11am-6pm Sun.) features a well-curated selection of outdoor gear and may be the friendliest little outdoor store you've ever shopped in. Everyone here is outdoorsy—active in hiking, mountain biking, white-water rafting, kayaking, paddleboarding, fly-fishing, rock climbing, you name it—and can help you get set up for just about any activity. Next door, the store operates **BCOutdoors Taproom** (10am-9pm Mon.-Sat., 11am-7pm Sun.), offering a dozen beers on tap—mostly North Carolina brews as well as some other regional beers—plus a great selection of bottles and cans. It's a fun place to hang out, enjoy a pint, swap trail stories or fish tales, and figure out tomorrow's adventure.

There are a number of T-shirt and souvenir shops in Bryson City, but **Appalachian**

1: fly-fishing on the Tuckasegee River **2:** rafters on the Nantahala River

Mercantile (158 Everett St., 828/488-2531, www.appalachianmercantile.net, 10am-6pm daily Apr.-Oct., call for hours Nov.-Mar.) is top on the list. Their selection doesn't overwhelm, and there's not as much souvenir flotsam as you'll find elsewhere; instead, the foodstuffs, playing cards, games, and toys have been winnowed down to the best in each category. The owner, Lance, was a backcountry guide in the area and then a location scout for the film industry; now he's an author of local histories and a shopkeeper, and he's ready with a story if you've got a minute to listen.

FOOD

The Bistro at The Everett Boutique Hotel (16 Everett St., 828/488-1934, www.theeveretthotel.com, 4:30pm-9pm Wed.-Sun., $10-38) serves an excellent dinner that is contemporary Appalachian in nature but includes one or two vegetarian-friendly dishes, typically noodle bowls. Regardless of what you order, the flavors will be on point and you'll find a cocktail, wine, or North Carolina beer to pair with it.

You can't beat breakfast at **Everett Street Diner** (126 Everett St., 828/488-0123, www.brysoncityrestaurant.com, 7am-2pm Mon. and Wed.-Sat., 7:30am-2pm Sun., $5-14), featuring filling options that won't weigh you down on the trail, like fluffy pancakes or biscuits and gravy. For lunch, you'll find great burgers, and the light lunch—a salad and half a sandwich—is a bargain. For a real treat—Bryson City gossip and local news—sit at the counter in back.

The Appalachian Trail passes only a few feet from **River's End Restaurant** (13077 U.S. 19 W., 828/488-7172, www.noc.com, 11am-7pm Wed.-Sun., $8-23) at the Nantahala Outdoor Center. Given its proximity to the trail (really a footbridge over the river, but on the trail nonetheless) and to the center's rafting, paddling, and hiking nexus, it's a popular spot for outdoorsy sorts. The menu reflects this with dishes like the Sherpa bowls (rice, veggies, and optional meat) that are packed

with protein, calories, and carbs to fuel you through a day on the trail.

For coffee and a quick breakfast, lunch, or snack, visit **Mountain Perks Espresso Bar & Café** (9 Depot St., 828/488-9561, www.mtnperks.com, 7am-3pm Sun.-Mon. and Thurs., 7am-4pm Fri.-Sat., $2-16). They make a good cappuccino, and the quiche, wraps, and bagel sandwiches hit the spot whether you eat them in-house or take them on your park adventure.

Nantahala Brewing Brewpub (116 Ramseur St., 828/585-5885, www.nantahalabrewing.com, 3pm-10pm Mon.-Fri., noon-11pm Sat., noon-10pm Sun. Jan.-Feb., noon-10pm Sun.-Fri., noon-11pm Sat. Mar.-Apr., noon-11pm Sun.-Thurs., noon-midnight Fri.-Sat. May-Aug., noon-10pm Sun.-Thurs., noon-11pm Fri.-Sat. Sept.-Dec., $7-25) carries a full slate of Nantahala Brewing beer but also a menu of elevated pub grub. The salads are sizable and fresh, the pot roast and brown ale chicken are pleasant surprises, and the tacos and shareable plates exceed your bar food expectations.

Speaking of bars and bar food, **Mountain Layers Brewing Company** (90 Everett St., 828/538-0115, www.mountainlayersbrewingcompany.com, noon-9pm Mon.-Sat., noon-8pm Sun.) has an excellent rooftop deck overlooking the Tuckasegee River and a board of tasty beers to go with it. The Russian Imperial Stout, Dragon Tamer New England IPA, and Hazel Creek Blonde Ale are top-notch. Local food trucks stop by to trade food for money with hungry imbibers.

ACCOMMODATIONS

Bryson City has a surprising number of high-quality inns and bed-and-breakfasts. Overlooking Bryson City is the **McKinley Edwards Inn** (208 Arlington Ave., 828/488-9626, www.mckinleyedwardsinn.com, from $159), a lovely 12-room house and inn built in 1922. The grounds are magnificent, and breakfast, a drink, or just quiet time on the deck gazing at the mountains will convince you to come back again.

Built in 1923 and on the National Register

of Historic Places, the ★ **Fryemont Inn** (245 Fryemont St., 828/488-2159, www.fryemontinn.com, mid-Apr.-late Nov. $190-345, includes meals, late Nov.-mid-Apr. $115-215, no meals) has a cozy, rustic feel with chestnut-paneled guest rooms and an inviting lobby with an enormous stone fireplace. Suites and a log cabin that sleeps six are available.

★ **The Everett Boutique Hotel & Bistro** (16 Everett St., 828/488-1934, www.theeveretthotel.com, $219-369) has 10 suites, a rooftop hangout area, and an excellent on-site restaurant. Rooms are spacious, comfortable, and mountain chic, and the beds are so comfortable you might just want to move in. The hotel is in the former Bryson City Bank, built in 1908, and you can still see the vault door in the restaurant. It's as lovely a place to stay as you can imagine, and everything Bryson City has to offer is within a 10-minute walk.

Some river outfitters provide lodging, which can be a cheap way to pass the night if you don't mind roughing it. Many of the outfitters also offer camping on their properties. The **Rolling Thunder River Company** (10160 U.S. 19 W., 800/408-7238, www.rollingthunderriverco.com, $10-12 pp) operates a large bunkhouse with beds for its rafting customers. For large groups of 15 or more, it offers a free night in the bunkhouse Monday-Thursday. No alcohol is permitted here. **Carolina Outfitters** (715 U.S. 19, Topton, 828/488-9819, www.carolinaoutfitters.com, $80-100) offers a variety of accommodations, including two-room cabins, two-bedroom apartments, and three-bedroom cabins suitable for a large group.

Nantahala Cabins (580 Nantahala Cabins Lane, 828/488-1433, www.nantahalacabins.com, $175-325) has 10 cabins to rent, ranging from studios to three-bedroom cabins fit for a family or group. A few minutes down the road from Bryson City proper, closer to Almond, **Watershed Resort** (137 W. Watershed Rd., Bryson City, 877/784-0688, www.watershedresort.com, $90-700) rents cabins in just about any size, style, and configuration imaginable. There are pet-friendly cabins, cabins with a modern flair, small cabins, and cabins fit for a family reunion. Want a hot tub or a jaw-dropping view? They've got you covered. You'll find some short-term openings here and there, but if you're planning on staying for a week or more, you'll want to book well in advance. These are excellent properties, and folks snap them up quick.

Camping

Among the nicest camping options available in Nantahala National Forest is **Standing Indian Campground** (90 Sloan Rd., Franklin, campground 828/524-6441, reservations 877/444-6777, www.recreation.gov, Apr.-Oct., $20-75). It has a nice diversity of campsites, from flat grassy areas to cozy mountainside nooks. Drinking water, hot showers, flush toilets, and a phone are all available on-site, and leashed pets are allowed. The campground is close to the Appalachian Trail and sits at an elevation of 3,400 feet.

Another nice campground is the **Deep Creek Tube Center and Campground** (1040 W. Deep Creek Rd., 828/488-6055, www.deepcreekcamping.com, Apr.-late Oct., campsites $31-60, cabins $99-325), with more than 50 campsites, 18 cabins, and access to Deep Creek. The creek runs right by many campsites, and you can go tubing ($7 per day). You can also go gem "mining" here, a great mountain tradition; bags and buckets of gem-enriched dirt are sold in the camp store. The best part is that the campground is within walking distance of Great Smoky Mountains National Park.

DEEP CREEK

Just south of Cherokee and just north of Bryson City, Deep Creek is a spot more popular with locals than visitors, but it's worth a stop. Deep Creek is relatively placid, aside from a couple of waterfalls farther upstream. If you're not into wading or tubing, don't worry; this is a lovely place to picnic and hike or even camp away from the crowds in some of the more popular spots in the park.

At the end of Deep Creek Road you'll find

the trailheads leading to the waterfalls. You'll also find the **Deep Creek Campground** (877/444-6777, www.recreation.gov, mid-Apr.-late-Oct., $25). There are nearly 100 campsites, many of which fill up with locals. If you want to camp here, arrive early or reserve well in advance.

Deep Creek Tube Center and Campground (1040 W. Deep Creek Rd., Bryson City, 828/488-6055, www.deepcreek-camping.com, campsites $31-60, cabins $99-325) is a charming collection of tent and RV campsites and cabins for rent; the two largest cabins sleep 10, and one is pet-friendly. As the name implies, they rent tubes (all-day $7) for use on Deep Creek. Rentals are cheap, so you can play in the water as long as you like.

There are two nice waterfalls to see here. **Juney Whank Falls** (yes, that's its name) is less than 0.5 miles from the Deep Creek Campground and cuts an impressive figure as it drops a total of 90 feet in two stages. **Indian Creek Falls,** 1 mile from the campground, is a stunning set of falls and cascades some 60 feet high.

ROAD TO NOWHERE

An odd place to visit is the so-called Road to Nowhere. Just south of the Deep Creek entrance outside Bryson City is a short stretch of highway leading north into GSMNP. Lonely, even spooky, the road is all that remains of a parkway planned to trace a path through the Smokies along Fontana Lake. Though construction was started on the parkway, it was abandoned. Today, the road stops quite abruptly about six miles inside the park, at a constructed stone tunnel. Hard feelings over the failed parkway have softened, but many families still hold a grudge against government officials who vowed to build a road along the lake to provide access to old family cemeteries.

Cars are prohibited from using the tunnel at the end of the Road to Nowhere, but visitors on foot can stroll through. After you pass through the tunnel, there's a marathon-length hike—seriously, it's 26 miles—weaving along the northern bank of Fontana Lake.

GETTING THERE AND AROUND

Bryson City can be reached via U.S. 19 and U.S. 74, if you're coming south from Maggie Valley (45 minutes) and Cherokee (15 minutes). It's 20 minutes to the Great Smoky Mountains National Park's Oconaluftee Visitor Center, just north of Cherokee. Asheville is 1 hour and 20 minutes east via U.S. 74 and I-40.

Waynesville and Vicinity

Waynesville, just west of Asheville and east of Cherokee, is the very definition of the word *quaint*. Writers have compared it to a Norman Rockwell painting with its storybook Main Street, busy with shops and lined with brick sidewalks and iron lampposts. This is an artistic little community where the art and craft galleries and studios are seemingly endless. In nearby Cullowhee, Western Carolina University is one of the mountain region's leading academic institutions as well as the location of the Mountain Heritage Center museum and Mountain Heritage Day festival.

WAYNESVILLE

Waynesville's downtown can keep a gallery-hopper or shopper happy for hours. Main Street is packed with studio artists' galleries, cafés and coffee shops, and a variety of boutiques.

Sights

One interesting stop in Waynesville is the Museum of North Carolina Handicrafts (49 Shelton St., 828/452-1551, www.sheltonhouse.org, 10am-3pm Thurs.-Sat. Apr.-Oct., $7 adults, $5 students, free under age 6). Consisting of a farmhouse, a barn, and gardens, the museum opened in 1980 and shows off the work of Native American and North Carolina heritage artists. This means mountain musical instruments, ceremonial items and crafts from Native American tribes, basketry, woodcarvings, quilts, and even antique farm tools. Tours of the museum are guided, so you'll hear plenty of stories to go with the items you see.

Shops and Galleries

Waynesville's galleries are many and varied, although the overarching aesthetic is one of studio art with inspiration in the environment and folk arts. Shops in the area feature local gems and necessities.

Blue Ridge Books & News (428 Hazelwood Ave., 828/456-6000, www.blueridgebooksnc.com, 9am-4pm Mon.-Fri., 9am-3pm Sat.) is a nice bookstore with specialties of regional interest and good coffee. A number of prominent Southern authors come through here to read and sign books, so check their schedule and ask about signed copies.

One of the several locations of Mast General Store (63 N. Main St., 828/452-2101, www.mastgeneralstore.com, 10am-6pm Mon.-Sat., 11am-6pm Sun. spring-fall, hours vary in winter) in Waynesville. While the stores are perhaps best known among vacationers for making children clamor for the candy kept in big wooden barrels, old-time dry-goods-store style, they have an even larger selection of merchandise for adults, including camping gear, such as top-brand tents, cookware, maps, and outdoors-oriented upscale clothing and shoes.

Twigs and Leaves (98 N. Main St., 828/456-1940, www.twigsandleaves.com, 10am-5:30pm Mon.-Sat., 1pm-4pm Sun., hours vary seasonally) carries splendid art furniture that is both fanciful and functional, pottery of many hand-thrown and hand-built varieties, jewelry, paintings, fabric hangings, mobiles, and many other beautiful and unusual items inspired by nature.

Artist Gretchen Clasby displays her work alongside the works of 83 additional artists at Cedar Hill Studio (196 N. Main St., 828/421-6688, https://cedarhillstudio.com, noon-5pm daily). This is the largest fine-arts gallery in Waynesville and the artists represented are from town, nearby, and the region, and their works span media and styles, so you're sure to find something that catches your eye.

The work at Curatory Gallery (120 Miller St., 828/356-5585, https://curatorygallery.art 4pm-9pm Thurs.-Fri., noon-5pm Sat., Sun. by appointment) is on constant rotation, but one thing stays the same: the artists here are

Waynesville

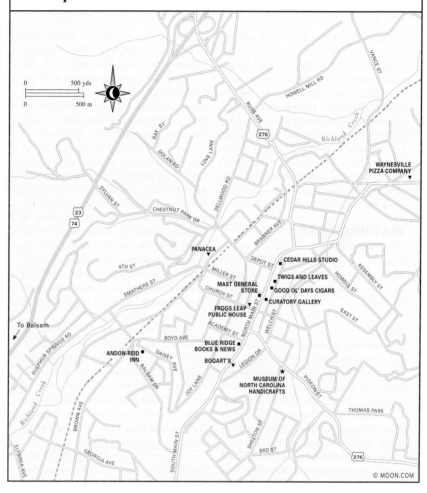

0 ___ 500 yds
0 ___ 500 m

© MOON.COM

pushing their limits. Underrepresented artists, artists from marginalized communities and backgrounds, and artists who have a distinct voice and distinct message are found here, so come expecting some challenging, dazzling, conversation-starting pieces.

Food

Waynesville's ★ **Frogs Leap Public House** (44 Church St., 828/456-1930, http://frogsleap-publichouse.com, 5pm-9pm Tues.-Sat., $8-29)

serves an interesting menu that's quite sophisticated but not afraid of its Southern roots. Dishes like the wood-grilled sirloin tip in a bourbon-shallot demi and the spicy Korean pork belly sliders show a real adventurous spirit that diners appreciate, not just because it's ambitious but because it's excellent.

Waynesville Pizza Company (32 Felmet St., 828/246-0927, www.waynesvillepizza.com, 11am-9pm Mon. and Wed.-Fri., noon-10pm Sat., noon-9pm Sun., $7-13) makes some hand-tossed pizzas that have folks in these parts talking. Well, they're talking about the pizza when they're not devouring a Buffalo chicken sandwich, a classic reuben, or a burger from this casual spot.

The ever-popular **Bogart's** (303 S. Main St., 828/452-1313, www.bogartswaynesville. com, 11am-8pm Sun.-Thurs., 11am-9pm Fri.-Sat., $7-23) is locally famous for its filet mignon, although their local trout also has a good reputation. The menu is huge but very steak house-y; vegetarians will have a tough time, although a few dishes, like the chipotle black bean burger and the grilled portobello salad, are options.

If you're just passing through town and need a jolt of good strong coffee, visit **Panacea** (66 Commerce St., 303 S. Main St., 828/452-6200, http://panaceacoffee.com, 9am-3pm Wed.-Sun., $5-11) in the funky Frog Level neighborhood downhill from downtown. The proprietors give back to their community and trade fairly with those who supply their coffee. They stock beans, blends, and brews from all around the world.

Accommodations

Waynesville has quite a selection of luxury inns. The **Andon-Reid Inn** (92 Daisey Ave., 828/452-3089, www.andonreidinn.com, from $160, no pets or children) is a handsome turn-of-the-20th-century house close to downtown with five tranquil guest rooms, each with its own fireplace, and a sumptuous breakfast menu that could include sweet-potato pecan pancakes and pork tenderloin, homemade cornbread with honey butter, or the intriguing baked lemon eggs. With advance notice they can cater to special dietary needs.

For absolute tip-top luxury, try **The Swag** (2300 Swag Rd., 800/789-7672, www.theswag. com, starting at $885). Superb guest rooms and cabins of rustic wood and stone each have a steam shower, and several have saunas, wet bars, and cathedral ceilings. The menu is decidedly country and upscale, two things you wouldn't think go together, but they do, and quite nicely. The inn is at 5,000 feet elevation in a stunning location at the very edge of the Great Smoky Mountains National Park.

Up on the Blue Ridge Parkway above Waynesville and quite close to Asheville is the fantastic ★ **Pisgah Inn** (Milepost 408.6, Blue Ridge Pkwy., 828/235-8228, www.pisgahinn.com, Apr.-Oct., $138-182), with motel-style accommodations surrounding an old lodge with a large family-style dining room and a Parkway gift shop. The inn is on a nearly 5,000-foot-high mountaintop, so the view is sensational. Trails lead from the inn to short pretty strolls and challenging daylong hikes. The restaurant (7:30am-10:30am, 11:30am-4pm, and 5pm-9pm daily) has a mesmerizing view and an appetizing and varied menu (breakfast $3-9, lunch $9-20, dinner $10-27) of both country cooking and upscale meals. The guest rooms are simple but comfortable, each with its own balcony and rocking chairs overlooking the valley, and with a TV but no telephone. The Pisgah is a perfect spot for resting, reading, and porch-sitting.

Information and Services

The **Haywood County Tourism Development Authority** (1110 Soco Rd., 800/334-9036, http://visitncsmokies.com) has a wealth of information about visiting Waynesville and surrounding towns. **MedWest Haywood** (262 Leroy George Dr., Clyde, NC, 828/456-7311, www.myhaywoodregional.com), accessible from the Lake Junaluska exit off U.S. 23/74, is the region's hospital.

SYLVA

The small town of Sylva, southwest of Waynesville, is crowned by the pretty Jackson County Courthouse, an Italianate building with an ornate cupola, kept under wistful watch by the requisite courthouse-square Confederate monument. Visitors should stop by the **Jackson County Visitor Center** (773 W. Main St., 800/962-1911, www.mountainlovers.com, 9am-5pm Mon.-Fri.) or visit them online to learn more about the communities here.

Sights

South of Sylva, the mysterious **Judaculla Rock** (off Caney Fork Rd., www.judacullarock.com) has puzzled folks for centuries. The soapstone boulder is covered in petroglyphs estimated to be at least 500 years old. The figures and symbols and squiggles are clearly significant, but as of yet are not understood. I'm fascinated with petroglyphs, and these are some of the most mysterious I've encountered. The soft rock has eroded and the pictures are not as clear as they were in generations past, but many of them can still be discerned. To reach the rock, drive south on Highway 107 eight miles past the intersection with Sylva's U.S. 23 Business. Make a left on Caney Fork Road (County Rd. 1737) and drive 2.5 miles to a gravel road. Turn left, and after just under 0.5 miles you'll see the rock on the right and a parking area on the left.

Shopping

Sylva's City Lights Bookstore (3 E. Jackson St., 828/586-9499, www.citylightsnc.com, 10am-6pm Mon.-Sat., 10am-3pm Sun.) is hardly a knockoff of the monumental Beat establishment in San Francisco with which it shares a name. Instead, it's a first-rate small-town bookstore with stock that has the novelty sought by vacationers and the depth to make regulars of the local patrons. In addition to the sections you'll find in any good bookstore, their selection of books of regional interest, including folklore, nature, recreation guides, history, and fiction and poetry by Appalachian and Southern authors, is excellent.

Founded by a pair of Appalachian Trail through-hikers, **Black Balsam Outdoors** (562 W. Main St., 828/631-2864, 10am-6pm Mon.-Sat., noon-5pm Sun.) will get you geared up for a trip into the woods whether you're looking for hard-core trail gear to use on your own through-hike or if you're in the market for a day-hike kit that will serve you for this trip to the Smokies and many more. They know their gear, how to use it, and where to go to give it a good workout, so don't hesitate to inquire about their favorite hikes in the area and the national park.

Food

The North Carolina mountains are experiencing a booming organic foods movement, and you'll find eco-aware eateries throughout the area. **Lulu's On Main** (678 W. Main St., 828/586-8989, www.lulusonmain.com, 11:30am-3pm and 5pm-8pm Mon.-Thurs., 11:30am-3pm and 5pm-9pm Fri.-Sat., $11-30) is one of the most acclaimed restaurants in the area. The menu is American gourmet at heart, with splashes of Mediterranean and Nuevo Latino specialties. Try the cheese ravioli with tofu, the beef short ribs, or the paella. They have plenty of vegetarian options.

At ★ **Ilda** (462 W. Main St., 828/307-2036, www.ildainsylva.com, 5pm-9pm Thurs.-Sun., $16-22) you'll find rustic Italian dishes with a little bit of Appalachian twang on a menu that's perfectly representative of chef Santiago Guzzetti and sommelier Crystal Pace, a husband-and-wife duo who found their way back to her hometown. The food here is nothing short of spectacular. Seasonal availability drives the individual ingredients in dishes, and the mushroom risotto, *mafaldini* (lamb bolognese with local greens), and rigatoni with nasturtium sausage all take advantage of what's fresh and on hand, but even in the depths of winter, the menu shines.

City Lights Café (3 E. Jackson St., 828/587-2233, www.citylightscafe.com, 8am-3pm Mon.-Sat., 9am-3pm Sun., breakfast $2-8, lunch and dinner $5-12), downstairs from the bookshop, has some excellent crepes, a mighty good biscuit, and fun tacos, and they serve wine and beer. It's a cool, casual spot to dine and relax with your book and a bottle of wine, or to see a small local act.

If you're in the mood for coffee and something light, try **White Moon** (545 Mill St., 828/331-0111, www.whitemoonnc.com, 8am-3pm Tues.-Sun., $3-11). White Moon is one street over from the main drag, so it would be easy to overlook, but that would be a mistake. Friendly folks serve coffee, café drinks, and a small but tasty breakfast and lunch menu. When you need your avocado toast fix, a savory breakfast bowl, or a sandwich, this is the spot.

Nightlife

It's a small town, so there's not a whole lot in the way of nightlife, but **Innovation Brewing** (414 W. Main St., 828/586-9678, www.innovation-brewing.com, noon-10pm Sun.-Thurs., noon-midnight Fri.-Sun.) has 22 beers in their regular rotation, with 10 on tap at any time. The Nitro Irish Stout, Nut Brown, and Midnight Rye-der Black IPA are mainstays, but they also make a few sours. Keep an ear out for live music in the taproom, as bands drop by often. If you're hungry, you're in luck: **Cosmic Carry-Out** (828/506-2830, www.cosmiccarryout.com, noon-9pm Mon.-Thurs., noon-10:30pm Fri.-Sat., 11am-9pm Sun., $4-12) has burgers, tacos, grilled-cheese sandwiches, and fries for your dining enjoyment.

Balsam Falls Brewing (506 W. Main St., 828/631-1987, www.balsamfallsbrewing.com, 11am-10pm Mon.-Thurs., 11am-midnight Fri., 10am-midnight Sat., 10am-10pm Sun.) came to Sylva by way of the Tampa, Florida, home-brew scene, where owners Corey and Laure Bryson got their start. But Balsam Falls is far from home brew. The pair went on to get their Cicerone certification (think sommelier for beer), and Corey's a certified beer judge, so the brews they put on draft are topnotch. Every beer has a fun name—Elvis Has Left the Brewpub, Fergus the Rat Chocolate Milk Stout, Petrified Dragon—and the variety runs the gamut from IPAs to barley wine to Russian imperials to lightly hopped American pale ales.

Lazy Hiker Brewing (617 W. Main St., 828/349-2337, www.lazyhikerbrewing.com, noon-10pm Mon.-Thurs., noon-11pm Fri.-Sat., noon-9pm Sun.) is based in Franklin, North Carolina, but has a taproom in Sylva. They keep a dozen taps flowing with styles across the spectrum, each well done, and each appealing to different palates and preferences. Sour fans will find a black cherry sour as well

as a gose and a berlinerweiss on tap, but dedicated IPA fans will find drafts highlighting different hops. If you like something in between, they have brown ales, blonds, and other brews to choose from.

DILLSBORO

Next door to Sylva is Dillsboro, a river town of rafters and crafters. **Dogwood Crafters** (90 Webster St., 828/586-2248, www.dogwoodcrafters.com, 10am-6pm Mon.-Sat., 10am-4pm Sun.), in operation since 1976, is a gallery and co-op that represents around 100 local artists and artisans. While the shop carries some of the ubiquitous country-whimsical stuff, mixed in is the work of some very traditional Blue Ridge weavers, potters, carvers, and other expert artisans, making the shop well worth a visit.

In November, Dillsboro's population grows significantly when potters and pottery lovers descend on the town for the annual **Western North Carolina Pottery Festival** (828/586-3601, www.wncpotteryfestival.com). This juried pottery show features more than 40 potters, a street fair, and the Clay Olympics. The Clay Olympics are timed competitions to make the tallest cylinder or widest bowl, as well as blindfolded pot making. The competition may seem odd, but the crowd and the artists get into it, making the one-day festival worth seeing.

Recreation

Dillsboro River Company (18 Macktown Rd., 828/507-2428, www.northcarolinarafting.com, 9:30am-5:30pm daily May-Oct., tubing $20, guided trips $27-37), across the river from downtown Dillsboro, will set you afloat on the Tuckasegee (tuck-a-SEE-jee) River, a comparatively warm river with areas of Class II rapids; it's often referred to simply as "the Tuck." Dillsboro River Company rents rafts, "ducks," and inflatable and sit-on-top kayaks. If you'd like to hire a river rat, guides will be happy to lead you on tours twice daily, and for an extra fee you can share a boat with the guide. There are minimum weight restrictions

for these watercraft, so if you are traveling with children, call ahead to ask if the guides think your young ones are ready for the Tuck.

Nightlife

Sylva's Innovation Brewing has an outpost in Dillsboro, **Innovation Station** (40 Depot St., 828/226-0262, www.innovation-brewing.com, noon-midnight Mon.-Thurs., 11am-midnight Fri.-Sun.). Housed in a former train depot, it's got the right feel for this railroad town, and their generous taps—there are nearly three dozen—mean plenty of brews to choose from. Innovation also has a barrel-aging program here, and Dillsboro is home to their pilot brewhouse, so you'll likely find a few experimental brews to sample.

Food

★ **Haywood Smokehouse** (403 Haywood Rd., 828/631-9797, www.haywoodsmokehouse.com, 11am-8pm Wed.-Thurs., 11am-9pm Fri.-Sat., $8-26) is a funky little barbecue shack serving some fine western North Carolina 'cue, craft beers, and house-made smoked barbecue sauces. The menu is small, but if it's pork or chicken and it can be barbecued, it's here. The Haywood Smokehouse is biker-friendly, so don't be surprised if you see a line of Harleys outside.

It's not surprising to find a restaurant bragging about their farm-to-fork philosophy these days, even in a town as small as Dillsboro, but it is surprising to find one living up to that boast and delivering great food. ★ **Foragers Canteen** (42 Depot St., 828/631-4114, www.foragerscanteen.com, 11am-8pm Mon. and Wed.-Thurs., 11am-3pm Tues., 11am-9pm Fri., 10m-9pm Sat., 10am-8pm Sun., $8-25) has fried (or grilled if that's your thing) chicken sandwiches, some inventive tacos, great salads, and bowls (steak tips over mashed potatoes or smoked gouda grits? Yes, please).

1: Sylva's historic and lovely courthouse
2: Dogwood Crafters 3: signs in Dillsboro
4: finishing the glaze on pottery at the Western North Carolina Pottery Festival

Chow down on some Greek goodness at **Kostas Express Restaurant** (489 Haywood Rd., 828/631-0777, www.kostasexpress.com, 11:30pm-8pm Mon.-Thurs., 11:30am-8:30pm Fri.-Sat., $7-28). Not everything here is expressly Greek, but it's all done with a Greek twist. Gyros, pita wraps, and baklava share menu space with burgers, pasta dishes, steak, and even barbecue, and whatever you order, you'll leave full (maybe even with leftovers) and happy to come back for another meal.

If your sweet tooth is calling, give it a little satisfaction with a stop at **Dillsboro Chocolate Factory** (28 Church St., 828/631-0156, www.dillsborochocolate.com, 10am-5pm Mon.-Tues., 10am-7pm Wed.-Sat., noon-5pm Sun.). They have truffles, chocolate, fudge, candy, and other assorted sweets, many of which they make in-house.

Accommodations

The **Best Western Plus River Escape Inn & Suites** (248 WBI Dr., 828/586-6060, www.bwriverescape.com, from $135 Mar.-Aug., from $185 Sept.-Oct., from $115 Nov.-Feb.) isn't what you think of when you think chain hotel; it's much more. The rooms are more attractive and comfortable (and more frequently updated) than you'd expect, the big patio overlooking the river includes a firepit area, and the hotel is close to Dillsboro (walkable, in fact), the road to Cherokee, and the national park.

The ever-charming ★ **Dillsboro Inn** (146 N. River Rd., 828/586-3839, www.dillsboroinn.com, $125-225) sits perched on the banks of the Tuckasegee River, giving every room in the place great views. Rooms range from spacious efficiencies to suites to something more akin to a small apartment (which means plenty of room to spread out). There are nightly fires on the deck overlooking the river, a couple of the rooms are pet-friendly, and it's walkable to Dillsboro, making a visit to Innovation Station or Foragers Canteen that much easier.

CULLOWHEE

The unincorporated village of Cullowhee ("CULL-uh-wee"), on Highway 107 between Sylva and Cashiers, is the home of Western Carolina University (WCU). The university's **Mountain Heritage Center** (Hunter Library, WCU campus, 828/227-7129, www. wcu.edu, 10am-4pm Fri.-Mon., 10am-7pm Thurs.) is a small museum with a great collection that will fascinate anyone interested in Appalachian history. The permanent exhibit *Migration of the Scotch-Irish People* is full of artifacts like a 19th-century covered wagon, wonderful photographs, and homemade quilts, linens, and musical instruments. The Mountain Heritage Center also hosts two traveling exhibits in addition to the permanent installation as well as the annual **Mountain Heritage Day** (www.mountainheritageday.com) festival (late Sept.), which brings together many of western North Carolina's best and most authentic traditional musicians and artisans in a free festival that draws up to 25,000 visitors.

GETTING THERE AND AROUND

Waynesville is easily reached from Asheville by heading west on I-40 and then taking either U.S. 23 or U.S. 74. The Blue Ridge Parkway also passes a little to the south of the town, near Balsam. Sylva is to the southwest of Waynesville on U.S. 23, and from there, Cullowhee is an easy drive down Highway 107.

Robbinsville and the Valley Towns

Between Robbinsville and the Georgia state line is another region at the heart of Cherokee life. Snowbird, not far from Robbinsville, is one of the most traditional Cherokee communities, where it's common to hear the Cherokee language and the arts, crafts, and folkways are flourishing. The burial site of Junaluska, one of the Eastern Band's most prominent leaders, is here.

As moving as it is to see the memorial to one of the Cherokee heroes, the town of Murphy is forever linked with tragedy for the Cherokee people and a dark incident in American history—the Trail of Tears. Around 16,000 Cherokee people, including warriors and clan leaders, men, women, children, the elderly, and the infirm, were forced to leave their homes in North Carolina, Tennessee, and Georgia. They were arrested and marched under guard to Fort Butler, here in Murphy, and from Fort Butler they were forced to walk to Oklahoma. You'll find the names of these people, many of whom died along the way, inscribed in Cherokee on a memorial at the L&N Depot in Murphy.

In addition to places of historic significance in Cherokee culture, this farthest southwestern corner of North Carolina has other compelling sights. Brasstown, a tiny village on the Georgia state line, is the home of the John C. Campbell Folk School, an artists' colony founded in 1925, where visitors can stroll among studios and along trails and stop at a gallery shop with some of the most beautiful crafts you'll find in the region. Back up toward Robbinsville, the relentlessly scenic **Cherohala Skyway** (www.cherohala. org) crosses 43 miles of the Cherokee and Nantahala National Forests. This road is a major destination for motorcyclists and sports-car drivers as well as day-trippers and vacationers.

ROBBINSVILLE

The whole southwestern corner of North Carolina is rich with Cherokee history and culture, and the Robbinsville area has some of the deepest roots of great significance to the Cherokee people. In little towns and crossroads a few miles outside Robbinsville, several hundred people known as the Snowbird community keep alive some of the oldest Cherokee ways. The Cherokee language is spoken here, and it's a place where some of the Eastern Band's most admired basket makers, potters, and other artists continue to make and teach their ancient arts. If you're visiting and want to enjoy an adult beverage, you'd better bring your own, as Graham County is North Carolina's one and only dry county.

Sights

Outside Robbinsville, in the ancient Stecoah Valley, is an imposing old rock schoolhouse built in 1930 and used as a school until the mid-1990s. It has been reborn as the **Stecoah Valley Center** (121 Schoolhouse Rd., Stecoah, 828/479-3364, www.stecoahvalleycenter.com), home of a weavers' guild, a native plants preservation group, a concert series, several festivals, and a great **Gallery Shop** (828/497-3098, 10am-4pm Mon.-Sat.) with local artisans' work. Concerts in the Appalachian Evening summer series, featuring area musicians, are preceded by community suppers of traditional mountain cuisine.

On Robbinsville's Main Street is the **Junaluska Memorial** (Main St., 0.5 miles north of the Graham County Courthouse), where Junaluska, a 19th-century leader of the Eastern Band of the Cherokee, and his third wife, Nicie, are buried.

Down a winding country road 14 miles outside Robbinsville, **Yellow Branch Pottery and Cheese** (1073 Old Yellow Branch Rd., 828/479-6710, www.yellowbranch.com, noon-5pm Tues.-Sat. Apr.-Nov., or by appointment) is a beautifully rustic spot for an afternoon's excursion. Bruce DeGroot, Karen Mickler, and their herd of Jersey cows produce graceful, functional pottery and prize-winning artisanal cheeses. Visitors are welcome at their farm and shop.

Recreation

The **Joyce Kilmer Memorial Forest** (5410 Joyce Kilmer Rd., 828/479-6431, www.grahamcountytravel.com), off Highway 143 west of Robbinsville, is one of the largest remaining tracts of virgin forest in the eastern United States, where 450-year-old tulip poplar trees have grown to 100 feet tall and 20 feet around. The forest stands in honor of Joyce Kilmer, a soldier killed in action in France during World War I. His poem "Trees" inspired this living memorial. The only way to see the forest is on foot, and a two-mile loop or two one-mile loops make for an easy hike through a remarkable forest.

a trail in Joyce Kilmer Memorial Forest

Junaluska

One of the most important figures in the history of the Eastern Band of the Cherokee is Junaluska, who was born near Dillard, Georgia, in 1776. During the wars with the Creek Indians 1812-1814, the Cherokee people fought beside U.S. forces, and it's said that the fierce young Junaluska saved the life of Andrew Jackson at the battle of Horse Shoe Bend in Alabama.

Twenty years later, Jackson, by then president, repaid Junaluska's bravery and the loyalty of the Cherokee people by signing the Indian Removal Act, which ordered that they, along with four other major Southern nations, be forced from their homelands and marched to the new Indian Territory of Oklahoma. Junaluska traveled to Washington and met with Jackson to plead for mercy for the Cherokee nation; his pleas were ignored, and in 1838, Junaluska joined 16,000 members of the Cherokee nation, who were force-marched close to 1,000 miles to Oklahoma. Midway across Tennessee, he led a failed escape attempt and was captured and chained; he completed the march in leg irons and manacles. It was during this time that Junaluska supposedly said, "If I had known what Andrew Jackson would do to the Cherokees, I would have killed him myself that day at Horse Shoe Bend." In 1841 he was finally able to leave Oklahoma and made the 17-day trip to North Carolina on horseback.

He spent his final years in Cherokee County, on land granted to him by the state of North Carolina. He and his third wife, Nicie, are buried at Robbinsville, at what is now the Junaluska Memorial and Museum. His grave was originally marked according to Cherokee tradition—with a pile of stones—but in 1910 the Daughters of the American Revolution commissioned a marker for his gravesite. During the dedication ceremony, Reverend Armstrong Cornsilk delivered a eulogy in the Cherokee language:

He was a good man. He was a good friend. He was a good friend in his home and everywhere. He would ask the hungry man to eat. He would ask the cold one to warm by his fire. He would ask the tired one to rest, and he would give a good place to sleep. Juno's home was a good home for others. He was a smart man. He made his mind think well. He was very brave. He was not afraid. Juno at this time has been dead about 50 years. I am glad he is up above [pointing upward]. I am glad we have this beautiful monument. It shows Junaluska did good, and it shows we all appreciate him together—having a pleasant time together. I hope we shall all meet Junaluska in heaven [pointing upward] and all be happy there together.

The Joyce Kilmer Memorial Forest abuts the Slickrock Wilderness Area, and **Slickrock Creek Trail** is one of its longest trails. This 13.5-mile (one-way) trail starts out easy, but the final 5.5 miles are fairly strenuous. *Backpacker* magazine named this one of the toughest trails in the country several years ago, in part because the hike can be a 21.7-mile loop by connecting with the **Haoe Lead, Hangover Lead,** and **Ike Branch** trails. Be forewarned that this is a big trip, but it's rewarding, with views of waterfalls (the first is only a few miles in, on the easy part) and rhododendron thickets. Its name is apt: The rocks here can be incredibly slick.

On the **Hangover Lead South Trail,** the trailhead is adjacent to the parking area at Big Fat Gap (off Slick Rock Rd., about 7 miles from U.S. 129). The trail is only 2.8 miles long, but it's strenuous. The payoff is the view from the Haoe summit at 5,249 feet. There are backcountry campsites here, and the rule is to keep campsites 100 yards from streams and practice Leave No Trace guidelines.

A handy collection of trail maps for Joyce Kilmer Memorial Forest, Slickrock Creek, Snowbird Back Country, and Tsali Recreation Area is available from the Graham Chamber (http://grahamchamber.com). The maps provide a rough idea of the locations and routes of these trails, but they are not a replacement for topographic maps, which you should have with you while on any of these rugged or isolated trails.

Entertainment and Events

Every year on the Saturday of Memorial Day weekend in late May, the Snowbird Cherokee host the **Fading Voices Festival** in Robbinsville. The festival features a mound-building ceremony along with typical festival attractions—music, dancing, storytelling, crafts, and lots of food—but in the deeply traditional forms carried on by the Snowbird community. Contact the Junaluska Museum (828/479-4727) for more information.

Food and Accommodations

You can grab a really good steak or burger at **Moonshiner's Steakhouse** (2645 Tallulah Rd., 828/479-0708, www.moonshiners-steakhouse.business.site, 5pm-9pm Fri.-Sun., $10-26), one of the only steakhouses around. As at many of the restaurants and accommodations in these parts, you're likely to see a lot of motorcycles and sports cars in the parking lot because folks come from all over to ride several of the twisty mountain roads. Belly up to the big outdoor bar and enjoy some live music, or sit inside with your fellow travelers and talk bikes, road trips, and what your neighbors ordered.

The **Snowbird Mountain Lodge** (4633 Santeetlah Rd., 11 miles west of Robbinsville, 828/479-3433, http://snowbirdlodge.com, $310-525, meals included) was built in the early 1940s, a rustic chestnut-and-stone inn atop a 3,000-foot mountain. The view is exquisite, and the lodge is perfectly situated among the Cherohala Skyway, Lake Santeetlah, and the Joyce Kilmer Memorial Forest. Guests enjoy a full breakfast, picnic lunch, and four-course supper created from seasonal local specialties.

Another pleasant place to stay 15 miles north of Robbinsville is the **Tapoco Lodge Resort** (14981 Tapoco Rd., 828/498-2800, www.tapoco.com, rooms and suites $179-329, cabins $149-249). Built in 1930, the lodge is on the National Register of Historic Places, and it has the feel of an old-time hotel. Guest rooms in the main lodge and surrounding cabins are simple but comfortable, and the resort overlooks the Cheoah River, a legendary run for rafters several times each year when controlled releases of water form super-fast rapids. Dine here at **Tapoco Tavern** (828/498-2800, 11am-8pm Sun.-Thurs., 11am-9pm Fri.-Sat., $9-36) on pizzas, steaks, trout, fried chicken, sandwiches, and salads.

The 39-acre **Iron Horse Motorcycle Lodge** (1755 Lower Stecoah Rd., 828/479-3864, www.ironhorsenc.com) caters to motorcyclists here to ride the Tail of the Dragon, Cherohala Skyway, and Blue Ridge Parkway and to explore a number of other notable routes in the area. A lodge ($99-165), bunkhouses ($36), fully outfitted cabins ($420-1,250) that sleep up to 20, covered wagons ($110), and tent ($20-30) and RV ($45-55) camping are available.

If you're RVing your way through the Smokies, the **Simple Life Campground** (88 Lower Mountain Creek Rd., 828/788-1099, www.thesimplelifecampground.com, Mar.-Nov., cabins $38-194, RVs $48-58, tents $22, pop-up campers $32) has cabins, RV sites, and tent sites with access to hot showers and Wi-Fi. This campground is near the Cherohala Skyway, Joyce Kilmer National Forest, and Lake Santeetlah.

HAYESVILLE, BRASSTOWN, AND MURPHY

Between Hayesville and Brasstown, you can get a really good sense of the art that has come out of this region over the years. These three small towns are along the Georgia border on U.S. 64.

Murphy River Walk

The **Murphy River Walk** is a three-mile trail along the Hiwassee River and Valley River, winding from Konehete Park to the Old L&N Depot through the charming tiny town of Murphy. It gives you the chance to see the town up close, and it's a great way to stretch your legs after a long ride.

After a walk along the river, take a look in some of the many antiques stores in Murphy.

Marketplace Antiques (41 Peachtree St., Murphy, 828/837-1060, 10am-5pm Mon.-Thurs., 10am-6pm Fri.-Sat., noon-4pm Sun.) and **Black & White Market** (40 Valley River Ave., Murphy, 828/516-1634, www.black-and-white-market.com, 10am-5pm Mon.-Sat.) will have you covered in the antiques department, and **Serenity Mountain Gift Shop** (35 Tennessee St., Murphy, 828/361-7543, 10:30am-5:30pm Tues.-Fri., 10am-5pm Sat.) has all the shirts, souvenirs, and gifts you'll want. If you're looking for beer, wine, or cigars, swing by **The Murphy Co.** (50 W. U.S. 64, Murphy, 828/516-1630, 12:30pm-5:30pm Mon.-Fri., noon-4pm Sat.).

John C. Campbell Folk School

One of North Carolina's most remarkable cultural institutions, the **John C. Campbell Folk School** (1 Folk School Rd., Brasstown, 800/365-5724, www.folkschool.org) was created by Northern honeymooners who traveled through Appalachia 100 years ago to educate themselves about Southern highland culture. John C. and Olive Dame Campbell, like other high-profile Northern liberals of their day, directed their humanitarian impulses toward the education and economic betterment of Southern mountain dwellers. John Campbell died a decade later, but Olive, joining forces with her friend Marguerite Butler, set out to establish a "folk school" in the Southern mountains that she and John had visited. She was inspired by the model of the Danish *folkehøjskole,* workshops that preserved and taught traditional arts as a means of fostering economic self-determination and personal pride in rural communities. Brasstown was chosen as the site for this grand experiment, and in 1925, the John C. Campbell Folk School opened its doors.

Today, thousands of artists travel every year to this uncommonly lovely remote valley, the site of an ancient Cherokee village. In weeklong and weekend classes, students of all ages and skill levels learn about the traditional arts of this region, such as pottery, weaving, dyeing, storytelling, and chair caning, as well as contemporary and exotic crafts such as photography, kaleidoscope making, bookmaking, and paper marbling. The website outlines the hundreds of courses offered every year, but even if you're passing through the area on a shorter visit, you can explore the school's campus. Visitors are asked to preserve the quiet atmosphere of learning and concentration when viewing the artist studios, but you can have an up-close look at some of their marvelous wares in the school's **Craft Shop** (bottom floor of Olive Dame Campbell Dining Hall, 10am-5pm Mon.-Wed. and Fri.-Sat., 10am-6pm Thurs.), one of the nicest craft shops in western North Carolina; you'll be wowed by what you find here. Exhibits about the school's history and historic examples of the work of local artists of past generations are on display at the **History Center** (8am-5pm Mon.-Sat., 1pm-5pm Sun.), next to Keith House.

There are several nature trails on campus that thread through this lovely valley. Be sure to visit the 0.25-mile **Rivercane Walk,** which features outdoor sculpture by some of the greatest living artists of the Eastern Band of the Cherokee. In the evenings you'll often find concerts by traditional musicians, or community square, contra, and English country dances. A visit to the John C. Campbell Folk School, whether as a student or a traveler, is an exceptional opportunity to immerse yourself in a great creative tradition.

Harrah's Cherokee Casino opened a location in Murphy in 2015: **Harrah's Cherokee Valley River Casino & Hotel** (777 Casino Pkwy., Murphy, 828/422-7777, www.caesars.com, $99-499) has 300 rooms and a huge 50,000-square-foot gaming floor with 70 table games and more than 1,000 slot machines. The dining options are mostly national chains. (Still, who comes to a casino to eat?)

Food

The western terminus of the North Carolina Barbecue Trail is in Murphy, and **Herb's Pit Bar-B-Que** (15725 W. U.S. 64, Murphy, 828/494-5367, 11am-7pm Thurs., 11am-8pm

Fri.-Sat., 11am-3pm Sun., $2-30) should be your first or last stop on it. Here you can sample more than the 'cue that pit masters in the deep mountains make—you can also order plates of tasty fried trout and chicken and thick steaks off the grill.

When you're hungry for something that's not barbecue, **Bistro Twenty Nine** (29 Tennessee St., Murphy, 828/361-0524, www.murphybistro29.com, 4pm-9pm Tues.-Sat., $9-32) serves some upscale but affordable meals in a surprisingly chic dining room. Warm lights, exposed brick, and local art make the perfect setting for a night out. On the menu you'll find steaks, crab cakes, burgers, shrimp scampi, and appetizers to satisfy a hungry hiker or someone ready to settle in for some good food, good company, and good conversation.

At **The Daily Grind & Wine** (46 Valley River Ave., Murphy, 828/835-7322, www.thedailygrindandwine.com, 8am-2pm Mon.-Tues. and Sat., 8am-8pm Wed.-Fri., breakfast $2-7, lunch $4-11), you'll find plenty of coffee and a great, cheap breakfast menu as well as a more filling lunch and snack menu loaded with sandwiches and salads, a very tasty, spicy black bean burger, and a Guinness beer brat that's top-notch. They also have a wine shop and bar serving wine and regional craft beer.

In nearby Hayesville, 15 miles east along U.S. 64, there are two spots to keep on your radar. **The Copper Door** (2 Sullivan St., Hayesville, 828/389-8460, http://thecopperdoor.com, 5pm-10pm Tues.-Sat., $16-48) is an upscale joint serving a nice selection of seafood, steaks, and other meat-centric dishes, but they can accommodate vegetarians and vegans. This elegant restaurant is run by a chef from New Orleans, and his influence is all over the menu, from crawfish to mussels to other French- and Creole-inspired creations.

Over at **Nocturnal Brewing Company** (893 U.S. 64 Business, Hayesville, 828/305-7337, www.nocturnalbrewing.com, 4pm-9pm Thurs.-Fri., 2pm-9pm Sat., $5-25), they have a solid burger, a really good lentil sloppy joe, and tempeh tacos if you're hungry, and the beer—saisons, goses, pale ales, and *bières de garde*—is proof positive that in North Carolina, there's a great brewery anywhere you go.

Tiger's Department Store & Chinquapins Ice Cream & Soda Bar (42 Herbert St., Hayesville, 828/389-6531, www.tigersandchinquapins.com, 9:30am-6pm Mon.-Sat.) has, in addition to clothing and gear, an **old-fashioned soda counter** (under $10) that provides some tasty refreshments.

GETTING THERE AND AROUND

This is the most southwestern corner of North Carolina, in some places as close to Atlanta as to Asheville. The drive from Murphy to Asheville is 2.5 hours along U.S. 74 and I-40, and to Atlanta the drive is closer to 3 hours. Robbinsville and Murphy are about 45 minutes apart along U.S. 129 and U.S. 74. It's 1 hour from Murphy to Bryson City, and the drive from Murphy to the Oconaluftee Visitor Center in Cherokee is 1.5 hours.

Background

The Landscape

GEOGRAPHY

North Carolina encompasses more than 50,000 square miles of land and water; within that space are three distinct geographic regions. The **Mountain Region** forms the western border of the state, with the Blue Ridge and Great Smoky Mountains, both subranges of the long Appalachian Mountain Range, undulating like the folds of a great quilt, running northeast to southwest from Virginia along the border with Tennessee and into the southwestern corner where the inland tip of North Carolina meets Georgia. This is a land of waterfalls, rivers

and fast-flowing creeks, and beautiful rugged peaks of smaller mountain configurations. Hemmed in among the peaks and hollows of the Blue Ridge and the Smokies are the Black Mountains, the Pisgah Range, and the Unka Range. The Black Mountains are only about 15 miles wide and are confined mostly to Yancey County, but they're the highest in the state, and 6 of the 10 tallest peaks in the eastern United States are here, including Mount Mitchell, the highest, at 6,684 feet.

Since the mid-19th century, the **Piedmont** has been the center of the state's population and industry. Most of North Carolina's major cities are in the Piedmont, including Charlotte, Winston-Salem, Greensboro, and the Raleigh-Durham metro area. In the late 19th century and most of the 20th century, the textile mills, furniture factories, and tobacco fields of the Piedmont ruled the state's economy. Today, most of the textile mills have been shuttered, and the furniture factories have mostly vanished thanks to economic globalization. The earliest mills were generally water-powered, harnessing swift rivers as they charged toward the coast. Changes in the tobacco industry have led farmers to give up the former cash crop, and the fields that were once thick with tobacco are now growing corn and soybeans.

The **Coastal Plain** is the third region, and though I-95 is commonly regarded as its western boundary, geologically the Sandhills section of the state is part of the Coastal Plain. Wedged between the Piedmont and the wetlands-rich Cape Fear Valley (the delta stretching from Fayetteville to Wilmington), the Sandhills are a zone of transition between the rich soil and rolling topography of the Piedmont and the sandy soil and dune systems of the Coastal Plain. The Sandhills are a range of sand dunes that mark where the coast was several million years ago. Since then the ocean has retreated a hundred miles or so to the coastline we know today.

The sandy soil, immense freshwater and saltwater wetlands, deep rivers, wide shallow sounds on the northern coast, and a chain of barrier islands stretching from Virginia to South Carolina make eastern North Carolina's landscape distinct. Among the wetlands are pocosins and Carolina bays, two distinct types of wetlands. Pocosins are wet, peaty expanses of moist ground that are slightly elevated in the center. Carolina bays are ovoid bodies of water on diagonal axes, unexplained but beautiful; they dot the landscape across the southeastern corner of the state.

The **Outer Banks** make a giant sweeping arc from Virginia to the north out to the point at Cape Hatteras; they then turn almost due west, forming the Bogue Banks, also known as the Crystal Coast. Along this northerly half of the North Carolina coast, the barrier islands work with wide complexes of sounds and marshes to protect the mainland from hurricanes and smaller storms. To the south, the barrier islands are closer to the mainland but also work with marshes, creeks, and rivers to absorb the brunt of a storm's strength. At all points along the coast, from the Outer Banks to the southern border, hurricanes can change the shape and structure of the protective islands in an instant, although the northerly barrier islands, which tend to be longer and thinner than those in the south, are often impacted more dramatically when wind and water join forces to rearrange geography.

CLIMATE

Generalizing about North Carolina's climate is difficult. It's not as hot as at the equator and not as cold as at the poles, but beyond that, each region has its own range of variables and has to be examined separately.

The mountains are much cooler than either the Piedmont or the coast, and winter lasts longer. Towns like Asheville and Boone can be blanketed in snow while less than 100 miles away the trees in Piedmont towns aren't even

---

Previous: Wild horses on the beach in North Carolina's Outer Banks.

showing their fall colors. The coldest temperature ever recorded in North Carolina, -34°F, was recorded in 1985 on Mount Mitchell. Spring and fall can bring cool to temperate days and chilly nights, while summer days can hit the 80s, and the evenings bring a welcome relief.

The Piedmont, on the other hand, can be brutally hot during the summer and quite warm on spring and fall days. The hottest temperature recorded in the state—110°F—was at Fayetteville in 1983. Add to that the stifling humidity of the summer months, which is more intense than along the coast because there the ocean breezes mitigate its effects, and you have some uncomfortable heat. Winter afternoon temperatures often peak in the 50s, although there are many nights when the temperature stays below freezing. It snows, but not as heavily or as frequently as in the mountains, and the counties east of this area are more likely to see rain during winter storms.

Along the coast, temperatures are more moderate than in the Piedmont. The warm Gulf Stream washes past not far off shore, keeping temperatures from getting too frigid in winter, bringing spring early, keeping water warm near shore and pushing storms farther inland in summer, and extending the fall season, making it a pleasant time to be here. It's windy along the coast, and these breezes help mitigate summer's heat and make the humidity more bearable.

North Carolina gets its fair share of hazardous weather to go along with beautiful summer days and crisp fall nights. Along the Outer Banks, which jut far out into the Atlantic, **hurricanes** are a particular threat. It's not just the Outer Banks that are vulnerable to these powerful storms; the coastline south of the Banks suffers plenty of hits, and even inland, hurricanes that make landfall in South Carolina can curve up through the Lowcountry and into North Carolina's Piedmont, bringing high winds and heavy rains to inland cities and dangerous floodwaters to coastal towns. Hurricane season

is June-November, but it's toward the end of summer and the start of fall that the risk becomes greatest. Wind and rain are the first effects of a hurricane, but the storm surge and high waves can cause massive damage to barrier islands, dune systems, and sensitive estuarine complexes. Flooding from inland rains as well as the coastal deluge can spell disaster. In 1999, Hurricane Floyd killed 35 people in North Carolina, caused billions of dollars of property damage, and permanently altered the landscape in places. During this storm, rivers in eastern North Carolina reached 500-year flood levels, leaving one-third of Rocky Mount under water and causing devastating damage to Tarboro, Kinston, and other towns in the region. Princeville, the oldest African American town in the United States, was nearly destroyed. Today, many towns in eastern North Carolina still carry scars to their infrastructure and economies due to Floyd.

Tornadoes, most common in the spring, can cause trouble any time of year. A rare November twister touched down in 2006, smashing the Columbus County community of Riegelwood, killing eight people and leaving a seven-mile swath of destruction. Even plain old **thunderstorms** can be dangerous, bringing lightning, flash flooding, difficult driving conditions, and even hail. **Snowstorms** are rare and usually occur in the mountains. The Piedmont sees more snow than the coast, which sees flurries once or twice each winter and the occasional dusting of snow. Outside the mountains, most North Carolinians are woefully inexperienced snow drivers, and the state Department of Transportation doesn't have the equipment in coastal counties to handle much more than a little snow. Along the coast, the humorous rule of thumb is that for every inch of snow that is predicted, banks, schools, and government offices shut down for a day, and for every inch of snow that actually falls, it's two days. As soon as the meteorologists mention flurries, there's a run on the most valuable snowstorm essentials: milk, bread, and toilet paper.

Plants

In the early 1700s, John Lawson, an English explorer who would soon be one of the first victims of the Tuscarora War, wrote of a magnificent tree house somewhere in the very young colony of North Carolina. "I have been informed of a Tulip-Tree," he wrote, "that was ten Foot Diameter; and another, wherein a lusty Man had his Bed and Household Furniture, and liv'd in it, till his Labour got him a more fashionable Mansion. He afterwards became a noted Man, in his Country, for Wealth and Conduct." Whether or not there was ever a tulip poplar large enough to serve as a furnished bachelor pad, colonial North Carolina's forests must have seemed miraculous to the first Europeans to see them.

FORESTS

Today, after generations of logging and farming across the state, few old-growth forests exist. In the Smoky Mountains, stands of old-growth timber, like the Joyce Kilmer Forest, are a sight to behold, and some of the trees almost validate Lawson's anecdote. Across the state, scores of specialized ecosystems support a marvelous diversity of plant and animal life. In the east, cypress swamps and a few patches of maritime forest still stand; across the Sandhills are longleaf pine forests; in the mountains are fragrant balsam forests and stands of hardwoods.

Because the state is so geographically and climatically varied, there's a greater diversity in tree species than anywhere in the eastern United States. In terms of land area, more than half of the land is still forested in the Piedmont and eastern North Carolina. Coastal forests are dominated by hardwoods—oaks of many varieties, gum, cypress, and cedar—and the barrier islands have a few remaining patches of maritime forest where the branches of live oak trees intertwine to shed storm wind and their roots sink deep to keep islands stable. The best and largest remaining example of a pristine maritime forest is on Bald Head Island, where the Bald Head Island Conservancy provides education and studies the form, function, and future of barrier islands, including these important maritime forest ecosystems. In the Piedmont, oak and hickory dominate the hardwoods alongside bands of piney woods. In the mountains, oak and hickory are also the rule, but a number of conifers, including pine and balsam, appear.

The science and profession of forestry were born in North Carolina: In the 1880s and 1890s, George W. Vanderbilt, lord of the manner at Biltmore, engaged Frederick Law Olmsted, who designed New York City's Central Park, to plan a managed forest of the finest, healthiest, and most hardy trees. Vanderbilt hired Gifford Pinchot and later Carl Shenck to be the stewards of the thousands of wooded acres he owned in the Pisgah Forest south of Asheville. The contributions these men made to the nascent field are still felt today and are commemorated at the Cradle of Forestry museum near Brevard.

Longleaf Pine

Arguably, the most important plant in North Carolina's history is the longleaf pine, sometimes called the pitch pine. This beautiful tree is something of a rare sight today, as the longleaf pines that formerly blanketed the eastern part of the state were used extensively in the naval stores industry in the 18th and 19th centuries, providing valuable turpentine, pitch, tar, and lumber. The overharvesting of this tree has a lot to do with the disappearance of North Carolina's once legendary pine barrens, but an unanticipated ancillary cause is the efficiency of modern firefighting. Longleaf pines depend on periodic forest fires to clear out competition from the underbrush and provide layers of nutrient-rich singed earth. In the 20th century the rule was to put out forest fires, cutting down on smoke but disturbing the natural growth cycles of these trees. In some nature preserves today, controlled burns keep the longleaf piney woods alive and healthy as crucial habitats for several endangered species, including the red cockaded woodpecker and the pine barrens tree frog.

A great place to get a feel for this ecosystem that once covered so much of the Southeast is Weymouth Woods-Sandhills Preserve, near Southern Pines. Some of the longleaf pines here are believed to be almost 500 years old. Many of these centuries-old trees bear scars from the days of the naval stores bonanza, when turpentine makers carved deep gashes in the bark to collect the resin that bled out. The tallest and oldest longleaf pine in the state is here, and at over 130 feet tall, it's a sight.

FLOWERS

Some of North Carolina's flora puts on great annual shows, drawing flocks of admirers—the gaudy **azaleas** of springtime in Wilmington, the **wildflowers** of the first warm weather in the hills, the **rhododendrons** and **mountain laurel** of the Appalachian summer. The Ericaceae family, a race of great woody bushes with star-shaped blossoms that includes azaleas, rhododendrons, and laurel, is the headliner in North Carolina's floral fashion show. Spring comes earliest to the southeastern corner of the state, and the Wilmington area is explosively beautiful when the azaleas are in bloom. The **Azalea Festival,** held annually for more than 50 years, draws hundreds of thousands of people to the city in early-mid-April, around the time that public gardens and private yards are spangled with azaleas.

The flame azalea makes a late-spring appearance on the mountainsides of the Blue Ridge and Great Smokies, joined by its cousins the mountain laurel and Catawba rhododendron in May and June. The ways of the rhododendron are a little mysterious; not every plant blooms every year, and there's no sure-fire way of predicting when they'll put on big

shows. The area's widely varying elevation also figures into bloom times. If you're interested in timing your trip to coincide with some of these flowering seasons, your best bet is to call ahead and speak with a ranger from the Great Smoky Mountains National Park or the Blue Ridge Parkway to find out how the season is coming along.

Around the end of April and into May, when spring finally arrives in the mountains but the forest floor is not yet sequestered in leafy shade, a profusion of delicate flowers emerges. **Violets** and **chickweed** emerge early on, as do the quintessentially mountainous white **trillium** blossoms and the wake robin, also a trillium, which looks something like a small poinsettia. Every year since 1950, around the end of April, the Great Smoky Mountains National Park has hosted the **Spring Wildflower Pilgrimage,** a week-long festival featuring scores of nature walks that also reveal salamanders, birds, and wild hogs, along with workshops and art exhibits. Visit www.springwildflowerpilgrimage.org for upcoming events.

Surprisingly, one of the best places in North Carolina to view displays of wildflowers is along the major highways. For more than 20 years the state's Department of Transportation has carried out a highway beautification project that involves planting large banks of wildflowers along highways and in wide medians. The displays are not landscaped but are allowed to grow up in unkempt profusion, often planted in inspired combinations of wildly contrasting colors that make the flowerbeds a genuinely beautiful addition to the environment. The website of the state's **Department of Transportation** (www.ncdot.org) offers a guide to the locations and seasons of the wildflower beds.

FALL FOLIAGE

Arriving as early as mid-September at the highest elevations and gradually sliding down the mountains through late October, autumn colors bring a late-season wave of visitors to western North Carolina. Dropping

Horticultural Havens

North Carolina's natural scenery provides inspiration for constructed landscapes of almost equal beauty. Wilmington, the Triangle, and Asheville are home to great botanical gardens, touchstones of the state's horticultural heritage.

WILMINGTON AND ENVIRONS

It's hard to imagine anywhere more beautiful than Wilmington in the springtime. The old port city is a year-round knockout, but the floral fireworks of spring are really special. **Airlie Gardens** is a century-old formal garden with a stunning azalea collection, a 500-year-old oak tree, and a sculpture garden dedicated to longtime gatekeeper Minnie Evans, a renowned visionary artist.

The **Cape Fear Botanical Garden** in Fayetteville is simply gorgeous. On a 78-acre strip of land between the Cape Fear River and Cross Creek, more than 2,000 varieties of ornamental plants flower and fruit throughout the year, and miles of walking trails provide a chance to stretch your legs.

THE TRIANGLE

The urban Raleigh-Durham region might not be an obvious destination for garden lovers, but if you look in the right places, you'll find a horticultural heaven. First, there are the formal gardens: Chapel Hill's **North Carolina Botanical Garden,** the Southeast's largest botanical garden, with plants ranging from herbs to carnivorous species; Raleigh's **J. C. Raulston Arboretum,** devoted to the development of ornamental plants that thrive in Southern climates; and the **Sarah P. Duke Gardens** in Durham.

AROUND ASHEVILLE

Asheville is the home of the **North Carolina Arboretum,** a garden of more than 400 acres that borders the Pisgah National Forest and the Blue Ridge Parkway. Special collections include the National Native Azalea Repository and more than 200 bonsai. You can tour the arboretum on foot, by Segway, or on your bike, and you can even bring your dog on some of the trails.

At the **Biltmore Estate,** Frederick Law Olmsted created formal gardens of beauty to match the opulent mansion, and architect Richard Morris Hunt designed the conservatory where young plants are still raised for the gardens. Self-guided tours of the conservatory—and the walled, shrub, Italian, vernal, and azalea gardens—are all included in admission to the estate.

Asheville is also an excellent home base for excursions to other garden spots in the mountains. Don't miss the **Rivercane Walk** at the John C. Campbell Folk School in Brasstown, where modern Cherokee sculptures line a path along Little Brasstown Creek. The **Mountain Farm Museum** at the edge of Great Smoky Mountains National Park demonstrates gardening methods used on the early mountain homesteads. The **Cradle of Forestry** in Pisgah National Forest explains how the science of modern forestry was born here in western North Carolina.

temperatures change trees' sugar production, resulting in a palette of colors, while simple fatigue causes the green to fade in others, exposing underlying hues. Countless climatic factors can alter the onset and progress of leaf season, so the mountains blush at slightly different times every year. The latter weeks of October tend to be the peak; during those weeks it can be difficult to find lodging in the mountains, so be sure to plan ahead. Some of the best places for leaf peeping are along the Blue Ridge Parkway and in the Great Smoky Mountains National Park.

CARNIVOROUS PLANTS

You've probably seen **Venus flytraps** for sale in nurseries, and maybe you've even bought one and brought it home to stuff with kitchen bugs. Venus flytraps grow in the wild only in one tiny corner of the world, a narrow band of counties between Wilmington and Myrtle Beach, South Carolina. The flytraps and their dozens of carnivorous Tar Heel kin, including Seuss-like sundews and pitcher plants, the abattoirs of the bug world, are fondest of living in places with nutrient-starved soil, like pine savannas and pocosins, where they have little competition for space and sunlight and can feed handsomely on meals that come right to them.

There are many species of **pitcher plants,** a familiar predator of the plant world. Shaped like tubular vases with a graceful elfin flap shading the mouth, pitcher plants attract insects with an irresistible brew. Unsuspecting bugs pile in, thinking they've found a keg party, but instead find themselves paddling in a sticky mess from which they're unable to escape, pinned down by spiny hairs that line the inside of the pitcher. Enterprising frogs and spiders that are either strong or clever enough to come and go safely will often set up shop inside a plant and help themselves to stragglers. Another local character is the **sundew,** perhaps the creepiest of the carnivorous plants. Sundews extend their paddle-shaped leaf-hands up into the air, hairy palms baited with a sticky mess that bugs can't resist. When a fly lands among the hairs, the sundew closes on it like a fist and gorges on it until it's ready for more.

There are several places where you can see wild carnivorous plants in North Carolina. Among the best are the **Bluethenthal Wildflower Preserve** at the University of North Carolina Wilmington, **Carolina Beach State Park,** and the **Green Swamp Preserve** and **Ev-Henwood Nature Preserve** in Brunswick County. There's also a good collection of them on display at Chapel Hill's **North Carolina Botanical Garden.**

Animals

Among the familiar wildlife most commonly seen in the state, **white-tailed deer** are out in force in the countryside and in the woods; they populate suburban areas in large numbers as well. **Raccoons** and **opossums** prowl at night, happy to scavenge from trash cans and the forest floor. **Skunks** are common, particularly in the mountains, and are often smelled rather than seen. They leave an odor something like a cross between grape soda and Sharpie markers. There are also a fair number of **black bears,** not only in the mountains but in swamps and deep woods across the state.

In woods and yards alike, **gray squirrels** and a host of familiar **songbirds** are a daily presence. Different species of **tree frogs** produce beautiful choruses on spring and summer nights, while **fireflies** mount sparkly shows in the trees and grass in the upper Piedmont and mountains. Down along the southeast coast, **alligators** and **turtles** sun themselves on many a golf course and creekside backyard.

The town of Brevard, in the Blue Ridge south of Asheville, is famous for its population of ghostly **white squirrels.** They're regular old gray squirrels that live all over North America, but their fur ranges from speckled gray and white to pure bone white. They're not albinos; it's thought that Brevard's white squirrels are cousins of a clan that lives in Florida and that their ancestors may have found their way to the Blue Ridge in a circus or with a dealer of exotic pets in the early 20th century.

The Carolina woods harbor colonies of **Southern flying squirrels.** It's very unlikely that you'll see one unless it's at a nature center or wildlife rehabilitation clinic because flying squirrels are both nocturnal and shy. They're also almost unspeakably cute. Fully extended, they're about nine inches long snout to tail, weigh about four ounces, and have super-silky fur and pink noses. Like many nocturnal animals, they have comically long whiskers and huge, wide-set eyes that suggest amphetamine use. When they're flying—gliding, really—they spread their limbs to extend the patagium, a membrane that stretches between their front and hind legs, and glide along like little magic carpets.

Also deep in the Smokies are some herds of wild hogs, game boar brought to the area about 100 years ago and allowed to go feral. The official line among wildlife officials is that mountain lions—in this region called panthers—have been extinct in North Carolina for some time. But mountain dwellers claim there are still panthers in the Blue Ridge and Smokies, and most people here have seen or heard one—their cry sounds like a terror-filled scream. There are even tales of a panther in the inland woods of Brunswick and Columbus Counties on the southeast coast.

WILD PONIES

Small herds of wild ponies have called several barrier islands in the Outer Banks home for more than 400 years. Locally known as Banker ponies but more properly as feral horses, they're descendants of Spanish horses, a fact established by extensive DNA testing. No one's quite sure how they arrived here, but the consensus is that they've been here since the 1500s. They may have arrived with early English colonists or with even earlier Spanish explorers. Stories passed down here for hundreds of years say they swam ashore from long-ago shipwrecks. Today, the primary herds are on Shackleford Banks in the Cape Lookout National Seashore and in Corolla, at the extreme north end of the Outer Banks, near the Virginia border. Since they roam freely in areas open to public visitation, you may find one staring you down from behind a sand dune or a stand of scrubby cedar trees. Remember to use caution around the Banker ponies; they may resemble domestic horses, but they are wild animals. Feeding them or approaching them only ends up hurting the herd in the long run. They also pose some

physical danger; all it takes for them to show you who's boss is one swift kick. You can learn more about the horses and their history at http://shacklefordhorses.org and www.corollawildhorses.com.

REINTRODUCED SPECIES

In the 1990s and early 2000s a federal program to reestablish red wolf colonies in the Southeast focused its efforts on parkland in North Carolina. Red wolves, thought to have existed in North Carolina in past centuries, were first reintroduced to the Great Smoky Mountains National Park. They did not thrive, and the colony was moved to the Alligator River National Wildlife Refuge on the northeast coast. The packs have fared better in this corner of the state and now roam several wilderness areas in the sound country.

The Smokies proved a more hospitable place for the reintroduction of elk. Now the largest animals in the Great Smoky Mountains National Park, elk, which can grow up to 700 pounds, are most often observed in the Cataloochee section of the park, grazing happily and lounging in the mist in the early morning and at twilight.

BIRDS

Bird-watchers flock to North Carolina because of the great diversity of songbirds, raptors, and even hummingbirds across the state—a 2013 count put the number of species at 473—but the state is best known for waterfowl. In the sounds of eastern North Carolina, waterfowl descend en masse as they migrate. Hundreds of thousands of birds crowd the lakes, ponds, trees, marshes, and waterways as they move to and from their winter homes. Many hunters take birds during hunting season, but they're outnumbered by birdwatchers. Birders say that one of the best spots for birding in the state is around large shallow Lake Mattamuskeet in the Mattamuskeet National Wildlife Refuge on the central coast, with 40,000 acres of water to attract incredible numbers of snow geese and tundra swans, Canada geese, and ducks. Just a few miles away, **Swanquarter National Wildlife Refuge** is also a haven for ducks, wading birds, shorebirds, and their admirers.

While in eastern North Carolina, bird fanciers should visit the **Sylvan Heights Bird Park,** a remarkable park in the small town of Scotland Neck that's a conservation center and breeding facility for rare waterfowl from across the globe. Visitors can walk through the grounds, where large aviaries house bird species that, unless you're a world traveler and a very lucky birder, you're unlikely to see elsewhere. There are more than 170 species, and you can get quite close to most of them. Bring your camera; you'll have the chance to take shots you could never get in the field.

There are many books and websites about birding in North Carolina. One of the most helpful is the North Carolina Birding Trail, both a website (www.ncbirdingtrail.org) and a series of print guidebooks. Organized by region, these resources list dozens of top sites for bird-watching and favorite bird-watching events throughout the state. Another good resource is the **Carolina Bird Club** (www.carolinabirdclub.org).

AMPHIBIANS

Dozens of species of **salamanders** and their close kin, including **mudpuppies, sirens,** and **amphiumas,** call North Carolina home, and Great Smoky Mountains National Park harbors so many that it's known as the Salamander Capital of the World. Throughout the state, **frogs** and **toads** are numerous and vociferous, especially the many species of dainty **tree frogs.** Two species, the gray tree frog and the spring peeper, are found in every part of North Carolina, and beginning in late winter they create the impression that the trees are filled with ringing cell phones.

Hellbenders are quite possibly the strangest animal in North Carolina. They are enormous salamanders—not the slick little pencil-thin five-inch salamanders easily spotted along creeks, but hulking brutes that grow to more than two feet long and can weigh five pounds. Rare and hermetic, they live in rocky mountain streams, venturing out from under rocks at night to gobble up crayfish and minnows. They're hard to see even if they do emerge in the daytime because they're lumpy and mud-colored, camouflaged against streambeds. Aggressive with each other, the males often sport battle scars on their stumpy legs. They've been known to bite humans, but as rare as it is to spot a hellbender, it's an exponentially rarer occurrence to be bitten by one.

REPTILES

Turtles and **snakes** are the state's most common reptiles. **Box turtles,** found everywhere, and **bog turtles,** found in the Smokies, are the only land terrapins. A great many freshwater turtles inhabit the swamps and ponds, and on a sunny day every log or branch sticking out of fresh water will become a sunbathing terrace for as many turtles as it can hold. Common water turtles include **cooters, sliders,** and **painted turtles. Snapping turtles** can be found in fresh water throughout the state, so mind your toes. They grow up to a couple of feet long and can weigh more than 50 pounds. Not only will they bite— hard!—if provoked, they will actually initiate hostilities, lunging for you if they so much as disapprove of the fashion of your shoes. Even the tiny hatchlings are vicious, so give them a wide berth. Finally, we are visited often by **sea turtles,** a gentle and painfully dwindling race of seafarers. The most frequent visitor is the **loggerhead,** a reddish-tan living coracle that can weigh up to 500 pounds and nests as far north as Ocracoke. Occasional visitors include the **leatherback,** a 1,500-pound goliath at its largest, along with **hawksbills, greens,** and **olive ridleys.** The Bald Head Island Conservancy on Bald Head Island has been protecting the turtles and their nests since the mid-1980s, gathering data on birth rates, nest numbers, and the mother turtles. During the nesting season, conservancy members can tag turtles alongside ecologists and interns and watch them lay their eggs.

There are not many kinds of **lizards** native

to North Carolina, but those that are present make up for their homogeneity with ubiquity. **Anoles,** tiny scaly dragons that dart along almost any outdoor surface, are found in great numbers in the southeastern part of the state, up the coast, and along the South Carolina state line to west of Charlotte. They put on great shows by puffing their ruby-red dewlaps and by vacillating between drab brown and gray or lime-Slurpee green, depending on the color of the background on which they hide. The ranks of lizard kind are rounded out by several varieties of **skinks** and **glass lizards,** also called glass snakes because they look like snakes, although they're not, and **fence lizards.**

There are plenty of real **snakes** in North Carolina. The vast majority are shy, gentle, and totally harmless to anything larger than a rat. There are a few species of venomous snakes that are very dangerous. These include three kinds of **rattlesnake:** the huge diamondback, whose diet of rabbits testifies to its size and strength; the pigmy; and the timber or canebrake rattler. Other venomous species are the beautiful mottled **copperhead** and the **cottonmouth or water moccasin,** famous for flinging its mouth open in hostility and flashing its brilliant white palate. The **coral snake** is a fantastically beautiful and venomous species.

Most Carolina snakes are entirely benign to humans, including old familiars such as **black racers** and **king snakes** as well as **milk, corn,** and **rat snakes.** One particularly endearing character is the **hognose snake,** which can be found throughout North Carolina but is most common in the east. Colloquially known as a spreading adder, the hognose snake compensates for its total harmlessness with amazing displays of histrionics. If you startle one, it will first flatten and greatly widen its head and neck and hiss most passionately. If it sees that you're not frightened by plan A, it will panic and go straight to plan B: playing dead. The hognose snake won't simply lay inert until you go away, though; it goes to the dramatic lengths of flipping onto its back, exposing its pitiably vulnerable belly, opening its mouth, throwing its head back limply, and sticking out its tongue as if it had just been poisoned. It is such a devoted method actor that should you call its bluff and poke it back onto its belly, it will fling itself energetically back into the mortuary pose and resume being deceased.

Alligators make their reptilian kin look tiny. Tar Heel gators are most abundant in the area south of Wilmington, but they've been seen the full length of the state's coast—note how far north the Alligator River is—and as far inland as Merchants Millpond State Park near the Virginia state line. The biggest ones can reach 1,000 pounds and measure 10-15 feet long. Smaller gators are more common, and the 6- and 8-foot females are small in comparison to the massive bull gators. They have a mouthful of sharp teeth, and even hatchlings can pack a nasty bite. These amazing prehistoric-looking amphibious assault machines appear to spend most of their waking hours splayed out in the sun with their eyes closed, or floating motionless in the water. Don't fall for it; it's their fiendishly clever, or perhaps primitively simple, ploy to make you come closer. They can launch themselves at prey as if spring-loaded and are more than capable of catching and eating a dog, cat, or small child. It happens very rarely, but given the chance, large gators can and will eat an adult human. The best course of action, as with most wildlife, is to admire them from a distance.

History

ANCIENT CIVILIZATION

By the time the first colonists arrived and called this place Carolina, the land had already sustained some 20,000 years of human history. We know that Paleo-Indians hunted these lands during the last ice age, when there were probably more mammoths and saber-toothed tigers in North Carolina than people. Civilization came around 4000 BC, when the first inhabitants settled down to farm, make art, and trade goods. By the first century, Southern Woodland and Mississippian Indians were also living in advanced societies with complex religious systems, economic interaction among communities, advanced farming methods, and the creation of art and architecture.

When the Europeans arrived, there were more than a dozen major Native American groups within what is now North Carolina. The Cherokee people ruled the mountains while the Catawba, Pee Dees, Tutelo, and Saura, among others, were their neighbors in the Piedmont. In the east, the Cheraw, Waccamaw, and Tuscarora were some of the larger communities, while many bands occupied land along the Outer Banks and sounds.

CONQUEST

The first Europeans to land here were Spanish. We know conquistador Hernando de Soto and his troops marched around western North Carolina in 1539, but they were just passing through. In 1566, another band of Spanish explorers, led by conquistador Juan Pardo, came for a longer visit. They were making a circuitous trek in the general direction of Mexico, and along the way they established several forts in what are now the Carolinas and Tennessee. One of these forts, called San Juan, has been identified by archaeologists outside present-day Morganton in a community called Worry Crossroads. Although the troops who were garrisoned for a year and a half at Fort San Juan eventually disappeared into the woods or were killed, it's theorized that they may have had a profound impact on the course of history, possibly spreading European diseases among the Native Americans and weakening them so much that, a couple of decades later, the indigenous people would be unable to repel the invasion of English colonists.

The next episode in the European settlement of North Carolina is one of the strangest mysteries in American history: the Lost Colonists of Roanoke. After two previous failed attempts to establish an English stronghold on the island of Roanoke, fraught by poor planning and disastrous diplomacy, a third group of English colonists tried their luck. Sometime between being dropped off in the New World in 1587 and one of their leaders returning three years later to resupply them, all of the colonists—including Virginia Dare, the first English person born in the Americas—had vanished into the woods. To this day, their fate is unknown, although a host of fascinating theories are still debated and probably always will be.

The disappearance of the Roanoke colonists did little to slow the process of the European conquest of North America. After the establishment of the Virginia colony in 1607, new English settlers began to trickle southward into Carolina, while Barbadians and Europeans from Charles Town (in present-day South Carolina) gradually began to populate the area around Wilmington. The town of Bath was established in 1706, and New Bern was settled shortly thereafter. The bloody Tuscarora War followed, and after a crushing defeat near present-day Snow Hill, in which hundreds were killed, the Tuscarora people retreated, opening the land along the Neuse River to European colonization.

COLONIALISM

The conflict between Europeans and Native Americans wasn't the only world-changing cultural encounter going on in the Southern colonies. By the middle of the 18th century, nearly 100,000 enslaved people had been brought to North Carolina from West Africa. By the end of the 18th century, many areas, especially around Wilmington, had populations where enslaved Africans and enslaved Americans of African descent outnumbered whites. Although North Carolina did not experience slavery on as vast a scale as South Carolina, there were a number of plantations with more than 100 enslaved workers, and many smaller plantations and town homes of wealthy planters, merchants, and politicians with smaller numbers of enslaved people. Africans and African Americans were an early and potent cultural force in the South, influencing the economy, politics, language, religion, music, architecture, and cuisine in ways still seen today.

In the 1730s the Great Wagon Road connected Pennsylvania with Georgia by cutting through the Mid-Atlantic and Southern backcountry of Virginia and North Carolina. Many travelers migrated south from Pennsylvania, among them a good number of German and Scottish-Irish settlers who found the mountains and Piedmont of North Carolina to their liking. Meanwhile, the port of Wilmington, growing into one of the most important in the state, saw a number of Gaelic-speaking Scots move through, following the river north and putting down roots around what is now Fayetteville. Shortly before the American Revolution, a group of German-speaking religious settlers known as the Moravians constructed a beautiful and industrious town, Salem, in the heart of the Piedmont, which would later become Winston-Salem. Their pacifist beliefs, Germanic heritage, and artistry set them apart from other communities in colonial North Carolina, and they left an indelible mark on the state's history.

The 18th century brought one conflict after another to the colony, from fights over the Vestry Act in the early 1700s, which attempted to establish the Anglican church as the one official faith of the colony, through various regional conflicts with Native Americans and events that played out at a global level during the French and Indian War. At mid-century the population and economic importance of the Piedmont was growing exponentially, but colonial representation continued to be focused along the coast. Protesting local corruption and lack of governmental concern for the western region, a group of backcountry farmers organized themselves into an armed posse in resistance to colonial corruption. Calling themselves the Regulators, they eventually numbered more than 6,000. Mounting frustrations led to an attack by the Regulators on the Orange County courthouse in Hillsborough. Finally, a colonial militia was dispatched to crush the movement, which it did at the Battle of Alamance in 1771. Six Regulators were captured and hanged at Hillsborough.

REVOLUTION AND STATEHOOD

Many believe the seeds of the American Revolution were sown, tended, and reaped in New England, but the southern colonies, particularly North Carolina, played important roles before and during the rebellion. In 1765, as the War of the Regulation was heating up, the residents of Brunswick Town, the colonial capital and the only deep-water port in the southern half of the colony, revolted in protest of the Stamp Act. They placed the royal governor under house arrest and put an end to taxation in the Cape Fear region, sending a strong message to the crown and to fellow patriots hungry to shake off the yoke of British rule. In the ensuing years, well-documented events like the Boston Tea Party, the Battles of Lexington and Concord, and the signing of the Declaration of Independence occurred, but North Carolina's role in leading the rebellion was far from over.

After the Battles of Lexington and Concord, the colonies were aflame with patriotic fervor, and Mecklenburg County (around Charlotte) passed the first colonial declaration rejecting the crown's authority. By this time, North Carolina, like the other colonies, had formed a provincial government, and it was busy in the tavern at Halifax writing the Halifax Resolves, the first official action in the colonies calling for independence from Britain. On April 12, 1776, the resolves were ratified and delegates carried them to the Second Continental Congress in Philadelphia. Other delegates were so inspired that more such resolves appeared. Ultimately the Declaration of Independence was written and ratified, and the revolution was on in earnest.

Although North Carolina may have been the first to call for independence, the state was divided in its loyalties. Among the most noteworthy Loyalists was the community of Highland Scots living in and around modern-day Fayetteville. Men from this community were marching to join General Cornwallis near Brunswick Town and Southport (then Smithville) when Patriots ambushed them at the bloody battle of Moore's Creek, killing 30 Scots and routing the Loyalist force.

North Carolinians fought all over the eastern seaboard during the Revolution, including about 1,000 who were with Washington at Valley Forge. The year 1780 brought fighting back home, particularly in the area around Charlotte, which a daunted General Cornwallis referred to as "the hornets' nest." The battle of Kings Mountain, west of Charlotte, was a pivotal moment in the war and particularly costly to the Loyalist forces. Cornwallis received another blow at the Battle of Guilford Courthouse; although technically a British victory, it weakened his forces considerably. By the time the war ended, thousands of North Carolinians were dead, and the treasury was far in debt—but North Carolina was now a state with the business of statehood to attend to. The capital was moved inland to Raleigh, and 20 miles away at Chapel Hill, ground was broken for the establishment of the University of North Carolina, the first state university in the country.

THE FEDERAL ERA

The early 19th century in North Carolina was a good deal more peaceful than the previous hundred years had been. The first decade of the 1800s saw a religious awakening in which thousands of North Carolinians became devout Christians. At the same time, the introduction of the cotton gin and bright-leaf tobacco were economic boons in the state, particularly the eastern counties. Railroads and plank roads made trade immeasurably more efficient, bringing new prosperity to the Piedmont.

There was also conflict, of course, in the early 19th century. Andrew Jackson's administration presided over the passage of the Indian Removal Act in 1830, which assigned reservations in the Indian Territory of present-day Oklahoma to the "Five Civilized Tribes" of the southeastern United States—the Cherokee, Choctaw, Creek, Chickasaw, and Seminole. Thousands of Cherokee people were forced out of western North Carolina, northern Georgia, eastern Tennessee, and Alabama and marched west on the Trail of Tears. About 4,000 died along the way. Another 1,000 or so Cherokee people, through hiding, fighting, and negotiation, managed to win the right to stay in North Carolina—an act of resistance that was the birth of the modern Eastern Band of the Cherokee, still centered around the town of Cherokee on the Qualla Boundary in North Carolina's Great Smoky Mountains. The Eastern Band of the Cherokee tell the story of their relocation in the enlightening outdoor drama *Unto These Hills*.

THE CIVIL WAR

Compared to South Carolina and a few other Southern states, North Carolina was considered politically moderate in the mid-19th century because it was less invested economically and politically in enslavement. Combined with the knowledge that if secession became a reality, war would follow and North Carolina's tobacco and cotton fields would quickly become battlefields, secession was on the lips of everyone across the South. As some states voted to remove themselves from the Union, North Carolina's voters stayed true to unity and rejected a ballot measure calling for treason: a secession convention. As grand a gesture as that victory may have been, when fighting erupted at Fort Sumpter in Charleston Harbor, North Carolina's hand was forced and its secession was a reality. The traitorous Secessionist governor John Ellis rejected Lincoln's call to federalize state militias, instead seizing control of the state and all federal military installations within its boundaries as well as the Charlotte Mint. North Carolina officially seceded on May 20, 1861, and a few weeks later Union ships began to blockade the coast. Roanoke Island in the Outer Banks fell, and a freedmen's colony (a home for enslaved people who had been freed or escaped) sprung up. New Bern, which fell in the spring of 1862, became a major focal point of Union military strategy and a thriving political base for freed and escaped African Americans. To the south, Fort Fisher, on the Cape Fear River just south of Wilmington, guarded the river's inlet and was crucial to the success of the blockade runners—smugglers whose speedy boats eluded the Union blockade. Fort Fisher kept Wilmington in Confederate hands until nearly the end of the war. When it finally did fall to Union forces in February 1865, it required what would be the largest amphibious assault in American military history until World War II. Wilmington was the last major port on the Confederacy's eastern seaboard, and its fall severed supply lines and crippled what remained of the Confederate Army in the area.

The varying opinions felt by Southerners about the Civil War, in the South also called the War between the States, was particularly strong in North Carolina, where today you'll still hear whites refer to it as the War of Northern Aggression or the War of Yankee Aggression. A symbol of the Lost Cause and of racial oppression—the Confederate flag—is flown with pride rather than the shame it deserves. More than 5,000 African Americans from North Carolina joined and fought in the Union Army, and there were pockets of strong Union sentiment and support among white North Carolinians, especially in the mountains. Some 10,000 North Carolinians fought for the Union. Zebulon Vance, who won the 1862 gubernatorial election and served as governor through the duration of the war, was a native of Weaverville, near Asheville, and felt acutely the state's ambivalence toward the Confederacy. Much to the consternation of Richmond, the Confederate capital, Governor Vance was adamant in his refusal to put the interests of the Confederacy over those of his own state. Mountain communities suffered tremendously during the war from acts of terrorism by deserters and rogues from both armies.

The latter years of the Civil War were particularly difficult for North Carolina and the rest of the South. Approximately 4,000 North Carolina men died at the Battle of Gettysburg alone. After laying waste to Georgia and South Carolina, General William T. Sherman's army entered North Carolina in the spring of 1865, destroying homes and farms. His march of fire and pillage spared Wilmington, which is one reason the town contains such an incredible collection of Federal architecture. The last major battle of the war was fought in North Carolina, when General Sherman and Confederate General Joseph Johnston engaged at Bentonville. Johnston surrendered to Sherman in Durham in April 1865.

By the end of the war more than 40,000 North Carolina soldiers were dead—a number equivalent to the entire present-day population of the city of Hickory, Apex, or Kannapolis.

RECONSTRUCTION AND THE NEW SOUTH

The years immediately after the war were painful as well, as a vast population of newly free African Americans tried to make new lives for themselves economically and politically in the face of tremendous opposition and violence from whites. The Ku Klux Klan was set up during this time, inaugurating an era of horror for African Americans throughout the country. Federal occupation and domination of the Southern states' political and legal systems also exacerbated resentment toward the North. The state's ratification of the 14th Amendment on July 4, 1868, brought North Carolina back into the Union.

The late 1800s saw large-scale investment in North Carolina's railroad system, launching the industrial boom of the New South. Agriculture changed in this era as the rise of tenancy created a new form of enslavement for many farmers—Black, white, and Native American. R. J. Reynolds, Washington Duke, and other entrepreneurs built a massively lucrative empire of tobacco production from field to factory. Textile and furniture mills sprouted throughout the Piedmont, creating a new cultural landscape as rural Southerners migrated to mill towns.

THE 20TH CENTURY AND TODAY

The early decades of the 1900s brought an expanded global perspective to North Carolina, not only through the expanded economy and the coming of radio but as natives of the state scattered across the globe. About 80,000 North Carolinians served in World War I, many of them young men who had never before left the state or perhaps even their home counties. Hundreds of thousands of African Americans migrated north during what became known as the Great Migration. The communities created by Black North Carolinians in the Mid-Atlantic and the Northeast are still closely connected by culture and kinship to their cousins whose ancestors remained in the South. The invasion of the boll weevil, an insect that devastated the cotton industry, hastened the departure of Southerners of all races who had farmed cotton. The Great Depression hit hard across all economic sectors of the state in the 1930s,

but New Deal employment programs were a boon to North Carolina's infrastructure, with the construction of hydroelectric dams, the Blue Ridge Parkway, and other public works.

North Carolina's modern-day military importance largely dates to the World War II era. Installations at Fort Bragg, Camp Lejeune, and other still vital bases were constructed or expanded. About 350,000 North Carolinians fought in World War II, and 7,000 of them died.

A few old-timers remember World War II quite vividly because they witnessed it firsthand: German U-boats prowled the waters off the coast, torpedoing ships and sinking them with frightening regularity. These German submarines were often visible from the beach, but more often the evidence of their mission of terror and supply-chain disruption—corpses, wounded sailors, and the flotsam of exploded ships—washed up on the shore. More than 10,000 German prisoners were interned in prisoner-of-war camps, in some parts of the state becoming forced farm laborers. In Wilmington, just a few blocks from downtown, is an apartment complex that was part of a large prisoner-of-war compound for U-boat officers.

In the 1950s and 1960s, African Americans in North Carolina and throughout the United States struggled against the monolithic system of segregation and racism enshrined in the nation's Jim Crow laws. The Ku Klux Klan stepped up its pro-segregation efforts with political and physical violence against Native Americans as well as African Americans; in the famous 1958 Battle of Maxton, 500 armed Lumbee people foiled a Klan rally and sent the Knights running for their lives. Change arrived slowly. The University of North Carolina accepted its first African American graduate student in 1951 and the first Black undergraduates four years later. Sit-ins in 1960 at the Woolworth's lunch counter in Greensboro began with four African American men, students at North Carolina A&T. On the second day of their protest they were joined by 23 other demonstrators; on the third day there were 300, and by day four about 1,000. This was a pivotal moment in the national Civil Rights Movement, sparking sit-ins across the country in which an estimated 50,000 people participated. You can see the counter today at the International Civil Rights Center and Museum in Greensboro. Even as victories were won at the level of Congress and in the federal courts, as in *Brown* v. *the Board of Education* and the 1964 Civil Rights Act, actual change on the ground was inexorably slow and hard-won. North Carolina's contribution to the Civil Rights Movement continues to be invaluable for the whole nation.

The 2020 census showed that North Carolina's population is at 10.44 million and growing, making it the ninth most populous state in the country. The state continues to adapt and contribute to the global community, thanks in large part to larger cities like Charlotte and the university-, research-, and tech-rich Raleigh, Durham, and Chapel Hill area. It is now a place of ethnic diversity, growing especially quickly in Latino residents. In 2014 an estimated 9 percent of North Carolinians were Latino, and that number is still climbing. There are also significant communities of Dega, Hmong, and Montagnard people from Southeast Asia as well as Eastern Europeans, among many others.

Government and Economy

POLITICAL LIFE
Liberal Enclaves

Although historically a red state, North Carolina's large population of college students, professors, and artists has created several boisterous enclaves of progressive politics. The outspoken archconservative U.S. Senator Jesse Helms supposedly questioned the need to spend public money on a state zoo in North Carolina "when we can just put up a fence around Chapel Hill." The Chapel Hill area is indeed the epicenter of North Carolina's liberalism, with its smaller neighboring town of Carrboro at its heart. Would-be Democratic presidential candidates and politicians on the campaign trail regularly stop here to bolster support in the state.

Although you'll find a mixture of political views statewide, the Triangle is not the only famously liberal community. In Asheville, lefty politics are part of the community's devotion to all things organic and DIY. Significant pockets of liberalism also exist in Boone, the cities of the Triad, and Wilmington.

MAJOR INDUSTRIES

Over the last 20 years, North Carolina has experienced tremendous shifts in its economy as the industries that once dominated the landscape and brought wealth and development declined. The **tobacco** industry ruled the state's economy for generations, employing innumerable North Carolinians from field to factory and funding a colossal portion of the state's physical and cultural infrastructure. The slow decline of the tobacco industry worldwide from the 1980s changed the state dramatically, especially the rural east, where tobacco fields once went from green to gold every fall. Other agricultural industries, especially **livestock**—chickens and hogs—are still important in the east. The **textile** industry, a giant for most of the 20th century, suffered the same decline as manufacturers sought cheaper labor overseas. Likewise, the **furniture** industry slipped into obscurity. Today, the once-thriving **fishing** industry is in steep decline, largely due to globalization and overfishing.

While these staple industries have fallen off, new industries and fields have sprouted across the state. **Pharmaceutical** and **biotech** companies have set up in the Research Triangle, formed by Raleigh, Durham, and Chapel Hill. The **film industry** has made Wilmington a hub of feature film production, Charlotte is a major production center for television programming and commercials, and Raleigh is home to a number of visual-effects studios that contribute to films and TV. **High-tech** leaders such as Apple have set up in North Carolina, and other tech giants have followed, locating database and network centers here. Charlotte is second only to New York City among the country's largest **banking** centers. **Tourism** continues to grow and contribute in a major way to the state's economy. **Agriculture** remains relevant, though it is increasingly becoming more specialized, especially as demand for organic products and locally and regionally sourced products continues.

Tourism

North Carolina has always drawn visitors to its mountains, waters, beaches, and cities. As the economy evolves, tourism has become even more important. Mountain and beach landscapes sell themselves, but competition is strong to be the town visitors think of first. The Yadkin Valley's **wine industry** and **wine trail** and the boom in **NASCAR** tourism are well-established examples of niche destinations, but the niche tourism trend continues to evolve. As **culinary tourism** gains momentum, so too do foodie destinations like **Asheville,** which was named "Beer City USA" 2009-2012 and boasts some two dozen breweries and specialty beer shops along with more than 250 independently owned restaurants. **Raleigh** and **Durham** continue to build foodie credentials as chefs and breweries rack up impressive awards and prestigious nominations. It seems that every city, large or small, celebrates some sort of "Taste of the Town" or restaurant week. **Heritage tourism** is also enormously important, with a number of guidebooks and driving trails established or under development to promote

history, traditional music, folk arts, and literary achievements. The state's Department of Commerce estimates that nearly 46 million people visit North Carolina every year, bringing in more than $19 billion, and that close to 200,000 state residents work in industries directly related to and dependent on tourism.

DISTRIBUTION OF WEALTH

For the most part, North Carolina is basically working-class. Pockets of significant wealth exist in urban areas, and as more and more retirees relocate to North Carolina, there are moneyed people in the mountains and coastal counties. Extensive white-collar job availability makes the Triangle a comparatively prosperous region, with average household incomes in 2010 exceeding $60,000, much higher than the state's median household income of just over $46,000.

The state also experiences significant **poverty.** The proportion of people living in poverty has been rising in recent years, partly due to the derailment of many of North Carolina's backbone industries. As recently as a generation ago, a high school graduate in small-town North Carolina could count on making a living wage in a mill or factory; nowadays those opportunities have dried up, and the poverty rate in 2017 was 14.7 percent. Even more distressing, the number of children living in poverty is just over 24 percent, climbing to 28 percent for children under age six.

The northeastern quadrant of North Carolina is the most critically impoverished, which points to **financial inequality** correlating to race, as the region has a significant African American population. Broken down by ethnicity, the data reveal that 10 percent of urban and rural whites live in poverty, while 20-30 percent of rural and urban Latinos, African Americans, and Native Americans live in poverty.

Several hardworking organizations and activists are trying to alleviate the economic hardship found in North Carolina. National organizations like **Habitat for Humanity** (www.habitat.org) and regional groups like the **Southern Coalition for Social Justice** (http://southerncoalition.org) and the **Institute for Southern Studies** (www.southernstudies.org) bring community activism and research to the state. There are also excellent North Carolina-based advocates in groups such as the **North Carolina Rural Economic Development Center** (www.ncruralcenter.org), the **North Carolina Justice Center** (www.ncjustice.org), the **Black Family Land Trust** (www.bflt.org), and **Student Action with Farmworkers** (http://saf-unite.org).

People and Culture

DEMOGRAPHICS

The ninth most populous state in the union, North Carolina's population of 10.44 million residents is slightly more than Michigan and New Jersey and slightly less than Georgia. More than two-thirds of North Carolinians are white, primarily of German and Scottish-Irish descent, and not quite one-quarter are African American. The state is about 9 percent Latino and has the seventh-largest Native American population of any state.

More than 40 percent of North Carolinians are between the ages of 25 and 59, but the older population is steadily rising, due in large part to the state's popularity with retirees. The majority—about 70 percent—of North Carolinians live in family groups, with married couples constituting about half of those and married couples with children making up almost one-quarter of households. Of the remaining one-third of the state's population who live in "nonfamily households"—that is, not with blood relatives or a legally recognized spouse—the vast majority are individuals living on their own. Unmarried couples, both straight and gay, have a much lower rate of cohabitation here than in more urban parts of the United States, but such households are common and accepted in the Triangle, Asheville, Charlotte, and other urban areas.

Indigenous People

Many Americans have never heard of the **Lumbee people,** despite the fact that they are the largest Native American nation east of the Mississippi. This is in part due to the federal government's refusal to grant them official recognition, although the state of North Carolina does recognize them. The Lumbee are primarily based in and around Robeson County in the swampy southeastern corner of the state, their traditional home. In the Great Smoky Mountains, the town of Cherokee on the Qualla Boundary, which is Cherokee-administered land, is the government seat of the **Eastern Band of the Cherokee.** The Eastern Band are largely descended from those Cherokee people who escaped arrest during the deportation of the Southeast's Native Americans on the Trail of Tears in the 19th century, or who made the forced march to Oklahoma but survived and walked home to the mountains again. The Lumbee people and Cherokee people are both important cultural groups in North Carolina. Several other Native American communities are indigenous to the state as well; those recognized by the state are the **Waccamaw-Siouan, Occaneechi Band of the Saponi Nation, Haliwa-Saponi, Coharie, Sappony,** and **Meherrin.**

Latinos

North Carolina has one of the fastest-growing Latino populations in the United States, a community whose ranks have swelled since the 1990s, in particular as hundreds of thousands of **Mexican and Central American laborers** came to work in the agricultural, industrial, and formerly booming construction trades. Their presence in such large numbers makes for some unexpectedly quirky cultural

How Can You Tell a Tar Heel?

> What manner of man is a North Carolinian? How can you tell a Tar Heel? What ingredients went into his making? Is he different, and if so, how and why? There is no slide-rule answer to these questions, but it may be interesting to explore them. The Tar Heel is not a distinct species, but he may have some distinguishing marks. [We are] independent, courageous, resourceful, democratic, gregarious and individualistic, although we would use plainer words than these Latin terms to describe ourselves.... There is a progressive strain in this Tar Heel, a realistic and resourceful determination to get ahead with the work for a better way of life for himself and his fellows.... There is often a kindness in the voice which covers a lot of humanity in its acceptance of all sorts and conditions of men.... But there is no pouring Tar Heels into a mold. The point is that we are by preference and habit individualists, or what we call "characters."
> Blackwell P. Robinson, ed., *The North Carolina Guide*, UNC Press, 1955.

juxtapositions, as in small rural towns that are now majority Latino, or in Charlotte, where the Latino population has made Roman Catholicism the most common religion.

Other Immigrants

Significant numbers of non-Latino immigrants also live in North Carolina. Charlotte is a dizzying hodgepodge of ethnicities, where native Southerners live and work alongside **Asians, Africans,** and **Middle Easterners,** where mosques and synagogues and *wats* welcome worshipers just down the street from Baptist churches and houses of prayer. Many **Hmong** and other **Southeast Asian** immigrants have settled in the northern foothills and the Piedmont Triad, and the dense thicket of universities in the Triangle attracts academics from around the world.

RELIGION

As early as the 17th century, North Carolina's religious landscape foreshadowed the diversity we enjoy today. The first Christians in North Carolina were Quakers, soon followed by Anglicans, Presbyterians, Baptists, Moravians, Methodists, and Roman Catholics. Native American and African religions, present in the early colonial days, were never totally quashed by European influence, and Barbadian Sephardic Jews were here early on as well. All of these religions remain today,

with enrichment by the presence of Muslims, Buddhists, and an amazing mosaic of other Christian groups.

North Carolina claims as its own one of the world's most influential modern religious figures, Billy Graham, who was raised on a dairy farm outside Charlotte and experienced his Christian religious awakening in 1934. After preaching in person to more people around the world than anyone in human history, and being involved with every U.S. president since Harry Truman, Graham died at his home in Montreat, outside Asheville, in 2018, and is buried at the Billy Graham Library in Charlotte.

LANGUAGE

Few states can boast the linguistic diversity of North Carolina. North Carolina speech varies widely by region and even from county to county. These variations have to do with the historical patterns of settlement in a given area—whether Scots-Irish or German ancestry is common, how long Native American languages survived after the arrival of the Europeans, the presence or lack of African influence—as well as other historical patterns of trade and communication.

Of our distinct regional accents, the **Outer Banks brogue** is probably the best known. Much like the residents of the Chesapeake islands in Maryland and Virginia, "Hoi

Toiders," as Outer Bankers are jokingly called, because of how they pronounce the phrase "high tide," have a striking dialect that resembles certain dialects in the north of England. "I" is rounded into "oi," the r sound is often hard, and many distinctive words survive from long-ago English, Scottish, and Irish dialects. Not dissimilar is the Appalachian dialect heard through much of the mountains. The effect is more subtle than in the Outer Banks, but "oi" replaces "I" in Appalachian English too, and r's are emphasized. A telltale sign of upcountry origins is the pronunciation of the vowel in words like bear and hair, which in the mountains is flattened almost inside-out so that the words are pronounced something like "barr" and "harr." This is similar to mountain accents in Tennessee, West Virginia, Virginia, and Kentucky.

Piedmont Carolinians have a wide spectrum of linguistic influences. The heart of the state has been a cultural and commercial crossroads since the days of the Great Wagon Road, which brought 18th-century white settlers into the Southern backcountry; the magnetic influence of jobs in cigarette factories and textile mills drew rural Southerners from all over the region. The product of this linguistic mix-and-match is probably the closest thing in North Carolina to the generic Hollywood version of "the Southern accent," but Piedmont speech is far from homogenous within the region. For example, native central Carolinians are equally likely to call the Queen City "CHAR-lit" or "SHOLL-utt."

There are a great many smaller linguistic zones peppered throughout the state. Folks from up around the **Virginia border** in eastern North Carolina may have a distinctively Virginian accent. Listen for the classic telltale word *house.* Southside Virginians and their neighbors south of the state line will pronounce it "heause," with a flat vowel. **Cherokee English,** heard in the Smokies, combines the Appalachian sound with a distinctively Cherokee rhythm, while **Lumbee English,** spoken in and around Robeson

County in the southeast, combines sounds somewhat like those of the Outer Banks or deep mountains with a wealth of unusual grammatical structures and vocabulary of unknown origin. Oft-cited examples are the Lumbee construction "be's," a present-tense form of "to be," and words like *ellick* for coffee and *juvember* for slingshot: "Get me some more ellick, please, if you be's going to the market." Residents of the **Sandhills** area, bounded by the Uwharries to the west, Sanford to the north, and Southern Pines to the southeast, have a highly unusual rhythm to their speech—a rapid, soft, almost filigreed way of talking, delivered in bursts between halting pauses. Down around Wilmington and south to the South Carolina state line, African American English, and to a lesser extent white English, have some of the inflections of the **Gullah language** of the Lowcountry. These are only a few of the state's dialects, and even these have subvariations. Old-timers can pinpoint geographical differences within these categories—whether a Lumbee speaker is from Prospect or Drowning Creek, for example, or whether a Banker is from Ocracoke or Hatteras.

Of course, English is hardly the only language spoken here. If you visit Cherokee, you'll see that many street and commercial signs bear pretty, twisty symbols in a script that looks like a cross between Khmer or Sanskrit and Cyrillic; **written Cherokee** uses the script famously devised by **Sequoyah** in the early 19th century. Cherokee also survives as a spoken language, mostly among the elders in traditional communities such as Snowbird, near Robbinsville, and many younger Cherokee people are determined to learn and pass on their ancestral tongue, but the small pool of speakers points to the slow death of the language. **Spanish** is widely spoken throughout the state as the Latino population continues to grow rapidly, and within Latino communities here are many national and regional dialects of Spanish. Some Central American immigrants who speak indigenous languages

Understanding Local Lingo

North Carolina speech features delightful and sometimes perplexing regional vocabulary and grammar. Following are some of the common Carolinianisms most likely to stump travelers.

- **bless your/his/her heart:** A complex declaration with infinitely varied intentions, interpreted depending on context or tone. In its most basic use, "Bless your heart," is a sincere thank-you for a favor or a kindness paid. It's also an exclamation of affection, usually applied to children and the elderly, as in, "You're *not* 92 years old! You are? Well, bless your heart." Frequently, though, hearts are blessed to frame criticism in a charitable light, as in, "Bless his heart; that man from New York don't know not to shout."

- **buggy:** a shopping cart, as at a grocery store.

- **carry:** convey, escort, give a ride to. "I carried my mother up to the mountains for her birthday."

- **Coke:** any soft drink; may be called "pop" in the mountains.

- **come back:** often uttered by shopkeepers as a customer leaves, not to ask them to return immediately, but simply an invitation to patronize the establishment again someday.

- **dinner:** the midday meal.

- **evening:** not just the twilight hours, but all the hours between about 3pm and nightfall.

- **fair to middling:** so-so, in response to "How you?"; a holdover term from North Carolina's moonshining days, the term originally applied to grading 'shine by examining bubbles in a shaken mason jar.

- **fixing to:** about to or preparing to do something. "She's fixing to have a baby any day now."

- **holler:** hollow, a mountain cove.

arrive unable to understand English or Spanish. Anyone who doubts that newcomers to this country are dedicated to the task of integrating into American society need only consider the incredibly difficult task faced by such immigrants, who must first learn Spanish before they can enroll in ESL programs to learn English.

The Arts

As much as North Carolinians like to brag about the beaches and mountains and college sports teams, it's the artists across the state who help North Carolina distinguish itself. There is an incredibly rich and complex cultural heritage here that has strong support from the North Carolina Arts Council and a vast network of local and regional arts organizations. These groups have supplied inspiration, financial and emotional support, and sustenance for generations of remarkable musicians, writers, actors, and other artists.

LITERATURE

Storytelling seems to come naturally to Southerners. From the master storytellers of Jack Tales in the Blue Ridge to the distinguished journalists we see every night on television, North Carolinians have a singular gift for communication. Thomas Wolfe

- **Kakalak:** Carolina. Also Kakalaky, Cakalack.

- **mash:** press, as a button. "I keep mashing the button, but the elevator won't come."

- **mess:** discombobulated, in a rut, not living right. "I was a mess until I joined the church."

- **mommocked:** exhausted, worn out. Used especially on the Outer Banks and in rural southeastern North Carolina.

- **piece:** a vague measure of distance, as in, "down the road a piece" (a little ways down the road) or "a fair piece" (a long way).

- **poke:** a bag, such as a paper shopping bag. Used especially in the mountains.

- **reckon:** believe, think. Often used in interrogative statements that end in a falling tone, as in, "Reckon what we're having for dinner." (That is, "What do you suppose is for lunch?")

- **right:** quite, very. Variations include "right quick" (soon, hurriedly), "right much" (often), and "a right many" or "a right smart of" (a great quantity).

- **sorry:** worthless, lame, shoddy. "I wanted to play basketball in college, but I was too sorry of an athlete."

- **supper:** the evening meal (as opposed to "dinner," the midday meal).

- **ugly:** mean or unfriendly, spiteful. Sometimes referred to as "acting ugly." "Hateful" is a common synonym.

- **wait on:** to wait for.

- **y'all:** pronoun used to address any group of two or more people.

- **yonder:** over there.

was an Asheville native, and O. Henry, whose real name was William Sidney Porter, was born and raised in Greensboro. Tom Robbins (*Even Cowgirls Get the Blues*) was born in Blowing Rock. Charles Frazier (*Cold Mountain*) is from Asheville. Sarah Dessen (*Just Listen*) is from Chapel Hill. Kaye Gibbons, Lee Smith, Fred Chappell, Randal Kenan, and Clyde Edgerton, leading lights in Southern fiction, are all natives or residents of North Carolina. Also closely associated with the state are Carl Sandburg, David Sedaris, Armistead Maupin, and Betsy Byars, who have all lived here at some point. Arts programs focused on creative writing have sprung up across the state, imbuing the literary scenes in towns like Wilmington, Greensboro, Asheville, and Chapel Hill with talented undergraduate and graduate students and their professors. Notable writers teaching creative writing programs include poet A. Van Jordan, essayist David Gessner, and novelist and short story writer Jill McCorkle. In 2021, a North Carolina novelist became the second in the state to receive the National Book Award (Charles Frazier was the first with *Cold Mountain*) when Jason Mott received the National Book Award for his novel, *One Hell of a Book,* making him the first Black author, second novelist, first graduate of UNC Wilmington's MFA program, and the first friend of mine to take home such an honor.

North Carolina has also given the world some of the giants of 20th-century journalism. Edward R. Murrow, Charles Kuralt, David Brinkley, and Howard Cosell were all sons of Carolina.

MUSIC

It's hard to know where to begin when describing the importance of music to North Carolinians. Since the earliest days of recorded country music, North Carolinians have shared their songs with the world. Charlie Poole and Wade Mainer were among the first to record and became influential artists in the 1930s. By 1945, a banjo player named Earl Scruggs was helping to create what would become the quintessential sound of **bluegrass** music, particularly his three-fingered picking style. Bluegrass greats like Del McCoury helped further define the sound. Today, bluegrass is alive and well in North Carolina; Steve Martin's collaboration with the Steep Canyon Rangers sold out concerts around the world and garnered many awards, and the late Doc Watson's annual **MerleFest** is still going strong. **Country** musicians like Ronnie Milsap, Donna Fargo, Charlie Daniels, and Randy Travis made big names for themselves from the 1970s to the 1990s; more recently, Kellie Pickler and Scottie McCreery of *American Idol* fame as well as Eric Church have made waves on the country charts.

The growth of **jazz** and **funk** would be unimaginably different if not for a number of notable innovators that make North Carolina nearly as important as New Orleans to the development of these genres. John Coltrane was raised in High Point, Thelonious Monk was a native of Rocky Mount, Nina Simone hails from Tryon, and Dizzy Gillespie grew up just over the South Carolina state line but contributed greatly when he studied music in Laurinburg. In terms of funk music, what would the genre be without George Clinton, founder of Parliament and Parliament-Funkadelic? Saxophonist Maceo Parker and his brother, drummer Melvin Parker, played with Clinton and with South Carolina's favorite son and the Godfather of Soul, James Brown. Together they developed the classic funk sound and influenced the groove-driven side of **soul** music.

In North Carolina, you're never far from some good **gospel** music. On the coast, African American choirs blend spirituality and faith with showmanship and serious talent to perform beautiful, inspired sets. In the mountains, you're more likely to find gospel quartets and old-time gospel music, which is more inspired by bluegrass and traditional music, at camp meetings and gospel sings on weekend nights. The state's Native American communities also have thriving gospel traditions of their own.

Artists that include James Taylor, Tori Amos, Clay Aiken, the Squirrel Nut Zippers, the Avett Brothers, Fred Durst (from Limp Bizkit), rapper and producer Jermaine Dupri, Corrosion of Conformity, Ben Folds Five, Daughtry, Southern Culture on the Skids, and Megafaun have all had a hand in shaping the state's musical legacy.

THEATER

Regional theater companies such as the venerable Flat Rock Playhouse near Hendersonville make great theater accessible in small towns and rural areas. Wilmington is home to Thalian Hall and the Thalian Association, a group founded in 1788 that was named the Official Community Theatre of North Carolina thanks to their long-running commitment to the arts in Wilmington. The North Carolina School for the Arts in Winston-Salem mints great actors and filmmakers, among other artists. The film and television industries have long recognized North Carolina as a hotbed of talent as well as a place with amazing filming locations.

For some reason, **outdoor historical dramas** have long flourished in North Carolina. The most famous is North Carolina playwright Paul Green's *Lost Colony,* which has been performed every summer since 1937 on Roanoke Island, except during World War II when German U-boats lurked nearby. The Cherokee people depict emblematic episodes in their history in the outdoor drama *Unto These Hills,* in production since 1950. The community of Boone has presented *Horn* *in the West* since 1952, and it is joined by Valdese and several other communities in North Carolina in turning to performance tableaux to commemorate their heritage. It's especially important to note that among the characteristics of outdoor drama in North Carolina is the fact that the cast, crew, and often the producers and playwrights are members of the communities whose stories the plays tell.

ARTS AND CRAFTS

Folk art and studio crafts show vitality in North Carolina. Several communities are known worldwide for their local traditions. Countless individual artists, studios, and galleries can be found across the state.

Seagrove, a minuscule town at the geographical center of the state, has been the home of hundreds of **potters** since the 18th century. What began as a commercial enterprise to turn out utilitarian products made for trade on the Great Wagon Road became an increasingly artistic form in the early 20th century. Skilled potters still work in Seagrove today, many of them descendants of founding members of the community. Wilson, between Raleigh and Wilmington, was home to Vollis Simpson, a folk artist and maker of internationally admired whirligigs that were named the Official Folk Art of North Carolina.

Cherokee craft is an important aesthetic school comprising a wide range of techniques and media such as wood- and stone-carving, fiber arts, traditional weaponry, and avant-garde sculpture and painting. **Qualla Arts and Crafts Mutual,** located in the town of Cherokee, has a wonderful sales gallery that will dazzle lovers of fine craft.

Asheville is an epicenter of the arts, the heart of a vast community of artists that stretches throughout western North Carolina and includes such major folk schools as **John C. Campbell** in Brasstown, near the Georgia state line, and **Penland,** close to Tennessee in the northeastern mountains. In Asheville you can see and purchase an infinite variety of crafts that include handmade baskets, quilts, furniture, clothing, jewelry, and iron architectural elements. The **Southern Highland Craft Guild** (www.southernhighlandguild. org), an old and accomplished organization, deserves a lot of the credit for the thriving health of the craft movement in western North Carolina. Its website has a great deal of information about contemporary master crafters and their work. On the coast, Wilmington, New Bern, Hatteras, and other towns have folk-art and fine-art artists and galleries.

As people become more accustomed to a world in which almost every object we see and use was mass-produced far away, we develop a deeper appreciation for the depth of skill and aesthetic complexity that went into the production of everyday objects in past generations. North Carolinians have always been great crafters of utilitarian and occupational necessities. As you travel through the state, keep an eye out for objects that you may not immediately recognize as art—barns, fishing nets, woven chair bottoms—but that were made with the skill and artistry of generations-old traditions. In North Carolina, art is everywhere.

Food

You'll probably have heard of North Carolina's most famous specialties—**barbecue, Brunswick stew,** and **hush puppies**—but are you brave enough to venture deeper into the hinterlands of Carolina cooking? Few snacks are more viscerally craved by locals, and more revolting to non-Southerners, than **boiled peanuts.** The recipe is simple: Green peanuts are boiled in their shells in bulk in water as salty as the chef deems necessary. Once they're soft and slimy, the peanuts are dumped into a strainer and are ready to eat. All you need to make them is a big kettle and a fire, so boiled peanuts are often made and sold in small bags at roadside stands, primarily in the Lowcountry and coastal plain, but increasingly in the mountains as well. Often these roadside stands are themselves folk art, with handmade signs reading "Bolit P-Nuts Here," with a collection of carvings or sculptures for sale in the bed of a truck nearby. To eat a boiled peanut, pick it up by the ends with your thumb and forefinger and place it lengthwise between your front teeth. Gently crack open the shell—don't bite through it—and detach the halves. Pry off half of the shell, and nip or slurp the peanuts out as if you're eating an oyster (boiled peanuts often show up at Lowcountry oyster roasts). Toss the shell out the window—chances are you're driving as you eat—and have another. Be sure you have a lot of something to drink close at hand, because you'll soon get thirsty.

Many cultures have a recipe that makes thrifty use of the leftover meat scraps that are too small, too few, or too disgusting to be served alone. For upper Piedmont Carolinians, particularly those of German ancestry raised in the wavy ribbon of towns between Charlotte and Winston-Salem, that delicacy is **livermush.** Some folks say that if you're from the Mid-Atlantic and are familiar with scrapple, you'll have a pretty good idea of what livermush is like. That's not true—livermush is much worse and tastes like some bitter combination of burning hair and pepper. Under North Carolina law (really), livermush must contain at least 30 percent hog liver, which is supplemented with sundry scraps from hog heads, sometimes some skin, and cornmeal. At the factory, it's mashed up and cooked in loaves. In the kitchen, it's sliced and fried. You can eat it at breakfast like sausage, in a sandwich, or even on a stick if you go to the annual livermush festivals in Drexel and Shelby. Should you try it? Yes, at least a bite; plenty of people like it.

In the eastern part of the state, a similar aesthetic underlies the creation of **hog hash,** best made directly after an old-time hog killing, when the animal's organs are pulled steaming hot out of the carcass in the frosty fall morning. The liver, lungs, and a variety of other organs and appendages are dumped in a kettle with potatoes, a liquid base (broth, milk, or just water), and some vegetables and seasonings. Unlike livermush, hog hash is served in bowls or tubs as a dark, musky stew; it's not common.

Up in the Blue Ridge Mountains, and across Appalachia, for that matter, the early spring is the season for **ramps,** sometimes called skunk cabbage—very pungent wild onions that grow along creek beds in the deep mountains. They're another of those foods passionately defended by those who grew up eating them but greeted with trepidation by outsiders. The reason they're feared by the uninitiated is their atomically powerful taste, which will emanate from every part of your body for days if the ramps are too strong or not prepared correctly. Ramps taste like a cross between regular onions, garlic, leeks, shallots, and kryptonite. When they're young, they're perfectly pungent—not too overwhelming, but still powerful enough to let you know they're in the dish. Folks skillet-cook them, fry them up in grease, boil them with fatback, or just chomp on them raw. For a special treat and a gentle introduction to ramps, stop in at the Stecoah Valley Center near Robbinsville, pick up a bag of the Smoky Mountain Native Plants Association's special cornmeal mix with dried ramps, and make yourself a skillet of deliciously tangy cornbread. You can also try them at the local ramps festivals held in Robbinsville and Cherokee in spring. A growing number of restaurants from Asheville to Wilmington are buying ramps and morel mushrooms from mountain foragers and preparing them every way from skillet-fried to pickled, so ramp lovers can get a taste of this springtime mountain delicacy even on the coast.

You can read all about these and other acquired tastes at NCFOOD (www.ncfolk.org) or Our State Eats by *Our State* magazine (www.ourstate.com), two food blogs devoted to Carolina cooking, or on the Southern Foodways Alliance (www.southernfoodways.com) and Dixie Dining (www.dixiedining.com) websites.

Vegetarians and devotees of organic food, fear not; North Carolina is an unusually progressive state when it comes to healthy and homegrown grub. Nevertheless, if you want to avoid meat, you have to be cautious when ordering at a restaurant: Make sure the beans are made with vegetable oil rather than lard, ask if the salad dressing contains anchovies, and beware of hidden fish and oyster sauce. Traditional Southern cooking makes liberal use of fatback (cured pork fat) and other animal products; greens are often boiled with a strip of fatback or a hambone, as are most soups and stews. Even pie crusts are still made with lard in many old-time kitchens.

In the major cities, you'll find organic grocery stores. Earth Fare and Whole Foods are the most common chains, but there are also plenty of small independent markets. Farmers markets and roadside stands are so plentiful that they almost have to fight for space. Visit the state Department of Agriculture's North Carolina Farm Fresh (www.ncfarmfresh.com) for directories of farmers markets and pick-your-own farms and orchards.

Essentials

Getting There

AIR

The state where air travel began has more than 70 public airports, almost 300 privately owned airfields, and about 20 fly-in communities where residents share an airstrip and have their own hangar space. Nine airports have regularly scheduled passenger service, and two of them host international flights. The state's Department of Transportation estimates that more than 35 million people fly in and out of North Carolina every year. The main hubs are North Carolina's international

airports in Charlotte, Greensboro, and Raleigh-Durham; Wilmington has more limited service.

The eighth-busiest airport in the country, **Charlotte Douglas International Airport** (CLT, 5501 Josh Birmingham Pkwy., Charlotte, 704/359-4013, www.cltairport. com) has more than 730 daily departures and is served by dozens of airlines. There are nonstop flights to 140 U.S. cities as well as international flights to Latin America and the Caribbean, London, Frankfurt, Munich, and Toronto. Parking is abundant and inexpensive, with parking shuttle buses operating from 5am. **Raleigh-Durham International Airport** (RDU, 2400 W. Terminal Blvd., Morrisville, 919/840-2123, www.rdu.com), located in Wake County about midway between Raleigh and Durham, has flights to most domestic hubs as well as London, Toronto, and Cancún, Mexico. Hourly and daily parking is available for reasonable rates within walking distance of the terminals and in satellite lots linked by shuttle buses. **Piedmont Triad Airport** (GSO, 1000 A Ted Johnston Pkwy., Greensboro, 336/665-5600, www. flyfrompti.com) serves the Greensboro and Winston-Salem area with flights to domestic destinations in the South, Midwest, and Mid-Atlantic.

There are several smaller airports around the state with regularly scheduled domestic passenger service, including **Wilmington International Airport** (ILM, 1740 Airport Blvd., Wilmington, 910/341-4125, www.fly-ilm.com), **Asheville Regional Airport** (AVL, 61 Terminal Dr., Fletcher, 828/684-2226, www.flyavl.com), and **Fayetteville Regional Airport** (FAY, 400 Airport Rd., Fayetteville, 910/433-1160, www.fayettevil-lenc.gov). **Pitt-Greenville Airport** (PGV, 400 Airport Rd., Greenville, 252/902-2025) has flights to Charlotte, and New Bern's **Coastal Carolina Regional Airport** (EWN, 200 Terminal Dr., New Bern, 252/638-8591,

www.newbernairport.com) has flights to Atlanta and Charlotte. **Albert J. Ellis Airport** (OAJ, 264 Albert Ellis Airport Rd., Richlands, 910/324-1100, www.flyoaj.com), near Jacksonville and Richlands, has flights to Atlanta, Charlotte, and Washington DC.

Private aircraft can fly to any of the state's 75 regional, county, and municipal air strips statewide; **NC Airports Association** (www. ncairports.org) has a full list with contact details, navigational information, airstrip specifications, and aerial photos. For historical reasons there are more municipal airports in the central and western parts of the state. When the state government started handing out grants for small public airstrips in the 1950s, there were already many surplus military airfields in the eastern part of the state, a legacy of World War II.

CAR

Several major interstate highways run through North Carolina, so if you're driving and would prefer that your trip be efficient rather than scenic, you've got several choices. From anywhere along the eastern seaboard, I-95 slices through the eastern third of the state, providing easy access to the beaches, which are mostly one or two hours east of I-95, and to the Triangle area, under an hour west of I-95 via U.S. 64, U.S. 70, or I-40. From the north, you may choose to veer southwest at Richmond, Virginia, on I-85; this is an efficient route to Durham and Chapel Hill as well as to the Triad and Charlotte regions.

I-40 starts in Wilmington and runs west to Barstow, California. It's a fast road all the way through North Carolina, although weather—ice in the fall, winter, and spring, and fog any time of year—may slow you down considerably between Knoxville, Tennessee, and Asheville. U.S. 64 and I-77 connect North Carolina to the Midwest. I-77 cuts through the toe of Virginia in the mountains and runs straight to Charlotte, while U.S. 64 meanders east through the Triangle all the way to Roanoke Island and the Outer Banks. From the Deep South or Texas, the best bet is I-20 to Atlanta, and from there I-85 to Charlotte, or U.S. 19 or U.S. 23 if you're going to the mountains.

There are no checkpoints at the state line to inspect vehicles for produce or animals, but sobriety checkpoints are established and staffed throughout the year.

BUS

Travel around North Carolina can be accomplished easily and cheaply by bus. Greyhound (800/231-2222, www.greyhound.com) offers daily service to many towns and cities, with the exception of the Outer Banks and mountain towns other than Asheville, but you can access that region via the Tennessee cities close to the state line, including Knoxville and Johnson City. Before you reserve bus tickets, be sure to check out special discounts on the Greyhound website. There are often regional promotions as well

as special "Go Anywhere" fares as low as $29 each way with 14-day advance booking, for example, as well as regular discounts for students and seniors.

These days, the large buses used by Greyhound and its local subsidiaries are clean and comfortable, and if you make a reservation ahead of time, you can choose your seat. One word of caution is that some bus stations are located in seedy parts of town, so make sure taxi service is available at your destination station after dark.

TRAIN

Although it does not currently serve the mountains or the coast, Amtrak (800/872-7245, www.amtrak.com) is a great way to get to and around central North Carolina. The main New York-Miami *Silver Service* and *Palmetto* trains pass through North Carolina following the I-95 corridor. The New York-New Orleans *Crescent* stops at both Winston-Salem and Charlotte. The *Carolinian* runs from New York to Charlotte by way of Raleigh.

Getting Around

CAR

North Carolina's highway system, with the largest network of state-maintained roads in the country and a good interstate highway grid, provides access to the whole state. I-95 crosses north-south, demarcating the eastern third of the state, and I-85 runs northeast-southwest from north of the Triangle area through Charlotte. I-40 is the primary east-west route, from Wilmington through the Smoky Mountains to Knoxville, Tennessee. The highest speed limit, which applies to some rural interstate highways and four-lane roads, is 70 mph. Highways in developed areas have much lower speed limits, and in residential areas it's a good idea to keep it under 25 mph.

You can take your pick of car-rental agencies at the major airports at Charlotte, Winston-Salem, and Raleigh-Durham; there

are fewer choices at smaller regional airports. There are also car-rental pickup and drop-off offices in many towns. Rental car companies in North Carolina include Alamo (800/462-5266, www.alamo.com), Avis (877/222-9075, www.avis.com), Budget (800/218-7992, www.budget.com), Dollar (800/800-4000, www.dollar.com), Enterprise (800/261-7331, www.enterprise.com), Hertz (800/654-3131, www.hertz.com), National (877/222-9058, www.nationalcar.com), Thrifty (800/847-4389, www.thrifty.com), and Triangle Rent-A-Car (800/643-7368, www.trianglerentacar.com). To rent a car you must be at least 25 years old and have both a valid driver's license and a credit card, although some companies will accept a cash security deposit in lieu of credit.

For getting around town in every city of a

Driving Trails

The state of North Carolina and a variety of regional organizations have created a wonderful network of automobile "trails"—thematic itineraries showcasing North Carolina's treasures. Check out the destinations on this sampling of trails.

- **Asheville Ale Trail:**
  http://ashevillealetrail.com

- **Blue Ridge Music Trails:**
  www.blueridgemusic.org

- **Cherokee Heritage Itinerary:**
  www.ncfolk.org

- **Civil War Traveler:**
  www.civilwartraveler.com

- **Core Sound Itinerary:**
  www.ncfolk.org

- **Discover Craft North Carolina:**
  www.discovercraftnc.org

- **Family Frolic in Winston-Salem:**
  http://visitwinstonsalem.com/Family

- **Haw River Wine Trail:**
  www.hawriverwinetrail.com

- **Historic Albemarle Tour**:
  www.historicalbemarletour.org

- **Homegrown Handmade Art Roads and Farm Trails:**
  www.homegrownhandmade.com

- **North Carolina Scenic Byways:**
  www.ncdot.gov/travel/scenic

- **North Carolina Wine Country:**
  www.visitncwinecountry.com

- **Pottery Itinerary for the Seagrove Area:** www.ncfolk.org

- **Quilt Trails of Western North Carolina:** www.quilttrailswnc.org

- **Trail of Tears National Historic Trail, North Carolina Chapter:**
  www.arch.dcr.state.nc.us/tears

- **Western North Carolina Cheese Trail:** http://wnccheesetrail.org

- **Yadkin Valley Wine Country:**
  www.yadkinvalleywinecountry.com

reasonable size, you can always use rideshare services like Uber (www.uber.com). Service will be limited in small towns and rural areas, but check the website or the app for available drivers in your destination.

Driving to and through the Outer Banks can be a bit complicated, depending on your destination, because there are not many bridges. The northern banks are linked to the mainland by bridges between Point Harbor and Kitty Hawk and from Manns Harbor over Roanoke Island to just south of Nags Head. There are no bridges to Hatteras and none until you get all the way to the southern end of the banks, where bridges link Morehead City and Cedar Point to the towns along Bogue Banks. The state's excellent ferry system connects the Outer Banks to the mainland; it's a fun way to travel. Detailed information is available from the state Department of Transportation (www.ncdot.gov/ferry). Several ferries link mainland points across sounds and rivers, while ferries from Currituck to Knotts Island, and from both Swan Quarter and Cedar Island to Ocracoke, will carry you to the Outer Banks.

On the other side of the state, driving in the Great Smoky Mountains and Blue Ridge can be difficult in bad weather, and roads can be icy in winter. The major interstate highways that cross the mountains are fast, and if you're traveling from one major town to another, U.S. 19, U.S. 74, and U.S. 421 are also fast. On smaller highways, count on much slower traveling. The Blue Ridge Parkway, while geographically direct, is very slow. The maximum speed is 45 mph, but there are few stretches of the Parkway where it's safe to drive that fast; add to that the frequent braking of sightseers, and traffic can crawl. Numbered roads in the mountains are often similar, with surprise hairpin turns and narrow cliff-side shoulders. Allow plenty of time to get from point to point; on some roads it'll take you an hour to cover 20 miles. In the mountains you have to take it slow and be alert to weather and wildlife. If you find a local driver tailgating you, find a place to pull over and allow the faster drivers to pass.

Highway Safety

Write "*HP" (*47) on a sticky note and affix it to your dashboard. That's the direct free hotline to the North Carolina Highway Patrol, which will send help if you're trouble. North Carolinians don't hesitate to report aggressive, reckless, or drunk motorists to the highway patrol, and you might be reported by another driver if you're tailgating, speeding, weaving, or driving aggressively. What passes for normal driving in many parts of the United States is regarded as aggressive driving in the South.

Pull well off the road and turn on your hazard lights if you have an accident. If you can't safely pull your vehicle out of traffic, at least get away from the roadway. A distressing number of motorists with disabled vehicles as well as pedestrians are struck and killed by cars every year.

Some rules to remember while driving in North Carolina: Wearing your seat belt is required by law; child safety seats are mandatory for anyone under age 8 or weighing less than 80 pounds; and if it's raining hard enough to need windshield wipers, you must also use your headlights.

Weather Considerations

If you're driving in the mountains in the morning or at night, you may run into heavy **fog.** Because the clouds perch on and around mountaintops, you may find yourself in clear weather one moment and only seconds later in a fog with little visibility. It can be dangerous and frightening, but if this happens, slow down, keep an eye on the lines on the road, watch for other cars, and put on your low beams. As in any kind of bad weather, it's always best to find a safe place to pull off the road and wait for the weather to improve. Fog can dissipate as quickly as it appears.

In the winter you could encounter icy roads in any part of the state, and up in the mountains you may hit **ice and snow** three seasons of the year. Many Southerners on the coast

and in the Piedmont tend to panic when snow is forecast; folks in the mountains manage to keep their wits about them no matter the weather. In anticipation of a half-inch dusting of snow, schools and businesses may close, fleets of sand and salt trucks hit the highway, and residents mob the grocery stores. This overreaction to snow makes the roads a little safer because many folks are more likely to stay home, but those who do drive in winter weather are less likely to know how to drive on ice than the average Yankee or Midwesterner. That can make the roads hazardous, so even if you are an experienced snow driver, stay alert.

While North Carolinians from the mountains are more experienced at driving in snowy or icy weather, the roads themselves can be dangerous. The safest plan is to avoid driving in the mountains in bad weather. If you must go, keep in mind that mountain roads, even highways, may close—especially those maintained by the National Park Service, including the Blue Ridge Parkway and the roads in Great Smoky Mountains National Park. The National Park Service offers the following advice: "When driving downhill on slippery mountain roads, shift to a lower gear (2, 1, or L on automatic transmissions) to avoid using brakes more than necessary. Leave extra room between you and the vehicle in front of you. Be aware that icy sections persist on mountain roads even when the weather is warm in the lowlands."

The other weather concern is rain. In spring and fall, you can encounter thunderstorms in all parts of the state, and these are usually run-of-the-mill storms, but heed any weather warnings you hear or see. Summer and early fall is hurricane season, and while most people think of hurricanes as coastal events, the torrential rains brought on by a hurricane (or tropical system of any sort) can cause flash flooding, high winds, and heavy rains as these systems move inland. Whether you're on the coast or in the mountains and you learn there is a hurricane on the way, follow the directions of civil authorities and be safe. If you're on the coast, familiarize yourself with hurricane evacuation routes (they're marked on highways and in local literature) and follow directions.

Wildlife on the Road

A final note about highway travel: Be conscious of wildlife. Deer, rabbits, turtles, foxes, coyotes, raccoons, and opossums litter the highways. Head-on collisions with deer can be fatal to both species, and smaller animals die because drivers are going too fast to avoid them. If you see an injured animal and are able to help it without putting yourself in danger, you'll find a phalanx of wildlife rehabilitators throughout the state to give it the care it needs.

The large number of deer in urban and rural areas makes them frequent victims of highway accidents. In clear weather when there's not much oncoming traffic, use your high beams so that you'll see them from farther away. If you see a deer cross the road in front of you, remember that they usually travel in small herds, and there may be several more nearby.

Road Etiquette

Certain informal rules of road etiquette apply in North Carolina, and they help make driving less stressful. North Carolina drivers willingly let other vehicles get in front of them, whether merging onto the highway or exiting a parking lot. Wave to say thanks when someone lets you in; positive reinforcement helps keep these habits alive. Folks will often wave at drivers in oncoming traffic on two-lane country roads, and there is an expectation of a quick wave from drivers and pedestrians as well. It's not a big production; simply lift two or three fingers off the steering wheel. A general rule of thumb is that if you're able to discern the facial features of someone outside your car, waving to that person is appropriate.

Drivers are legally obligated to pull over to let emergency vehicles pass. There's also an old tradition of pulling over to allow funeral processions to pass. Very few drivers are willing to merge into or cross a train of cars headed for a funeral, but in rural areas you will still see drivers pulling all the way off the road and waiting for a procession to pass before resuming driving. It's meant as a gesture of respect to the deceased and the mourners.

In all of these situations, safety should be the top priority. You don't need to wave or make eye contact with someone you feel is threatening, and don't pull off the road if there's no safe place to do so. But if you show courtesy to other drivers when you're able, you'll find that traffic karma will work its way back around to you when it's needed.

BUS

Municipal bus services operate in larger towns and some of the more popular tourist areas. The state **Department of Transportation** (www.ncdot.gov/nctransit) maintains information on the state's 99 public transportation systems, including those that serve rural counties.

BICYCLE

Before the Wright brothers made history as the first aviators, they were bicycle men. With its temperate climates, abundance of scenic roads, and full spectrum of terrain, North Carolina is bicycling heaven. There are hundreds of organized bicycling events every year, many of them in support of charities, and they welcome participants from all over. The most popular bike events are held spring to fall, including a six-day Ocracoke Vacation Tour from New Bern to the tip of the Outer Banks, regular scenic rides through wine country, and rides along the Blue Ridge that include a five-day bicycling vacation starting in Blowing Rock.

Each month except December has as many as a dozen public cycling events, including January's New Year's Day Breakfast Ride in Jacksonville, February's Frostbite Tour in Raleigh, and March's Rumba on the Lumber 5K Run and Bike Ride in Lumberton. In April there's the annual Circle-the-Bald Bike Ride, starting in Hayesville, and in May,

Wilkesboro's Burn 24 Hour Challenge, a team relay endurance challenge. June has bicycling events as part of the North Carolina Blueberry Festival in Burgaw; July has North Wilkesboro's Hurt, Pain, and Agony Century Race; and August has a Beginner Skills Bicycling Camp in Asheville. In late September is the state-spanning Annual Mountains to the Coast Ride that even goes to the islands of the Outer Banks by ferry; approximately 1,000 cyclists take part. In October there's Rutherfordton's Tour de Pumpkin, and in November, the North Carolina Horse Country Tour takes place. For a full roster of routes, trails, and events, see the **Traveling by Bicycle** page maintained by the North Carolina Department of Transportation (www.ncdot.gov).

Baggage cars on **Amtrak**'s *Piedmont* trains are equipped with bicycle racks; call 800/872-7245 to reserve bike space on a train. You can also take your bicycle on any of the seven **North Carolina Ferries** (800/293-3779, www.ncdot.gov/ferry).

TRAIN

North Carolina has good rail connections among the major cities in the central part of the state. **Amtrak** (800/872-7245, www.amtrak.com) serves North Carolina with its *Silver, Carolinian, Crescent,* and *Palmetto* trains; cities served include Raleigh and Durham, High Point, Winston-Salem, Gastonia, Kannapolis, and Charlotte. *Piedmont* trains connect Raleigh to Charlotte twice daily with stops in several Piedmont towns in between.

FERRY

For hundreds of years, ferries were a crucial link between points on North Carolina's coast, and they still provide an essential service today. The **North Carolina Department of Transportation's Ferry Division** (877/293-3779, www.ncdot.gov/ferry) operates seven primary ferry routes along the coast. All ferries have restrooms, and some can accommodate cars and allow pets. Commercial ferries also operate throughout the coastal region.

Conduct and Customs

GREETINGS

Common courtesy, such as saying "please" and "thank you," being deferential to the elderly, and demonstrating concern for others, is hardly particular to the South. No matter where you're from, chances are your parents raised you to "act like folks," as people say here. The difference is that in North Carolina and elsewhere in the South, manners are somewhat more ritualized.

If you're unfamiliar with Southern ways, the thing you may find strangest is the friendliness of strangers. When passing a stranger on the sidewalk or in a corridor, riding together in an elevator, or even washing hands in the restroom, eye contact and a quick greeting are usually in order. Most common greetings are "Hey," "How you doing," and "How you," spoken as a statement rather than a question. The reply is usually equally casual: "Doing good, how about you," pronounced with just four syllables, "Doin' good, 'bout you," again spoken as a statement rather than a question. Often that's the end of the conversation, although passengers on elevators sometimes wish each other a good day when one gets out. In these encounters, eye contact needn't be lingering, there's no expectation of false pleasantries, and there is certainly no obligation to engage someone who makes you uncomfortable.

It's standard courtesy in a retail or similarly casual transaction to inquire as to the well-being of the person serving you. It takes little time, especially when delivered in the spoken shorthand most Southerners use. For instance, a cashier at McDonalds in another part of the country might greet you with "What would you like?" or simply wait for your order and not speak until asking for your money. The transaction here would more likely start with the "How you," "Doin' good, 'bout you," exchange. With that two- or three-second dialogue, a bit of human warmth and mutual respect is shared.

It's expected that people hold doors open for each other and thank each other for doing so. In addressing someone elderly that you don't know well, the standard courtesy is to use a title, Mr. or Ms., with the last name, or in friendlier situations, Mr. or Ms. with the first name. The South was way ahead of the curve in adopting the "Ms." designation;

Southerners have always pronounced both "Mrs." and "Miss" as "miz." North Carolinians will likely address you as "ma'am" or "sir" regardless of your age; it doesn't mean they think you're old.

TIPPING

Besides restaurant servers, tip motel and hotel housekeeping staff, bartenders, cab drivers, bellhops, redcaps, valet parking staff, and other service workers. Standard tipping rates are 20 percent for meals, 15 percent for a taxi ride, and $1 per piece of luggage for a redcap or porter, although tipping extra for good service is always gracious and appropriate.

Travel Tips

TRAVELERS OF COLOR

North Carolina is a predominantly white state, with just a touch over 70 percent of our population of 10.44 million identifying as white. Nearly a quarter, 22 percent, identify as Black, 9.8 percent as Latino, 2.3 percent as Asian, and 1.6 percent as Native American. Generally, more rural areas tend to have higher populations of white residents, lower concentrations of other races and ethnicities, and more conservative worldviews. The urban areas—the cities and communities with large university or college presences—are more diverse and politically liberal.

Visitors of color will find themselves welcome and warmly received in every part of the state, though I can't say they'll find every individual in every community welcoming them with open arms. The unfortunate truth is that too many North Carolinians take pride in flying the flag of the Confederate army and espousing political sentiments that aren't in keeping with the richness and diversity that makes the United States great. Fortunately, these troubling truths do not make the state unsafe for visitors. There are no significant instances of violence against visitors or in general.

In Asheville, the **Racial Justice Coalition** (www.rjcavl.org) maintains a list of organizations working on race- and equality-based issues. These include the Asheville-Buncombe NAACP, which maintains an active social media presence; SONG, an acronym for **Southerners on New Ground** (www.southernersonnewground.org); and the **ACLU of Western North Carolina** (www.acluofnorthcarolina.org). The North Carolina Chapter of the **NAACP** (866/626-2227, www.naacpnc.org) has resources in every corner of the state.

LGBTQIA+ TRAVELERS

North Carolina offers no legal protection against discrimination based on sexual orientation or gender identity, and, like in most states, hate-crimes statutes do not address violence targeting victims because of their sexual orientation or gender identity. Despite all this, don't close the book on North Carolina. While some laws may be retrogressive, the people are not; much of North Carolina is LGBTQIA+-friendly.

Despite being a red state, North Carolina has a strong purple streak. Metropolitan areas have active and open queer communities with numerous organizations and social groups, publications, human rights advocacy services, and community centers. Like anywhere in the United States, smaller and more rural communities are less likely to be gay-friendly, although there are exceptions and pleasant surprises. As a general rule, a same-sex couple will attract little attention holding hands on Durham's 9th Street, Asheville's Patton Avenue, or Weaver Street in Carrboro, but they may not be received warmly at Big Al's Shuckin' Shack in Back Water Creek (not a real place, but you get the idea).

Gay, lesbian, bisexual, and transgender travelers planning to visit North Carolina can learn a great deal about community resources and activities at QNotes (www.q-notes.com), North Carolina Pride (www.ncpride.org), and NC Gay Travel (http://ncgaytravel.com).

SENIOR TRAVELERS

North Carolina has attracted a tremendous number of retirees in recent years, especially in the mountains and coast. It's also an increasingly popular destination for older travelers. For those who want to visit the state through organized programs, Road Scholar (www.roadscholar.org) is a great choice. Tours and classes are available throughout the state; the offerings in the mountains are particularly rich, with a great variety of courses and hands-on workshops about Appalachian culture and crafts. The North Carolina chapter of AARP (866/389-5650, www.states.aarp.org) is a good resource for senior issues and information.

VisitNC (800/847-4862, www.visitnc.com) can also answer questions about activities and accessibility.

WOMEN TRAVELING ALONE

Women from other parts of the country might find male strangers' friendliness a little disconcerting, but keep in mind that while some of them may be flirting with you, it's just as likely that they are simply being courteous. When a Southern man holds a door open for you, offers to help you carry something, or even calls you "honey," "darlin'," or "dear heart," it usually implies no ulterior motives and isn't intended to be condescending; he's probably just showing that he was raised up right. Again, manners should never preclude safety, so if some sketchy character is coming on to you in a way that gives you the creeps, trust your instincts.

TRAVELERS WITH DISABILITIES

Access North Carolina (800/689-9090, TDD 919/733-5924, www.ncdhhs.gov) is an excellent up-to-date guide on the accessibility of hundreds of cultural, recreational, historical, environmental, and commercial sites of interest and a goldmine for travel planning. Download a copy or phone to ask for the current edition, published by the state Department of Health and Human Services. The guide is set up by region and county, and sites and venues are described and rated in terms of accessibility.

Health and Safety

CRIME

As nice a place as North Carolina is, it's not immune to crime. Common sense about safety applies, particularly for women. Lock your doors immediately when you get into the car, park in well-lit areas as close as possible to your destination, and don't hesitate to ask a security guard or other trustworthy type to see you to your car. Don't carry too much cash on you. Pepper spray might save your life if you're attacked, whether by a person or by a bear.

Note that 911 emergency phone service is available everywhere in the state, but cell phone signals are not dependable everywhere. The deep mountains and more remote parts of western North Carolina and isolated stretches of the coast are more likely to have cell-phone dead zones.

SPECIAL WEATHER CONCERNS
Hurricanes

Hurricanes are a perennial danger, but luckily there tends to be plenty of warning when one is approaching. The Atlantic Hurricane season runs June-November, but North Carolina generally sees the highest hurricane activity late in the season, in September-October. Evacuation orders should always be heeded, even if they are voluntary. It's also a good idea to leave sooner rather than later to avoid being trapped in traffic when the storm hits. The state **Department of Crime Control and Public Safety** (www.nccrimecontrol. org) posts a map online every year showing evacuation routes. You'll also see evacuation routes marked along the highways.

Tornadoes

Tornadoes can happen in any season and have killed people here in recent years. Pay close attention to tornado watches and warnings, and don't take chances: Find a safe place to shelter until the danger is over.

Rip Currents

More than 100 people die every year on U.S. beaches because of rip currents. Also called riptides, these dangerous currents can occur on any beach and can be very difficult to identify by sight. In rip current conditions, channels of water flow swiftly out toward deep water, and even if you are standing in relatively shallow water, you can suddenly be swept under and out into deep water. Rip current safety tips are available on the National Oceanic and Atmospheric Administration's **National Weather Service** (www.ripcurrents.noaa.gov). Among their advice: "Don't fight the current. Swim out of the current, and then to shore. If you can't escape, float or tread water. If you need help, call or wave for assistance." Heed riptide warnings, and try to swim within sight of a lifeguard. Even good swimmers can drown in a rip current, so if you have any doubts about your swimming abilities or water conditions, play it safe and stay close to shore.

ANIMAL THREATS

There are a handful of dangerous creatures across the state, ranging in size from microscopic to monstrous, that can pose risks to health and safety. Be on the lookout for mean bugs: **Ticks** can carry Lyme disease and Rocky Mountain spotted fever, both serious and lingering conditions. Most likely to climb on you if you are walking through brush or bushes but liable to be lurking about anywhere, ticks come in many sizes and shapes, from barely visible pinpoint-size to that thing that looks like a grape hanging off your dog's neck. Wear insect repellent if you're going to be tramping around outside, and check your body and your travel companions thoroughly—your clothing as well as your skin—for stowaways. They'll attach themselves to any soft surface on your body, but they particularly like people's heads, often latching on to the scalp an inch or so

Coronavirus in North Carolina

At the time of writing in 2022, North Carolina had mostly stabilized from the effects of the coronavirus, but the situation is constantly evolving.

Now more than ever, Moon encourages readers to be courteous and ethical in their travel. Be respectful to residents and mindful of the evolving situation in your chosen destination when planning your trip. **Get vaccinated** if your health allows, and if possible, test regularly before, during, and after your trip to ensure you continue to test negative for Covid-19.

On the whole, North Carolina weathered the coronavirus storm well, with widespread—but not total—mask use, social distancing, and reduced hours/capacity for businesses; the state's appetite for vaccines and boosters varied (with mask and vaccine use drawn roughly along political and urban/rural lines), but today most residents are vaccinated and boosted. Predictably, the hospitality industry was hit hard by quarantines and shutdowns forcing the closure of smaller businesses and the delay of new business openings, but also impacting staffing at hotels, restaurants, breweries, bars, and more (a problem that endures today).

LOCAL CONDITIONS AND RESTRICTIONS

Check local websites for **local restrictions** and the overall health status of your destination and your point of origin. If you're traveling to or from a Covid-19 hotspot, or anticipate potential cancellations or quarantine requirements, you may want to reconsider your trip.

Some destinations **may require proof of vaccination** or a recent, negative Covid test result before arrival; other tests and potentially a self-quarantine period, once you've arrived; or proof of a negative test to re-enter your original point of departure. You may also be required to wear a mask and/or provide proof of vaccination or a negative Covid test to enter indoor businesses such as restaurants, bars, and museums. For proof of a negative Covid test, a PCR test is often required. It's a good idea to research places that offer tests in your destination, and possibly make some testing appointments, before your trip.

TRAVEL REQUIREMENTS

If you plan to fly, **check with your airline** and the destination's health authority for updated travel requirements. Some airlines may be taking more steps than others to help you travel safely. Check their websites for more information before buying your ticket, and consider an early or late flight to limit exposure. Flights may be more infrequent, with increased cancellations.

At present, mask requirements for visitors are few and far between. Airlines and airports are following CDC guidance and internal policies, meaning that masks are optional for travelers, and on public transportation, it's much the same. Many rideshare and public transportation drivers and employees will wear masks, but they're not required for you.

PLANNING YOUR TRIP

Check the website of any venues you wish to patronize to confirm opening hours and to learn about any specific visitation requirements, such as testing, mask, and vaccination policies; mandatory reservations; or limited occupancy. Check Google, the venue's website, and even their social media to get the most up-to-date information on hours and whether they're open. And when in doubt, reach out to a business and ask; most are responsive to queries about their hours over social media.

behind the ears. If you find a tick on you or on a human or canine companion, don't remove it roughly, no matter how freaked out you are. Yanking can leave the tick's head buried in your skin, increasing the risk of infection. Grasp the tick in a pinching motion, and pull slowly but firmly. You may have to hang on for several moments, but eventually it will decide to let go. Dab the bite with antiseptic, and over the next several weeks be alert for a

More than ever, it's a good idea to plan your meals and accommodations and **make reservations** well in advance. You may want to consider restaurants with outdoor dining options picnic areas and parks for to-go meals, or find accommodations where you can cook meals on your own (which is another great way to connect with your destination). Small towns and out-of-the-way destinations (like the villages and hideaways on the coast, along the Blue Ridge Parkway, and in the deep mountains) continue to have issues with staffing at restaurants, bars, and similar businesses, so arrive early, be patient, and be flexible with your plans. Service disruptions and difficulty landing a table isn't limited to small businesses, though, and it's possible you'll experience these in cities and at typically well-staffed destinations. For those must-see places and must-eat restaurants, do yourself a favor and make reservations before you arrive.

Expect general disruptions. Events may be postponed or cancelled. Some tours and venues may require reservations, enforce limits on the number of guests, operate during different hours than the ones listed, or be closed entirely. Be diligent and continue to research all the way up to your time of departure, as things are likely to change. Across most of North Carolina's outdoor destinations—our beaches, state and national parks, and in forests and on trails—you'll find increased use, which means limited parking and more folks sharing the great outdoors with you.

WHAT TO PACK

Pack **hand sanitizer,** a **thermometer,** and plenty of **face masks**. Though cloth masks may be sufficient for local requirements, a well-fitting N95, KN95, or KF94 mask is generally considered more effective at reducing the risk of transmission of Covid-19. If possible, stock up on at-home rapid tests to take throughout your travels.

Be prepared for possible closures and reduced services over the course of your travels. Consider packing snacks, bottled water, a cooler, or anything else you might need to limit the number of stops along your route.

RESOURCES

- **World Health Organization:** https://www.who.int/emergencies/diseases/novel-coronavirus-2019/travel-advice

- **CDC:** https://www.cdc.gov/coronavirus/2019-ncov/travelers

- **International Air Transport Organization:** https://www.iatatravelcentre.com/world.php

- **U.S. State Department:** https://travel.state.gov/content/travel/en/traveladvisories/ea/covid-19-information.html

- **New York Times Coronavirus Map:** https://www.nytimes.com/interactive/2020/world/coronavirus-maps.html

- **North Carolina Department of Health and Human Services COVID-19 information page:** https://covid19.ncdhhs.gov

- **State of North Carolina COVID-19 information hub:** https://www.nc.gov/covid19

bull's-eye-shaped irritation around the bite and for flu-like symptoms such as fever, achiness, malaise, and fatigue. If you have any of these signs, visit your doctor for a blood test.

Mosquitoes can carry West Nile virus, La Crosse encephalitis, and eastern equine encephalitis. Wear insect repellent and clothing that covers your arms and legs to avoid bites. Although not disease vectors, **fire ants** are among the state's most feared insects. It's easy to stumble onto one of their nests, and before you realize what you've stepped in, they can be swarming up your legs and biting you. Certainly this is a painful and frightening experience, but it's also potentially dangerous if you're allergic. There have been documented cases in recent years of adult humans being swarmed and killed by fire ants. Watch where you step, and keep an eye out for areas of disturbed ground and turned-up soil. Sometimes their nests look like conventional anthills, sometimes like messy piles of dirt, and other times just soft spots on the ground.

Another reason to mind where you tread: snakes. The vast majority of snakes in North Carolina are harmless and shy, but we do have a few pit vipers. **Copperheads** are quite common in every part of the state and in wooded or semi-wooded terrain—even in backyards, where they can lurk in bushes and leaf piles, under porches and in storage sheds, and in the walls of a house. They have a gorgeous pattern of light and dark brown splotches, which makes them incredibly difficult to spot against the ground in fall. Copperheads are usually less than three feet long. Their bite is poisonous but usually not fatal.

Found in the eastern half of the state and up into the Sandhills, **cottonmouths**—also called water moccasins—are very dangerous. They range in color from reddish brown to black, can grow up to 5.5 feet long, and are easily mistaken for harmless water snakes (and vice versa). They sometimes venture into the woods and fields, but cottonmouths are most commonly seen on or near water. Be especially careful walking along creek beds or in riverside brush. When threatened, they display the inside of their mouths, which are a startling and beautiful cottony white. Their bite is potentially lethal.

Coral snakes are endangered in North Carolina, but if you're going to be in the woods in the southeastern quarter of the state, keep an eye out. These jewel-toned snakes are generally small and slim, rarely more than a couple of feet long. Like the harmless scarlet king snake and scarlet snake, coral snakes have alternating bands of red, yellow, and black. The way to tell coral snakes from their harmless kin is to note the order of colors. On coral snakes, the yellow bands separate the black and the red, whereas on their imitators, red and black touch. An adage advises, "Red and black, friend of Jack; red and yellow, kill a fellow." Coral snakes can also be identified by their sinister black snouts, making them look like cartoon burglars, whereas scarlet snakes and scarlet king snakes have red clown noses. That's a lot to remember in that instant of panic when you notice a coil of red and yellow and black stripes at your feet looking up at you testily. Rather than stopping to figure out if the snake is friend or foe, it's better just to quickly step away. Coral snakes' venom works on its prey's respiratory system, and it can kill humans. They're cousins of cobras and are some of the most beautiful snakes in these parts, but locals fear them more intensely than the huge, lumpy-headed, tusky-fanged vipers that appear more threatening.

There are also three poisonous native rattlesnakes: The **eastern diamondback rattlesnake** is the largest of rattlesnakes and can grow to nearly six feet long and as fat around as an adult human's arm. They are extremely dangerous—powerful enough to catch and eat rabbits, and willing, if provoked, to kill a person. Eastern diamondbacks are rare but can be found in the southeastern sandy swamp counties. Also large are **canebrake rattlers,** more formally known as timber rattlers. They are found throughout the state, including the mountains. Their bite can be fatal to humans. To make them even scarier, they too can grow to nearly six feet in length, and in cold weather they like to congregate in large numbers to hibernate. **Pygmy rattlesnakes** are found along the state's coastline, up into the Sandhills, and around Crowder's Mountain. Generally up to about 1.5 feet long, pygmies are also venomous.

Alligators are incredible creatures, scaly submarines that can exceed 15 feet snout to tail (females generally mature at around 10 feet) and can weigh 1,000 pounds, with a steel-trap maw of 75-80 fangs. They are found through much of eastern North Carolina, as far north as Merchants Millpond State Park near the Virginia border, but they are most common from Wilmington south. You don't have to trek into the depths of a swamp to see gators; they like to sun themselves on golf courses, next to roadside drainage ditches, and even in yards that adjoin fresh water. Their behavior is deceptive: they seem to spend 90 percent of their time in a motionless stupor, but they can awaken and whirl around to grab you before you have time to back away. They also spend much of their time submerged, sometimes entirely underwater, and more often drifting just below the surface with only their nostrils and brow ridges visible. Be aware of floating logs, as they may have teeth attached. Alligators will gladly eat dogs that venture too close, so it goes without saying that small children should never be allowed to wander alone near potential alligator habitats. An adult alligator can kill an adult human, and even the cute little ones will be only too happy to help themselves to your foot, so don't tempt fate for the sake of a photo or a closer look. If you're determined to get a close-up picture, visit one of the state's aquariums.

Bear attacks are rare and usually defensive, but considering that the creatures can weigh up to 800 pounds, caution would seem to be indicated. They are present in the woods in various parts of the state, especially up in the mountains and in the deep swamps and pocosins along the coast. They're quite shy and apt to gallop into the brush if they see a human coming. They will investigate potential meals, though, so securing your food when camping is crucial. If your car is nearby, lock the food in it; otherwise, hoist it into a tree with a rope, too high to reach from the ground and out of reach from the tree trunk. The National Park Service recommends the following course of action if a bear approaches you. First, try backing away slowly. If the bear follows, stand your ground. If it continues to menace you, try to scare it: Make yourself look bigger and

more threatening by standing on a rock or next to your companions. Try waving sticks and throwing rocks. In the extremely unlikely event that you actually find yourself in hand-to-hand combat with a bear, remember the Park Service's advice to "fight back aggressively with any available object." Your chances of seeing a bear in North Carolina, much less being threatened by one, are pretty slim.

DISEASES AND NATURAL THREATS

Among the invisible villains here is **giardia,** a single-celled protozoan parasite that can be contracted by drinking untreated water. Hikers and campers should avoid drinking from streams unless they first boil the water vigorously for at least one minute. Filtering water with a filter of 0.1-1 micron absolute pore size or chemically treating it with iodine or chlorine is less reliable than thorough boiling.

There's a fairly high incidence of **rabies** in North Carolina's raccoons, bats, foxes, groundhogs, and skunks. If you're bringing a pet into the state, be sure that its vaccinations are up to date. If you plan to go hiking with your dog, it may even be wise to bring a copy of its rabies vaccination certificate in case you have to prove its immunity. If you are bitten by a wild animal, seek medical help immediately, even if you're out in the woods. Rabies is deadly to humans, and it's extremely important to start treatment immediately.

HEALTH PRECAUTIONS
Emergencies

As elsewhere the United States, calling 911 in North Carolina will summon medical help, police, or firefighters. On the highway, blue road signs marked with an "H" point the way to hospitals, but if you're experiencing a potentially critical emergency, it's best to call 911 and let the ambulance come to you. There are plenty of rural places in the state where cellphone coverage is spotty to nonexistent, so if you have a medical condition from which an emergency could arise, keep this in mind.

Summer Weather

Heat, humidity, and air pollution often combine in the summer to create dangerous conditions for children, the elderly, and people with severe heart and lung conditions. Even if you're young and healthy, don't take chances in the heat. Carry drinking water with you, avoid exertion and being outside in the hottest part of the day, and stay in the shade. Even young, healthy people can die from the heat. Remember that even if it doesn't feel very warm outside, children and pets are in grave danger when left in cars. Temperatures can rise to fatal levels very quickly inside closed vehicles, even when it's not terribly hot outside.

Information and Services

MONEY

For international travelers, currency-exchange services can be found in the big cities at some major banks and at currency-exchange businesses. Numerous money-transfer services, from old familiars like Western Union to a multitude of overseas companies, are easily accessible. The easiest place to wire or receive money is at a grocery store—most have Western Union or a proprietary wiring service—or at a bank. Banking hours vary by location and chain, but most are closed on Sunday and federal holidays. ATMs are located at most bank branches as well as in many grocery stores and convenience stores.

COMMUNICATIONS AND MEDIA
Newspapers and Radio

North Carolina has several major newspapers, the largest of which is the Pulitzer Prize-winning *Charlotte Observer* (www.charlotteobserver.com). In addition to the print edition, the *Observer* has extensive online-only content for travelers. The Raleigh *News & Observer* (www.newsobserver.com) serves the Triangle area and much of central Carolina. Other prominent newspapers include the Wilmington *Star-News* (www.starnewsonline.com) and the Asheville *Citizen-Times* (www.citizen-times.com). Alternative papers like the *Mountain Xpress* (www.mountainx.com) and the Triangle-area *Independent Weekly* (www.indyweek.com), available in print and online, cover the state's counterculture. Among the many local and regional radio stations are a number of NPR affiliates. There are few parts of the state where you won't be able to tune in to a clear NPR signal.

Magazines

Our State magazine (www.ourstate.com) is a widely distributed monthly that tells the stories of people, places, and history across North Carolina. As a travel resource, it will give you a feel for the people you're likely to encounter, but it will give you an even better idea of places to eat and towns you may not have thought to visit. Their website has an extensive collection of archived stories arranged by topic. In most larger cities in North Carolina it isn't hard to find magazines covering the local arts scene or guiding area parents to the best the town has to offer for kids. Look at news racks outside grocery stores and on street corners to pick up free publications like *North Brunswick Magazine* in and around Brunswick County; *Wilma!* And *Wrightsville Beach Magazine* in Wilmington; and *O. Henry Magazine* in Greensboro. Online, there's no better resource than *NC Tripping* (www.nctripping.com), a travel-centric website run by dear friends.

Internet Access

Internet access is widespread. Coffee shops are always a good place to find Wi-Fi, usually free but sometimes for a fee. A few small towns have free municipal wireless access. Most chain motels and major hotels offer free wireless access, and smaller hotels and bed-and-breakfasts often do too. This is true for some remote areas as well. The deep mountains are the most difficult place to get a reliable internet connection, but you'll probably be able to get online at your place of lodging or the coffee shop in town.

Cell Phones

Cell phone coverage is not consistent across North Carolina. You'll get a signal in all of the cities and most areas in between. You may hit dropout spots in central North Carolina, but there aren't many. On the other hand, service can be spotty in the eastern and western parts of the state. Up in the mountains, you may have a good signal on one side of a ridge and none on the other. Driving along the Blue Ridge Parkway, you'll find that signals come and go. This is also true on the coast and in rural eastern North Carolina. Along the sounds, and certainly on the Outer Banks, there are plenty of areas where you could drive 20 miles before finding any reception. Spotty cell-phone coverage is a safety issue; if you're treed by a bear or run out of gas on a backwoods track, 911 may be unreachable.

MAPS AND VISITOR INFORMATION

Among the best sources for travel information in North Carolina is the state's tourism website, **VisitNC** (www.visitnc.com). They maintain an up-to-date list of festivals and events, tours and trails, and almost anything else you may want to know. Also excellent is the magazine *Our State* (www.ourstate.com), available at grocery stores, drugstores, and bookshops. Their website monitors upcoming events as well.

North Carolina Welcome Centers, located at several major highway entry points to the state, are sources for more free brochures and maps than one person could carry. They are located at the Virginia state line on I-77 near Mount Airy, on I-85 in Warren County, and on I-95 in Northampton County; at the Tennessee state line on I-26 in Madison County and on I-40 in Haywood County; and along the South Carolina state line on I-26 in Polk County, I-85 in Cleveland County, I-77 just outside Charlotte, and I-95 in Robeson County.

For basic planning, the maps on the VisitNC website will give you a good sense of the layout of the state and its major destinations. Many areas are experiencing rapid growth, particularly around Charlotte and the Triangle, so if your map is even a little out of date, you may not know about the newest bypass. For features like mountains, rivers, back roads, and small towns that don't change, atlas-style books of state maps are useful. My own favorite is DeLorme's *North Carolina Atlas & Gazetteer*.

Resources

Suggested Reading

TRAVEL

Daniels, Diane. *Farm Fresh North Carolina.* Chapel Hill: UNC Press, 2011. This guidebook will help you find the perfect place to pick apples, cut Christmas trees, visit a pumpkin patch, pick a bushel of blueberries, and shop at every farmers market across the state. You'll find recipes from chefs and farmers as well.

Duncan, Barbara, and Brett Riggs. *Cherokee Heritage Trails.* Chapel Hill: UNC Press, 2003; online companion at www.cherokeeheritage.org. A fascinating guide to both the historic and present-day home of the Eastern Band of the Cherokee in North Carolina, Tennessee, and Georgia, from ancient mounds and petroglyphs to modern-day arts co-ops and sporting events.

Eubanks, Georgann. *Literary Trails of the North Carolina Mountains: A Guidebook.* Chapel Hill: UNC Press, 2007. This book and its companion books, *Literary Trails of the North Carolina Piedmont: A Guidebook,* 2010, and *Literary Trails of Eastern North Carolina: A Guidebook,* 2013, introduce fans of Southern literature to the places that produced and inspired various scribes. Also included are the best bookstores and book events across the state.

Fussell, Fred, and Steve Kruger. *Blue Ridge Music Trails of North Carolina: A Guide to Music Sites, Artists, and Traditions of the Mountains and Foothills.* Chapel Hill: UNC Press, 2013. A guide to destinations—festivals, restaurants, oprys, church singings—in the North Carolina mountains where authentic bluegrass, old-time, and sacred music can be experienced by visitors. An accompanying audio CD allows you to continue to hear the music. The exceptional photography by Cedric N. Chatterley in this book and in *Cherokee Heritage Trails*—reproduced in full color—and the depth of context conveyed make these two guides worth buying even if you're not touring the region.

NC Tripping. www.nctripping.com. Useful, constantly updated, and focused on the best of what the Tar Heel State has to offer, this is a great resource for visitors. Follow Carl and Christina and their family across the state. Responsive in their community on social media, they are always fun to run into on the road.

North Carolina Atlas and Gazetteer. Yarmouth, ME: DeLorme, 2012. Since I was a Boy Scout, I have always been partial to DeLorme's state atlases. This series represents in great detail the topography and other natural features of an area, giving far more useful and comprehensive information than the standard highway map.

Our State. www.ourstate.com. For a lively and informative look at North Carolina destinations and the cultural quirks and treasures you may find in your travels, *Our*

State magazine is one of the best resources around. The magazine is easy to find, sold at most bookstores and even on grocery store and drugstore magazine racks. It covers arts, nature, folklore, history, scenery, sports, and lots of food, all from a traveler's perspective.

HISTORY AND CULTURE

Cecelski, David. *The Waterman's Song: Slavery and Freedom in Maritime North Carolina.* Chapel Hill: UNC Press, 2001. A marvelous treatment of the African American heritage of resistance in eastern North Carolina, describing how the region's rivers and sounds were passages to freedom for many enslaved people.

Powell, William S. *North Carolina: A History.* Chapel Hill: UNC Press, 1988. A readable, concise account of our fascinating and varied past.

Powell, William S., and Jay Mazzocchi, editors. *Encyclopedia of North Carolina.* Chapel Hill: UNC Press, 2006. A fantastic compendium of all sorts of North Carolina history, letters, and politics. If you can lift this mammoth book, you'll learn about everything from Carolina basketball to presidential elections to ghosts.

Setzer, Lynn. *Tar Heel History on Foot: Great Walks through 400 Years of North Carolina's Fascinating Past.* Chapel Hill: UNC Press, 2013. This book sends you on a series of short walks in all parts of the state—coastal and mountain, city and country, historic sites and state parks—to discover the history of the state. The walks are arranged by theme and location, making it simple to find one near you.

Wright, David, and David Zoby. *Fire on the Beach: Recovering the Lost Story of Richard Etheridge and the Pea Island Lifesavers.* New York: Oxford University Press, 2002. The riveting tale of the first African American captain of a U.S. Life-Saving Station and his all-African American crew. Spanning the time from just before the Civil War to the turn of the 20th century, it's a fascinating look at life for enslaved people and the formerly enslaved on the Outer Banks.

SPORTS

Blythe, Will. *To Hate Like This Is to Be Happy Forever: A Thoroughly Obsessive, Intermittently Uplifting, and Occasionally Unbiased Account of the Duke-North Carolina Basketball Rivalry.* New York: Harper, 2007. A highly entertaining book about the hatred between partisans of UNC and Duke, describing how the famous basketball rivalry brings out the best and worst in the fans.

Thompson, Neal. *Driving with the Devil: Southern Moonshine, Detroit Wheels, and the Birth of NASCAR.* New York: Broadway Books, 2008. The creation story of a great sport, the rise of stock-car racing from moonshiners' getaway wheels to a multibillion-dollar industry.

Internet Resources

NEWSPAPERS

North Carolina newspapers have unusually rich online content and are great resources for travel planning.

Charlotte Observer
www.charlotteobserver.com
This website is packed with information about the arts, food, newcomer issues, and more.

Raleigh News & Observer
www.newsobserver.com
Raleigh's paper of record.

Asheville Citizen-Times
www.citizen-times.com
A good online edition for this Asheville-based paper.

Mountain Xpress
www.mountainx.com
Also covering the Asheville area, with a politically progressive and artistically countercultural bent—much like Asheville itself.

Mountain Times
http://mountaintimes.com
Weekly newspaper covering Boone and the High Country.

Independent Weekly
www.indyweek.com
A great source for the Triangle on the local music scene, politics, food, and more.

Fayetteville Observer
http://fayobserver.com
News and culture from Fayetteville and the surrounding towns.

StarNews
www.starnewsonline.com
Providing daily news coverage of Wilmington and neighboring towns.

Outer Banks Sentinel
www.obsentinel.com
News and events pertinent to Outer Banks towns.

ARTS AND CULTURE

North Carolina's arts and history have an ever-growing online dimension, telling the story of the state in ways that paper and ink simply can't.

North Carolina Folklife Institute
www.ncfolk.org
The website will fill you in on the many organizations across the state that promote traditional music, crafts, and folkways. You'll also find a calendar of folk life-related events in North Carolina and travel itineraries for weekends exploring Core Sound, the Seagrove potteries, and Cherokee heritage in the Smokies.

NCFood
www.ncfolk.org/category/food
This wonderful food blog, maintained by the Folklife Institute, features articles about the culinary back roads of the state.

North Carolina Arts Council
www.ncarts.org
The Arts Council provides information about performing arts, literature, cultural trails, galleries, and fun happenings.

North Carolina ECHO
www.ncecho.org
ECHO stands for "Exploring Cultural Heritage Online," and this great site has links to hundreds of online exhibits and brick-and-mortar museums.

Carolina Music Ways
www.carolinamusicways.org
A lively guide to the extremely varied musical traditions of the North Carolina Piedmont.

Blue Ridge Heritage Area
www.blueridgeheritage.com
This resource has a huge amount of mountain-area travel information and an ever-growing directory of traditional artists of all kinds in the Carolina mountains.

Southern Highland Craft Guild
www.southernhighlandguild.org
An Asheville-based regional arts giant with an extensive online guide to craftspeople throughout the region.

Creative Loafing Charlotte
http://clclt.com
A creative, enlightening, and sometimes irreverent look at Charlotte life, art, culture, news, and events.

Thrillist Charlotte
www.thrillist.com/Charlotte
A hip millennial look at arts, culture, and happenings in Charlotte and across North Carolina.

Our State
www.ourstate.com
The online companion to this print publication provides expanded coverage of the history, people, food, and arts across North Carolina. An extensive archive of stories lets you look back several years for the best the state has to offer.

OUTDOORS
Great online resources exist for planning outdoor adventures in North Carolina, where rich arts and blockbuster sports are matched by natural resources.

North Carolina Sierra Club
http://nc2.sierraclub.org
Find information about upcoming hikes and excursions as well as an overview of the state's natural areas and environmental issues.

North Carolina Birding Trail
www.ncbirdingtrail.org
Covering bird-watching across the state, this site contains information about dozens of pristine locations and active flyways along the coast, in the Piedmont, and in the mountains.

Carolina Canoe Club
www.carolinacanoeclub.com
A clearinghouse of statewide canoeing resources.

Carolina Kayak Club
www.carolinakayakclub.org
A repository for flat-water kayaking information, resources, trails, and activities across the state.

CanoeNC
www.canoenc.org
A nice starting point for planning a flat-water paddling trip in eastern North Carolina.

North Carolina Sportsman
www.northcarolinasportsman.com
Covering hunting and fishing news, destinations, and seasonal trends across the state.

Friends of the Mountains-to-Sea Trail
www.ncmst.org
Find details, hike-planning tools, and resources for a day or longer on the 1,000-mile-long Mountains-to-Sea Trail that crosses North Carolina.

NC Hikes
www.nchikes.com
All things hiking-related, including trails in every corner of the state, books, and trip recommendations.

Index

A

Abrams Falls Trail: 452
accessibility: 524
Ackland Art Museum: 230
Actor's Theatre of Charlotte: 302
Admiral, The: 24, 406
Adventure Center of Asheville: 386, 394
adventure parks: Northern Blue Ridge 357; the
    Triangle 220; Wilmington and Cape Fear
    178–179
African American Cultural Trail of Greenville-Pitt
    County: 89
Airborne and Special Operations Museum: 185
Airlie Gardens: 144
air travel: 516–517
Alamance Battleground: 276
Alamance County: 276–277
Alexander Dickson House: 239
Allanstand Craft Shop: 384
Alligator River National Wildlife Refuge: 30, 32, 85
Alum Cave: 453
American Dance Festival: 224
American Tobacco Historic Campus: 217
American Tobacco Trail: 220
Amusement Center: 200
amusement/theme park: 83
Andrews Bald: 452
Andy Griffith Museum: 326
Andy Griffith Playhouse: 326
Andy Griffith's boyhood home: 326
Angeline's: 25, 310
Angry Troll Brewing: 334
animals: 496–499
anoles: 145
Antler Hill Village: 394
Appalachian Mountain Brewery: 345
Appalachian Ski Mountain: 343
Appalachian Trail: 23, 385, 447
AQUA Restaurant and Spa: 30, 49
aquariums: general discussion 32; Crystal Coast
    127; Outer Banks 55; Wilmington and Cape
    Fear 167–168
Archetype Brewing: 392, 405
Arch Rock: 453
Arsenal Park: 185
Art in Bloom: 30, 156
Art of Cool Fest: 224
Art on the Mountain: 340
arts: 510–513
Arts of the Albemarle: 76

Artsplosure: 207
Asheboro: 279–280
Asheville: 23–25, 26, 28, 206, 376–413; maps 374,
    374–379, 380, 399
Asheville and Southern Blue Ridge: 372–437;
    maps 374, 423
Asheville Art Museum: 24, 377
Asheville Ballet: 393
Asheville Brewery Tours: 392
Asheville Community Theatre: 393
Asheville Outdoor Center: 387
Asian Festival: 303
ATMs: 530
Attmore-Oliver House: 98, 100
ATV/OHC areas: Central Carolina 281; Crystal
    Coast 104–105; Wilmington and Cape Fear 186
auto travel: 517–521
Avalon Pier: 46
AvidXchange Music Factory: 303
Avon: 63
Avon Fishing Pier: 67, 69
Ayr Mount Historic Site: 239, 241
Azalea Festival: 149

B

Backing Up Classics Museum: 315
Backstreet Park Concert Series: 340
Bald Head Island: 32, 173–176
Bald Head Island Conservancy: 174
Balsam Falls Brewing: 481
Banktown: 303
Banner Elk: 350
Banner Elk Winery & Villa: 350
barbecue: 13, 22
Barbecue Festival: 25, 278–279
Bascom Lamar Lunsford "Minstrel of the
    Appalachians" Festival: 419
Bath: 86–87
BBQ Festival on the Neuse: 108
beach driving: 64, 66
beaches: Crystal Coast 104, 122, 124, 126, 127;
    Northern Blue Ridge 370; Outer Banks 40, 41,
    42, 62, 63, 64, 66; the Triangle 200; Wilmington
    and Cape Fear 141, 148, 163–164, 165, 166–167,
    173, 175, 176–177, 182
Bear Pen Gap Trail: 461
Beasley's Chicken + Honey: 29, 212
Beaufort: 33, 110–116; map 111
Beaufort Historic Site: 112, 114
Bechtler Museum of Modern Art: 25, 294

List of Maps

Photo Credits

Get inspired for your next adventure

Follow @**moonguides** on Instagram or
subscribe to our newsletter at **moon.com**

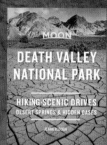

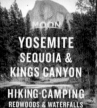

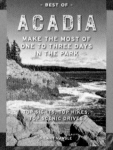

MOON

Plan your parks adventure!

USA RV ADVENTURES
25 EPIC ROUTES
BONNIE & GRANT SINCLAIR

MOON
USA NATIONAL PARKS
THE COMPLETE GUIDE TO ALL 63 PARKS
BECKY LOMAX

MOON
USA STATE by STATE
The Best Things to Do in Every State for Your Travel Bucket List

MOON
- BEST OF -
GRAND CANYON
MAKE THE MOST OF ONE TO THREE DAYS IN THE PARK
TOP SIGHTS, TOP HIKES, TOP SCENIC DRIVES
TIM HULL

MOON
- BEST OF -
YELLOWSTONE & GRAND TETON
MAKE THE MOST OF ONE TO THREE DAYS IN THE PARKS
TOP SIGHTS, TOP HIKES, TOP SCENIC DRIVES
BECKY LOMAX

MOON
- BEST OF -
YOSEMITE
MAKE THE MOST OF ONE TO THREE DAYS IN THE PARK
TOP SIGHTS, TOP HIKES, TOP SCENIC DRIVES
ANN MARIE BROWN

MOON
- BEST OF -
ZION & BRYCE
MAKE THE MOST OF ONE TO THREE DAYS IN THE PARKS
TOP SIGHTS, TOP HIKES, TOP SCENIC DRIVES
JUDY JEWELL & W. C. McRAE

ROAD TRIP GUIDES

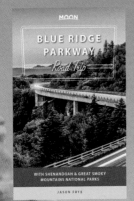

MOON
BLUE RIDGE PARKWAY
Road Trip

WITH SHENANDOAH & GREAT SMOKY
MOUNTAINS NATIONAL PARKS

JASON FRYE

MOON
CALIFORNIA
Road Trip

SAN FRANCISCO, YOSEMITE, LAS VEGAS,
GRAND CANYON, LOS ANGELES,
& THE PACIFIC COAST HIGHWAY

STUART THORNTON

MOON
NASHVILLE TO NEW ORLEANS
Road Trip

NATCHEZ TRACE PARKWAY • MEMPHIS •
TUPELO • MISSISSIPPI BLUES TRAIL

MARGARET LITTMAN

MOON
NEW ENGLAND
Road Trip

SEASIDE SPOTS, MAJESTIC MOUNTAINS &
FALL FOLIAGE, COZY GETAWAYS

MILES HOWARD

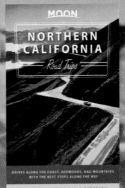

MOON
NORTHERN CALIFORNIA
Road Trips

DRIVES ALONG THE COAST, REDWOODS, AND MOUNTAINS
WITH THE BEST STOPS ALONG THE WAY

STUART THORNTON & KAYLA ANDERSON

MOON
OREGON TRAIL
Road Trip

HISTORIC SITES, SMALL TOWNS, AND
SCENIC LANDSCAPES ALONG THE LEGENDARY
WESTWARD ROUTE

KATRINA EMERY

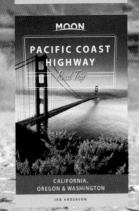

MOON
PACIFIC COAST HIGHWAY
Road Trip

CALIFORNIA,
OREGON & WASHINGTON

IAN ANDERSON

MOON
PACIFIC NORTHWEST
Road Trip

OUTDOOR ADVENTURES AND CREATIVE CITIES
FROM THE COAST TO THE MOUNTAINS

ALLISON WILLIAMS

MOON
ROUTE 66
Road Trip

JESSICA DUNHAM

MOON.COM | ROADTRIPUSA.COM

MOON

SOUTH FLORIDA & THE KEYS
Road Trip

WITH MIAMI, WALT DISNEY WORLD, TAMPA & THE EVERGLADES

JASON FERGUSON

MOON

SOUTHERN CALIFORNIA
Road Trip

DRIVES ALONG THE BEACHES, MOUNTAINS, AND DESERTS WITH THE BEST STOPS ALONG THE WAY

IAN ANDERSON

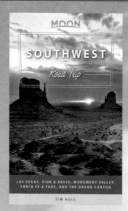

MOON

SOUTHWEST
Road Trip

LAS VEGAS, ZION & BRYCE, MONUMENT VALLEY, SANTA FE & TAOS, AND THE GRAND CANYON

TIM HULL

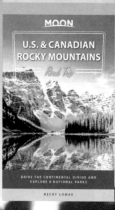

MOON

U.S. & CANADIAN ROCKY MOUNTAINS
Road Trip

DRIVE THE CONTINENTAL DIVIDE AND EXPLORE 9 NATIONAL PARKS

BECKY LOMAX

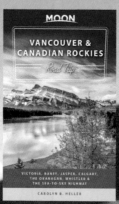

MOON

VANCOUVER & CANADIAN ROCKIES
Road Trip

VICTORIA, BANFF, JASPER, CALGARY, THE OKANAGAN, WHISTLER & THE SEA-TO-SKY HIGHWAY

CAROLYN B. HELLER

MOON

YELLOWSTONE TO GLACIER NATIONAL PARK
Road Trip

JACKSON HOLE, CODY, THE GRAND TETONS & THE ROCKY MOUNTAIN FRONT

CARTER G. WALKER

MOON

BASEBALL *Road Trips*

TIMOTHY MALCOLM

THE COMPLETE GUIDE TO ALL THE BALLPARKS, WITH BEER, BITES, AND SIGHTS NEARBY

the OPEN ROAD

50 BEST ROAD TRIPS *in the* USA

From Weekend Getaways to Cross-Country Adventures

JESSICA DUNHAM

MOON

Road Trip USA
25TH ANNIVERSARY EDITION

CROSS-COUNTRY ADVENTURES ON AMERICA'S TWO-LANE HIGHWAYS

Jamie Jensen

BAJA

CARTAGENA
& COLOMBIA'S
CARIBBEAN COAST

CHILE

COSTA RICA

ECUADOR
& THE GALÁPAGOS ISLANDS

TRIP OF A LIFETIME
MACHU PICCHU

OAXACA

YUCATÁN PENINSULA

MOON
Alaska

MOON
Arizona
& THE GRAND CANYON

MOON
Coastal Maine
WITH ACADIA NATIONAL PARK

MOON
Montana & Wyoming
WITH YELLOWSTONE, GRAND TETON, AND GLACIER NATIONAL PARKS

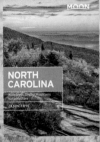
MOON
New Mexico

MOON
NORTH CAROLINA

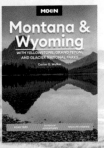
MOON
TENNESSEE

MOON
UTAH

BAHAMAS
MARIAH CAINE HOYLE

DOMINICAN REPUBLIC
LEBAWIT LILY GIRMA

JAMAICA
OLIVER HILL

PUERTO RICO
SUZANNE VAN ATTEN

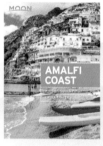
AMALFI COAST
LAURA THAYER

AMSTERDAM
BRUSSELS & BRUGES
KARLA ZIMMERMAN

EGYPT
SARAH SMIERCIAK

Greek Islands
& ATHENS

ICELAND
JENNA GOTTLIEB
WITH A ROAD TRIP ON THE RING ROAD

IRELAND
CAMILLE DeANGELIS

MOROCCO

NORMANDY & BRITTANY
CHRIS NEWENS
WITH MONT-SAINT MICHEL

PRAGUE, VIENNA & BUDAPEST
JENNIFER D. WALKER & AUBURN SCALLON

ROME,
FLORENCE & VENICE
ALEXEI COHEN

Scotland

SOUTHERN ITALY
LINDA SARRIS & LAURA THAYER
SICILY, PUGLIA, NAPLES & THE AMALFI COAST

AMSTERDAM
BRUSSELS & BRUGES

MOON
CANADIAN
ROCKIES
WITH BANFF & JASPER NATIONAL PARKS

SCENIC DRIVES · WILDLIFE
HIKING & SKIING

ANDREW HEMPSTEAD

MOON

COSTA
RICA

NIKKI SOLANO

MOON

EGYPT

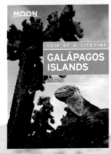

MOON

TRIP OF A LIFETIME

GALÁPAGOS
ISLANDS

MOON

Japan

MOON

TRIP OF A LIFETIME

MACHU
PICCHU

RYAN DUBE

MOON

MOROCCO

More Great Travel Guides from Moon

MOON

NEW
ZEALAND

JAMIE CHRISTIAN DESPLACES

MOON

NORMANDY
& BRITTANY

WITH MONT-SAINT MICHEL

MOON

OAXACA

MOON

PRAGUE, VIENNA
& BUDAPEST

MOON

ROME,
FLORENCE
& VENICE

MOON

Scotland

MOON

SOUTHERN
ITALY

SICILY, PUGLIA, NAPLES & THE AMALFI COAST

MOON

UTAH
With Zion, Bryce Canyon, Arches,
Capitol Reef & Canyonlands
National Parks

W. C. McRAE & JUDY JEWELS

MAP SYMBOLS

▦ Expressway	○ City/Town	✈ Airport	⚲ Golf Course
▦ Primary Road	◉ State Capital	✈ Airfield	Ⓟ Parking Area
▦ Secondary Road	⊛ National Capital	▲ Mountain	⬟ Archaeological Site
⬚ Unpaved Road	◉ Highlight	✦ Unique Natural Feature	⬧ Church
- - - Trail	★ Point of Interest		⬦ Gas Station
⋯ Ferry	● Accommodation	🝞 Waterfall	Glacier
✖ Railroad	▼ Restaurant/Bar	⬆ Park	Mangrove
▦ Pedestrian Walkway	■ Other Location	⬧ Trailhead	Reef
▥ Stairs	⬛ Campground	⛷ Skiing Area	Swamp

CONVERSION TABLES

°C = (°F - 32) / 1.8
°F = (°C x 1.8) + 32
1 inch = 2.54 centimeters (cm)
1 foot = 0.304 meters (m)
1 yard = 0.914 meters
1 mile = 1.6093 kilometers (km)
1 km = 0.6214 miles
1 fathom = 1.8288 m
1 chain = 20.1168 m
1 furlong = 201.168 m
1 acre = 0.4047 hectares
1 sq km = 100 hectares
1 sq mile = 2.59 square km
1 ounce = 28.35 grams
1 pound = 0.4536 kilograms
1 short ton = 0.90718 metric ton
1 short ton = 2,000 pounds
1 long ton = 1.016 metric tons
1 long ton = 2,240 pounds
1 metric ton = 1,000 kilograms
1 quart = 0.94635 liters
1 US gallon = 3.7854 liters
1 Imperial gallon = 4.5459 liters
1 nautical mile = 1.852 km

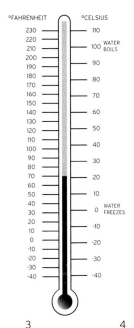

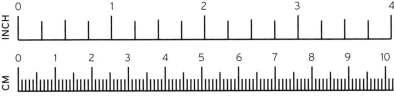

MOON NORTH CAROLINA

Avalon Travel
Hachette Book Group
1700 Fourth Street
Berkeley, CA 94710, USA
www.moon.com

Editor: Kimberly Ehart
Acquiring Editor: Nikki Ioakimedes
Series Manager: Kathryn Ettinger
Copy Editor: Christopher Church
Graphics and Production Coordinator: Rue Flaherty
Cover Design: Toni Tajima
Map Editor: Kat Bennett
Cartographers: Erin Greb, Natalie Higginbotham, John Culp, Stephanie Poulain
Indexer: Greg Jewett

ISBN-13: 978-1-64049-731-3

Printing History
1st Edition — 1999
8th Edition — March 2023
5 4 3 2 1

Front cover photo: Bunker Hill Covered Bridge, Catawba County, North Carolina © Tetra Images / robertharding.com
Back cover photo: Bodie Island Lighthouse © Daveallenphoto | Dreamstime.com

Printed in Malaysia for Imago